SmartWare® Tips, Tricks, and Traps

2nd Edition

Andrew N. Schwartz

SmartWare® Tips, Tricks, and Traps

2nd Edition

Library of Congress Catalog No.:LOC 90-62952

ISBN 0-88022-543-2

93 92 91 4 3 2 1

Interpretation of the printing code: the rightmost double-digit number is the year of the book's printing; the rightmost single-digit number, the number of the book's printing. For example, a printing code of 91-1 shows that the first printing of the book occurred in 1991.

SmartWare Tips, Tricks, and Traps, 2nd Edition, is based on Smart, version 3.10, and SmartWare II, version 1.02.

About the Author

Andrew N. Schwartz

Andrew N. Schwartz received his B.A. from Amherst College and his M.B.A. from the Amos Tuck School of Business Administration at Dartmouth College. He is president of his own computer consulting and development company in St. Louis, Missouri. The firm specializes in database management and information analysis applications. Previously, he was a consulting manager for Tymshare, Inc., a computer services company.

The author is president of the St. Louis Users Group for the PC and a member of the Independent Computer Consultants Association.

The author of *Using Smart, Using SmartWare II*, and the first edition of *Smart Tips, Tricks, and Traps*, published by Que Corporation, Mr. Schwartz has written several articles for *PC Magazine* and is a frequent contributor to *SmarTimes* and computer publications in the St. Louis area. He is on the faculty of the University of Missouri and lectures regularly on Smart, SmartWare II, and other software topics.

Publishing Director

Lloyd J. Short

Acquisitions Editor

Karen A. Bluestein

Product Director

Shelley O'Hara

Project Manager

Paul Boger

Production Editor

Betty A. White

Editors

Lori Lyons
Elizabeth A. Hoger

Technical Editor

Rudolf E. Wolf

Indexer

Sherry Massey

Book Design and Production

Hilary Adams
Jeff Baker
Scott Boucher
Martin Coleman
Joelynn Gifford
Sandy Grieshop
Denny Hager
Betty Kish
Bob LaRoche
Howard Peirce
Cindy L. Phipps
Joe Ramon
Tad Ringo
Dennis Sheehan
Suzanne Tully
Johnna VanHoose
Mary Beth Wakefield
Lisa A. Wilson

Composed in Garamond and OCRB
by Que Corporation.

Contents at a Glance

Introduction 1

Part I The Smart System

Chapter 1 Installation, Configuration, and Startup 11

Part II The Database

Chapter 2 Creating, Modifying, and Working with Files and Views 35
Chapter 3 Viewing Files and Arranging Data 93
Chapter 4 Finding Your Data and Working with Multiple Files 123
Chapter 5 Entering and Deleting Data 149
Chapter 6 Producing Reports 187
Chapter 7 Interfacing Files and Using the Dummy Facility 233

Part III The Spreadsheet

Chapter 8 Setting Parameters and Entering Data 299
Chapter 9 Operating the Worksheet 333
Chapter 10 Functions 359
Chapter 11 Printing, Reporting, and Integrating the Spreadsheet 385
Chapter 12 Graphics 407

Part IV The Word Processor

Chapter 13 Using the Word Processor 417

Part V Project Processing

Chapter 14 Project Processing 453
Chapter 15 Communications and Commands Used throughout Smart 519

Appendix A Database Project Files 547
Appendix B Iterative Recalculation in the Spreadsheet 561
Appendix C Word Processor Project Files 563
Index 567

Table of Contents

Introduction 1

Smart Version 3.10 and SmartWare II Version 1.0 2
Additional Reference 2
How To Use this Book 2
- Using the SmartWare System 2
- The Smart Database 3
- The Smart Spreadsheet 5
- The Smart Word Processor 6
- Project Processing 6
- Communications and Common Commands 6
- Appendixes 7

Conclusion 7

I The Smart System

1 Installation, Configuration, and Startup 11

System-Wide Tips 11
- Installing Smart 12
- Entering the System 12
- Using Expanded Memory 17
- Virtual-File Facility 17
- Using Text Editors 18
- Using the DOS Window 19

Main Menu 19
- Configuring Smart 20
- Printer Setup 25
- Networking Smart 30

II The Database

2 Creating, Modifying, and Working with Files and Views 35

Creating Files and Views 35
- Declaring Fields 38
- Field Rules 45

Bar and Pop-up Menus 49
Alpha Field Masks 51
Using Calculated Fields 53
Using Running-Total Fields 63
Using Counter Fields 64
Choosing Numeric or Alphanumeric Fields 68
Replicating Fields and Files 72
Multiple File Views 73
Loading Files 75
Using Subdirectories 79
Using the Virtual-File Facility 81
Activating Files 81
Using Screens and Views 82
Protecting Screens with Passwords 87
Safeguarding Data 89
Project Processing and Database Files 91

3 Viewing Files and Arranging Data 93

Viewing Files 93
Browsing through Files and Views 93
Working with Multiple Windows 96
Splitting Windows 96
Zooming and Closing Windows 97
Changing Windows 99
Linking Files 99
Arranging Your Data for the Best Results 102
Using Keys 102
Sorting Your Data 114
Changing the Order of the Data 118

4 Finding Your Data and Working with Multiple Files 123

Using the Find and Data Find Commands 123
Working with Multiple Files 130
Relating Two Files into a Third 130
Passing Transactions from One File to Another 138
Using Utilities To Restructure and Concatenate 142

5 Entering and Deleting Data 149

Entering and Updating Records 149
Advancing between Fields and Records 152
Using Custom Screens 154
Repeating Data from Record to Record 158

Project File Data Entry and Update 164
Looking Up Data from One File to Another 165
Loading Lookup Definitions 168
Automatic versus Manual Mode 169
Validating Entries 172
Trapping Duplicates 174
Deleting Data 176

6 Producing Reports 187

Creating Quick Reports 187
Creating Formal Reports 191
Page Length Specifications 192
Form and Table Specifications 193
Driver versus Driven Files 194
Handling Page Overflow 195
Defining Tables 195
Field Selection 196
Calculated Fields 198
Table Report Headings 202
Multiple Print Lines 203
Breakpoints 207
Defining Forms 212
Using Fields 212
Using Labels 213
Calculated Fields 217
Defining Page Numbers 218
Form Text 218
Using Report Techniques 219
Creating Similar Definitions 220
Using One Report Definition with Multiple Databases 220
Combination Reports 225
Special Techniques 230

7 Interfacing Files and Using the Dummy Facility 233

Reading Data from an External Source 233
External File Types 234
Field Formats 235
Reading a Partial Field List 238
Efficiency Techniques 239
Writing Data to an External Destination 241
Creating Detail Files 241
Writing Summarized Data 245
Creating a Summarized Report with a Project File 248

Sending Data to Another Smart Module 249
Creating a Summarized Database 250
Changing a Summarized Definition 253
Using a Partial Option 254
Row and Column Specifications 255
Testing a Send Summarized Definition 257
Using the Query Command 260
Using Field Names 260
Using Date Specifications 263
Using AND and OR Operators 266
Fast Query Definitions 268
Using Special Alpha Fields 270
Formula Writing Techniques 271
Copying Query Definitions 278
Documenting Query Definitions 278
Using the Replace Facility 280
Deleting and Activating Records with a Query 284
Performing Queries on a Network 287
Query by Example 288
Special Query Topics 291

III The Spreadsheet

8 Setting Parameters and Entering Data 299

Setting Parameters 299
Entering Data into the Spreadsheet 306
Command Mode versus Enter Mode 306
Using the Cursor Key or the Enter Key 306
Constructing Formulas with the Cursor Key 307
Absolute versus Relative Address 309
Entering Text 312
Using the F-Calculator 312
Using Blank Cells 313
Project-File Data Entry 314
Recalculating the Worksheet 319
Circular References 321
Protecting the Worksheet 326
Incorporating Data from the Database 328

9 Operating the Worksheet 333

Copying Parts of the Worksheet 333
Using Absolute Address 333

Copying a Block of Text 334
The Effect of Copying to the Destination Block 339
Preformatting a Block 339
Using External References 340
Moving Portions of the Worksheet 340
The (Edit) Copy Command Compared to the (Edit) Move Command 341
The Effect of the (Edit) Move Command on External References 341
Operating the Worksheet 343
Using Named Worksheet Blocks 343
Using the Fill Command 345
Using the Matrix Commands 346
The Matrix Transpose Command 346
The Matrix Parallel Command 347
The Linear Regression Command 347
Using the File Combine Command 356
Sorting the Worksheet 356
Forcing Zeros to Blanks 357

10 Functions 359

Using the Lookup Functions 359
Smart versus 1-2-3 Lookups 359
Alphabetic versus Numeric Lookups 361
Error Handling 363
Using Worksheet Position Functions 365
Validating Worksheet Contents 366
The NA Function 366
The ISNA Function 367
The ISBLANK Function 367
Using Date and Time Functions 370
Formatting and Selection Functions 371
Numeric Conversion Functions 374
VAL and STR 374
Making Block References 375
Statistical Database Functions 376
Text Functions 379
The FIND and MATCH Functions 379
Substituting Parts of Strings 380
Miscellaneous Functions 380

11 Printing, Reporting, and Integrating the Spreadsheet 385

Controlling Worksheet Appearance 385
- Underscoring Entries in the Spreadsheet 385
- Controlling Column Width 388

Printing the Worksheet 388
- Printing Formulas 388
- Selecting Output Destinations 389
- Changing the Print Line Width 390

Using the Report Command 391
- Duplicating a Report Definition 391
- Report Headings and Footings 391
- Report Width Specifications 392
- Report Output Destinations 393
- Block and Print Group Destinations 394
- Page Numbering 396
- Changing Report Definitions 396

Integrating the Spreadsheet with Other Modules 398
- Using an All-Formula Spreadsheet 398
- Using Project Files to Reformat Data 400
- Using Parameters in Project Files 402
- Sorting 403
- Sending and Writing Data from the Spreadsheet 403
- Using the Read and File Import Commands 405
- Interfacing with 1-2-3 Releases 1A and 2.0 406

12 Graphics 407

Creating Graph Definitions 407

Graph Operations 410
- Printing Edited Graphs 412
- Histograms versus Bar Charts 413

IV The Word Processor

13 Using the Word Processor 417

Starting the Word Processor 417

Editing and Formatting Documents 421
- Using Footnotes 423
- Reformatting Documents 425
- Multiple Columns 426

Using Dictionaries 426

Printing Documents 430

Headers and Footers 432
Printer Settings 434
Merge-Printing 437
Inserting Graphics 441
Miscellaneous Tips, Tricks, and Traps 442

V Project Processing

14 Project Processing 453

Creating a Project File 453
Using the Beep Command 455
Error Handling 455
Adding Comments 457
Compiling Project Files 458
Spreadsheet-Related Topics 458
Editing Project Files 460
Database-Related Topics 460
Executing Project Files 464
File-Access Commands 466
Using IF Statements in Project Files 471
Using the INCHAR and NEXTKEY Functions 476
Jumping to a Project File Statement 477
Using Let Statements in Project Files 478
Direct Printing from a Project File 480
Using Menu and Screen Commands 483
Command Line Substitution 488
Procedures and Functions in Project Processing 494
Using Quiet Settings 496
Testing for the End of a Data File 497
Editing Project Files 497
Repainting the Screen 499
Singlestep Settings 501
Halting Project-File Execution 501
Using Variables in Project Files 502

15 Communications and Commands Used throughout Smart 519

Commands Used Throughout Smart 519
Windows and Borders 519
The DOS Window (Secondary Command Processor) 520
File Commands 520

Input Screens 525
Macros and Quick Keys 527
Zooming Windows 531
Functions 532
The PrtSc Key 537
Fonts 537
The Communications Module 537
Capturing and Storing Data 539
Dialing the Modem 540
Using Files in Communications 542
Profiles and Settings 543
Emulating VT100 and VT52 Terminals 544

A Database Project Files 547

Project Files To Delete All Records from a Database 547
Project File To Find and Change a Date in a Smart 3.10 Report Heading 548
Forcing Generation of a New Form in a Smart 3.10 Combination Report 549
Series of Smart 3.10 Project Files To Construct and Execute a Query 551
Project File 1 551
Project File 2 551
Project File 3 552
Project File 4 553
Project File 5 553
Project File 6 554
Project File To Simulate the Browse Command 554
Project Files To Simulate the Find and Data Find Commands 556
Project File To Add a Record to an Index 558

B Iterative Recalculation in the Spreadsheet 561

C Word Processor Project Files 563

CONVERT.PF2: The Main File 563
FILENAME.IS2: Called by CONVERT 565
FORMAT.IS2: Called by CONVERT 565
INTRO.IS2: Called by CONVERT 566

Index 567

Foreword

This book covers both Smart, version 3.10, and SmartWare II, version 1.02. I wrote the first edition of *Smart Tips, Tricks and Traps* after having used Smart 3.10 for three years with many clients. This second edition includes not only the Smart 3.10 material, but also hundreds of new items on both Smart 3.10 and SmartWare II. While some topics pertain to only one product or the other, many apply to both; use the following icons in the margin as your guide:

3.10 ***SW II*** ***Both***

The following statistics will give you an idea how much new material is contained in this second edition:

- 700 New Tips, Tricks, or Traps
- 450 Items on SmartWare II
- 250 New items on Smart 3.10
- 280 SmartWare II Database items

When I develop client applications, as I discover a helpful tip, clever trick, or dangerously lurking trap, I jot it down. My most difficult task in writing this book was to organize all this information into a form that would be easy to use and would provide just the right amount of detail.

As in the first edition, I have grouped the book into parts that correspond to each of the major Smart and SmartWare II modules. A quick scan of the book shows my major emphasis on the Database and Project Processing. In my work with the two products, I have found that these areas deserve the greatest amount of coverage, due to both their power and complexity. The Database, in particular, has so many options and capabilities that it is easy to become confused or get caught up on a small item. Pay particular attention to the tricks in this section because you will learn ways of getting around many of the restrictions.

How you use this book depends on your stage of application development. If you are just getting started with Smart or SmartWare II, you should probably read completely through a chapter before beginning to work on the topics it covers. You may be able to save yourself hours of frustration or avoid making decisions that you would later find limiting.

If you have been using the Smart products for a while, you will appreciate the tricks you can use to enhance your applications. You will want to make extensive use of the index to this book to find a subject quickly. The index includes references to the specific modules and explanatory phrases that help you to identify the desired topic quickly.

If your Smart applications are already in production, read this book to identify possible traps that may be causing problems. If you occasionally experience anomalies in your system, this book may offer an explanation. Also, be alert for efficiency-related items; many of the entries in this book offer solutions that can make your existing applications run faster and more smoothly.

If you are converting from Smart 3.10 to SmartWare II, you will find many items in this book that will ease the transition. Where there are differences between the products or where a capability has been improved in SmartWare II, I have tried to point that out.

Both Smart 3.10 and SmartWare II offer extensive capabilities and features. As with any sophisticated product, there are often several ways to accomplish the same task, but some techniques are better (or faster or more accurate) than others. This book highlights these alternative methods and helps you select the best one for your purposes. And, as bug-free as the SmartWare products are, there are some things you want to avoid. These are the "traps"; watch for them.

I hope that your use and enjoyment of Smart 3.10 and SmartWare II are enhanced by reading this book. If I can save you an afternoon of frustration, help you develop an application days earlier, or forestall losing days' worth of data, then I will have accomplished my objective.

Andrew N. Schwartz

ACKNOWLEDGMENTS

My thanks to the following employees of Informix Software for their thoughts, suggestions, contributions, and encouragement.

First Edition:

Bruce Barr
John Beveridge
Stan Christ
Wanda Boliere
Bobby Brim
Doug Boyce
Mona Brower
Dave Cearley
Bob Dodge
Mark Drake
Allan Duarte
Mike Gillespie
John Marks
Julia Meyer
Kim Pheffer
Diane Phillips
Lesa Pohl
John Purpura
Gene Rebman
Russ Sarbora
Diana Sexton
Lisa Vanover

Second Edition:

Louise Bergeron
Jim Cote
Mark Drake
John Green
Jeff Jordan
Dennis Kelleher
Kevin Mayfield
Roger McKenzie
Jeff Renshaw
Diana Sexton
Ken Vrana
Rick Vreeland
John Enslein
Amy Livingood-Rogers
Karl Rose
Lisa Spradling
Larry Worster

Trademark Acknowledgments

Que Corporation has made every reasonable attempt to supply trademark information about company names, products, and services mentioned in this book. Trademarks indicated below were derived from various sources. Que Corporation cannot attest to the accuracy of this information.

1-2-3 and Lotus are registered trademarks of Lotus Development Corporation.

dBASE and dBASE III are registered trademarks of Ashton-Tate Company.

EPSON is a registered trademark of Epson America, Inc.

Intel is a registered trademark of Intel Corporation.

LaserJet is a trademark of Hewlett-Packard Co.

Microsoft is a registered trademark of Microsoft Corporation.

Rampage is a registered trademark of AST Research, Inc.

Smart is a copyright of Innovative Software.

Introduction

The wide variety of sophisticated capabilities available in the Smart and SmartWare II products has prompted the need for this book of tips, tricks, and traps. You may not yet be using all of SmartWare's features; but if your application is straightforward, either the software manual, *Using Smart* or *Using SmartWare II* provides enough information to construct and use your database, build your spreadsheet, or use the Word Processor. This book is for users who want to extend their applications beyond the elementary.

Before you begin using this book, you should know what makes up "tips," "tricks," and "traps." All tips are based on standard features of the SmartWare Systems. An item is considered to be a tip if it helps you use the software more efficiently or quickly. I discovered some tips simply by using the SmartWare Systems. Other tips are mentioned in the documentation but deserve highlighting because they are valuable or need emphasis. Still other tips are included for further explanation of complex subjects.

A trick helps you get around a problem or streamline the use of the program. Naturally, not all software programs can address every need; the tricks in this book help you accomplish your tasks in ways that exceed SmartWare's intended or documented capabilities. In some cases, a trick may be a standard Smart or SmartWare II feature used in an unintended or inapparent manner. In other cases, a trick relies upon a unique combination of SmartWare and DOS components to get around a restriction or to enhance the software capabilities.

A trap is an item that can result in loss of data or cause serious problems impeding your use of the program. Watch out for the traps—you may never encounter the conditions that cause them; but, on the other hand, knowing where they lie may save you hours (or days) of work. Fortunately, SmartWare is 99 percent bug free, so you will find far fewer traps than tips and tricks in this book.

Sometimes you may wonder why I have classified an item as a "tip" rather than a "trap." Usually my classification depends on the severity of the consequences and the action I recommend you take. If, by adhering to my suggestion, your system starts running faster and you find your development time is reduced or that you can accomplish more—the item becomes a tip. However, if by not following the suggestion, you can suffer serious consequences, such as loss of data or loss of significant hours of time, the item is a trap.

The book is divided into parts corresponding to the individual modules of the SmartWare Systems. Project processing is covered in a major chapter by itself rather than being covered within each module section. You'll find that the emphasis has been placed on the Database and Project Processing.

Smart Version 3.10 and SmartWare II Version 1.02

The material in this book covers version 3.10 of the Smart System and version 1.02 of SmartWare II. Icons in the margin indicate whether the item applies to Smart, SmartWare II, or both. In many cases, where the item applies to both, the only difference lies in the command structure. In these instances, I have supplied the commands for both products.

Additional Reference

If you find that, in addition to the tips, tricks, and traps covered in this book, you want more information about the SmartWare Systems, refer to *Using Smart* or *Using SmartWare II*, also published by Que. These books are specifically aimed at new SmartWare users and cover the concepts and commands you need to get your applications up and running.

How to Use This Book

With a few exceptions, the examples in this book are short, focusing on the specific topic at hand. I kept them short for two reasons: first, the shorter they are, the easier it is to grasp the essence of the tip or trick. Second, I want to encourage you to not just read about the tip, but actually try it on your computer and in your application. The real value of these tips is their use in your applications.

Here is a chapter-by-chapter preview of *SmartWare Tips, Tricks and Traps.*

Using the SmartWare System

This part of the book covers the topics that you address when you first install your system or that are found on the Main Menu. A number of these tips will help you install and use your printer to full advantage. I also discuss the various option switches you can use when you enter Smart.

The Smart Database

The Database receives special attention in this book for four reasons.

First, if you have not used a database previously, you will find many of the items in this book of great value. While the elemental concepts of database management (fields, records, files, sorting, reporting, and so on) are often the same in different software, Smart's use of the commands to invoke these components may require some additional explanation.

Second, while you can see much of what the Database does, many tasks and activities take place "behind the scenes." Because you cannot readily observe this hidden processing, some explanation is required to help you understand what is happening so that you can use the commands to best advantage.

Third, sophisticated database management systems are inherently more complex than either spreadsheets or word processors. Even if you have used another system previously, the particular features and capabilities of the Smart Database deserve special coverage.

Fourth, many features and components of the Smart Database system work together in myriad ways; so the usage of various commands may seem unclear when you look at the manual or even *Using Smart* or *Using SmartWare II*. Frequently, you can accomplish the same task several ways, but one may be more applicable to existing conditions than another. While one command sequence may yield correct results in one circumstance, the same set of commands can produce invalid or erroneous results under other conditions.

Here is a preview of the topics covered in the chapters on the Database.

Chapter 2 is devoted to creating files and custom screens and views. You will find several tips and traps on using passwords and why a password may not give you complete data protection. You will also find out how to load more files in Smart 3.10 than your system seems to allow. I then offer several suggestions for creating new, matching, or similar files. Finally, I give some tips to help you forestall losing any of your data.

Chapter 3 covers the commands you use to specify ways to view your files and rearrange your data. I discuss the subject of working with multiple windows and the requirements for windows with some commands and not with others. I delve into the use of keys and compare this to the use of the Sort commands. (Some features require keys and some work faster with keys, but having too many keys can be detrimental.)

The first part of Chapter 4 is dedicated to the use of the Find commands and the ways they can help you locate specific records in your database. I compare the Find commands to the Query commands and tell you when you must use one or the other. (Sometimes these commands produce identical results, but one may work faster.)

The second half of Chapter 4 discusses those commands dealing with multiple files that work together within the Database. In Smart 3.10, these commands are named Relate, Transactions, and Utilities Concatenate and Restructure. In SmartWare II, they are Data Relate, Data Transact, and Data Utilities Append. You will find out why a Relate command may not always work correctly, or why a transaction may seem incomplete. The Utilities Concatenate and Restructure commands may seem similar, but they have very different uses; you will discover why. The Data Utilities Append command in SmartWare II takes the place of both of these Smart 3.10 commands.

Read Chapter 5 to learn more about entering and deleting data. I cover the Enter and Update commands and offer several tips and tricks with custom screens and views, macros, and the F-Calculator. I present a detailed discussion on the subject of handling fields that repeat from record to record. I also present the use of the Smart 3.10 Lookup command for both retrieving data from another file and validating entries. I discuss how to accomplish, in SmartWare II, the same effect as the Lookup command, but with more certainty and capability.

The last portion of Chapter 5 covers deleting data by using both the Delete and the Query commands. Some commands in the Database will proceed to process deleted records, and others will ignore them—find out which these are.

The entire subject of reporting is consigned to Chapter 6. Using the Print command for "quick and easy" reporting is covered in the first portion of the chapter—determine why decisions you made early in the application or the Smart installation may affect the output of this command.

The Table, Form, and Combination report formats are discussed in great detail. I explain the workings of these commands, and how you can tailor them to your needs. In this chapter and in Appendix A, I provide several tricks you can use to expand the capabilities of the Report and Print Report commands.

If you need either to read data from an external source or write out data from the Database, you will want to read Chapter 7. Some types of external files provide greater flexibility when reading data, but there are a couple of tricks you can employ to get around some restrictions.

The final portion of Chapter 7 is devoted to the Query commands and the SmartWare II Query by Example facility. Because of the wide variety of uses of Query and its expansive definition capability, many Smart users have had trouble with this command. In this chapter, I not only explain the Query facility, but also illustrate its usage with many examples. Rely on this chapter to master the Query command.

The Smart Spreadsheet

The section on the Smart Spreadsheet covers not only areas in which Smart is different from other spreadsheets, but also specific techniques that you can employ right now to make your application faster and easier to use. Some topics are included because they deserve additional explanation; they may be more complex than most, or they may provide an outstanding capability. Other topics, such as Matrix Regression (Chapter 9), have been included in great detail because there simply was not enough space in either the software manual or in *Using Smart* or *Using SmartWare II* to provide the coverage this subject deserved.

Here is a preview of the topics covered in the Spreadsheet section.

Chapter 8 covers tips and tricks for entering data into your spreadsheet, either manually from a project file or by sending the data from the Database. I discuss the topic of relative versus absolute addressing and the effect on the Copy commands.

The last part of the chapter is allotted to the construction of formulas, using the normal entry mode, cursor keys to help you enter cell addresses, and the two formula editors.

If you want to unravel the mysteries of using the iterative mode of worksheet recalculation to solve recursive scenarios, be sure to read this chapter.

Chapter 9 deals with operating your worksheet, using the Copy and Move commands, and external worksheet references. Also covered are named blocks and the Fill commands.

A major portion of this chapter is devoted to the Matrix Transpose, Parallel, and Regression commands. An entire forecasting model complete with seasonality analysis is provided as an example of the use of the Matrix Regression facility.

New functions introduced with SmartWare II and existing functions that deserve further explanation are covered in Chapter 10. I deal with the Lookup functions in detail, comparing the 1-2-3 versions with SmartWare equivalents. You will be surprised to discover that you may want to use the 1-2-3 versions rather than the SmartWare versions.

Error handling has its own section in this chapter: how to find errors, correct them, and display them.

If you are using your spreadsheet as a database, the statistical database functions presented in this chapter will be of interest to you.

Chapter 11 is devoted to reporting from your spreadsheet and integrating it with other SmartWare modules. The Print commands are quick and easy; and although there are some unique features of these commands, there are some surprising restrictions, too.

The Report commands are used for formal reporting; by careful definition, you can achieve outstanding results. However, there are some traps to watch out for.

If you are integrating your spreadsheet with either the Word Processor or the Database, be sure to read this chapter.

Smart Spreadsheet graphics is covered in Chapter 12. I discuss not only techniques for defining graphs but also considerations for printing them. Determine how to print an edited graph in this chapter.

The Smart Word Processor

The Word Processor is covered in Chapter 13; major topics include the Dictionary, Footnotes, and Merge. A significant portion of this chapter is devoted to printing documents and setting the necessary options.

Project Processing

Chapter 14 is dedicated to Project Processing. I cover both the module specific commands and those which are common to all modules. Major topics include:

Error codes
Compiling project files
Entering spreadsheet data
File access commands
The four types of IF statements
Assignment statements
Direct printing
Menus
Parameters and variables
Execution efficiencies

If you are developing applications to run from project files, do not miss this chapter.

Communications and Common Commands

In Chapter 15, I cover the SmartWare Communications and those commands that are common to all of the modules.

In the communications portion of this chapter, you will discover how to debug a communications session, switch between data and voice communications, and utilize the VT100- and VT52-emulation facilities.

Of the common commands, the subjects of the DOS window, file commands, and macros receive the most attention.

Appendixes

The three appendixes contain additional material on the Database, Spreadsheet, and Word Processor, respectively.

In Appendix A, I provide project files to

1. Delete all records from a database in a few seconds
2. Change a date in a Smart 3.10 table report heading
3. Force the generation of a new combination report form on every page
4. Construct a Query from a project file
5. Simulate the Browse command
6. Add a record to an index in Smart 3.10

Appendix B gives an example of a spreadsheet designed to use the iterative-recalculation mode.

Appendix C provides a project file to strip all carriage returns from a text file and load it into the Word Processor.

Conclusion

The tips, tricks, and traps included in this book result from my use of Smart and SmartWare II to create hundreds of databases, spreadsheets, documents, and project files. These techniques and suggestions are based on real, everyday business situations. By reading this book, you will be able to rely on my tips, implement the tricks, and avoid the traps.

Part I

The Smart System

Includes

Installation, Configuration, and Startup

1

Installation, Configuration, and Startup

This chapter covers tips, tricks, and traps that you can use in installing the Smart System and configuring it for your own applications. Hints are offered for customizing an application configuration and for changing the configuration as you switch from one application to another. You learn how to make Smart take advantage of your computer's processing capability and how to circumvent some of Smart's restrictions.

Many of the items contained in this chapter apply to all modules of the Smart System; they appear here so that you will not miss them. Particular attention is paid to printer configuration. Tips relating to the main menu's commands and facilities are also included in this chapter.

Finally, if you are using Smart on a network or plan to move a single-user application to a network environment, the tips, tricks, and traps presented here are very helpful.

System-Wide Tips

Regardless of the module you use the most, some tips apply to the entire Smart system. Using them can help to make your application more powerful, easier to use, and more flexible. The entry switches can tie the DOS and the Smart environments together, and the DOS window, invoked with Ctrl-O, can provide a temporary facility for executing DOS commands from within Smart.

Smart version 3.10's virtual-file facility is introduced in this chapter, and the discussion is developed further in Chapter 2.

Installing Smart

Both

1.1 Trick: By positioning certain files in a separate subdirectory, you can customize a unique configuration for each application.

If copies of any of the following files are in an application subdirectory, the Smart System uses these files instead of the corresponding files in the Smart subdirectory:

CONFIGURE (3.10)
PSETUP.DEF
PRINTER.DSC (3.10)
PRINTxx.DSC (3.10)
PARAMx (3.10)
Module Preference Files (SmartWare II)
Modem Definitions (SmartWare II)
REPORT.DEF
WPPRINT.DEF
SPELL.DEF
DISPLAY ADAPTER DRIVER
GRAPHICS ADAPTER DRIVER
PLOTTER DRIVER

Entering the System

Both

1.2 Tip: Use the -d entry switch, followed by a pathname, to specify a data path.

In Smart 3.10, the path for each application module can be specified within the main menu Configure command (refer to fig. 1.6, later in this chapter). No method exists, however, to specify the path of files to be accessed from the main menu itself. To specify such a path, use the -d switch upon entry into Smart:

```
-d\account
```

Files that you access from the main menu usually are text and project files.

In SmartWare II, the -d switch overrides the default data paths in the SmartWare II module or Global preferences.

Note: Do not confuse the -D entry switch with the D argument, which initiates the Database.

Both

1.3 Tip: Use the -e entry switch to prevent Smart from using expanded memory if you want to reserve expanded memory for use by another program.

If you have an expanded memory board in your computer, Smart automatically recognizes it and uses the expanded memory for system memory and paging. Use the -e switch if you plan to use the DOS window facility (Ctrl-O) to invoke a secondary command processor and run software requiring expanded memory.

If you are running only Smart on your system, or if a program you execute in the DOS window does not use expanded memory, you should not use this switch.

1.4 Tip: Use the -r entry switch to reserve RAM for the DOS window. ***Both***

If you plan to use the DOS window facility, you may want to reserve RAM for use by the programs to be run in the window. Reserving memory may not be necessary for minor DOS commands invoked from within the Database or the Spreadsheet. But because all available RAM is allocated to the Smart 3.10 Word Processor, you cannot invoke DOS from the Word Processor without having reserved some memory for the DOS window. If you specify

```
SMART W -r64
```

then Smart does not use 64K of memory. The 64K is reserved for your other application program running in the DOS window.

1.5 Trick: On some computers, simply reserving 1K of memory increases the amount of memory available to a secondary command processor by a significantly greater amount. ***SW II***

The -r entry switch is used to reserve additional memory to be used by a secondary command processor when you temporarily exit to DOS, using the Tools OS command or the Ctrl-O Quick Key. The amount of memory you reserve, however, is subtracted from the memory available to the application. On some computers, if you reserve just 1K (-r1), the memory available for the secondary command processor increases by almost 20K. Try this trick to see if it works on your computer.

1.6 Trap: The -a and -p entry switches are mutually exclusive. These switches cannot be used together. ***Both***

The -a entry switch is used to execute a command at the command level. The -p switch is used to designate a project file to be executed upon entry to the Smart System. If you need to do both, the first line of the project file should contain the command you would have specified with the -a switch.

In SmartWare II, you can also specify project files to run on entry to individual modules; use the Tools Preferences menu for each module. Using the Tools Preferences Global selection menu, you can specify project files to run both on entry and exit of SmartWare II.

3.10

1.7 Tip: Use the -a switch instead of the -p switch if you want a project file to run in memory.

When you specify -p and a file name, you cannot specify that you want the project file to run in memory. Therefore, the project file runs from the file. As discussed in Chapter 14, running from a file can be much slower than running in memory. If you use the -a switch with the full command, however, you can run the project file in memory:

```
Smart d -aExecute Loadall in-memory
```

SW II

1.8 Tip: Use the -oe entry switch to run all default project files in memory.

In some cases, you cannot specify whether a project file is to be run from memory or from a file. These are called "default" project files. If you use the -oe switch, all project files are run in-memory. The instances in which you cannot specify to run project files in-memory are the following:

1. Projects run with the -p entry switch
2. Entry project files selected in the Tools Preferences of individual modules
3. Entry and Exit project files in Global Preferences
4. Quit and Send project files
5. Projects you execute with your own keywords, using SMART.MNU

3.10

1.9 Trap: If you have an IBM PC AT computer, you may need to use the -n entry switch to initiate the Smart session.

The -n switch is used to prevent Smart from using the math coprocessor. If your system does not have a math coprocessor chip (8087 or 80287), you can have problems entering Smart when using some AT models with some Smart 3.10 versions. If you find that your system hangs or gives an error, try using the -n switch as follows:

```
SMART -n
```

SW II

1.10 Tip: Create your own commands by using a SMART.MNU file.

If you create a file called SMART.MNU, you can add extra commands to various SmartWare II module menus. By executing these new commands just as you execute regular commands, you can execute a project file.

Create your SMART.MNU file with the text editor. Each line of the file contains 5 entries:

1. Module Number. This entry is represented as follows:

   0 Main Menu

   1 Spreadsheet

   2 Wordprocessor

   3 Database

   4 Communications

2. Keyword #. This entry indicates the location and menu on which the new keyword is added. The keyword numbers are reserved as follows:

   1-5 Top menu of the module

   6-9 Quit menu of the module

   10-14 Tools menu

   15 Help menu

   16 Remember tools menu

3. Keyword. The command name to appear on the menu. A keyword is limited to 31 characters. If you want to be able to select the keyword by just the initial letter, make sure that no other commands on the menu begin with that letter.

4. Project file to run when the keyword is selected.

5. Autohelp explanation. You may explain your commands with up to 79 characters. When you move the highlight block to the command, this text appears on the autohelp line.

Three ways exist to invoke the SMART.MNU facility when you initiate a SmartWare II session.

1. On the command line, when you initiate Smart, use the following switch:

   ```
   -om
   ```

   When this switch is used, Smart searches for a file called SMART.MNU in the current directory or the system directory.

2. At the bottom of the Global Preferences menu, a selection reads:

   ```
   Look for menu keyword file on entry to Smart:
   ```

   If you have selected Yes, Smart looks for the SMART.MNU file.

3. You can also specify your own file on the command line with a switch:

```
-omC:\account\own.mnu
```

Make sure to include the path if the file is in a subdirectory other than the current subdirectory.

Chapter 14 has an example of a project file that you can use to change your subdirectories easily. The following is an example of a SMART.MNU file that adds this command/project file to the main menu of the Spreadsheet module.

```
1,1,New-Directory,newsub.rf1,Change Default Data Path
```

Notice that the text is not contained within quotation marks, and that commas are used as separators between the entries on the line. Figure 1.1 shows the new command:

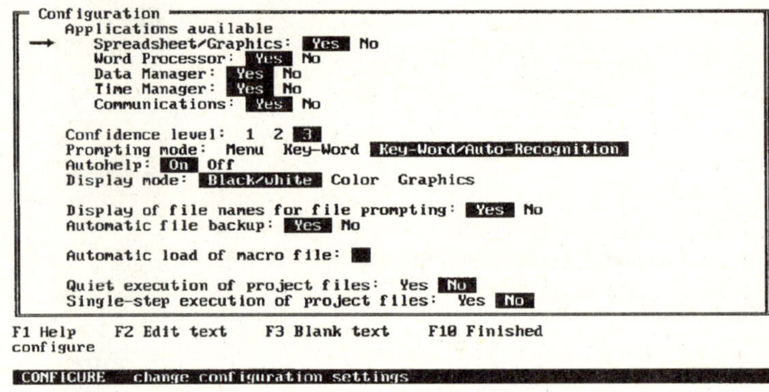

Fig. 1.1.
An additional menu command.

Remember that project files that omit any module-specific commands may be used from any module. In this example, you can execute this same project file from any module and still reference an RF1 file.

Both

1.11 Tip: If you have Smart 3.10 and SmartWare II on your computer, use batch files to run one or the other.

To run Smart 3.10, you can have a batch file similar to the following:

```
C:\SMART\SMART.EXE %1 %2 -sc:\SMART -fVIRTUAL
```

To run SmartWare II, use the following batch file:

```
C:\SMARTII\SMART.EXE %1 %2 -sc:\SMARTII
```

The parameters %1 and %2 enable you to pass an argument to the batch file, such as D, to go right into the database, or -r32 to reserve 32K of extra memory. The -s switch is used to indicate the location of the Smart software, regardless of the current DOS path.

Using Expanded Memory

1.12 Tip: Installing an expanded-memory board can increase the capabilities of your application. *Both*

Expanded-memory boards running under the Lotus-Intel-Microsoft standard add only 47K of system memory (RAM) to your configuration; AST Rampage boards add 200K to 400K of usable RAM. Because of the design of expanded-memory boards, a portion of the memory on each type of board can be used as additional system RAM. The memory beyond the portion used as system RAM is used automatically for paging large worksheets or documents. In Smart 3.10, The extra memory is not used by Database applications.

1.13 Tip: To use the Intel Above Board(TM) in an IBM PC AT, you must use DOS 3.0 or a later version. *Both*

Support for memory extension was not available in previous versions of DOS.

1.14 Tip: Use an inexpensive RAM disk card for paging instead of a more expensive expanded memory card. *Both*

Because most of the memory on an expanded memory card is used only for paging, you can save some money by purchasing a card that can be configured as a RAM disk. You then can specify (in the Configure command on the main menu of Smart 3.10 or the Tools Preferences Global menu of SmartWare II) that the system paging be directed to this RAM disk. Figure 1.6 shows this command. This approach accelerates your applications without the expense of purchasing an expanded memory card.

Virtual-File Facility

1.15 Trap: You cannot open as many files on a network as you can on a single-user system. *3.10*

When Smart is used under DOS, 20 files can be open at a time. This DOS limitation applies not only to your application files, but also the Smart system files, index files, project files, and any other files you need to run the application. Because DOS uses 6 of the 20 files, the number available to Smart is 14. Using the Virtual File Facility increases this limit from 14 files to 100.

If you are operating Smart on a single-user computer, use the -f virtual-entry switch to invoke a Smart facility that circumvents the 20-file restriction. On a network, however, the switch is not available, so the restriction applies.

The entry switch is

```
-fVIRTUAL
```

The file VIRTUAL.DVR must be resident in the subdirectory containing your Smart system files. The VIRTUAL.DVR file is not automatically copied to the disk during the installation process; you must copy the file yourself.

If you have developed an application on a single-user machine that opens many files simultaneously, and you plan to transport the application to a network environment, you must rewrite portions of the application to avoid exceeding the DOS open-file limitations. If you plan to upgrade to a network, you should keep this restriction in mind.

SW II

1.16 Trap: The -f entry switches in SmartWare II and Smart 3.10 have completely different meanings.

Used with SmartWare II, -f disables the network driver. Begin the session in SmartWare II by typing:

```
Smart -f
```

On a network, this command disables the installed network driver, forcing the single-user mode. Although this may have advantages for some database administration maintenance procedures, you should be aware that in a normal network situation, this switch should be avoided.

Using Text Editors

Both

1.17 Trick: Use the Alt-F3 key sequence to read any text file into any editor in the Smart system.

Because most Editors within the system are identical, you can read an external ASCII file into the work space. The editors include the Formula editor (Alt-K), Query definition, Create-field-calculation definition, Project-file editor, Text-editor, and the Spreadsheet large-cell editor (Alt-F).

To read a file into the work space, use Alt-F3 and enter a file name at the prompt. You must supply the full file name and extension. You must enter the drive and path specification if they are not current.

Using the DOS Window

1.18 Trap: To use the DOS window facility with a two floppy-disk system, you must copy the COMMAND.COM file to the data disk in the B: drive and set the COMSPEC environment variable to recognize the file's location. *3.10*

Copy the COMMAND.COM file from your boot disk to each data disk that you plan to use with your system. (The system and program disks do not have enough room for this file.) Then issue the following command prior to entering Smart:

```
SET COMSPEC = B:\COMMAND.COM
```

This command tells the system to search for the COMMAND.COM file on the B disk drive when you use Ctrl-O to invoke the DOS-window secondary command processor.

Main Menu

Properly configuring the Smart System can make a big difference in the performance of your applications. Because configuring printers often causes the most frustration when installing Smart, many of the tips and tricks in this section address this crucial subject, as well as other important configuration settings.

Figures 1.2 through 1.6 show the five screens of options for the Smart 3.10 Configure command.

```
Configuration
  Applications available
→    Spreadsheet/Graphics: Yes No
     Word Processor: Yes No
     Data Manager: Yes No
     Time Manager: Yes No
     Communications: Yes No

  Confidence level: 1 2 3
  Prompting mode: Menu Key-Word Key-Word/Auto-Recognition
  Autohelp: On Off
  Display mode: Black/white Color Graphics

  Display of file names for file prompting: Yes No
  Automatic file backup: Yes No

  Automatic load of macro file:

  Quiet execution of project files: Yes No
  Single-step execution of project files: Yes No

F1 Help    F2 Edit text    F3 Blank text    F10 Finished
configure

CONFIGURE - change configuration settings
```

Fig. 1.2.

The first screen of the 3.10 Configuration menu.

```
Configuration
→ Time format:  AM/PM  24-hour

  Date1 format:  99-mmm-99  99 mmm 99  99.mmm 99
  Date2 format:  99-99-99  99/99/99  99.99.99  99/99-99
  Date style:  MMDDYY  DDMMYY  YYMMDD

  Currency symbol:  $
  Currency symbol location:  Before-amount  After-amount
  Decimal separator:  Period  Comma
  Thousands separator:  Comma  Period  Blank
  Division by zero is:  Zero  Error

  ---------------------------- Printers ----------------------------
  1 IBM Graphics/Proprinter    18 Okidata 192                 40 Brother HR25
  2 Epson MX                   19 Okidata 2410                48 DWP 220
  3 Epson FX                   20 IDS Color(DP 8050/8070)     49 DWP 510
  4 Epson RX                   22 IBM Color(DP 8052/8072)     60 AT&T 455
  5 Epson LQ-1500              23 IBM Color Jetprinter        61 AT&T 470
  6 Epson JX                   25 HP LaserJet                 62 AT&T 475

F1 Help    F2 Edit text    F3 Blank text    F10 Finished
configure

CONFIGURE - change configuration settings
```

Fig. 1.3.

The second screen of the 3.10 Configuration menu.

```
Configuration
  3 Epson FX                  20 IDS Color(DP 8050/8070)     49 DWP 510
  4 Epson RX                  22 IBM Color(DP 8052/8072)     60 AT&T 455
  5 Epson LQ-1500             23 IBM Color Jetprinter        61 AT&T 470
  6 Epson JX                  25 HP LaserJet                 62 AT&T 475
  10 Okidata 84-s2            26 HP LaserJet Plus            64 AT&T 477
  11 Okidata 92/93            30 Diablo 630                  89 DMP 120
  12 Okidata 82/83            32 IBM Wheelprinter E          91 DMP 2100P
  13 Okidata 182              35 NEC 3530                    92 DMP 430
  14 Toshiba 1340/50/51       36 NEC 3550                    99 Generic
  ---------------------------------------------------------------------
  Printer number:  1
  Printer port:  Parallel 1  Parallel-2  Serial-1  Serial-2  PRN  AUX
  For serial printers:
     Baud rate:  300  600  1200  2400  4800  9600
     Word length:  7  8
     Parity:  Even  Odd  None
     Stop bits:  1  2
  Characters per line:  80
→ Lines per page:  66

F1 Help    F2 Edit text    F3 Blank text    F10 Finished
configure

CONFIGURE - change configuration settings
```

Fig. 1.4.

The third screen of the 3.10 Configuration menu.

Configuring Smart

Both

1.19 Tip: Select printer output as PRN to force Smart to write to the printer through DOS.

Interfacing to the printer through DOS is mandatory with some networks and printers. If you must force printer output through DOS, select PRN on the Configure command at the main menu. If you select Parallel-1 or Parallel-2, however, Smart accesses the printer hardware directly (see fig. 1.4). In SmartWare II, the direct connection printers are called LPT1, LPT2, and LPT3.

```
Configuration
      Word length:  7  8
      Parity:  Even  Odd  None
      Stop bits:  1  2
   Characters per line:  80
   Lines per page:  66

   --------------------------- Plotters ---------------------------
   1 HP 7470 A                 4 HI DMP-40           7 Calcomp M84
   2 HP 7475 A                 5 HI DMP-29           8 Amdek Amplot II
   3 HP 7550 A                 6 IBM XY/749          9 Polaroid Palette
   ----------------------------------------------------------------
   Plotter number:  99
   Plotter port:  Parallel-1  Parallel-2  Serial-1  Serial-2  PRN  AUX
   For serial plotters:
      Baud rate:  300  600  1200  2400  4800  9600
      Word length:  7  8
      Parity:  Even  Odd  None
      Stop bits:  1  2
-> Plotter pen speed (1-10):  10

F1 Help     F2 Edit text     F3 Blank text     F10 Finished
configure

CONFIGURE - change configuration settings
```

Fig. 1.5.

The fourth screen of the 3.10 Configuration menu.

```
Configuration
   Plotter pen speed (1-10):  10

   ------------------ Graphics Display Screens ------------------
     1 IBM Color Display Adapter        6 Apricot-xi
     2 AT&T 6300                      102 IBM EGA - RGB
     3 IBM 3270 PC                    103 IBM EGA - enhanced/monochrome
     4 Hercules                       110 Tandy 2000
     5 STB Graphics Plus II(color)    201 IBM Monochrome
   ---------------------------------------------------------------
   Graphics display screen number:  4

   Paging file path:

   Application data paths
      Spreadsheet/Graphics:
      Word Processor:
      Data Manager:
      Time Manager:
->    Communications:

F1 Help     F2 Edit text     F3 Blank text     F10 Finished
configure

CONFIGURE - change configuration settings
```

Fig. 1.6.

The fifth screen of the 3.20 Configuration menu.

Similarly, selecting Serial-1 and Serial-2 (COM1 and COM2) causes Smart to address the hardware directly, whereas selecting AUX causes Smart to address the COM1 serial port through DOS (see Tip 1.25).

1.20 Tip: Switch printers during a single session by changing the entry in the Configure command in the main menu. *3.10*

When you first install your system, the driver for the selected printer is copied to your Smart subdirectory (see fig. 1.4). Because printer drivers are not copied to a unique file name during installation, multiple printer drivers can coexist in your Smart subdirectory. When you switch printers, you must make sure that the appropriate drivers are available.

You can copy additional printer drivers (DVR) from the Graphics Drivers disk and additional font files (FNT) from the Printer Fonts disk. The names of the files on each disk, with a description of each file's use, are listed in Chapter 3 of *The Smart Release Notes* booklet in your documentation.

You cannot switch printers in midsession, however, if you have made entries in the Printer-Setup Printer-Codes menu. Changing printers is impossible because the PRINTxx.DSC file is read only when you enter Smart. (For more information on PRINTxx.DSC files, look at Tip 1.24 and Trick 1.38)

3.10 **1.21 Trap:** You cannot switch printers in midsession if you have changed your printer codes.

By executing the Printer-Setup Printer-Codes, you create a file named PRINTxx.DSC, where xx is a two-digit number corresponding to the number of the current printer selected on the Configure menu (see Tip 1.31). When you initiate a Smart session, this PRINTxx.DSC file is read, and the appropriate printer codes are stored in RAM. The inclusion of the printer number as part of the name of this description file indicates that the codes contained in the file refer to the corresponding printer.

If you decide to change printers during a Smart session, you can change the designation on the Configure menu. This action does not automatically revoke the code descriptions read when the session was initiated, nor does it cause a new PRINTxx.DSC file to be read. A new description file can be utilized only if it is read when you start a new Smart session.

If you need to use multiple printers in different Smart sessions, refer to Trick 1.38.

In SmartWare II, you can change printers on the Tools Preferences Hardware menu. Position the cursor next to the printer selection and press F6 to display a list of the available printers you selected during the installation.

3.10 **1.22 Trap:** The installation program can assign printer ports incorrectly if you are operating on a network.

In the default configuration, for instance, the Hewlett-Packard LaserJet printer is installed as Serial-1. On a network, however, you should execute the Configure command on command list 3 to change to Parallel-1.

Because a network-system printer is addressed by a user as a parallel printer, the actual connections between the file server and the printer can be parallel or serial, depending on the type of printer.

1.23 Trap: Peripheral settings redefined in the Configure command on the main menu do not take effect immediately. *3.10*

The settings you choose on the Configure menu are read only at the beginning of the session. If you change any peripheral's settings, such as printer or plotter port assignments (see figs. 1.4 and 1.5), you must press F10 to quit Smart and then initiate a new Smart session. All other changes to the Configure menu take place immediately, so you do not have to quit Smart for other changes to take effect.

1.24 Tip: If you select Serial-1 or Serial-2 for your serial printer, you must select the appropriate communications settings on the Configure menu. ***Both***

Selecting Serial-1 or Serial-2 (see fig. 1.4) causes Smart to write directly to the serial port, bypassing DOS. The DOS MODE command has no effect on the communications settings. You do not have to issue a matching MODE command at the DOS level.

If you select PRN as the printer port for your serial printer, however, you must issue one MODE statement for the communications settings and another to redirect the printer output to the communications port. For example, the following settings can be used for the Hewlett-Packard LaserJet printer:

```
MODE COM1:9600,N,8,1

MODE LPT1: = Com1:
```

These commands should be issued before starting Smart (see Tip 1.25).

1.25 Tip: To direct printer output through DOS to COM1, select AUX. ***Both***

By selecting AUX, you are still printing through DOS, but the extra step of directing output from LPT1 to COM1 is not needed (see Tip 1.24). You need only one Mode statement at the DOS level:

```
MODE COM1:9600,N,8,1
```

This command must be issued before you begin the Smart session.

1.26 Tip: The Characters Per Line setting in the Configure command at the main menu level only affects commands that print without an explicit line-length option. *3.10*

Commands such as Print in the Database and Print in the Spreadsheet lack options for specifying line length. The default line length for these commands is taken from the selection in the main menu Configure command. The Report commands, however, require a definition that includes a line-length setting—

report commands ignore the Configure line length. Your line length for these commands can be less than or greater than the Configure specification (see fig. 1.4, tip 6.12, and tip 11.14).

3.10

1.27 Trap: When you establish a paging file path in the main menu Configure command, the system does not check your entry for accuracy (see fig. 1.6).

If your paging path is entered incorrectly, no error occurs until the system tries to use the paging path when a Word Processor or Spreadsheet file overflows. Take great care when establishing your paging path, or you can lose part of your work.

If you enter the paging path incorrectly, the following error message can appear:

```
Page file creation failure
```

```
Emergency recovery #3-1: Paging problem - press any
key
```

The system does not freeze, but you cannot proceed with your work until the problem is corrected. The system advises you to exit as soon as possible.

In SmartWare II, you cannot enter into the Tools Preferences Global menu a paging path that does not exist. If you do so, you get the following error message:

```
Path not accessible (c:\pathname\)
```

When you press Esc, however, the Tools Preferences Global command is concluded, and the incorrect path selection is saved. This incorrect path selection is ignored.

3.10

1.28 Trap: If you do not specify a paging path on a two floppy-disk system, you cannot work with extremely large spreadsheets or documents.

If the paging path is left blank, the default is the root directory in drive A. Because little disk space is available on the system and program disks, which must be in drive A, you probably will get a paging error message if your application has to page to disk. If you have a two floppy-disk system, set your paging path to

```
B:\
```

so that paging occurs on your data disk in drive B.

Both

1.29 Trick: Press Alt-156 to use the British pound symbol for currency.

The standard IBM character set represents the ASCII code 156 as the British pound sign. To enter this screen character as your currency symbol (see fig. 1.3), select Currency Symbol, then hold down the Alt key and enter 156 on your numeric keypad while the pointer is adjacent to the Currency Symbol. When you release the Alt key, the symbol is entered on the menu.

Although this technique displays the British pound sign as the currency symbol on all Smart screens, you may need the dollar sign in some instances. In the Spreadsheet, for example, you must preface the entry with a dollar sign to enter a money figure into a cell.

Your printer may not be able to handle the new symbol correctly, so refer to your printer's manual for information. You may be able to define a printer macro to generate the correct code on your printer.

1.30 Trap: Date-style selection is crucial if you are using the Database. *3.10*

The date style defines how numeric dates are displayed and stored in the Database (see fig. 1.3). A Date field in the Database is actually a special alphanumeric field; the numerals are stored in the field in the style of the date selected on the Configure menu. If you change your mind later and want to change the display order, you must create a complex Query Replace definition to rearrange the numbers.

Fortunately, the default date style is MMDDYY, the most commonly used date style in the United States.

In SmartWare II, dates are stored as numbers in the Database; the numbers represent the number of days since the beginning of the 20th century. Day 1 is January 1, 1900. You can display the date fields in a wide variety of formats; use the Field Display Format selection to enter the options.

Printer Setup

1.31 Tip: Create a PRINTxx.DSC file with special codes or macros for your printer. *3.10*

In the Printer-Setup Printer-Codes command on the main menu, you can create a file named PRINTxx.DSC if you press Enter in response to the prompt for the printer number. The xx represents the two-digit current printer number as designated in the Configure menu (see fig. 1.4). This number does not represent the printer number you selected during installation.

If you already have such a file, the Printer-Setup Printer-Codes command is used to edit the file. The original file contents are derived from the file PRINTER.DSC. You also can create a PRINTxx.DSC file for a printer other than your default printer by supplying the printer number.

After you have changed the new file, it is stored in the subdirectory with the original PRINTER.DSC file. Remember that the PRINTxx.DSC file is read by the system only when you first enter Smart. Therefore, any changes you make will not be reflected immediately. You must exit Smart and then initiate a new session (see Trap 1.21).

3.10 **1.32 Trick:** Break a printer macro in two if it exceeds 15 characters.

Printer macros are limited to 15 characters (bytes) in the Printer-Setup Printer-Codes command at the main menu. If your macro is longer than 15 characters, you can split the macro in two and use one macro key to generate the first part and a second key to generate the second part. With some printers, the first part of many macros is repetitive (macros for font selection, for instance). You can take advantage of this repetition and use one macro as a preface for several other macros.

3.10 **1.33 Tip:** Use custom fonts 1 and 2 for commonly used alternate fonts, such as the letter-quality font.

If you like to print letter-quality text at some times and draft-quality text at others, you can assign custom fonts 1 and 2 (called 11 and 12 in the Font command) to invoke the mode you want. This feature is especially useful if you cannot select letter-quality printing from your printer's front panel or if the printer is not close at hand.

In addition to using custom fonts 1 and 2, you also can redefine the definitions of any standard font. For example, if you never use small caps, you can insert your own set of codes instead.

Refer to your printer's manual for the proper codes. Be sure to enter the codes to turn off letter quality, and move the highlighted block to indicate that both fonts are supported.

Although you can use a printer macro to accomplish the same task, the Font command is more straightforward, especially for common font selections.

3.10 **1.34 Tip:** Use the Printer-Setup Init-Sequences command to define and send initial codes to your printer (see fig. 1.7).

The Init-Sequences command lets you send initialization codes to your printer. The codes activate certain characteristics that you cannot create within the application command or from your printer's front panel. This command is entered from the main menu Printer-Setup menu.

For example, if you want to print in compressed mode in the Database, you can define and send the codes to your printer to activate the compressed type style. The codes you insert in the Init menu are the same as those you would use to set up a printer macro. Printer macros, however, can accept only 15 characters, but the Init sequences can accept 64 characters.

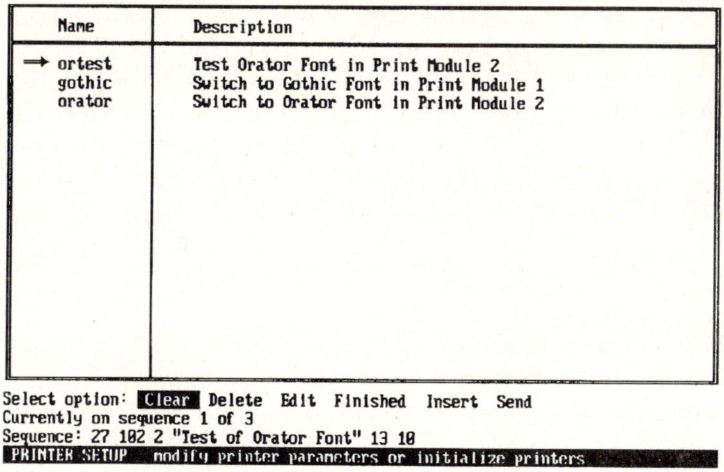

```
 Name       Description

→ ortest    Test Orator Font in Print Module 2
  gothic    Switch to Gothic Font in Print Module 1
  orator    Switch to Orator Font in Print Module 2

Select option: Clear Delete Edit Finished Insert Send
Currently on sequence 1 of 3
Sequence: 27 102 2 "Test of Orator Font" 13 10
PRINTER SETUP   modify printer parameters or initialize printers
```

Fig. 1.7.

Init Sequences.

The name you associate with the Init sequence can be up to eight characters long. Any uppercase characters you enter are converted automatically to lowercase. The verbal description of the Init sequence can be as long as 50 characters in upper- and lowercase.

You can enter text surrounded by quotes, ASCII codes, or hex numbers, preceded by an uppercase H. Refer to the Lprint command in Chapter 14 for an alternative method for sending codes from within an application module.

1.35 Trick: To test your printer codes, include a temporary text line in your Init-Sequence specification.

3.10

The control codes for some printers can be tricky, and the printer documentation can be complex. To test an Init sequence, enter sample text within quotation marks following the Init sequence to determine whether the code is correct. This trick eliminates the necessity to initiate an application module to test the code sequence. After you know the Init sequence is correct, edit it to remove the sample text.

Some printers do not print a line until they receive a carriage return and line feed. You may have to insert ASCII codes 13 and 10 following the text to force the return and line feed. Refer to the sample sequence at the bottom of figure 1.7.

1.36 Tip: Use printer macros to embed special codes in your text for activating special printer functions.

3.10

Printer macros can be defined in the Printer-Setup Printer-Codes command on the main menu. A printer macro is a set of codes that is sent to the printer in lieu of the single code you enter in your document. Use a high ASCII code not normally used in a text file; any number above 127 will work unless the number is used by another function.

When you establish the printer macro on the Printer-Codes menu, you enter the ASCII number that represents the special character. However, when you use the printer macro in a document, you must hold down the Alt key as you type the ASCII number of the printer macro on the numeric keypad. If you do not hold down the Alt key, you just enter numbers into your text. When you release the Alt key, the symbol is entered.

The macro itself can be entered in ASCII format or as text, depending on the examples in your printer documentation. Although you can enter text in double quotation marks, the menu shows that the Smart system has translated all entries to ASCII codes.

3.10 **1.37 Trap: The total number of Printer-Macro characters in the Printer-Setup Printer-Codes definition is 255.**

Each macro itself is limited to 15 characters. Therefore, if all your macros are 15 characters long, you can have up to 17 macros (15 × 17 = 255).

Although you can enter printer-macro definitions exceeding the 255-character limit, the system recognizes only the first 255 characters. A total of 64 printer macros can be defined.

3.10 **1.38 Trick: Use a batch file to select from among a set of PRINTxx.DSC FILES.**

If you need some macros at some times and other macros at other times, but all your macros combined exceed the 255-character limit, you can use a batch file to select the appropriate PRINTxx.DSC file when you enter Smart:

```
COPY   PRINT25.%1   PRINT25.DSC

SMART W
```

When you make entries to the Printer-Setup Printer-Codes menu, the PRINTxx.DSC file is created if you are executing this command for the first time. The PRINTxx.DSC file is changed if this is a later execution. The xx corresponds to the printer you have currently selected in the Configure menu on command list 3 of the main menu.

If your configuration indicates printer 25, for example, the system searches for the PRINT25.DSC file when you initiate a Smart session and inserts the printer codes into RAM. If your application calls for certain printer macros or other settings at some times and different settings at other times, you can use the DOS batch-file facility to make sure that the necessary description is available as the current PRINT25.DSC file.

Suppose that you need one set of printer codes for the Database and a different set of printer codes for the Word Processor. The following is a batch file to select the proper DSC file:

```
echo off
if !%1 == !w goto wp
if !%1 == !W goto wp
if !%1 == !d goto dm
if !%1 == !D goto dm
echo Bad Argument .. please restart
goto alldone
:
:wp
copy printwp.dsc print25.dsc > nul
smart w
goto alldone
:
:dm
copy printdm.dsc print25.dsc > nul
smart d
:
:alldone
```

The PRINTWP.DSC and PRINTDM.DSC files are printer code description files created by using the Printer-Setup Printer-Codes menu. After you create the first set of codes for the Database, quit Smart and rename the PRINT25.DSC file to PRINTDM.DSC. Use the Printer-Setup Printer-Codes menu to create the codes you want to use for the Word Processor. You should then rename the description file PRINTWP.DSC.

If you use this technique, you must remember to initiate Smart through the batch file rather than the directory, because the existing version of the PRINT25.DSC file will be the one leftover from the last time. For example, if you entered the Database previously through the batch file, the description file is the one needed for that module. Now, if you enter the Smart Word Processor directly, you'll have the wrong DSC file.

You also can select different printer code description files with different subdirectories, as outlined in Trick 1.1 in this chapter.

1.39 Trick: Use a batch file to select different printers. *3.10*

If you use different printers in the running your application, you can use a batch file to select the appropriate configuration at the time you initiate the Smart session:

```
echo off
if !%1 == !l goto laser
if !%1 == !L goto laser
if !%1 == !e goto epson
if !%1 == !E goto epson
echo Bad Argument .. please restart
goto alldone
:
:laser
copy c:\smart\configur.l c:\smart\configur > nul
smart %2
goto alldone
:
:epson
copy c:\smart\configur.e c:\smart\configur > nul
smart %2
:
:alldone
```

If you execute the batch file with argument E, the configuration for the Epson printer is used. Argument L uses the configuration for your laser printer. You must set up the configurations separately in the Configure menu on command list 3 of the main menu. Then exit the Smart system and copy the CONFIGUR file to the file CONFIGUR.E or CONFIGUR.L, for Epson or laser printers, respectively.

Even if you have executed the Printer-Setup Printer-Codes command to create PRINTxx.DSC files, the appropriate description file is read because the printers specified in the configuration files have different numbers. The description file for the Epson FX series is PRINT03.DSC, and the file for a Hewlett-Packard LaserJet is PRINT25.DSC (see fig. 1.3).

3.10

1.40 Trap: Do not attempt to use the Init-Sequences key to override the font-selection codes that Smart sends to the printer.

Sending the Init sequence for letter-quality mode is useless if your printer codes are set so that selecting the standard font always resets the printer to draft mode.

Although the code is sent to the printer from the main menu, selection of the standard font resets the printer to draft mode—if the appropriate codes are in the printer-codes file when you start printing a document.

Networking Smart

Depending on your application requirements and your budget, there are two ways you can install Smart in a network. The more expensive method performs better than the less expensive method—you get what you pay for.

1.41 Tip: To ensure best performance, install separate copies of Smart software on each computer in your network.

Both

With individual copies of Smart on each computer's hard disk, the Smart programs do not have to be transmitted over the network. Network traffic is limited to transmitting data records, documents, and worksheets. All the Smart programs, message files, overlays, configuration files, and so on, can be retrieved faster from a local hard disk than from a network file server. Network and file access contention is reduced, causing the programs to load faster. Smart runs at higher speeds when the Smart program is on your hard disk instead of a file server.

1.42 Tip: For greatest economy, install the Smart system on the file server, and purchase only LAN User Access modules for each workstation.

Both

If economy is more important than operating speed, installing the User Access modules on each workstation is less expensive than installing the complete system on each computer. Also, the individual computers do not need a hard disk to operate as a workstation.

Installing the User Access modules makes sense if your application does not call for heavy, simultaneous access to the same files. Using the modules is also more appropriate if users are unlikely to be executing the same module at the same time.

1.43 Tip: On a network, use your local hard disk as much as possible.

Both

Passing data and programs back and forth on a network can slow you down, so you want to try to use the hard disk of your work-station when possible. Keep on the network only those programs and files that are shared by multiple users. The following should be on local hard disks:

The paging path; use the Tools Preferences Global.

Temporary files, including database index files or temporary databases.

Wordprocessor custom dictionaries.

Part II

The Database

Includes

Creating, Modifying, and Working with Files and Views

Viewing Files and Arranging Data

Finding Your Data and Working with Multiple Files

Entering and Deleting Data

Producing Reports

Interfacing Files and Using the Query Facility

2

Creating, Modifying, and Working with Files and Views

The heart of a successful application is a good file design: one that matches the requirements of the job and that works in concert with the Database module. This chapter covers techniques for creating files and views and for loading or activating them so that your applications can work with them. Custom screen and view features are also covered. Techniques for loading and activating your database files and views are discussed. Other topics covered in this chapter include passwords, subdirectories, and the virtual-file facility.

Creating Files and Views

If you have more than a minimal application, you need to employ the virtual file facility of the Smart 3.10 Database. This topic, introduced in Chapter 1, is further developed here. Field declarations, their types, names, and positions within the file are discussed in this section. Several alternatives to using Counter fields also are presented.

2.1 Tip: Use the File-Specs (Smart 3.10) or Data Utilities Information (SmartWare II) commands to display and print file and field declarations as you develop your application.

Both

The Smart Database offers no data dictionary to govern the field characteristics throughout your application. You therefore need to keep track of common field names and declarations when the same fields are used in different files. Be sure to use the documentation facilities of these commands to view and print the details of your file as you build your databases. Your system is easier to work with if fields that have the same meaning in different files also have the same declarations.

SW II

2.2 Tip: In SmartWare II, use the Data Utilities Information command to display information about the current view. Look for the display of the field input masks to the right of your screen, beyond the initial visible display on most monitors.

If you want to see the input mask specifications, press the Ctrl-Right key when the cursor is on the Field header line.

SW II

2.3 Tip Use some of the Text-Editor function keys to help you locate and view portions of the Data Utilities Information display.

When you execute the Data Utilities Information command, the display is viewed in a mode similar to the Tools Text-Editor. Although you cannot change what you see on-screen, you can use some of the function keys. Use F3 to find a string, Alt-G to go to a specific line, or F9 to repeat either of these commands.

SW II

2.4 Trick: Use a project file to return certain information about the current file and view.

The trick is to execute the Data Utilities Information command, write the information to a disk file, then use the Fread command to read portions of the file and enter it into variables. The following is an example of reading the name of the current view:

```
local $inline $filename
tools file erase "fileinfo.dat"

Data utilities information
keys Alt-W,"fileinfo.dat",enter,esc

fopen "fileinfo.dat" as 1
fread 1 into $inline
let $filename = mid($inline,17,64)

message "The view name is: "|$filename
```

If the view has been loaded from a different subdirectory, the path is included with the file name.

3.10

2.5 Trap: If you are in Confidence Level 1, you can create a file with only Alpha, Numeric, or Date fields.

The other field types are not available at Confidence Level 1. To declare other field types, escape from the Create command and change your confidence level (command list 5).

3.10

2.6 Trap: You can create a database file with only 40 fields if you are in confidence level 1.

If you need to create a file with a greater number of fields, you should change the confidence level to 2 or 3.

2.7 Tip: Use fixed-length rather than variable-length files to reduce the number of open files. *3.10*

When a file is declared as fixed length, no PIX file is used. The number of open files therefore is reduced. Limiting the number of open files can be important when using Smart on a network or when the -FVIRTUAL switch is not used on a single-user system.

2.8 Tip: In Smart 3.10, variable length files minimize the storage of all fields types, not just alpha fields. In SmartWare II, only alpha and inverted fields are variable. ***Both***

You normally use a variable length file to save space if you have alpha fields whose contents vary greatly in length from record to record. Actually, however, all field types are considered to be variable in length in Smart 3.10. This includes date fields, numbers, SSN, and Phone. If the fields are empty, minimal disk space is used for them.

In SmartWare II, only alpha and inverted fields save you space in a file. Any numeric fields or fields that are based on numbers, such as date and time fields, do not save any space if they are empty.

2.9 Trap: If you add a field to a variable length file, even though the file is rewritten completely, "dead" spaces are not recovered. ***SW II***

In a variable length file, "dead" spaces occur if you increase the length of the contents of an alpha field. Because the records are variable in length, when you increase the size of the contents of an alpha field, the entire record is copied to the end of the file and the original location becomes "dead" space. Although files are rewritten completely when you add or subtract fields, the rewriting process does not recover the dead spaces. You must use Data Utilities File-Fix Data-File to reclaim this dead space in a variable length file.

2.10 Trap: If you create a new version of a database, using the old DBS file causes garbled data. *3.10*

If you create a file similar to an existing one and then restructure the data, erase the old file, and rename the new one, make sure that you use the new DBS file and not the old one. Using the old DBS file causes garbled data to appear and can damage your file.

2.11 Trap: The Create command does not flag as an error the declaration of multiple fields with the same name; therefore, unpredictable results can occur. *3.10*

If you declare multiple fields with the same name, you encounter problems in identifying fields and need to use field numbers rather than field names. When using a file created with the Relate command, identification can be uncertain.

Matching of fields in the Utilities Restructure command is awkward and unnecessarily time-consuming. You therefore should keep field names unique within a single file.

If you plan to upgrade to SmartWare II, be aware that duplicate field names absolutely are not allowed. If you have duplicates in Smart 3.10, you will have *major* problems when you convert to SmartWare II.

Declaring Fields

Both

2.12 Trick: Declare the most frequently used key field as the first field.

In a pop-up menu of field names, the cursor points by default to the first field name (see fig. 2.1). If the most frequently used key field is first, you therefore need only press Enter when executing the 3.10 command Order Key, Link, and Find, or SmartWare II commands Order Change Key, Window Link, or Data Find.

```
DEP  4
DEG AB
CAR  3
STREET 6 Greenville St
CITY Yarmouth
ST MA
ZIP 02675
 Available fields
 → k   1 SSN          2 FIRST        3 LAST        4 AGE
       5 SEX          6 MS           7 DEP         8 DEG
       9 CAR         10 STREET      11 CITY       12 ST
      13 ZIP         14 WAGE        15 STATUS     16 SKILL
   k  17 DEPT        18 PHONE       19 EMPDATE    20 PCT

[
F6 will select the current field
File: person3   Window: 1                    Page: 1  Rec: 7  ( 7 )  Act: Y
PRINT - print the current file, page or record
```

Fig. 2.1. *Field names displayed in a pop-up menu.*

Both

2.13 Tip: Position all frequently used or viewed fields at the beginning of the file or view.

If frequently used fields are at the beginning of the file, you can see these fields together on the first screen of a multiple-screen file when using the standard screen. You may be able to see all those fields together in browse mode when you specify Browse All.

3.10

2.14 Trap: Beware of conflicting field names and field abbreviations.

The Smart Database accepts not only field names, but also abbreviations in response to field prompts, as in figure 2.1. If you have an address (STREET) and state (ST) in a database, for example, you cannot use the field name ST for the state field if its declaration follows that of the STREET field, because Smart recognizes ST as an abbreviation for STREET.

2.15 Tip: Keep field names as short as possible for ease of use. *Both*

You can define a field name as long as 16 characters in Smart 3.10, or 20 characters in SmartWare II. In a very complex application, you sometimes must use all available characters to differentiate similar fields. Whenever possible, however, I recommend keeping the field names as short as you can. Field names are easier to type if they are short, and you are less likely to make mistakes.

2.16 Tip: In SmartWare II, you can use field numbers, rather than names, when referring to fields in a calculation or selecting them in a pop-up menu, but this is potentially dangerous. *SW II*

Using field numbers may help after converting from Smart 3.10 if you have used field numbers in your project files and Query definitions. In the long run, however, you should avoid using field numbers because a field's number may change if you add another field to a view or change the input order of the fields.

2.17 Trick: Keep field names as short as possible for maximizing output in the Print command. *Both*

When you use the Print...Report command in Smart 3.10, or Print View Report in SmartWare II, the default width of the column is the greater of the declared field width or the number of characters in the field title. In figure 2.2, the fields STATUS, SEX, and MS are 1-byte alphanumeric fields. Note that the STATUS field uses 5 columns because of the length of the field title.

```
SSN         STATUS SEX MS
-------------------------
345-98-7593 Y      M   M
498-48-3900 Y      F   S
239-87-8876 2      M   M
208-23-0300 2      M   D
887-63-5498 Y      M   M
598-44-5922 2      F   W
876-33-0989 Y      F   M
987-65-7653 2      M   D
387-59-8374 1      M   M
498-34-5998 2      F   S
776-39-8763 Y      M   M

Enter any key to continue

File: person3   Window: 1                    Page: 1  Rec: 1  ( 1 )  Act: Y
PRINT - print the current file, page or record
```

Fig. 2.2. The effect of field-name widths in the Print command.

2.18 Trap: A trailing blank in a field name is treated as part of the name and causes recognition problems. *3.10*

A trailing blank in a field name is not easy to spot. Much of the time the trailing blank does not cause a problem, but you can have difficulty under certain circumstances. When using the Merge command of the Word Processor to pick up data from a file sent from the Database, for example, no match is found to the field name in the first line of the data file unless you include the trailing blank inside the Ctrl-J...Ctrl-K delimiters. The other choice is to edit the data file and remove the trailing blank from the field name that is enclosed in quotation marks.

It is best not to have a trailing blank on a field name at all. Be careful, when declaring fields, to press Enter without pressing the space bar first.

SW II

2.19 Tip: Create a view with only project processing fields to take advantage of the features that a view has to offer. This technique may be easier and faster than writing the project processing code to accomplish the same tasks.

One way to prompt for values to go into Project Processing variables is to write a project file and use the Screen Print and Screen Input statement. You must type the row and column screen location positions and background and foreground color numbers. You can draw boxes by using the Screen Draw Box command. However, another way to accomplish this same task is to use a custom view.

In a custom view, for example, field positions can be assigned visually, without writing coding statements to locate specific rows and columns. Notes and boxes are easy to create and change. Rules for jumping, changing color, and error trapping are created easily. Depending on the complexity, these tasks may be easier in a project processing program.

When entering data, moving the cursor from field to field (or back to a previous field) is readily accomplished in a custom view; this may be difficult in a project file because you must write the code to accomplish each step.

SW II

2.20 Tip: The default value for a project processing variable field is assigned only when you update a record of the view. If you want the field to have a default value as soon as the view is loaded, use a project processing program to set the value prior to loading the view.

The field initially appears blank when you load the view. When you update or enter a new record and type a value into the field, the value is assigned to the variable and is available in all records of the view. A default value may be offered when updating or entering a record; you may accept the value or type a new one, as needed. If you want to have a default value without updating the view, you must use a project file to assign the value to the variable.

2.21 Trap: Project processing variables used in a view are declared Public with Module Lock. As with variables in project files similarly declared, the variables continue to exist after you return to the command level. Unlike variables declared in project files, variables created in a view cannot be unlocked while you are in the Database module.

SW II

Project processing variables declared via a view are unlocked when you quit the Database module. If the variables were created originally in the view, however, you cannot unlock them in the Database module or change them to a System lock. The Unlock command has no effect.

If you want project processing variables used in a view to have a System lock, rather than just a Module lock, you must declare the variables in a project file *prior* to being used in the view. When you quit to a different module, the variables continue to exist. You then may unlock them by name in a project file in a different module.

2.22 Tip: Omit a data entry message if you want to display the Enter/Update function keys.

SW II

When you create a field, the extended options offer the opportunity to add your own data entry message. This optional message can be used to provide a long explanation of the field, or may give allowable codes. The maximum length of the message is 100 characters. If you provide a message, however, the message replaces the Enter/Update function key display on the command lines. On the other hand, if you create notes in your view, you still can provide this additional information and not lose the function key display.

2.23 Tip: When creating a custom view and a database simultaneously, the field attributes are recorded in the custom and standard views. Later, you can modify either view independently of the other.

SW II

When you initially create a custom view and a database, you do not have separate questions about the characteristics or options for the display of the fields in the standard view versus the custom view. One set of responses establishes the display and operating features of the fields in both views.

After you save the view and file definitions, you may modify either the custom view or the standard view independently of the other to alter the appearance or characteristics of the fields in the view.

2.24 Tip: Move the cursor to the desired field before selecting the file creation or modify subcommand, because identifying the field by location rather than by name is easier.

SW II

If the cursor is already on the field, you press Enter to select the field. Among the subcommands to which this tip applies are:

Move Item Field
Delete Item Field

Edit Field
Create or Edit Calculation
Create or Edit Rule

SW II

2.25 Tip: When modifying a standard view, position the cursor on the field you want as the default first field when the view is loaded.

If you want the 5th field as the default first field when you load a standard view, for example, modify and then save the view while the cursor is on this field. When you load a standard view, if the cursor initially is on the wrong field, modify the view, move the cursor to the field you want, and press F10.

SW II

2.26 Tip: You cannot change the input order of fields in a standard view. You can move them to a new location, however, if you want to change the order.

If you want to change the prompt order of the fields in a standard view, you must move the fields to the new location, rather than changing the input order. Remember that a field is moved to the location after the destination column, not before the column.

SW II

2.27 Trap: If you want to make actual changes to a data file, not just changes to the appearance of a view, make sure the file is not loaded. An actual change to a data file takes place if you add a new field or change the size of an alpha field, for example.

If the file you are trying to change is loaded in another view, you are not warned of this fact until you try to save your changes. The error message you see is:

```
Unable to modify: Data-file in use elsewhere
```

You have to abandon your work (press Escape), unload the file, and begin all over again.

SW II

2.28 Tip: To delete several fields at the same time from a custom view, use the Delete Block subcommand. Despite the appearance of the prompt, you can delete only one field at a time if you use the Delete Item Field command.

To use the Delete Block subcommand, begin by moving your cursor to the upper left corner of the block. When you issue the command, you are prompted:

```
Move to corner and press Enter to mark area.
```

After you move your cursor and press Enter, you are prompted:

```
Are you sure? (y/n)
```

This prompt appears regardless of what is being deleted within the block. If the block contains fields, you also are prompted:

```
Delete fields from data-file also? (y/n)
```

Press *y* if the fields are to be deleted from the data file.

If you execute the Delete Item Field subcommand, however, a pop-up window displays the list of the fields, with the following notations at the bottom of the screen:

```
F2 Mode   F6 Select fld   F7 Remove fld
```

This leads you to believe that you can select several fields at the same time. Using this subcommand, you must select fields individually, however. As soon as you press F6 at the first desired field, field selection is terminated, and you are prompted if you want to delete the field from the Data file or just from the view.

2.29 Tip: When you are modifying a file and deleting fields, you are warned about the potential loss of data only for the first field you delete from the data file. *SW II*

The message you see is:

```
Warning: Some data may be lost when file is restructured,
press any key
```

If you delete another data-file field, the same potential for loss of data exists, but you are not warned. If you continue and conclude the modification of your file, the database is rewritten, eliminating the fields you deleted. If you change your mind, however, you can Escape from the File Modify command.

2.30 Tip: When changing the input order of fields in a view, fields with a length of 1 byte display only the first digit of the current order, which may be misleading. *SW II*

In figure 2.3, the Status field shows an input order of `1`.

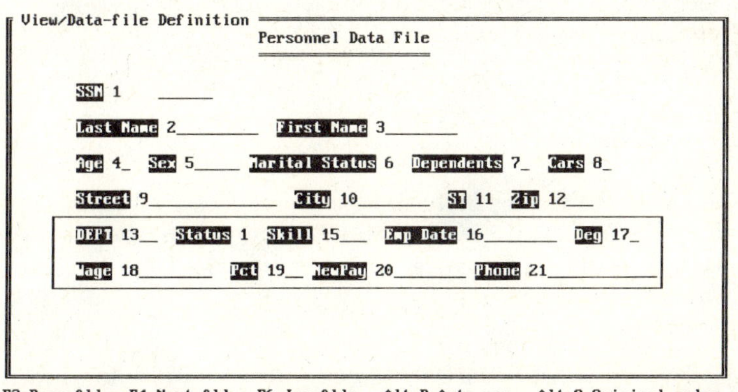

Fig. 2.3.
Truncated display of the input order of a short field.

Because the fields are in the Auto-Row order and because the field falls between numbers 13 and 15, it is safe to assume that the Status field is number 14. When you press F4 and pass through the field, the entire order number is displayed and remains displayed throughout the remainder of the execution of the Input-Order subcommand.

Be careful if you are changing the input order of the fields and have a 1-byte field with a two-digit order number. If you press Alt-R to change the input order automatically, any truncated field numbers are not repainted. The same number possibly may appear two times, as seen in figure 2.4:

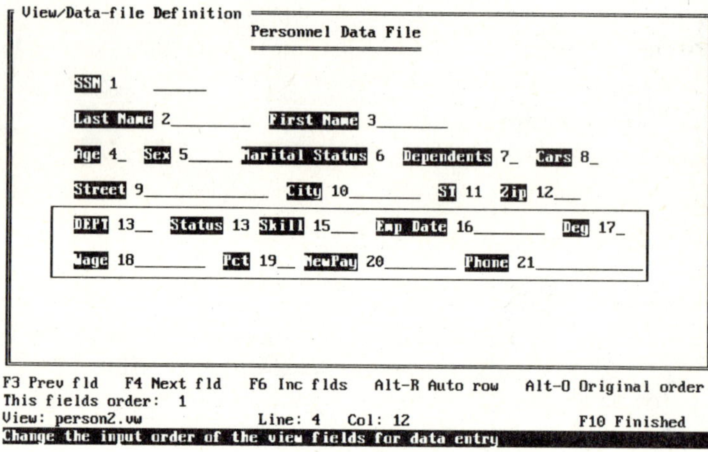

Fig. 2.4.
Duplicate display of input order of a short field.

To create this example, field 1 was changed to number 14, and then the Auto-Row order was invoked with Alt-R. Note that the DEPT and Status fields are numbered 13. You have to assume that the Status field actually is number 14.

SW II

2.31 Tip: When modifying a view, you have two opportunities to change the width of an alpha field, but they have different purposes.

When you edit an alpha field to change it, you are prompted:

```
Move to corner and press Enter to mark area. Lines: x Cols: y
```

This initial prompt refers to the display of the field within the view. It is possible to display less of an alpha field on the view than actually exists in the file. To increase the display width of the field, move the cursor to the right. To decrease the display width, move the cursor to the left.

Whether or not you change the display width, when you press Enter, the field options are displayed. On the second line is the specification for the field width. Change this value if you want to change the actual size of the field in the file.

Having a display width that is longer than the actual size of the field in the file is somewhat pointless. However, you may want to conserve space in the view by having a display width shorter than the actual width. When you enter data into an alpha field that has a display width shorter than the actual field width, the data in the field scrolls as you enter the data.

2.32 Trap: If you accidentally change the file width of an alpha field when modifying a file, the file is reconstructed even if you correct your mistake. *SW II*

When you change the actual width of the field, you are warned that some data may be lost. Even if you change the value back to its original setting, the file is rebuilt when you complete the file modification. Although this may not be time-consuming for a small file, if the file is large, the rebuilding may take some time. If you do not want the file rebuilt and if you will not have lost many other changes, press Escape to abort the File Modify command and return to the command level.

2.33 Tip: When modifying a view, if you delete a field accidentally, you can create the field again with the same name without losing any of the data. *SW II*

As long as the names are the same, you can recover from the inadvertent deletion of a field by creating a new one with the same name. A change in the field declaration usually does not destroy any data, unless you change from an Alpha field to one that is Numeric, Date, or Time. Even if you change from a numeric field to an alpha, the data is preserved, but in an alpha format.

Field Rules

2.34 Tip: Although you can create a jump rule to bypass a mandatory field, you cannot exit the record unless the mandatory field is completed. *SW II*

Although you may have a special reason for doing so, you probably do not want to design a view in which you jump over a mandatory field.

2.35 Tip: Create a Jump Rule to make a field conditionally mandatory. The rule should jump back to a previous field if that field is blank and if a specified condition exists. *SW II*

For example, suppose you must enter a [Spouse_Name] if the [Marital_Status] is "M". On the field following [Spouse_Name], create the following jump rule:

```
trim([Spouse_Name]) = null and [Marital_Status] = "M"
```

If both of these conditions are true, jump back to [Spouse_Name]. If the conditionally mandatory field is the last field in the view, you can create a "dummy" final field for the jump rule; create the dummy field as a 1 byte alpha field with a calculation of a single blank character (not a default calc).

2.36 Tip: Create a jump rule to validate field entries against a reference file just as the Lookup facility does in Smart 3.10. *SW II*

If you want to validate a code or other field in one database against a key field in another database, follow these steps:

1. Attach the reference database to the view. For example, if you have a personnel file as the main database of the view and you want to validate departments, attach the department data file to the personnel view.

2. Attach a field to display from the reference data file—Department Name, for example.

3. Edit this display field to make it read-only.

4. Create a rule to jump back to the link field. In this example, create a rule on the department name field to jump back to the department code if the following formula is true:

   ```
   isblank([])
   ```

   You also can use this formula:

   ```
   trim([]) = null
   ```

5. Edit the links between databases to complete the process of attaching one file to another.

Because the department name field is read-only, you cannot type anything into the field. The only way the field can get a value is from the Department file. The only way a value can be retrieved from the department file, however, is by typing a correct department code in the department code field. Therefore, unless you type a correct department code, you cannot continue with the entry of the record.

For best results, make sure that in the input order of the fields, the department name immediately follows the department code field.

SW II

2.37 Trick: Use a dummy view field to enable you to create a rule to jump to the next record.

Jump rules are used to jump to a specific field if a test condition is true. If a certain field value enables you to bypass the remainder of the fields in the view, create a final field on the view and jump to the field. This field should be read-only and can be a dummy alpha view field of 1 byte. If you do not display the title, you never even see the field.

In a table area, you can use this same technique to advance to the next record in the table. The dummy field should have a calculation of a single space, or the cursor stops on the field and blinks. You have to reboot your computer to get the cursor to stop. Use an underscore as the dummy field name to make the field as inconspicuous as possible.

2.38 Tip: Use a dummy field and a jump rule to advance from the last table record to the next main data file record.

SW II

First, create a dummy view field in the main data-file area, in a sequence after the fields in the table. This dummy field should be 1 byte in length, read-only. Then create a jump rule in the table testing both a condition and whether you are on the last table record. An example of a jump formula is:

```
[sex] = "F" and tablecount([sex]) = tablerec([sex])
```

The TABLECOUNT function provides the total number of records in the current table containing the field specified. the TABLEREC function provides the number of the current record in the table. If the two counts are equal and if the other condition is true, the rule causes a jump to the final dummy field in the view, and on to the next main data file record.

2.39 Tip: Use a dummy field and a jump rule to avoid being prompted to enter new data when you are updating data in a table area.

SW II

First, create a dummy, read-only view field following the table area. Then, create a rule on the last field of the table to jump to this dummy field if the following condition is true:

```
tablerec([]) = tablecount([])
```

Therefore, if the current record number in the table is the same as the total number of records in the table, the jump to the dummy field outside the table is taken, and the next main data-file record is displayed.

2.40 Tip: When creating a file, simple rules can omit the field name, but compound rules must specify complete field names.

SW II

If you are testing the field called [sex], for example, your rule can be:

```
= "F"
```

Note that the field name is not specified—the current field is assumed as the default. If the condition involves multiple fields, however, you must use either of the following two formulas:

```
[sex] = "F" and [Marital_Status] = "M"

[] = "F" and [Marital_Status] = "M"
```

The empty square bracket represents the current field. In these examples, the order of the field condition tests is unimportant.

2.41 Trap: The order in which you declare rules is the order in which they are executed. You cannot change the rules' orders without deleting rules and declaring them again.

SW II

If you have two jump rules for a field, for example, the first rule you create is executed before a second rule. If you decide later that you need to switch the order of evaluation of the rules, you have to delete the first rule and set it up again, this time as the second rule.

SW II

2.42 Trap: Field rules that are too complex may not be accepted when you try to create them.

The following rules for a field called [rate] are acceptable:

```
[] < 5.35
[rate] < 5.35
not ( [rate] < 5.35 )
[rate] < 5.35 or [rate] > 8.55
( [rate] < 5.35 or [rate] > 8.55 )
```

The following rule formula, however, is not acceptable:

```
not ( [rate] < 5.35 or [rate] > 8.55 )
```

If you try to create this rule, you get the following error message:

```
Invalid rule on field [rate]
```

The restriction applies to a compound condition negated with the NOT function.

SW II

2.43 Trap: An error rule is evaluated only when you enter data into the field to which the rule is attached. If you simply pass through a field that violates the rule, no error message results.

The order in which you enter or update data in a record can seemingly violate an error rule. For example, suppose that you have fields [field1] and [field2] with an error rule for [field2], such that an error results if the following rule is violated:

```
[] <= [field1]
```

If you enter the number 5 into [field1] and the number 6 into [field2], an error results because [field2] (6) is not less than or equal to [field1] (5). Of course, you can correct the error by entering 4 into [field2] and continue with the entry of the other fields in the record.

Potential problems arise if you update the record at a later time. If you change [field1] to a value of 3, you can press F4 or Enter to pass through [field2] without an error. In this case, [field1] is less than [field2], but no error message is displayed. Even if you retype the number 4 in [field2], no error results—only if you type a number greater than 3 in [field2] do you get an error.

SW II

2.44 Tip: Create a color rule on an important field to show if the record is deleted.

A record that is marked for deletion displays `DEL` in the lower right corner of the screen. Although this flag is displayed in red on a color monitor, the flag still is easy to miss if you are not looking for it. By having a color rule to indicate the deleted status, it is more obvious that the record is marked for deletion. The rule is:

```
Deleted
```

Use this rule to display the SSN or Part Number or some other important field in red if the record is deleted.

Bar and Pop-up Menus

2.45 Trick: Use a bar or pop-up menu to display more than you need to store in a field. The number of bytes stored in the field will be equal to the size of the field and you will not get an error. By displaying more than the field will hold, the menus can be more explanatory than they would be otherwise. *SW II*

An example of such a menu for an A1 field called [job] is as follows:

```
Cook Wait Liquor/Bar Bus Dishwash Host Manager
```

In this example, only the initial letters of the items in the menu are stored in the file. Just make sure that the initials are unique, or you will not be able to distinguish between the entries. If necessary, you can use numbers to identify the entries, as in the following:

```
1-Bus 2-Bar 3-Waiter 4-Cook 5-Host 6-Dishwash
```

In this example, an A1 field stores the digits 1 through 6.

2.46 Tip: Bar menu entries that are in uppercase appear in proper case in the menu, but they actually are entered in uppercase in the database. *SW II*

If you want uppercase data entered from a bar menu, the items must be typed in uppercase when you create the menu. You cannot use a mask to convert the items to uppercase at the time the record is entered.

2.47 Trap: Make a field mandatory even if there is a bar or a pop-up menu. *SW II*

A field with either a bar or pop-up menu defaults to the first item in the menu. With the cursor or the highlight block on any menu item, that item is entered into the field if you press Enter. If you press F4 to advance to the next field or F6 to advance to the next record, however, you are able to bypass the menu selection. Therefore, if the field is important and required on each record, make the field mandatory in addition to creating the bar or pop-up menu.

2.48 Tip: Position the most frequently used entries in a pop-up or bar menu near the beginning to make their selection faster. *SW II*

The menu entries are not alphabetized automatically, therefore enabling you to arrange them in any desired order. If the most frequent choice is first, for example, selection is easy because you simply press Enter—you do not have to move the cursor.

SW II

2.49 Tip: Write the pop-up menu contents to a file for documentation purposes. No standard provision exists to display this information after the file is created.

The command Data Utilities Information supplies much of the information about a view, but does not display the contents of the pop-up menus. While you are creating your pop-up menus, use the Alt-W key to write the menu contents to a file, which you then can print at a later time and save with your system documentation.

SW II

2.50 Tip: A field in a standard view cannot have a bar menu. Although you are not prevented from selecting a bar menu, the system defaults to a pop-up menu.

To use a bar menu, all selections must be able to be displayed across the view. A standard view, however, usually has no room. When you select Bar, the pop-up menu editor is displayed.

SW II

2.51 Tip: When using a bar menu for a field, display a data entry message to make the cursor position evident. Without this message, determining the location of the cursor often is difficult.

At all other times in data entry, you have no doubt about the cursor position. If you use a pop-up menu, the menu pops up when the cursor is on the field. If the field has no menu at all, the field is highlighted when prompted. If you use a bar menu, however, you may not know when the cursor is on the field. A data entry message will provide this information.

SW II

2.52 Trick: Use a project file to update the contents of a pop-up menu, based on the contents of another database.

Unfortunately, pop-up menus are not designed to be updated dynamically. The types of selections in a pop-up menu normally are relatively static items that do not change every day. For example, you are more likely to have job categories in a pop-up menu (Wait; Bus; Cook; Dishwash; Manager) than customer names. If you have a field that changes occasionally, however, you can use a following project file to make the pop-up menu changes for you (see fig. 2.5).

Window 1 contains a personnel file with a field called [DEPT] that holds a department code and has a pop-up menu that lists all the valid codes. Window 2 shows a department file. The following project file writes the department codes from the department file to an external file, modifies the personnel view, and imports the new department code list into the pop-up menu.

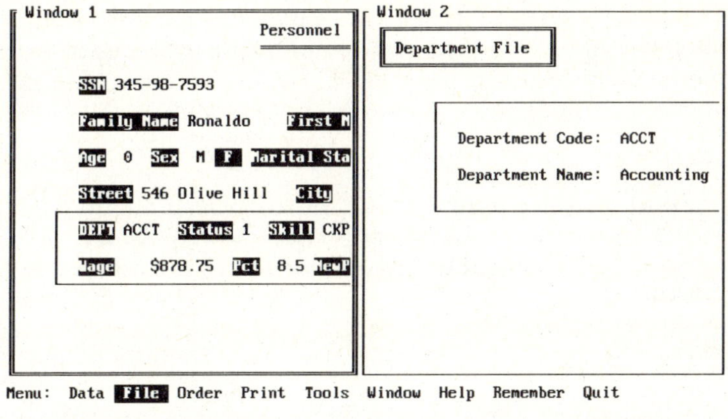

Fig. 2.5.
File examples for automated pop-up menu changes.

```
'go to the department file
data goto window 2
order change key "[DEPT]"
tools file erase "dept.dat"

'export the department codes text format
file export text row-format "[DEPT]" file "dept.dat"

'go back to the personnel file
data goto window 1
file modify custom-view "person6.vw"

'edit the popup menu for the DEPT field
keys "em","dept",Enter,"p"

'clear old menu items and read new ones
keys Alt-F2,"y",Alt-F3,"dept.dat",Enter,F8,F10,F10
```

On the last line of the project file, the previous pop-up menu list is cleared with the Alt-F2. Notice, also, that the first line of the new list is deleted with the F8 key; this is the field name that is generated by the File Export Text command.

Alpha Field Masks

2.53 Tip: Use braces {} in a field mask to indicate an optional entry. The location of the braces can have different meanings. If any entry is made inside the braces, the entire entry in the braces must be completed.

SW II

The following example is a mask for a phone number that is optional:

```
{###}-{###}-{####}
```

This mask allows entry of a phone number without the area code, because the braces surround each element of the phone number individually. None of the three elements of the phone number may be partially completed. If you want to require the area code, use the following:

```
{###-###-####}
```

In this example, the whole phone number must be entered if anything is entered at all. If you want a phone number, but don't always require the area code, use the following. This mask ensures that you must have at least the last seven digits of the number:

```
{###-}###-####
```

Finally, if you sometimes want just a "1" as a prefix, as for phone numbers in your same area code, use the following:

```
{{##}{#}-}###-####
```

In this example, you can move the cursor to the right to skip the first two positions of the area code and then enter just a 1.

SW II

2.54 Tip: If a default field value does not conform to the mask of the field, the default will be blank.

No error message is generated at the time you enter the new record, and no error is displayed at the time you save the field definition.

SW II

2.55 Tip: Because database keys use the ASCII sorting sequence, use a mask to force key fields to be the same case so that similar entries remain adjacent.

Most of the SmartWare II system uses the collation sorting sequence. Database keys use the ASCII sorting sequence, however, in which all uppercase letters sort before the lowercase letters. Therefore, any key field beginning with a lowercase "a" appears after an entry beginning with the uppercase letter "Z". To avoid this situation, use a mask to enforce case standards. For example, the following mask indicates 4 bytes, alphabetic, forced to uppercase:

```
*4au
```

If the length of the field may be less than 4 bytes, use the following:

```
*4{au}
```

Masks may be used only with alpha fields.

SW II

2.56 Tip: For a field mask to exclude two ranges, you must use the exclamation point once for each range.

If you want to exclude a-e and A-E throughout a 5-byte field, the mask must be as follows:

```
*5[!a-e!A-E]
```

You cannot use the following:

```
*5[!a-eA-E]
```

This second mask rejects letters in the range a-e, but allows those from A-E.

Using Calculated Fields

2.57 Tip: Set the recalculation mode to Immediate to view the results of field calculations as you enter the calculation factors. ***Both***

In Smart 3.10, use the Parameter command (command list 5) to set the recalculation mode of the Database. If you set the mode to Immediate, you can view the calculations as they take place. If the recalculation mode is set to Wait, the cursor stops at the calculated field, and you must press Enter, F6, F10, or [down arrow] to cause the calculation to be performed and to proceed to the next field.

In SmartWare II, the recalculation mode of each calculated field can be set individually. The three options are:

```
Immediate   Wait   Manual
```

During data entry or update, if the calculation is to take place as soon as the cursor enters the field, select Immediate. The cursor advances automatically to the following field. If you select Wait, you must press Enter to perform the calculation and exit the field. Manual calculation requires you to press Alt-F5, which displays and enables you to change the value.

2.58 Tip: If you add a calculated field to an existing file, use the Data Utilities Recalc-All command to enter the calculated values for calculation types that are Immediate or Wait. ***SW II***

Calculated fields normally are assigned a value during the data entry or update process. When the cursor passes through a calculated field, the result is inserted into the field. If you add a calculated field to an existing database, however, you do not want to go back and update each record manually.

One alternative is to write a replacement Data Query that performs the calculation. However, an easier way is to execute the Data Utilities Recalc-All command to figure the Immediate and Wait calculations. Manual calculation types are not calculated. If the view is ordered by an index, only the calculations in the available records are affected. The calculated fields do not have to be in the current view to be recalculated.

2.59 Tip: Position a calculated field after the fields that are the factors of the calculation. ***Both***

The position of a calculated field within your database or custom screen does not really matter, but placing calculated fields after the fields that are factors in the calculation may be beneficial. The calculation is performed correctly in any case, provided you have defined the calculation correctly. If you position the calculated field after all the factor fields, however, the resultant value will appear in the calculated field as soon as your cursor passes through the calculated fields. Seeing this calculation before proceeding with the rest of the record can be desirable, useful, or even necessary.

In SmartWare II, this tip is even more significant, because a calculated field may be classified as Manual, in addition to Immediate or Wait. If the field is manual, you must press Alt-F5 for the calculation to take place. If the factors of the calculation have not been entered, the calculation will be incorrect. In SmartWare II, use the Input-Order subcommand to set the entry order of the fields in the view.

Both

2.60 Trick: Do not place a calculated field in the final position on a screen.

If you want to be sure to see the calculation, don't make the calculated field the final field on the custom screen. If you do so and your parameter option is set to proceed to the next field when a field is full, the display immediately proceeds to the next record—and you have only a fleeting glimpse of the calculation. If you can observe the calculation, you may realize that one of your factor entries is wrong, and you can go back and correct the entry.

In SmartWare II, this suggestion applies only if the calculated field is Immediate. If the field is Wait or Manual, you must press Enter to exit the field, and therefore you have a chance to see the result of the calculation.

SW II

2.61 Trap: Define a view field as an Immediate or Wait type calculation if the field is based on other fields in the record.

If a view field is calculated immediately, each time a new record is accessed, the calculation is displayed. If you define the view field as Manual, the same value appears in all records of the file, regardless of the value of the factors in each record.

3.10

2.62 Tip: Calculated fields need not be displayed on a custom screen.

If you don't need to see calculation results, you don't need to allocate a position for them on your custom screen. Even when the field is omitted from the screen, the calculation is performed in the background when the factor fields of the calculation are filled in.

SW II

2.63 Trap: The factors of a calculation must exist in the view. Because this is not true in Smart 3.10, it may be a trap for you only if you are converting to SmartWare II.

If you use the program DBS_Conv to convert files and screens from Smart 3.10 to SmartWare II, the conversion process terminates abnormally if you have a calculated field that references other fields not available in the custom view. In

SmartWare II, this is not allowed. If it is necessary to minimize the display of the factor fields, you can make the fields read-only and 1 byte in length, located away from the primary viewing area.

2.64 Trick: Concatenate values from two fields to create the effect of a compound lookup key. *3.10*

When you define a lookup, you are validating a screen entry or retrieving data from another file. The linkage from the current file to the Lookup file, however, can use only a single field.

But what do you do if you need to use a combination of fields? Suppose that the combination of a Store Code and a Job Code at that store defines the rate of pay. You can create your RATE file with the following four fields:

```
Store Code
Job Code
Store/Job (a calculated concatenation)
Pay Rate
```

Make the Store/Job field the key field for the purposes of the lookup.

Your transaction file—file of job openings at various stores, for example—can have the same four fields as well as any other necessary fields. The lookup is defined so as to link the two files using the concatenated Store/Job field and to insert the rate into the job-openings file.

This technique will work with as many concatenated fields as you need, but remember that both the factor fields (the Store Code and the Job Code, in this case) and the concatenated field consume space in your detail file.

2.65 Trick: You must include a calculated field on a custom screen if the field is to be used as a linking field in a lookup to another file. *3.10*

If you use the technique outlined in Trick 2.64, the concatenated field used as the link-from field must be included on the custom screen. This field cannot be omitted from the screen, even though the field will have been calculated correctly nonetheless.

If you want to hide the field from view, you can position the field on page 2 of the custom screen, where the field is not as obtrusive.

2.66 Trap: Do not use a recursive calculation—the field will be calculated twice. *3.10*

A recursive calculation is one whose result is itself a factor in the calculation. If a calculated field is recursive, the evaluation actually is performed twice within each Update command: once at the beginning of the update of the record and again upon completion. Even if you update a record only once, you at least have a double calculation. And if you update the record subsequently, the results are even more inaccurate. Although the Smart Database does not flag a recursive field calculation as an error, you will not be satisfied with the results.

Both

2.67 Tip: Syntax errors in calculated fields are caught at the time of creation.

Syntax errors are recognized when you try to exit the calculation-edit screen. If you omit a square bracket from a field name, for example, the system buzzes and flashes a syntax error message at you.

Both

2.68 Trap: Field name errors in calculated fields are not caught until you attempt to complete the file definition.

If you misspell a name or enter the name of a field that does not exist, the system does not catch the error until you try to save the file by pressing F10. At that time, the following message appears:

```
Invalid field in equation for calculated field xx
```

The `xx` represents the number of the field. In SmartWare II, the name of the field is displayed.

3.10

2.69 Trap: Errors in complex calculations may not be caught until you try to execute the Enter command.

If you have an IF statement in the calculation, a misspelled field name on the right side of the equation may not be flagged. You may discover this only when you attempt to enter data. The error checking of calculated fields is not perfect, so be careful.

Both

2.70 Trick: Define a calculated field in the YYMM format to aid in monthly data analysis.

An alpha field defined in the YYMM format (for example, 8702) greatly aids you in monthly analysis. If you plan to aggregate detail files such as orders, invoices, or time and billing records, and send them to the Spreadsheet module, such a field is handy for monthly totals.

Because the year (YY) makes up the first part of the field, you also can sort the results into proper order. This field is calculated from an appropriate date in your file, such as the invoice date or order date.

You can use the following calculation in Smart 3.10 to calculate the YYMM field:

```
right([invdate],2) | left([invdate],2)
```

This calculation concatenates the two rightmost characters of the invoice date field (the year) and the two leftmost characters (the month). The text-concatenation operator (|) works here because a date field is simply an alphanumeric field, albeit a very special one.

This type of month-identification field can be used as the Row Field of a Summarized Write or Send definition, summarizing all records for the month. Queries are made easier because you can perform a test similar to the following:

```
[YYMM] = "8702"
```

rather than the more complex format using a regular date field:

```
days([date]) >= days("02/01/87") and days([date]) <= days("02/28/87")
```

In SmartWare II, use the following formula:

```
right(date2([date]),2) | left(date2([date]),2)
```

This assumes that you have configured the DATE2 function in your Tools Global Preferences to generate a date in the format MM/DD/YY or MM/DD/YYYY. Note that the DATE2 function is required in SmartWare II, because date fields are stored physically as numbers in the database. In Smart 3.10, dates are stored as alpha.

Note that this YYMM field must be an actual Data-File field and not just a view field, if you intend to make this field a key for use in optimized searches. You cannot create a key from a view field.

2.71 Tip: If you want to group dates by week, use a calculation to determine the Friday week-ending date of any other date field.

Both

The calculation is:

```
days([date]) + ( 6 - mod(days([date])-6 , 7 )
```

This formula provides a number that represents the Friday following (or equal to) the [date] field. If you need to display the number in a date format, use the formula as an argument to one of the Date functions:

```
date2(days([date]) + ( 6 - mod(days([date])-6 , 7 ))
```

2.72 Trick: Database field calculations can contain variables and functions.

Both

You don't have to restrict yourself to using only a field or constant in a field calculation. As shown in some of the previous examples, any of the valid functions are perfectly acceptable. You also can use variables or parameters in your calculations.

Take, for example, the problem of determining the tax for an item sold at retail. You can include the actual tax rate in the following field calculation:

```
[amount] * .05725
```

As we all know, however, taxes change. If you actually have the tax rate in the field calculation, you have to create a new file every time the tax rate changes or you sell an item to someone in another state. The following user-defined variable provides a better way to handle this situation:

```
[amount] * $taxrate
```

You set the value of the $taxrate variable in your start-up project files or in your invoice-printing project file.

Both

2.73 Trap: A variable used in the calculation of a field causes the value of the field to change if the variable changes. The following technique can prevent this from happening.

As covered in the previous trick, you can calculate the amount of a [tax] field by the following calculation:

```
$taxrate * [amount]
```

But what happens when the tax rate changes and you have to update the record? The [tax] field changes. Consider, however, the following calculation:

```
if [tax]+0 = 0 then $taxrate * [amount] else nochange
```

If a value already is in the field, the value does not change if you update the record. In SmartWare II, you can use this formula in a field calculation, or you can establish a default calculation:

```
$taxrate * [amount]
```

A default calculation takes effect only when a field is blank, but does not change the value of the field.

SW II

2.74 Tip: If converting to SmartWare II from 3.10, change the use of NULL in any calculations to BLANK.

For example, a record creation date calculation in Smart 3.10 can be as follows:

```
if [date] = NULL then today else nochange
```

Change this calculation in SmartWare II to the following:

```
if [date] = BLANK then today else nochange
```

In Smart 3.10, a field that has no content is NULL; in SmartWare II, it is BLANK.

SW II

2.75 Tip: Use different views if the calculation of a field will vary under different circumstances.

The calculation of a field is a function of the view, and not of the Database itself, because calculations are defined in individual views. If you want a field to be calculated automatically sometimes, use a view with a defined calculation. If you want to enter the value into the field manually, use a view without a calculation for the field. If the field is to be calculated in different ways at different times, you again can use different views. By contrast, in Smart 3.10, calculations are built into the database definition itself.

3.10

2.76 Trap: Field calculations cannot be changed without creating a new database.

After you complete the definition of a file, a field calculation cannot be changed. If the calculation needs to be changed, you must create a similar file, change the calculation, and restructure the data from the original file to the new one.

2.77 Trick: Use the Replace feature of the Query command in lieu of a calculated field. *Both*

By using the Replace feature of the Query command, you can insert data (either a constant or the result of a calculation) into a field. You have a great deal of flexibility when you use the Query. You decide which records are to be affected, what calculation is to be performed, and when the calculation is to be done.

The calculation used in Trick 2.72, for example, can be expressed as the following Query definition:

```
replace [tax] = [amount] * $taxrate
```

2.78 Trap: Using a query is slower than using a calculated field. *Both*

If you use a query instead of a calculated field, you must perform several additional steps, each of which is time-consuming. In Smart 3.10, if you can use a key field to identify the records upon which to use the Query command, you must perform the Key Update, order the file by the key, and finally perform the replacement query.

If you cannot use a key field, you can perform an initial Query to identify the new records, an Order to select them, and then the replacement Query. As an alternative, you can include the record selection as part of the replacement Query.

In SmartWare II, use the Data Query command.

2.79 Trick: Use the Let statement in a project file to assign a field value. *Both*

Under control of a project file, you can assign a value to a field. If you are entering records under control of a project file (see Tip 2.103), you can use the Let command to enter a value into a field.

2.80 Trick: A field in a calculation sometimes can be used as a "switch," rather than as a factor in the calculation. *Both*

If some customers are taxable and some are not, for example, you can have a field in your customer file that is a 1-byte alpha code in which you enter Y or N, indicating whether this customer is taxable.

In your invoice file, using the customer number, you then can perform a Lookup, extract the Yes/No alpha code, and use the following to help determine the tax:

```
if [taxcode] = "Y" then [amount] * $taxrate else 0
```

Both

2.81 Trick: Use a numerical field as an automatic switch.

Rather than using an alpha code, as in Trick 2.80, you can use a numeric code of 1 or zero and accomplish several tasks at the same time. Arithmetic rules define that a number multiplied by zero is zero, but that same number multiplied by 1 is equal to itself. By using a numeric switch of 1 or zero, the switch itself can act as the trigger for the calculation of the tax.

In this example, a 1 in the field indicates a taxable customer and a zero indicates no tax applied. The calculation in the invoice file then can read:

```
[taxcode] * [amount] * $taxrate
```

If the taxcode contains 1 (taxable), the tax is calculated as the amount multiplied by the taxrate. If the taxcode is zero, the result of the entire calculation is zero.

In Smart 3.10, an added benefit of the one/zero approach is that in the field-range specification of the custom screen in the customer file, you can specify a range of zero to one. Range checking in custom screens is discussed further in Tip 2.134.

Both

2.82 Trap: When defining field calculations with IF statements, be sure to repeat the full test condition for each sub-expression of the conditional clause.

For example, the following calculation may look right:

```
IF ( [CATEGORY] = 10 OR 85 OR 170 OR 172 OR 174 OR 176 OR
       608 OR 610 OR 700 )
THEN 0 ELSE INT(([MGPRICE]*.128*10))/10+.09
```

In fact, this calculation does not result in an error; the result will never be zero, however. The rounding following the ELSE always will be performed.

The correct way to test for multiple equality conditions on the same field is to treat them as if they were separate fields, as shown in the following example:

```
IF ( [CATEGORY] =  10 OR [CATEGORY] =  85 OR [CATEGORY] = 170
OR   [CATEGORY] = 172 OR [CATEGORY] = 174 OR [CATEGORY] = 176
OR   [CATEGORY] = 608 OR [CATEGORY] = 610 OR [CATEGORY]=  700)

THEN 0 ELSE INT( ([MGPRICE] *.128 * 10) ) / 10 + .09
```

This is a long way of writing the calculation, but it works correctly.

Both

2.83 Trick: Use the CASE function instead of a series of multiple-condition IF statements.

Another way you can do the same calculation as shown in Trap 2.82 is to use the CASE function, as shown in figure 2.6.

```
Formula Editor
IF ( case [CATEGORY] (10,1) (85,1) (170,1)
(600,1) (610,1) (700,1) else 0 ) = 1 then 0 else
INT(([MGPRICE]*.120*10))/10+.09
```

Fig. 2.6.
Using the CASE function in lieu of multiple-condition IF statements.

In the example, the CASE function returns 1 if the category is equal to one of the specified values in the parentheses, or zero if the category is not equal. The IF statement evaluates the 1 or zero condition, performing the calculation only if the result of the CASE is a zero. If not, the calculation itself results in zero.

2.84 Tip: Calculate alpha fields from numerics or numeric fields from alphas without having to use the STR, FIXED, VAL, or VALUE conversion functions.

SW II

An alpha field calculated equal to a numeric field contains the value displayed in the numeric field, provided the field is large enough. If the alpha field is too small, the content is truncated. If the display format of the numeric field rounds the number, the alpha field truncates the value unrounded if the field size necessitates.

Numeric fields also can be calculated equal to alphas. If the alpha field contains a valid number, the numeric field reflects the value of the number. If the field is all alphabetic, the result is zero. If the alpha field begins with a number, conversion is from left to right, and halted at the first non-numeric character, similar to the VAL or VALUE functions.

2.85 Tip: Use the FETCHFIELD function in a default equation so that a field repeats the contents from the same field in the previous record.

SW II

Consider the following field default equation:

```
fetchfield([dept])
```

This equation repeats the [dept] field from record to record. Because the equation is only the default, rather than a calculation, you can change the contents when a new department is encountered. A view with this equation saves you from having to press F9 to repeat from the previous field.

If you are starting with an empty database, you do not want to try to repeat when you are entering the first record of the file. You should use the following equation:

```
if record > 1 then fetchfield([dept]) else blank
```

This equation prevents an error message when entering the first record.

SW II

2.86 Trap: The FETCHFIELD function in a calculation references data from the record last *accessed*, not necessarily the record immediately prior in the logical or physical order of the file.

If you go from record 10 to record 9, the FETCHFIELD function references fields from record 10, rather than from record 8. This may be an advantage in certain applications, but you need to be aware that the reference is not to the record located immediately before the current record, but to the one accessed immediately prior to the current record.

SW II

2.87 Trick: Replicate a field calculation by writing it to a file and then reading the file contents into the calculation definition of the new field.

When you create the calculation of the first field, before you press F10 to save the calculation, press Alt-W and write the calculation to a file. (It must be a new file.) Now press F10 and proceed to the next field.

When you are in the calculation formula editor of another field, press Alt-F3. You are prompted for a file name, and you should type the name of the file you just created. The definition is read from the external file. Make any necessary changes and press F10 to save the file.

SW II

2.88 Tip: Do not create a jump rule to bypass calculated fields if you expect to see the results of the calculation appear within the view.

The result of an immediate calculation appears only if the cursor can pass through the field. If you jump over the field, you don't see the result, but the calculation is performed when you advance to the next record. The only thing you lose is the visual verification of the calculation result.

SW II

2.89 Tip: Create a manually calculated view field if you want the same value to appear in the field in all records of the file.

If a view field has a manual calculation, after you perform the calculation (press Alt-F5), the value is assigned to the field in every record of the view while the view is loaded. When the view is unloaded, the value is cleared. When you load the view again, the calculated view field is blank.

SW II

2.90 Trap: In a project file, the Recalc command cannot display the recalculated value of a field that is not available in the view or has not been selected in a Data Browse Fields command.

Although you have a calculated field in your file and have changed the factors of the calculation, if the field is not available, the Recalc command has no effect and you do not get an error message.

If you use the Data Browse command to display only certain fields of your file and exclude the calculated field, you must change the display to include the field by using the Data Browse Off command or by issuing a new Data Browse Fields command.

Not all the factors of a calculation have to be available, however. If a field that is a destination of an assignment statement has not been selected in the browse, the error message to the assignment is:

```
Invalid LET or command target
```

The calculated field remains unchanged. If an unchanged factor field is not available in the selection of browsed fields, the calculation proceeds without error, as if the field is present.

2.91 Trap: The NA function in a database calculation can be used to indicate missing data, but does not block the summation of a report grand total. SW II

For example, you can create a view field with the following calculation:

```
if isblank([WAGE]) then na else [wage]
```

The field displays and prints NA if the [wage] field is blank. In the Spreadsheet, a cell with NA causes a calculation using the cell also to appear as NA. In the database, however, this is not true. The following is a report with an NA field:

DEPT	*WAGE*	*NA Wage*
MKTG	$2,564.33	$2,564.33
MFGR		NA
ACCT	$3,365.86	$3,365.86
SALE	$2,626.61	$2,626.61
DATA	$654.34	$654.34
Grand	$9,211.14	$9,211.14
Total	========	=====

If the NA function worked in the Database as it does in the Spreadsheet, the grand total of the left column of the report would be NA.

Using Running-Total Fields

2.92 Tip: Declare a numeric field with a running total to maintain a total of that field for all records of the database. 3.10

If you include a Running Total declaration with a numeric field, the system maintains a running total of the contents of this field (see fig. 2.7). Through use of the Totals function or the Running-Totals option of the File Specs command, the running total can be readily accessible through a project file or the F-Calculator.

A running total may be useful in a checkbook application (like the one in fig. 2.7) or in any other application in which a running total of a field's contents throughout the file would be meaningful. If you have a separate file of invoice data for each year, for example, the running total of the TOTAL field represents

Fig. 2.7.

A file declaration with a running total.

```
Creating file
    Fld No | Title      | Type | Length | Running Total
       1   | DATE       | D    |   8    |
       2   | PAYEE      | A    |  20    |
       3   | NOTATION   | A    |  25    |
       4   | DEBIT      | N2   |   8    |      Y
       5   | TAXFLAG    | A    |   1    |
       6   | STATUS     | A    |   1    |

F3 Calc fld  F7 Insert field  F10 Exit     PgUp Prev page   Home First entry
F4 Del calc  F8 Delete field  Esc Abandon  PgDn Next page   End  Last entry
Title can be up to 16 characters long

CREATE - creates a new file or screen
```

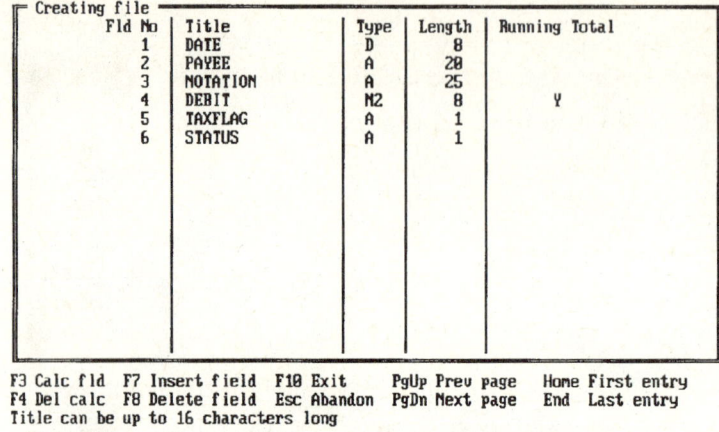

your year-to-date figure. Similarly, in an accounting application, you typically expect the running total of the debits and credits to be zero. A non-zero total indicates that your accounts are out of balance.

3.10 **2.93 Trap:** The running total declaration cannot be used to subtotal on a break field.

If your database contains data for multiple years, you cannot use the running-total facility to obtain separate totals for 1986 and 1987. To obtain such totals using this facility, you must have a separate database for each year. Even the use of an index to limit your view of the database does not change the total calculation.

Using Counter Fields

Both **2.94 Tip:** A counter field can be declared to increment automatically for each new record entered into the database.

As you enter records into your database, the system increments the counter field for you. Typically, you may use this type of field in an accounts-payable or check-writing application, or in any application with preprinted numbers on forms such as invoices. If you needed to sequentially number applicants, books, or parts, you can use counter fields, which are declared as six digits.

When you first create a file containing a counter field, the counter field of the first record you enter contains 1, the next record contains 2, and so on. If you need to begin the count with a number other than 1, look at the following tip.

2.95 Tip: In Smart 3.10, use the Utilities Alter-Count command (command list 2) to change the count value. In SmartWare II, the command is Data Utilities Change-Count. *Both*

The prompt for the count is:

```
Enter the new count:
```

The two options are:

```
Next Renumber
```

If you choose Next, the counter field in the next record you enter will contain the number you entered as a response to the prompt. If you choose Renumber, the counter field in the first physical record in the file will contain the number, and each sequential record will be incremented by 1. The increment is always 1; you have no choice about this.

The setting of the Next number is file-dependent. Other files loaded currently that have counter fields are not affected. The Next setting is retained with the file between Smart Database sessions. You don't need to reset the count each time.

2.96 Tip: Use the Utilities Alter Count Renumber command to change a counter field on a network by loading the database without the network driver. *3.10*

On a network, you ordinarily cannot renumber counter fields when databases are loaded using the network drivers. If you enter Smart without the network driver, however, you can renumber these counter fields.

2.97 Trap: The values in a counter field change if the field is used in a Relate command. *Both*

In Smart 3.10, after a counter field is transferred to a new file by means of the Relate command, the numbers in the counter field change their values and you are unable to tie the numbers back to the original settings.

If you are using a counter field as an invoice number, for example, the invoice number will be different when the field is copied to a new file in a Relate command. The original field contents are not retained in the new file. Therefore, a report containing invoice numbers is confusing if the report is printed from this new file.

In SmartWare II, although the correct counter field values are carried forward into the new file as a counter field, the count of any new records begins with 1. Therefore, you may have duplicates if you add any records.

2.98 Trick: Use a Query to save the value of a counter field permanently. *Both*

If you declare one field as a counter field and another as a regular six-digit numeric field, your database can store the value of a counter field permanently. After the day's records are entered, you can perform a query such as:

```
replace [realcount] = [counter]
```

where [realcount] is the ordinary numeric field and [counter] is the counter field.

This useful solution solves the problem of counter fields changing, although it is a little wasteful of disk space. Unless you use a query to get a subset of the files to limit your view of the file to just those new records, the replacement query can take a long time.

Both

2.99 Trick: Use two almost identical files to avoid the problem of a counter field changing values.

The two different files should be of identical structure, except that one is a real numeric field and the other is a counter field. Enter the new records into the temporary file with the counter field. The system increments the values in the counter. At the end of the day's entries, you can restructure the temporary file onto the permanent one, thus freezing the invoice numbers into the real field. In Smart 3.10, you must perform a Utilities Restructure command instead of concatenating the files, because a concatenation requires that the two files have identical structures.

Both

2.100 Tip: Use the Utilities Purge command to delete records from a temporary file and maintain counter values. In SmartWare II, the command is Data Utilities Purge.

If you use the method in Trick 2.98, use this technique to make sure the temporary file begins with the correct counter value in the next Smart Database session. Use the Query command to delete all records, then purge the records with the Utilities Purge command. The starting record count will be maintained the next time you load the file. Although this operation can be time-consuming, it is probably the safest way.

Both

2.101 Trick: Use a Query employing the record number to establish an incrementing field.

Rather than declare a counter field, you can declare a regular numeric field (for an invoice number, for example) and enter your data into the new record just as you would normally. Leave the invoice number field null. After you enter as many records as needed, perform two queries. The first query limits the view to those records you just entered. The query could look like the following:

`[invoice] = null` (Smart 3.10)

`[invoice] = blank` (SmartWare II)

The second query would look like the one in figure 2.8.

```
Query Editor

    replace [invoice] = precords + record - records
```

Fig. 2.8.

A query to create sequentially numbered fields.

The Smart functions in the query have the following significance:

- Records is the number of physical records in the file.
- Record is the logical number of the record within the indexed view.
- Records is the number of records in the indexed view.

If you already have 100 records in your file and add two more, the formulas evaluate as follows:

Additional record	Invoice	Precords	Record	Records
First	101	102	1	2
Second	102	102	2	2

2.102 Trick: Sequential numbering of a numeric field can be controlled within a project file.

Both

If you are entering new records under the control of a project file, you can use another way to enter a field similar to a counter. You can maintain a file on your disk that has the number of the counter (or invoice or check) last used. Within your project file, you can use the file access commands to read this number and write the number back out, having incremented the number for each of the new records.

The following is an example of such a project file in Smart 3.10:

```
fopen "invoice.num" as 1
fseek 1 0
fread 1 into $invoice

let $invoice = val($invoice)
let %1 = $invoice
message Most recently used invoice was %1 ...\
    press any key to continue
input $yn Do you want to change it?
if upper($yn) = "N" then jump nudder
input $invoice Enter Number of most recent invoice:

label nudder
let $invoice = $invoice + 1
enter blank
update only-one
let [invnum] = $invoice
```

```
input $yn Do you want to enter another?
if upper($yn) = "Y"then jump nudder

fseek 1 0
fwrite 1 from $invoice
fclose 1
```

Note that the project file adds one record and then displays the screen for updating just that record. When the update is done, the invoice number is set equal to the newly incremented user variable $invoice.

Both

2.103 Tip: You can use a calculated field as a substitute for a counter field.

The following is a substitute calculated field:

```
if [recno] = null then precords else nochange
```

If the record number ([recno]) of the current record is null, the record number of the new record is inserted into the field. (In SmartWare II, test the field equal to blank.) After this value is calculated, the value cannot change.

This technique avoids most counter field problems, but be aware of some other potential problems. If you delete and purge some records, you have duplicate counter fields. For example, by deleting record number 1, record 10 becomes 9. If you had 10 records to begin with, the next record you enter becomes number 10.

Note that if you plan to enter the records with the Read (3.10) or File Import (SmartWare II) command, rather than the Enter command, the formula must be

```
if [recno] = null then precords + 1
```

The formula must be different, because the first new record will not have been recognized in the sequence to be used correctly by the calculation.

Choosing Numeric or Alphanumeric Fields

Both

2.104 Tip: Declare ZIP code fields as alpha rather than numeric, so that leading zeros are retained.

If you already have defined the field as numeric, create a new file with the field declared as alpha and perform a Utilities Restructure command.

In SmartWare II, if you change the field type from Numeric to Alpha, the values are retained. You do not have to perform a Data Utilities Append command to transfer the data into a new file.

3.10

2.105 Trick: Use a companion alpha field to display commas if a numeric field is so large that commas are needed for clarity.

Commas cannot be included in numeric fields in the Smart Database. In some circumstances, however, your numerics can be so large that you need commas in order to read the fields clearly. You can specify the printing of commas for numeric fields in the report generator. If you want to display numbers with commas in your file, however, you must use a calculated alpha field. The following is an example of such a calculation for numbers between 1,000,000.00 and 9,999,999.99:

```
left(fixed([field1],2) ,1) | "," |
mid(fixed([field1],2) ,2,3)  | "," |
right(fixed([field1],2) ,6)
```

In SmartWare II, use the display format of the extended field options to display commas in a numeric field.

2.106 Trick: Save disk space by using an alpha field to store numbers.

SW II

Numeric fields always consume 8 bytes in a database, regardless of the size or type of number stored. In most cases, this may not be a problem. If you have a large database with a numeric field that is always small, however, you may use an alpha field to store the number. If you have a number that does not go over 99, you can declare an alpha field of 2 bytes. In this example, you save 6 bytes for each record of your database. Use a mask of "##" to guarantee that the contents are numeric. You also may want to make the field right-justified, so that the digits align as in numeric fields.

You cannot use an alpha field in a calculation, even if the alpha field does contain a number. You can declare a view field that is calculated as the value of the alpha field, however. You then can multiply the view field by another value or use the field in other numerical calculations, such as a report breakpoint or a cross tab.

If the alpha field is named [alpha_value], for example, the calculation for the numeric, view field would be:

```
value([alpha_value])
```

If the number possibly may ever be numeric, be sure to allow an extra byte in the alpha field for the minus sign.

2.107 Trick: Save disk space by using binary fields to store numbers.

SW II

As mentioned in the previous trick, numeric fields always consume 8 bytes in a database record. If you have a number that may be as large as five or six digits, you may not want to bother storing the number in an alpha field, because you would not save as many bytes.

However, you also may store a number in binary format. Using this technique, you can store a positive integer up to the value of 255 in 1 byte, and up to 65,535 in 2 bytes. The trick lies in recognizing that each byte in a computer file can have

256 values. Although entering (and remembering) the character representation of each of the 256 ASCII values would be awkward, you can enter the value into a view field and calculate the actual alpha field.

You probably also want a calculated view field to translate the value of the alpha field from base 256 back into base 10, using the ASC function.

The following are file declarations for using a 1-byte alpha field to hold a positive integer with a maximum value of 255. (Remember that zero makes the 256th value.)

1-byte field:

Field	Data-file Table	Data Type	Length	Entry Status	Display Format
bo_In		N	8	R/W	0r
bo_bin	binstor	A	1	R/W	
Calc: if isblank([bo_in]) then nochange else chr([BO_In])					
bo_out		N	8	R/W	0r
Calc: asc([bo_bin])					

The fields [bo_in] and [bo_out] are view fields; field [bo_bin] is the only field actually in the database. Notice that the calculation of [bo_bin] uses the function CHR to convert the number in [bo_in] into a 1-byte character. If you enter the number 42 into [bo_in], for example, the character "*" is stored in [bo_bin]. On the output side, the number 42 is displayed in the [bo_out] field, because ASC("*") = 42. In this example, you may want to have an error rule on the [bo_in] field to prevent the entry of a value greater than 255. If you need to store a positive number larger than 255, you need larger alpha fields. Following are the declarations for a 2-byte field needed for a number up to 65,535, and a 3-byte field needed for a number up to 16,777,215.

2-byte field:

Field	Data-file Table	Data Type	Length	Entry Status	Display Format
oh_in		N	8	R/W	0r
oh_bin2	binstor	A	1	R/W	
Calc: if isblank([oh_in]) then nochange else chr([oh_in]/256)					
oh_bin1	binstor	A	1	R/W	
Calc: if isblank([oh_in]) then nochange else chr(mod([oh_in],256))					
oh_out		N	8	R/W	0r,
Calc: asc([oh_bin2])*256 + asc([oh_bin1])					

3-byte field:

Field	Data-file Table	Data Type	Length	Entry Status	Display Format
ann_in		N	8	R/W	0r
ann_bin3	binstor	A	1	R/W	
Calc: if isblank([ann_in]) then nochange else chr([ann_in]/(256*256))					
ann_bin2	binstor	A	1	R/W	
Calc: if isblank([ann_in]) then nochange else chr([ann_in]/256)					
ann_bin1	binstor	A	1	R/W	
Calc: if isblank([ann_in]) then nochange else chr(mod([ann_in],256))					
ann_out		N	8	R/W	0r,
Calc: asc([ann_bin3])*256*256 + asc([ann_bin2])*256 + asc([ann_bin1])					

In each of these examples, the numbers are positive integers. The following is an example of a positive number with two decimal digits, such as you may have with a price field. The maximum value in this example is 655.36.

Field	Data-file Table	Data Type	Length	Entry Status	Display Format
price_in		N	8	R/W	2r
price_bin2	binstor	A	1	R/W	
Calc: if isblank([price_in]) then nochange else chr(100*[price_in]/256)					
price_bin1	binstor	A	1	R/W	
Calc: if isblank([price_in]) then nochange else chr(mod(100*[price_in],256))					
price_out		N	8	R/W	2r$
Calc: asc([price_bin2])*256/100 + asc([price_bin1])/100					

Finally, if you possibly may have to store a negative number as well as a positive number, you have to give up one bit. In 2 bytes, you can store +/– 32,767. Note that this is half of the number you can store if the number is always positive. The declarations are as follows:

Field	Data-file Table	Data Type	Length	Entry Status	Display Format
mo_in		N	8	R/W	0r
mo_bin2	binstor	A	1	R/W	
Calc: if isblank([mo_in]) then nochange else chr((abs([mo_in])/256) + (([mo_in] < 0) * 128))					
mo_bin1	binstor	A	1	R/W	
Calc: if isblank([mo_in]) then nochange else chr(mod(abs([mo_in]),256))					

Field	Data-file Table	Data Type	Length	Entry Status	Display Format
mo_out		N	8	R/W	0r,

```
Calc: if ( asc([mo_bin2]) >= 128 ) then
      -1 * (( asc([mo_bin2]) -(asc([mo_bin2]) >= 128) * 128 ) * 256
      + asc([mo_bin1])) else
      asc([mo_bin2])*256 + asc([mo_bin1])
```

If you use these techniques, the savings in disk space can be considerable. If you have a record with 36 numeric fields, for example, but you need to store only +/–10,000 in each field, you need 2 bytes per alpha field, instead of 8 bytes for an actual numeric field. This is a savings of 6 bytes per field, which is 216 bytes per record. If you have 10,000 records, this totals 2,160,000 bytes saved. Not only do you save disk space, but, on a network, you have to transfer fewer bytes from the server to each workstation.

Of course, such an approach is not without drawbacks. The process of using alpha fields to store numbers in binary format is complicated, and time-consuming to create. And because you must use a view field to calculate a decimal number to use in your application, the calculation of the view fields consumes computing resources.

Replicating Fields and Files

SW II

2.108 Tip: When you replicate a data file in SmartWare II, the key declarations from the original file are retained.

By contrast, in Smart 3.10, when you create a similar file, the keys are not declared automatically in the new file. In a project file you translate from Smart 3.10 to SmartWare II, if you replicate a file, delete the Order Key Add commands for the new file.

SW II

2.109 Trap: You may not be able to use the Tools File Copy command to copy a database file (DB) and a view (VW or VWS) to create an entirely new database; you run the risk of destroying the original data!

When you create a view, you embed within the view not only the names of the databases that are attached to the view, but you also may specify the subdirectories in which the databases are located. You observe the names of the database subdirectories when you execute the Data Utilities Info command. If you have a view that is attached to a file named \hres\PERSON.DB and you use the Tools File Copy command to make a copy of the view, for example, the new view still is attached to the original file \hres\PERSON.DB. If your intent is to make a second copy of the database and then delete the data from the new view, you find that you have deleted the data from the original file! Fortunately, if you also copied the DB file, you have an intact copy of the data.

If you attach a file without specifying a subdirectory, the default subdirectory is that from which the view is loaded. In this case, you have no problem about copying the view and database to a new subdirectory.

To safely make a new view and a new database without any records, use the File Create command with the replicate option. If you want a copy of the data that was in the original file, use the Data Utilities Append command. As a shortcut, you also can copy the DB file from the original name to the new database name, overlaying the file you created during the replicate process.

For a shortcut method of emptying a database of all records, refer to Appendix A.

2.110 Tip: Use the F9 and Alt-X keys when creating or modifying a view. The keys work with the file creation subcommands just as they do at the menu level of the Smart modules. *SW II*

If you have several Notes to move, for example, rather than pressing MIN (Move Item Note) for each note, after you have moved the first note, just move the cursor to the next note you want to move and press F9. This repeats the most recent subcommand. Similarly, if you want to execute a subcommand that is similar to the previous subcommand, but needs some editing, use the Alt-X to display the command to make the command available for editing.

Multiple File Views

2.111 Trick: You can control the default display fields in a table by positioning the fields before you save the table. *SW II*

A view table does not have to display all the fields at one time. If you do not necessarily want the field in column 1 displayed in the table as a default, when creating the table, shift the display of the fields in the table so that the desired column is shown on the left before you press F10 to save the table definition. The selected field and the other fields to the right are displayed as a default, filling the table area as much as possible. Additional fields to the left and right of the table area are available if you go to the table and use the right and left cursor keys or the Ctrl-Right and Ctrl-Left keys.

2.112 Trick: Create a new standard view for a file to be used in a table if you don't like the standard field names. *SW II*

You are not restricted to only one standard view for a file. When you define a table within a view, you are prompted for the name of a standard view to display in the table, *not* for the name of the data file. Therefore, if you want to display alternate field names for the columns of the table, attach an alternate standard view, one in which you have changed the names of the fields. Because this new standard view reflects the desired file, the correct data is displayed in the table.

SW II

2.113 Trick: Chain multiple files together to create a view that displays data several levels deep.

Consider the following files in an application:

Sales File	**Inventory File**	**Mfgr File**
Part Number—>	Part Number	
	Mfgr Code——>	Mfgr Code
		Mfgr Name

Using these files, you can create a view in which the sales file is primary, and the name of the Manufacturer is shown. First, attach the Inventory File, displaying the Mfgr Code and linking to the Sales file via the Part Number.

Next, attach the Mfgr file and display the Mfgr Name, linking to the view via the Mfgr Code. In this view, the Inventory file is used as a conduit between the Sales File and the Mfgr File.

The chain may go even deeper. For example, if the Mfgr File contains a state abbreviation, you can attach a State file and display the name of the state.

SW II

2.114 Tip: Fields linking two files in the same view must be the same length, but do not need to have the same names.

The length that is important is the actual length in the databases, not the displayed length of the field in the view. If necessary, you may need to create an additional field in the main or secondary file so that the field is the correct length for linkage. Linkage fields must be data file fields.

SW II

2.115 Tip: Follow a precise set of steps to add a field to a table in a custom view.

1. Edit the table to increase the size, allowing generous space for the new field.
2. Position the cursor on the field *after* which the new field is to be added. If the field is to be added as the last column, position the cursor on the last field on the right. If you want the new field to be first, you have to insert the new field after the first, and then move the first field after the new, second field.
3. Attach the field, selecting the correct file. Press F3 or F4 to display the fields from an alternate file.
4. Edit the table to adjust the size back to the proper size, if needed.

SW II

2.116 Tip: Specify the subdirectory when creating a data file or attaching an existing data file to a view.

When you load a view, the default location for any attached databases is the subdirectory from which the view is loaded. If you specify the database subdirectory when creating the view, however, the database is loaded from that location, regardless of the subdirectory from which the view is loaded. By using this technique, you can keep databases in their own subdirectories, separate from programs and views, for ease of maintenance and backup.

Loading Files

Before you can use a file in the Database, you first must load or activate the file. This section gives several tips and tricks for loading files both from the current subdirectory and from alternative subdirectories.

2.117 Trick: Use a macro to supply a password when loading a password-protected database under control of a project file. ***Both***

Although you cannot include a password within a project file, you can use a macro to supply the password as an argument. Because keystrokes from a macro are presented to the Smart command processor just as if they had been typed from the keyboard, the password is stored in the keyboard buffer until the password is requested. The following Smart 3.10 macro is an example of this:

```
F8CrawlCr1234
```

The F8 key is the quick key for Execute. The project file, in this case, is named Crawl, and the password to the file loaded by the project file is 1234.

Note that the carriage return is not provided after the password 1234 in Smart 3.10 because you do not press Enter when you supply a password. In SmartWare II, you must press Enter at the end of the password.

2.118 Trick: You can use a project file if you want to know whether a database is loaded. ***3.10***

The following project file can be used to determine whether a database is loaded:

```
quiet off

%1 Enter Name of database
let %2 = "%1" ".dbu"
if file(%2) = 1 then jump okfile
message File %1 is not loaded .. press any key ..
jump alldone

label okfile
let %0 = "%1" ".dat"
command /c dir %2 > %0     'redirect to <filename>.dat
fopen "%0"as 1
```

```
fread 1     into $line        'fifth line of .DAT file
fread 1     into $line        'has .DBU file name & size
fread 1     into $line
fread 1     into $line
fread 1     into $line
fclose 1

let $size = mid($line,13,9) 'file size starts in column 13
let $vsize = val($size)

if $vsize = 4
message     File %1 is open and unchanged
else
message     File %1 may be open and changed
endif

label alldone
```

The expression `let %0 = "%1" ".dat"` builds a file name by concatenating the user's entry with the extension `.dat`. If a file with that name exists, execution transfers to the line labeled `okfile`. Otherwise, execution transfers to the end of the file and no further action is taken. In the lines following the label `okfile`, the DOS command DIR is issued and its output is redirected to a file. The first four lines of that file then are read and "thrown away," because the fifth line of the DIR command output has the needed information. The expression `let $size = mid($line,13,9)` extracts the file size string from the contents of `$line`, and the next line converts the string to a numeric value. If this value—the size of the DBU file—is equal to 4, then the user is informed that the file is open and has not been changed.

When a database file is loaded, the update file (DBU) for the database is opened. If the DBU file does not exist, you can be certain that the file is not loaded. If the DBU file contains 4 bytes, the file is loaded but has not been changed. You can tell that no changes have been made because no updated Record key data has been written to the file to increase its size beyond the original 4 bytes.

If the DBU file exists but is larger than 4 bytes, the file may be loaded. It is possible, however, that the file is not loaded, and that your keys were not updated after the last Enter or Update command.

3.10

2.119 Tip: Use variables to keep track if files are loaded. This is particularly useful on a network, because you cannot tell by the existence of the DBU if the file is loaded.

On a single-user system, you usually can determine if the file is loaded by the fact that the DBU file exists (refer to Tip 2.118). On a network, however, the DBU files always exist, so this technique does not work. The following project files demonstrate the use of user variable "switches" to help you keep track of whether the files are loaded.

```
'Name:   Loadit
if $file == "state"
      if $state = null
            load state screen standard
            let $state = "x"
      else
            goto file state screen standard
      endif
elseif $file == "person3"
      if $person3 = null
            load person3 screen standard
            let $person3 = "x"
      else
            goto file person3 screen standard
      endif
else
      'no action
endif
```

This project file must be called by another project file similar to the following:

```
input $file File Name:
execute loadit in-memory
```

If you plan to unload files during the course of the application, be sure to set the switch variable to null, in case you need to load the file again. Initializing the switch variables to null during a start-up routine at the beginning of the application also is important.

2.120 Trick: You can use a project to test for an open database on a network. *3.10*

To test for an open database on a network, use the following project file:

```
Fopen "account.db" as 1
Fread 1 length 5 into $test
if cerror <> 0
      beep
      message File is Open
endif
fclose 1
```

The Fread command fails and yields a non-zero cerror code if the database is open.

2.121 Tip: Use the left-arrow key to select from the end of a pop-up menu, rather than pressing the right and down arrows multiple times to get to the end. *Both*

The process of selecting from a pop-up menu "wraps around." If you go too far, you are back at the beginning again. If you are at the beginning and want to go to the end, press the left arrow to take you to the end immediately. Even if you need the second to the last entry, pressing the left arrow twice is frequently faster than pressing the right and down arrows multiple times.

This tip applies not only to the Load and File Load commands, but to any command that displays a pop-up menu.

SW II

2.122 Tip: In a project file, whether you specify Standard-view or Custom-view doesn't matter, as long as you use the correct file extension—VW or VWS.

The file extension VW indicates a custom view; VWS is used for standard views. When using the File Load command in a project file, if you specify the name of the view with the correct extension, the command can refer to the view as either a standard or custom view. The following two commands provide equal results:

```
File Load Custom-view "person2.vw"

File Load Standard-view "person2.vw"
```

Both of these commands specify a file extension of VW and load the custom view.

SW II

2.123 Tip: If a key file is damaged, you may not be able to load the view. In this case, use the Data Utilities File-Fix Data-File command to repair the damage to the key file.

The Data Utilities File-Fix Data-File command attempts to repair both damaged data files and key files. In this case, if only the key file is damaged, the file is rebuilt, and you can load the file.

If the key file is missing altogether, you are able to load the view, but you cannot perform any command that uses the keys. Use the Order Key Rebuild command to reconstruct the key file if you are able to load the file.

SW II

2.124 Trick: On a network, it is possible to load a file in the Exclusive mode so that others cannot load the file while you are working with it.

To load a file in the Exclusive mode, and thus making it impossible for others to load the file while you are working with it, use the following trick:

At the command level, press Alt-X to display the most recent command, if any. Press F8 to clear the line. Now type the following on the command line:

```
File Load Custom-View "datafile.VW" Exclusive
```

(Be sure to include the quotation marks around the name of the view.) When you press enter, the view is loaded and you have exclusive use of the data files attached to the view. When you conclude your need for exclusive use of the files, be sure to unload the view so that others may use them.

Using Subdirectories

2.125 Trick: Locate databases that do not change in a separate subdirectory to facilitate backing up only those files that change on a regular basis. *Both*

When you load a database file, the file is opened for both reading and writing. You cannot open a file as "read-only" within the Database. This normally does not cause a problem, until you consider backing up your data. All files open for writing are marked by DOS as having been changed, whether or not you have used the Enter or Update commands.

When you back up your primary subdirectory, establish any static files in a separate subdirectory to avoid having to back up files that you have not actually changed. You then can use the Backup command with the /M option to back up only those files that have changed.

In an accounting application, for example, you typically have a chart of accounts, which does not change very often, and a ledger file to which you add records every day. When Smart opens the ACCOUNTS file, however, the DOS archive bit is set and is backed up, even though you use the /M switch on the Backup command.

To segregate the files, store them in different subdirectories as follows:

```
c:\account\account.db
c:\ledger\ledger.db
```

To back up just the LEDGER file, without backing up the ACCOUNT file, perform the following:

```
cd\ledger
backup c: a: /m
```

To load databases from alternative subdirectories, refer to the following tip.

2.126 Tip: Use the F5 key to identify databases in other subdirectories. *3.10*

If you spread your application among several subdirectories, the Load command normally does not display the names of databases in these other subdirectories. To display the names of these files in the pop-up window as if they were in the current subdirectory, type an entry like this in response to the prompt for a file name:

\ACCOUNT.DB*

Instead of pressing Enter, press F5. The pop-up menu displays the names of all files with a DB extension in the alternative subdirectory. Be sure to specify the DB extension. If *.* is used, Smart displays the names of every file, not just the database files. Selecting a file that is not a database results in a Load error.

SW II

2.127 Tip: With careful use, you can use the F4 key to search for a database to load from another subdirectory.

When you issue the File Load command for either a Custom or Standard view, the appropriate view names from the current subdirectory are displayed. A function key prompt also appears at the bottom of the screen. By following these steps, you can use the F4 function key to help you successfully load a view from another subdirectory.

1. You must have a custom view and a standard view with the same file name in the other subdirectory.

2. When you execute the File Load command, select either Custom-View or Standard view, depending on which type of view you want to load.

3. When the list of the view names from the current subdirectory is displayed, press F4. You are prompted:

```
Enter the file specification:
```

Type as much of the file specification for the view as you know. Be sure to include the path of the other subdirectory. For example, if you know that the view begins with the letter "d" and is in the \account subdirectory, you should type:

\account\d.vw*

You can search for just the VW file extension. The name of each file matching the specification will be displayed on the command line in the following format:

```
File was found in <\account\data.vw> - Continue searching? (y/n)
```

If this is the file you are seeking, press `n`. It does not matter that only the custom view extension is displayed, even if you want to load a standard view.

5. A pop-up menu displays two occurrences of the file name. Press Enter to select the first file name.

Both

2.128 Tip: Project files can load databases from alternative subdirectories when the path is specified.

If your application runs under the control of project files, the Load command within your project file can contain a statement similar to the following Smart 3.10 statement:

```
load \mg\ORDER screen ORD1
```

With the appropriate path specified, the file is loaded just as if the file were in the current subdirectory. There is no other effect on the application or the user.

Remember that loading a file from an alternative subdirectory does not automatically give you access to any associated files, such as Query or Report definitions. The only files that are "brought along" with the database file are the screen (DBS) file and any key files. If you want to use any other files or definitions from other subdirectories, you must specify the appropriate path.

Using the Virtual-File Facility

2.129 Tip: Enter Smart with the -FVIRTUAL switch to load multiple files and avoid the error message `Too many files open.` *3.10*

To use the virtual-file facility, copy the file VIRTUAL.DVR from your Communications disk to your Smart subdirectory. Use the command

```
SMART D -FVIRTUAL
```

to enter the Database.

The virtual-file facility permits as many as 100 files to be opened simultaneously on a single-user system. Without this feature, you may be able to open only four or five files at the same time.

Although DOS currently allows only 20 files to be open at any one time, this does not mean that you can work with 20 databases simultaneously. From the 20 files, you must subtract 6 for use by DOS and the Smart system. This leaves 14 files for your use within the Smart Database.

Each open database accounts for at least three files: the database file itself (DB); the screen file (DBS); and the database update file (DBU). If you order the file by a key or an index, you have another file. Using a Query or a Sort definition consumes yet another file each during the time they are in use. Therefore, if you have 4 files open, with 2 of them ordered by keys, all 20 files are used.

Because the Database must open individual files for each database and individually predefined operation (Query, Sort, Write or Send Summarized, Report, and so on), you quickly run out of available files in even a medium sized application. For this reason, the FVIRTUAL facility is provided with the system.

Activating Files

The Smart 3.10 Activate command (File Activate in SmartWare II) is used whenever you want to open a database file for processing, but you do not want (or need) to display that file in the current window.

2.130 Tip: Use the Activate (File Activate in SmartWare II) command to open a file for use without displaying the file in the current window. *Both*

Some commands within the Smart Database require only that the file be opened for usage. If you do not want to displace the file visible in the current window, but you need to open another file, use the Activate command. Its operation is the same as that of the Load command, but Activate does not display the file.

Both

2.131 Trick: Activate all password-protected files at the beginning of an application to consolidate password prompting.

Getting all the password prompting out of the way at the outset can be more convenient than scattering database password prompts throughout the application. Additionally, if your files have different levels of access authorization, you should ensure that the user is authorized to open all files necessary for the application.

Both

2.132 Trick: Activate all files at the beginning of your application so that you can use the Goto command to access needed files.

If you activate all the files you need, you can use the Goto command safely to access any files you need during the course of the application. In Smart 3.10, there is no certain way to test whether a file is loaded, but by loading all files at the outset, you eliminate the need for such a test.

In SmartWare II, the command to work with a different loaded view in the current window is Data Goto View.

Using Screens and Views

Each database you create in Smart 3.10 has at least one screen. The default screen you get initially is referred to as the "standard" screen within the Database. This standard screen displays the names and contents of all fields in the order in which they were declared during file creation.

In addition to the standard screen, you can create up to nine custom screens for a file. Custom screens enable you to display and use a screen that is better looking than the standard screen, to suppress the display of selected fields, to change the order of prompting, and to introduce certain editing and validation characteristics.

In SmartWare II, each database has at least one standard view and may have an unlimited number of custom views. Custom views can display data from several different files at one time.

3.10

2.133 Trap: Custom screen names are case sensitive; be careful how you use and assign them.

The fact that custom screen names are case sensitive is not much of a problem if you are loading your file manually. The names of the screens are displayed for

Fig. 2.9.
Custom screens with similar names.

you in the pop-up menu, and you can select one of the names by using the cursor keys and pressing Enter. Figure 2.9 shows two custom screens defined: DEPT1 and dept1.

2.134 Trick: Use numbers for custom screen names to avoid case confusion. *3.10*

Screen names are case sensitive, but you do not have to remember whether the names are in uppercase or lowercase if you use numbers for the screen names in a project file. You also avoid having to press the Shift key on your keyboard to type the correct name.

2.135 Tip: You cannot have a blank in the middle of a screen name. *3.10*

If you leave a blank in a screen name, you get the error message:

```
Incorrect command syntax
```

If you want to have two words, use an underscore or a dash as a separator.

2.136 Tip: Keep custom screen names unique and with no more than 8 characters if you ever plan to convert to SmartWare II. *3.10*

The program to convert Smart 3.10 applications to SmartWare II converts custom screens into custom views. In SmartWare II, each custom view is a separate DOS file, and as such, the file names must be a maximum of 8 characters. Within the same subdirectory, you are not allowed to have two views with the same name. Although custom screen names in Smart 3.10 are case sensitive, custom view names in SmartWare II are not. Therefore, upper- and lowercase versions of the same name are considered duplicates in SmartWare II.

2.137 Tip: Initiate the execution of the Load command to view a list of the screen names declared for a file. *3.10*

When you execute the Load command and select a file, a pop-up menu displays the names of the associated screens, as in figure 2.9. The names of all screens are displayed, both loaded and unloaded.

3.10 **2.138 Trick: Conceal a custom screen by assigning the screen a name that will not be displayed.**

If you use a custom screen name made up of an Alt-255, the very existence of the screen is not apparent. When you are creating the screen and are prompted for the name, hold down the Alt key and type *255* on the keypad section of your keyboard, and then release the Alt key. Later, when loading a file, the character represented by the Alt-255 will not appear in the pop-up box when you are prompted for a screen name. If this special screen is declared after all the other custom screens, an open "hole" will not appear in the pop-up list of screens.

Both **2.139 Tip: Use the Index command to view a list of only the screens currently loaded. In SmartWare II, the File Display-Active command shows you the names of the views and the files currently loaded.**

The File Display-Active command shows the names of the files and screens currently open (see fig. 2.10).

Fig. 2.10.

An index of open database files.

Window 1

Index of Open Data Files

View	File	Order	Records
depper.vw	dept	Physical	6
	person3		13
person2.vw	person2	Physical	13
dept.vw	dept	Physical	6

3.10 **2.140 Trick: Use the project file listed in figure 2.11 to "change" a custom screen.**

The project file in figure 2.11 prompts you for the name of the current database and of the screen you want to change. Both must be current in your window. Be sure to type the name of the screen in the proper case (upper or lower). If you are in doubt, execute the Index command on command list 4 (see fig. 2.10).

The Create Screen Editor is invoked twice; you can make your changes either time—or both, if you want. This routine runs quickly and is much easier than changing your project files and report definitions to recognize the name of a new screen.

Both **2.141 Tip: Draw a box in a custom screen to highlight certain areas.**

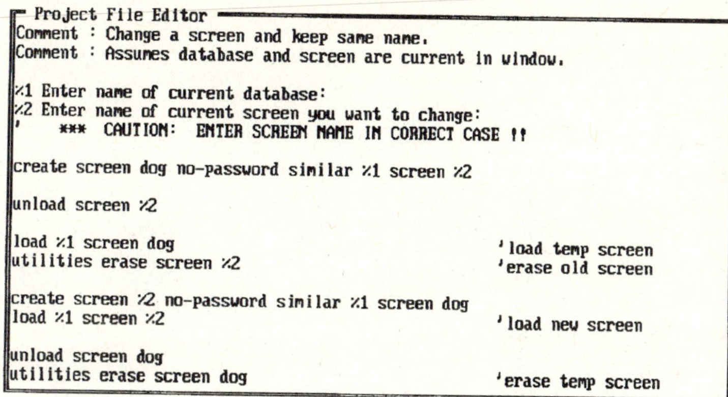

```
Project File Editor
Comment : Change a screen and keep same name.
Comment : Assumes database and screen are current in window.

%1 Enter name of current database:
%2 Enter name of current screen you want to change:
'    *** CAUTION:  ENTER SCREEN NAME IN CORRECT CASE !!

create screen dog no-password similar %1 screen %2

unload screen %2

load %1 screen dog                               'load temp screen
utilities erase screen %2                        'erase old screen

create screen %2 no-password similar %1 screen dog
load %1 screen %2                                'load new screen

unload screen dog
utilities erase screen dog                       'erase temp screen
```

Fig. 2.11.

A project file to switch screens.

In Smart 3.10, you can draw a box in a custom screen by first positioning your cursor at the upper left corner of the desired box position (see fig. 2.12). Press F4, then move the cursor to the lower right corner. When you press Enter, the box is displayed. A box can be used to highlight certain parts of your screen or to mark off special areas. After the box is drawn, you can type over portions of the box to include comments or instructions. You do not need to consume an additional line of the screen for this purpose.

```
Mandatory Data Entry
Last Name: ________   First: ________
Social Security Number: _________

Optional Data Entry
Sex: _  Race: _  Date of Birth: ______
```

Fig. 2.12.

Custom screen boxes.

In SmartWare II, use the Create Box subcommand. You may select a box with either a Double or Single border and an optional foreground color.

2.142 Tip: For ease of use, change the order of field access in a custom screen. ***Both***

In Smart 3.10, you can change the input order of the fields on your custom screen from the order in which the fields were declared to the order in which they appear on-screen. Notice that in the lower right corner of figure 2.12, the symbols `IO:P` appear. This means that the input order has been changed to the positional order of the fields.

Pressing Alt-F3 changes the P to a #, indicating numerical order. In positional order, the fields are prompted in order from left to right and top to bottom. The default order is numerical (#), however, so don't forget to change the order before saving your screen if you want positional order. (See also Tip 5.16.)

In SmartWare II, use the Input-Order subcommand. The Alt-R key sets the field order to Left-to-Right, Top-to-Bottom. If you press F6, the sequence number of each field increments by 1. If you change the order of an individual field by retyping it, the individual field swaps orders with the field having the number you just typed. Press Alt-O if you want to start over with the original order.

Both

2.143 Tip: Establish field ranges within a custom screen to help ensure the accuracy of your data.

An additional advantage of using a custom screen is the ability to define a range over which a field is valid. If you press Alt-F8 when the cursor is positioned on the field, you are prompted for both the low and the high values of the range. For example, if the current-year salary increase percentages in a personnel application are all under 10 percent, then the low end of the range is zero and the high end is 10.

A valid range must be contiguous, however. Using range checking, you cannot, for example, specify that the contents of the SEX field be either an M or F. If you require the validation of a discontinuous range, you must use the Lookup facility, which is discussed in Tip 5.21.

In SmartWare II, use a mask or field rules to establish valid ranges or entries.

3.10

2.144 Tip: Use the F8 key to blank text and delete fields while creating a custom screen.

Although you can use the space bar to blank text, when the cursor reaches a field, the system beeps, and you are required to use the F8 key to delete a field. Using the F8 key accomplishes both purposes.

SW II

2.145 Trick: Add a note on the last line of the last page of a multiple page view to maintain consistency when using the PgUp and PgDn keys.

At the menu level, the PgUp and PgDn keys may be used to move from page to page of a multiple page view. On all pages but the last, the movement is one full page at a time. On the last page, however, the view advances only as far as the final contents of the page. Therefore, if the last item on the last page goes to only line 12, for example, you see the last page plus the bottom half of the preceding page. This will look really messy, especially if you have carefully designed each page of the view.

You can solve this problem if you add a note at the bottom of the last page. This note forces the display of the full last page without showing any of the preceding page. Any note will do—a line, a dash, or even a period. If you do not want the note to be seen, make the note the same color as the background of the view.

Protecting Screens with Passwords

Some applications require greater degrees of data security than others. Indeed, some portions of an application may be more sensitive than others.

The Smart Database has password facilities for protecting the database and also each individual screen or view. You may choose to forgo passwords altogether or to assign a password only to the screens showing sensitive data.

When establishing passwords, you must take care to make sure you achieve the protection you require. This section covers tips you should know and traps to watch out for.

2.146 Tip: Protect your databases and screens/views with passwords. ***Both***

In Smart 3.10, if the data in your file is sensitive, select the Password option with the Create File or Create Screen command. When you execute the Load or Activate commands, you are prompted to enter a password. After three failed attempts at entering the password, the command is terminated.

When you create a view in SmartWare II, you may assign a password to the view itself, a database you create, or both. Passwords in SmartWare II are more flexible than in Smart 3.10 because they can be as long as 16 characters and may include spaces and special characters.

2.147 Trick: Use numbers for your passwords to avoid having to remember whether the password characters are upper- or lowercase. ***Both***

Remember that passwords are case sensitive; *PASS* is not equivalent to *pass*. Because numbers do not have an upper- or lowercase, the use of numbers simplifies password specification.

Do not forget the password to your file. You cannot recover the data if you forget the password.

2.148 Trap: In Smart 3.10, if you don't assign passwords to a file and to its screens, you do not have complete security. The same potential security breach exists in SmartWare II if you assign a password to a data file, but not to a custom view that uses the data file. ***Both***

In Smart 3.10, assigning a password to a file when you use Create File does not prevent access to that file through the use of custom screens. For maximum security, you must use passwords for all custom screens, as well as the file itself. A file password really protects only the standard screen. Access to the file can be achieved through any custom screens not protected by password. Similarly, using a password with only your custom screens does not prevent access to your standard screen unless your standard screen also is protected by a password.

Both

2.149 Tip: Database passwords cannot be embedded in Smart 3.10 project files, but can be included in SmartWare II project files.

In Smart 3.10, if a database screen is protected by a password, you cannot embed the password in the project file, either by making a literal entry or using a parameter. You must type the password from the keyboard.

In SmartWare II, use the Keys statement to supply a password from a project file, as in the following example:

```
file load standard-view "account.vws"
keys "abracadabra",Enter
```

Note that because a view password in SmartWare II may be any length up to 16 characters, you must use the Enter key.

3.10

2.150 Trap: The Utilities New-Password File Password command does not add a password to a file and therefore does not restrict access.

The effect of the Utilities New-Password File Password command is to restrict access only to the structure of the file, therefore preventing the creation of a similar file by unauthorized personnel. This command is not a substitute for the password you introduce when you initially create a file.

Both

2.151 Tip: In Smart 3.10, use the Utilities New-Password Screen Password command to add a password to the standard screen, thus preventing access by unauthorized individuals. In SmartWare II the command is File Password.

If you decide you want to restrict access to a file after you have created the file, use the Utilities New-Password Screen Password command to add a password to a screen, including the standard screen. If passwords are assigned to all screens, the file cannot be loaded unless the appropriate password is provided at Load time.

In SmartWare II, use the File Password command to add a password to either the data file or the view.

3.10

2.152 Trap: Contrary to the appearance of the command, selecting the Password option in the Create File Similar or Matching command does not restrict access to the file.

The Password option of the Create File Similar or Matching command does not add a password to the standard screen or any of the custom screens. The function of this option is to prevent access to only the structure of the file, not to the data.

If, after creating the Similar or Matching file, you want to limit access to viewing or changing the contents of the file, use the Utilities New-Password Screen command (command list 2) to add a password to the standard screen. You then are fully protected.

2.153 Tip: Change the password of your standard view for greater security after you have created a new view and file. *SW II*

In the File Create command, you may assign passwords separately to the view and the data file. The password you assign to the data file is assigned to the standard view. If you want to increase security, you can change the password for the standard view after you complete the File Create command. You then have separate passwords for the custom view, the standard view, and the data file.

Commands that work with just the data file, and none of the views, prompt for the password of the data file. These commands include Data Utilities File-Fix Data-File and Data Utilities Purge.

Safeguarding Data

Although the Smart System provides for protecting the integrity of your data while you are running your application, Smart does not provide automatic safeguards against power failures and other mishaps. You can take several steps, however, to guard against losing data due to physical malfunctions or operator error.

2.154 Tip: Execute the Save command periodically to flush the file buffer and write all records to disk. *Both*

Depending on the size of the records in your database, several records can be stored in a buffer without having been written to disk. Executing the Save command flushes the buffer, writing all records to disk. If the power goes off or the computer malfunctions, you do not lose these records.

2.155 Trap: Unload your view and load it again to update the File Allocation Table. On a single-user system, the FAT is not updated when you issue the File Save command. *SW II*

Even after you save your file, if your computer locks up, you lose much of the data you had just entered. When you save a file, the new records in memory are written to disk. Because the File Allocation Table has not been updated, however, the new data is stored in "lost clusters" and is inaccessible and unrecoverable if the computer freezes and you have to reboot. Even the Data Utilities File-Fix command cannot recover the lost data.

This problem does not exist on a network—the File Allocation Table is updated correctly.

SW II

2.156 Trap: Use the following project file to unload and reload the current view to simulate the File Save command and ensure that the File Allocation Table is updated.

```
local $filename

repaint off
tools file erase "save.txt"

data utilities information
keys Alt-W,"save.txt",Enter,Esc

fopen "save.txt" as 1
fread 1 into $filename
fclose 1

let $filename = mid($filename,17,80)

file unload view $filename
file load custom-view $filename
```

Note that the name of the current view is read from the file created by the Data Utilities Information command.

Both

2.157 Tip: Always be sure to exit the Smart Database by pressing the F10 key and Quit to return to DOS.

Several records can be in the file buffers, and you can lose these records if you just turn the power off. Pressing the F10 key and Quit performs a Save command before exiting Smart.

3.10

2.158 Trap: The Save and Key Update commands are independent of each other; executing one does not automatically execute the other.

When you save a file or quit the Database, your keys are not updated automatically. Similarly, updating a key does not save the file for you. To protect your data, issue the Save command. If you concluded an Enter or Update command without updating the keys and you now need to work with the keys, perform the Key Update command.

SW II

2.159 Tip: If you copy a database temporarily to a different subdirectory so that you can test the original and still have a good copy, copy the KEY file, too.

When you add records or change a key field, the KEY file is updated. When you finish your testing and the time has come to copy the original database back into your working subdirectory, unless you have preserved the original KEY file, you get errors reading the database and you have to perform the Data Utilities File-Fix Data command to reconstruct the KEY file. If your database is large or if you have many keys, this can be time-consuming.

Project Processing and Database Files

Several tips, tricks, and traps are provided in this section to help you work with databases in project files. Chapter 14 of this book is devoted entirely to Project Processing. For additional database project-file listings, refer to Appendix A.

2.160 Tip: Compile project files without line numbers and execute them with Quiet On to reduce the number of open files. *3.10*

If Quiet is On and the project file has been compiled without line numbers, the PF3 file is not accessed during execution of the project—only the RF3 file is used for execution. The number of open files, therefore, is reduced. Minimizing open files can be important on a network or when the -FVIRTUAL switch is not used on a single-user system.

2.161 Trick: Use the project file in figure 2.13 to change the structure of an existing database. *3.10*

```
Project File Editor
comment Switch files when no custom screens exist
'Original file must be loaded and Temp file must have already been created
%5 Enter name of Original File:
%6 Enter name of Temporary File:

unload file %5
unload file %6
utilities erase file %5

let %1 = "%6"!".db"
let %2 = "%6"!".dbs"
let %3 = "%5"!".db"
let %4 = "%5"!".dbs"

file rename %1 to %3
file rename %2 to %4
load %5 screen standard
```

Fig. 2.13.

A project file to switch files.

The database structure actually cannot be changed. However, you can create a similar file, transfer the existing data, and change the file names.

Before executing this project file, be sure to create your new file and any associated screens. You also must perform the Utilities Restructure command before executing the project file, because line 8 erases the original file. Be careful.

2.162 Trap: A database file must be in sequential order when you use the Enter Blank command in a project file. *3.10*

If you use the technique outlined in Trick 2.102, be absolutely certain that your file is in sequential order rather than ordered by an index or by a key. If the file is not in sequential order, the newly entered blank record is appended to the physical end of the file, but you update a different record altogether.

3.10

2.163 Trap: The Update and Enter commands used in a project file do not update the keys automatically.

You must issue the Key Update command separately in the project file.

SW II

2.164 Trap: Although the command Czbreak Off disables the use of Ctrl-Z to cancel or suspend the execution of a project file, Czbreak Off does not affect the ability to cancel a report.

When a report is executed in a project file, the following message is displayed on the second command line:

```
Ctrl-Z to Cancel
```

You may use Ctrl-Z to halt the execution of the report, whether Czbreak is On or Off. You can, however, suppress the display of the message if you set Repaint Off.

3.10

2.165 Trick: Use the Menu Print command to overlay portions of a custom screen to display additional information or calculations. The screen can appear to vary, as if additional data is in the file, but you do not consume space in the file.

In a project file, you may want to display a custom screen showing database information, but you also need to show additional data. You can use the Menu Print command to display calculations or information in the middle of the custom screen.

This technique is valid only if you are displaying data on-screen. The information is maintained as you press F6 or F5 to go from record to record. If you update the record or zoom the window, however, the data from the Menu Print is lost.

3

Viewing Files and Arranging Data

This chapter explores some of the techniques you can use to view your Database files on the screen and in windows—including working with and linking multiple windows. A project file is introduced that will permit you to simulate the Browse mode while you're working within an application that is completely driven by project files.

In addition, this chapter compares the use of keys and sorts and looks at the question of which one to use. Finally, a number of tips and tricks are presented for use with the Order command.

Viewing Files

This section begins with a Browse project file that simulates the actual Browse command (you'll find the listing of the project file in Appendix A) followed by tips and tricks you can use to create and use multiple windows. The Link command is discussed, and a solution is presented to the problem of linking more than two windows simultaneously.

In SmartWare II, the corresponding commands are Data Browse and Window Link.

Browsing through Files and Views

3.1 Trick: Use a project file to simulate the Browse command. ***Both***

If you have an application that runs under the control of a project file, and you also want to be able to browse through the file, you can use a project file to simulate the Browse command. This project file is listed in Appendix A.

Both

3.2 Tip: If you specify incorrect fields in the Browse command, there is no error message. The result will be the same as if you had used the Browse All command, but you can fix the problem easily.

If you notice that all fields are displayed, rather than the ones you specified, you probably typed the field names incorrectly during the execution of the command. To check your entries, press Alt-X to display the Browse command on the first command line. Simply edit the command to correct your mistakes and press Enter.

In SmartWare II, if the fields are incorrect in a Data Browse Fields command, you will get this error message:

```
Invalid field entered
```

The list of fields you specified will be displayed automatically for you to edit when you press any key to clear the error.

Both

3.3 Tip: In Smart 3.10, use a custom screen if you want to display fields in an order different from numerical order when you execute the Browse All command. The field order will correspond to the prompting order on the screen. In SmartWare II, use a custom view to alter the order of the fields displayed by the Data Browse All command.

If you're using a standard screen or view, the order of the fields across the screen will be the same as the order in which you declared them when creating the file. However, if you're using a custom screen or view, the order of the fields displayed in the Browse All mode will match the order on the screen.

In Smart 3.10, remember that when you are creating a custom screen, you can establish positional order by using the Alt-F3 key to display `IO:P` in the lower right corner of the screen. In SmartWare II, use the Input-Order subcommand to change the order of the fields.

In either Smart 3.10 or SmartWare II, only the fields available on the custom screen or view may be viewed in the Browse mode.

Both

3.4 Trick: Press Alt-B twice to return quickly to the first field when you are in the Browse mode.

In the Browse mode of Smart 3.10, you can view fields to the right of those currently on your screen by pressing the right arrow key; the left arrow key returns you to previous fields. In SmartWare II, you can use the right and left arrow keys to view fields individually. Press Ctrl-Right or Ctrl-Left to view a full screen.

In neither product is there a single keystroke that will return to the first field, however. Because the first field is the default when you first execute the Browse All command, if you press Alt-B twice (once to Browse Off and again to Browse All), you will return quickly to the first field.

3.5 Tip: You will consume more system memory in the Browse mode than you will in the unbrowsed mode of the same view.

SW II

Not only will a browsed view use more memory, but the more fields you display, the more memory you will use. Therefore, to conserve memory, avoid displaying views in the Browse mode. You can display system memory by pressing Ctrl-F1.

3.6 Trap: Only those fields selected in the Data Browse command may be used in subsequent commands; many commands will operate as if the other fields do not exist.

SW II

For example, in a personnel application, if you execute the Data Browse command to display only Last Name and First Name, you cannot sort by Department. When you execute the Order Sort command, only the names of the browsed fields will be displayed in the popup window of field names. The system behaves as if you had a custom view with only the browsed fields attached to it.

You can access all fields if you are entering or updating data or executing the Data Browse command.

Because fields not selected in a Data Browse command will be unavailable to most subsequent commands, you should perform any commands requiring those fields first. In the personnel example, you would perform the sort by Department before the Data Browse to display the first and last names.

In Smart 3.10, this restriction does not apply. You can use any fields in the screen at any time, whether or not they have been selected in the Browse command.

3.7 Trap: A browsed SmartWare II view that is displaced from a window will retain its browsed status when displayed again. In a project file, you cannot expect the view to revert to the unbrowsed mode, as is the case in Smart 3.10.

Both

In Smart 3.10, when one file is displaced by another and is relegated to the background, it automatically reverts to the unbrowsed mode. In SmartWare II, this is not true. Not only will the file still be in the browsed mode when it is displayed again (use the Data Goto View command), but only the browsed fields will be available for use by other commands.

If you have converted project files from Smart 3.10, you may have assumed that the view would be unbrowsed when displayed again. To display the view in the unbrowse mode, use the command Data Browse Off.

Working with Multiple Windows

Often when your are working with multiple views or screens, it is necessary or useful to split the monitor screen into two or more windows. This section takes a look at the uses and pitfalls of using multiple windows.

Splitting Windows

Both

3.8 Tip: Maximize the number of windows available by observing the minimum window sizes.

When you split a window in the Smart Database, you must maintain certain minimum window sizes. If you split a window horizontally, you must move the cursor down at least three lines in order to leave at least two lines visible in the old window. You must have at least three visible lines in the new window, as well. If you move the cursor down too far, you will get the error message

```
Window too small.
```

This message refers to the new window rather than the old one.

Similarly, if you split a window vertically, you must move the cursor over at least 13 positions (hit the right-arrow key 13 times) so that 13 columns are visible in the old window. Oddly enough, the column requirements for the new window are less than those for the old window; you must leave at least 12 visible columns in the new window.

Both

3.9 Trick: Increase the number of lines you can see in any window by turning off the border.

The Border (Smart 3.10) or Window Border (SmartWare II) commands are toggles that remove or restore the border around a given window. If you want many windows but need to see more within them, you can turn the border off and see three lines instead of just the minimum two.

However, you may find the view confusing because a clear demarcation no longer exists between one window and the next when borders are removed from both windows. Removing the border also removes the window-number legend that otherwise appears in the top line of the border. One solution would be to turn off the border of every other window; then, at least, you would have some borders left to mark the boundaries.

Both

3.10 Tip: When splitting a window in a project file, the row and column numbers must be included as arguments to the command.

Although you won't find this in the Smart documentation, both the Split Horizontal and Split Vertical commands require two numerical arguments, separated by spaces. If you look closely at the command line when you execute these commands, you will see that the row and column numbers appear briefly. (The equivalent commands in SmartWare II are Window Split Horizontal or Vertical.)

These numerical arguments represent the cursor position at the instant the Split command is executed. If, for instance, you were to split window 1 and leave the minimum two lines in the window, the actual Smart 3.10 command would be:

```
Split Horizontal 5 2
```

You do not type the 5 and 2 (the row and column numbers, respectively, of the cursor position). You simply move your cursor to that position and press Enter. (If you use the Remember Start mode to record your keystrokes, these numbers will be inserted into your project file.)

In SmartWare II, the equivalent command is:

```
window split horizontal 5
```

Zooming and Closing Windows

3.11 Trap: Within a project file, determining whether a screen is zoomed is impossible. Using the Split or Close commands when the screen is zoomed will cause errors.

Both

The Zoom command (command list 3) fills the entire screen of your monitor with the current window so that you can see more of the contents. Zoom is a toggle; execute it again, and you will see all your windows. The Zoom command has no argument, such as On or Off.

If you are executing your application from the command level, you obviously can see whether your screen is zoomed. But if you are operating your system under control of a project file, you may be unable to determine whether the screen is zoomed. Some commands, such as the Split and Close commands, are illegal if the screen is zoomed.

If you have constructed a project file that expects the screen to be zoomed (or not zoomed), you cannot control the zoom because you cannot determine its current status. You must issue a prompt that asks whether the screen is zoomed and then change the Zoom status accordingly (see fig. 3.1).

Even with this test, there is no way you can be certain that the question has been answered correctly. I try to avoid using the Split and Close commands in project files.

In SmartWare II, check the Cerror code after a command to determine if the window was zoomed. For example, Cerror code 3744 is generated if you attempt to close a zoomed window.

Fig. 3.1.

A project file to query the user about screen status.

```
Project File Editor
input $yn Is the Screen Zoomed?
if upper($yn) = "N" then jump nozoom
zoom
label nozoom
```

Both

3.12 Tip: You can execute the Goto Window command in the Database while the screen is zoomed.

The Smart 3.10 Word Processor and the Spreadsheet require that the screen be unzoomed before you go to another window. In the Database, however, this restriction does not exist. (Refer to Tip 13.10 to learn how to overcome this restriction in the Word Processor and the Spreadsheet modules.)

In any module of SmartWare II, you can go to another window while the screen is zoomed.

Both

3.13 Tip: It will appear as if the current file has been unloaded if you close the current window and the other windows are empty. For example, if you have a file in window 2 and window 1 is empty, window 1 will be blank when you close window 2.

Closing a window does not automatically unload a file. But it may appear that way if you have two windows and close the current one without a file visible in the other. Use the Goto File (3.10) or Data Goto File (SmartWare II) commands to display one of the loaded files or views in the current window.

Both

3.14 Tip: Use the cursor keys to view additional portions of your screen even when you have multiple windows; you do not necessarily have to Zoom to be able to view more of the screen display.

Ordinarily, when you have multiple windows, you can see only a portion of each window, either the upper portion, the left portion, or the upper left corner. The Zoom (Window Zoom in SmartWare II) command allows you to fill the entire monitor screen with the entire window, but when you do this, you cannot see the other windows. However, even if you do not Zoom, you can view other portions of the window if you use the cursor keys to reposition the screen within the window.

3.10

3.15 Trap: In a project file, the Zoom command will not work while the repaint is off if you are working on an 8088 computer.

The Repaint Off setting prevents the Zoom command from executing if you are on an 8088 computer. If you are on an 80286 or 80386 computer, you will not have this problem. To avoid the problem on an 8088 machine, issue the Repaint On command before the Zoom command.

Changing Windows

3.16 Tip: The execution speed of the Data Goto Window command is affected by the type and order of the view. A custom view is usually faster, but not always. *SW II*

If you have a standard view or a custom view in the Browse mode, either of which is ordered by a key, there can be a noticeable delay when you go to the window containing the view. The delay is less if the views are in physical order, and the delay is minimal if the custom view is displayed in the unbrowsed mode, regardless of the order. In a project file, the delay is not affected by the repaint status.

3.17 Trick: Use the command Data Goto Window Next to advance to the next sequentially numbered window. *SW II*

Using the "Next" argument to a Goto Window command is valid in only the Database module. At the command level, however, rather than typing the word *next*, it is easier and faster to use the Quick Key F8. The command Data Goto Window Previous also is valid in the Database.

In a project file, you may use either window numbers or the words *next* or *previous* in the Data Goto Window command.

Linking Files

3.18 Trick: Create a macro to build multiple simultaneous links between windows in the Data Base. *3.10*

The Link command is used to join two windows whose files share a common field. For instance, in figure 3.2, you might want to link the DEPT field in window 1 to the DEPARTMENT field in window 2. Thus, when you change from record to record in window 1, you can see the full name of the person's department in window 2.

Unfortunately, you can execute only one Link command at a time. You cannot link from the department (DEPT) field in window 1 to window 2 and, at the same time, from the state (ST) field to window 3.

You can develop a macro that first links to one file and then to the other. The record in window 2 will not change if you link to window 3; so, in effect, you can display both correct records. You can define a macro key as follows:

```
F6Li2Cr17CrLi3Cr12Cr
```

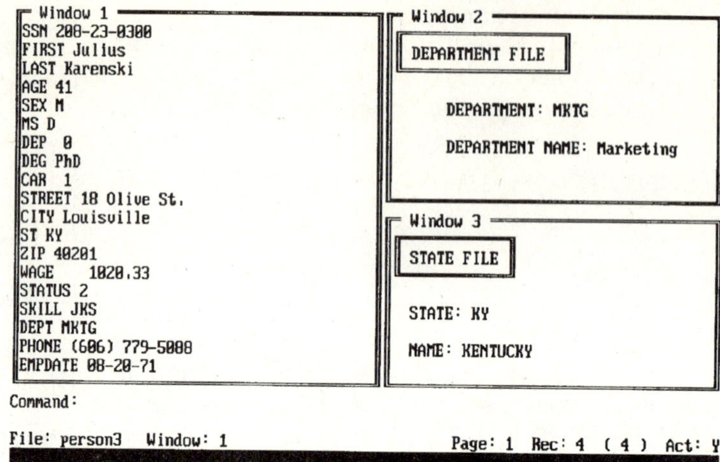

Fig. 3.2.
Multiple linked windows.

The macro is interpreted as follows:

F6	Advance to next record
li	Invoke the Link command, confidence level 5
2	Window 2
Cr	Return
17	Field 17 in window 1
Cr	Return
li	Link
3	Window 3
Cr	Return
12	Field 12 in window 1
Cr	Return

If you operate at a confidence level other than 5, alter this macro accordingly. I used the F6 key at the beginning of the macro both to advance to the next record and to create the linkages. You also could set up a macro to go to the previous record and perform the links.

This example shows two linkage windows; the same concept would work with as many windows as you want. Remember that your link-to files must be ordered by the keys that are used for the linkages.

SW II

3.19 Tip: Link multiple views simultaneously in a series for a coordinated display.

Several files may be linked together in a network in which changing the record of the first view changes the record display in all other views. If you go to the next record in view 1, this changes the record in view 2, which changes the record in view 3, and so on. Figure 3.3 will help to illustrate the point:

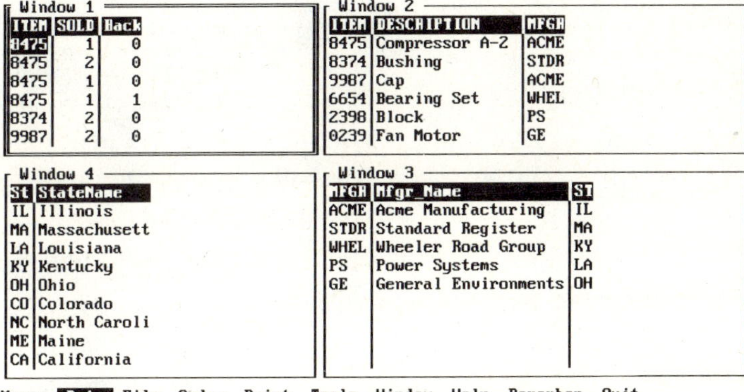

Fig. 3.3.

A network of linked views.

The ITEM field in the SALES view in window 1 is linked to the ITEM field in the Inventory view in window 2. The MFGR field in window 2 is linked to the MFGR field in the Manufacturer view in window 3. And the STATE field in window 3 is linked to the STATE field in the view in window 4. If you change to a different record in window 1, it is possible to cause the records in the other three windows to change at the same time.

A view in one window may be linked to only one other window at a time, however.

3.20 Trap: Links between files can be broken easily, causing unexpected results or preventing the printing of combination reports. ***3.10***

The Link command establishes the link from one window to another; the Unlink command breaks the link.

Actually, linkage is so transitory that the Unlink is practically not necessary. If you change the order of the link-to file, the linkage will be broken even if you revert to key-field order. If you update the link-to file and then update the keys when you finish, the link is broken. Linkage can be maintained only if you update a non-key field and choose not to update the key.

3.21 Tip: As long as link fields have the same contents, they do not have to have the same data type to be linked successfully. ***Both***

Thus, a numeric field that contains the number 47 will link correctly to an alphabetic field that also contains the number 47. In the same way, field names do not have to be identical or have the same length.

In SmartWare II, the field types must match for a link to be successful. Field sizes and names do not have to be identical.

Both

3.22 Tip: In Smart 3.10, the case of the contents of alphabetic linkage fields is immaterial; the Link command works correctly, regardless of case. In SmartWare II, this is not true.

Since Smart Version 3.10 uses the collation sorting sequence, lower- and upper-case letters have the same value, and thus will match in the Link command.

In SmartWare II, due to the use of the strict ASCII sequence in key maintenance, lowercase fields will not link with upper case fields containing the same letters.

3.10

3.23 Tip: Always execute the Link command in a project file before printing a combination report.

Linkage is mandatory when you print a combination report; you must link from the window with the driver file to the window with the driven file. If you are executing your combination report under control of a project file, establish the linkage before you execute the report rather than assuming that the linkage is in effect.

Arranging Your Data for the Best Results

The use of keys within the Database provides a powerful means for both arranging your data and performing lightning fast selections through the Find and Query commands. In SmartWare II, the commands are Data Find and Data Query.

In some commands, the presence of a key is mandatory; in others, a key is helpful; and in some, it can be detrimental.

In some cases, either a sort or a key can be used. The decisions governing which technique to use are presented in several tips and tricks in the following sections.

Using Keys

Both

3.24 Tip: You can have multiple fields within a single key.

A key does not have to consist of just one field. For instance, you might want to focus on the most recently hired employee in each department. You can do this by defining a key field (see fig. 3.4) as a combination of the DEPT and the EMPDATE fields and designating the EMPDATE field as Descending. To change from the default of Ascending to Descending, move the cursor to the appropriate line and press D.

Figure 3.5 shows the result of a Browse command after the file is ordered by the DEPT key field. Notice that within each department, the employees are listed in descending order by the date of employment.

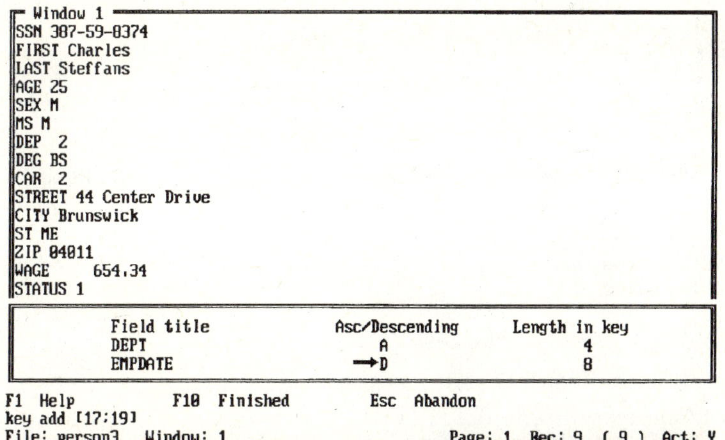

Fig. 3.4.

Assignment of multiple key fields.

3.25 Trick: If you have multiple key fields in the link-to file, the Link command displays the first record that matches the link field. ***Both***

In the example in Trap 3.24, you can move from department to department and display the record of the most recently hired employee. To do this, use the personnel file as the link-to file and DEPT file as the link-from file.

This technique helps you find information quickly. See Chapter 7 on the Query command to read about another way.

3.26 Tip: Use of a multiple-field key lets you perform counts quickly. ***3.10***

Continuing the personnel example, the command Query Count will print a count of the number of employees within the department. To use this tip, you must order your file by the key field that is used as the major aggregation category. The report in figure 3.5 shows a count of employees by department.

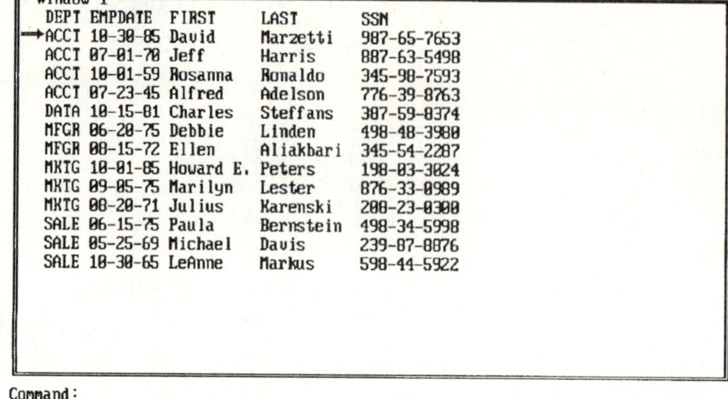

Window 1

DEPT	EMPDATE	FIRST	LAST	SSN
ACCT	10-30-85	David	Marzetti	987-65-7653
ACCT	07-01-70	Jeff	Harris	887-63-5498
ACCT	10-01-59	Rosanna	Ronaldo	345-98-7593
ACCT	07-23-45	Alfred	Adelson	776-39-8763
DATA	10-15-81	Charles	Steffans	387-59-0374
MFGR	06-20-75	Debbie	Linden	498-48-3980
MFGR	08-15-72	Ellen	Aliakbari	345-54-2287
MKTG	10-01-85	Howard E.	Peters	198-03-3024
MKTG	09-05-75	Marilyn	Lester	876-33-0989
MKTG	08-20-71	Julius	Karenski	208-23-0300
SALE	06-15-75	Paula	Bernstein	498-34-5998
SALE	05-25-69	Michael	Davis	239-87-8876
SALE	10-30-65	LeAnne	Markus	598-44-5922

Command:

File: person3 Key: 17 Window: 1 Page: 1 Rec: 1 (8) Act: Y

Fig. 3.5.
Number of employees by department.

If, for example, you frequently need a count of employees in each department by sex, you can set up a multiple-key field of department and sex and use the Query Count command.

Both

3.27 Trick: Establish a dummy field so that you can effectively use the same field twice as the major sort of two keys.

Because the first field of a multiple-field key is designated as the key-selection field, you cannot use it twice. That is, you could not use the two multiple-key fields DEPT-SEX and DEPT-EMPDATE. If you need two keys like these, define a dummy one-byte alpha field calculated as a blank (or some other constant), and use that field as the major field in a multiple-field key.

By calculating the constant value for each record, you ensure that it has no effect when designated as the major sort key. The first minor key (DEPT in this example) then acts as the major sort:

	First set of keys	**Second set of keys**
Major	DEPT	DUMMY
Minor	SEX	DEPT
		EMPDATE

The extra byte wastes a bit of space, but this trick can solve the problem.

Both

3.28 Tip: Add keys to eliminate sorting.

Usually, you designate a key at the time you create your file. But you also can add a key later, using the Key Add command on command list 2 (Order Key Add in SmartWare II).

If your project requires that you frequently sort the file by the same set of keys, add a key to substitute for the sort. When you are finished with the project, you can delete the key. Using the additional key will not interfere with the operation of any other project file or command.

3.29 Tip: Whenever possible, force all key fields to be entered and maintained in the same case, either upper or lower. *SW II*

The SmartWare II b-Tree key structure maintains key fields in ASCII order, which differentiates the cases. Because the b-Tree order is strict ASCII, not the Smart collation sequence, all lowercase letters will sort following uppercase letters. Thus, in an ascending sort, deWinter sorts below Rebecca and van Horn may not be adjacent to VAN HORN.

In your custom views, use masks to enforce case standards. For example, a mask of `*10{au}` on an alphabetic field of 10 characters will ensure that each character is alphabetic and is forced to uppercase.

3.30 Tip: Do not create unnecessary keys because the key files in SmartWare II are much larger than those for Smart 3.10. *SW II*

In SmartWare II, the key file for a database contains both the field data values and the datafile record numbers. Depending on the number of records, and the number and size of the key fields, the KEY file can be quite large. In one instance, the KEY file in SmartWare II was *ten* times as large as the corresponding key file in Smart 3.10.

3.31 Tip: Delete unneeded keys. *Both*

If a key is no longer needed or is rarely used, delete it. Extra keys slow the Key Update process after an Update or Enter command. In SmartWare II, significant amounts of disk space can be saved if you delete unnecessary keys.

3.32 Tip: Do not establish your keys immediately if you are creating a new version of an existing file. *3.10*

If you are creating a file similar to an existing one and you intend to restructure your data, erase the old file, and rename the new file. Do not create any keys for the temporary file. You only waste space and time because after the renaming, the system rejects the key file and you have to perform a Key Organize command anyway.

3.33 Tip: To save space and time, define a shortened key length for an alpha field. *Both*

When you add a key for an alpha field, the default is the entire field length or 100, whichever is lower. The longer the field, the greater the time necessary to update the keys and the more space the key file consumes on your disk. If your application makes it possible, shorten the key.

To shorten the key, move the cursor over to the key length column (see fig. 3.6) and down to the appropriate field line, then enter a number less than the field length shown on the screen.

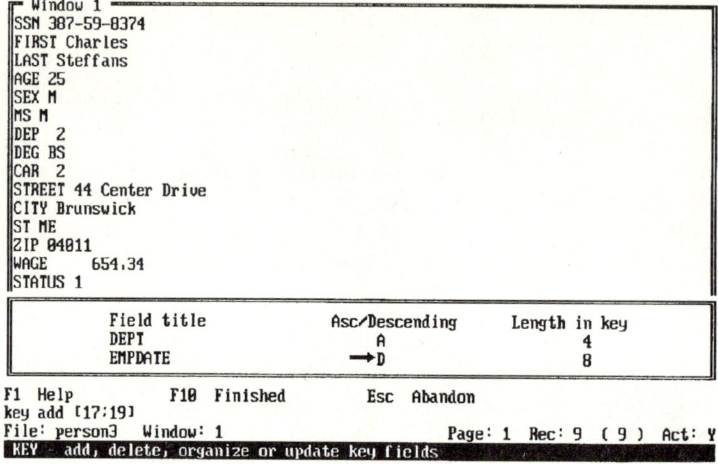

Fig. 3.6.

Assignment of multiple key fields.

Shorter key lengths save time and space but this technique may be a disadvantage if your application requires the entire field length to present the records in the desired order.

This technique would be useful if, for instance, you have a field in which the important variations fall within the first 10 characters. In such a case, set the key length at 10. Even if a few duplicates result, the design of your application might allow you to select the correct record manually.

Both

3.34 Tip: Execute the File-Specs Key-Fields command to view the names of all fields that constitute a key.

A popup menu of your fields—such as the menu that appears when you execute the Order command—displays a `k` next to the field number but does not tell you whether there are any other fields within this key. After you have added the key, the only way to find out if other fields are within the key is to execute the File-Specs Key-Fields command, on command list 2 (see fig. 3.7).

In SmartWare II, use the Data Utilities Information command.

3.10

3.35 Trap: Some commands can change key values but do not prompt you to update your keys. Failure to update them will cause your files to appear out of order.

When you enter new records or update existing records from the command level of the Smart 3.10 Database, you are prompted

```
Do you wish to update keys now (y/n)
```

```
Key Field Information
       Field number  Title            Asc/Descending  Key length

major        1       SSN                   A              11

major       17       DEPT                  A               4
minor       19       EMPDATE               D               8
```

Fig. 3.7.
Executing the File-Specs Key-Fields command.

This prompt reminds you that keys may need to be updated. Sometimes, you may enter or change data in a file without being prompted to update your keys. You should know the commands that do not prompt for a key update so that you can manually execute the Key Update command. The following commands do not prompt for updating your keys:

Utilities Restructure
Utilities Concatenate
Query . . . Replace
Project File Statements
    Let [field]
    Enter
    Update
    Update Only-One

Take care to issue the Key Update command within your project files after performing any of these operations. If you fail to update your keys after any changes to key fields, your Order Key commands will not work accurately.

3.36 Tip: When in doubt, execute the Key Update command. *3.10*

To make sure that your keys are updated, issue the Key Update command even if it may not be needed. If the keys do not require updating, no time is lost because the system recognizes immediately that the keys have not changed. Control is quickly returned to the command level.

3.37 Tip: Do not always update your keys. *3.10*

If you are alternating between updating and entering data, you may not need to update your keys each time you finish a command. Updating keys, in this instance, can be time-consuming and unnecessary. When you complete a data-maintenance session (at the end of the day, for instance), perform the Key Update command.

3.38 Trick: Keys do not have to be updated to perform many tasks within the Database. *3.10*

Even if you have finished updating certain records, you do not necessarily have to update your keys to continue working productively within the Database. The Key Update command is something of a misnomer because if you have used the Update command to change only data fields (as opposed to key fields) and have not added any new records, the key files on your disk are still valid. Each record is still in its correct position and can be found with the appropriate key. Unfortunately, the Database does not differentiate between changing a key field and changing a data field. The system recognizes only that a record has been changed. Therefore, you are prompted to update your keys after you end the Update command.

It can be disconcerting, however, when the Report command presents you with the following error message:

```
File contains un-updated records. Continue (y/n)
```

If you are certain that you have changed only data fields and no key fields, you can proceed with no problem. If you are unsure, answer `N` to the prompt and perform a Key Update.

3.10 **3.39 Trap:** If you do not update your keys after you change key field data, your file will be out of order.

If you forget to update your keys after changing key fields, what happens? When your file is ordered by a key field and you change a key-field value so that the record falls in a different order, the file is then out of order. Figure 3.8 shows a record out of place because the keys were not updated—even though the key field for the department code for Data Processing was changed from DATA to PROC. Note that the file is ordered by the key in field 1. Updating the keys keeps the files in order.

Fig. 3.8.

The result of not updating keys.

```
 Window 1
  DEPT DEPNAME
  ACCT Accounting
→PROC Data Processing
  MDSE Merchandising
  MFGR Manufacturing
  MKTG Marketing
  SALE Sales

Command:

File: dept   Key: 1   Window: 1                 Page: 1  Rec: 2  ( 5 )  Act: Y
```

3.40 Trap: If you do not update your keys after entering new records, those records do not appear when you order by a key. 3.10

For example, imagine your key file contains 100 records, and you enter 10 records without updating the keys. When you order by a key, you have access to only the original 100 records. If, however, you use the Order Sequential command, you can work with the complete file. To have access to the entire file as ordered by a key, however, you must update your keys.

3.41 Trap: In a project file running on a network, the Key Update command has no effect if another user has the file loaded. 3.10

On a network, you cannot update the key if someone else has the same file loaded. If you try to update the keys from the command level, you receive the error message:

```
File in use by another station, cannot perform key operation
```

In a project file, no error message appears, but the keys are still not updated because another user has the file loaded.

3.42 Tip: Do not execute the Key Organize command unless you are prompted to do so. 3.10

Whereas the Key Update command modifies existing key files, the Key Organize command completely rebuilds the key file. If you ever need to run the Key Organize command, the system displays an error message telling you to execute this command.

3.43 Tip: Use the following project file to rebuild the keys of all the databases in the current subdirectory. SW II

```
local $databases $count
let $databases = getfnames("*.db",1)
let $count = 1
file unload all
while group($databases,$count) <> null
    data utilities file-fix datafile group($databases,$count)
    let $count = $count + 1
end while
```

3.44 Tip: If the key file is in the proper format but does not accurately reflect the current status of the file, the file loads, but you cannot enter new records. SW II

When you try to enter a new record, you receive the error message:

```
Error reading data-file
```

Press Esc several times until the Database menu returns. Then execute the command Order Key Rebuild to reconstruct the key file.

Both

3.45 Tip: Use of key fields is mandatory for certain operations.

Keys must be declared to be able to use the following 3.10 commands:

Link
Lookup
Combination Reports
Query Count and High-Low
Transactions
Relate

In SmartWare II, the following commands and features require keys:

Window Link
Combination Reports
Multiple File Views
Data Transact
Data Relate
Filelookup function

Both

3.46 Tip: Using key fields allows certain commands to work faster.

The Query and Find commands operate much faster if the object field of the command is a key field. (In SmartWare II, the commands are Data Query and Data Find.) For example, you can use the query command to perform the replacement

```
[partno] = $partno
```

even if the file is ordered sequentially. In this example, the search will be performed sequentially, from the top of the file to the bottom. If, however, you have established [partno] as a key field, then you should write your query as

```
where [partno] = $partno
```

and order the file by the key field [partno]. Performing such a query will take a matter of seconds; the equivalent sequential search generally takes much more time.

The search technique used with key fields is a "binary search," the computer equivalent of guessing a number between 1 and 1000 by systematically guessing in the middle of the available range. In SmartWare II, this is known as an optimized search. The system uses the key file (which is small, compared to the data file) to perform the binary search to locate the address of the data record. Once the address is found, the record at that address is retrieved immediately. Using key fields, the Smart Database can locate any record from a file of 32,000 records in fewer than 15 searches through the key file.

3.47 Tip: The Find command automatically performs a binary (optimized) search if the file is ordered by the field being searched. *Both*

You must specify the Equal option and cannot select either the Ignore Case or Whole Words Only commands. (Global and Backward options are ignored.)

In SmartWare II, you can perform an optimized Data Find even if the view is not ordered by the key; you must use the Global option.

3.48 Tip: Considerations apply when you decide between establishing a key and using a sort. *Both*

1. *Frequency of use*: How often do you need to view or work with your file in the different order? If you need the file in the field order every few minutes, then you probably need a key. On the other hand, if you need the file in order by the field once a month, then a sort may work just fine.

2. *Size of the file*: If the file is small, little extra time is necessary to perform a key update. Remember that each extra key requires processing time to update the key and that key files consume disk space. For a small file, these overhead items can be insignificant; for a large file, they can be monumental in Smart 3.10.

3. *Frequency of changes to the file*: If the file does not change frequently, key-update time becomes less important. On the other hand, you could create an index as a result of the sort and continue to use the index throughout the period of time in which the file remains static. After you enter new records into the file or change any key on which the sort was based, you have to perform the sort again to refresh the index. A key is dynamically maintained; after every Enter or Update command in Smart 3.10, you are prompted to update your keys.

4. *Effects of the key (or the sort) on the person using the system*: If the application causes you to sit idle while the computer updates an optional key, you lose time. You also lose time during a long sort but can order your file instantly with a key.

5. *Need for a sorted subset of the file*: Although a key provides a means for quickly organizing your file in an order sorted by one or more fields, the entire file is available when you order by a key. Frequently, you can begin with a key order, and subsequently use a query to limit the view (see Tip 3.72). Sometimes, though, perform a query first on a sequentially ordered file and then execute a sort.

You may be able to structure the tasks so that idle time is minimized. Suppose that a certain report, requiring a special sort order, is needed once a day. The file is large, and you have to perform frequent updates. Do you keep a key for just this report? What if you could use a project file to run the report during lunch, with the system performing a sort and printing the report? The work would all be done when you got back to your desk.

3.10 **3.49 Trick:** Because of the similarity of structures, you can use an index as a temporary substitute for a key if you need to restrict the driven file in a multiple file command.

In the Relate command, for example, File 1 (the driven file) must be ordered by a key. You are allowed to perform a Query to restrict the records in File 2, but not File 1. However, an Index and a Key file have structures that are similar enough to allow you to temporarily substitute an Index for a key on File 1.

Figure 3.9 shows a sales file in window 2 and an inventory file in window 1.

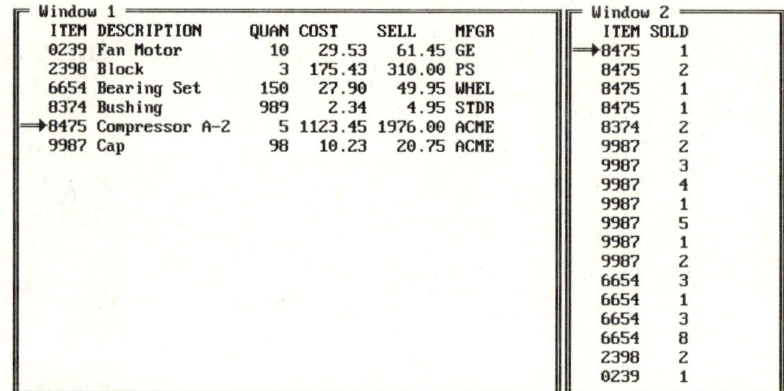

Window 1

ITEM	DESCRIPTION	QUAN	COST	SELL	MFGR
0239	Fan Motor	10	29.53	61.45	GE
2398	Block	3	175.43	310.00	PS
6654	Bearing Set	150	27.90	49.95	WHEL
8374	Bushing	989	2.34	4.95	STDR
→8475	Compressor A-2	5	1123.45	1976.00	ACME
9987	Cap	98	10.23	20.75	ACME

Window 2

ITEM	SOLD
→8475	1
8475	2
8475	1
8475	1
8374	2
9987	2
9987	3
9987	4
9987	1
9987	5
9987	1
9987	2
6654	3
6654	1
6654	3
6654	8
2398	2
0239	1

Fig. 3.9.
Example files for the Relate command.

Using the Relate command between the two files, you can create a third which contains only the ACME items sold. The following project file performs a Relate command in which File 1 is ordered by a key that has been created to use only one record from the file. An index is used as a temporary substitute for the key.

```
goto window 1
order key [item]                             'order by item
query predefined ACME index IND1             'select only ACME Mfgrs

unload file INVENTRY                         'unload the file
file rename inventry.i01 to inventry.sav     'save the real key file
file rename ind1.idx to inventry.i01         'rename the index as the key
load INVENTRY screen standard                'load file back again
order key [item]                             'order by index/key

erelate predefined ACME intersect acme       'execute the query for acme
unload file INVENTRY                         'unload the Inventry file
file rename inventry.i01 to ind1.idx         'clear the substitute key
file rename inventry.sav to inventry.i01     'restore the real key file
load INVENTRY screen standard                'load the inventory file
```

```
order key [item]                          'check the real key

load ACME screen standard                 'load the ACME file
```

Notice that the index is used as a substitute for the key for the Inventory file. Although you are not allowed to order the driven file of a Relate command by an index, this substitution method works just as well. The file must be unloaded to rename the key files.

3.50 Tip: Add a key only when needed instead of continually updating keys.

Both

In Smart 3.10, after an Enter or Update command, updating the keys takes time. If a key is needed infrequently, it may be more efficient to add the key only when needed, rather than maintaining the key as you enter new records or update current ones. When you update keys, the record numbers of the newly entered records (from the .DBU file) are inserted in place in the key files. If the number of entries in the .DBU file grows beyond a certain size (determined by a formula of field size, record size, number of current updates, and previous updates), the system will perform a Key Organize command, rather than the Key Update.

At a certain size, the system computes that using Key Organize is more efficient than using Key Update. In other words, the time to organize a key is the same as adding the key initially. Therefore, if your application is performing the Key Organize option most of the time, you may just as well add the key only when you need it. (The screen message `sorting` indicates that the Key Organize option is taking place.)

In SmartWare II, the more keys you have, the more disk space is consumed. If you ever need to rebuild the keys, more keys require more time.

3.51 Tip: Add a key when needed if you are entering blank records within a project file and assigning the values of the data fields.

3.10

Because the .DBU file does not keep track of the numbers of the records entered with the Enter Blank command in a project file, using a Key Update command on such a file always performs the Key Organize function. This process takes the same amount of time as the Key Add function. If a key is needed only infrequently, consider performing a Key Add and Key Delete option when the key is actually needed to avoid wasting updating time in the intervening periods.

3.52 Trap: In alphabetic key fields, watch out for trailing blanks which will cause the Link command and combination reports to fail inexplicably.

Both

In an alphabetic field, you may not always fill the field completely. For instance, after defining a five-byte Department Code, you might enter only ACCT and then proceed to the next field. What happens to the last character in the Department Code? The character is null (ASCII 0) if you advance to the next field immediately with a carriage return or an F6 keystroke. The character is an actual blank (ASCII 32) if you hit the space bar. You can tell the difference between the null character and blank on the screen only in Update mode. Identical-looking fields with and without trailing blanks are not the same.

This problem is particularly vexing when you are using linkages. If you have a trailing blank in the sample personnel file, the system cannot find a link in the DEPT file, which has a trailing null. If you define a Lookup command to match the fields, you will get an error message that indicates:

```
Cannot find data for field 17
```

If you anticipate this problem, you should be able to avoid it. However, it is possible to ignore the warning and proceed with the Enter or Update command without the Lookup being performed.

If a trailing blank in the current file causes the Lookup to fail, press F3 to return to the field and use the delete key to eliminate any trailing blanks.

To get rid of any trailing blanks with the TRIM function, use the following query:

```
replace [field] = trim([field])
```

The TRIM function will strip off any leading or trailing blank characters. In Smart 3.10, be sure to update the keys after running this query.

Both

3.53 Tip: Manually correct alpha key fields with trailing blanks.

If you inspect the suspect records in update mode, one or more underscore characters at the end of the field show trailing nulls. Nothing at the end of the field indicates trailing blanks in the file. If your application standard is to maintain trailing nulls, then use the delete key to remove the trailing blanks, and you should be OK. Pressing the F7 key also deletes the character at the cursor location and all characters to the right.

Both

3.54 Trick: Use the Relate...Subtract command to isolate records that do not match on keys. (In SmartWare II, the command is Data Relate.)

If you have too many records to locate manually, perform a Relate...Subtract Command to create a file of records from the detail file (in the example, the personnel file) that do not match the standard file (the DEPT file). Include an identifying field, such as SSN, so you can locate the offending records quickly and correct the situation.

Sorting Your Data

Both

3.55 Tip: Create a sort definition to mix ascending and descending sort orders.

Performing the sort with the NOW option requires that all fields be sorted in either an ascending or descending sort sequence.

When using the Define option of the Sort command, you are given the choice, by field, of ascending or descending sort order. You can also specify the length of the field to use if the sort field is an alpha field (see fig. 3.10).

```
Window 1
  SSN         FIRST      LAST       AG S M DE DEG CA STREET           CITY
→345-98-7593 Rosanna    Ronaldo    52 M M  3 BA   2 546 Olive Hill   Oak Park
 498-48-3980 Debbie     Linden     29 F S  1 MA   2 409 Pleasant St Amherst
 239-87-0876 Michael    Davis      61 M M  1 MBA  2 100 Lewis Ave.   Covington
 208-23-0300 Julius     Karenski   41 M D  0 PhD  1 18 Olive St.     Louisvill
 887-63-5498 Jeff       Harris     34 M M  4 BA   5 1201 Horton Rd. Lyndhurst
 598-44-5922 LeAnne     Markus     48 F W  1 MBA  1 14 Crumpet Ave. Alamosa
 876-33-0989 Marilyn    Lester     55 F M  4 AB   3 6 Greenville St Yarmouth
 987-65-7653 David      Marzetti   47 M D  0      1 20 Grayln Dr.    Wilmingto
 387-59-8374 Charles    Steffans   25 M M  2 BS   2 44 Center Drive Brunswick
 498-34-5998 Paula      Bernstein  30 F S  3 MA   3 18 Worcester St Beaumont
 776-39-8763 Alfred     Adelson    60 M M  0 BA   1 14 Spring St.    Hartford
 345-54-2207 Ellen      Aliakbari  35 F S  0      1 2171 University Westfield
 198-03-3024 Howard E.  Peters     18 M S  0      1 10 Dennis Drive Winnfield

          Field title              Asc/Descending      Length in key
          DEPT                           A                   4
          WAGE                          →D                   10

F1  Help          F10  Finished         Esc  Abandon
sort define SORTSAM fields [dept:wage]
File: person3   Window: 1                    Page: 1  Rec: 1  ( 1 )  Act: Y
SORT - sort the current file and create a temporary index
```

Fig. 3.10.

Selecting sort sequence.

3.56 Trap: **When defining a sort, be sure your current screen or view displays all the fields you may need for a complete field-selection menu.**

Both

The menu of fields for sorting is screen-dependent. If necessary, you may have to load the file's standard screen or view to define the sort. The actual sort must take place with all the selected sort fields in the screen. If all sort fields are not in the screen, you will receive an error message:

```
Invalid field in sort definition file
```

3.57 Trick: **If several calculated view fields or multiple databases are attached to the custom view, use the standard view instead of a custom view to sort a database if possible.**

SW II

If all the fields you require for the sort of the main data file exist in the standard view, the standard view will sort faster. When the index has been created as a result of the sort, return the standard view to physical order and then order the custom view by the index. Of course, if the sort requires one of the view fields or one attached from another database, this technique cannot help you.

3.58 Trap: **The field identification in the sort-definition file is maintained by field number, not by name. If field numbers change at a later time, you must redefine the sort.**

3.10

If adding fields to a file causes existing fields to be renumbered, your sort will not work because the wrong fields will be addressed in the sort and the field lengths will differ from those originally defined.

3.10

3.59 Tip: If you need to add a field to a file, add it at the end of the file so that the numbers of the other fields are not changed.

Sort definitions (among other definitions) are dependent on field numbers rather than names. When you change your file by adding a field, add it at the end of the file instead of in the middle. By adding the field at the end, you ensure that the numbers of the prior fields do not change, and you avoid having to re-create your sort definitions.

3.10

3.60 Trick: The same sort definition can be used on multiple files, provided the files have the same structure.

The name of the file for which the sort was originally defined is not stored with the definition. If you have several files with the same structure, you need not define multiple sorts. Using the same sort definition works if the files have the same field numbers and record lengths.

SW II

3.61 Trick: One sort definition may be applied to different views if the field names and sort criteria are the same.

Using the same sort definition on different views may save effort and disk space, and make system maintenance easier. The views do not have to have the same number of fields or the same total number of bytes in each record, as in Smart 3.10.

3.10

3.62 Tip: Use the Shift-PrtSc key sequence to document your sort definition.

Unlike most other definitions in Smart, a sort definition cannot be inspected after it is defined. If you forget the specifications or take over a system that someone else has developed, you are at a loss.

To document your sort definition, perform a Print Screen just before you save the definition. The final screen will be similar to the one in figure 3.10; hold down your Shift key and press the Print Screen key. You may get some strange characters on the printer because of the way your printer represents the screen graphics, but you do have a record of the definition. Save this printout with your other system documentation and label it with the name of the sort definition.

Both

3.63 Tip: Use Sort Now (3.10) or Order Sort Now (SmartWare II) in a project file, rather than a predefined sort, for clarity of documentation and ease of maintenance.

In a project file, if you use Sort Now and specify the field names, the program becomes self-documenting. This procedure is particularly important in version 3.10 because as soon as a predefined sort has been created, you cannot view the sort definition.

One disadvantage to using a Sort Now is that you cannot mix ascending and descending sort orders. For that feature, you have to create a predefined sort.

The other disadvantage is that if you decide to change a common set of sort rules for the same file in several project files, you must edit each program individually.

3.64 Tip: Create an extra numeric field to use as a sort field in a nonstandard sorting situation.

Both

If you need to sort your file in a way that does not correspond to the regular sorting sequence within Smart, you can use an extra numeric field as a substitute. If you want to use the extra field for multiple purposes, use a Query with replace to enter the contents into the field. For example, the query definition creates a special sorting order for the Department field in a file:

```
replace [sortfield] = case [dept]
("DATA",1)  ("ACCT",2) ("SALE",3) ("MDSE",4) ELSE 5
```

If the special sort field has just one purpose, then you can use a calculated field. In SmartWare II, use a view field with a calculation; you do not have to store the data in the file.

This technique also can be important if you want to sort on an alpha field that mixes text and numbers. Consider the following examples of entries in several records:

```
JE11 JE22 JE31 JE2 JE3
```

Sorting the file using this field yields the following order, since an alpha field sorts from left to right:

```
JE11 JE2 JE22 JE3 JE31
```

However, if you really want the fields in numerical order, you could use the following query to insert a number into the sort utility field:

```
replace [sortfield] = value(mid([field],3,2))
```

By sorting on this numeric field, the records will be in the following order:

```
JE2 JE3 JE11 JE22 JE31
```

Notice that the query extracts the numerical portion of the field contents.

3.65 Tip: Even though you may elect to display an alpha field as right-justified, it still sorts left-justified.

SW II

Consider the following set of codes:

```
1,2,3,11,12,13,21,22,24,31,32
```

Displaying the codes right-justified in the field, as if they were actually in a numeric field might be important. Of course, if it were really a numeric field, it would sort in numeric order. However, an alpha field sorts from left to right, even though you are displaying the field contents right-justified. Thus the fields in this example would sort in the following order:

```
1,11,12,13,2,21,22,24,3,31,32
```

3.10

3.66 Trap: You cannot halt a sort in progress with a Ctrl-Z; you must wait until the sort is completed.

If the sort is executed within a project file, the Ctrl-Z will be accepted, but takes effect only after the completion of the sort, and applies to the cessation or suspension of the project file, not of the sort itself.

In SmartWare II, use Ctrl-Z to cancel the Order Sort command.

Changing the Order of the Data

Both

3.67 Tip: In Smart 3.10, you must perform the Order command after you execute a Sort or Query command that creates an index. In SmartWare II, this step is unnecessary.

If you do not order your file by the index you have created, your results will not meet your expectations. The Sort and Query commands create index files containing the physical numbers of the records in your data base that either meet the criteria specified in your query or are arranged in the specified sort order. When you perform the Order command, these record numbers are used to select both the records to display on your screen and the sequence in which they appear.

In SmartWare II, the Order Change Index command is performed automatically, following a successful Data Query or Order Sort command.

Both

3.68 Trick: No Smart Database command exists to specifically erase an index; use the File Erase command on command list 4 in Smart 3.10, or the Tools File Erase command in SmartWare II.

In Smart 3.10, use the File Erase command to erase an index file:

```
File Erase ins1.idx
```

You must remember to supply the file extension. If no index files are in use, erase all index files with this command:

```
File Erase *.idx
```

In SmartWare II, use the following command:

```
Tools File Erase *.idx
```

Index files can also be erased from DOS with the equivalent commands:

```
ERASE IND1.IDX
ERASE *.IDX
```

You may, of course, effect a temporary window to DOS by using the Ctrl-O quick key.

3.69 Tip: Re-use your index files. ***Both***

Because index files are generally used temporarily and then erased, you can set up two or three index files to use over and over again. (I call them IND1 and IND2, but the names are immaterial.) The Smart Database readily writes over the contents of an exiting index without prompting you to indicate whether it is OK to do so.

3.70 Trap: Do not order a file by an old index if database changes have made the index obsolete. You run the risk of producing incorrect reports or altering the wrong portions of your database. ***Both***

Even if you have not added to your database but have altered data that would change the result of the Query or Sort commands, do not use the index. In this instance, Smart will not prevent you from using an outdated index file.

3.71 Trick: If you are certain that conditions have not changed, you can retain index files and reuse them without having to execute the Query or Sort command again. (In SmartWare II, the commands are Data Query and Order Sort.) ***Both***

This technique works with files that are relatively static. For instance, in a file of a parts inventory, you might add new parts to the file only once or twice a year. You could create index files to identify parts by product line, price class, vendor, and so on. Then, just by using the Order command, you could easily switch to one or the other views of your data.

This example points out one important difference between using a key and an index file. A key, by definition, must span all records of your data base. An index file, however, may address only a subset of your data. In the parts inventory, your query could select only those parts in price class A, which might be only a fraction of the total number of parts on file. You could establish multiple index files on your disk, one for each price class.

3.72 Tip: Use your keys and index files together for efficient operations. ***3.10***

For example, for a report that is sorted by SSN but represents only those employees in the ACCT department, perform the following steps:

1. Order Key [SSN]
2. Query [dept] = "ACCT" index ind1
3. Order Index ind1
4. Report

The following sequence of steps produces the same result:

1. Order Sequential
2. Query [dept] = "ACCT" index ind1
3. Order Index ind1
4. Sort by [SSN] index ind2
5. Order Index ind2
6. Report

In this example, the first sequence would be more efficient because you do not have to sort the data. The sequence of the data is not disturbed during a query.

In SmartWare II, key order is not retained during the execution of a Data Query command; you must use the Order Sort command after you select the desired records.

Both

3.73 Trick: For efficiency, try to order your data base physically in the same sequence as the key you use most often.

If your data in a physical sequence is vastly different from the logical key sequence, your computer must do a great deal of searching and reading of multiple data-file clusters to present the order you want to see. This process is like trying to read a book in alphabetical sequence, using the index as a guide.

In Smart 3.10, when the data is loaded, you can create a new database in which the physical order matches your most commonly used logical order. For instance, after loading the data from a personnel data base, you can order the data by the key of the SSN (if that is the most frequently used key) and then concatenate the data into a new data base. With this technique, the physical order of the new database matches the SSN key, and your file access is much faster.

To complete the reorganization, create a new file that matches your old file. Load the new file in one window and the old file in another. Then—and this is important—order the old file by the key you want to specify as the new physical order. Go to the window that contains the new file and use the Utilities Concatenate command. The physical order of the new file now matches the logical (or key) order of the old file.

Once the data has been moved over to the new file, do not forget to create any custom screens similar to those of the old file. If necessary, unload the files, return to the DOS level with either the Ctrl-O DOS window or an F10 and Quit, and erase and rename files as follows:

```
ERASE OLDFILE.*
RENAME NEWFILE.* OLDFILE.*
```

When you return to the Smart Database, add the keys needed for the file.

Obviously, as you add and lose employees, the physical order will no longer match the logical order, but you can go through the erasing and renaming process periodically.

To provide an example of the benefits of this technique, I ran a query through a database of 5000 records, both ordered by the same key. One database was in the same physical order as the key and the other was in random order. The query took five times as long in the random file!

3.74 Trick: When not using a file, order it sequentially (instead of by a key or an index), to reduce the number of open files. ***Both***

If you order your file sequentially, the key file or the index file does not have to be open and the number of files open at any one time is decreased. Having few open files is important when operating on a network or not using the -FVIRTUAL switch on a single-user system in Smart 3.10.

3.75 Trap: Loaded views that are not in windows will retain their orders. If a view is going to be displaced from the window by another view, change the order to Physical to release the index. ***SW II***

By contrast, in Smart 3.10, when a file is displaced from its window by displaying another file, the first file automatically reverts to sequential (physical) order, releasing the index. In SmartWare II, the first file continues to be ordered by the index, even if it is in the background and not visible. If you attempt to use this index name while it is still in use, you receive the following error message:

```
Filename in index file does not match current file
```

If you are converting Smart 3.10 project files to SmartWare II, you may have problems if you assumed the release of the index files when a database was displaced from a window.

3.76 Trap: Be careful not to order two files in different windows by the same index. ***3.10***

After the first file is ordered by the index, you can go to another window, perform a Sort or Query command into the same index, and then order it by the index. No error message appears, and the files remain operable if you do not change their orders. If you return to the first file, order it sequentially, and then attempt to order it by the index again, you see this message:

```
A view is already ordered by this index file
```

On a network, you are prohibited from ordering two files by the same index.

SW II

3.77 Tip: In project files you have translated from Smart 3.10, delete the Order Change Index commands following the Data Query command.

The TRANSLAT program translates your Smart 3.10 programs to the SmartWare II format on a line-for-line basis. Although the 3.10 Order Index commands are translated to Order Change Index commands, they are superfluous because a Query that creates an index also orders the view by the index in SmartWare II. You receive no error message, however, if you do not delete the commands and order the view by an index by which it is already ordered.

3.10

3.78 Trick: Use the project file in Appendix A to add a record to an existing index.

Under normal circumstances, once an index has been created, you cannot change it. If you want a subset of the records, you can execute a Query to select those you need and create a new index. There is no provision within Smart, however, to *add* records to an existing index. The project file in Appendix A may be used to increase the number of records in an index.

Finding Your Data and Working with Multiple Files

To use your data, you must know where to find the records you need and be able to locate them quickly and accurately. The Find command (Smart 3.10) and Data Find command (SmartWare II), covered in this chapter, are used to locate records. Some methods of using the Find commands are faster than others—if you use them incorrectly, however, a search could take 10 times as long.

After providing several tips and tricks on the use of the Find commands, this chapter covers the use of the Relate and Transactions commands. These commands can seem complex to those who have not used them much, but this chapter is intended to take the mystery out of these commands and to make their use easier and more effective. In SmartWare II, the commands are Data Transact and Data Relate.

Using the Find and Data Find Commands

The Find (3.10) or Data Find (SmartWare II) commands can help you locate a given database record quickly and easily. If the conditions are right, Find utilizes a binary (or optimized) search technique to locate a record in a matter of seconds. If you are not careful, however, the same search can take minutes, or even hours.

Several other tips and tricks are presented to make your use of the Find command easier. Finally, a project file is listed that can simulate the Find command.

4.1 Tip: If the conditions are right, the Find (3.10) or Data Find (SmartWare II) commands can quickly locate a key field. *Both*

First, if you are using Smart 3.10, order your file by the key field you are searching. (This tip applies only if your search field is a major key field; if not, you have to perform a sequential search.) Next, execute the Find command on command list 1 of Smart 3.10, or the Data Find in SmartWare II. For both systems, the Quick Key is F3.

You must adhere to the following rules for this fast, optimized search to be effective:

1. The field you want to search for must be the major field of the key.
2. The file must be ordered by that key field if you are using Smart 3.10.
3. The search must apply only to that single field.
4. You must specify the Equal operator.
5. You must not select any options if you are using Smart 3.10. In SmartWare II, use the G (Global) option for an optimized search if your view is not ordered by the key.

If you adhere to these conditions, the Find command executes quickly. If you happen to select the I (Ignore Case) option, however, the Find command is executed sequentially and does not use the key.

Both

4.2 Trap: In Smart 3.10, if you forget to order your file by the key field, the Find command executes sequentially. The same thing happens if you also forget to use the Global option in SmartWare II.

Unlike the Query command, in which you can use the "where" modifier only if the file is ordered by the key field, no special notation is needed to use the binary-search feature of the Find command. You will realize you forgot to order the file by the key field only when execution of the command takes much longer than you expected. You can always stop the Find operation with a Ctrl-Z, order by the key, and use the Alt-R quick key to repeat the most recent Find command.

In SmartWare II, you can correct the problem by adding the G option to the command. Press the Alt-X to display the Data Find command, then edit the line to insert the G at the end of the command, within the quotation marks. Press Enter to execute the command.

Both

4.3 Tip: When executing the Find command to search on a key field, you can specify an abbreviation.

If you specify an abbreviation for the search string, the Find command locates the closest match (see fig. 4.1). This feature can be a great time saver if the first few characters of the key field are significant and unique.

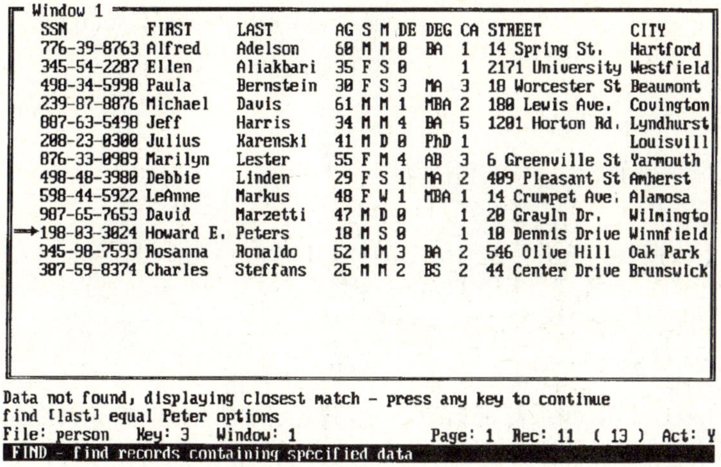

```
┌ Window 1 ─────────────────────────────────────────────────────────────────────
  SSN         FIRST      LAST       AG S M DE DEG CA STREET           CITY
  776-39-8763 Alfred     Adelson    60 M M 0  BA  1  14 Spring St.    Hartford
  345-54-2287 Ellen      Aliakbari  35 F S 0      1  2171 University Westfield
  498-34-5998 Paula      Bernstein  30 F S 3  MA  3  18 Worcester St Beaumont
  239-87-8876 Michael    Davis      61 M M 1  MBA 2  180 Lewis Ave.   Covington
  887-63-5498 Jeff       Harris     34 M M 4  BA  5  1201 Horton Rd.  Lyndhurst
  208-23-0300 Julius     Karenski   41 M D 0  PhD 1                   Louisvill
  876-33-0989 Marilyn    Lester     55 F M 4  AB  3  6 Greenville St Yarmouth
  498-48-3980 Debbie     Linden     29 F S 1  MA  2  409 Pleasant St Amherst
  598-44-5922 LeAnne     Markus     48 F W 1  MBA 1  14 Crumpet Ave.  Alamosa
  987-65-7653 David      Marzetti   47 M D 0      1  20 Grayln Dr.    Wilmingto
→198-03-3024 Howard E.  Peters     18 M S 0      1  10 Dennis Drive Winnfield
  345-98-7593 Rosanna    Ronaldo    52 M M 3  BA  2  546 Olive Hill   Oak Park
  387-59-8374 Charles    Steffans   25 M M 2  BS  2  44 Center Drive Brunswick

Data not found, displaying closest match - press any key to continue
find [last] equal Peter options
File: person   Key: 3   Window: 1              Page: 1  Rec: 11  ( 13 )  Act: Y
 FIND - find records containing specified data
```

Fig. 4.1.
Finding the closest match.

4.4 Tip: The Partial operator and the Whole Words Only option often are confused.

Both

Looking at the screen in figure 4.1 can help explain the differences and similarities between the Partial operator and the Whole Words Only option.

By using the Partial operator, you indicate that you want to find your search string within a larger alphanumeric field. Look at the STREET field in figure 4.1, for example. If you are searching for someone living on a street (St) rather than a road (Rd) or a drive (Drive), you need to use the Partial operator instead of the Equal operator. Equal does not work because you are supplying only part of the field contents (St) rather than the entire field contents. The Partial operator is similar to the Contains operator that you specify in a query with the exclamation point (!).

The Whole Words Only option identifies records in which the specified search string is bounded by blanks or appears as a separate word at the beginning or end of the field. If you want to use St as the search string but want to avoid finding the St of Stanton in the address 4228 Stanton Dr., you should specify the Whole Words Only option because the St in Stanton is not bounded by a blank on both sides. The complete Smart 3.10 command is

```
find [street] partial St option w
```

The Partial operator and the Whole Words Only option frequently are used in conjunction, as in the preceding example. You can use the Partial operator by itself if you think you may miss the record you want and are willing to tolerate the display of a few records you do not want to see. For example, if you include the Whole Words Only option in this example, you miss the records in which St is followed by a period. To find the records containing St. and St, issue the following command:

```
find [street] partial St options
```

Specifying just the Whole Words Only option without the Partial operator would be meaningless.

Both

4.5 Tip: The greater-than and less-than Find command operators, although usually applied to numeric fields, also can be applied to date and alpha fields.

By using these operators on date fields, you do not have to resort to the DAYS function, which sometimes is needed in the Query command. If you can use the Find command, the structure of a statement with a Date field is less complicated than a Query. (In SmartWare II, if you are using the Query by Example facility, you can enter dates directly, without using the DAYS function. Refer to Chapter 7.)

Figure 4.2 shows the result of a Find operation on the EMPDATE field of the Person file.

Fig. 4.2.

Using Find on a Date field.

```
Window 1
  EMPDATE  LAST        FIRST
  07-23-45 Adelson     Alfred
  10-01-59 Ronaldo     Rosanna
  10-30-65 Markus      LeAnne
  05-25-69 Davis       Michael
  07-01-70 Harris      Jeff
  08-20-71 Karenski    Julius
  08-15-72 Aliakbari   Ellen
  06-15-75 Bernstein   Paula
  06-20-75 Linden      Debbie
→ 09-05-75 Lester      Marilyn
  10-15-81 Steffans    Charles
  10-01-85 Peters      Howard E.
  10-30-85 Marzetti    David

Data found in [EMPDATE], continue search (y/n)
find [empdate] greater-than 7/23/75 options g
File: person   Index: IND1   Window: 1          Page: 1  Rec: 10  ( 7 )  Act: Y
FIND   find records containing specified data
```

A query to accomplish a similar search is more complex, and the result is slightly different because the query selects all records with an employment date greater than 7/23/75. In the Smart 3.10 query and the SmartWare II View Expression query, you must use the DAYS function to convert the date to a sequential number indicating the number of days from the beginning of the 20th century (January 1st, 1900, is day 1). The query is shown in figure 4.3.

```
Query Editor

      days([empdate]) > days("7/23/75")
```

Fig. 4.3.
A similar Query on a Date field.

Additional Query command examples are presented in Chapter 7.

4.6 Tip: Use the following technique to find the next key field after a prompt value. *3.10*

When a file is ordered by a key, the Find command can be used to locate very quickly the first occurrence of a key field value. If you really want the *next* key record, your task is easy if only one record exists per key value; simply go to the next record.

If the key fields have multiple occurrences, the task is more difficult. Although you can use "Greater-Than," you have to perform a sequential search rather than a fast, binary search. The following project file may be used to locate the next key field following a prompted value.

```
input $field Field Value:
let $len = len($field)

Let %2 = left($field,$len-1) | chr((asc(right($field,1))+1))

find [dept] equal "%2" options
```

In this example, the program finds the next [dept] field following the value entered in response to the prompt.

4.7 Trap: Using the Find...Equal command on an alpha field in Smart 3.10 disregards the field case. This is not true in SmartWare II. *Both*

In figure 4.4, you can see that searching for the last name in uppercase finds the last name in mixed case.

The Data Find command in SmartWare II is case-sensitive.

4.8 Tip: Use the Find...Partial command on an alpha field to force case recognition. *3.10*

Although ignoring case sometimes can be a benefit, you may have occasions when finding the right case is important. If you do not want to ignore case, use the Partial operator instead of the Equal operator. You cannot, however, perform a binary search if you select the Partial operator.

4.9 Tip: If you are executing the Find command within a project file, use a command error (CERROR) code 3002 to check whether the find was successful. *3.10*

```
Window 1
 EMPDATE  LAST       FIRST
 07-23-45 Adelson    Alfred
 10-01-59 Ronaldo    Rosanna
 10-30-65 Markus     LeAnne
 05-25-69 Davis      Michael
 07-01-70 Harris     Jeff
 08-20-71 Karenski   Julius
 08-15-72 Aliakbari  Ellen
 06-15-75 Bernstein  Paula
 06-20-75 Linden     Debbie
 09-05-75 Lester     Marilyn
 10-15-81 Steffans   Charles
→10-01-85 Peters     Howard E.
 10-30-85 Marzetti   David

Data found in [LAST], continue search (y/n)
find [last] equal PETERS options g
File: person   Index: IND1   Window: 1          Page: 1  Rec: 12  ( 13 )  Act: Y
FIND - find records containing specified data
```

Fig. 4.4.

Ignoring case with the Find...Equal command.

The following is an example of checking the error:

```
find [last] equal Peters options g
if CERROR = 3002
      beep 2
      message Command error ... press any key ...
      stop
endif
```

The more error checks you put into your project files, the more foolproof your files will be.

In SmartWare II, the equivalent CERROR number is 3716.

3.10 **4.10 Trap: When using a search-string parameter with the Find command in a project file, you get an error if the parameter contains a blank and you omit the double quotation marks.**

If you use the Find command in a project file and the search string is contained in a parameter, you should write your statement like this:

```
find [street] partial "%1" options g
```

The Find command can work perfectly well without the double quotation marks around the parameter. If, however, the parameter contains two or more words, you get a syntax error because the Smart Database interprets the space between the two words as a delimiter in the command. Better play it safe and include the quotation marks. Even if your field is a numeric field, the quotation marks will not hurt, but the marks are not needed.

3.10 **4.11 Trap: If the current record meets the criteria of the Find command, the record is accepted and the pointer remains on the current record.**

If you are executing Find from the command level, you can answer the prompt to proceed to the next acceptable record, if you want. If you are executing Find in a project file, however, the fact that the current record is acceptable can cause your project file to remain in an endless loop. The loop develops because subsequent executions of the same Find command keep finding the same record. To avoid this problem, use the Goto Record Next command, as shown in the following Smart 3.10 project file:

```
goto record rec-number 1

label begin
find [empdate] greater-than 7/1/75 options
if cerror <> 3002 then jump okfind
beep 2
message No record found ... press any key ...
jump alldone

label okfind
lprint [last]
if record = records then jump alldone
goto record next
jump begin

label alldone
```

4.12 Tip: The Find and the Query...Screen commands are similar, but they also have subtle differences that can be useful. *3.10*

The Find command appears similar to the Query...Screen command, and in many ways the commands are alike. Both commands can be used to locate records in your database according to the field value. These commands have differences, however.

The Find command accepts a single value, which is measured by one of four operators against one or more fields. Find is easy to execute, does not require a special modifier to utilize key fields, and can begin in the middle of a database.

Query...Screen, on the other hand, can accept as complex a search criterion as you care to write, going far beyond the scope of the Find command. You can specify multiple fields and comparison values. The more complex the query, however, the more difficult the query is to write. And—this is important—the Query...Screen command must search the entire range of the file or index because the command cannot begin at the current record or work backwards through the file. Alternating between a Query...Screen and an Update command, for example, is time consuming because each new query returns to the same first record.

4.13 Tip: You can specify multiple search fields in the Find or Data Find commands. *Both*

To specify multiple fields, separate the fields with semicolons on the command line as you enter the field names, or use the F6 key to identify the fields. The search will be successful if either field matches the criteria. The following SmartWare II example displays the command to search for personnel records in which the Wage or NewPay is greater than 900.

```
data find [Wage;NewPay] greater-than 900 options
```

As a qualifying record is found, a message similar to the following is displayed:

```
Data found in [NewPay]. Continue search? (y/n)
```

Note the display of the name of the field satisfying the criterion.

Both

4.14 Tip: When using the Find command on an inverted field, you should enter the search string in its uninverted form, as displayed on-screen.

If the inverted field contains the name *Gloria Granite*, for example, the Find statement should be:

```
find [Name] equal "Gloria Granite" options f
```

Unlike the Query command, the Find command does not require you to use the REINVERT function or to enter the search string in its inverted format.

In SmartWare II, the Data Find command accepts the inverted field contents in the same order as in Smart 3.10. However, in the Data Query command, unlike 3.10, you do *not* use the invert function, but simply enter the string as displayed on-screen.

Both

4.15 Trick: Refer to Appendix A for project files that simulate the command-level Smart 3.10 Find and SmartWare II Data Find commands.

Working with Multiple Files

The Relate and Transactions commands are used when you need to process two database files together. In SmartWare II, the commands are Data Relate and Data Transact. The Relate command is used to combine two files into a third, based on one or more link fields. In the Transactions command, data from one file is either moved, added, or subtracted from fields in another file.

These powerful commands sometimes are confusing if you do not use them frequently. The tips and tricks in this section are intended to make your use of the Relate and Transactions commands easier, and to point out ways in which you can take full advantage of their capabilities.

Relating Two Files into a Third

Both

4.16 Tip: Use the Relate (3.10) or Data Relate (SmartWare II) commands to combine two files into a new one.

To perform the Relate command, you must have a Link field common to both files. If you combine two files in the examples, the DEPT code would be the Link field between the Person file and the Dept file (see fig. 4.5).

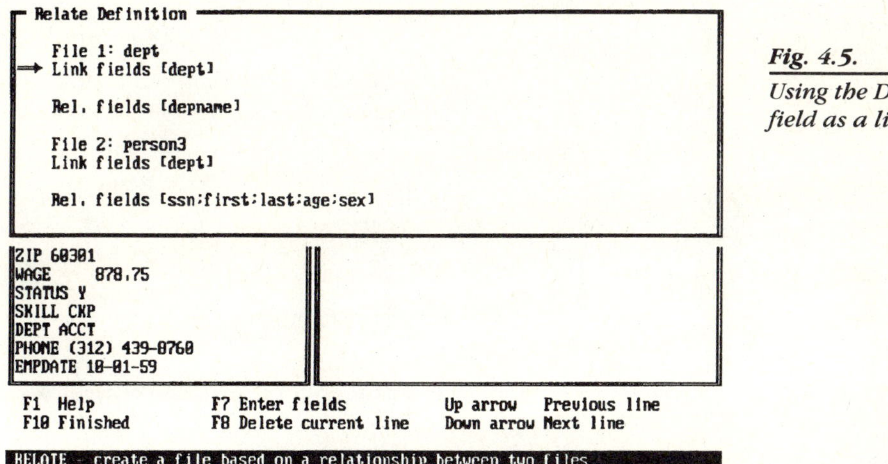

Fig. 4.5.
Using the DEPT field as a link.

In the example, the Dept file is the number 1 file (driven) and Person is the number 2 file (driver). You always must designate the Link field in the number 1 file as a key field, and the file must be ordered by that key. (This is one case in which you must have a key field; just sorting a file by the field will not suffice.)

(In SmartWare II, the nomenclature has changed—File 2 is the driven file and must have the key.)

The driver file doesn't need to be ordered by a key or even sorted by the link field. If the driver file is in order by the link field, however, the resulting output file will be in the same order.

Your Relate command actually may run more slowly if you sort the driver file by the link field. If the link field in the driver file happens to be a key field, the speed loss is not as great, but still is greater than if the file is in purely sequential order. The best situation is to have the physical order match the key order.

You don't always want to match all the records in the driver file with those of the driven file. Although you cannot restrict the number of records in the driven file (the file must be ordered by the link field key), you can limit the number of records in the driver file by a query and an order by an index. Naturally, the fewer records you have in the driver file, the faster your command will execute.

In Smart 3.10, the driver file must be current when you execute the Relate Predefined command. In SmartWare II, either file may be current.

A comparable relation definition screen is shown in figure 4.6.

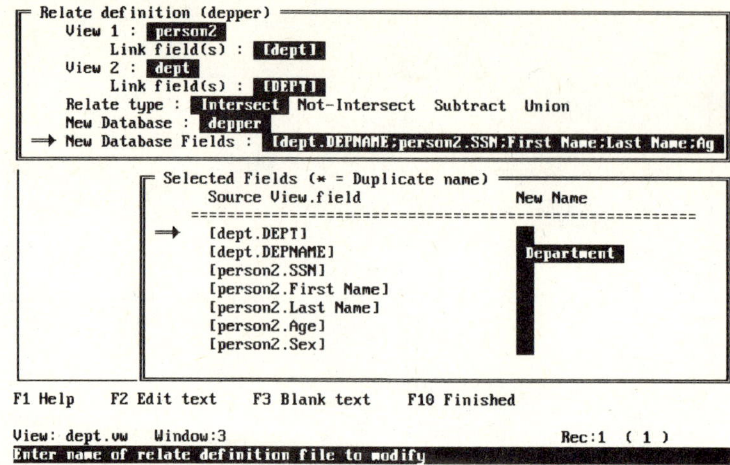

Fig. 4.6.

The same Data Relate definition in SmartWare II.

Note that the type of the relation and the name of the new file are included within the definition in SmartWare II. The driven view is called View 2, rather than View 1. You also have the opportunity of changing the names of any of the resulting fields. You *must* change a name if you have a duplicate, which is noted by the display of an asterisk.

3.10

4.17 Trap: If you specify a field range when defining your relation, take great care to use the vertical bar (|) rather than the colon (:). Although no error message will be issued, the results will be incorrect.

The vertical bar and the colon look similar enough that you can mistake one for the other. Smart does not catch the error, but only the fields before the colon are included in the resulting file. You will wonder what happened to the remaining fields.

In SmartWare II, if you use the colon rather than the vertical bar, you get the message `Invalid field entered`.

Both

4.18 Tip: After using a file created by the Relate command, you may want to unload and erase the file so that you can perform the exact Relate command again without an error. In SmartWare II, the command is Data Relate.

The Relate command issues an error message if the output file already exists. If you think you might perform the Relate command to create the same file again during the same session, unload the file and erase it. In SmartWare II, the error message is:

```
Data-file already exists
```

In Smart 3.10, if you are performing the commands manually, you must perform Utilities Erase File before executing the Relate command to create the same file again.

In SmartWare II, use the Tools File Erase command to erase the existing database and standard view. In Smart 3.10, use the Utilities Erase File command.

4.19 Trap: If you are executing the Relate or Data Relate commands from a project file, make sure the output file does not exist. Existence of the output file causes an error that halts the project file.

Both

In Smart 3.10, you may want to use the following statement just before the Relate command:

```
if file("outfile.db") = 1 then utilities erase file outfile
```

With this statement, any existing output file is erased. In SmartWare II, use the following:

```
tools file erase "depper.db"
tools file erase "depper.vws"
```

These commands erase the database and the standard view

4.20 Trap: A Data Relate (SmartWare II) or Relate (3.10) command that results in zero records does not generate a CERROR code. You must check the file for the number of records.

Both

```
If records = 0
     sound 200 .5
     message "Zero records created .. press any key"
end if
```

These SmartWare II statements check for zero records in a view.

4.21 Tip: After executing the Relate command in Smart 3.10, you must load the output file.

3.10

In Smart 3.10, the Relate command does not load the output file for you. In SmartWare II, the view is loaded automatically at the conclusion of the Data Relate command.

4.22 Tip: You can specify multiple link fields to define further matching conditions in the Relate or Data Relate commands.

Both

If additional fields are needed to specify a unique match, you can designate the fields as secondary link fields. The field numbers, lengths, types, and numeric-precision definitions must match exactly, although the field names do not have to match. In the driven file, the secondary link fields must be minor keys of the primary key field.

Use this tip when the primary key field is not sufficient to identify a record uniquely. For example, just matching on [lastname] between two files is insufficient; you may have to add [firstname] as a secondary link field. You even may need to add the middle initial as a third field.

If you defined Relate with three link fields, the field contents must be identical in records in both files for the match condition to be true.

Both

4.23 Tip: You can specify multiple link fields in the driver file of a Relate definition to create a match if any link fields match the single link field in the driven file.

If an individual personnel file record contains the codes of three departments for which an individual can work (see fig. 4.7), you can establish all three fields as the links in the driver file and create a maximum of three records in the resulting output file.

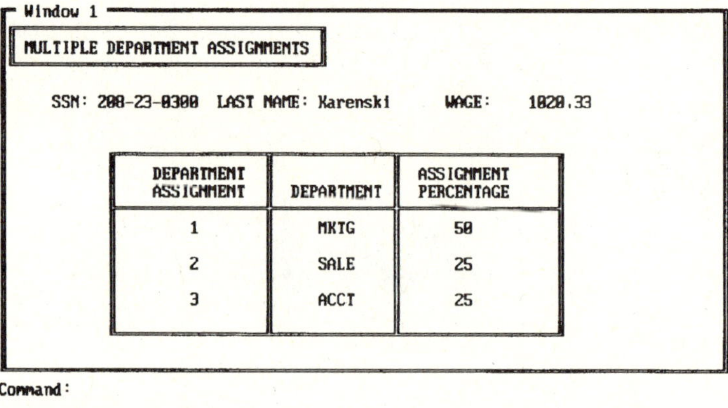

Fig. 4.7. *A personnel record with multiple departments.*

The definition in figure 4.8 relates the DEPT field in the DEPT file to the fields DEPT1, DEPT2, and DEPT3 in the MULTDEPT file.

The file resulting from the execution of the Relate command is shown in figure 4.9. Note that employee Karenski (at pointer) now has three records, one for each of his departments. Employees working for only one department have only one record in the resulting file.

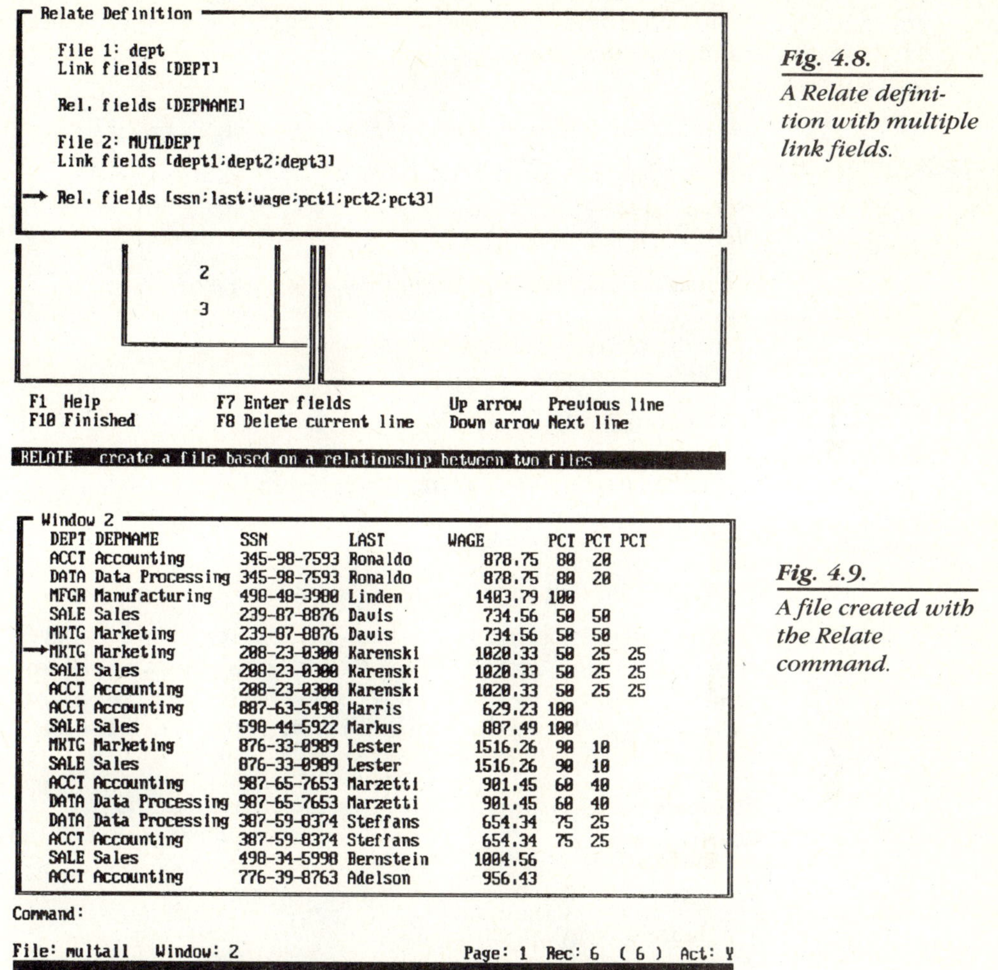

Fig. 4.8. *A Relate definition with multiple link fields.*

Fig. 4.9. *A file created with the Relate command.*

The data fields retrieved from the driver file, such as LAST, SSN, and WAGE, repeat from record to record for the same individual.

4.24 Tip: In Smart 3.10, the case of the contents of the linkage fields is immaterial—the Relate command will work correctly, regardless of case. In SmartWare II, this is not true. ***Both***

Because Smart Version 3.10 uses the collation-sorting sequence, lower- and uppercase letters have the same value and, therefore, match in the Relate command.

In SmartWare II, the Data Relate command does not work the same way because key fields are maintained in strict ASCII sequence. In an ASCII sequence, upper- and lowercase letters have different values.

Both

4.25 Trap: In the Relate and Data Relate commands, records marked for deletion in either file are not processed by the command.

If you are not getting all the records you expect in your output file, check the active status of the records in your files.

3.10

4.26 Trap: You must remember the screen for which a Relate definition was created. Although an error message may not appear if you use the wrong screen for file 2 in the execution of a Relate command, you may get many more records than you expected.

Relate definitions are screen-dependent for file 2. If more than one screen is loaded at the time you create the definition, you are prompted to identify the screen to use. When you execute the Relate, the definition attempts to use the required screen. If the screen is not loaded, you get the following error message:

```
Screen used in definition for second file not open
```

If the required screen is in the "background," however, the screen is used, even though another screen for the same file may be visible in the window and ordered by an index. In such an instance, all records for file 2 are considered in the Relate—not just those records available through the index used on-screen in the window.

There is no available documentation to identify the file 2 screen defined for the Relate—you must remember the screen you selected at the time you created the definition.

Both

4.27 Tip: Press your Print Screen key to document the Relate definition and save this with your system information.

Just before you press F10 to save the Relate definition, if you print the definition, you can refer back to the definition in the future. No built-in facility is provided for documenting these definitions. On the printout, write the names of the Relate definition, the date, and the screens used.

In SmartWare II, documenting the Data Relate definitions is particularly important because the type of the relation (Intersect, Union, Subtract or Not-Intersect) and the output file name are contained within the definition. (In Smart 3.10, these selections are provided at the time of execution.)

3.10

4.28 Trap: You can change a Relate definition accidentally if you recall the definition and specify the wrong files.

Display the Relate definition with the Relate Define command. With this command, however, if you forget the file name you specified for file 2 and select the wrong one, the name of the incorrect file is inserted on the definition screen as file 2. You have no way of knowing if this was the original file in the definition.

If the Relate fields were specified by numbers, rather than by names, the numbers will still appear in the Relate fields list, although they may represent incorrect fields if the file is incorrect.

4.29 Tip: Enter the field names for the Relate fields, rather than the field numbers, when creating a Relate definition. *3.10*

The following are several reasons for using field names instead of numbers:

- The screen print is easier to read.
- If you later add fields to your files, the Relate definition still is valid because field names have been used rather than numbers.
- If you recall the definition accidentally and specify the wrong file, the field list is blank if any fields do not match the file 2 field list. The blank field list tips you off that something is wrong.

In SmartWare II, you must use field numbers.

4.30 Trick: Use an existing Relate definition as a template for a new definition. *Both*

If you want to duplicate an existing Relate definition, copy the original to a new name. You cannot use the Relate Define or Data Relate Create command to create a relation definition similar to an existing one.

The file extension of a Relate definition is DFX. In Smart 3.10, use the File Copy command; in SmartWare II, use Tools File Copy.

4.31 Trap: If you specify a counter field to be selected in a Relate command, the field value changes when carried into the new file. *3.10*

For alternatives to using a counter field, refer to the suggestions in the section "Using Counter Fields," in Chapter 2.

4.32 Tip: A calculated field that is written to the output file during a Relate command no longer is calculated in the new file, but is an actual, real database field. *Both*

You do not have to select the fields that are the factors of the calculation to write out a calculated field. If you do, the value of the formerly calculated field does not change even if you change the factor fields.

4.33 Trick: Specify an extra relation field if you need an additional field in the output file. *Both*

You cannot add a brand new field to a file during the Relate command; you can select only fields that exist in either file 1 or file 2. If, you need an additional field, however, you can select a field to use as a surrogate even though you already may have selected the field. Relate does not prohibit you from selecting the same field twice.

You should select a field that matches the type, size, and degree of precision you need—the name is immaterial. In Smart 3.10, if you have selected the same field twice, however, you should refer to the fields by their numbers when using the output file because that file then has two fields with the same name.

You can specify the following field list in the SmartWare II Data Relate definition:

```
[person2.ssn|street;street]
```

In this example, you are selecting the `[street]` field twice.

After you have your extra field in the output file, you can perform a replacement Query with the additional fields as a target. (In this case, the fact that Report definitions in Smart 3.10 store field numbers rather than field names can be an advantage.)

In SmartWare II, if you use this trick and select the same field twice, you must provide a new name for one of the fields.

SW II

4.34 Trick: Create a file with both new and existing database fields by using the Data Relate command.

When creating a Data Relate definition, you can assign new names to fields in the output file. This has the effect of replicating existing database fields and retaining the attributes of the originals. After the new file has been created, you can use a Query to blank the contents of the new fields or assign values to them.

3.10

4.35 Trick: Use an index as a substitute for a key on file 1 in the Relate command to save processing time.

File 1 normally must be ordered by the key when executing a Relate command. File 2 may be ordered by an index to select only the records you want. If you want to base the selection on fields in file one, however, you usually must extract the necessary fields during the Relate and Query them after the new file is created.

Refer to Chapter 3 for an example of using an index as a substitute for a key for file 1 to reduce the processing time of a Relate command.

Passing Transactions from One File to Another

Both

4.36 Tip: In a Transaction (3.10) or Data Transact (SmartWare II) command, the file that causes the action to take place is the driver.

Any transaction must contain both a driver and a driven file, and the distinction can be confusing. The file that causes action to take place is the driver file. For example, if you have a parts-inventory file and a file of sales transactions for the day, you designate the sales-transactions file as the driver file if you want to update the inventory based on the parts quantities sold during the day (see fig.

4.10). Generally, the file that has only one record for each link-field occurrence is the driven file, and the file that can have multiple link fields or none at all is the driver file.

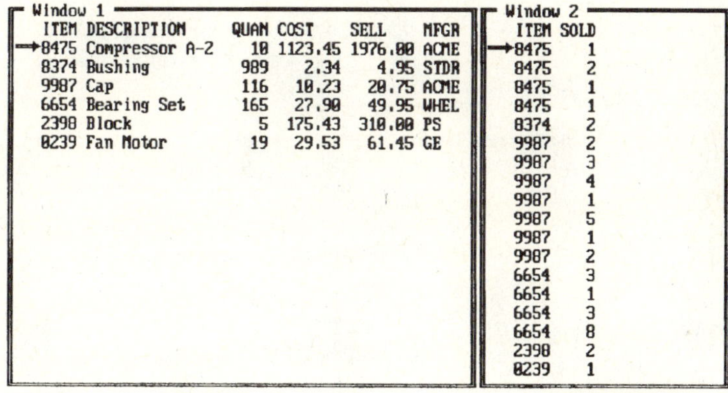

Fig. 4.10.

The driver file (Window 1) and the driven file (Window 2).

4.37 Tip: The destination file in a transaction can be the driver or the driven file. *Both*

Designating files as Source and Destination also can be confusing. When you decide which file is to be the driver, you must decide where the data is to be moved.

In the example cited in Tip 4.36, the source file is the driver; that is, the sales-transaction file is the source of data (sales quantities) and also is the driver because you want to update the inventory quantities in the parts file for each sale entered into the sales file. Because the Sales file is the source, the Parts Inventory file is the destination.

The driver file also can be a destination. If you have an empty cost field in the sales file, you can move cost data from the parts file to the sales file to prepare a daily profitability-analysis report. In this case, the sales file still is the driver and also the destination.

In Smart 3.10, a transaction may go only one direction at a time. The driver file may be the source or the destination, but not both. In SmartWare II, the driver may be the source and the destination simultaneously.

4.38 Tip: In a transaction, the link field in the driven file always must be a key field. In Smart 3.10, the file must be ordered by the key, but in SmartWare II, this is not necessary. *Both*

In the example, the parts file is used throughout the application. You most likely would establish the item number as a key field—not only for performing transactions, but also for using the Relate command, for using the binary search capabilities of the Find and the Query commands, and for performing Lookups.

Both

4.39 Tip: In Smart 3.10, the case of the contents of the linkage fields is immaterial—the Transaction command works correctly, regardless of case. In SmartWare II, this not true.

Because Smart Version 3.10 uses the collation sorting sequence, lower- and uppercase letters have the same value and therefore match in the Transactions command.

In SmartWare II, this is *not* true because keys are maintained in ASCII sequence, in which upper- and lowercase letters are not equal.

Both

4.40 Trap: If you do not specify that all driver files are to be marked for deletion during the transaction, you risk using them more than once.

For example, if you have the driver files marked for deletion, you cannot accidentally subtract from inventory twice. In the previous example, however, in which the driver file (Sales) was going to be used as a transaction destination for the cost-data loading so that you could run a profitability report, you would not want to delete the driver records. (The Report command ignores deleted records.)

Both

4.41 Trap: A driver record in a transaction will not be used if the link record in the driven file is deleted.

If a record in the driven file is deleted accidentally, any transaction to that record does not occur. If a driver record exists with the matching link field, the record is not deleted after the transaction.

This situation presents both a Trap and a Tip. It is a Trap if you are unaware of the accidental deletion of the record in the driven file. Because the driver record was not processed, however, you do not want the record to be marked for deletion.

You can take several steps to prevent this occurrence. To make sure no driven records are deleted accidentally, perform a Query command to activate all records. Alternatively, you can purge all deleted records from the driver file after the transaction, load the file again, and report any records still existing in the file.

3.10

4.42 Tip: When you define a transaction, the current window must contain the destination file. The source file must be loaded, but need not be in a window.

The Transaction command prompt asks for the file that will be used as the source. It is assumed that the current file is the destination.

4.43 Trap: If you try to define a transaction with a name longer than eight characters, the command terminates inexplicably without an error message. *3.10*

All other commands in which you create a definition provide an error message indicating that the file name is invalid. The Transaction Define command does not issue an error message if the name is too long and the command terminates without any explanation, returning you immediately to the command level.

4.44 Tip: When you execute a predefined transaction, both files must be loaded in windows and the driven file must be in order by the link field. *3.10*

You do not, however, have to execute the Link command to link the driver file to the driven file. The transaction can be executed from any window on your screen—the window need not contain a file involved in the transaction.

In SmartWare II, neither of the views have to be in windows to execute the Data Transact command.

4.45 Tip: After performing the transaction, perform a Key Update command on the destination file. *3.10*

If you update a field that is only a data field and not a key field, however, you do not necessarily have to update the keys. When you run a report, you are warned:

```
File contains unmerged records. Continue (y/n)
```

This message is only a warning. If you are sure that the only fields you have changed since your last key update have been data fields, you can proceed safely. If, however, you have changed a key field or entered new records and have ordered your file by a key, then your report may be missing some records or may be out of its expected order. For further discussion of this subject, refer to Chapters 6 and 7.

4.46 Tip: You cannot target a transaction into a calculated field. No error message will appear, nor will there be any result. ***Both***

A calculated field is derived from its factors and cannot be changed on its own. If you try to direct a transaction into a calculated field, an error message does not appear when the Transaction definition is created or when the Transaction is executed.

4.47 Trap: If the driven file in a transaction is active in more than one window, you may be prevented from performing the Transaction, due to system confusion about key fields. *3.10*

Even if the driven file is ordered by a key in one of the windows, and not in the other, you may get the following message:

```
Field x of C:\database.db is not the current key field
```

This indicates that the driven file is not ordered by the key field. When you execute a Predefined transaction, each window is checked in sequence, beginning with window 1. If the driven file is found in one of the windows and is not ordered by the key, the error message results.

This is true even if the current window contains the driven file and *is* ordered by the key. For example, if the current window is number 3, and window 2 contains the driven file in sequential order, the error message is displayed.

SW II

4.48 Tip: Deleted driven file records are processed by the Data Transact command, but generate a No-Match condition. In the audit report, nothing indicates that the match failed because the records were deleted.

Deleted records in the driver file are not processed and do not generate messages in the audit file.

Using Utilities To Restructure and Concatenate

3.10

4.49 Tip: Transport data between files with the Utilities Restructure command.

The Utilities Restructure command generally is used after you add a field to a file or change a field declaration. Because you cannot simply add a field to a file, you must create a file similar to the old file, add the new field or change the declaration, and then move the data from the old file to the new file.

Utilities Restructure matches fields between the old file and the new file by the field names. If the names match, the restructure definition is completed for you (see fig. 4.11). This command is a great convenience and time saver.

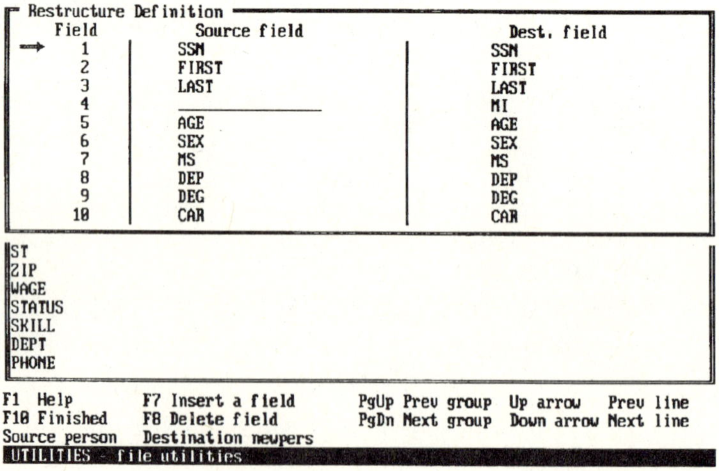

Fig. 4.11.

Adding a field with Utilities Restructure.

```
Restructure Definition
   Field          Source field                       Dest. field
 →   1         SSN                                  SSN
     2         FIRST                                FIRST
     3         LAST                                 LAST
     4         _______________                      MI
     5         AGE                                  AGE
     6         SEX                                  SEX
     7         MS                                   MS
     8         DEP                                  DEP
     9         DEG                                  DEG
    10         CAR                                  CAR

ST
ZIP
WAGE
STATUS
SKILL
DEPT
PHONE

F1  Help          F7 Insert a field      PgUp Prev group  Up arrow    Prev line
F10 Finished      F8 Delete field        PgDn Next group  Down arrow  Next line
Source person     Destination newpers
UTILITIES - file utilities
```

4.50 Tip: In the Utilities Restructure (3.10) or Data Utilities Append (SmartWare II) definitions, use the F7 key only if you have added a field or changed a field name.

Both

The F7 key is used to insert a field name in the source-file field list. In the example in figure 4.11, a field for a middle initial has been added to the personnel file. Because the old file does not contain a field with the name MI, the line is left blank in the source-file list of field specifications.

If you change the field name from MIDDLE to MI, you move the cursor to the fourth line, press F7 to display a list of fields from the source file, and select one. Although the opportunity exists to enter more than one field name in the command line, the system accepts only the first one. You cannot use this command to concatenate two fields.

4.51 Trap: Make sure the last screen loaded for a file contains all the fields you want to transfer to the new file. If it doesn't, you cannot transfer all fields.

3.10

The source screen for the Utilities Restructure command is the last one loaded for the file, regardless of which is visible in a window. If you have two screens loaded, the second screen is used as the source. If the screen does not contain all the fields, you cannot transfer all fields. For best results, your screen should contain all fields. Preferably, use the standard screen, which you know has all fields.

4.52 Trap: Field names do not match if they are not in the same case, even if they are spelled correctly. You have to select fields manually if they do not match.

3.10

Normally, whether field names are in upper- or lowercase (or both) does not matter. The Utilities Restructure command, however, initializes the field matching from the source file to the destination file based on identical spelling of the field names and their case. If the fields do not match, you have to use the F7 key to indicate corresponding fields for the restructure.

In SmartWare II, this problem does not exist.

4.53 Trick: Use a Query (or Data Query in SmartWare II) to assign values to fields whose names do not match those in the destination database when using the Utilities Restructure (3.10) or Data Utilities Append (SmartWare II) commands.

Both

If you are executing these commands from the command (or Menu) level, you always have the opportunity to select the source and destination fields manually, or accept the transfer based on field name matches. In a project file you cannot do this. However, if the destination file has two fields, one of which matches the source file, you can use a Query to move the data to the desired field.

For example, if you have a source file with a field called WAGE and you want to transfer the data into a file in which the field is called PAY, you can accomplish this in a project file if the destination file has both WAGE and PAY. The Utilities Restructure command or Data Utilities Append command matches WAGE with WAGE. You then can execute the following query in the destination file:

```
replace [PAY] = [WAGE]
```

This assigns the value in the WAGE field to the PAY field.

Both

4.54 Tip: Use the F8 key to delete the source-field specification from the Utilities Restructure (3.10) or Data Utilities Append (SmartWare II) definition.

If you have changed field names so that the system matches fields inappropriately, use the F8 key to delete the source-field specification at the current cursor position. The source-field line then is left blank.

3.10

4.55 Trap: After performing the Utilities Restructure command, be sure to perform the Key Update command if your file has any key fields.

The Utilities Restructure command does not update the keys for you.

Both

4.56 Tip: When using the Utilities Restructure (3.10) or Data Utilities Append (SmartWare II) commands, order the source file by an index to select the records to transfer.

Only the available source file records are transferred to the destination file when using the Utilities Restructure command. If you want to transfer only some of the records from the source file, perform a Query (Data Query in SmartWare II) to select just the records that you want, and order the file by an index before performing the Utilities Restructure command.

In Smart 3.10, the source file must be in a window so that the file can be ordered by an index.

Both

4.57 Tip: The Utilities Restructure (3.10) or Data Utilities Append (SmartWare II) commands do not eliminate deleted records automatically.

If you want to prevent deleted records from being transferred to the destination file, use the Query (Data Query in SmartWare II) command to create an index that omits deleted records.

Both

4.58 Tip: Use Utilities Restructure (Data Utilities Append in SmartWare II) to append records to an existing file.

The command does not assume that the destination file is empty, nor does Utilities Restructure delete any data that already exists in the destination file. You therefore can use Utilities Restructure to add records to an existing file.

To take advantage of this feature, execute the Utilities Restructure command as you normally would, with the source file loaded and the destination file as your current file in the current window. If the source file is to be ordered by an index, the source file also must be in a window in Smart 3.10.

4.59 Trick: You can use the Utilities Restructure command to change data types, but you should be careful of some details. *3.10*

- Alpha fields are padded with null characters if the new field is longer than the old alpha field. If the new alpha field is shorter, the data may be truncated.
- If you change from a numeric field to an alpha, the new field contains the number represented as an alphanumeric string, rather than a number on which you can perform computations.
- If you change from an alpha field to a numeric, the result is a zero value, not a null value.
- If you decrease the length of a numeric field, the system drops the least significant digits, but with some unexpected results. For example, if the field contains 1516.26 and the new field has a length of 6 and a precision of 2, the resulting field will appear as 1516.2. This is only temporary, however, because if you try to address the field in an update, the following error message appears:

```
Number is too large for this field
```

If you are shortening a numeric field, you must take great care that you can accommodate the largest number in your file.

4.60 Tip: The Utilities Concatenate (3.10) or Data Utilities Append (SmartWare II) does not destroy the field reform of a multiple line alpha field if you retain the same field size and screen configuration. *Both*

When you manually enter data into multiple line alpha fields, the F8 key in Smart 3.10 or the F7 key in SmartWare II is used to reform the field for word wrapping. (In 3.10, blanks actually are inserted into the field.) If you do not change the field sizes or screen configurations when using the Utilities Concatenate or Data Utilities Append commands, you do not have to reform the fields. If you change the field size or space allocated on the screen or view, however, you have to manually reform each large alpha field during an Update command. You cannot automatically reform a large alpha field in a Query or other command.

4.61 Trap: In the Utilities Restructure command, NULL numeric fields are converted to zeros. Because null fields are not used in the computation of averages, but zeros are, a table report in which breakpoint averages are computed gives you different answers before and after the Utilities Restructure command. *3.10*

By contrast, the Utilities Concatenate does not convert NULL numeric fields to zeros.

In SmartWare II, you do not have this problem. Blank fields are brought forward into a new file as blanks, not as zeros.

3.10

4.62 Trick: Use this trick to preserve Null values when performing a Utilities Restructure command. (See Trap 4.61.)

If you change null values to a unique value before performing a Utilities Restructure command, you can identify the unique values later and change them back to null.

Because all null values are changed to zero during a Utilities Restructure, you lose the significance of null entries. Perform a query before you perform the restructure so that all null values are changed to a unique, identifiable value, as in the following example:

```
[field] = null replace [field] = -99999
```

After the restructure, you can query again to return the original fields to their Null status:

```
[field] = -99999 replace [field] = null.
```

Make sure the temporary value is unique and normally is not found as a real value in any record.

Both

4.63 Tip: The source file order in a Utilities Restructure (Data Utilities Append in SmartWare II) command determines the physical order of the destination file.

In Smart 3.10, if you want the destination file's physical order to be the same as the source file's logical order, the source file must be in a window and must be ordered by an index or a key. Otherwise, the destination file will be in the same sequential order. In SmartWare II, a view may be ordered by an index even if the view is not displayed in a window.

As pointed out in Chapter 3, file access time is reduced greatly if the file's physical order closely matches the logical order of your most frequently used key.

3.10

4.64 Trap: If ordering the source file by a key, make sure your keys are updated when performing the Utilities Restructure command. If your keys are not updated, you will not transfer all records.

If your source file is ordered by a key, but the key is not updated to include any newly entered records, these new records are not be transferred to the destination file.

3.10

4.65 Tip: Utilities Restructure and Concatenate are similar in many respects.

Both commands can add records from one file to another, but Restructure can operate on files that are different in structure. The Concatenate command must use files of identical structures.

Both commands transfer deleted records from the source file to the destination. If you want to omit deleted records, you must have the old file in a window and order the file by an index you have created in a query specifying that deleted records are to be ignored.

4.66 Tip: Use Utilities Concatenate to append data from one file to another file with an identical structure. *3.10*

The Utilities Concatenate and Restructure commands yield identical results if the source and destination file structures are identical. Given the choice, use the Concatenate option rather than Restructure. Setting up the Concatenate command does not take as long because that command does not have a field-matching screen, which the Restructure command does have, and the actual execution of the command takes less time.

4.67 Trick: In the Utilities Concatenate command, the field names themselves need not be the same in the source file and the destination file *3.10*

Only the field structures and the order in which they appear must be the same. The data concatenation is accomplished by field position rather than by field name.

4.68 Trap: When you use the Utilities Restructure command and create a new file version, new fields or fields with changed names or sizes are not included on any custom screens. *3.10*

You must add any new or changed fields to the custom screens. The names of the fields not yet assigned appear on the status line of the screen-creation editor. Even if you have changed only the field names, those fields still are dropped from the Similar screen.

4.69 Tip: Use the Write All and Read commands in a project file instead of Utilities Restructure to avoid multiple password prompts in a project file. *3.10*

If the source file in a Utilities Restructure command is passworded, you are prompted for the file password when you execute the command, even though you had already entered the password when you loaded the file. From the command level, this may be a minor annoyance, but in a project file, this prompt can interrupt the smooth flow of processing. You are prompted regardless if the loaded screen is custom or standard.

You can circumvent this annoyance if you execute the command Write All to write the data to a file, and then read the data into the new file with the Read command. Refer to the following example:

```
if file("temp.dat") = 1
file erase temp.dat

endif

goto window 1
write all [1|20] ascii temp.dat
goto window 2
read ascii temp.dat fields [1|20]

file erase temp.dat
```

No password prompt appears when you execute the Write All command.

SW II

4.70 Tip: In a project file, issue the command Keys F10 following a Data Utilities Append command to allow the project file to continue automatically.

The Data Utilities Append command requires the issuance of an F10 key to conclude the match of fields in the source and destination files. This is true whether the command is executed from the command level or within a project file. In a project file, because you probably will want to continue without having to manually press F10, the statement Keys F10 immediately following the Data Utilities Append command will have the desired effect.

5

Entering and Deleting Data

This chapter covers techniques for entering data into and removing data from your database. In Smart 3.10, the Enter and Update commands are used for entering and changing data. In SmartWare II, use the Data Enter command for new data, or press Esc to update the view. This chapter discusses advancing to successive fields and records, using custom screens and views to best advantage, and repeating selected data fields from record to record.

The Lookup facility of Smart 3.10 is reviewed in detail, and several tips and tricks for using this powerful feature are presented. Finally, this chapter discusses deleting and activating records and the effect of deleted records on Database commands.

Entering and Updating Records

This section presents tips and tricks to use when you are entering new records or updating existing ones. Command-level and project-file operations are discussed. This section also reviews using custom screens and views and calculated fields in detail. Several solutions to the problem of repeating fields from record to record are presented.

5.1 Tip: Use the F-Calculator in Enter and Update modes to perform calculations and insert the results into your file. *3.10*

Rather than reaching for your pocket calculator when entering data, you can use the F-Calculator to perform the calculation for you. Just press Alt-K to display the F-Calculator screen and then enter your calculation, observing all the Smart calculationrules. You can use the standard calculation operators (+, –, *, /, and ^) and the Smart functions. Variables and fields from the current record can be used in the calculation. Press F2 to display the results of your calculation on the status line.

After the calculation has been performed, you can enter the results automatically into a Database field. Exit the F-Calculator with F10 (do not use the Esc key) and press Ctrl-C to enter the result into the current field. Press Enter to proceed to the next field.

SW II

5.2 Tip: Create a macro to make calculating a field value easier during data entry.

The built-in calculator of the Data Entry mode in SmartWare II is awkward. If you perform the task manually, you must follow these steps:

1. With the cursor on the field, press Alt-T to display the Field Text Editor.
2. Enter the formula or calculation.
3. Press F5 to perform the calculation and display the results on the status line.
4. Press F8 to delete a single-line formula, or Alt-F2 to delete a multiple-line formula.
5. Press Ctrl-C to insert the result.
6. Press F10 to insert the calculation into the field.

The following macro makes this task much easier:

```
Alt-T,until,enter,up,F5,F8,look,Result,F10
```

After you type the calculation on the top line of the field text editor, press Enter. The macro proceeds from there. The term `Result` is similar to Ctrl-C, inserting the calculation result onto the first line of the calculator. `Result` is like a macro in itself, which is why the `Look` statement is needed.

Both

5.3 Tip: Visually locate a record to update while you are in Browse mode.

When you are in Browse mode, you can spot a record you need to update easily. When you see the record you want to change, you do not need to execute Browse Off (Data Browse Off in SmartWare II) before updating the record. You can perform an update directly from Browse mode.

Both

5.4 Tip: Reforming a long alphanumeric field is screen or view dependent. The field may look acceptable on one screen, but on another screen the field will be jumbled.

In Smart Version 3.10, press F8 to reform an alpha field; in SmartWare II, press F7. Smart 3.10 does not word wrap automatically and frequently splits words in the middle. Press F8 before you advance to the next field. In SmartWare II, word wrapping takes place automatically, and unless you edit the field, you may not have to press F7 to reform the field.

5.5 Tip: Reforming a large alpha field (F8) in Smart 3.10 deletes any blanks that you may have inserted purposely; in SmartWare II, your blanks remain when you reform (F7).

Both

In Smart 3.10, actual blank characters are inserted at the ends of the lines to effect the word wrapping; intervening multiple blanks on the line are reduced to one blank when you reform. In SmartWare II, a special character is inserted at the end of each line to create the word wrapping effect, and multiple blanks within the lines are not stripped out when you reform the field.

5.6 Tip: If you have disallowed duplicate keys in a file, the duplication is checked only at the completion of the entry.

SW II

If you have not allowed duplicate SSNs in an employee file, for example, only at the completion of the entry is the file checked for duplicate keys. If the file has many fields, you may waste a considerable amount of time entering data that may have to be discarded if you already have entered the employee's record. The error message is:

```
Key value "xxxx" for data file "data-file already exists."
```

If you have mistyped the key value, you can correct the value and proceed to the next record.

5.7 Tip: In a project file, use the following coding to allow the entry of one record, simulating the Enter Only-One command of Smart 3.10. This technique allows you to enter just one record at a time.

SW II

```
Reply On Char "N" to 3015  'allow escape half way through
order change physical        'physical order
data goto record last        'last record
if isblank([ssn]) = 0        'a mandatory or other imp field
     data enter blank        'enter blank if the last
end if                       '..record is not blank


     data delete no          'make sure not deleted
     data update only-one    'update the single record

if isblank([ssn]) = 1        'is important field blank?
     data delete yes    'if so, delete the record
end if
```

Note that if the record is blank after the update, the record is deleted to prevent processing by other commands.

5.8 Trap: You will destroy data in your file if the custom screen is read-only and you attempt to enter a blank record and make field assignments in a project file.

3.10

You cannot enter a blank record in a project file if all the fields in the screen are read-only. Although the fields are read-only, the project file allows you to make field assignments. If you proceed to make field assignments after the failure to enter a blank record, you overlay data that exists in your file. Perform a test as follows to prevent this problem:

```
order sequential
let $precords = precords      'number of records at start
enter blank
if $precords = precords       'if record count same
     beep
     message Screen is Read-Only
else
     let [field] = $value     'make assignments
endif
```

If the number of physical records has not changed, the Enter Blank command has failed.

SW II

5.9 Tip: If a field has a mask, using the Delete key blanks only the current character and does not shift the remaining characters to the left.

If a field has no mask, when you delete a character in a field, characters to the right are shifted left by one position. If the field has a mask, the shift does not occur because any characters to the right may not pass the masking restrictions of the current position.

Advancing between Fields and Records

3.10

5.10 Tip: To advance to the next field when the current field is full, select `Yes` for the automatic return option on the Parameters menu.

The choice on the Parameters menu is as follows:

```
Automatic return on full field: Yes No
```

Because the Enter command is issued automatically when the field is full, you don't have to press Enter. This feature can be a significant time-saver if you are likely to have many full fields in your database. Select the extended field options.

In SmartWare II, this option may be selected individually by field when you create a view.

Both

5.11 Tip: An automatic return on a full field may yield undesirable results.

If you advance automatically to the next field when the current field is full, the condition may take effect when you do not expect it. If you seldom have full fields in your database, you might issue your own Enter command, in addition to the automatic Advance command. The result will be that you skip the field after the full field, and have to return to the field with the F3 key.

If the full field is the final one on-screen, the system advances automatically to the next record. While this may not present a problem in some situations, you do lose the opportunity of reviewing the screen before proceeding. If you are updating a record, you can return to the previous record by pressing F5. If you are in Enter mode of Smart 3.10, you must terminate Enter mode and execute the Update command to view the record just completed. In SmartWare II, you can use the F5 key even if you are entering new records.

5.12 Trap: After advancing to the next record, you cannot return to the preceding record while you remain in Enter mode. *3.10*

If you want to see or change the preceding record, terminate Enter mode by pressing F10 and do not update the keys. If you select Update mode immediately, you can change the last record you entered. When the data is correct, finish Update mode with an F10 (again, do not update the keys) and execute the Enter command again.

5.13 Tip: If you have an alpha field that spans multiple lines on your view, use the F4 key rather than the Enter key to advance to the next field. *SW II*

If you press Enter, as you can do with a single-line field, the cursor advances from line to line within the field. If the cursor is located in the middle of an existing line, the line splits when you press Enter. If the cursor is located at the beginning of the line, a blank line is inserted. If the multiple line alpha field is the final field of the view, pressing F4 returns the cursor to the first position of the field. To advance to the next record, press F6.

5.14 Tip: If you need to change key values in a series of records, update the view while the view is sorted by the key field. If you order the view by the key, you lose your place. *SW II*

If the file is ordered by the key you want to change, after the value has changed, the logical order of the record is altered immediately. Although your current record is the same one you changed, the next record no longer is the same "next" record as before, because your record now is in a new logical location. Rather than having to reposition your cursor each time, if you sort by the key field, the index maintains the logical order during your update process, allowing you to advance to each record in succession.

5.15 Trap: When using a standard view to update records, do not use PgUp or PgDn without pressing Enter, F5, or F6 first. If you just use PgUp or PgDn, the change looks like it has been made to the field, but the change will not have been made. *SW II*

Note that if you press PgDn and Esc after a change, you are prompted:

```
Save Current changes to record (y/n)?
```

In this case, the record referenced is the one you changed just prior to the PgDn. If you have made a change to the current record and have not moved to another field, pressing `n` discards the changes in both records. When you move the cursor to another field in the second record, the change to the original record is retained, even if you press Esc.

Using Custom Screens

Both

5.16 Tip: Design custom screens and views to make data entry easier.

As discussed in Chapter 1, field order can be dictated by several considerations. One valid reason for deciding on field order is the ease of data entry. If you are using only a standard screen or view, you may want to place the most frequently entered or updated fields at the beginning of the screen because you can view and access the fields easily—the update begins with the first field in the screen. When you have reached the last field you wish to enter or update, you can press F6 to proceed to the next record, rather than pressing Enter several times to step through the remaining fields.

If you create a custom screen, you can change the order in which the fields are entered. In Smart 3.10, after designing your screen and before pressing F10 to complete the definition, press Alt-F3 to change the input from the field-declaration numerical order to an order based on the fields' screen positions. The symbol `IO:#` on the right side of the status line indicates numerical order. When you press Alt-F3, the symbol changes to `IO:P` for positional order.

In SmartWare II, use the Input-Order subcommand when you create a custom view. Press Alt-R to set positional order, left to right, top to bottom. You also may assign the order of each field individually.

Both

5.17 Trick: Use additional custom screen and view pages to provide help or instructions.

Instead of providing instructions or code listings in printed system documentation alone, you can provide help information on the custom screen or view pages that are not used for data entry. Just as many software programs (including Smart and SmartWare II) provide help screens, you can provide help for yourself or others using your application by placing information on the secondary pages of a screen. This information can be an explanation of data, codes, optional entry instructions, and so on. An example is shown in figure 5.1.

If you employ this technique, make sure that required fields do not interfere; you cannot proceed to a later page of a screen if you have not satisfied the mandatory-field requirements on the current page.

SW II

5.18 Tip: Make a temporary entry into a mandatory field to return to previous fields in the same record.

```
TITLE CODE       DESCRIPTION
----------       -----------
   BAGR          Bagger
   BKPR          Bakery Production
   BKSL          Bakery Sales
   BULK          Bulk
   CHKR          Checker
   CKCE          Cook - Chef Express
   CKGR          Cook - Grill
   CKSC          Cook - Scratch
   DELI          Deli / Seafood
   DRVR          Driver
   DWCE          Dishwasher - Chef Express
   DWRT          Dishwasher - Restaurant
   FLRL          Floral
   GMCK          General Merchandise Clerk

                           ... continued on next page ...

F1 Help  F3 Ins. w/o title F5 Prior fld  F7 Ins fld  AF7 E-status F9 Clr Page
F2 Next Menu F4 Box/Line    F6 Next fld   F8 Del fld  AF8 Range     F10 Exit
 Field 16 SKILL  Length 5                 Pg:1  Ln:1  Ps:1       IO:P
 CREATE - creates a new file or screen
```

Fig. 5.1.

Displaying help information on a custom screen.

If you have created a mandatory field in SmartWare II, you cannot back up to a previous field unless you have entered something into the field. If you press F3, you get the following message:

```
Mandatory entry. Please enter something into field [fieldname]
```

If you want to go back to a previous field immediately, make an entry into the current, mandatory field, and rather than pressing Enter or F4 to go the next field, press F3 to go to the previous field. If necessary, you can make a single letter a temporary entry if you are not ready to complete the entry for the current field.

5.19 Tip: In a project file, if you have any mandatory fields in a view, you cannot escape from the entry of new records unless you change the default reply. ***SW II***

At the command level, when you are entering a new record and press Esc half way through the entry, you are prompted:

```
Save current changes to record? (y/n)
```

You must answer the question. In a project file, however, the default reply is `y`. If any mandatory fields have not been completed, however, conflict occurs because you cannot save the changes without entering the mandatory data. To resolve this problem, use the following statement:

```
Reply on char "N" to 3015
```

Insert this statement at the beginning of the project file to change the default reply to `n` for any Data Enter or Data Update commands throughout the program.

Both

5.20 Tip: Create separate custom screens or views for different data entry or update situations.

In the Smart Database, the data is independent from the ways in which you view the information. You can control field selection and order by using different custom screens. One screen format may be just right for the original data entry, but may be totally inappropriate for subsequent updates. For example, you may find that an update is faster if the fields to be updated are at the top of the screen, instead of the bottom, so that you can access the fields quickly.

An order-entry application provides a good example of using multiple custom screens. At the time you accept the order, you may not know the invoice number or the invoice date. Display these fields at the bottom of the original data-entry screen. The fields more important for order acceptance, such as the quantity ordered, description, customer code, and purchase-order number, are at the top of the screen.

Figure 5.2 shows an example of a screen you can use for order entry. Figure 5.3 shows a screen you can use easily at the time you invoice the order. Finally, figure 5.4 shows a screen that eases the entry of payment data.

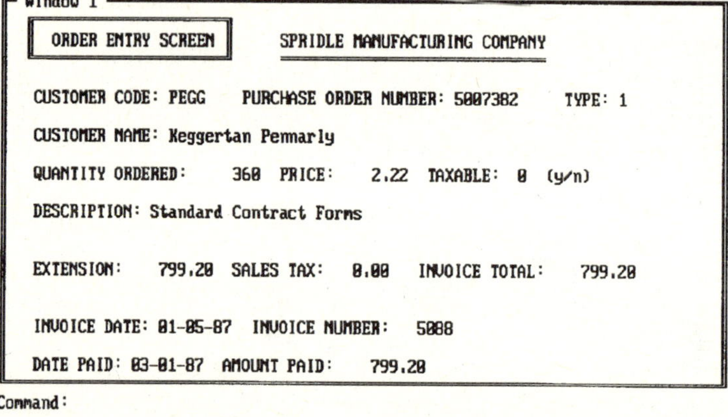

Fig. 5.2.
An order-entry screen.

Both

5.21 Tip: Field position is important if you want to view the result of a calculation.

You need not worry whether the calculation is going to be performed—and performed correctly—if you have defined it right. Careful positioning of a calculated field can help you verify its accuracy or get information from the field as you enter or update a record.

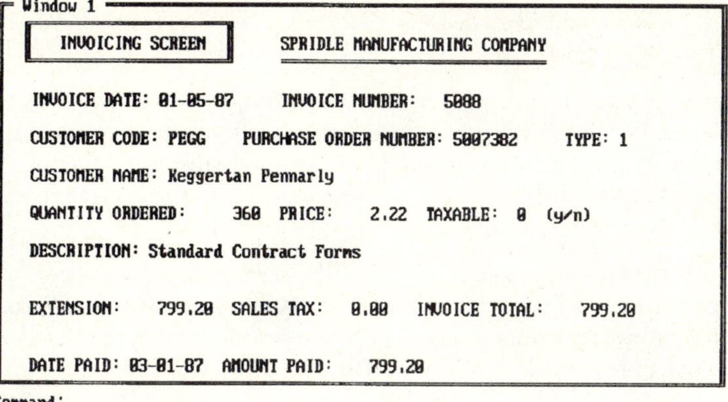

Fig. 5.3.
An invoicing screen.

```
Window 1
PAYMENT SCREEN          SPRIDLE MANUFACTURING COMPANY

DATE PAID: 03-01-87     AMOUNT PAID:    799.20

INVOICE DATE: 01-05-87     INVOICE NUMBER:   5008

CUSTOMER CODE: PEGG    PURCHASE ORDER NUMBER: 5007382     TYPE: 1

CUSTOMER NAME: Keggertan Penmarly

QUANTITY ORDERED:     360  PRICE:    2.22  TAXABLE: 0  (y/n)

DESCRIPTION: Standard Contract Forms

EXTENSION:     799.20  SALES TAX:   0.00   INVOICE TOTAL:    799.20

Command:
File: ACCREC   Window: 1                    Page: 1  Rec: 1  ( 1 )  Act: Y
```

Fig. 5.4.
A payment screen.

The result of a calculation does not appear on your screen until all the calculation factor fields have been entered. (Even if the calculation is additive, partial additions are not computed because the missing value is not considered to be equivalent to a zero.)

If you want to view the result of a calculation, therefore, you should position the calculation-factor fields prior to the calculation-result field in the prompting sequence. The sequence can be the default field-number sequence or, if you have created a custom screen or view, the screen-position sequence.

In Smart 3.10, if one of the calculation-factor fields is retrieved in a Lookup operation, the retrieved factor is available for use in the calculation as soon as the Lookup takes place. The availability of the factor, in this case, does not depend on its location in relation to the calculated field.

Both

5.22 Tip: Do not locate a calculated field in the final position on your screen.

If the final field on your screen is a calculated field and the preceding field is a factor, you have only a fleeting glimpse of the calculated value if you have specified automatic return on a full field (see Tip 5.11). As soon as you key in the final factor and press Enter, the calculation is performed and the next record appears on-screen.

When updating or entering records in SmartWare II, you can press F5 to return to the previous record. But in Enter mode of Smart 3.10, you cannot return to the previous record easily. You must finish Enter mode, view the results on-screen, and then select Enter mode again (see Trap 5.12).

In Smart 3.10, if you establish your Parameters settings so that you proceed to the next field when the current field is full, position at least one field on-screen after the calculated field so that you can view the calculation results. The results sometimes will indicate that you have made a mistake in one of the factors.

In both 3.10 and SmartWare II, a calculated field can be `Wait` rather than `Immediate`, so you can always view calculation results. To proceed to the field following the calculation, press Enter.

Repeating Data from Record to Record

Both

5.23 Tip: Use F9 to repeat an entry from the current field of the previous record.

If you are entering a series of orders from the same customer, for example, and the customer code must be included in every order file record, use the F9 key to repeat the code from the previous record. No carriage return is issued, even if you set your parameters for automatic return on full field.

SW II

5.24 Tip: The F9 key retrieves data from the last accessed record just as the FETCHFIELD function references data from the record last accessed.

If you go to record 9 from record 10, however, F9 retrieves fields from record 10, rather than from record 8. This represents a major change from Smart 3.10, in which F9 always retrieves from the record immediately preceding in the file order.

Both

5.25 Tip: Establish a macro to perform both the F9 and Enter keystrokes for you.

The Ctrl-F9 keystroke is easy to execute and bears some similarity to the normal F9 quick key, so Ctrl-F9 might be a logical keystroke for such a macro. If the repeating field is the first field on-screen, you can use the following Smart 3.10 macro when you enter the final field on-screen:

```
Ctrl-F9 = CrF9Cr
```

The first return enters the final field, the F9 repeats the first field of the preceding record in the new record, and the last return enters the first field and proceeds to the second field.

In SmartWare II, the same macro is:

```
Ctrl-F9 = Enter,F9,Enter
```

5.26 Tip: Use the following macros to help you in data entry. *SW II*

- `Tab = F4`
  `Shift-Tab = F3`

  To advance to the next field from a multiple line field, you must use the F4 or F10 keys; you cannot use Enter. If you do use Enter, you add extra lines to the field. Rather than reaching up to the function key row to press F4 or F10, using the Tab key may be easier. F4 (now Tab) does not advance to the next row of a table; however, here you still must press Enter. The Shift-Tab is redefined as F3 to access the previous field.

- `F7 = F7,^End`

  In SmartWare II, F7 reforms a multiple line alpha field, but the cursor returns to the beginning of the field. By adding Ctrl-End, the cursor goes to the end of the field so that you can continue typing easily.

- `F12 = F6,esc`

  Use this macro to terminate data entry. You cannot always use the F10 key, because F10 completes a multiple line field and the entry of data into a table. This macro advances to the next record and then Escapes back to the command mode.

5.27 Trick: Use the F9 key in the first record of an Enter command session to repeat values from the last record you entered in a previous Enter command session. *3.10*

The last record you entered is at the end of the file if your file is in sequential order. Even if the file order is based on a key or an index, using F9 on the first record in Enter still copies from the last sequential record in the file because sequential order is implied in an Enter session.

5.28 Trick: Use the F9 key in the first record of an Update command session to repeat values from the previous record in the order you have selected. *3.10*

In the Update command, the record considered to be "previous" depends on the current order of the file. The file may be ordered sequentially or can be ordered by an index or a key. Pressing F9 repeats values from this previous record. The Enter command, however, ignores the logical order, defaulting to sequential order during the execution of the command (see Trick 5.27).

If you are addressing the first record in logical order, however, you have no previous record from which to repeat. Pressing F9 for a field in this record results in the following error message:

```
Cannot repeat field in first record
```

For the second and subsequent records, the repetition for both Update and Enter commands follows the previously addressed record. The implication is that in the Enter command, the default order is sequential (even though your file was ordered by a key or an index at the time you executed the Enter command) and the order for the Update command is, in fact, the actual order you had specified—Key, Index, or Sequential.

Both

5.29 Trick: If you are entering new records under control of a project file, you can assign a value to a repeating field.

Consider the example shown in figure 5.5. If you are using the standard screen with this project file, you have to press Enter to advance to the field after the COMPCODE field. If you set up a custom screen, however, you can define the field as Read Only, and the system will skip that field during the update.

Fig. 5.5.

A Smart 3.10 project file for filling a repeating field.

```
Project File Editor
'enter multiple orders

quiet on

order sequential

label begin
input $compcode Enter Company Code:

label nextord
enter blank
let [compcode] = $compcode
update only-one

wait ,1 Another Order (y/n)
if inchar = asc("Y") then jump nextord

F1 Help     F3 Find     F5 Replace       F7 Insert line      F9 Repeat
F2 Calc     F4 Goto     F6 List fields   F8 Delete line      F10 Finish
                                   Line:    1  Column:  1    Insert: ON
REMEMBER - create a new project file or modify an existing file
```

A drawback to this method is the extra keystroke required to answer the question `Another Order`. You can use the INCHAR function, as in the example, which eliminates the need for pressing Enter after pressing `y` or `n`.

Both

5.30 Trick: To enter a repeating value automatically into newly entered records, define a field as calculated equal to a value stored in a variable.

For example, you can use the following as your calculation of the COMPCODE field:

```
[compcode] = $compcode
```

Your project file, then, looks like the Smart 3.10 file shown in figure 5.6.

```
Project File Editor
'enter multiple orders

quiet on

input $compcode Enter Company Code:

enter
```

Fig. 5.6. *Using a calculation to fill a repeating field.*

This technique works well and is somewhat simpler than the previous example. Note that the project file in figure 5.6 has only two significant statements. If you think ahead a bit, however, you may be able to spot a danger in Smart 3.10.

The technique is fine for the original data entry, but what about updating your existing records? If COMPCODE is a calculated field, then the value may change when you perform an Update, depending on the contents of the $compcode at that time. You can have a project file similar to the one in figure 5.6, which prompts you for the $compcode value and then updates just that one record. Such a project file would require unnecessary input, however. A solution for this problem is given in the next Trick.

In SmartWare II, rather than using this formula for a field calculation, use the formula as the default calculation. You then do not have the problem of the value possibly changing when you update the record at a later time.

5.31 Trick: To repeat data easily from record to record, define a field in which the calculation applies only to newly entered records.

Both

The best solution to the potential problem of data changing, as noted in Trick 5.30, is a formula that enters data into an empty field but does not change the value in a field that is not empty. The field calculation in figure 5.7 is designed to address this problem.

```
Calculated Field Equations

Field 1 [COMPCODE] =
if [compcode] = null then $compcode else nochange
```

Fig. 5.7. *Using a calculation to fill null fields only.*

In Smart 3.10, if the COMPCODE field is null (the default condition of fields in newly entered records), the value of COMPCODE is taken from the user-defined variable $compcode. If the field is not null, the value is not changed. (In SmartWare II, an empty field is blank.)

This method has another advantage. The COMPCODE field is skipped because the field is calculated, even if you are using the standard screen. In Smart 3.10, you do not have to create a custom screen and define the field as Read Only. In SmartWare II, the field can have a calculation in one view and not in others.

3.10 **5.32 Trick:** You must use a project file to change a calculated field similar to the field in figure 5.7.

Such a field is not easy to change after the field contains data. You must write a project file that specifically replaces the field value:

```
let [compcode] = "TUBE"
```

You cannot change the field with the Update command.

3.10 **5.33 Tip:** Use a temporary file to ease the entry of repeating data.

The temporary file would calculate the repeating field (COMPCODE in the example) with the following formula:

```
[compcode] = $compcode
```

Enter your data into the temporary file, using the project file shown in figure 5.6. When you are done, use the Utilities Concatenate command to transfer the data from the temporary file to the permanent file all at once. The COMPCODE field in the permanent file is not a calculated field, and therefore can be changed easily in the Update command at a later time.

The following is a Smart 3.10 project file illustrating the use of this technique:

```
'using a temporary file to enter repeating data

input $compcode Enter Company Code:

'company code is calculated equal to $compcode in tempcomp
goto file tempcomp screen standard

enter

'company code is not a calculated field in compsale
goto file compsale screen standard

utilities restructure tempcomp

'purge records already added to permanent file
goto file tempcomp screen standard

'query definition is: replace delete
query predefined delall neither

unload file tempcomp
utilities purge tempcomp
```

For the final record in the Enter command, press F10 (without pressing Enter) immediately after you enter the last field. If you press Enter, calculation of the company code begins the creation of an extra record, and you will have an extra record you do not want. If you forget and press Enter, you can press Esc to abandon the final record.

5.34 Trick: Use a Query (3.10) or Data Query (SmartWare II) command to set the value of a repeating field. *Both*

When you finish entering new records, perform the following query:

```
[compcode] = null replace [compcode] = $compcode
```

This query says, "If the COMPCODE field is null, replace it with the value in the user-defined variable $compcode."

This solution is not without problems, however. If your file is very large, the query can take a few minutes and will take longer each day as the file grows. If you forget to perform the query from the last entry session, you will have records in your file for two different customers, both with null COMPCODE fields. You then have to sort the records with individual queries and replace the COMPCODE values.

In SmartWare II, use the following query statement:

```
[compcode] = blank replace [compcode] = $compcode
```

Empty fields in SmartWare II are BLANK, not NULL.

5.35 Tip: Entering new records into a temporary file as a batch, rather than directly into the main database, has many advantages. *3.10*

Batch processing, or handling a number of records together at one time, has advantages in certain applications (see in Tip 5.33). If you need to maintain the keys within a permanent file at all times, and new data from the temporary file is not needed until the end of the day (or whenever you execute the batch process), then using the batch method may make sense.

For example, updating keys can take a few minutes or more if the permanent file is very large. You may not be able to spare the time if, throughout the day, you enter each record into the main Database.

The batch-entry method also is useful if you need to run various reports from newly entered data. Because the data is segregated in a temporary file, you can identify the data readily without having to perform a time-consuming query to isolate the data within a large permanent file.

Using the temporary-file method has some potential disadvantages, however. You must remember to delete and purge the records from the temporary file after the records have been concatenated to the permanent file. Otherwise, you will have duplicates in the permanent file. Also, you may need duplicate Lookup definitions—one for the temporary file (for original data entry) and another for the permanent file (for subsequent updates).

Project File Data Entry and Update

Both

5.36 Tip: Use the Lock-Record command in project processing to speed operations when you make multiple assignment statements.

If you are performing multiple assignments in a project file, such as

```
let [first] = $fname
let [last] = $lname
```

insert the Lock-Record command prior to the first assignment. The entire set of assignments is held in RAM until you finish with the record, resulting in faster operation of your project file.

3.10

5.37 Tip: On a network, the following is the correct command sequence to enter a blank record.

```
Enter Blank
Lock-Record
```

If you execute the commands in reverse order (in a project file), unpredictable data is entered into the file.

3.10

5.38 Tip: Use the Goto Record Next command in a project file on a network to unlock the current record after updating the record.

To update a record on a network in a project file, you must issue the Lock-Record command. There is no unlock command, however. If the program is doing nothing else to this file immediately, you should unlock the file so that other users on the network are not prevented from updating the record. Even if you are on the final record in the file, the Goto Record Next command will unlock the record and not cause an error.

3.10

5.39 Trap: In a project file on a network, the statement `Lock Record` (without the intervening dash) has no effect.

For the command to work correctly, you must insert the dash between the two words:

```
Lock-Record
```

The command does not work without the dash, but no error message is generated while the program compiles. Only when the program runs and the record locking is required is an error message displayed:

```
Record must be locked to do assignment
```

Make sure you include the dash in the command.

5.40 Trap: Go to a different record in a project file to ensure that field assignments are retained. *3.10*

Refer to the following sequence:

```
let [field] = 2
let [field] = if "A" = "B" then 1 else nochange
```

The result of these two commands is zero. However, consider the following statements:

```
let [field] = 2
          goto record next
          goto record previous
let [field] = if "A" = "B" then 1 else nochange
```

In this example, the value of the field is 2, because the original value actually is assigned to the field when a different record is addressed.

5.41 Trick: Assign a value to a field that is not on your custom screen, therefore allowing the entry of new data but preventing the viewing of existing data. *3.10*

In a project file, you may want to allow the entry of sensitive data, but prevent the operator from viewing existing data. The following example works successfully even if the [salary] field is not contained in the custom screen:

```
Enter only-one
input $salary Enter New Salary:
let [salary] = $salary
```

Even if the operator cancels the project file and returns to the command level, the screen still is loaded, but the [salary] field is not visible on any record.

Looking Up Data from One File to Another

The Smart 3.10 Lookup command is a powerful and truly relational feature of the Smart Database. Using Lookup, you can retrieve data from multiple reference files simultaneously while executing the Enter or Update commands. If retrieval is unnecessary, you can perform validations of key fields.

In SmartWare II, the Lookup command does not exist because a view may have multiple files attached to it and may display fields from those files and fields from the main file of the view. You also may use the FILELOOKUP function in a calculation or default calculation to display or insert data from other files. For tips on these topics, refer to Chapter 2.

This section explores many of the features of the Lookup facility and provides tips and tricks to make its use even more powerful.

3.10 **5.42 Trick:** A Lookup can perform "hidden" retrievals from source files, without displaying the retrieved fields on-screen.

The Lookup Definition screen displays the names of all the fields in the destination file—not just those fields available through the current screen. By selecting a destination field that is not visible on the current screen, you can define a hidden retrieval.

The Lookup definition menu displays only the names of source-file fields that appear on-screen, but you can type the name or number of any data field. All fields from the source file are available for extraction to the destination file, even if the fields are not displayed on the custom screen.

3.10 **5.43 Trap:** A calculated field used as the link in a Lookup retrieval or validation must be displayed on-screen.

If you need to retrieve a wage rate that depends on the combination of job title and store, for example, you declare a calculated field that is a concatenation of the two fields:

```
trim([Jtcode]|[Store])
```

This calculated field must be declared in both the destination and source files. In the source file, the key is this concatenated field. Other fields contain the actual wage rate, the job title, and the store code. Be sure to display the concatenated field on the destination-file screen, but do not mark the field as "read only." Because the field is calculated, the Update or Enter command skips over the concatenated field.

By using the TRIM function, any blanks entered mistakenly at the end of either field are stripped off.

3.10 **5.44 Trick:** To hide fields in the Lookup source file, place the fields on the second page of a custom screen.

If you want a cleaner looking screen, or if you want to hide the fields you are using for a Lookup source, you can position the fields on the second page of a custom screen. You also can use the Zoom command so that the source file is not visible. Because the file must be ordered by a key, the Lookup source file must be in a window. A file cannot be ordered by a key unless the file is in a window.

3.10 **5.45 Trick:** Display user messages or text information on the first page of a custom screen to hide data on subsequent screens.

Using a Lookup requires that the source file be located in a window. If you do not want the user to view any data in the window, however, you can create a multiple-page custom screen, with the link field displayed only on the second page. As long as the link field is present, you can define and use the Lookup without the source field being displayed anywhere in the custom screen. All fields from the source file are available for extraction to the destination file, even if the fields are not displayed on the custom screen (see Trick 5.42).

5.46 Trap: Lookup definitions are not unloaded automatically when you unload the files.

3.10

When you unload your files, the associated Lookup definitions are not removed (unloaded) automatically. Many applications have an initial project file that loads all files and Lookup definitions. If you Unload your files and then execute this project file later, the files will be loaded, but you will get an error message at the load of the Lookup definitions because they still are loaded from the previous execution of the project file. The error is not fatal, however; execution of the project file continues.

5.47 Tip: Use a Lookup command rather than a Relate command for a "snapshot" picture of data in the Lookup file.

3.10

You frequently must use a Lookup rather than a Relate command to combine data from two files. An inventory quantity, existing at the moment of order entry, may be needed in your destination file. Using a Relate command at some later time to retrieve the quantity may not be effective, because the quantity may have changed by then.

5.48 Trap: A Lookup cannot be used for display only. You must store the result in your file.

3.10

If you need to display a value from a Lookup file, you have no other choice than to use a Lookup. Unfortunately, you cannot just perform a "display only" Lookup without actually storing the retrieved value in your file. The result of this restriction is the duplication of data, files that are larger than they need to be, and processing that is slower than necessary because larger amounts of data are handled.

5.49 Trap: The Lookup command does not differentiate between upper- and lowercase values in the link field.

3.10

For example, "MKTG" matches a record in the source file with the value "mktg." Fortunately, the Link command and the Relate command also treat these values as being equal, so this feature can have benefits. You should be aware of this condition, however, so that you do not try to use upper- and lowercase letters to distinguish between different records.

Sometimes whether an entry is in upper- or lowercase does not matter. For example, the Find command with the Equal option ignores the case of the field. If you use the Partial option, the case is recognized (see Trap 4.7 and Tip 4.8 in Chapter 4). The Query command also recognizes the case of field contents unless you specifically override case recognition.

3.10 **5.50 Tip:** Define a Lookup again to document or review the definition. The Lookup must not be loaded if you want to define it again.

Although the Lookup Index command enables you to review the names of the files and the linkage fields, you cannot see the detail rules of the Lookup. To review the entire definition, remove the Lookup from memory and proceed as if you were defining the Lookup again—the existing definition will be displayed for you.

Make sure that you use the Lookup Remove command to release the definition from memory. Do not use the Lookup Undefine command because this command erases the definition from the disk.

Loading Lookup Definitions

3.10 **5.51 Tip:** Multiple Lookup definitions can be invoked simultaneously for one destination file.

With the Lookup facility, you can extract data from several source files into a common destination file. (Contrast this with the Link command, which can link to only one other file at a time.)

The Lookup definitions are separate. Each Lookup definition is established for the destination and source file. You must define them separately and each Lookup must be loaded separately.

3.10 **5.52 Trick:** By selective loading of Lookup definitions, you can use the Lookup facility to exercise control over the fields to be extracted during an Enter or Update command.

At different times during your application, you may need all or only some Lookup definitions active. You have the choice of loading only those Lookup definitions you need at that stage and ignoring the others. If a Lookup definition you don't want is already loaded, use the Lookup Remove command to deactivate the definition.

3.10 **5.53 Trap:** If source-file records have duplicate major-link keys, a Lookup retrieves data from the first source-file record with a link field matching the destination file.

Having duplicate keys in your particular application may not be incorrect, but be aware that in a Lookup, the retrieval of data is based on the fields in the first record in the set.

3.10 **5.54 Tip:** When defining a Lookup, make certain that the current window contains the destination file and another window contains the source file.

At the time of definition, the source file does not have to be ordered by the key field, but the source file must be ordered by that field when the Lookup is used during an Enter or an Update command. The Lookup definition process does require, however, that the link field in the source file is defined as a key field.

Automatic versus Manual Mode

5.55 Tip: After you have loaded Lookup definitions, they are automatically in effect when you update a record. *3.10*

The automatic condition is noted at the bottom of the screen by the legend `Mode: AUTO` on the status line (see fig. 5.8). In most cases, using automatic mode is appropriate because you want to make sure that your data is correct and synchronized with the other files in your application. The Lookup command not only validates the link field you enter, but also extracts field values from the corresponding file and inserts them into your current file.

```
Window 1

        DEPARTMENT NAME RETRIEVAL

        SSN:198-03-3024

        LAST NAME:Peters____

        FIRST NAME:Howard E.

        DEPARTMENT CODE:MKTG

        DEPARTMENT NAME:Marketing______

Insert ON  F3 - Prev fld   F5 - Prev rec   F7 - Fld delete   F9  - Repeat fld
F2 - Date  F4 - Next fld   F6 - Next rec   F8 - Fld reform   F10 - Finished
File: DEPEMP Lookups: 1 Mode: AUTO           Page: 1 Rec: EOF  ( 13 )  Act: Y
UPDATE - allows editing of the current record
```

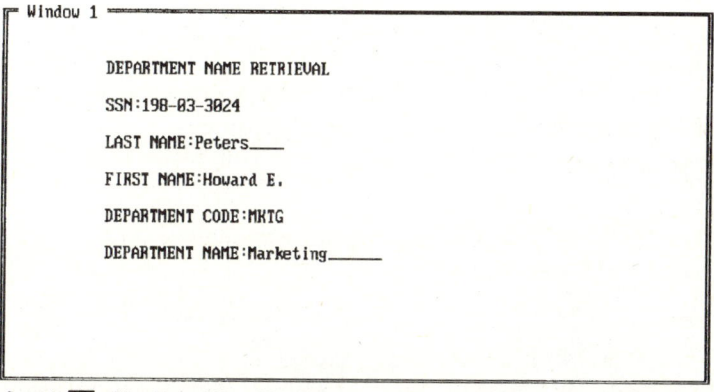

Fig. 5.8. *Mode: AUTO indicating automatic Lookup mode.*

5.56 Tip: Turn off automatic Lookup mode to disable it temporarily. *3.10*

You sometimes may want to turn off the automatic Lookup mode for manual operation. To turn off automatic Lookup mode, press Ctrl-A while in Update or Enter mode. The word `AUTO` on the status line changes to `MAN`. You then can perform the Lookup manually by pressing Ctrl-L. The Lookup can be performed for all fields in which the link value has been entered.

Why would you want to perform the Lookup manually? Suppose that you have a personnel system in which the link field from the destination file is the entry-level job code for the employee when hired. The source file may contain the starting rate of pay. Over the years, the starting rate of pay for that particular job changes, but you do not want to change the field that contains the actual pay rate at which the individual began working for the company.

Even after beginning the Update process, unless you move the cursor through the link field, the Lookup will not be performed even if the mode is set to automatic Lookup. Therefore, you can perform an automatic Lookup selectively.

3.10 **5.57 Trap:** The manual Lookup setting does not prevent the Lookup from taking place into destination fields omitted from the current custom screen.

You can turn off the automatic Lookup with Ctrl-A, which carries forward to other Enter or Update executions within the same session, unless you turn automatic Lookup back on with the same keystroke. If a screen has a Lookup link field and does not contain the destination field, when you press Ctrl-L, the Lookup takes place nonetheless and the value is inserted into the destination field.

3.10 **5.58 Tip:** A Lookup is performed only in Enter or Update mode, not when you are viewing the record.

The function of the Lookup facility is to extract data from a reference file and insert the data into the current file during the Enter or Update commands. This extraction does not take place if you are simply advancing from record to record at the command level.

To tie the current file to reference files when you are viewing data at the command level, use the Link command (see Chapter 3).

3.10 **5.59 Tip:** In manual mode, you can perform a Lookup selectively.

In Update or Enter mode, pressing Ctrl-A toggles the Lookup mode to manual (see Tip 5.56). Pressing Ctrl-L performs a manual Lookup for any link field that is filled in at that time. If you have more than one Lookup defined, with more than one link field, you can perform selective Lookups by purposely leaving blank those fields that you do not want looked up.

Pressing Ctrl-L, however, performs the Lookup for the entire record. The Lookup does not depend on the cursor position at the time you press Ctrl-L. Any Lookups depending on fields that are null are ignored, and no error messages are issued. If the data in any link field does not match the assigned link field in the link-to file, you receive the following error message:

```
Cannot find data for field <n>
```

The field number <n> represents the field's numeric position in the current file rather than the field's position on the current screen.

3.10 **5.60 Tip:** The Automatic or Manual setting for Lookup status remains in effect between Update or Enter commands during the current session.

You must initiate the Update or Enter mode to change the setting. The setting cannot be changed from the command level of Smart or from within a project file.

5.61 Tip: The Automatic or Manual Lookup setting applies simultaneously to all Lookups to the current file and any other files in your current application. *3.10*

The Lookup setting, either Automatic or Manual, applies to all Lookup definitions and files at the same time and does not vary among files, windows, or Lookup definitions.

5.62 Trap: Establishing a Lookup does not prevent the entry of erroneous values in link fields. *3.10*

Although you may need to enter only correct codes into your file (customer codes or item codes, for example), you cannot rely on the Lookup facility to guard against incorrect values. If you enter a link field that does not match the Lookup source-file key, the system beeps and displays the following error message:

```
Cannot find data for field <n>
```

Your next keystroke advances the cursor to the following field, regardless of your Parameters settings, and the incorrect code is accepted into the link field. Any fields whose contents were to have been extracted with the Lookup contain null values unless you make a manual entry.

This condition can have its advantages, as well as the obvious disadvantages. Because you can enter a code that does not exist in the source file, you can, for example, enter a code for a new customer that you have not yet established. You then can enter the name and address and any other fields that are to be entered by means of the Lookup. When you finish with the data entry in your current file, you can go back to the source file and enter the new customer code.

The disadvantages, of course, are that you may enter a code you did not intend to enter, or you may misspell an existing code. If you are not careful, you can continue entering data and not realize that the error condition exists. If you turned off the Beep error indicator, you get the error message only and not the audible tone, which also signifies the error.

5.63 Trap: Do not put a Lookup link field in the final position on your screen. *3.10*

When an error has been detected by the Lookup definition, your next keystroke advances the cursor to the next field in the defined order. If your link field is the final field in the order of entry and no additional fields are on the screen, Enter mode advances to the next record. Enter mode does not offer the capability of returning to the previous record. To correct the mistake, you must exit Enter mode and invoke the Update command. This sequence can be awkward and time-consuming (see Trap 5.12).

3.10 **5.64 Trick:** Use a macro to help correct Lookup link-field errors.

An error in a Lookup causes the cursor to advance to the next field as soon as you press a key. To return to the previous field, you must press F3. To delete the field contents, you must press F7. You can define a macro to perform these steps for you:

```
Ctrl-F3 = F3F3F7
```

Using Ctrl-F3 as the macro key seems appropriate. The first F3 only clears the error, the next F3 returns to the previous field, and the F7 clears the field so that you can enter the correct value.

Validating Entries

3.10 **5.65 Tip:** Use a Lookup to verify the validity of a code or field in a source file ordered by the corresponding key field.

Although the primary purpose of a Lookup is to retrieve selected data fields from the source file and insert them into the current (destination) file during an Enter or Update command, you can establish the Lookup solely for the purpose of validating the link field entry.

If you are retrieving a field, you normally enter the field selection on the Lookup Definition screen. In this case, however, because you do not want to retrieve a field, you press F10 when the definition screen appears. No fields are retrieved during the Lookup, but the link field is validated against the source file nonetheless.

3.10 **5.66 Trick:** Retrieve the Lookup linkage field to guarantee that the field in the destination file is the same case as in the source file.

Because the Lookup relies on the collation sequence to evaluate if the linkage fields match, an uppercase field matches with a lowercase field. If you retrieve the linkage field along with data fields, you can ensure that the case is the same in both files. Even if you are using the Lookup to validate, and you are not retrieving any data fields, use this technique to guarantee case equality. This technique also solves the problem of erroneous equality matching of special characters, discussed later in this section.

3.10 **5.67 Tip:** The Lookup command does not reject deleted records.

Data from deleted records can be retrieved by the Lookup facility. You cannot assume that a successful Lookup also guarantees that the data is retrieved from active records.

3.10 **5.68 Tip:** Use a project file to validate code entries.

Rather than using the Lookup facility to validate a code against a reference file, the following project file may be used for the same purpose.

```
'code validation in a project file

label begin
%1 Enter Department Code:
if %1 == "done" then jump alldone

goto window 2
find [dept] equal "%1" options
if cerror = 0 then jump okdept
beep 2
message Department < %1 > not found ... \
    hit any key to continue ..
jump begin

label okdept
goto window 1
enter blank
let [dept] = upper("%1")
update only-one
jump begin

label alldone
```

Using a project file to validate a code ensures that no invalid codes are entered. The Lookup facility permits the entry of codes not found in the reference file (see Trap 5.62).

5.69 Trick: Use a Read-Only field and a calculated field to make a Lookup foolproof.

3.10

When performing a Lookup during data entry or update, if the Lookup fails, although you get an error message and a beep, if you are not paying attention, you possibly may bypass the field. The next keystroke clears the error and advances to the next field.

Follow these steps to construct a foolproof Lookup:

1. Create the Lookup so that the [destination] field is Read-Only on a custom screen. Although the field is Read-Only, the Lookup still works.

2. Create a mandatory 1 byte calculated field with the following calculation:

   ```
   left([destination],1)
   ```

Because the second field is mandatory, you cannot proceed unless something is in the field. The only way to have something in the field, however, is from the [destination] field. Because the [destination] field is Read-Only, the only way for the field to have a value is from the Lookup. Therefore, unless the Lookup is successful, you cannot proceed with the entry of this record.

3.10 **5.70 Trap:** In the Lookup command, many of the special characters are equated to each other because of the collation sequence evaluation method of Smart.

For example, a slash (/) is evaluated the same as a minus sign (–) in the Lookup command. Therefore, if an account number is supposed to be "2402–02" and you type "2402/02" by mistake, the Lookup command does not reject this entry. The slash (/) is entered into your file without any warning.

This situation may create problems in other commands within your application that do not equate a slash with a dash. For example, in a Query, "2402–02" is not equal to "2402/02".

This problem is solved if you also retrieve the link field along with any data fields.

Trapping Duplicates

3.10 **5.71 Trick:** Use a surrogate file to help prevent duplicate key fields.

Although the Smart 3.10 Database has no explicit way to prevent the entry of duplicate records, you can use the Lookup capability to search a second file for the field (SSN, for example) and respond with an "error" if the field is not found. In this example, however, the error is a positive message because you do not want duplicates in your first file. If you don't get an error message, the system has found an occurrence of the key field in the second file, and you need to check your entry.

This solution entails many problems. First, you cannot perform a Lookup from a file into itself—one file cannot be both the source and destination of a Lookup. If you use this method, you therefore need to establish a second file with the SSNs, maintain the key of the SSN, and be sure to order the file by the key when performing an Enter or Update using the Lookup. The auxiliary file needs only one field (the SSN); you do not have to duplicate all fields in the whole file.

Although these technical obstacles can be overcome, an even more serious problem with this approach is the human one. If you use this method, "no news" is "bad news." Normally, you hear a beep and see an error message if something is wrong. With Smart and most other systems, you come to expect this relationship. With this technique, however, you get a beep and an error message if the SSN is new (a good condition), but no indication, other than the immediate acceptance of the entry, if the SSN already is in your system. If you use this method, you also have to change your thinking about error conditions. The project file in the following Trick addresses the problem of duplicate keys.

3.10 **5.72 Trick:** Use a project file to prevent the entry of duplicate key-field entries.

The following is an example of such a project file:

```
'add an applicant, preventing duplicate SSN's

goto window 1
goto file APPLY screen AP1
order key [ssn]

label begin
menu clear 7 0
menu print 8 25 9 0
Enter SSN of Applicant or "DONE"
menu input 10 35 9 17 11
text1 let %1 = text1

if upper(text1) = "DONE" then jump alldone
find [SSN] equal %1 options
if cerror = 3002 then jump newapp
beep 2
message Duplicate SSN .. please check .. press any key
jump begin

label newapp
order sequential
enter blank
let [ssn] = text1
update only-one
order key [ssn]
jump begin

label alldone
order sequential
key update
order key [ssn]
```

In this example, the file is ordered by the key field SSN, allowing the use of the fast binary-search Find command. Before the record is entered for the new applicant, however, the file is ordered sequentially. This step is extremely important when using the Enter Blank command in a project file. If you do not order the file sequentially, you indeed enter a blank record. The following Update command, however, does not update the new record, but updates some other record.

The SSN field is assigned before issuing the Update Only-One command. This assignment prevents having to enter this file manually again on the Update screen. If the field is designated Read-Only on-screen, the cursor skips over the field and you do not have to press Enter to proceed to the next field.

Deleting Data

A record marked for deletion may or may not be processed by a Smart command. This section covers the effect of deleted records on various commands and how you can use the deleted status of a record to your advantage.

Both

> **5.73 Tip:** The Delete (Data Delete Record in SmartWare II) command does not remove a record from a database—it only marks the record for deletion.

If you execute the Delete command, the current record's delete status changes. Note that this command is a toggle: if you execute the command, the status changes to the opposite condition. If you execute the command again, the status changes again. At the far right of the status line in figure 5.9, you can see the designation `ACT: Y`, which indicates that the record is active in Smart 3.10.

```
DEPT SALE
PHONE (303) 797-5939
EMPDATE 10-30-65

Command list 1:  Autohelp  Browse  Create  Delete  Enter  Find  Goto  Help
                 Print  Query  Report  Scroll  Update
File: person    Window: 1                       Page: 1  Rec: 6  ( 6 )  Act: Y
DELETE - deletes or activates the current record (toggle)
```

Fig. 5.9.

`Act: Y` indicating that a record is not deleted (3.10).

Figure 5.10 shows the marker for a deleted (not active) record in SmartWare II. The screen designation reads `DEL`.

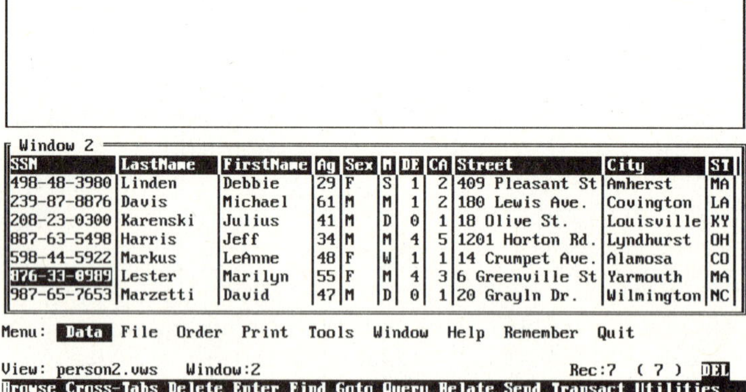

Window 1

Window 2

SSN	LastName	FirstName	Ag	Sex	M	DE	CA	Street	City	ST
498-48-3980	Linden	Debbie	29	F	S	1	2	409 Pleasant St	Amherst	MA
239-87-8876	Davis	Michael	61	M	M	1	2	180 Lewis Ave.	Covington	LA
208-23-0300	Karenski	Julius	41	M	D	0	1	18 Olive St.	Louisville	KY
887-63-5498	Harris	Jeff	34	M	M	4	5	1201 Horton Rd.	Lyndhurst	OH
598-44-5922	Markus	LeAnne	48	F	W	1	1	14 Crumpet Ave.	Alamosa	CO
876-33-8989	Lester	Marilyn	55	F	M	4	3	6 Greenville St	Yarmouth	MA
987-65-7653	Marzetti	David	47	M	D	0	1	20 Grayln Dr.	Wilmington	NC

Menu: Data File Order Print Tools Window Help Remember Quit

View: person2.vws Window:2 Rec:7 (7) DEL

Browse Cross-Tabs Delete Enter Find Goto Query Relate Send Transact Utilities

Fig. 5.10.

`DEL` indicating that a record is deleted (SmartWare II).

The record is marked for deletion, but not physically removed from the file.

Both

> **5.74 Tip:** Many Smart 3.10 and SmartWare II Database commands will process deleted records.

The following commands will process deleted records:

Smart 3.10	*SmartWare II*
Find	Data Find
Goto Record	Data Goto Record
Link	
Lookup	
Print	Print View
Query	Data Query
Save	File Save
Send	
Sort	Order Sort
Update	(updating records)
Utilities Concatenate	Data Utilities Append
Utilities Restructure	Data Utilities Append
Write	
Delete	Data Delete
Browse	Data Browse

Note that the Print (Print View in SmartWare II) command prints deleted records. If you specify the List format rather than the Report format, both the physical record number and the Active status are printed on the first line, as shown in figure 5.11.

```
AGE: 34
SEX: M

Record #: 6  Act: N
SSN: 598-44-5922
FIRST: LeAnne
LAST: Markus
AGE: 48
SEX: F


Record #: 7  Act: Y
SSN: 876-33-0989
FIRST: Marilyn
LAST: Lester
AGE: 55
SEX: F

Enter any key to continue

File: person   Window: 1                      Page: 1  Rec: 6  ( 6 )  Act: N
PRINT - print the current file, page or record
```

Fig. 5.11.
Displaying record number and active status with Print...List.

Print is the only command in which you can print the Active status of a record.

5.75 Tip: The Query (3.10) or Data Query (SmartWare II) command does not reject deleted records automatically. ***Both***

If you want to make certain that the records you select in a query are not deleted, you must include the following in your definition:

```
not (deleted)
```

The request must be made this way because no corresponding statement called *active* exists. To select just the deleted records, the Query definition is:

```
deleted
```

Both

5.76 Trap: The Replace Activate and Replace Delete Query statements are not toggle functions.

Unlike the Delete command in Smart 3.10 or Data Delete in SmartWare II, which change the record status from one condition to the other each time you execute them, a Replace Activate Query definition forces the selected records to be active, and Replace Delete forces the selected records to be deleted, regardless of the record status prior to the Query execution. For an example of the use of this Query definition, refer to Tip 5.82. For more Query examples, refer to Chapter 7.

Both

5.77 Tip: The Report (3.10) or Print Report (SmartWare II) command does not process deleted records.

You do not have to perform a query to extract active records. You may find that this feature saves you some time during the running of your application.

Both

5.78 Tip: The Relate (3.10) or Data Relate (SmartWare II) command does not process deleted records in file 1 or file 2.

Again, this can be a time-saver because you do not have to make a separate pass to extract only the active records.

Both

5.79 Trick: Temporarily delete certain records to perform a Relate command for only a subset of the driven file.

In a Relate command in Smart 3.10, the driven file is file 1, which must be ordered by the key. In SmartWare II, the driven file is file 2, which does not have to be ordered by the key during the execution of the Data Relate command, but cannot be ordered by an index. You may, however, want to perform the relation for only a subset of the records in the driven file. To do so, temporarily delete those records you want to exclude from the relation and then order the file by the key field. Because the command does not process the deleted records, in effect you perform the relate operation on a subset of your data.

For example, if you are matching daily sales records (driver file) to the master inventory file (driven file) but want the resulting file to contain records for only those products with a cost greater than $1,000, you can perform the following Query to temporarily delete the records for products you do not want to consider:

```
[cost] <= 1000 replace delete
```

When you perform the Relate or Data Relate commands, only the active records from the driven file are matched to the driver. When you complete the Relate command, perform the following Query to reset the active status of the deleted records:

```
deleted replace activate
```

One caution about this method, however. If all records in the driven file normally are active (not deleted), you should not have any problem reactivating the deleted records. If some records, however, actually have been marked for deletion, you could have problems. In this case, include in your file a Status field, which you can use to indicate whether the record is to be considered deleted or active. On the basis of the Status field, you can execute a Query command to change the record's Delete condition:

```
[status] = "A" replace activate
```

5.80 Tip: The Transactions (3.10) or Data Transact (SmartWare II) command does not process deleted records. ***Both***

In fact, one option on the Transactions definition menu specifies that records from the driver file are to be marked for deletion after they have been used in the transaction. Transactions are not processed against any deleted records in the driven file, even if eligible transactions exist in the driver file. Because the unprocessed driver records are not used in the Transactions command, they are not deleted from the driver file.

If the driven file contains records marked for deletion, the problem of preventing their reactivation can be solved by purging them prior to temporarily marking any other records for deletion (see Trap 4.41 in Chapter 4 for further explanation).

5.81 Trick: Use the Delete feature as a substitute for ordering by an index in the Transactions command. In SmartWare II, the commands are Data Delete and Data Transact. ***Both***

In Smart 3.10, as in the Relate command, the Transactions command requires that one file (the driven file) be ordered by the link-field key. By temporarily deleting those records against which you do not want to have transactions posted, you can control the driven file as if the file were ordered by an index. Be sure to activate the records again at a later time.

In SmartWare II, the driven file cannot be ordered by an index, although you do not have to order the file by the key to execute the Data Transact command.

5.82 Tip: If you want to delete all records in a file, delete only the active records. ***3.10***

If you ever need to delete all records in a database file, the Query

```
not (deleted) replace delete
```

may execute much faster than

```
replace delete
```

Although the result is the same, the second query reads and writes all records, regardless of whether they already are deleted. The first example reads all records but writes out only those records that need to be deleted.

Even if you use the second method, the more records that already are deleted, the faster the query runs. Deleting an active record can take up to twice as long as "deleting" a record that already is deleted. This ratio also holds true if you are activating records.

In SmartWare II, no action is taken if you specify the deletion of a record that already is deleted.

SW II

5.83 Tip: In a project file, when using the statements Data Delete Yes or Data Delete No, no change is made to the file if the record already is in the desired state. The system does not reset the delete status indicator in the record.

For example, a record in the file is not forced active if the file already is active. If this were not true, you would want to minimize disk access by checking the delete status before issuing the Data Delete command.

SW II

5.84 Tip: If the delete status of a table linkage is tied to the main record, the delete status of the individual table records does not always toggle on and off with the status of the main record.

The Data Delete Record command usually is a toggle—execute the command, and the record is deleted. Execute the command again, and the record is made active again. Although this condition holds true for the main view record, if some of the table records already are deleted, they remain deleted when you delete the main view record, rather than becoming active. If you activate the main view record again, all the table records become active.

SW II

5.85 Tip: If you do not allow duplicate keys, deleting an existing record does not allow the entry of a new record with the same key.

The key values of both active and deleted records are considered in the evaluation of uniqueness of the file keys. If you want to add a new record to replace a deleted record with an identical key, you must execute the Data Utilities Purge command to eliminate any deleted records physically.

3.10

5.86 Tip: When using the Utilities Duplicates Delete command, an existing deleted record is ignored when evaluating subsequent records to mark for deletion.

If you have two records with the same key field, if the first record already is deleted, the second record is not marked for deletion by this command.

5.87 Trap: Uppercase and lowercase keys are not considered equal in the Utilities Duplicates Delete command. *3.10*

Whether a key is in upper- or lowercase normally does not matter. Because of the use of the collation sorting sequence, a lowercase "a" is equal to an uppercase "A." In the Utilities Duplicates Delete command, however, they are not equal. Therefore, if you have a department file in which each department is supposed to have just one record, this command allows records with both "ACCT" and "acct" department codes. If you have multiple occurrences of the same key, and if adjacent records do not have the same case structure, no records with the following codes are deleted:

ACCT
acCt
acct
aCCt
acCT
ACCT
Acct

In this example, if the department codes happen to appear in this order when ordered as a key, the Utilities Duplicates Delete command does not delete any of these records. If you change the spelling to all uppercase (or all lowercase), all records but the first are deleted.

5.88 Trick: Create a concatenated field, combining several fields, if you want to delete records based on the duplication of more than one field. *3.10*

The Utilities Duplicates Delete command operates on only the major field of a key. If your file legitimately has duplicates of the major field, therefore, you cannot use this command to delete the duplicates. You may not want to allow duplicates of multiple field keys, however. If you have a file with Manufacturer numbers and Product Categories, for example, you may allow duplicate Mfgrs or duplicate Categories, but not duplicate Mfgr/Category combinations.

To clean up your file, create a concatenated field, such as the following example:

```
upper(trim([mfgr]|[category]))
```

With this new field as a key, you can use the Utilities Duplicates Delete command to delete records with duplicate combinations of the fields.

5.89 Tip: Use the FETCHFIELD function in a Data Query definition to delete records with duplicate fields. *SW II*

An example of a Data Query definition is:

```
[dept] = fetchfield([dept]) replace delete
```

Before executing the Data Query, sort the file by the field you are examining. This Query deletes the second or any successive record that is a duplicate of a prior record, because the FETCHFIELD function refers to the previous record.

This Query is useful if you want to add a unique key to a file, but cannot because duplicates exist. After the duplicate records have been deleted and purged, load the file and add the key. If two or more fields together are to define a unique record, create a view field that is a concatenation of the individual fields, and then use this view field in the Data Query.

Both

5.90 Trick: Use the following project file to purge deleted records from a file, rather than using the standard Utilities Purge command. Using the project file can be faster.

In Smart 3.10, prior to executing the Utilities Purge command, you occasionally must run the Utilities File-Fix Data command. Even on a single-user computer, you sometimes must run this command to clear an erroneous indication that someone else is using the file. This can be a time-consuming procedure. In this project file, this step is not necessary.

The Utilities Purge command writes the data "in place," to conserve disk space. Therefore, if the electricity goes off during the command, you must restore the file from your backup disks. With the project file, because a new database is created and is swapped at the completion of the process, loss of electricity does not destroy your original data.

Note that this project file makes certain assumptions:

- You *must* have two windows open.
- The file is fixed length and does not have a password.
- Keys are deleted; you must use the Key Add command to create them again.
- Disk space is sufficient for another copy of the database.

The project Smart 3.10 file is as follows:

```
'assumes 2 windows !!!!
unload all
%1 Database Name:
let %2 = "%1"|".db"
let %3 = "%1"|".dbs"

goto window 1
load %1 screen standard
let $precords = precords                'number of records
```

```
if file("kill.db") = 1
    utilities erase file kill
endif

goto window 2
create file kill fixed-length no-password matching file %1

goto window 1
query predefined active index ind1      'not (deleted)
if cerror = 0                           'if there are some active
     order index ind1
     if $precords = records             'none deleted if same
          beep
          message No Records to delete ... press any key
          unload file kill
          utilities erase file kill
          order sequential
          jump alldone
     endif

     goto window 2
     utilities concatenate %1           'get active records

endif

goto window 1
unload all
file erase %2                           'original DB file

file rename kill.db TO  %2              'database file
file erase kill.dbs

load %1 screen standard

beep 2
wait 60 All deleted records purged .. press any key

label alldone
```

The SmartWare II equivalent of this same project file is as follows:

```
local $file $precords

file unload all
screen shortinput $file "Database Name:"

tools file erase "kill.*"

file create "kill" similar standard-view $file no-password
keys "rd",Enter,"kill",Enter,"fn",F10

file load standard-view $file:".vws"
let $precords = precords                     'number of records

data query execute "active" index "ind1"     'not (deleted)
keys esc
if cerror = 0                                'if there are some
active
```

```
      if $precords = records                          'none deleted if same
           beep
           message "No Records to delete ... press any key"
           file unload view "kill.vw"
           tools file erase "kill.*"
           order change physical
           jump alldone
      end if

      data goto view "kill.vw"
      data utilities append $file|".vws"      'get active records
      keys F10
end if

file unload all
tools file erase $file|".db"                          'original db file

tools file rename "kill.db" to $file|".db"   'database file
tools file erase "kill.vws"
if file("kill.key") = 1
      tools file erase $file|".key"
      tools file rename "kill.key" to $file|".key"
end if

file load standard-view $file|".vws"

beep 2
wait 60 "All deleted records purged .. press any key"

label alldone
```

In SmartWare II, you do not need to rebuild the keys—this is done automatically in the File Create command.

3.10

5.91 Tip: Reserving memory at the time you begin your Smart Database session usually prevents the following error message.

```
Warning: Someone else may be using this file
```

This error message occurs when you try to execute the Utilities Purge command, and is caused by a flag that is attached accidentally to a datafile when you exit to DOS while the file is loaded. To clear the flag, you must execute the Utilities File-Fix Data command, which is a time-consuming procedure. You can exit to DOS temporarily if you press Ctrl-O from the command level or use the Command statement in a project file. Reserving memory when you begin the Smart session (-r32 or -r64) usually prevents this problem.

SW II

5.92 Tip: In SmartWare II, when you execute the command Data Utilities Purge, the keys are rebuilt automatically.

In Smart 3.10, however, the keys are deleted when you execute the Utilities Purge command. You then must load your file and execute the Key Organize All command.

5.93 Trick: Use the File Erase command to erase a database if the Utilities File Erase command does not work.

3.10

A database sometimes becomes corrupted so badly that you cannot erase the database with the Utilities File Erase command. This is most likely to happen if the power goes off during a critical process or if you have a hardware malfunction. When you try to use the Utilities File Erase command, you get the following error message:

```
Unexpected end of file
```

To delete the file from your disk, use the File Erase command on command list 4. Erase the following files:

filename.db*	(DB and DBS)
filename.i*	(key files)
filename.pix	(PIX file of a variable length database)

5.94 Tip: Use the general purpose Tools File Erase command to erase a database and associated files individually from your disk. There is no special command for this as there is in Smart 3.10.

SW II

In Smart 3.10, you use the Utilities Erase File command to erase a database and its associated files at the same time. In SmartWare II, the Tools File Erase command must be used to erase each file individually. Erase the following files:

filename.db*	(database)
filename.vw*	(standard view and custom view)
filename.key	(key file)
filename.pix	(PIX file of a variable length database)

6

Producing Reports

While it may be well and good to maintain files and display data on your screen, at some point you need to communicate your results to others by printing a report. This chapter covers the reporting capabilities of the Smart Database, from the elementary print command to the more complex combination reports.

As comprehensive as any report-generation facility may be, there are always needs for additional capabilities. This chapter shows you how to customize your work. Several tips and tricks point out little-known facts about Smart's report-generation facilities.

Finally, this chapter shows you how to get around many of the inherent restrictions in the Report command. Sample project files are included in this chapter and in Appendix A.

Creating Quick Reports

Use the Print (3.10) or Print View (SmartWare II) commands when you need data on paper in a hurry, but you don't need all the special formatting features of the Report or Print Report commands.

6.1 Tip: Use the vertical bar (|) to specify a range of fields. ***Both***

Instead of typing individual field names or numbers separated by semicolons, use the vertical bar to specify a range when you have several consecutive fields:

```
[field1|field9]
```

In Smart 3.10, you also can use field numbers:

```
[1|9]
```

You can specify an individual field and a range at the same time:

```
[1¦9;11]
```

You will save space on the command line (or your project file) and make fewer errors.

Both

6.2 Trap: Output from the Print or Print View commands cannot be saved to a file; you can print only to the printer or the screen.

If you need disk-file output, you must use the Report (3.10) or Print Report (SmartWare II) commands, because you cannot save output from the Print command to a disk file. Figure 6.1 shows the two destination output options from the Print command.

```
SKILL CKP
DEPT ACCT
PHONE (312) 439-8760
EMPDATE 10-01-59

Select option: Screen Printer
print file report [1:2:3]
File: person   Window: 1                          Page: 1  Rec: 1  ( 1 )  Act: Y
PRINT - print the current file, page or record
```

Fig. 6.1.
Print destination options.

Both

6.3 Tip: The Print and Print View commands can display the active status of each record.

Unlike the Report command, the Print command in Smart 3.10 prints both deleted and active records. (In SmartWare II, the commands are Print Report and Print View.) In addition to the active status, the physical (not logical) record number is printed. (An example of the Print...List command's output is shown in figure 5.11.) This display is available only if you select the List format, in which each field is shown on a separate line. In the Report format the fields are displayed side by side across the page.

Both

6.4 Tip: Use the Print...List format to display, in an easy-to-read format, more data than you can view in the Report format.

In the Report format (do not confuse this format with the Report or Print Report commands), lines longer than the width of your printer or screen will wrap around, but the display can be difficult to read. The screen shown in figure 6.2 displays 20 fields in the Print...Report format.

The Print...List command prints fields one above the other, for ease of reading records with multiple fields.

Both

6.5 Tip: Keep field names as short as possible to maximize output when using the Print...Report command in Smart 3.10 or print View...Report in SmartWare II.

```
SSN          FIRST     LAST       AGE SEX MS DEP DEG CAR STREET
CITY         ST ZIP        WAGE STATUS SKILL DEPT PHONE           EMPDATE  PCT
------------------------------------------------------------------------------
345-98-7593 Rosanna    Ronaldo     52 M   M  3   BA  2   546 Olive Hill
Oak Park    IL 60301     878.75 Y     CKP    ACCT (312) 439-8760 10-01-59 5.3
498-48-3900 Debbie     Linden      29 F   S  1   MA  2   409 Pleasant St
Amherst     MA 01002    1403.79 Y     SDL    MFGR (413) 886-3498 06-20-75 4.5
239-87-8876 Michael    Davis       61 M   M  1   MBA 2   100 Lewis Ave.
Covington   LA 70433     734.56 2     PWJV   SALE (318) 997-6621 05-25-69 8.7
208-23-0300 Julius     Karenski    41 M   D  0   PhD 1   18 Olive St.
Louisville  KY 40201    1020.33 2     JKS    MKTG (606) 779-5000 08-20-71 1.6
887-63-5498 Jeff       Harris      34 M   M  4   BA  5   1201 Horton Rd.
Lyndhurst   OH 44124     629.23 Y     KPR    ACCT (614) 776-3398 07-01-70 9.2
598-44-5922 LeAnne     Markus      48 F   W  1   MBA 1   14 Crumpet Ave.
Alamosa     CO 81101     887.49 2            SALE (303) 797-5939 10-30-65 6.5
876-33-0989 Marilyn    Lester      55 F   M  4   AB  3   6 Greenville St
Yarmouth    MA 02675    1516.26 Y     ZOBY   MKTG (617) 873-0979 09-05-75 4.3

Enter any key to continue

File: person   Window: 1                      Page: 1  Rec: 1  ( 1 )  Act: Y
PRINT - print the current file, page or record
```

Fig. 6.2.

Lines wrapping with the Print File...Report command.

When you use the Print command in the Report format, column width is determined by which is largest—the field width or the length of the field name. Figure 6.3, for example, shows a printout of several fields. The STATUS field is actually defined as a one-character alpha field; but because the field name is six characters long, the field consumes six columns rather than just one.

```
SSN         LAST       STATUS MS AGE
------------------------------------
345-98-7593 Ronaldo    Y      M  52
498-48-3900 Linden     Y      S  29
239-87-8876 Davis      2      M  61
208-23-0300 Karenski   2      D  41
887-63-5498 Harris     Y      M  34
598-44-5922 Markus     2      W  48
876-33-0989 Lester     Y      M  55
987-65-7653 Marzetti   2      D  47
387-59-8374 Steffans   1      M  25
498-34-5998 Bernstein  2      S  30
776-39-8763 Adelson    Y      M  60

Enter any key to continue

File: person   Window: 1                      Page: 1  Rec: 1  ( 1 )  Act: Y
PRINT - print the current file, page or record
```

Fig. 6.3.

Default Report field widths determined by field names and contents.

6.6 Tip: Use the Smart 3.10 Report form/label facility rather than the Print...List command to print multiple columns of fields one above the other. In SmartWare II, the command is Print Report.

Both

Although the List format of the Print command prints the fields over each other, only one column of data is available. You cannot print two or three columns side by side with fields over each other. If you want to have this type of output, you should use the Report Form Label option, as shown in figure 6.4. You can print a maximum of four fields next to each other on any line.

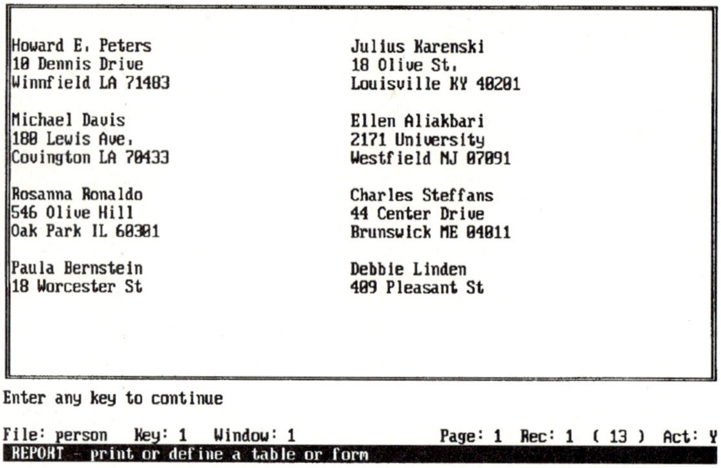

Fig. 6.4.

Creating labels with the Report Form Label.

```
Howard E. Peters                    Julius Karenski
10 Dennis Drive                     18 Olive St.
Winnfield LA 71483                  Louisville KY 40201

Michael Davis                       Ellen Aliakbari
100 Lewis Ave.                      2171 University
Covington LA 70433                  Westfield NJ 07091

Rosanna Ronaldo                     Charles Steffans
546 Olive Hill                      44 Center Drive
Oak Park IL 60301                   Brunswick ME 04011

Paula Bernstein                     Debbie Linden
10 Worcester St                     409 Pleasant St

Enter any key to continue

File: person   Key: 1   Window: 1              Page: 1  Rec: 1  ( 13 )  Act: Y
REPORT - print or define a table or form
```

Both

6.7 Tip: The Print command has no capability for specifying print line width.

In Smart 3.10, the line width is governed by the page width specified in the main menu Configure command. If you switch your printer to compressed print and find that you are still getting only an 80-column report, increase the number of characters per line in the Configure command.

In SmartWare II, line width is controlled by the paper width setting in the Tools Preferences Global command. The entry should be made in inches, not print positions.

Both

6.8 Tip: Preview your Print (3.10) or Print View Report (SmartWare II) output on your monitor to check for correct field and fit before you print.

Sometimes you can't be sure the fields you have selected are the ones you want or even that the output will fit without wrapping around. If you execute the Print (Smart 3.10) or Print View Report (SmartWare II) command, directing the output to the screen, you can preview your result. If the output is correct, press Alt-X to display the Print command, and edit it, changing the output device from Screen to Printer. Press Enter to execute the newly changed command.

6.9 Tip: Use the following project file to display the sum of any numeric field in a database. *SW II*

```
local $field

screen clear 7 0
screen input 5 10 0 7 12 $field
evaluate ( "screen print 7 10 0 7 filesum([" | $field | "])" )

message "Press any key to continue..."
```

When you run this project file, the name of the field is entered into the $field variable, which then will be used in the Filesum calculation. The evaluate statement constructs the full screen print command.

6.10 Tip: Here is another project file to display the sum of a numeric field in a database. *SW II*

```
local $field

screen clear 7 0
screen print 5 10 7 0 "Field name:"
screen input 5 22 0 7 12 $field

tools file erase "qnow.dfq"

fopen "qnow.dfq" as 1
fwrite 1 from "field ["|$field|"] filesum"
fclose 1

data query execute "qnow.dfq"
```

Note that this program uses the QBE facility of the Data Query command to display the result of the Filesum function.

Creating Formal Reports

Use the Report (3.10) or Print Report (SmartWare II) commands when you want to produce formal reports that you cannot obtain with the Print command. With these commands, you can print Tables, Forms, or reports that combine both Tables and Forms.

This section describes many little-known features of the Report command and presents methods of circumventing some of the command's restrictions. Useful project files are presented as examples, so that you can easily implement these suggestions. The options for the Report command are shown in figures 6.5, 6.6, and 6.7.

```
Page Definition
   Page length (in lines): 66
-> Page width (in characters): 80
   Page numbers:  Left  Right  Center  Left-right  Right-left  No-numbers
   Start page number: 1

   Lines per inch: 6  8
   Characters per inch: 10  12  17


   IS THERE A FORM ON THIS PAGE: Yes  No
     Location of upper left corner of form
       line: 1
       column: 1
     Location of lower right corner of form
       line: 5

Loaded File-Screens
   dept standard                              person3 standard

F1 Help    F2 Edit text    F3 Blank text    F10 Finished

Report: DEPTREP                      F10 Finished  ESC Cancel
REPORT - print or define a table or form
```

Fig. 6.5.

Report Page Layout options.

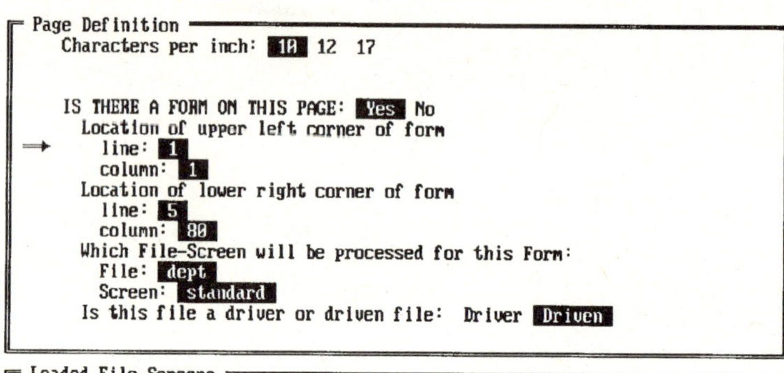

```
Page Definition
   Characters per inch: 10  12  17


   IS THERE A FORM ON THIS PAGE: Yes  No
     Location of upper left corner of form
->     line: 1
       column: 1
     Location of lower right corner of form
       line: 5
       column: 80
     Which File-Screen will be processed for this Form:
       File: dept
       Screen: standard
     Is this file a driver or driven file:  Driver  Driven
```

```
Loaded File-Screens
   dept standard                              person3 standard

F1 Help    F2 Edit text    F3 Blank text    F10 Finished

Report: DEPTREP                      F10 Finished  ESC Cancel
REPORT - print or define a table or form
```

Fig. 6.6.

Report Page Form options.

Page Length Specifications

Both

6.11 Tip: Set page length to the physical length of your paper.

In Smart 3.10, default page length is determined by the number of printer lines per page specified in the Main Menu Configure command. In SmartWare II, the default is derived from paper length, specified in inches when you execute the Tools Prefererences Hardware command.

If you are using 8 1/2 x 11-inch paper and specifying 6 lines per inch, the page length default is 66 lines (11 inches x 6 lines per inch). If you plan to print your report at 8 lines per inch, the page-length setting should be 88 (11 inches x 8 lines per inch).

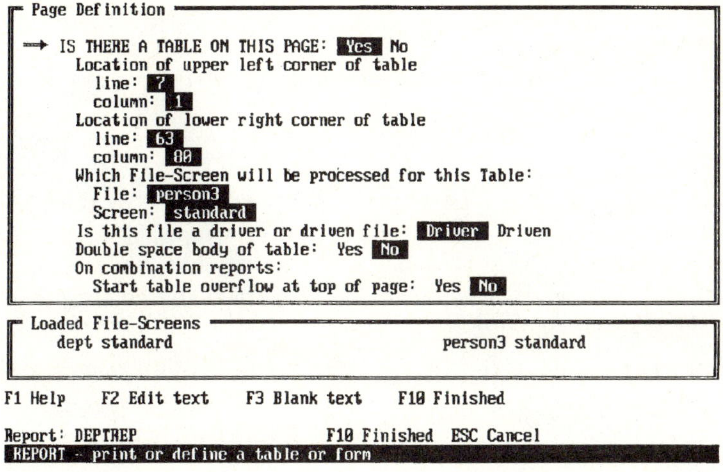

Figure. 6.7.
Report Page Table options.

6.12 Tip: Page width is related to the pitch you select. ***Both***

In Smart 3.10, the default page width is governed by the page width specified in the Configure command in the main menu. In SmartWare II, the default is derived from the paper width, specified in inches when you execute the Tools Preferences Hardware command.

If the print width is 8 inches and you are printing at 10 characters per inch (10 pitch), a page-width setting of 80 characters is correct. If, on the other hand, you plan to print your report in compressed print mode (17 characters per inch) on 8-inch-wide paper, set the page width to 132 characters.

Form and Table Specifications

6.13 Trick: Adjust your table location and paper position to accommodate the page number. ***Both***

If you specify page numbers in the Page definition menu, they will be printed close to the bottom of the page; and you cannot change the line location. For a page length of 66 lines, the page number is always printed on line 64. Unless your paper is positioned exactly, the page number could appear at the top of the following page.

Even if your paper is positioned exactly, you may want to leave more of a margin between the page number and the perforation. Do not change the page length, however, because the system must match the defined page length with the physical length of the paper. You can "fool" your printer into leaving a greater margin at the bottom of the page if you roll the paper downward in the printer, thus ending the page several additional lines before the perforation.

If you use this trick, remember to adjust the upper left corner of the Table area so that the printing does not begin on the bottom of the previous page. If the upper line of the table had been line 1, for example, and you roll the paper down four lines, the upper line should be changed to line 5.

3.10 **6.14 Tip:** File and screen names must be saved in the Report definitions.

Because file and screen names are embedded in the Report definition, there is no prompt for them when you run the report. This may save typing the names every time you want to run the report, but it also means that your Report definition is bound to a specific file and screen. (Tips on getting around this restriction are provided in Tricks 6.86, 6.87, and 6.88 in this chapter.)

You must have the correct file and screen loaded if you want to edit the Report definition. If they are not loaded, you will see the following error message

```
File-screen ff-ss must be loaded
```

where `ff` is the file name, and `ss` is the screen name. If the report is a combination, both files must be loaded.

3.10 **6.15 Trap:** Screen names in a Report definition must be entered in the correct case.

Screen names are case-sensitive; if the incorrect case is used, an error will result. To help you enter screen names correctly, the names of currently loaded files and screens are displayed at the bottom of your definition screen. The current file and screen are entered into both the Table and Form specifications as a default. If you need to change a screen name, be sure you use the case that matches the display.

Driver versus Driven Files

3.10 **6.16 Tip:** Decide which file will be the Driver and which will be the Driven.

If your report consists of only a form or table, you don't have to select a driver or driven file; the default for both types of reports is driver. But if you are creating a combination report, you must designate one as the Driver and the other as the driven. Like the Transactions command, which also uses two files, the Report command requires that you decide which file will govern the production of the report.

In the example used in figure 6.8, there is a personnel file in the table portion of the report and a department file in the form. One page of the report is shown in the figure. The personnel file is designated as the Driver to make sure the report includes all employees, even though a department record may be missing. If a separate page were required for each department, regardless of whether any employees were working in that department, the Department file would be the Driver, and the personnel file would be the Driven file.

```
                ABERDEEN MANUFACTURING CORPORATION
                        Department Listing

                    Department:   Manufacturing
                              01-10-87

     LAST        FIRST                    EMPLOYMENT
DEPT NAME        NAME       SSN           DATE        WEEKLY PAY HOME PHONE
------------------------------------------------------------------------------
MFGR Linden      Debbie     498-40-3980 06-20-75        1403.79 (413) 886-3498

     Aliakbari   Ellen      345-54-2287 08-15-72         997.66 (201) 727-9242

                                                      ----------
                                         Total         2401.45
                                                      ==========
```

Fig. 6.8.

A combination report.

6.17 Trap: Selecting Double Space Yes causes double spacing between every output line in a Table report.

Both

The selection of double spacing will leave one blank line between each physical line of the report's table section. While this may be a perfect format for instances in which you are printing on only the first of the four output lines, you may not want double spacing if there are multiple physical lines for each database record.

Trick 6.44 and Tip 6.50 provide ways to solve this problem.

Handling Page Overflow

6.18 Trap: You cannot reprint the form portion at the top of a subsequent page if the table portion overflows.

3.10

Leaving the top of the second page blank is the best way to avoid printing on top of a preprinted form. (Appendix A contains a project file you can use to cause the Form to reprint.)

In SmartWare II, you *can* reprint the form when the Table overflows.

Defining Tables

A Table is a report in the row-and-column format. Although it is similar to the results of the Print...Report command, there are many differences, as well as options you can use to customize your printed output.

In addition to pointing out some of the lesser-known features of the Table Report facility, this section presents several tricks and traps to make your use of this feature more productive.

Field Selection

SW II

6.19 Trap: Field names are case sensitive in report table definitions. In all other commands and features of SmartWare II, field names are not case sensitive.

Although report definitions are independent of the view, the table field declarations are case sensitive. The field [wage] is not the same as a field named [WAGE]. If you attempt to modify or execute a report definition that contains the field [wage], but the current view contains [WAGE], you will see an error message:

```
Field [Wage] is not on current view
```

You can modify the report definition to substitute the field [WAGE], or modify the view to change the name of the field. However, in columns the field names are not case sensitive.

SW II

6.20 Tip: If columns for numeric fields are not wide enough, they will display as asterisks. Follow these rules to make sure your numeric columns are the right size.

For example, if the field contains the number 1000.00, the field must be at least 8 columns wide, assuming the following settings:

Display:	Formatted
Precision:	2
Special Formatting:	None
Negative Formatting:	Minus
Use Commas:	No

Add one column for Dollar formatting or commas, or add two for both. If the field will ever be negative, add one column. No columns have to be added if you are using parenthesis, credit, or debit negative formatting.

Both

6.21 Tip: Insert and delete a temporary calculation in your table definition to close a gap.

When defining a table report, if you decrease the width of a column, there will be unused space to the right of the field; the gap is not closed automatically. Although you can do a series of Moves, an easier way is to insert and then delete a calculation of one space (" ") with a width of 1. Once it is declared, the gap is closed when you Remove it.

Make sure you leave a space before this temporary calculated entry, or the fields will run together. The Remove subcommand takes out the field itself and the following blanks, if any. If there is a gap of only 2 blanks, insert the calculation in the second blank location; this will leave the first blank in position.

6.22 Trick: Move a field to the 2nd line of the Table definition temporarily to make it easier to rearrange the fields on the first line.

Both

When moving a field from the left of the line to the right, you will get the following message if the line is already full:

```
Move would cause line overflow
```

To avoid the problem, move the field out to the 2nd line temporarily, and then move it back where it needs to go. If you are moving from the right to the left under the same conditions, there is no error message and you will have no problem.

6.23 Tip: If you have selected a numeric field, the degree of precision (number of decimal places) defaults to the value declared in the field definition.

If you decide on fewer decimal places, the displayed values are rounded. Of course, any calculation using the field will rely on the unrounded number, and hence you may see a report that does not seem to calculate correctly.

Actual calculation:	6.4 x 3 = 19.2
Apparent calculation:	6 x 3 = 19

In this example, if the number 6.4 is shown as just 6 with no decimal positions, and if the result is also shown without a decimal, it appears that the computer cannot multiply correctly.

6.24 Tip: Truncate or wrap alpha fields that are longer than the defined column.

Both

Choose this option on the field-selection options menu. If you have a very long alpha field, you may want to define the report field as shorter than the actual field; setting the report field to the same length as the database field might cause you to run out of room before defining all the fields you want on the report. You can elect to truncate the alpha field or, if you want to see the entire field contents, to wrap it around. In Smart 3.10, the maximum number of wrapped lines is 10, however. In SmartWare II, the field may wrap all the way down the page, if necessary.

Defining a numeric field as shorter than any given value is not a good idea; asterisks are displayed in place of any value that is too wide for the field, regardless of whether you selected truncation or wrapping.

6.25 Tip: Specify No Justification in a table report column heading if you want to position the heading in a special location.

Both

When you choose No Justification, you can insert leading spaces to position the headings exactly where you want them. The report generator will not trim the leading spaces.

Both

6.26 Tip: The multiple line display of a long alpha field in a table report is unrelated to the field reform usage during data entry or update.

Reforming a field by pressing F8 in Smart 3.10 (or F7 in SmartWare II), ensures that words are not split between lines and that you can view the maximum amount of the field on the screen or view. In a table report, a long alpha field may be printed on multiple lines by wrapping around, but it does not matter if the field was reformed on the current screen/view or another screen/view. However, if you have purposely inserted multiple blanks in SmartWare II, they will be included in the report.

SW II

6.27 Tip: You may safely use a proportional font for left-justified text in a report, but you should use a monospaced font for numerics.

With text material, there are no decimal points to align. Left-justified text begins printing at the specified location. However, if you are printing numeric fields, which are usually right justified, using a proportional font destroys the alignment of the decimal points.

Use the Set-Font option to establish the font to an individual column item or for new items you are going to declare.

Calculated Fields

Both

6.28 Trap: Calculated alpha fields cannot wrap around.

Calculated alpha fields will truncate automatically, even if you select the wrap option. Refer to the next tip for advice on circumventing this restriction.

SmartWare II does support the wrapping of calculated fields.

3.10

6.29 Tip: Use multiple field calculations to simulate the wrapping of calculated alpha fields.

Although calculated alpha fields cannot wrap around like fields that come directly from the database, you can simulate the wrap feature by defining up to three additional calculated fields, each of which extracts an additional portion of the original field.

For example, suppose you have a 100 byte field containing a part description. You would like to concatenate onto the beginning of the field a message that says New Item. If you want to print the new concatenated field in 40 columns on the report, you should create three defined fields as follows:

```
Line 1: "New Item: "|[description]
Line 2: mid([description],31,40)
Line 3: mid([description],71,30)
```

The calculation on the second line will extract the characters from 31 to 70 from the description, and the final calculation will display characters 71 to 100. (The first calculation will truncate at the 40-character field width.)

If the last line is null because of a short item description, the line will not be printed, as long as no other field on the line is specified (see Tip 6.45).

Be sure to specify left justification for the calculated fields. To look best, any heading you supply for a calculated field should be on the same line as other headings in the report and should be left-justified (see Trap 6.42).

6.30 Tip: Use the & (ampersand) to leave a single blank between fields when calculating an item in a report. *Both*

Examine the following example:

```
[first]&[last]
```

This calculation leaves a single blank character between the first name and the last name. Any trailing blank characters on the first name are stripped off; you do not have to use the Trim function to delete any trailing blanks.

6.31 Tip: Use a calculation of a period to represent "Not Available" rather than null, blank, or zero. *3.10*

If it is significant that a value is not available, other than zero, do not display a zero; this would be misleading. And although you can display a null or a blank in these cases, your report may be easier to read if there is a period there.

In the following two reports, a calculation is used for each data column. The calculation for the first column of the first report is:

```
if [dept] = "ACCT" then [wage] else "."
```

In the second version of the report, a NULL is printed instead of the period. Note that the first version is much easier to read than the second version.

Version 1:

Wages by State and Department

State	Acct	Data	Mfgr	Mktg	Sale
CA	.	.	.	.	1,004.56
CO	956.43	.	.	.	.
.	956.43	.	.	.	.
IL	878.75	.	.	.	.
KY	.	.	.	.	.
LA	.	.	.	1,020.33	734.56
LA	.	.	.	1,544.00	.
MA	.	.	1,403.79	.	.
MA	.	.	.	1,516.26	.
ME	.	654.34	.	.	.
NC	901.45	.	.	.	.
NJ	.	.	997.66	.	.
OH	629.23	.	.	.	.
TOT:	3,365.86	654.34	2,401.45	4,080.59	2,626.61

Version 2:

Wages by State and Department

State	Acct	Data	Mfgr	Mktg	Sale
CA					1,004.56
CO					887.49
CT	956.43				
IL	878.75				
KY				1,020.33	
LA					734.56
LA				1,544.00	
MA			1,403.79		
MA				1,516.26	
ME		654.34			
NC	901.45				
NJ			997.66		
OH	629.23				
TOT:	3,365.86	654.34	2,401.45	4,080.59	2,626.61

SW II

6.32 Tip: Do not define a calculated numeric field with a default of BLANK or NULL if you plan to total the field in a breakpoint or grand total. The report usually will fail to run.

If you want a totally blank space on the paper and the condition is not true, you might be tempted to create a calculated field similar to the following:

```
if [dept] = "ACCT" then [wage] else BLANK
```

You can create the report definition without incident. However, you will get the following error message when a record is encountered in which the calculation evaluates to BLANK:

```
Trying to total an alpha calculation
```

You will get the same result if you use NULL as a default. Neither BLANK nor NULL are considered to be numeric. If you want to have a blank on the paper, use the following formula:

```
if [dept] = "ACCT" then [wage] else 0
```

Then, in the options for the calculated field, when you select a formatted display, the last option should be:

```
Blank when the Value is Zero:  Yes
```

With this option set at Yes, a blank will be printed instead of the zero default for the calculation. The only problem with this solution is that an actual field value equal to zero will also display as a blank, and it will not be possible to distinguish this from the default for the calculation.

6.33 Trap: Changing the number of fields in a file could cause your reports to be incorrect. *3.10*

If you never add a field to your file, this trap should not bother you. But if you add a field, you may have problems, depending on where you add the field in your file. (You cannot, of course, actually add a field to your file; you must create a new file that is similar to the original file, and then rename it.) Because Report definitions refer to fields by their numbers, not their names, a field should be added to the end of the file to avoid changing the numbers of the prior fields.

6.34 Tip: Using Data Cross-Tabs, create a temporary file to generate totals for use when calculating percentages in a report. *SW II*

Although you can use the FILESUM function in a calculation, it is time consuming to generate the total repeatedly for each record. If you use the Data Cross-Tab command to create a temporary file, you can use the Filelookup command to retrieve the totals for use in the calculation. Consider the following report.

```
                                         Pct to      Pct to
DEPT Last Name                   Wage    Dept        Company
-------------------------------------------------------------
ACCT   Adelson              $956.432    8.4%           8.2%
       Harris               $629.231    8.7%           5.4%
       Marzetti             $901.452    6.8%           7.8%
       Ronaldo              $878.752    6.1%           7.6%
                           ----------
       Total ACCT          $3,365.86
                           ==========
```

In this sample report, the percent to the department total is calculated as:

```
[wage]/filelookup([depwage.dept],[depwage.wage],[dept])
```

The file DEPWAGE, which contains total wages for each department, was created prior to running the report. The calculation for the percentage to the company total is:

```
[wage]/$totwage
```

The variable $totwage was assigned a value by the following project file statement:

```
let $totwage = filesum([depwage.wage])
```

Although the Filesum formula could have been used in the actual report calculation, rather than the variable, it would have been time-consuming to recalculate the sum of the wages for each record on the report.

Table Report Headings

SW II

6.35 Trap: When creating a table report, if you plan to include a variable in a heading or footing calculation, that variable must exist and be locked.

In a heading of a table report, you can create a calculation if the first character is an equal sign (=). The calculation must be alpha; use the STR or FIXED function to convert any numeric fields to alpha. The entire calculation may be a variable, or you may include a variable within the calculation:

```
="From "|$begdate|" to "|$enddate
```

But if the variable is not locked, you will be prevented from saving the calculation with the titles. If you temporarily delete the equal sign, you can continue with the definition. Later, when you have declared and locked the variable, you can edit the report definition and repair the title calculation.

SW II

6.36 Tip: In the heading of a table report, a calculation using a database field will reference the first record on the page. On each successive page, the first record on the page becomes available for use in heading calculations.

Compare this feature to that of table record references in the form of a combination report, in which the available record is the first in the *table* not on the page. (For more information, refer to the section on Combination reports later in this chapter.

SW II

6.37 Tip: An undefined variable in the heading of a table report will not prevent the printing of the report and may not even cause an error message.

For example, you may have a heading of a report containing the following formula:

```
=$date
```

In this case, you will be able to run the report even if the $date variable no longer exists. A blank line will be printed in the heading where the variable would have been.

SW II

6.38 Trick: Use a combination of the Key and Keys statements to change the column headings in a table report.

In the following report, the column headings need to change to reflect the current month:

```
                    Gletsch & Grimsel, Inc.
                      Year to Date Sales
                                       Month        YTD
          Description                 May 90     May 90
          Fan Motor                        1          1
                                           2          4
                                           1          2
                                           5          7
          Total                            9         14
```

The following project file can be used to change the column headings, depending on the response to the prompt:

```
local $date
screen shortinput $date "Date: "

'key will contain Feb 90 or Mar 90, etc.
key define "#1000" chr(34)|format($date,"Dmon yy")|chr(34)

print report modify "ytdsales"

'table columns
keys "tc"

'update and change the columns headings
keys Tab,Tab,"u",Down,Down,Look,#1000,Enter,F10
keys Tab,Tab,"u",Enter,Down,Down,Look,#1000,Enter,F10

keys F10,F10,F10

key remove "#1000"
```

Note that the date, in month and year format, is inserted into the special macro key #1000. The Keys statement is then used to update the column headings of the report.

6.39 Trick: In a table report, if you have proportional fonts in column headings that will not align with their respective columns, enter the headings in the form section of a combination report. *SW II*

Create a form to print just the column headings. Although you will have to adjust the position of the text manually, you will have the flexibility to position the headings exactly where you need them. Just remember to reprint the form on each new page.

Multiple Print Lines

6.40 Tip: Four detail lines can be printed for each input record in the table. *Both*

Each line is as long as is specified in the Page definitions. How do you get access to these additional lines? Simply move the cursor out past the final print position of the first line, and you will move automatically to the second line. (The Tab key will move the cursor quickly; the Home and End keys will move the cursor to the first or last column of each line.) Both the column and line numbers are displayed on the status line. If you move the cursor past the final print position, the line number changes.

Not only can you now squeeze more data into your reports, but now they can be more interesting and complete.

3.10

6.41 Trick: Embed printer macros in calculated or text fields to control your printer.

In the same way that printer macros can be used in the Word Processor to insert underlining, boldface, italics, or other fonts, printer macros can be inserted in text or calculated fields of Report definitions to perform similar functions. (See Chapter 13 for a discussion of printer macros.)

The same printer macros can be used in the Database as in the Word Processor. To insert a printer macro into a report Text item, hold down the Alt key while entering on the numeric key pad the ASCII code for the printer macro. When you release the Alt key, the macro will be entered.

The printer macro may be entered conditionally if it is in a calculated field. For example, if you want to boldface any sales figures over 1000, your calculation would be

```
if [sales] > 1000 then "x" else " "
```

where x is the printer macro that activates the boldface font. Once the code has been sent to the printer, the next field will appear in boldface; you could print the name of the sales representative, the actual sales figures, or any other report item you want to stand out.

To return to the normal font, create a text field that contains the printer macro to turn off the boldface font. Even if boldface has not been turned on previously, turning it off unnecessarily will have no detrimental effect.

Both

6.42 Trap: Extra detail lines create extra heading lines.

At least one extra heading line is added for each additional detail line. Leaving them blank will not preclude them.

Let's take the example of a table report with two lines of information. If you have just one line of headings for the fields on the first line and no headings at all for the fields on the second line, then there will be a total of two heading lines for the table—one for each line of data. If you add a heading line for the second line of the report and the heading line is specified on the same line as the first data line, there will still be only two lines of headings on the report.

The following table specifies the number of heading lines under several conditions:

Table 6.1.
Heading Positions

Line 1	*Line 2 Position of Heading Line*			
Position of Heading Line	Blank	1 Head	2 Heads	Both Heads
Heading Line 1	2	2	4	4
Heading Line 2	2	4	2	4
Both Heading Lines	4	4	4	4

6.43 Trick: The additional detail lines can be useful work space during the construction of a Report definition.

Both

If you need to move columns around and want to set one or more aside for the moment, you can move some fields out to a secondary line temporarily, then move them back when you are ready. Doing this prevents having to remove a field and enter it again.

6.44 Trick: Calculate a special field on a secondary table line to double space only between records.

Both

In your Page definition, you have the option of specifying that you want your table double spaced. If you choose this option and you have multiple lines within the table, you will find one blank line between detail lines as well as between records. There is no documented way to double-space between records only, but you can employ a trick.

If you have defined three detail lines, for example, and you want a blank line between the last detail line and the first detail line of the next record but you want no blank lines between detail lines within a record, you can establish a text field on the fourth line as a "place holder," while specifying single-spacing in the Page portion of the Report definition. The Smart Database does not allow you to enter a blank as a text item by itself, although this would seem a good choice. Unfortunately, Smart's programmers decided to protect you from entering such a character by mistake.

If you enter some other character that will print as a blank on your printer, that character will have the same effect. Many printers recognize ASCII code 255 or 160 as a blank; you will have to read your printer manual carefully (this information is usually in an ASCII table in the back) and do some experimenting.

To enter an ASCII 255 into a text field, select Text from the Table Columns menu (see fig. 6.9). Insert the special code on the first line that is labeled Text. With the cursor pointing to this line, hold down the Alt key and enter 255 on the numeric key pad. When you release the Alt key, the character is entered.

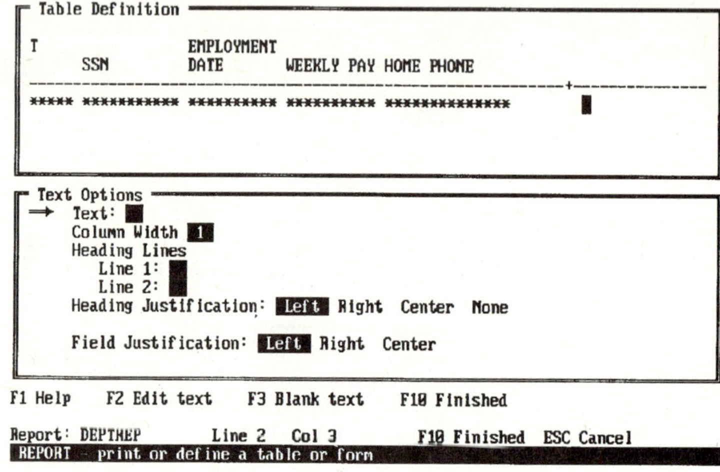

Fig. 6.9.

Entering Table text.

Do not enter any heading lines; you need not change the column width or justification specifications. If the ASCII character is the right code for your printer, you will find that you can now print "paragraphs" of data within the Table Report environment.

Although this technique is not perfect, it can help you in some circumstances. It has two drawbacks. Because there is now an extra line on your report, there are also extra lines of blank headings that can make your report look peculiar. The other drawback is that you have no visible evidence of this hidden field. If you need to edit your Report definition, you will not know the field location. If you use this trick, I suggest placing the hidden field in column 1 so that you will always know the location of the hidden field.

Both

6.45 Tip: Secondary table lines are not printed if the contents are null in Smart 3.10 or blank in SmartWare II.

If you organize your report to take advantage of this feature, you can add some variety to the report format and perhaps make it more meaningful. In a personnel database, for example, if you plan to print Spouse Name and Birth Date on the second line, the line will not print if these fields are null.

Breakpoints

6.46 Trap: You cannot use a calculated report column in the definition of a breakpoint.

Both

A breakpoint must refer to an actual field in the file. To circumvent this restriction, refer to Tip 6.47.

6.47 Tip: Create a calculated view field to be used in the definition of a breakpoint.

SW II

Although you cannot use a calculated column in the report as a breakpoint field, you can get around the problem by creating a calculated view field. Then use this field as the breakpoint field in the report.

6.48 Tip: Establish a breakpoint using a field that is not in the table.

SW II

When you add a breakpoint, you are prompted:

```
Move to break key field and press Enter or press F6 to list fields
```

If you simply move the cursor, you are limited to the fields declared in the table. However, if you press F6, a popup menu displays all the fields in the view. Select the field you would like to use as the breakpoint, and press Enter. The breakpoint field does not have to be printed on the report.

6.49 Trick: Hide a breakpoint field by making the width zero.

SW II

Another way to hide a breakpoint field is to set the field width at zero without a column heading, the field will still be recognized as being used in the report, but will not print.

BE CAREFUL: Once you change the width to zero, you cannot update or remove the field within the columns option. You may, however, update or remove the breakpoint specification for the field.

6.50 Tip: Use a breakpoint to double-space between records.

Both

If you are printing several lines for each database record, a field that you know is different from record to record (such as an invoice number) can be designated as a breakpoint, causing a single-line skip at the break. If you have selected no double spacing on the Page menu, you can have single spacing within each "paragraph" on the report and double spacing between paragraphs.

If there is no identifiable field that you know will be different from record to record, use the method presented in Trick 6.44.

6.51 Tip: The order of declaration for breakpoints defines the order of importance. The first field you define is the major breakpoint, the next is the intermediate, the third is the minor, and so on.

Both

In Smart 3.10, apart from the order in which the breakpoints are defined, there is no other means of establishing the order of importance. If you later need to add a breakpoint to a Report definition, however, you will have to remove any breakpoints falling below the order of the new definition, and declare those breakpoints again.

In SmartWare II, you can insert a new breakpoint in the sequence prior to an an existing breakpoint. When you add breakpoints, the default breakpoint number is displayed at the top of the screen; if you already have one breakpoint, the display will read:

```
Break  2:
```

Observe, also, that at the bottom of the screen, there is the following message:

```
Press Enter to add at current break position

F3 Previous break   F4 Next break
```

If you want the new breakpoint to be number one, and the existing breakpoint to be two, press F3. This will change the breakpoint number at the top of the screen to:

```
Break 1:
```

The name of the field currently assigned to Break 1 is also displayed. When you press Enter, you are prompted:

```
Move to break key field and press Enter or press F6 to list fields
```

Now move your cursor to the new field you would like to assign to break 1, and press Enter. The new field you have selected will become break 1, and the original field will become break 2.

Similarly, if you remove a breakpoint, the breakpoint numbers of any lower breaks are increased by one.

SW II

6.52 Trick: Assign a breakpoint to a temporary field to swap the breakpoint orders of two fields.

If you currently have break 1 assigned to [field1] and break 2 assigned to [field2] and you want to swap the breakpoint assignments, temporarily assign break 1 to [field3]. Then you can assign [field2] as break 1, and finally assign [field1] as break 2.

When you update breakpoints, the last breakpoint number is shown at the top of the screen, along with the name of the field to which it is currently assigned. If break 2 is shown and you want to up date break 1, press F3 and Enter to edit the current break. Now you are prompted:

```
Move to break key field and press Enter or press F6 to list fields
```

Move the cursor to the field you want as break 1 and press Enter. You can edit any of the options, or simply press F10 to retain the current options. Now that break 1 has been reassigned to a temporary field, you can proceed to reassign break 2 to the desired field and finally reassign break 1 again.

6.53 Tip: Insert an extra breakpoint to prevent duplicate field printing. ***Both***

Suppose you have a report sorted in the following order:

Wage
Department Code
Department Name
LastName

If you need subtotals at each department break, you may want to suppress the repeated printing of the department name. Declare a breakpoint on the department name field, with the sole purpose being to prevent the duplicate printing.

6.54 Tip: Create two breakpoints for the same break field in a table report if you want two different types of summary calculations for the same data field, such as SUM and AVERAGE. ***3.10***

The calculations at a table report breakpoint may be SUM, AVERAGE, MINIMUM or MAXIMUM. If you want both a sum and an average for the same field, however, you will have to set up two breakpoints for the same break field. The calculations will print in reverse order; the first breakpoint calculation you establish will print second. If you set up the SUM first, and then the AVERAGE, the SUM will print after the AVERAGE.

6.55 Trap: When editing a breakpoint, you cannot change the numerical-operation field selection. ***3.10***

If you have designated that one or more fields are to be summed, you cannot change this selection in the Breakpoints Edit subcommand. You must remove the breakpoint and then add it again. Be careful, however, because the newly added breakpoint will now be the minor break and may not match your desired breakpoint sequence.

6.56 Tip: In a Table Report, different summary types will print on different lines at a breakpoint. ***SW II***

Here is an example:

New DEPT	Last Name	Wage	New Wage
ACCT	Adelson	$956.43	$1,031.03
	Harris	$629.23	$687.12
	Marzetti	$901.45	$912.27
	Ronaldo	$878.75	$953.44
Summary:	Max	$956.43	
	Avg		$895.97

Note that the maximum and average are on separate lines at the breakpoint.

Both

6.57 Tip: A record with an empty numeric field is not counted when breakpoint averages are calculated for that field; the record is counted if the value is zero. In Smart 3.10, a field without an entry is NULL; in SmartWare II, it is BLANK.

In the following report, no values were entered for the missing figures in the fields shown in the first two wage columns; zeros were entered for the missing figures in the last two wage columns. Observe the differences in the calculations of the breakpoint averages.

DEPT	Wage Female	Wage Male	Wage Female	Wage Male
MKTG		1,020.33	0.00	1,020.33
	1,516.26		1,516.26	0.00
		1,544.00	0.00	1,544.00
AVG:	1,516.26	1,282.17	505.42	854.78

If you are tabulating a survey, you may wish to distinguish between an actual answer of zero and the lack of a response by leaving the no response fields without any entry whatsoever. When printing an average of a field at a breakpoint on a table report, the records with the empty fields will not be counted in the total number of records.

These same characteristics are true when calculating an average in a Data Cross-Tab command in SmartWare II.

Both

6.58 Tip: In a table report, if you need a breakpoint on a minor field, you do not necessarily need a break on the major field.

Ordinarily, to have a break on a minor field, you will have a break on the major field. But this is not always necessary. For example, if you have a file of students, you might want a roster printed in the following order:

Grade
Teacher

In this example, you can have a breakpoint on [Teacher] without having a break on the [grade] field. However, you must be careful, because if you happen to have two teachers with the same name teaching in consecutive grades, there will not be a break.

6.59 Tip: Calculations in a breakpoint Result Line Label must be text, not numbers. If you want to display a number, use either the STR or the FIXED function to convert it to text.

SW II

In the breakpoint definition, in the Result Line Label, enter an equal sign (=), followed by the formula you want to print when the break field changes. The following example prints a percentage of the total that is derived from department wages:

```
="Percent"|fixed(filelookup([depwage.dept],[depwage.wage],[dept])/ $totwage *100,2)
```

Note that the percentage has been converted to a string, using the FIXED function.

6.60 Trick: Use a text calculation to print a long breakpoint Result Line Label so that it will wrap around if there is not enough space.

SW II

In a Table Report, if there is not enough space for a long literal Result Line Label before the first summary value, you will get the following error message when you try to save the breakpoint:

```
Label overlaps first break field
```

If you change the literal label to a text calculation, the text will wrap around in the available space. In the following example report, the calculation is:

```
="Summary Statistics and Figures"
```

Note the quotation marks and the use of the equal sign (=) to denote a calculation.

```
                                            New
DEPT Last Name                  Wage        Wage
MFGR Aliakbari                $997.66   $1,040.56
     Linden                 $1,403.79   $1,530.13

Summary             Max     $1,403.79
Statistics          Avg                 $1,285.35
and Figures
```

6.61 Tip: A field used in the following calculation in a breakpoint Result Line Label references the first record in the breakpoint set.

SW II

In this example, the calculation used was:

```
="Wage: "¦Fixed([wage],2)
```

Observe that the wage printed in the breakpoint is that of the first record within the set:

DEPT	Last Name	Wage
ACCT	Ronaldo	$878.75
	Harris	$629.23
	Marzetti	$901.45
	Adelson	$956.43
Wage:	878.75	$3,365.86

Defining Forms

Use a Form Report when you want to print one record per page and you need to position fields on a page as if you were filling out a form. Not only can you print database fields, but you can include calculations, text, page numbers, and labels in the form definition.

The Label selection can be used to print mailing labels in an aesthetic format; you can print labels from several database records across the page, in a "two-up" or "three-up" format. Tricks for using labels are presented in this section.

Using Fields

3.10

6.62 Trap: If you have specified field names in a report form and have later deleted the fields from the file, there will be no error message when the report prints.

The fields will be blank on the report, but there will be no warning that an invalid field name is specified. If you use field numbers and delete the field with that number, the next field in the file will move up to assume the field number; in this case, the wrong field will print.

Of course, you cannot "change" a file, but you can create a similar one, restructure the data, and rename the file. Refer to Chapter 2 for a project file to help you change a database.

Both

6.63 Tip: In a form report, alpha fields will wrap onto additional lines.

For example, if you have an alpha field that contains 150 bytes, the field will wrap if you allow three lines of 50 bytes each. This is similar to the way long alpha fields will wrap in a table report. Because the system avoids splitting words in the middle, you should allow a little more size. In this example, you should probably allow three lines of 55 or 60 bytes in case extra space is needed. The longer the words, the more space will be needed to avoid splitting a word.

Using Labels

6.64 Tip: Labels are a special type of report format. *Both*

When you define a label area in the Report Form, blank lines are not printed and multiple labels can be printed across the page.

In figure 6.10, for instance, blank lines and null lines are treated alike; neither line is printed in a label, and successive lines within that label are moved up.

```
Rosanna Ronaldo                    Debbie Linden
546 Olive Hill                     409 Pleasant St
Oak Park IL 60301                  Amherst MA 01002

Michael Davis                      Julius Karenski
100 Lewis Ave.                     Louisville KY 40201
Covington LA 70433

Jeff Harris                        LeAnne Markus
1201 Horton Rd.                    14 Crumpet Ave.
Lyndhurst OH 44124                 Alamosa CO 81101

Enter any key to continue

File: person   Window: 1                    Page: 1  Rec: 4  ( 4 )  Act:
REPORT - print or define a table or form
```

Fig. 6.10.

Labels with variant numbers of lines.

Note that the second record in the right-hand column does not have a street address. Not only does the label look more professional without a blank line, but the alignment of other labels is not disturbed.

6.65 Tip: When printing multiple labels across the page, print fields from different records for each label. *Both*

One important option must be specified when you define labels that you want data from different records printed across the page. Note that in figure 6.11, the cursor is pointing to a question that states:

```
Obtain the next record before processing this label:
```

For the first label in the row, the answer to this prompt should be No; for all other label blocks, change the answer to Yes. If you forget to change this specification, you will find that all the labels on the row are exactly alike. If this happens, simply go back and edit the label blocks to the right of the first label and change your reply.

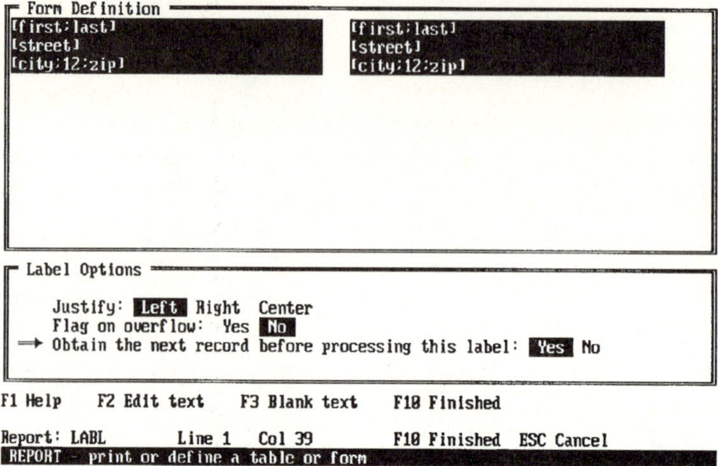

Fig. 6.11.

Selecting the "next record" option.

Both

6.66 Trick: Establish multiple adjacent labels to create the appearance of literals inserted into the label.

If you define a label in a report form, you cannot insert any literals within the label specification block. Sometimes, however, you need to include some additional explanatory information. Figure 6.12 shows an example of including literals in labels.

```
Form Definition
[first;last]                          [first;last]
[street]                              [street]
[city;12;zip]                         [city;12;zip]
Status: [   Degree: [deg]             Status: [   Degree: [deg]

Options

Select option: Calculated  Field  Label  Page-Number  Text
               Duplicate  Edit  Move  Remove
Report: lab12        Line 4    Col 62        F10 Finished  ESC Cancel
REPORT - print or define a table or form
```

Fig. 6.12.

Including literals in Report Form Labels.

There are actually three label definitions here: the top three lines make up the first label, the STATUS field is the second label (you can see only the left square bracket), and the DEGREE field is the third label. The text values are the words `Status:` and `Degree:`.

Notice that I have duplicated the label and text definitions on the right side of the screen so that I can print the Labels "two up." If you do this, don't forget to change the option for the second set to obtain the next record before processing the labels see (Tip 6.65).If you forget, the same data will be printed on both the right and the left labels.

6.67 Trick: Create a view field to insert text into a label. For example, create a view field consisting of a City field concatenated with a comma if the comma needs to be in the label.

SW II

Normally, when defining a mailing label, you can insert fields, but not literals. If you define the following:

```
[city;state;zip]
```

the label will look like this:

```
Amherst MA 01102
```

However, you can define a view field with the following calculation:

```
[city]|","
```

This will create a field with a comma after it, which then you can use in the label:

```
[commacity;state;zip]
```

and the result will be similar to the following:

```
Amherst, MA 01102
```

Note that there is a comma after the name of the city.

6.68 Tip: Use calculated view fields in a mailing label to provide variability.

SW II

For example, suppose you have a membership database with both home and business addresses, and a field indicating a mailing location preference. The [preference] field contains either "H" for Home or "B" for Business. Some members want the mail to go to their homes, and others want it to go to their businesses.

Create view fields to use for the printing of the mailing labels. The calculation of these fields will be either the home address or the business address, depending on the [preference] field. For example, the calculation for a [mail_street] field would be:

```
if [pref] = "H" then [home_street] else [bus_street]
```

The mailing labels will always print the correct address, and you do not have to print separate sets of labels.

Both

6.69 Tip: If you do not want to suppress blank lines, but still want the advantage of printing 2- or 3-up labels, you can define each line as an individual label.

Because blank line supression is effective only within each label definition, defining each line of output as an individual label allows you to avoid printing blank lines. This may be important if you are printing on preprinted forms, where fields must fall into specific locations. But by defining the lines or fields as individual labels, you can still print data from separate records across the page. Make sure that all label definitions to the right of the first definition obtain the next record before processing the label.

Both

6.70 Trick: Label blocks are useful not just for labels, but for other report forms, too.

For example, if you need to print names and addresses in the "bill to" and "ship to" portions of an invoice, use a label specification for these blocks. Your report will look better without any blank lines, and the vertical spacing will not be disturbed.

3.10

6.71 Trap: If you use a label area in the form area of a combination report, make sure you do not obtain the next record before processing the label; otherwise the label will not match with the table.

If you are printing a combination report, it is sometimes useful to include a label section within the form. For example, if you are printing invoices, you can print the "bill to" and "ship to" areas as labels; they will look better than if you print them as individual fields. But make sure that when the question appears:

```
"Obtain the next record before processing this label"
```

that you answer NO, or the label will not match with the data in the table of the report.

Both

6.72 Tip: If you print labels on a printer with continuous pin-fed labels, set the page length equal to the height from one label to the next.

The form height would be less than or equal to the page height. If you have specified only one row of labels across the page and you then go to a new page, the system will simply advance to the next label.

Both

6.73 Tip: When printing labels on a laser printer, you must define the entire page.

When using cut sheets, define your page size as the full paper size (for example, 60 lines for Hewlett-Packard's LaserJet printer), and define a form of the same size as the page. Using the Duplicate option, you can copy the label blocks not just across the page, but down the page as well. Both vertical and horizontal positioning will be critical, so you may want to run a test before completing the process of duplication. Remember that, for the first label at the top left of the page, you should answer No to the question about obtaining the next record before processing the label. For all other label blocks, answer Yes (see Tip 6.65).

6.74 Tip: To fill the page with identical label block copies, use the Duplicate option; it's called Dupe in SmartWare II. ***Both***

Duplicate the first label block, and then edit the duplicate, changing your response at the record-processing prompt to *Yes*. Once you have created this second copy, duplicate it throughout the page.

6.75 Tip: When specifying fields, calculations, or labels within the form, use the actual field names, rather than the numbers. ***Both***

If you later change your report, you can readily see the field names in use. Remember, though, that the form also uses field numbers rather than names so that even if a field's name is the same, the form must be redefined if the field's position has been changed. (Refer to the figures in this section of this chapter.) See Trap 6.62.

In SmartWare II, there are no field numbers, so using field names will make an eventual upgrade easier.

Calculated Fields

6.76 Trick: If a special condition exists on a report and you want to alert someone, create a calculated field to ring the printer bell. ***Both***

A calculation similar to the following will ring the bell on most printers:

```
If [terms] = "C.O.D." then chr(7) else null
```

The character chr(7) is the ASCII bell symbol. If you insert this formula into the calculated field of a report, when the condition is true, your printer's bell will ring when that page of the report is being printed. Other pages on which the condition is not true will not ring the bell.

6.77 Trick: If a special condition exists on a report and you want to highlight certain text, create a calculation to print lines of your report in emphasized type. ***Both***

A calculation similar to the following will print following text in emphasized type:

```
If [pastdue] >= 90 then chr(27)|"E" else null
```

In this example, this calculation generates an Escape-E, which on some printers will begin emphasized printing. (You should check your own printer's specifications, however.) If you insert this formula into the calculated field of a report, when the condition is true, emphasized printing will begin.

Following the print of the emphasized text, insert a calculation to return to normal weight printing. This calculation need not be conditional.

Defining Page Numbers

Both

6.78 Tip: Printing page numbers in the form rather than in the table gives you greater flexibility.

If you select Page-Number within your form, rather than on the Page specification screen, you can position the page number exactly where you want it. As I pointed out in Tip 6.13, if you select the page-number option on the Page definition screen, the number will be printed at the bottom of your page on line 64 (out of 66), leaving a very small margin.

However, if you are defining a combination report with the form at the top and the table below, and you require page numbers at the bottom of the page, then you have no choice but to specify the page numbers on the Page definition screen.

Form Text

Both

6.79 Tip: Centering form entries can be easy if you let the system do the work for you.

If you look at the entries on lines 1 and 2 of the form you saw in figure 6.13, you will see that the text entries for the company name and report title are not centered. When you establish the entries, however, specify that they should be centered.

```
Form Definition
ABERDEEN MANUFACTURING CORPORATION
Department Listing

                    Department:  [depname]
                          today

Options

Select option: Calculated Field Label Page-Number Text
               Duplicate Edit Move Remove
Report: DEPTREP       Line 1  Col 1          F10 Finished  ESC Cancel
REPORT - print or define a table or form
```

Fig. 6.13.

A sample Report Form definition.

If you need to center a field, calculation, label, page number, or text, and there is only one entry on the line, position your cursor at the far left and select the appropriate entry type from the menu. You are then prompted to

```
Move cursor to lower right corner of area to be defined
```

Press Ctrl-Right to move the cursor to the far right of your defined area, and press Enter to complete the definition of the area. Now, when you select the centering justification option for an area spanning from the far left to the far right, your entry is automatically centered on the page. If you have multiple lines within a block, each line is centered separately.

6.80 Trap: In a Report/Form, if you have an entry that is centered in an underscore font, the entry will be underscored from the left margin. *SW II*

The possible solutions to this problem are

1. Left-justify an entry with an underscore font.
2. Use a fixed number of dashes (—) to underscore text, in which the length does not vary. However, fields usually vary in length.
3. Use a calculation to vary the number of dashes, depending on the length of a field:

   ```
   repeat("-",len([field]))
   ```

4. Do not use an underscore font.

6.81 Tip: In a Report/Form, to center a double-wide expanded font, center the text in a box that is half the width of the form. *SW II*

The Report/Form does not recognize the width of specialized fonts. If you try to center a double-wide font as you would a single-wide font, the text will not be centered. But by centering the text or field within an area that is half the width of the form, the effect of double-wide centering is achieved.

6.82 Trick: When defining text areas in Form reports, you can use Alt-F3 to read frequently used text from an ASCII file. *SW II*

Rather than typing the same text repeatedly, such as your company name or address, you can use the Alt-F3 to read an ASCII file into the text area. You are prompted for the name of the file; you must type the file name and extension and press Enter.

Using Report Techniques

Once your Report definition has been created, there are several tips and tricks that will help you use the definitions more efficiently.

Creating Similar Definitions

3.10 **6.83 Trick:** Use the File Copy command to create a similar Report definition.

The Smart Database offers no explicit method of creating similar Report definitions. However, you may want to make a different version, or you may just want to try something new without disturbing the original version.

Report definitions have file extensions of .DFR. If you copy the file that contains the existing definition to a new file, you can then edit the new one and make your changes. Use the File Copy command to make the copy, or press Ctrl-O to exit temporarily to DOS.

3.10 **6.84 Trick:** Re-create a database temporarily if you want to use an existing report definition for another database but have erased the original database.

Once you have created a report definition, you can change it only if the database it uses is loaded. If you have erased the original database, and now find that you can use the report definition for another database, you should create a new database and screen with the original names. Once the database has been created again, you can change the file names in the Page specification. If the report is a table report, however, be careful, because the fields are identified by number.

Using One Report Definition with Multiple Databases

3.10 **6.85 Trap:** Report definitions are designed to report from specific files; you cannot select the file at the time you run the report.

The names of a specific file and screen are stored within the Report definition; if you have several files of identical structure, you must create a separate Report definition for each one. Some other definitions in the database, such as Query and Sort, are independent of the file; the Relate and Transactions definitions, like Report definitions, are file specific. Tricks 6.87, 6.88, and 6.89 offer methods for circumventing these restrictions.

3.10 **6.86 Trick:** To use one Report definition for multiple databases, rename your databases to reflect the name in the definition.

Within a project file, this renaming technique can work quite well. You must make sure the files are not loaded at the time, however.

Renaming your databases has some disadvantages. Any time you have a number of files, there will be overhead associated with them: Each database must have its own screen (.DBS) file; and on a hard disk, even the smallest file can consume 4K, and on some hard disks, 8K or more. The constant renaming of files is also bound to cause some confusion.

If you rename files, the key files will not be correct. In each key file, the associated database is identified. If you rename the databases, the keys will be unusable even if you rename the key files as well. If you try to use a key, you will get the error message:

```
Filename in index file does not match current file
```

The following project file illustrates the use of this trick:

```
'use the same report definition for several files

%1 Enter File Name
let %2 = "%1"|".db"
let %3 = "%1"|".dbs"

file rename %2 to descrip.db
file rename %3 to descrip.dbs

load descrip screen standard

report print descrip printer

unload file descrip

file rename descrip.db to %2
file rename descrip.dbs to %3
```

In your application, it may be faster to process smaller files individually than to process one large file. For example, you could maintain multiple years of sales records in one large file, or in separate files by year. If you usually report on only the current year, it would be faster to keep the years segregated so that you do not have to perform a Query to isolate the current year's records.

Using the technique described in this tip allows you to use one Report definition for each year's records, knowing that the files are all in the same format. (Of course, other considerations may require that all sales records be kept together.)

6.87 Trick: To use one Report definition for multiple databases, maintain databases with the same names in different subdirectories. *3.10*

Although DOS does not support multiple files with the same name in the same subdirectory, you can maintain different files with the same name in separate subdirectories. A project file can prompt you for the subdirectory name, and the file can be loaded just as easily as if it existed in the current directory. The project file would look something like this:

```
%1 Enter Subdirectory Name:
load \%1\order screen standard
```

Because the files in the separate subdirectories have identical names, you cannot load more than one file at a time. Because the files have similar names and structures, however, all of your project files and Report, Relate, and Transactions definitions will work correctly.

3.10

6.88 Trick: To use one Report definition for multiple databases, use the file-access commands within project processing to alter the Report definition file.

Because the database name is stored in the Report definition file, you can use the file-access commands of project processing to seek the location of the file name and change the definition file. The project file shown in figure 6.14 accomplishes this purpose.

Fig. 6.14.

A project file to change the database name in a report definition.

```
Project File Editor
'Change Table Database Name in Deptrep Report Definition

input $newfile Enter name of database file:

let %8 = len($newfile)

fopen "deptrep.dfr" as 1

fseek 1 72

fwrite 1 length %8 from $newfile

fclose 1
```

This method is quick and easy, but it requires some care because it is dangerous. If you are not careful, you can destroy your Report definition.

The location of the database name can vary among Report definitions. You must determine the precise location of the database name for every definition. In the example in figure 6.14, the name is stored at location 72; the seek statement on the fifth line addresses this location. If, by chance, you write to the wrong location in the file, you will destroy the definition file and you will be unable to return the file to its original condition with the Report Define command.

The following is a project file you can use to locate a string of characters in a file and replace it with another string. It can be used for changing the name of a database in a Report definition, for changing a heading in a table report (see Trick 6.89), or for any situation in which it would be difficult (or impossible) to use the Text-editor to perform the substitution manually.

Note that the original and replacement strings must be of equal length; the format of a variable-length Report definition file would be destroyed if a string of a different length were substituted.

```
'find and change a string in any file
quiet on

label askfile
%1 Enter Name of file
if file(%1) = 1 then jump okfile
beep 2
message File < %1 > does not exist ... press any key ...
jump askfile

label okfile
fopen "%1" as 1
let %3 = 0

label askhead
input $nowhead Enter Existing String in file:
input $newhead Enter New String:
let %8 = len($nowhead)
let $lenew = len($newhead)
let %4= $nowhead
let %5 = $newhead
if %8 = $lenew then jump askseek
beep 2
message String Lengths not equal . . . \
      press any key to continue . . . jump askhead

label askseek
let %3 = %3 + 1
fseek 1 %3
wait 0 File Location: %3
fread 1 length %8 into $test
if cerror = 0 then jump testit
beep 2
message End of File .. String < %4 > not found \
      ... press any key ...
jump alldone

label testit
if $test = $nowhead then jump writit
jump askseek

label writit
fseek 1 %3
fwrite 1 length %8 from $newhead
```

```
label confirm
beep
message String < %4 > replaced with < %5 > in \
      file < % > at location < %3 >

label alldone
fclose 1
quiet off
```

The database names you use must always be the same number of characters in length if you use this technique. The Report definition files are in a variable-length format, so if you try to substitute a name whose length differs from that of the original, the database will not be found. The Report definitions will be destroyed, and you will not be able to use the Report Define command to fix it.

Obviously, this technique is fraught with potential problems. Before you try it, be sure to make a copy of your original Report definition (.DFR) file, and keep it in a safe place.

3.10

6.89 Trick: Use the file-access commands of project processing to create a variable heading for a Table report.

You cannot specify a variable within the heading. The heading must be "hard coded" manually during definition of the Report Table Title.

If you want to specify a variable heading, you can employ the same technique outlined in the previous Trick: use the file-access commands of the project processor to overlay a portion of an existing heading. The same caution applies to this technique. You can destroy your carefully designed Report Definition if you are not cautious.

Appendix A contains a project file you can use to substitute a date within a Report Table heading. Note the care taken to make sure the dates are the same length. Although you can execute this project file by itself, once you find the location of the date in the heading, you can incorporate just the necessary commands in a larger project file. To change a heading other than a date, use the project file listed in Trick 6.88.

Both

6.90 Trick: Insert leading blanks in table footings to simulate centering.

In Table Reports, footings are always left-justified. However, if you insert blanks before the text you want printed, you can position the footing in the center of the page. You can use the space bar to insert the blanks in this case; you do not have to use the Alt-255 character.

Both

6.91 Tip: In Smart 3.10, right justification is the default for a calculated field, even if the field is alphanumeric. In SmartWare II, calculated fields default to left justification.

Be sure to check the justification for calculated fields if you want to adhere to the convention of left justification for alpha fields and right justification for numeric fields.

Combination Reports

6.92 Tip: In a combination report, choose between starting the table overflow at the top of the page and reprinting the form when the form overflows. You cannot do both. *SW II*

If you are printing on blank paper, you probably will want to start the table overflow at the top of the page; if you are printing on preprinted forms, reprinting the form when the table overflows may make more sense. If you answer Yes to both questions, however, you will get the following error:

```
Form and table will overlap on table overflow
```

Change one of the two selections to No and continue with the report definition.

6.93 Trap: A combination report must have a linkage between the driver and driven portions, and the link field must be used as the page breakpoint. *3.10*

The link field must be printed as a column field in the table portion of the report, but the linkage field does not have to appear in the form portion.

6.94 Trick: Mark table records as temporarily deleted when you are running a combination report to avoid having to create a new database. *SW II*

In a SmartWare II combination report, the table records derive from a table within the view. The linkage between the table and the main file of the view is accomplished by the key field of the table records, and thus you cannot order the table file by an index.

Frequently, however, you want to limit the records to be printed in the table. One way to do this is to create a new database with just those records you want, and then use a special view that references this new database. Another way of solving the problem is to delete certain table records temporarily, thus eliminating them from the report.

1. Have a delete flag field in the table file to keep track of the actual delete status of the record. To save space, make the flag field 1 byte, alpha.

2. Execute a Data Query in the table file to set the delete flag:

```
replace [flag] = if deleted then "1" else "0"
```

3. Query to delete the records you do not want in the report. For example, if you want only those employees earning over $900, the query would be:

```
[wage] <= 900 replace delete
```

4. Run the report, using the multiple file view.

5. Reset the original delete status in the table file. You want to activate all records that were not originally deleted:

```
[flag] = "0" replace activate
```

Although this technique requires two extra queries, it prevents having to create another file, duplicate the data, and add the key for the linkage.

SW II

6.95 Tip: In a combination report, the fields in the first record of the table are considered to be part of the main data file and may be printed in the form.

Even though you can print records from the first record of the table in the form portion of the report, if the table overflows onto successive pages, the table fields shown in the form will not change to reflect the values of the first table record on each page; they always will reflect the first record of the first table record in the view.

SW II

6.96 Tip: You can create a combination report even if the view does not have an embedded table. Although you can include data from the view in the form, most likely it will derive from variables or system calculations.

The data in the table of the combination report comes from the fields of the view. Although you may include data from the view in the form, the same data will be repeated on each page, because this data refers to the first record of the view. It may make more sense to display variables or calculations in the form of the report.

3.10

6.97 Trick: Define a special field that does not have to appear in the Report Table portion to create a breakpoint in a combination report.

If one of your breakpoints is defined to perform a page break, you must include the field in your table, of course. If you are defining a combination report, the field still must appear in the table, even though you may have displayed the field in the report form portion. For instance, if you are performing a page break on a customer code so that each customer begins a new page, the customer code must appear in the table, even though you have specified the code in the form. This requirement wastes space, makes for poor-looking reports, and can even confuse the readers.

The way around this restriction is somewhat involved. You can suppress the printing of the field in the table portion if you observe the following guidelines:

1. The field must be an alpha field, not numeric.
2. The field length must be one character longer than the longest value contained in the field.
3. The first position of the field must contain a character that will not be printed. Likely candidates are ASCII codes 160 and 255, but this may vary, depending on the characteristics of your printer. In fact, your printer may not support such a character at all. It is also important that the character you select prints a blank character, not just a null (see Trick 6.44).
4. When you establish the field in the table portion of your report, define the field as one character wide, without a heading. Set the overflow option to Truncate rather than Wrap.
5. In the breakpoint definition for this field, besides selecting New-Page, you should specify that duplicate field entries are to be suppressed.

What does all this mean? You are printing just the first character (the one that prints the Alt-255 blank) on the table report; the remainder of the field is hidden because you specified that overflow is to be truncated.

You are wasting one space on your report, but this is preferable to wasting the five or six spaces the actual code field would consume. Besides, because the field is blank, you do not have to leave a space between this field and the next field on the report. If you want, you can even print the first character of the heading over the "dummy" field and print the remainder over the adjacent field.

Why not just use a blank as a leading character in the code field and specify that the field is to be right-justified? This will not work, because the Smart Database is designed to protect you from potentially confusing situations. If the first character is blank, the first nonblank character is displayed in the table column, even though you selected right justification for the field contents.

I have used this technique in special situations; usually I define a calculated field that is one byte larger than the actual code field. The field contents are calculated as a concatenation of the special blank character (in my case, the Alt-255) and the contents of the code field. If the code field is numeric, you can use the FIXED function to convert it to an alphanumeric in the dummy field calculation.

One word of caution when using this trick: Remember that the form portion of a combination report is reprinted only on the first page. If there is a page overflow, you will not know on those successive pages what caused the page break—customer code, invoice number, and so on..

3.10

6.98 Trick: Print a break field off the page if you do not want it displayed; some printers, specifically most laser printers, will simply ignore any printing off the page.

Fields used as break points must be displayed in combination reports and table reports. Sometimes they are extraneous, such as the link fields in combination reports. Why take up several valuable printing columns, when you easily can show the link field in the form? If you define your line length just a little bit longer than the physical printing capabilities of your printer and move the break field off the page, some printers simply will ignore the field.

You can make the field 1 byte and truncate it, so that it does not wrap around. Do not move the field too far off the page or make it too big; you will disturb the centering of the titles.

SW II

6.99 Tip: In a a combination report, embed the table within the form, thus creating both a heading and a footing form on the same page.

If you define the areas of the form and table so that the top line of the table is below the top of the form, and the bottom line of the table is above the bottom of the form, the table will be embedded within the form. You will be able to establish the form surrounding the table.

Figure 6.15 shows the table and form page boundaries used in this example:

Fig. 6.15.

Page definition table and form specifications.

```
Page Definition
→ Is there a Form on the Page: Yes No
    Location of the Upper Left Corner of the Form
      Line: 1
      Column: 1
    Location of the Lower Right Corner of the Form
      Line: 19
      Column: 78

  Is there a Table on the Page: Yes No
    Location of the Upper Left Corner of the Table
      Line: 5
      Column: 5
    Location of the Lower Right Corner of the Table
      Line: 14
      Column: 72
↕
Tables
  parthist Sales

F1 Help    F2 Edit text    F3 Blank text    F10 Finished

Report: split                                         F10 Finished
Define page/table/form dimensions and general report information
```

Notice that the table is embedded within the form. The following is one page of the actual report:

GLETSCH and GRIMSEL, Inc.
Sales Report

Item Number: 8475 Description: Compressor A-2

	Quantity Sold	Gross Revenue	Gross Profit	Quantity Backordered
	1	$1,976.00	$852.55	2
	2	$3,952.00	$1,705.10	4
	1	$1,976.00	$852.55	5
Total item 8475	4	$7,904.00	$3,410.20	11

Manufacturer Code: ACME Name: Acme Manufacturing

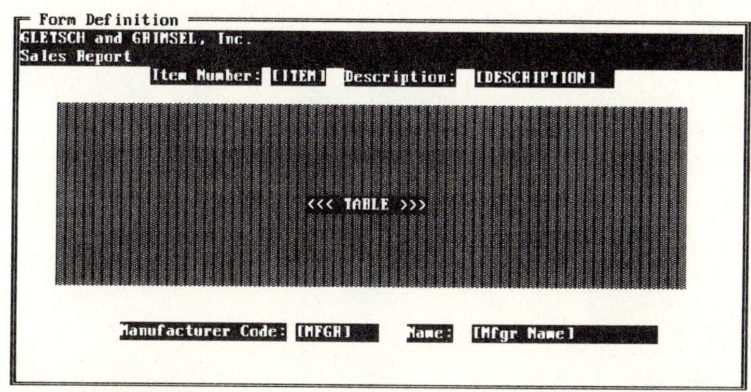

Fig. 6.16.

A table embedded within the form.

Note in figure 6.15 that the table does not have to extend the width of the form, thus allowing form data adjacent to the table.

6.100 Tip: Use the Move subcommand if you need to rearrange the design of a form report. ***Both***

Position your cursor at the upper left corner of the block and execute the Move command; then move the cursor to the new location and press Enter.

You may find that you must move a block out of the way in order to make room for the item to move. Just move the item temporarily to an unused portion of the form. Remember that the form is only as long as it's defined in the Page portion of the definition. If you need more room, you can return to the Page definition to make changes.

SW II

6.101 Tip: If you want to move a block in a Report Form, position the cursor on a blank area above or to the left of the block you want to move.

If you position the cursor on an item, you will be able to move only that one item. When you move a block, you are prompted to move the cursor to the lower right corner of the block and to press Enter to define the area.

Both

6.102 Tip: To duplicate a field, position your cursor anywhere in the field and press D.

You do not have to place the cursor at the upper left corner of the field to duplicate it. To position the new field, you should move the cursor to the upper left corner where the field is to appear.

Special Techniques

Here is a collection of special tips and tricks to use when printing reports.

3.10

6.103 Trick: Using the following project file, you can cause the printer to pause between individual pages of a report.

```
quiet off
%1 Report Name:
let %2 = "%1"|".prt"
if file(%2) = 1                              'erase the disk file
query undefine %2
endif

report print %1 disk %1

fopen "%2" as 1                              'open the file

label newpage
let $lineno = 0

message Insert new page.  Enter any key when ready.
menu clear box 22 1 22 80 7 0 no-border

  while $lineno < 66                          'for a 66 line page
  fread 1 into $line                          'read the whole line
  if cerror <> 0 then jump alldone
  lprint $line                                'print the line
  let $lineno = $lineno + 1                   'increment line counter
endwhile

jump newpage

label alldone
fclose 1                                      'close the file
```

6.104 Tip: Write your Report to a disk file while you are still testing it; this will save time.

Both

Rather than printing copies of test versions of your report, write them to a disk file, and then use the Text Editor to look at the result. You will save both time and paper. This tip is especially valuable if your printer is not located near you.

6.105 Tip: If you do not specify your own file extension, the default file extension is RPT when you write a report to a disk file.

Both

If the disk file already exists, the command will continue, but you are prompted:

```
File filename already exists.  Continue (y/n)
```

Press Y to continue. If you press N, the command is aborted.

6.106 Trick: By adjusting page sizes in report definitions, it is possible to print two or more reports on the same piece of paper.

3.10

Two or more reports in completely different formats can be printed on the same piece of paper if you can adhere to several rules.

1. Each report prints just one piece of paper—a single record form report, or a table with not enough records to go to the next page, for example.
2. The sum of the page lengths must add up to the actual paper length.

This trick works because Smart advances to the top of form at the completion of the printing of the report, not at the beginning of a new report. Thus, if the first report is designed so that the paper is 25 lines long, printing will begin on line 26 of the next page.

6.107 Trap: There is no double check when you remove a report definition; it is erased immediately. In Smart 3.10 the command is Report Undefine; in SmartWare II, it is Print Report Remove.

Both

Usually, when you remove or delete another type of definition, such as a query definition or a project file, you are prompted:

```
Are you sure? (y/n)
```

You must answer Y to erase the definition from the disk. However, in this case, there is no prompt when you remove or undefine a report definition.

7

Interfacing Files and Using the Dummy Facility

Because you may run programs other than Smart or SmartWare II and thus may need to either import or export data, Informix Software has included a broad set of commands to make these efforts quick and easy. A clear understanding of the capabilities of the Read and Write commands, coupled with some warnings and tips, will simplify your tasks. (In SmartWare II, the commands are called File Import and File Export.)

The more you use SmartWare, the less you will need to use outside programs; the different modules of Smart and SmartWare II will begin to fulfill more of your needs. In this chapter, I present several tips and tricks on sending data to other modules.

Probably no other Smart command is as powerful but as misunderstood as the Query command, or Data Query, as it's called in SmartWare II. The final section of this chapter deals extensively with this command and points out ways to use Query efficiently and safely. You will also find several warnings of traps for the unwary.

Reading Data from an External Source

Use the Read (or File Import) commands when you want to transfer data from another system; if the other system can create ASCII files, you can import the data into the Smart Database. If the external system is written in dBASE, you will have no problems—with one or two exceptions.

You will learn in this section that if you have the choice, some types of external files offer more flexibility than others, but there are ways around several of the obstacles.

External File Types

Both

7.1 Tip: The Read command in Smart 3.10 is used to import data from one of four different types of external DOS files. Using this command, you can transfer data from an external source into the Smart database in the current window.

In SmartWare II, the File Import command can also read databases from Smart 3.10 and create an entirely new SmartWare II database.

The four different types of external files are:

1. *ASCII*: Files in this format are comma-delimited, with alpha fields enclosed in double quotation marks (" "). In this context, alpha fields include date fields, Social Security numbers, and phone numbers.

2. *Fixed*: The fields in this format align with each other, much as they do in a report, with no delimiters. When you use the Write command to create an external file, the Text option creates a file in the fixed format, but with a header record containing the field name.

3. *SMART*: Just as in ASCII files, alpha fields in SMART files are enclosed in double quotation marks; however, the delimiter between fields is a space, rather than a comma.

4. *dBASE*: A dBASE file can be in either the dBASE II or the dBASE III format. A new database file is created with the same name as the dBASE file; you may not append to an existing file. If the dBASE field is longer than 1,000 characters, the field will be truncated in Smart 3.10.

Some comments about ASCII files are appropriate. Three of these files are in an ASCII configuration. If you were to display them on your screen using the DOS command TYPE, you would be able to read the files. You would not see funny characters or "smiling faces," and your PC would not beep at you unmercifully. These files can be created with a text editor (such as the one invoked with Smart's Text-Edit command) or from a database by means of the Write command.

The program developers at Informix Software have chosen to designate the ASCII format as "ASCII," and the other two as Fixed and SMART. These just happen to be the terms they have chosen, however, so don't be misled into thinking that the other two files are not in an ASCII format: from the DOS viewpoint, they are.

SW II

7.2 Trick: To match the widths of numeric fields, create a special view to use when importing fixed format files.

When you import a fixed format file, the field sizes define the boundaries of the data to be read into each database field. If the field is alpha, the external data must match the actual database field size, regardless of the field width displayed in the view. If the field is numeric, the width of the data in the external file must match the *display* width of the field in the view. If the numeric field widths in the views you ordinarily use do not match the widths of numeric fixed data you would like to import, create a view especially for this purpose.

There is no report available that will tell you the exact display width of each of the numeric fields. The Data Utilities Information command always displays 8 bytes for each numeric field, but this is the size of the field in the database, not the view display. To determine the display size of the numeric fields, place your finger on the monitor screen and start counting.

Field Formats

7.3 Tip: When reading internal data into your database, special alpha fields must conform exactly to the format specified in your file. Examples of special alpha fields are Social Security numbers, dates, and phone numbers, each of which is actually an alpha field but with special formatting and function characteristics. *3.10*

The special formatting becomes evident in the Enter and Update commands. You do not enter the delimiters, such as the slash (/) or dash (–) characters. Special functional characteristics are used when applying the date-handling functions in sorting on a date field.

In your external file, follow these formats:

SSN:	999-99-9999
DATE:	MM/DD/YY
PHONE:	(999) 999-9999

Be sure your files conform to these formats, including the edit characters (hyphens, slashes, and parentheses). Also, be sure to leave one space in the Phone field after the closing parenthesis of the area code.

7.4 Tip: Import a date that is in a string format into a date field which is stored internally as a number. *SW II*

If you read a date string from an ASCII or Smart format external file, the date should be in a format similar to the following:

"8/23/90"

Note that the field is enclosed within quotation marks, indicating that it is an alpha string. However, the File Import command will translate this alpha date representation into a sequential number to store in a Date field in a database as the data is read. You do not need to read the date into an alpha field first, and then create a date field.

Both

7.5 Trap: The Write (Smart 3.10) or File Export (SmartWare II) commands create a special header record containing field names when you write a file in either the Text (fixed) or Smart formats. If you are using the Write and Read (File Import in SmartWare II) commands to transfer data from one file to another, this can cause a problem.

In Smart 3.10, the Read command does not ignore these header records, and thus you will create an extra record in your database. If the field is an alpha field, it will contain all or part of the field name; if it is a numeric, SSN or Phone field, the contents will be null. If it is a Date field, the contents will be the actual field name; but it will be unusable as a date, of course.

In SmartWare II, a header record imported into a numeric or date field will create a zero; an alpha field will read the header.

In Smart 3.10, if you are using Write and Read to transfer data, use the Text-Editor to delete this header record. If you forget, you can mark the record for deletion, using the Delete command on list 1. In SmartWare II, use the Data Delete Record command. Some commands in the Smart Database inherently ignore deleted records. For a review of the treatment of deleted records, refer to Chapter 5.

Both

7.6 Trap: If you write to a Text file and attempt to read that file using the Fixed option, you must know the exact widths of fields.

When a file is written in the Fixed format, the width of each field is the greater of the field width in the source file and the number of characters in the field title. Thus, as seen in figure 7.1, the Status field takes up six columns, when, in fact, the field is actually only 1 byte.

```
Text Editor
SSN         LAST       STATUS SEX PHONE
345-98-7593 Ronaldo    Y      M   (312) 439-8760
498-48-3980 Linden     Y      F   (413) 886-3498
239-87-8876 Davis      2      M   (318) 997-6621
208-23-0300 Karenski   2      M   (606) 779-5088
887-63-5498 Harris     Y      M   (614) 776-3398
876-33-0989 Lester     Y      F   (617) 873-0979
987-65-7653 Marzetti   2      M   (704) 472-0042
387-59-8374 Steffans   1      M   (207) 878-4880
498-34-5998 Bernstein  2      F   (916) 475-4228
776-39-8763 Adelson    Y      M   (203) 739-3095
345-54-2287 Aliakbari  2      F   (201) 727-9242
198-03-3024 Peters     1      M   (318) 729-5060

F1 Help     F3 Find     F5 Replace       F7 Insert line     F9  Repeat
F2 Calc     F4 Goto     F6 List fields   F8 Delete line     F10 Finish
                                  Line:    1  Column:  1    Insert: OFF
TEXT-EDITOR - allows editing of a text file
```

Fig. 7.1.

A text file written in Fixed format.

When you use the Read command's Fixed option, the field width in the external file must exactly match the field widths in your database, because there are no delimiters. If the field widths in the external file are offset by a long field title, the correspondence of fields is destroyed. (This may be another reason for keeping field names short.) Even if you maintain short field titles, one extra column still remains between each field—this is something you must consider.

Unfortunately, simply deleting the header record from the Text file does not solve the spacing problem in this example. The spaces are there to stay, unless you go through the laborious task of deleting them manually. Even with short fields, the extra blank still exists.

7.7 Trap: When importing data, do not confuse an ASCII file with a Smart file. The formats are similar, but the results are not. If you read one type as another, there will be no error message, but the data will be incorrect. ***Both***

The SMART format external file has quotation marks around the alpha fields, as does an ASCII file, but the fields are separated by spaces rather than commas. The File Import command (SmartWare II) and the Read command (Smart 3.10) will not provide an error or warning message if you try to read a SMART file as an ASCII file, but the data probably will be unusable.

7.8 Tip: Delete the keys from a Smart 3.10 database before importing it into SmartWare II. Automatically converting the keys as the file is imported takes longer than if you add them later. ***SW II***

When you execute the File Import command and select 310-Smart, the command executes in two steps. First, the data is read, and then the keys are converted. Each step displays a message:

```
Importing 310 records
Converting 310 keys
```

If you have not already deleted the Smart 3.10 keys, press Ctrl-Z to halt the key conversion phase once the records have been read. Then use the Order Key Rebuild command to create the SmartWare II key file. Not only will the key file be created faster, but it may be smaller, as well.

7.9 Tip: If you import a Smart 3.10 file that has a password, you must assign a password to the SmartWare II file. ***SW II***

Although the password you assign to the new file does not have to be the same as the previous password, you must assign identical passwords to the database and the standard view. When you have finished importing the file, you can use the File Password...Remove command to remove the password on either the file or the view if you no longer want it.

7.10 Tip: After importing a Smart 3.10 datafile, change database calculated fields to view calculated fields to save disk space. ***SW II***

In Smart 3.10, calculated fields must be stored as data on the disk, even though their values are calculated by formulas. In SmartWare II, you have a choice. You can save the results of the calculation on the disk, or you can simply display the value as view fields. If you do not need to store the calculation results in the datafile, you can save disk space by modifying the view and datafile to create a view field. The steps are as follows:

1. Modify the view.
2. Replicate the calculated field as a view field, using a temporary name. The complete calculation will be replicated automatically.
3. Delete the original calculated field from the database.
4. Replicate the temporary view field as a view field with the same name as the original calculated field.
5. Delete the temporary view field.
6. Move fields and change input order, as necessary.

When you press F10 to complete the file modification, the database will be restructured, eliminating the database calculated field. You will save disk space, and still be able to view, print, and query the calculated view field as if it were a real database field.

SW II

7.11 Tip Importing a Smart 3.10 database does not eliminate deleted records.

Any records that are marked for deletion in the 3.10 datafile will be retained and marked for deletion in SmartWare II. If you do not want the deleted records, purge them in Smart 3.10 before importing the file. Of course, you can also purge them in SmartWare II.

Reading a Partial Field List

Both

7.12 Tip: If you want to Read Only certain fields from an external file, you must read from either an ASCII file or a SMART file because the delimiters define the field boundaries.

If you want to skip a field, enter a zero for the field number (see fig. 7.2).

Note that in the example, I have elected to read all fields from the file except the fourth field in each record. It may be a field I do not need or do not have in my database, or it may be an incorrect value I do not want to introduce into the file. Because there are delimiters in the external file, I can specify that I don't want this field to be read. If the file were in a Fixed format, however, I would have to read each field because columns, rather than delimiters, define field boundaries.

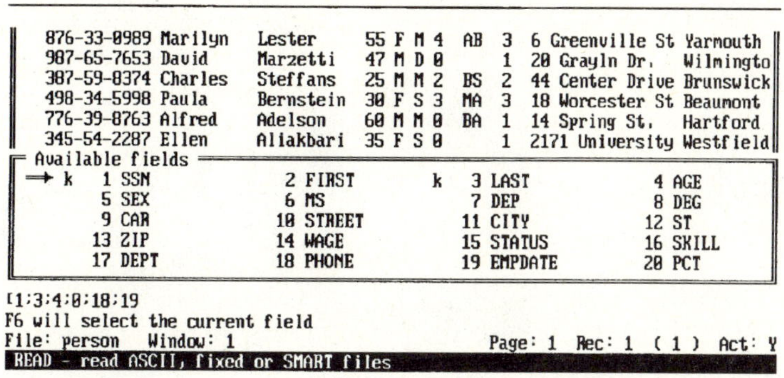

```
 876-33-8989 Marilyn   Lester      55 F M 4  AB  3  6 Greenville St Yarmouth
 987-65-7653 David     Marzetti    47 M D 0      1  20 Grayln Dr,   Wilmingto
 387-59-8374 Charles   Steffans    25 M M 2  BS  2  44 Center Drive Brunswick
 498-34-5998 Paula     Bernstein   30 F S 3  MA  3  18 Worcester St Beaumont
 776-39-8763 Alfred    Adelson     60 M M 0  BA  1  14 Spring St,   Hartford
 345-54-2287 Ellen     Aliakbari   35 F S 0      1  2171 University Westfield
 Available fields
 → k   1 SSN        2 FIRST        k   3 LAST       4 AGE
       5 SEX        6 MS               7 DEP        8 DEG
       9 CAR       10 STREET          11 CITY      12 ST
      13 ZIP       14 WAGE            15 STATUS    16 SKILL
      17 DEPT      18 PHONE           19 EMPDATE   20 PCT

[1;3;4;0;18;19
F6 will select the current field
File: person   Window: 1                        Page: 1  Rec: 1  ( 1 )  Act: Y
READ - read ASCII, fixed or SMART files
```

Fig. 7.2.

Specifying fields in the Read command.

Efficiency Techniques

7.13 Tip: On a network, import data in the single user mode, rather than the multiple user, network mode. ***SW II***

If you import data in the single user mode, the process will go faster because the system will not have to allow for the possibility that another user might add a record or change a key field. If you perform this task in the multiple user mode, there is a great deal of overhead associated with checking for other user activity. Once the file has been imported, unload the file and load it again in the multiple user mode to allow other users access to it.

7.14 Tip: Write data to a file to read into a database later, instead of using the Enter Blank command and making the assignments in a project file. The program will run faster and be cleaner. ***3.10***

If you are collecting data via project file Input or Menu Input statements and need to insert the data into a database, you can use the Fwrite command to write the data to an external file and the Read command to read it all in when you have finished. Your program will run faster and have a cleaner appearance, since the Enter Blank command flashes the screen each time it executes.

The following example shows the entry of debits and credits into an accounting journal:

```
  let $q    = chr(34)                  'quote marks
  let $c    = ","                         'comma
  let $qc   = $q|$c
  let $cq   = $c|$q
  let $qcq  = $qc|$q
  let $cqc  = $cq|$c

  if file("journal.dat") = 1
       query undefine journal.dat
  endif
```

```
fclose 1
fopen "journal.dat" as 1

label enter

menu clear 7 0
menu print 5 10 7 0 Transaction Date:
menu input 5 28 0 7 8 $date
if $date == "Z" then jump alldone
let $date = date2($date)

menu print 7 10 7 0 Debit Account Number:
menu input 7 32 0 7 3 $Caccount

menu print 9 10 7 0 Credit Account Number:
menu input 9 33 0 7 3 $Daccount

menu print 11 10 7 0 Amount:
menu input 11 18 0 7 8 $amount

menu print 13 10 7 0 Description:
menu input 13 23 0 7 25 $description

'write debit
let $account = str($Daccount)          'field is alpha
let $jamount = str($amount)            'fwrite alpha

call writit

'write credit
let $account = str($Caccount)
let $jamount = str(-1 * $amount)

call writit

jump enter

label alldone

fclose 1

read ascii journal.dat fields [date;account;amount;description]

end

procedure writit
   let $data = \
$q|$date|$qcq|$account|$qc|$jamount|$cq|$description|$q
   fwrite 1 from $data
return
```

Figure 7.3 shows the entry screen displayed by this program.

The entries displayed in the figure generate the following data in the external file:

```
"08/23/90","101",123.45,"Computer repair"
"08/23/90","409",-123.45,"Computer repair"
```

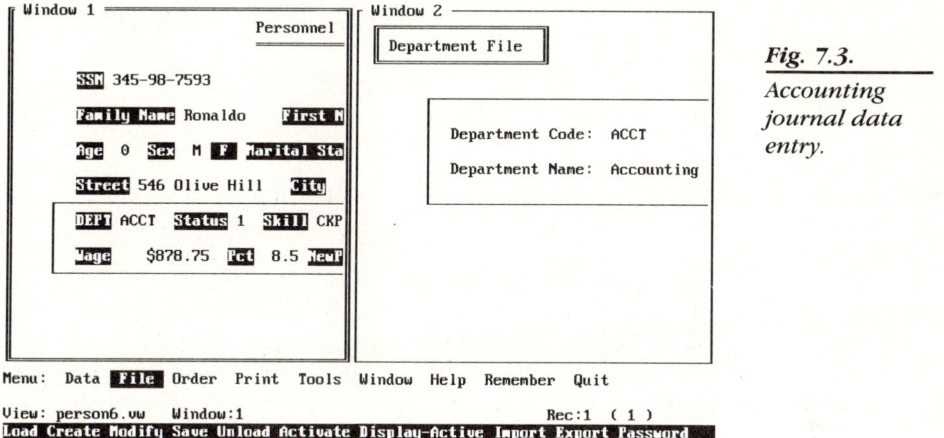

Fig. 7.3. *Accounting journal data entry.*

Note that this file is in the ASCII format. Two records, a debit and a credit, were generated from one set of input fields.

Writing Data to an External Destination

Although you would like to stay within the Smart System for all your computing needs, there are times when you have to write data to an external file. You may be running applications that have been developed in another system; or a colleague may not yet be using Smart but may need to use your data. Even if your colleague is using dBASE, you can create a suitable file with version 3.10 of Smart.

Creating Detail Files

7.15 Tip: Use the Write command to create dBASE III files; In Smartware II, use the File Export command. ***Both***

To write detail records to an external file in the dBASE III format, select 3-dBASE from the option list. A file will be created that can be used in the dBASE program.

If you try to convert more than 128 fields to the dBASE format, the command will terminate with the error message:

```
Too many fields for file format
```

Any alpha field exceeding 254 characters will be truncated.

7.16 Trap: Writing deleted records in the dBASE format yields unpredictable results. ***Both***

Make sure your file contains no deleted records when you use the Write All...3-dBASE command. Although the file is written and can be used successfully in dBASE, you will fail if you try to bring the file back into the Smart Database. You will receive the error message:

```
Error reading dBASE file
```

SW II

7.17 Trick: Create a special view to export data in the fixed format to provide greater control over spacing.

When you export a file in the Text format, the width of the field in the external file is the greater of the field width or the field name. To make sure you have only one blank column between each field, create a special view in which the lengths of all field names are shorter than their sizes. Even though these temporary field names are written into the first record of the external file, use the Tools Text-Editor to delete the line.

SW II

7.18 Tip: Create a special view without any numeric field editing characteristics when exporting fixed data to be read by another computer system.

When you export data, using the File Export Text command, any editing features of numeric fields are written to the file. These features may include dollar signs, commas, or special negative notations. If you are exporting the data to be read into another computer system, you do not want to have these editing features contained in the numeric fields in the external file. Create a new view that does not have any special numeric field editing features and use this when exporting for another computer system.

SW II

7.19 Trick: Use the Data Send Wordprocessor Data command to create an external Smart file in which numeric fields are bound by quotation marks.

The File Export command and the Data Send Wordprocessor Data command create external Smart files which are almost identical. In the Data Send command file, the numeric fields contain editing characteristics, and are bounded by quotation marks, as if they were text. The file created by the Data Send Wordprocessor Data command is temporary, and has an extension of IFF and a file name the same as the view.

In an external Smart 3.10 file created by the File Export command, the numerics are considered numbers, not text. When you execute the command, you are prompted for the file name; the file will reside on the disk until you erase it. Following are two examples:

Created by Data Send Wordprocessor Data:

```
"Last Name" "Wage" "DEPT" "Age" "Sex"
"Ronaldo" "$878.75 " "ACCT" "52 " "F"
"Linden" "$1,403.79 " "MFGR" "29 " "F"
```

Created by File Export Smart Row-Format:

```
"Last Name" "Wage" "DEPT" "Age" "Sex"
"Ronaldo" 878.75 "ACCT" 52 "F"
"Linden" 1403.79 "MFGR" 29 "F"
```

Note that the fields for Wage and Age are bounded by quotation marks in the Data Send Wordprocessor Data file, and that the Wage field contains editing characters.

The trick to creating the Data Send Wordprocessor Data file is to rename the temporary file after sending it to the Word Processor. If your database view is named "person," the Data Send Wordprocessor Data file will be named Person.IFF. Use the Tools File Rename command to rename the file.

If you quit from the Wordprocessor without renaming the IFF file, the file will be erased automatically.

7.20 Tip: To export a file as a SmartWare II database, use a defined query that will both select the desired records and give you the option to create a new database. *SW II*

When you execute a defined Data Query, you are prompted:

```
Index   Data-File
```

When you select Data-File, you are prompted for the name of the database to create and the fields it will contain. The records it will contain are based on the query criteria. At the successful completion of the command, the standard view of the new database is automatically loaded.

Note that you can create a new database only by using Data Query Execute; Data Query Now does not give you this option.

The options for the File Export command are: ASCII, Dif, M-Sylk, Smart, Text, and 3-Dbase. The "Smart" option does not mean a SmartWare II database, but rather an external file in the Smart format, with quotation marks around alpha fields and spaces as delimiters between the fields. However, if you execute a query, you are prompted to see if you want to create either an Index or a Data-File. Select Data-File to create a new SmartWare II database, which can include database fields and view fields.

7.21 Trap: The numbers you see in the view may not be the numbers written to the external file when using the File Export command. The view may show a rounded display of a number with more decimal positions. *SW II*

Just as in the Spreadsheet module, a number you see on your monitor screen may be a rounded display of the real, underlying number. For example, you may have the following calculation in a view:

```
[field1] / [field2]
```

If [field1] = 20 and [field2] = 7, the actual result is 2.85714285714286. However, if the calculated field has a display format of "2r," what you will see on the screen is 2.86, since the field is rounded to 2 decimal places. If you export the calculated field to a file, you get the full, underlying value of the calculation, up to 15 digits in length.

If you want the exported values to be the same as those displayed in the view, use the Round function in the calculation:

```
round([field1]/[field2],2)
```

If the calculation is rounded to the same number of decimals as the display format of the field, the displayed value and the underlying value will be the same.

3.10 **7.22 Trick:** Use the Report command as a substitute for the Write All command if you need to generate calculated fields that are not in your database.

The Write command will export calculated fields to an external file only if the calculated field actually exists in the database. If the calculated field does not exist, you can use the Report command to generate a disk file containing calculated fields that can then be read into the Spreadsheet.

To use this trick, there are certain rules you must follow:

1. Use quotation marks around any multiple word alpha fields. Create a calculated, one-byte field in which the formula is chr(34); this is the quotation mark.
2. The maximum record size (page width) in the external file is 255 characters. Set the page length at 255.
3. Numeric fields must be free of any editing characters, such as $, Cr, or %.
4. Column titles must be just one word each and must be on just one line.
5. In the Spreadsheet, column 1 will be too large, due to the line of dashes under the column headings; this should be deleted.

3.10 **7.23 Trick:** If you want to use dollar signs or commas in numeric fields to be used in a Word Processor merge, use the Report command instead of the Write command.

Use quotation marks around the numeric fields with editing characters as well as any multiple word alpha fields. The other rules outlined in Trick 7.22 apply.

Writing Summarized Data

7.24 Trap: Writing a Summarized dBASE file is not supported. 3.10

Although the option menu provides for selection of the 3-dBASE format and the Write Summarized...3-dBASE command executes without error, the external file is not generated in the dBASE format. The external file cannot be used in dBASE or be read back into the Smart Database.

7.25 Trick: Use the Write Summarized command to create a summarized database. 3.10

The Write Summarized command is used to create an external file summarizing a database. However, no automatic command creates a summarized database in Smart format. But if you are willing to perform a little manual labor, you can use the Write Summarized command to create an external file and then use the Read command to read that external file back into a new database. Figure 7.4 shows the Summary Definition that creates the ASCII file in figure 7.5.

```
Summary Definition
            COL FLD WAGE_____ DEP_____ ________ ________ ________
  ROW FLD
 DEPT_____

              PRINT WAGE_____ DEP_____ ________ ________ ________

 SEARCH      PRINT      1         2
UNIQUE____ UNIQUE____  1

F2 Match unique  F3 Match others  F4 Match all  F5 Count hits  F6 List fields
F7 Insert slot   F8 Delete field  F10 Finished   PgUp(left)  Pgdn(right)

WRITE - write data in ASCII, DIF, M-SYLK, SMART or text format
```

Fig. 7.4.
A Write Summarized definition.

```
"DEPT","WAGE","DEP"
"ACCT",3365.86,7
"MFGR",2401.45,1
"SALE",2626.61,5
"MKTG",4080.59,4
"DATA",654.34,2
```

Fig. 7.5.
An external ASCII file created with the Write Summarized definition.

Note that I have summarized the WAGE and DEP fields by the DEPT field. You also can see, however, that when you use the Write command's Summarized option instead of the All option, the header record is created. This is where the manual labor comes in. If you want to avoid creating such a record in the database into which you now read this data, you should use the Text-Editor to delete the first line of the external file.

If you really want to automate the entire process, you can read the file in its existing form into a temporary file, use the Query command to create an index that eliminates the first record, and concatenate the temporary file to the permanent file. Doing so makes a couple of extra steps, but allows you to automate the process.

When you have deleted the first line from the ASCII file, you are ready to create a new database and read in your data. Use either the ASCII or SMART formats because you don't have to be concerned about field-length problems caused by the title lengths.

3.10

7.26 Trap: The Write and Send Summarized definitions store field numbers, not field names.

Even though the field names appear when you define a summary definition, the numbers are stored. Thus, if you "change" a file and the field numbers change, you will have to recreate your definitions. For this reason, it is usually better to add a field at the end of a file than in the middle.

Both

7.27 Tip: Perform a Print Screen to record a copy of your Smart 3.10 summary definition or SmartWare II Cross-Tabs definition before saving it.

Although you usually can redefine a summary definition later without changing the contents, I recommend printing the screen and saving it with your documentation. (Hold down the Shift key and press the PrtSc key.) Also make a note of the file name; in 3.10, note whether the Summary Definition is Column/Row or Row, and whether the definition is Complete or Partial.

3.10

7.28 Trick: Write to a Fixed Text external file to create summary records broken out by multiple-sort fields.

Although I was able to create one summary line for each department in the previous example, I could not create a summary line for each department for each sex. (I could have used the Row/Column definition option, however, to create one record for each department, with a column for the Male wages and another column for the Female wages, but then I could not have included the number of dependents.)

In the Write definition, you cannot use a calculated field as the row specification; the field must be an actual database field. However, if you have in your file a calculated field that concatenates the DEPT and SEX fields, you can certainly use the calculated field as the row identifier. One row, therefore, would be created for each combination of DEPT and SEX, as shown in figure 7.6.

```
DEPSX        WAGE  DEP
ACCTM     3365.86    7
MFGRF     2401.45    1
SALEM      734.56    1
MKTGM     2564.33    0
SALEF     1892.05    4
MKTGF     1516.26    4
DATAM      654.34    2
```

Fig. 7.6.

Write summarized output using a calculated field.

7.29 Trick: Use "dummy" fields to ignore unneeded data from a fixed format file.

3.10

Sometimes, you have no choice about the type of external file you must read; if you have a fixed format file, such as the one in figure 7.6, you must find a way to ignore the columns you do not need.

To skip columns you do not want, you can read them into "dummy" fields you have included in your database. Since you can read several sets of columns successively into the same dummy fields, you don't need every combination of column widths. Figure 7.7 shows the layout of a file containing dummy fields.

Field No	Field Title	Type	Length	Key	Total	Status
1	DEPENDENTS	N0	3	N	N	N
2	WAGE	N2	10	N	N	N
3	DEPT	A	4	N		N
4	SEX	A	1	N		N
5	DUMMY6	A	6	N		N
6	DUMMY1	A	1	N		N

Fig. 7.7.

A file containing dummy fields.

Field 5 is a dummy field defined as 6 alpha characters, and field 6 is defined as 1 character. Because the dummy fields can be used as "place holders," the following statement can be used to read the file in figure 7.6 into this database:

```
read fixed DEPSEX fields [dept;sex;5;5;5;6;wage;6;depend]
```

Notice that field 5 is read three times, followed by field 6; the total number of columns skipped is therefore 19 (3 * 6 + 1).

Rather than having dummy fields in a permanent file, you may elect to use the Utilities Restructure command to transfer the important data to another file and purge the data from this temporary file.

If you do not want to define a dummy field, you also can read the same database field several times, using it as a placeholder. The final read will determine the resulting contents of the database field. The ability to use this tip is highly dependent on the order of the fields in the external file, however.

Creating a Summarized Report with a Project File

3.10 **7.30 Tip:** Use a project file to create a summarized report.

The example in the previous Trick may seem like a lot of work for accomplishing what should be a simple task, that of summing several numeric fields, broken out by 2 or more sort fields. You would like to be able to specify the following:

```
SUM WAGE AND NR_DEP
BY DEPT BY SEX
```

Although it may not be that easy in Smart, the following project file shows a method of producing such a summarized report:

```
'deptsex project file. Sum wage and dep by dept by sex
goto file person screen standard

sort predefined deptsex index ind1
order index ind1
goto record rec-number 1

let $wage = 0
let $dep = 0
let $dept = [dept]
let $sex = [sex]
let $deptsex = [dept]|[sex]
label nexrec
if $deptsex <> [dept]|[sex] then call breaker
let $wage = $wage + [wage]
let $dep = $dep + [dep]
if record = records then jump alldone
goto record next
jump nexrec

procedure breaker
let $lb = 10 - len(fixed($wage,2))
lprint $dept;" ";$sex;repeat(" ",$lb);fixed($wage,2);"";$dep
let $wage = 0
let $dep = 0
let $dept = [dept]
let $sex = [sex]
```

```
let $deptsex = [dept]|[sex]
return

label alldone
call breaker
```

To insert the data into a file, change the "breaker" procedure to the following:

```
procedure breaker

goto window 1
enter blank
lock-record
let [dept] = $dept
let [sex] = $sex
let [wage] = $wage
let [dep] = $dep
goto window 2

let $wage = 0
let $dep = 0
let $dept = [dept]
let $sex = [sex]
let $deptsex = [dept]|[sex]
return
```

Instead of printing a report, this project file inserts the data into a file in another window. Be certain, however, that the file in window 1 is in sequential order instead of being ordered by a key or an index. If the file is not in sequential order, the record into which you insert the values will not be the blank record inserted by enter blank. You will overlay existing data in some other record.

7.31 Trick: Align decimals when using the Lprint statement by repeating leading blanks. *3.10*

As an added trick, the lines

```
let $lb = 10 - len(fixed($wage,2))
lprint $dept;" ";$sex;repeat(" ",$lb);fixed($wage,2);" ";$dep
```

align the wage-field decimals. The first statement determines the length of the wage field with two decimals, and then subtracts this value from 10, which is the overall field length that I want on the report. The "repeat" function on the second line is used to print the number of space characters needed to align the decimals.

Sending Data to Another Smart Module

The tips and tricks in this section will increase your mastery of the Send command, which is used to transfer data to other modules of Smart.

Creating a Summarized Data Base

3.10

> **7.32 Trick:** Use the Send commands to summarize your data and to load it into a worksheet automatically. By sending the data back from the Spreadsheet, you can create a summarized database file.

If you use the Summary Definition shown in figure 7.4, you can send your data to the Spreadsheet. (The same Summary Definitions will work with either the Write command or the Send command.) In the Spreadsheet module, your worksheet will look like figure 7.8.

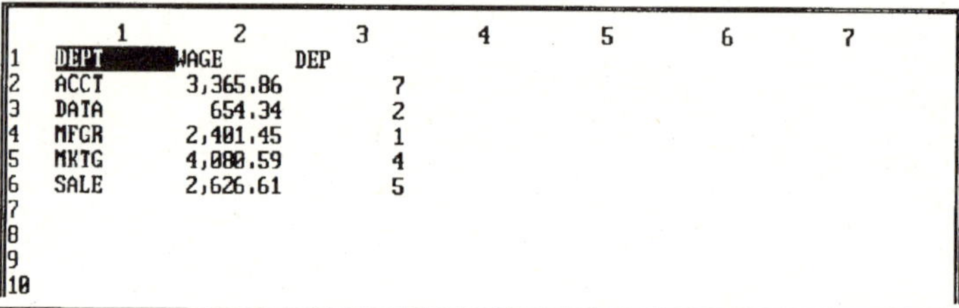

Fig. 7.8. *A data summary in the Spreadsheet module.*

Now, by using the Send command again, you can send your data back to the Database and have a file created automatically for you. The resulting file is shown in figure 7.9.

```
Window 1
 F001 F002     F
→ACCT 3365.86 7
 DATA  654.34 2
 MFGR 2401.45 1
 MKTG 4080.59 4
 SALE 2626.61 5
```

Fig. 7.9. *A database created from Spreadsheet data.*

You cannot specify field names when sending data from the Spreadsheet to the database, however. If the database is new, the field names created are F001, F002, and so on. Be sure, in the Spreadsheet, that your Send block does not include the top row, or this will be included in your database.

Also be sure to use the Newname command in the Spreadsheet to establish a new name not only for the worksheet, but also for the resulting database. The original worksheet name is the same as the database from which the data was summarized, and you would not want to read the data back into the original database.

If a database exists with the same name as the worksheet, the new records will be appended. The spreadsheet cell types must match the field types in the database in the order sent and received. Each spreadsheet row creates a record, and each column creates a field.

7.33 Tip: For faster operation, use the expert mode when defining a Cross Tab definition. *SW II*

Initiate the expert mode by pressing the Escape key. Once in the expert mode, with the cursor on any of the column summary entries, simply press any of the summary definition key letters to select the summary type. For example, press *S* for "Sum." You may then select a field from the popup window, if the type calls for it.

7.34 Trick: If you want a single output row from a Data Cross-Tab, just enter a title for the row; you do not have to enter an equation. *SW II*

If you do not enter either an equation or a title for the row, you will get an error message

```
No Rows or Automatic-Rows have been defined
```

7.35 Trap: When executing a Data Cross-Tab, if you accidentally omit the summary type, there will not be an error message, but the result will be zero. *SW II*

There is no error trap in either the creation or the execution of a Data-Cross tab to ensure that a summary type has been entered. If you see that you are getting all zeros in your output, check to make sure that you have entered a summary type in the definition.

7.36 Trick: Create a view field that concatenates two or more database fields to provide a multiple field automatic row or column in a Data Cross-Tab. *SW II*

Normally, when you specify automatic row or column generation, you may select only one field for the row or column. For instance, you may specify either [Dept] or [sex] for an automatic row field, but not both together.

However, define a view field, similar to this example:

```
"|chr(34)|trim([sex])
```

In a Data Cross-Tab, this will generate a double field automatic row. The output will look like the following:

```
"Dept" "Sex" "Wage"
"ACCT" "M" 3365.86
"DATA" "M" 654.34
"MFGR" "F" 2401.45
"MKTG" "F" 1516.26
"MKTG" "M" 2564.33
```

Note that this is the Smart external file format. The title of the Cross-Tab definition was created as:

```
Dept" "Sex
```

The outer quotation marks are added during execution of the Cross-Tab.

SW II

7.37 Trap: The maximum length of a field generated automatically in Data Cross-Tabs is 20 bytes. The title also is limited to 20 bytes.

This does not mean that the largest field may be 20 bytes, but any contents longer than this will be truncated without a warning.

SW II

7.38 Trap: When creating a Cross-Tab definition, if your criteria overlap, the same database record may be counted more than once.

For example, consider the following two criteria:

```
[wage] >= 25000
[wage] <= 25000
```

The record in which the wage is exactly equal to 25000 will be counted twice. There is no automatic exclusion of this event, nor will there be an error or warning message. Used properly, this feature of the Data Cross-Tab command can save time by combining several measurements within the same definition. However, be careful that you do not accidentally double count where you do not intend to.

SW II

7.39 Trap: Do not use column titles that begin with numbers if you are using the Data Cross-Tab command to create a new database, since field names that begin with numbers are not allowed.

When you use the Data Cross-Tab command to create a new database, the column title names become the database field names. Although you are not prevented from creating column titles that begin with numbers, database fields will not assume these titles. The execution of the Data Cross-Tab command is not aborted, but alternate field names are generated. If your first column is titled "1990," for example, the first field in the database will be called "F001-1990."

SW II

7.40 Trap: Do not use column titles that contain periods if you are using the Data Cross-Tab command to create a new database, since you must not have a field name with a period.

A period in a field name is used to separate the name of the view from the name of the field. Thus, [person2.dept] means the field [dept] in the Person2 view. Data Cross-Tab column titles are used as the field names when you create a new database. If you have used a period in the column title, it is converted automatically to an underscore; the command is not aborted, however.

SW II

7.41 Trap When using Data Cross-Tabs, do not use a view with a table to summarize data from the `main` file of a view. The data will be counted multiple times.

When you have a table in a view, the Data Cross-Tabs command operates as if each record of the table is attached to the main file. Thus, if there are 5 records in a particular table, the data from the main file will be counted 5 times, rather than just once, as you probably intended. For best results, use a single file view, or one in which the attached files do not comprise a table.

Changing a Summarized Definition

7.42 Trap: If you select the wrong options when changing a Write Summarized definition, you can alter your definition inadvertently. *3.10*

In order to edit a Summarized definition, you must remember and supply the following items of information:

The database to which the definition applies
Column/Row or Row

The database must already be loaded in the current window when you initiate the command. The definition is not screen-dependent. If you do not remember these items, you will receive the following error message:

```
Saved definition does not match command parameters
```

Rather than returning you to the command level of Smart, however, the definition continues as if you were starting from scratch. All previous entries in the definition are obliterated. If you really did intend to start from scratch, you can continue; but if you simply forgot the correct file name or the Column/Row selection, you should press Esc to abandon the definition, leaving your original intact.

You do not need to remember the database screen to which the definition applies in order to edit the specifications. Fields that are not available on the current custom screen will appear within the definition. You can delete any field, whether or not it appears on the custom screen; but because only the fields on the custom screen are available for selection, you cannot insert a field missing from the screen. Write and Send Summary Definitions are screen-independent.

7.43 Trap: Specifying Complete or Partial changes the Summarized definition to the option specified. *3.10*

The selection

```
Complete  Partial
```

is a function of the Write Summarized or Send definition instead of being specified when you execute the Predefined definition. When you edit a definition, there is no error message if you select the opposite choice from your original intention. Terminating the Define with the F10 key to save the definition redefines the Complete or Partial specification. There is absolutely no message or indication of this change until, of course, you see the results of your work.

Using a Partial Option

3.10 **7.44 Tip:** The Partial option in a Summarized Definition can have some useful applications.

For example, in figure 7.10, I have defined my specification to sum the wages and count the records by degree level.

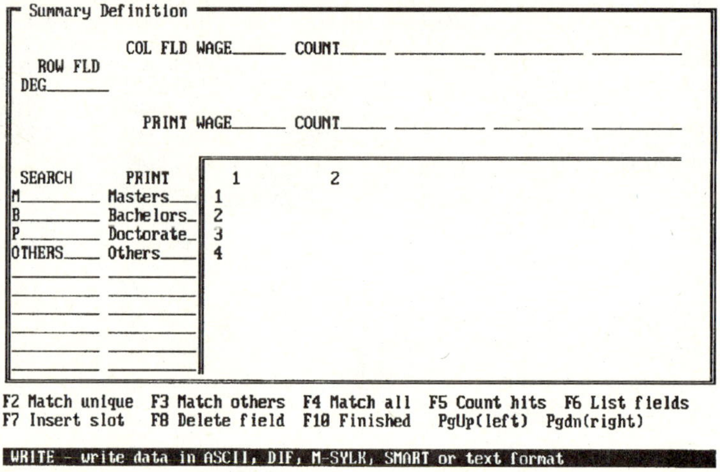

```
Summary Definition
            COL FLD WAGE______ COUNT_____ _________ _________ _________
  ROW FLD
 DEG______
              PRINT WAGE______ COUNT_____ _________ _________ _________

 SEARCH      PRINT       1          2
M________ Masters____  1
B________ Bachelors__  2
P________ Doctorate__  3
OTHERS___ Others_____  4

F2 Match unique  F3 Match others  F4 Match all  F5 Count hits  F6 List fields
F7 Insert slot   F8 Delete field  F10 Finished   PgUp(left)  Pgdn(right)

WRITE - write data in ASCII, DIF, M-SYLK, SMART or text format
```

Fig. 7.10. *A Summarized Partial definition.*

I have selected the significant letters from the degree abbreviations and have used these to pick up the degree level. Therefore, I am looking for an `M` to signify that the employee has a master's degree, a `B` for a bachelor's degree, and a P for a Ph.D. The fourth line, labeled `OTHERS`, was entered by pressing the F3 key; this enters the uppercase word `OTHERS` in the search column. If you are specifying individual row entries, as I have done, and you want to make sure you account for all records, use this OTHERS feature to accumulate the data for all the other records that do not match the specified conditions.

In the `PRINT` column, I have typed the labels I want to use as the titles for the rows. Figure 7.11 shows the results of this Write Summarized Row Partial command.

```
DEG             WAGE    COUNT
Masters      4030.40        4
Bachelors    4635.01        5
Doctorate    1020.33        1
Others       3443.11        3
```

Fig. 7.11.

Results of Summarized Partial by Degree Type.

Row and Column Specification

7.45 Trap: When using the Partial option of the Write (or Send) Summarized command, be careful of the order in which you specify your rows; changing the order can give you different results. *3.10*

In figure 7.11, I entered the Masters degree on the line before the Bachelors. Figure 7.12 shows the opposite entry, with the Bachelors first, and figure 7.13 shows the results.

```
Summary Definition
              COL FLD WAGE_____ COUNT____ ________ ________ ________
  ROW FLD
 DEG______

                PRINT WAGE_____ COUNT____ ________ ________ ________

 SEARCH     PRINT        1          2
B________ Bachelors_  1
M________ Masters___  2
P________ Doctorate_  3
OTHERS___ Others____  4
_________ __________
_________ __________
```

Fig. 7.12.

A Summarized definition in the wrong order.

```
DEG             WAGE    COUNT
Bachelors    6257.06        7
Masters      2400.35        2
Doctorate    1020.33        1
Others       3443.11        3
```

Fig. 7.13.

Incorrect Summarized results.

Instead of five individuals with bachelor's degrees and four with master's, we now show seven bachelors and only two masters. The difference appears because two employees on the payroll have MBA degrees. Notice that this degree abbreviation contains both the letters M and B. Because the search is ordered to find the B first, as shown in figure 7.13, the MBA is counted with the B row, rather than the M row. Neither definition is "wrong" from the viewpoint of Smart, however. If you use this feature, you need to know your data and the implications of the order in which you specify the matching.

3.10

7.46 Tip: Using the F2 key in the Summarized Definition causes each unique row field value to generate a new row in the output.

Rather than having to specify each individual department, press the F2 key for the first line in the SEARCH column. In figure 7.4, the word UNIQUE was inserted in both the SEARCH and PRINT columns. When, therefore, a new department is created in the company, you do not have to go back and change the definition.

If, however, you want the departments to appear in a certain order, then you must enter the department codes line by line. Just remember to modify the definition if you add a new department.

Both

7.47 Trap: Unique rows or columns in Write Summarized (Smart 3.10) or Data Cross-Tabs (SmartWareII) definitions are case sensitive. To solve the problem, use a query to ensure that the fields are in the same case.

In a Summarized definition, upper and lower case row field contents are not considered equal. Thus, in a field called [sex] for example, "F" is not equal to "f". If you specifically indicate the field contents equal to "F," you will omit any lowercase occurrences. If you generate rows based upon unique occurrences, you will get one row for "F" and another for "f".

Use the following query to make all the same case:

```
[sex] <> upper([sex]) replace [sex] = upper([sex])
```

Field case differences are less of a problem in SmartWare II, due to its ability to enforce case standards with field masks and to specify selection formulas within the Cross-Tabs definition. Thus, if you want to specify a field contents of "F" in either upper- or lowercase, the formula can be:

```
[sex] == "F"
```

The double equal sign indicates equality regardless of case.

SW II

7.48 Trap: The automatic generation of rows using numeric fields inserts a space following each number. This extra space makes spreadsheet processing awkward.

For example, if you have numeric account numbers which are 101, 102, and so on, and you use the automatic row (or column) generation feature of the Data Cross-Tab command, the rows will be labeled as in the following example:

```
"Account" "Amount"
"101 " 71591.66
"102 " 279676.94
"103 " 193000
```

Note that an extra space follows each number. When you import this file into the Spreadsheet module, the trailing space will be invisible, but will cause a VLOOKUP function to fail if the source linkage field does not have the space.

There are several solutions to the problem:

1. Use alpha fields for the account numbers, rather than numeric. The problem does not occur with alpha fields.
2. Create an alpha view field with the following calculation:

   ```
   str([account])
   ```

   This allows you to retain the numeric account number fields, but by using the alpha view field in the Data Cross-Tab, you avoid the problem of the extra space.
3. The source cell of a VLOOKUP function in the spreadsheet can be entered with a trailing blank. This will allow the function to operate without an error. This is awkward, however, because the trailing blank is invisible and easy to forget.
4. Create a formula in the spreadsheet that appends a trailing blank onto the original source cell; then use the formula version of the cell as the source for the VLOOKUP.

7.49 Tip: The automatic generation of rows from a numeric field will result in row identifiers that are alpha, rather than numeric. *SW II*

For example, if you have account codes 101, 102, and so on, when you generate automatic rows (or columns), the rows will be identified as "101 ", "102 ", and so on. Notice that quotation marks denote the contents as alphanumeric, rather than numeric. If you elect to generate a new data file, rather than create an external file, these automatically generated fields will be alphanumeric, rather than numeric, as they were in the original file.

Testing a Send Summarized Definition

7.50 Trick: Test a Send Summarized definition by using the definition first in a Write command. *3.10*

Both the Write and the Send Summarized commands use the same definition files. You can test the definition, while remaining in the Database, by using the Write command to write a text file. View your results with the Text-Editor to make sure the results look good. You then can execute the Send command if the results are as you expect.

If you execute the Send without first testing it, you will have unloaded all your files, losing any index settings, and invoked the Spreadsheet module perhaps only to find a simple mistake. You then must return to the Database, load your file again, and change your Send definition.

7.51 Trap: If you are not careful, you can easily Undefine a Summarized definition. *3.10*

The first menu within the Write (or Send) Summarized command is

```
Define Predefined Undefine
```

If you accidentally select Undefine when you had intended to select Define or Predefined, Smart immediately erases the definition for the selected name. There is no warning or double-check to protect against the wrong selection.

3.10

7.52 Trap: The Write Summarized command issues no warning if you are writing to a file that already exists.

If you were writing a report to a file, the following error message would appear:

```
File <name> already exists. Continue (y/n)
```

But there is no such message from the Write Summarized command. You run the risk of overlaying potentially valuable information.

SW II

7.53 Tip: Make sure the output file to be created by the Data Cross-Tab command does not already exist, or the command will fail.

If the file exists, you will get the error message:

```
Destination file already exists
```

Use the Tools File Erase command to delete the output file before you begin execution of the Data Cross-Tab command. In Smart 3.10, it is not necessary to erase the external file when using the Write command. You may need to edit your project files if you have translated them from Smart 3.10 to SmartWare II.

Both

7.54 Trap: You must supply your own file extensions when using the Write Summarized command.

The Write Summarized command does not automatically supply a file extension. Unlike most other commands that create files within the Smart system, you must provide your own file extension if you want one.

SW II

7.55 Tip: If you are using the Data Cross-Tab command to create a file to import into the Spreadsheet, use a file extension of DAT.

When you import Text files in the Spreadsheet module, those files with an extension of DAT will appear in a popup menu, and you can use the cursor to select the one you want. If the file you want to import does not have a DAT extension, you must type the name of the file in response to the prompt.

Both

7.56 Trick: Use the File Copy command to create a new variation of a Write or Send Summarized definition in Smart 3.10. In SmartWare II, use the Tools File Copy command to duplicate a Data Cross-Tabs definition.

If you copy the existing definition to a new file and execute the Write Summarized Define command to change the new file, you will have used the original definition as a template for the new definition. These summary definition files have the extension DFW.

In Smart 3.10, to copy the definition to a new file, you can exit temporarily to the DOS level with the Ctrl-O quick key or use the File Copy command on command list 4. Use Tools File Copy in SmartWare II.

Even if the new definition shares many characteristics with the old definition but will address a completely different file, you can alter the definition. The new file should be in the current window, and the old file should be active but not in the current window. When you define the new definition, all the existing specifications will apply. Change what you need and save the definition by pressing F10. Once it is saved, the definition will apply to the new file instead of the old file.

7.57 Tip: The number of rows or columns is limited only by the amount of available RAM when you use a UNIQUE search. *3.10*

If you specify the match strings in a Write or Send Summarized definition, you are limited to 99 rows and 20 columns. If you need to exceed these limits, you must create your summary in two or more steps, write the results to files, and combine the files in the Spreadsheet module.

If you are able to specify the UNIQUE selection criteria (by pressing F2), you are limited only by the amount of free RAM. Even if you have to delete some rows or columns once you have completed the Send to the Spreadsheet, you may still find it to your advantage to use the UNIQUE criterion.

7.58 Tip: Alter the order of your file to affect the order of the summarized rows when using the Unique feature of either the Write or Send Summarized commands. *3.10*

When the Write Summarized command is executed, each new row field value causes a new output row to be generated. Thus, if you want your output in alphabetical order, sort your file by the row field. If you have some other sort that makes sense (departments within divisions, for example) you can use a two-field sort to achieve the output order you want.

7.59 Tip: If data you send to the Spreadsheet is to be in date order, sort it before you send it to the Spreadsheet rather than after, since date fields become text cells in the spreadsheet. *Both*

In the database, date fields sort correctly. In Smart 3.10, date fields are special alpha fields; in SmartWare II, they are stored in numerical format, but displayed as dates. Fortunately, you do not have to treat dates specially when sorting, because their special status is recognized by the database sorting methods.

When date fields are sent from the Database to the Spreadsheet, however, they become like any other text data. In the Spreadsheet, these text cells will sort like any other text data, from left to right. Thus, all dates in January will be grouped together, since every date in January will begin with "01," regardless of the year. This is probably not what you would want.

To avoid this problem, sort the database records before sending them to the spreadsheet to make sure they are in the correct order.

SW II

7.60 Trick: Sort the database in descending order if you want the result in ascending order when generating rows automatically.

In the Data Cross-Tabs command, after processing all records, the data is written from memory to the disk file in last-in, first-out order. Thus, if the row with the lowest value is accumulated last, it will be written to the file first.

SW II

7.61 Tip: In the Data Cross-Tab command, if you select automatic row generation, the order of the output may not be what you expect.

Output records are generated for unique occurrences of the row field in the order in which they are encountered. If the file is in either Physical or Key order, the file is processed in physical order. If the file is ordered by an Index, the command will follow the order of the records in the index. Thus, if you want to make sure the output rows are in either ascending or descending order, you must sort the view, and not rely on the Key to determine the order.

SW II

7.62 Tip: When using the Data Cross-Tab command, numeric fields may not be written in the format in which they are displayed on the view.

Even though you see a numeric field displayed as having two decimal positions in the view, when the sum of the field is written to an external file, for example, it might be generated as 27982.7700000008 or in scientific notation as 4.00179889226138E-13.

To help prevent this problem, make sure that any calculated fields in a view are rounded to the number of decimal places displayed.

Using the Query Command

At first, the Query command of Smart 3.10 or Data Query of SmartWare II can be frustrating. The commands have so many capabilities, variations, and danger spots that it can seem to be an enigma. However, after you have used the Query command for a while, you will begin to appreciate its features.

This chapter is intended to increase your mastery of the Query command by providing both explanations and examples. I include an extensive discussion of working with date fields.

Using Field Names

3.10

7.63 Tip: Use field names rather than field numbers in Query definitions.

Using names rather than numbers has several advantages:

1. If you change a file by adding fields, a change to a field's position will not require you to change your Query Definition.

2. Your documentation is more easily understood. System documentation should include a printed copy of all Query definitions. Because definitions are ASCII files, you can print them easily.
3. The file name is not embedded in the Query definition. If you use the field names, you can apply the Query definition to any file where appropriate.
4. If you decide to upgrade to SmartWare II, field numbers are not used in this product. You will eventually have to change your query definitions.

7.64 Trick: Perform a Query using a field that is not available on the current screen. *3.10*

Even though a field may not be visible on the current custom screen, you still can perform a Query using the field. This can be a convenient feature, because you may not want to display the field, for reasons of security, but need to Query on it.

7.65 Trick: Use the Fwrite command to change a Query to vary the referenced field, since you cannot use a parameter in a Query definition. ***Both***

Occasionally, you may need to reference different fields in a Query. Although you can use a variable to vary the comparison value, there is no direct provision to vary field names.

For example, suppose your database contains the fields Month01, Month02, Month03 and so on. A Query might be as follows:

```
[Month01] > $amount
```

However, depending on the current month, you would like to vary the field. One choice is to have 12 separate query definitions. But with Fwrite, you can change the query as needed. Here is a short project file that will change the above query:

```
public $month $amount
lock system public

label askmonth
screen shortinput $month "Month number, leading zeros:"
if len($month) <> 2
     jump askmonth

else
     screen shortinput $amount "Amount:"
     fopen "month.dfq" as 1
     fseek 1 6
     fwrite 1 length 2 from $month
     fclose 1
```

```
        data query execute "month" index "ind1.idx"
    end if
```

Note that just the number portion of the field name is overwritten by the Fwrite statement.

Both

7.66 Trap: Make sure the file or view you intend to query is current at the time you define a replacement query. If it is not, you will not be able to save the definition, because the field name will not match.

When you save a Query definition in which you replace the contents of a field, the field name is verified against the current file or view. If the name does not match, or is misspelled, you will get the following error message:

```
Bad syntax        (SmartWare II)
Invalid field     (Smart 3.10)
```

Rather than discarding the query definition, you can temporarily change the field name to a number. This will allow you to save the definition and access the correct file or view. (Even in SmartWare II you can use field numbers, but you should not rely on them.) Finally, modify the query definition, inserting the correct field name.

3.10

7.67 Trick: Construct a very large Query definition using field numbers rather than field names to save space in the file and allow you to create larger Queries.

If your Query definition is too large, you will get the error message:

```
Expression too complex
```

There is a limit to the size of a query definition. The maximum size is determined by a number of factors, such as the complexity of the query and the amount of available RAM. If you change to field numbers, rather than names, the existing definition file will be smaller, and you will be able to add more to it.

SW II

7.68 Trap: To create or modify a Query definition, a view must be loaded in the current window.

If the window is empty, the error message will be:

```
No data-file in current window
```

If you want to modify a Query containing QBE conditions, the view must be the one for which the Query definition was originally designed or another that contains the same fields. If the query definition specifies fields not on the view, you will get an error message:

```
Invalid field [fieldname]
```

Press any key to abort the Data Query Modify command.

If the Query contains only a view expression, then usually any view may be loaded to allow you to modify the definition; most field names are not verified when saving the view expression Query. If the view expression contains a "**replace**" of a field that is not in the view, there is no error message when you modify the query definition. But when you press F10 to save it, you will get an error message:

```
Bad syntax
```

In general, the current view should be the one for which the query was originally created.

Using Date Specifications

7.69 Tip: Working with date fields in a Query requires some special attention. *3.10*

The DAYS function, when used with a valid date as the argument, returns a number representing the number of days from the beginning of the century. For example, January 1, 1900 is date number 1; June 20, 1965 is date number 23912. In a Query definition, the DAYS function is the only means of guaranteeing that dates will be compared accurately.

For example, you can have a query like the following:

```
days([empdate]) <= days("09-01-72")
```

Figure 7.14 shows the original data in window 1 and the selected data in window 2.

```
Window 1                                  Window 2
 EMPDATE  LAST       FIRST                 EMPDATE  LAST       FIRST
 07-23-45 Adelson    Alfred              →07-23-45 Adelson    Alfred
 10-01-59 Ronaldo    Rosanna               10-01-59 Ronaldo    Rosanna
 10-30-65 Markus     LeAnne                10-30-65 Markus     LeAnne
 05-25-69 Davis      Michael               05-25-69 Davis      Michael
 07-01-70 Harris     Jeff                  07-01-70 Harris     Jeff
 08-20-71 Karenski   Julius                08-20-71 Karenski   Julius
→08-15-72 Aliakbari  Ellen                 08-15-72 Aliakbari  Ellen
 06-15-75 Bernstein  Paula
 06-20-75 Linden     Debbie
 09-05-75 Lester     Marilyn
 10-15-81 Steffans   Charles
 10-01-85 Peters     Howard E.
 10-30-85 Marzetti   David

Command:

File: person   Index: IND1   Window: 1          Page: 1  Rec: 7  ( 12 )  Act: Y
```

Fig. 7.14. *Records selected by date of employment.*

If, however, you had used the following query statement:

```
[empdate] <= "09-01-72"
```

you would have selected the seven records shown in figure 7.15.

Fig. 7.15.

Selection on date without using the DAYS function.

```
Window 1
 EMPDATE  LAST       FIRST
 07-23-45 Adelson    Alfred
 05-25-69 Davis      Michael
 07-01-70 Harris     Jeff
 08-20-71 Karenski   Julius
 08-15-72 Aliakbari  Ellen
 06-15-75 Bernstein  Paula
→06-20-75 Linden     Debbie

Command:

File: person   Indcx: IND2   Window: 1        Page: 1  Rec: EOF  ( 2 )  Act: Y
```

On the surface, both Query statements look similar, and neither returned an error message. Yet the results are quite different. The first example selects only those employees whose dates of employment are before September 1, 1972. The second example selects employees with dates both before and after the target date.

Remember that a date field is a special case of an alpha field. If you look at the month numbers of the dates shown in figure 7.15, you will notice that they are all prior to the month of September (09), regardless of the year. What has happened is that when you compare dates without using the Date function, the date field is treated just like any other alpha field, and the comparison proceeds from left to right. To perform an accurate comparison, therefore, you must use the Date function.

3.10

7.70 Tip: Don't always use the DAYS function in a query involving date fields.

If your date field is also a key field and you are searching for records containing a particular date, you can use the following Query definition:

```
where [empdate] = "08-15-72"
```

If your file is ordered by the field specified, the key word `where` causes the Query to search with the key file rather than performing a sequential search. Thus you can use this structure if you are looking for a specific date. Using the

DAYS function with the `where` modifier invalidates the rules you must observe when using this feature; the Query definition will not be accepted if you try to use the DAYS function.

If you use the technique of comparison to a literal date, exercise some caution. For example, you cannot use any relational operator other than Equal (=) when you use the `where` modifier; but the purely alphabetic comparison (see fig. 7.16) would probably cause you to use Equal anyway. Also, the date must match exactly the way in which the field is stored in the database. If you used the DAYS function, the following date specifications would all be equal:

8-15-72
8/15/72
08/15/72

But because you are treating the date as you would treat any other alpha field, you must match the characters exactly.

Because you can use only one Equal comparison with `where`, you cannot specify more than one date for which to search. If you have several dates you want to retrieve, you may find it economical to make one sequential pass through the file with the DAYS function instead of making several searches using `where` each time.

7.71 Tip: If a date field is a key, some methods of performing a query are faster than others. *SW II*

From the command level, you can perform a QBE query such as the following:

```
DATE:   10/15/81
```

However, for a faster search, use the following:

```
DATE:   days("10/15/81")
```

This is a little more to type, but it's worth it. If the date is contained in a variable, it's best if the variable contains the days of the date, rather than the date in the "mm/dd/yy" format. If the variable contains the days value, the query definition would look like the following:

```
DATE: $begdate
```

If the variable contains the mm/dd/yy format of the date, use the following QBE expression:

```
DATE:   days($begdate)
```

In this instance, you cannot use the variable without the DAYS function.

In a view expression, you should use the `where` specification to execute an optimized query:

```
where [date] = days("10/15/81")
```

If the variable contains the days of the date, use this:

```
where [date] = $begdate
```

If the variable contains the date in the mm/dd/yy format, you must use the DAYS function:

```
where [date] = days($begdate)
```

If you forget to use the `where`, the query will still work, but it will be sequential, rather than optimized. You'll notice that it will run slowly. When you use `where`, it must be on the same line as the criterion, or you will get a syntax error.

SW II

7.72 Trap: If you use variables and the "double dot" notation to select records within a date range in the QBE editor, the variables must contain the `DAYS` of the date. If the variables contain dates in the "mm/dd/yy" format, use the View Expression editor.

The QBE editor will accept a date range selection in the following format:

```
DATE:   $begdate..$enddate
```

The contents of the variables must be numbers, representing the number of days sincc thc bcginning of the 20th century. (Date fields are maintained internally in this format.)

If the variables contain dates similar in format to "8/24/90", use the view expression editor and the DAYS function:

```
days($begdate) >= [date] and days($enddate) <= [date]
```

Do not use the DAYS function with the [date] fields, since they are stored internally as numbers anyway.

Using AND and OR Operators

3.10

7.73 Tip: To specify a range of dates, use a query similar to the one shown in figure 7.16.

```
Query Editor
days([empdate]) >= days("6/20/65") and
days([empdate]) <= days("6/20/85")
```

Fig. 7.16.
Querying for a range of dates.

Both

7.74 Tip: Use the AND operator if you mean "and at the same time."

The AND operator specifies that both conditions must be met at the same time by a single record if that record is to be included in the set. Think of what would happen if the OR operator had been used in figure 7.16; every record in the database would have been selected because the employment date in each record would always meet one condition or the other.

7.75 Tip: Pay attention to the greater-than (>) and less-than (<) symbols in range definitions.

Both

What if you wanted dates outside the same range? You would use a Query structure similar to the one shown in figure 7.17.

```
Query Editor
  days([empdate]) <= days("6/20/65") or
  days([empdate]) >= days("6/20/85")
```

Fig. 7.17.

Excluding a date range.

Notice that not only have the greater-than and less-than symbols been exchanged, but the logical operator has been changed to `OR` rather than `AND`. In this case, we want those records that meet one condition or the other: either less than the beginning date or greater than the ending date of the range. Clearly, no individual record could meet both conditions simultaneously; hence the use of the OR operator rather than the AND.

7.76 Tip: AND has a different meaning in English than it does in a Smart Query.

Both

For instance, we might say, "I want a list of all the employees in the accounting department and the data processing department." In English, that's fine; anyone would know what you mean. However, when you translate that into a Query request, you must be slightly more careful. You would not want to write the following Query:

```
[dept] = "ACCT" and [dept] = "DATA"
```

because any one individual cannot work for both departments simultaneously (within our system, anyway). The Query would have to be

```
[dept] = "ACCT" or [dept] = "DATA"
```

in which you search for individuals meeting one condition or the other.

7.77 Tip: Use the AND operator between specifications for two different fields.

Both

If you are searching on two different fields at the same time, that's a different story. Suppose you are looking for all individuals in the accounting department who live in Massachusetts. Use the following Query:

```
[dept] = "ACCT" and [state] = "MA"
```

In this instance, any individual record must meet both conditions to be included in the set. If you are willing to accept records meeting either condition, use the OR operator, rather than AND.

Both

7.78 Trap: Each element of a logical condition stands on its own; there is no carryover from one to the next.

Notice that the field name is repeated when performing a Query on one field for multiple contents. You may be tempted to use the following Query structure:

```
[dept] = "ACCT" or "DATA"
```

Absolutely do not use this shortcut! You won't get an error message, but only the records meeting the first condition will be selected. You may think you have selected everyone in accounting or data processing because there is no message to tell you otherwise. But, in fact, you will have selected only a subset of the records you wanted.

Fast Query Definitions

Both

7.79 Tip: Perform an optimized, binary search on a key field for an extremely fast Query.

The following conditions must be met:

1. The database is ordered by a key. (This is not necessary in SmartWare II.)
2. The key field is an element of the Query.
3. The logical operator on the key is Equal (=).
4. The reserved word WHERE precedes the key-field specification.
5. Only one condition is specified for the key field.

If you adhere to the preceding restrictions, a Query command can be extremely fast. For instance, in a personnel application, the SSN probably would be a key field in the primary file. An optimized, binary search can locate the record for any individual in a few seconds, whereas a sequential search can take several minutes.

For example, if you want to search for all individuals within a specific department, use the following Query:

```
where [dept] = "MFGR"
```

Both

7.80 Tip: A Query using `where` can be combined with another logical condition.

For example, consider this Query:

```
[state] = "MA" where [dept] = "MFGR"
```

Because the Query has no logical operator, the AND operator is not used. Using the key field and the equality search is similar to the special condition of the Find command that also performs a binary search. Refer to Chapter 4 for a review of the Find (3.10) and Data Find (SmartWare II) commands.

7.81 Trap: Make sure that the `where` condition is listed last in your Query. *Both*

If you were to reverse the previous Query so that it read

```
where [dept] = "MFGR" and [state] = "MA"
```

you would not get an error message, but no records would be retrieved. Yet this looks like a perfectly logical Query statement. Logical, maybe; correct, no! If you leave out the word `and`, all employees in the "MFGR" department will be selected.

7.82 Trap: An optimized search of a key field will be performed in a Query by Example (QBE) only if there is just one entry. If you search for two values for the field, using `OR`, a sequential search will be performed. *SW II*

Optimized searches, which use the internal binary search technique, will search for only one value at a time. For example, if you have a personnel file which has a key for the SSN field, an optimized search will be performed if you enter just a single SSN. However, if you enter two SSN's an optimized search will not be performed:

```
SSN: 498-48-3988 or 239-87-8876
```

You will recognize that a sequential search is being performed because it will run much slower than an optimized search. Depending on the number of records, it may be faster to perform multiple optimized queries.

7.83 Trap: A sequential Query will not always yield the same results as a binary, optimized Query, due to case differences. *Both*

Consider the following sequential Query:

```
[custid] = $custid
```

This may not give you the same results as the following optimized query:

```
where [custid] = $custid
```

Binary, optimized Queries are insensitive to case in Smart 3.10, due to the use of the collation sorting sequence. In the optimized Query, "SMITH" is equal to "Smith." Thus, if customer codes have been entered in upper case sometimes and in lower case other times, the binary search query will locate all of them.

Sequential Queries are sensitive to case, however. If you want to ignore case in a sequential Query, use the double equal sign:

```
[custid] == $custid
```

You may NOT use the double equal sign in an optimized query.

In SmartWare II, key fields are maintained in the ASCII sorting sequence, rather than the collation sequence. Since ASCII sorting is case sensitive, the same records will be selected when you use either the optimized or sequential query methods.

SW II

7.84 Tip: A Query performed using the record number is always optimized. If the view is ordered by a key or is in physical order, the number refers to the physical record. If the view is ordered by an index, it is the logical number.

An optimized Query works by the binary search method, the fastest search possible within the Database. If your Query specifies a record number, the search is optimized, even if the view is ordered by an index.

SW II

7.85 Tip: When developing and testing a Query, limit the number of records first, since testing on the record number performs a fast, optimized search.

If you have thousands, or even hundreds, of records in your database, and you want to test a query, the more records you have, the longer the test will take. In Smart 3.10, you can press Ctrl-Z and stop the Query halfway through, and you will have selected the records accepted up to that point.

In SmartWare II, however, if you do the same thing, the index will not be created, even if some records already processed would have passed the query criteria. Thus, select a few records to test the query, for example:

```
record <= 50
```

This query will select 50 into an index. Then test the new Query you are developing.

Using Special Alpha Fields

3.10

7.86 Tip: SSN and Phone fields are special alpha fields.

If you perform a Query using one of these fields, you must include the formatting characters that ordinarily you do not have to type when entering data. Some examples are:

```
where [ssn] = "419-93-7488"

[phone] ! "(413)"
```

Be sure to enclose the criteria in double quotes because you are treating these special fields as alpha fields. The second example performs a Query for all those employees with phone numbers in the 413 area code; the exclamation point (!) means "contains."

Formula Writing Techniques

7.87 Tip: Resist the temptation to begin a Query statement with `if`. *Both*

The if is implied, but do not use it. You will get syntax or other error messages.

7.88 Tip: When using the relational operators *greater than or equal to* or *less than or equal to*, make sure that the equal sign follows the "greater than" (>) or "less than" (<) sign. *Both*

```
[wage] <= 1000

[age] >= 65
```

The Query editor will catch this mistake and you will not be able to proceed until you have corrected it.

7.89 Tip: Use parentheses to control the order of evaluation in compound queries. *Both*

Sometimes, if you have complex, nested conditions, you must use parentheses to indicate your meaning. For example, consider what the Query in figure 7.18 means.

```
Query Editor
[age] < 40 and   [dept] = "ACCT" or [dept] = "MKTG"     or

[wage] >= 900 and [wage] <= 1100
```

Fig. 7.18. *A Compound Query.*

This Query selects six records from the sample database. Compare this definition to the one in figure 7.19.

```
Query Editor
( [age] < 40 and ( [dept] = "ACCT" or [dept] = "MKTG" )) or

( [wage] >= 900 and [wage] <= 1100 )
```

Fig. 7.19. *A Compound Query with parentheses.*

This Query selects seven records. If you find the Query in figure 7.18 confusing, just consider that Smart can have just as much difficulty in interpreting the definition as you do. To be sure you get what you want, use parentheses.

The Query in figure 7.18 is interpreted as

```
Select all records where
  either
       AGE is less than 40 and the DEPT is ACCT
  or
       either
             DEPT is MKTG
  or
             WAGE is between 900 and 1100
```

The Query definition in figure 7.19 is interpreted as

```
Select all records where
  either
       AGE is less than 40
       and
       DEPT is either ACCT or MKTG
  or
       WAGE is between 900 and 1100
```

3.10 **7.90 Tip: There is a difference between null fields and those that are blank or zero.**

A field is null if you have never entered a value or text into it. If you press F7 in Enter or Update mode, you can delete the contents of a field to return it to null status.

If an SSN, Phone, or Date field is filled with zeros, the field is considered to be null. When the record is created, the default value is zero; but even if you have entered zeros, the field is still null. But if, for some reason, blanks are introduced into these fields, the fields are not considered to be null.

It's not as easy to determine if an ordinary alpha field is null or blank; at the command level, they look exactly the same. In Update mode, however, you can tell the difference if you look closely. A null character is denoted by an underscore; this is the default condition of all fields in the Enter command. A blank character, however, will not have the underscore; the position will show nothing—it will be blank.

If you look closely at the third field in figure 7.20 (the field called LAST), you will notice that the first five characters of the field contents show nothing, but the remaining characters show an underscore. This is your clue that blank characters are actually in those first five characters.

```
Window 1
SSN 345-54-2287
FIRST Ellen____
LAST       _____
AGE 35
SEX F
MS S
DEP 0_
DEG ___
CAR 1_
STREET 2171 University
CITY Westfield_
```

Fig. 7.20. *Null and blank fields.*

Null numeric fields are much easier to identify; if a numeric field is null, it appears totally blank when viewed at the command level or underscored when viewed in the Update mode. If it contains zero, the numeral zero appears.

7.91 Tip: In SmartWare II, an empty field is BLANK, rather than NULL as in Smart 3.10. *SW II*

In SmartWare II, a Data Query to test for an empty field is as follows:

```
isblank([field]) = 1
```

If you tested for NULL in any Query definitions you have converted from Smart 3.10, you should change them to test for BLANK in SmartWare II.

7.92 Tip: In the Query command, you must specify blank text and null text separately, as well as zero numerics and null numerics. *3.10*

For instance, the two Query commands

```
[age] = 0
```

and

```
[age] = null
```

are not equivalent.

If you are referencing a numeric field, you can accomplish both at the same time with the expression

```
[age] + 0 = 0
```

or with the double condition

```
[age] = 0 or [age] = null
```

If the field is alpha, you can test for a null condition with the expression

```
[last] = null
```

To search for an alpha field that is either totally blank or that contains blanks and trailing null values, use a Query similar to the following:

```
trim([last]) = null
```

To identify fields that are not null, you must specify

```
[last] <> null
```

rather than using the *not* construct:

```
[last] not (null)
```

The preceding definition will result in the error message `Bad syntax` when you begin execution of the Query.

3.10

7.93 Trap: A date field of "00/00/00" will usually be evaluated equal to Null, but not always.

If the configuration of your Smart system uses the slash character (/) as the separator in a date field, the following Query definition will find all records in which the dates appear as "00/00/00":

```
[date] = null
```

However, if a colleague who uses dash (—) instead of a slash sends you a database in which the empty date fields are "00-00-00," these will not evaluate to null on your system, since your configuration looks for the slash character.

For a universal test for an empty date field, use the DAYS function as follows:

```
days([date]) = 0
```

This query definition will work if the date separator character is either slash or dash.

3.10

7.94 Tip: When defining and executing a Query, the fields you utilize need not be available on the screen in the current window.

Any database field can be used in the Query definition, even if it is not available on the current window. The pop-up menu, which shows the names of the fields when you press F6 in the definition screen, will show only the fields in the current window, however.

Both

7.95 Trap: Take extreme care in a Query if a number is contained in an alpha field.

If you have defined an alpha field (for example, a code field) in which you enter numeric codes, be careful how you create your Query definitions. To accurately execute a Query on such a field, you must enclose the numeric value in double quotation marks:

```
[status] < "2"
```

If you omit the quotation marks, the Query editor does not flag this as an error because numbers need not have quotation marks around them. Furthermore, the fact that the field is actually an alpha field is not noted in the Query editor.

If you were to omit the quotation marks, in this instance, you would select all records in your database. The reverse condition,

```
[status] > 2
```

would select no records. If you also have alpha codes in the same field, entering the Query definition,

```
[status] = Y
```

causes the Query editor to generate a `Bad syntax` error message.

The `Bad syntax` error message is generated because the letter Y, being an alpha literal, must have double quotes surrounding it. The number 2, however, is not an alpha character and thus does not bear this restriction. The type of the literal (alpha or numeric, in this example) is not compared to the type of the field in the Query definition process; the problems become evident only when the Query is executed.

7.96 Trap: In a Query, make sure that the data type of the variable matches the data type of the field; you cannot test a numeric field with an alpha variable. *SW II*

Even though you may prompt for a number (use Screen Shortinput or Screen Input), the resulting variable will be text. If you plan to use this variable in a Query to compare to a numeric field, you must first convert the contents to numeric:

```
let $amount = val($amount)
```

Then, in your Query, you can test against a numeric field.

7.97 Tip: You can perform range tests on alphabetic fields just as easily as on numeric fields. *Both*

If you want to perform a Query to work with only those individuals in the first half of the alphabet, you could use the following Query definition:

```
[lastname] < "N"
```

7.98 Trap: Alpha field ranges in the Query command are not sorted in accordance with the collation table. *Both*

Beginning with version 3.0 of Smart, alphabetic sorting followed the collation-table convention, in which upper- and lowercase fields were intermingled without regard to case, rather sorting lowercase after uppercase letters in an ascending sort. This convention has been almost universally adopted throughout the Smart system.

One notable exception to this collation-table convention is found in the Query command. For example, if you have both upper- and lowercase letters, such as codes, in a 1 byte alpha field, the following query

```
[status] >= "A" and [status] <= "G"
```

will exclude all lowercase codes falling within this range, even though a sort will display them in the proper sequence. In the Query command, all lowercase letters still sort after uppercase letters in an ascending-order sort.

To successfully identify the range in accordance with the collation-table sequence, use the following Query definition,

```
upper([status]) >= "A" and upper([status]) <= "G"
```

which converts all codes to uppercase for evaluation in the Query.

Both

7.99 Trick: The physical order of your database can have a significant effect on the speed of your Query commands.

You can speed the operation of your Query commands if you load your database so that the physical order matches the logical order of the key. Your computer will have to perform fewer I/O (input/output) operations to gather the records you want if each physical portion (cluster) of the disk file is read in its entirety before the rest is read.

Only certain applications lend themselves to this technique, however. For example, you could employ this method on a parts catalog that changes only infrequently. Even if the records are not originally entered in the key order, you can order your file, create a new one, and use the Utilities Concatenate command to transfer the data from the original, temporary file to the new, permanent file.

Although in theory you can use this technique with any database, the time it requires versus the benefit it yields may make it not worth your while.

Both

7.100 Trick:: In Smart 3.10, use the File Rename command to save the Query NOW definition in a permanent Query definition file.

The definition for Query Now is actually saved in a file named QNOW.$$$. Use the File Rename command to change the file specification to some other name of your choice, with an extension of DFQ. All permanent Query definitions have an extension of DFQ.

In SmartWare II, the Query Now definition file name is QNOW.DFQ; use the Tools File Rename command to rename it.

SW II

7.101 Trap: Use Alt-F2 to make sure that the specifications of a previous "Query Now" do not impact the current query and give you erroneous results.

When you perform a Data Query Now command, the specifications are stored in a file called QNOW.DFQ. If you perform a later Query Now command, these conditions will carry over if the view is the same or if another view has the same field names. You can add to the query criteria or edit them.

However, there is a potential drawback to the carry-over of the specifications. For example, if the new view is standard and the fields with the conditions extend beyond the viewing area of your monitor, you will not notice them. It is even possible to overlook specifications for small fields in a custom view. By pressing Alt-F2, you clear any previous Query Now criteria.

7.102 Trick: Test a Query definition by using the F2 calculate mode in the Query editor. If the result is 1, the current record will be selected by the Query; if it is 0, the record will be omitted.

Both

To test the Query, go to a record that you would expect to be selected by the Query. In the Query editor, once you have created the definition, press F2 to execute the calculation (F5 in SmartWare II). A result of 1 indicates "true," and that the current record will be selected. If the answer is 0, a false condition exists and the record will not be selected.

This technique is especially useful if you have a large and complex query. The definition does not need to be entirely on the first line; multiple line queries may be used with this technique. Many errors also will be flagged in this process, such as missing parenthesis and unbalanced IF...THEN statements.

In SmartWare II, this technique will work only in the view expression query editor but not QBE definition. If the view expression portion of a combined query is true and the QBE portion is false, the calculation will still be true, because the QBE expression is ignored.

7.103 Tip: Use the following procedures to select records based on the highest numerical value among records with identical breakpoint fields.

SW II

This example is a wage history file in which the important fields are:

SSN
Wage

The goal is to be able to print a report, showing the highest [wage] for each [ssn]. Begin by sorting the view by SSN and Wage in descending order; the highest wage will be the first record in each group of similar SSNs.

Next, perform the following query:

```
[ssn] = fetchfield([ssn]) replace delete
```

Note that in this query, every record but the first for each SSN is marked for deletion. The first is the record with the highest wage. If you do not want to mark the records for deletion, you can perform the following:

```
[ssn] = fetchfield([ssn]) replace [flag] = 1
```

Then query to select only the records in which the Flag field is not equal to 1.

Copying Query Definitions

Both

7.104 Trick: Use Alt-F3 to read an existing Query definition into the Query editor.

The NOW definition, as well as any other Query definition, can be copied in yet another way. When you are in the Query editor, press the Alt-F3 key combination. At the prompt for the name of a file to read, type *QNOW.$$$* and press Enter.

In Smart 3.10, at the end of each physical line of the Query definition is the tilde character (~), which marks a carriage return in the Query definition. For example:

```
[status] <= "2"~
```

The tilde character is generated automatically when you create the Query definition in the editor, but the character is not displayed. When you use Alt-F3 to read another Query into the editor, the tilde is read in along with the rest of the file. You must remove the tilde in order for the Query to work; if you do not remove it, you will get a bad syntax message when you press F10. At the same time, all characters beyond the tilde will be erased from the editor.

To read a predefined Query definition, use Alt-F3 and supply the Query name, including the DFQ extension.

Both

7.105 Tip: The Query command does not automatically ignore deleted records.

If you want to exclude deleted records in your Query definition, you must explicitly specify the condition:

```
[status] = "Y" and [dept] = "ACCT" and not (deleted)
```

This condition retrieves all active records with `Y` in the STATUS field and `ACCT` in the DEPT field. Because you have no other way of requesting active records, you must specify

```
not (deleted).
```

Similarly, you may wish to review all records marked for deletion prior to executing the Utilities Purge command. The following Query will select all deleted records:

```
deleted
```

Documenting Query Definitions

Both

7.106 Tip: Use the DOS Copy command to document your Query definitions.

1. At the DOS level, press Ctrl-P. Now, new text that is displayed on your monitor will also be printed on the printer.

2. Issue the following DOS command:

```
Copy    *.DFQ    CON
```

   This copy command will display all the DFQ Query definitions on the screen (CON). Since you have pressed Ctrl-P, the display is also directed to printer.

3. When all query definitions have been printed, press Ctrl-P again to turn off the echo of the screen display to the printer.

You will now have a hard copy of all query definitions, including the names.

7.107 Tip: Document Query definitions using the following Smart 3.10 project file. The program will write the name of the query and the definition into an external file. *3.10*

```
quiet off
if file("dfq.txt") = 1 then query undefine dfq.txt
command /c dir *.dfq | sort > dos.tmp

fclose 1
fclose 2
fopen "dos.tmp" as 1
fopen "dfq.txt" as 2

label readit
fread 1 into $inline
if cerror > 0 then jump alldone

if left($inline,1) = " " then jump readit

let $flname = trim(left($inline,8))
let $ext    = trim(mid($inline,10,3))

let $filid = $flname|"."|$ext
if  $filid = "." then jump readit
fwrite 2 from $filid
let %2 = $filid

'write the actual dfq contents here
fopen "%2" as 3

label readfq
fread 3 into $dfqline
    if cerror <> 0
        fclose 3
        jump readit
    endif
let $len = len($dfqline)
let $dfqline = left($dfqline,$len-1)
```

```
fwrite 2 from $dfqline
jump readfq

label alldone
fclose 1
fclose 2

file erase dos.tmp
```

Once the file has been created, you can load it into the Wordprocessor and rearrange it.

SW II

7.108 Tip: To document a Query definition, modify it and press Alt-P.

The entire Query specification will be printed, and will include the name, the date and time the query was last modified and when it was printed. Here is an example:

```
Query Definition: acct.dfq
Last Modified:    08/25/1989   13:19:16
Printed:          08/27/1989   10:23:47

field [DEPT] ACCT
not (deleted)
```

Entries from the QBE are followed by any view expression entries.

Using the Replace Facility

3.10

7.109 Tip: Use the Query command to replace the contents of your fields.

With the Query command's replace feature, you can replace field contents either throughout the file (if it is ordered sequentially or by a key) or within the current file view, if it is ordered by an index.

The modifying word for a replacement is replace. The following Query causes the DEPT field value to be replaced with ACCT:

```
replace [dept] = "ACCT"
```

Because you are performing a replacement operation, you do not want the Query results to be stored in an index or displayed on the screen. Thus, when prompted

```
Index Neither Screen
```

within the Query Now or Query Predefined commands, you should choose Neither.

The replace operation can be performed just for records within the database that meet certain conditions, such as

```
[dept] = "ACCT" replace [status] = "X"
```

You can perform multiple replacements simultaneously, as in

```
[dept] = "ACCT" replace [status] = "X", [wage] = 1000
```

Using the Smart functions, you can perform more sophisticated replacement Query commands. An example is shown in figure 7.21.

```
Query Editor
[status] = "Y" replace [wage] =
case [dept] ("ACCT",900) ("MKTG",1000) ("DATA",1100)
else [wage] * 1.1
```

Fig. 7.21.
A Query using Smart functions.

7.110 Trap: Do not insert a comma after the condition when performing a conditional Query replacement; the replacement will not be made, but there will be no error message. *3.10*

Examine the following Query:

```
[dept] = "ACCT" , replace [pct] = 5.9
```

The Query will perform the selection portion of the statement, but will not do the replacement. There is no error message or other indication that the replacement did not take place. Therefore, do not insert a comma after the condition.

7.111 Tip: Use the DATE2 function when replacing dates in a database. *3.10*

Using the DATE2 function guarantees that the format of the date will be correct in the field. Although

```
replace [fdate] = "5/2/43"
```

will work, it is more consistent to use the DATE2 function, as in

```
replace [fdate] = date2("5/2/43")
```

so that the result in the field appears as 05/02/43 rather than 5/2/43.

7.112 Tip: When replacing a date, using QBE, a variety of formats are available. *SW II*

Any of the following formats are acceptable:

```
DATE:   <- 6/20/65
DATE:   <- "6/20/65"
DATE:   <- days("6/20/65")
```

```
DATE:   replace 6/20/65
DATE:   replace "6/20/65"
DATE:   replace days("6/20/65")
```

Note that the "arrow" is formed by the "less than" symbol and a dash.

3.10

7.113 Trap: The Query command's Replace feature does not automatically update your keys and does not prompt you to do so.

Although there may be no problem if you choose not to update your keys when you have replaced only a data field, you may be surprised when you execute the Report command and get a warning message that your file contains unmerged records. This message indicates that your keys may not have been updated.

However, if you are replacing a key field in your database and you choose not to update your keys, your file will be in an incorrect order when you order it by the affected key. The previous order will still be in effect in the key file. If you want to order by the keys correctly, you must remember to perform the Key Update command.

3.10

7.114 Trap: Change a field that is not available in the current view by using a Query with replacement.

Even though the field may not be available on the current screen, you can nonetheless perform a Query replacement. You may reference the field by number or name, if known. This represents both a feature and a potential security weakness.

SW II

7.115 Trap: You cannot perform a replacement Query into read-only fields as is possible in Smart 3.10.

If the SmartWare II field is read-only and you try to assign a value to it, you will get the following error message:

```
Cannot assign value to field
```

If you are converting to SmartWare II and have taken advantage of the fact that you can assign values to read-only fields in Smart 3.10, make sure you use views in which the field is optional.

3.10

7.116 Trick Use a single Query definition to replace values in your database and create an index simultaneously.

The selection criteria in the Query definition will apply to both the field replacement and the creation of the index. Using this technique will save time, compared to performing two successive queries. But be careful if you convert to SmartWare II. This technique will not work because a replacement Query cannot be used to create an index.

3.10

7.117 Trap: Using the trim function in a replacement Query will reverse the effects of reforming a large alpha field key during either Enter or Update.

When entering or updating a record, the F8 key will insert blanks so that words in a large alpha field are not split between lines.

If you use the trim function in a replacement Query, the effects of the field reform are reversed because multiple blanks are removed, and you will have to reform each field manually during an Update command.

7.118 Tip: When entering several replacements in a QBE query, each replacement is independent. One cannot rely on the result of another, since each operates as if the others do not exist. *SW II*

For example, you cannot successfully perform the following in a QBE query:

PERCENT: <– 5.2
NEW WAGE: <– [wage] + [wage] * [percent] / 100

In this example, the second replacement should depend on the first. If you need to write a Query in which you have dependent replacements, use a view expression. A view expression equivalent to this QBE query is as follows:

```
replace [percent]  = 5.2 ,
     [new wage] = [wage] + [wage] * [percent] / 100
```

Replacements in a view expression will follow the order in which they have been written.

7.119 Tip: In a QBE query definition in which you are both selecting and replacing simultaneously, the "replace" specification must be entered into a field by itself. *SW II*

For example, if the goal is to replace a Percent field for those that are less than 5.2, the QBE statements would be:

ACCUM: [percent] < 5.2
PERCENT: replace 5.2

Note that the view expression format of the criterion is entered into another field in the QBE screen, not into the replacement field. You may be tempted to write the following:

PERCENT: < 5.2 <– 5.2

Zero matches will be found if you use this format. The following format will cause a syntax error:

PERCENT: < 5.2 replace 5.2

You may also use a combination of a QBE expression and a view expression. The QBE expression is:

PERCENT: < 5.2

The view expression is:

```
replace [percent] = 5.2
```

In this combination, the QBE performs the selection, and the view expression does the replacement.

SW II

7.120 Tip: Use the Fetchfield function within a Query to accumulate values from record to record, using a break field.

Let's say you have a file with multiple pay records for several employees, each record representing a pay period. The task is to accumulate the pay for each employee so that each record reflects not only the pay for that period, but also the year-to-date payments. This example uses the following fields in the file:

SSN
Date
Wage
Accum

Begin by performing a query to select the time period for the accumulation. Sort the file by SSN and date, ascending. Then execute the following query:

```
replace [accum] =
if record = 1 then [wage] else
if [ssn] <> fetchfield([ssn]) then [wage] else
[wage] + fetchfield([accum])
```

Note that there is special treatment for record 1, because a Fetchfield function from this record will yield NA (not available.)

Deleting and Activating Records with a Query

Both

7.121 Tip: Not only can you replace the contents of fields with the Query command, but also you can change the active status of records.

The format of a Query definition to delete records is similar to the following:

```
[dept] = "ACCT" replace delete
```

This command marks for deletion all records for which the department is ACCT. This facility is different from the Delete command because Query does not toggle the delete status. The "replace delete" definition forces a record to be marked for deletion, whether the record was previously deleted or not. You also can force selected records to be active. An example would be

```
[wage] > 1000 replace activate
```

3.10

7.122 Tip: For greater speed, do not delete records that are already deleted.

If you want to delete all records, you can issue the following Query:

```
replace delete
```

Although this command will have the desired effect, the following way is faster:

```
not (deleted) replace delete
```

This second method, in which only the active records are deleted, is faster because only the changed records have to be written back into the database. The larger the database, the more evident the time savings will be.

Refer to Appendix A for a project file that will quickly purge all records from a database.

7.123 Tip: For greater safety, perform a complex replacement in two steps. ***Both***

Although you can perform a Query replacement for selected records in one step (see fig. 7.22), you may find that the safer route is to perform the Query in two steps.

First, select the target records into an Index. You then can view these records to verify that your selection worked correctly. Once you are satisfied that the selection is accurate, perform the second Query with the actual replacement.

If your selection is complicated, I recommend this two-step procedure. When you have changed your database, you cannot change your mind.

7.124 Trap: When using the *replace delete* capability with a selection criterion, don't forget the word *replace*. ***Both***

If you omit the *replace*, the Query will be executed and the correct number of records will be displayed, but the deletion will not take place. The error is not caught by the Query editor or the command. However, if a Query consists of only the word delete instead of *replace delete*, without any qualifying criteria, the Query editor recognizes the query as a syntax error.

7.125 Tip: Use a Query...Neither command within a project file when validating a code (see fig. 7.22). ***3.10***

The record located will not be displayed; the purpose of the Query is simply to determine whether the record exists. Using the Neither option is slightly faster than using the Index option, in this case, because the index file does not have to be created.

7.126 Tip: Query definitions can contain variables. ***Both***

Look at figure 7.22. The Query used in the example is

```
where [ssn] = $ssn
```

This feature can help you automate your Query executions within project files. Use variables on the right side of your Query equations only.

Fig. 7.22.
Using a Query for validation in a project file.

```
Project File Editor
'find and validate an ssn in the file

goto window 1
order key [ssn]

label askssn
input $ssn Enter the SSN:

comment ** Query is: where [ssn] = $ssn
query predefined ssn neither
if cerror <> 3003 then jump okssn
beep 2
message SSN not found ... please enter again ... press any key
jump askssn

label okssn

F1 Help      F3 Find      F5 Replace        F7 Insert line       F9 Repeat
F2 Calc      F4 Goto      F6 List fields    F8 Delete line       F10 Finish
                                  Line:    1  Column:  1      Insert: ON
REMEMBER - create a new project file or modify an existing file
```

SW II

7.127 Tip In a project file, if you want to execute a Query definition containing a variable, the variable must be Public, not Global or Local. The variable does not have to be locked, however.

If the variable has been declared as Local or Global, the execution of the Data Query will generate the following error message:

```
Variable not found
```

3.10

7.128 Tip: Query definitions cannot contain parameters, but you can employ user-defined variables.

The following Query definition is legal:

```
[ssn] = $ssn
```

In your project file, you would assign a value to the $ssn variable, and perform this predefined Query. The following Query is not valid, however:

```
[ssn] = %1
```

Parameters have no significance outside project files because their function is to provide a facility for run-time substitution of statements in project files.

3.10

7.129 Trick: Construct a Query definition from a project file.

A Query definition is simply an ASCII file, with the addition of the tilde character to mark the end of a line. There is no reason you cannot construct a Query within a project file, using the file access commands, if you require a great deal of flexibility and control. Appendix A contains a series of six project files designed to construct and execute a Query. Note that the tilde character is actually inserted into the constructed Query definition file.

7.130 Tip: Perform a manual Query if the criteria are complex or your database is small. *3.10*

In a manual Query, you are prompted to indicate whether you want to select the current record (see fig. 7.23).

```
Window 1
  SSN         FIRST      LAST       AG S M DE DEG CA STREET           CITY
  345-98-7593 Rosanna    Ronaldo    52 M M  3 BA   2 546 Olive Hill   Oak Park
  498-48-3980 Debbie     Linden     29 F S  1 MA   2 409 Pleasant St  Amherst
  239-87-0876 Michael    Davis      61 M M  1 MBA  2 100 Lewis Ave.   Covington
  208-23-0300 Julius     Karenski   41 M D  0 PhD  1 18 Olive St.     Louisvill
  087-63-5498 Jeff       Harris     34 M M  4 BA   5 1201 Horton Rd.  Lyndhurst
->598-44-5922 LeAnne     Markus     48 F W  1 MBA  1 14 Crumpet Ave.  Alamosa
  876-33-0989 Marilyn    Lester     55 F M  4 AB   3 6 Greenville St  Yarmouth
  987-65-7653 David      Marzetti   47 M D  0      1 20 Grayln Dr.    Wilmingto
  387-59-8374 Charles    Steffans   25 M M  2 BS   2 44 Center Drive  Brunswick
  498-34-5998 Paula      Bernstein  30 F S  3 MA   3 10 Worcester St  Beaumont
  776-39-8763 Alfred     Adelson    60 M M  0 BA   1 14 Spring St.    Hartford
  345-54-2287 Ellen      Aliakbari  35 F S  0      1 2171 University  Westfield
  198-03-3024 Howard E.  Peters     18 M S  0      1 10 Dennis Drive  Winnfield

Select record (y or n)
Record 6 out of 13 - 4 records selected
File: person   Window: 1                         Page: 1  Rec: 6  ( 6 )  Act: Y
QUERY - select records meeting specified criteria
```

Fig. 7.23.
A manual Query.

From a practical point of view, you can perform a manual Query only on small files, because you must view each record and indicate with a Y or N whether the record is to be included in the index. Once you have begun, you can escape from the Query, but any selections made are discarded. You cannot use Ctrl-Z to terminate the Query and retain the prior selections. The manual Query always begins with the first record.

Performing Queries on a Network

7.131 Tip: On a network, create Query and Sort index files on your local hard disk, rather than in the application subdirectory on the network drive. *Both*

If you create the index files on the network in the application subdirectory, you run the risk of interfering with another user on the network writing the same index name at the same time. This is most likely to happen if you are running a project file, in which the index names are built into the program. Although you can write the index files to your own subdirectory on the network, if you use your local hard disk, access will be faster than via the network.

7.132 Tip: On a network, issue the Lock-Record command prior to performing a Query that replaces data in your file. *Both*

On a network, you must make sure that two users are not able to update the same record at the same time. But when performing a Query that replaces data, you cannot lock individual records. However, you must issue the Lock-Record command to protect the whole file as shown in the following example:

```
Lock-Record
Query Predefined Changit Neither
```

Query by Example

SW II

7.133 Tip: If the total number of characters in a QBE expression exceeds 255, use a view expression instead.

If the QBE expression is so extensive that it would exceed 255 characters, you must use a view expression. Press Alt-Q to bring up the view expression editor screen.

SW II

7.134 Tip: Use the F3 key to return to a QBE field to view a selection criterion that is too long to be seen in the field area itself.

A long QBE field criterion may not be visible within the field itself, especially if the field is short. For example, if you have an A2 field called [State], the following selection criterion will not be seen: MO or IL or TX or MA. If you want to view the criterion to check your work after you have typed it, press Enter and then press F3 to return to the field. The criterion will be shown on the second command line at the bottom of your screen; you'll be able to see the field specification all the way across your monitor screen.

SW II

7.135 Tip: The F8 key will clear the contents of the field in a Query QBE; however, the display of the definition that appears on the command line will not be cleared.

Even though the displayed definition is not cleared, pressing F8 actually does clear the criterion from the field. Don't worry about the display of the previous contents. After entering a new criterion, press Enter and F3 to display the new criterion on the command line.

SW II

7.136 Tip: In a QBE Query, alpha field search items usually do not need quotation marks around them, even if there are spaces. Occasionally, you *do* need quotation marks, however.

A list of state abbreviations that includes Oregon must use quotation marks because of the dual interpretation of "OR":

"IL" OR "OR" OR "MO" OR "MA" OR "LA"

A special character that might be interpreted as part of the query structure needs quotation marks. For example, if you are looking for a record in which the field contains an exclamation point, you need quote marks:

! "!"

Normally, however, you do not need quotation marks.

7.137 Tip: Combine QBE and view expression criteria within the same Query definition for flexibility and ease of entry. *SW II*

Straightforward conditions are easy to enter in QBE. Complex expressions are better entered in the view expression editor. If you have a compound set of criteria, enter the straightforward, equality tests in the QBE editor. Then press Alt-Q to enter the complex tests into the view editor. For a database record to be selected, it must pass the tests in both the QBE portion *and* the view expression at the same time.

7.138 Tip: Enter multiple summary statistic specifications in the same QBE field with commas between them. *SW II*

For example, if you want the sum, minimum, and average of a numeric field, enter the following in the field on the QBE screen:

```
filesum, filemin, fileaverage
```

The resulting summary display will show the values for all three statistics.

7.139 Tip: Screening criteria for summary statistics on multiple fields are additive; and the criteria apply to the whole file, not just the individual fields. *SW II*

Consider the following example:

Field	*QBE Expression*
Age	> 45 , fileaverage
Wage	< 1000 , filemax

The screening criteria operate on the file independent of the summary statistic functions. In this example, the only records considered are those in which the Age is greater than 45 *and* the Wage is less than 1000. Then the average age and the maximum wage for the selected employees are displayed.

7.140 Tip: Create a QBE Query definition by using the Tools Text-Editor; it may be faster and give you greater flexibility. *SW II*

The format of a QBE definition is as follows:

```
field [fieldname] value
```

For example, a query to test for a department equal to ACCT is:

```
field [dept] ACCT
```

If there are many fields, it may be faster to type the QBE definition, using the Tools Text-Editor, rather than using the QBE screen.

Any view expression entries must be listed after the QBE entries, as in the following example:

```
field [dept] ACCT
([degree] = "MS" or [degree] = "MBA") or
[skill] == "RS" and not (deleted)
```

In this example, the first line is the QBE expression, and lines 2 and 3 are view expressions.

SW II

7.141 Tip Browse only the fields you need to make field access faster when defining a QBE query.

In the Query by Example screens (QBE), addressing each field is sequential; you must press F4 (or Enter) to get from one field to the next. If you have only a few fields, this does not take much time. However, if you have many fields and you need to get to the last one, advancing from field to field can be time consuming.

If you use the Data Browse command to select only those fields that are significant in the Query, you will be able to address these fields quickly.

SW II

7.142 Tip: When defining a Query in which you want to create entries for table fields, execute the command Data Goto Table before beginning the Query definition.

If you go to the table before initiating the Query definition, the cursor will already be in the table area. If there are many fields in the view, or if there are multiple tables, this technique will save you some time.

SW II

7.143 Tip: A Data Query on custom view table fields selects records from the main file, not the table.

Refer to figure 7.24.

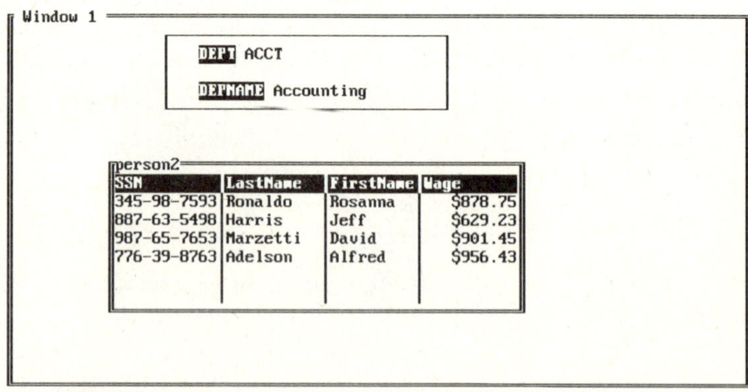

Fig. 7.24.

A table field Data Query.

Here is an example of a QBE query on the Wage field:

```
> 800
```

Because the Wage field is in the table area, the meaning of the query is: "Find all main view records which have at least one table record in which the wage is greater than 800." At the conclusion of the query, the record (visible in figure 7.24) will be included, because there are several table records that satisfy the criterion. All four table records will be available, even though one of them contains a wage less than 800.

If you want only those departments in which all employees are making more than 800, enter the following statement in any field *outside* the table area:

```
tablemin([wage]) > 800
```

In this example, the lowest wage of any table record must be greater than 800 for the main file to be accepted.

Special Query Topics

7.144 Trap: Due to trailing blanks, a Query in a project file may fail where the Find command will succeed. *3.10*

If there are trailing blanks in a field in one file but not in a corresponding field in another file, under project file control, a Find command succeeds in spite of the blanks:

```
goto window 1
let text1 = [field]
goto window 2
let %1 = text1
find [field] equal %1 options
```

This Find will succeed because the trailing blanks are not included in the parameter. In this instance, do *not* enclose the parameter in the find command within parenthesis. However, compare the following query :

```
[field] = text1
```

This query will fail, because the trailing blanks are retained in the variable. To strip any trailing blanks, use the following query definition:

```
trim([field]) = trim(text1)
```

This query will make sure that there are no trailing blanks in either the field or the variable.

7.145 Tip: In a project file, use the Keys Esc command to clear the Query summary from the screen. *SW II*

At the completion of a Query, a summary of the results is displayed on the screen. When you are operating at the command level, you simply press the Escape key to clear the summary display. In a project file, issuing the Keys Esc command after the Data Query statement will have the same effect.

```
data query execute "acct" index "ind1.idx"
keys esc

if cerror <> 0
     sound 200 .5
     message "No records retrieved ... press any key .."
     stop
end if
```

If you do not want the Query summary displayed on the screen, you should use Repaint Off. Check for any error codes after the Keys Esc command.

SW II

7.146 Trap: The cerror following a successful query should always be zero, but sometimes it is not. To be on the safe side, check for the specific cerror code, rather than a non-zero result.

Normally, you would expect the following statements to work successfully:

```
Data Query Execute "name.dfq" index "ind1.idx"
keys esc
if cerror <> 0
    'additional statements here
end if
```

And normally, this statement will work fine, and will execute the additional statements only if the Query does not find any matches. However, there have been instances in which matches have been found and in which the cerror is not equal to zero. Therefore, it is safer to test as follows:

```
if cerror = 3143
```

This error code means "no matches found."

SW II

7.147 Trap: The key order of a view is not maintained during a Query as it is in Smart 3.10; sort the view after executing a Data Query.

In Smart 3.10, if a file is ordered by a key, the index that results from a query will keep this same key order, but you will be working with fewer records, due to the selection process of the Query.

In SmartWare II, the key order is not maintained in the query. Thus, if you want your records to be in a certain order following a Query, you must execute an Order Sort command once the Query has completed. Unlike key order, however, if you have sorted the file to an index prior to the Query, this sort order will be retained.

7.148 Tip: Use a combination of the key and keys statements in a project file to query a database using wild card characters; you cannot use a variable to do this.

SW II

For example, if you want to develop a query to select those records in which the third letter of the [dept] field is a "T", the QBE entry would be:

```
??T?
```

This is fine if you always want to perform the same query, but if you would like to prompt for a different set of selection rules each time, you cannot have a variable that contains this string. The following is a project file which can be used to solve the problem:

```
local $string
order change physical
data browse fields "[dept]"
tools file erase "qnow.dfq"
screen shortinput $string "Screening string:"
key define "#1000" chr(34)|$string|chr(34)
suspendone command
keys "dqn",look,#1000,F10,esc
```

Note that the program prompts for the wild card selection string, which is then assigned to a macro key and used in the Keys statement, executing the Data Query Now command.

7.149 Tip: Use the FETCHFIELD function to find records in which a field is unique.

SW II

Sort the file by the field you want to identify. Then use the following Query.

```
[field] <> fetchfield([field])
```

Because the FETCHFIELD function references the previously accessed record, this Dat Query definition will compare the [field] in the current record to that of the previous record, and will select only those records unequal to the previous record. Note, that in order to use this technique, you must *sort* the file; you cannot simply order it by the key, because the query would ignore the key order and process the file in physical order rather than logical order.

7.150 Tip: Use the following project file and query to isolate the current record in an index by itself.

SW II

For example, if you want to print a report that consists of just the current record, you can isolate it easily by this project file and Query:

```
public $record
let $record = precord
data query execute "onerec" index "onerec"
keys esc
```

The Onerec query consists of the following:

```
record = $record
```

Note that this is an optimized query, and hence will run quickly.

SW II

7.151 Tip: In a project file, use the Order Manual command to quickly select the current record.

Refer to the following example:

```
Tools File Erase "ind1.idx"
Order Manual "ind1"
Keys F7,F10
```

The current record will be inserted into index Ind1 immediately; you do not have to perform a time-consuming Query to isolate just the current record.

SW II

7.152 Tip: In a project file, use the following code to allow a user to enter the specifications for a Query definition and then execute it.

```
Tools File Erase "qnow.dfq"
Data Query Now
Keys Until,F10
Keys Esc
```

By using this code, the QBE editor is displayed, allowing you to enter a Query definition. When you press the F10, execution resumes. Note that the Qnow.dfq file is erased, thus eliminating any previous Query Now definition.

If you want to use the Query view expression, you will have to select another key to indicate the end of the query, since the F10 key is needed to save the view expression.

SW II

7.153 Trick: Query the standard view and then apply the index to the custom view to save processing time.

Frequently, processing a standard view will be faster than a custom view for the same file. This is especially true if you have multiple files attached to the view or have several calculated view fields. If you have enough information in the standard view to perform the Query, you often can save time by executing the Query in the standard view, and then ordering the custom view by the resulting index. Here is an example:

```
data goto view "person2.vws"
data query execute "acct.dfq" index "ind1.idx"
keys esc
order change physical

data goto view "person2.vw"
order change index "ind1.idx"
```

You cannot use this technique if you need data from one of the attached files or view fields to perform the query.

7.154 Tip: Use a Query with database summary functions to create an ASCII file from a project file program. Use this in place of a Data Cross-Tabs.

SW II

Here is an example:

```
public $dept
tools file erase "depwage.dat"
screen shortinput $dept "Department code:"

data query execute "depwage"
keys Alt-W,"depwage.dat",Enter,Esc
```

The resulting file will be in the following format:

13 records searched
4 matches found
Sum of [Wage]: $3,365.86

Note that the field formatting is retained in the file. In this example, the query used was:

```
field [DEPT] $dept
field [Wage] filesum
```

Because the the program must be able to display the result on the screen, Repaint must be turned on prior to the Query command.

Part III

The Spreadsheet

Includes

Setting Parameters and Entering Data

Operating the Worksheet

Functions

Working with Multiple Files

Printing, Reporting, and Integrating the Spreadsheet

Graphics

8

Setting Parameters and Entering Data

This chapter covers some of the first tasks you perform in the Spreadsheet module: setting defaults and entering data. The way you set your defaults has an effect on the entry of data, so understanding the relationship between those tasks is important.

Setting Parameters

Spreadsheet parameters determine the default settings for new worksheets and for the operating environment during each session. Some Spreadsheet parameter settings take effect immediately, but others do not come into play until the next time you initiate a Spreadsheet session.

8.1 Tip: Establish default settings for new worksheets and each operating session with Spreadsheet parameters. *3.10*

The Parameters menu is shown in figures 8.1 and 8.2.

8.2 Tip: Most changes you make to the Parameters selections take effect immediately within the Spreadsheet environment or affect new worksheets created during the session. *3.10*

When you change parameters, existing worksheets are not affected. The automatic loading of macro files and worksheet files takes effect only when you begin a Spreadsheet session.

Default format settings and the column-width selection (see fig. 8.2) do not change the characteristics of even a blank worksheet. To cause these settings to take effect, you must Quit the Spreadsheet and begin again.

8.3 Tip: The default Recalculation mode can be set on either Automatic or Manual. ***Both***

Fig. 8.1.
Spreadsheet parameters (first screen).

```
Spreadsheet Parameters
→ Recalculation: Automatic Manual
  Display of recalculation counts: Yes No

  Confidence: 1 2 3 No-Change
  Prompting mode: Menu Key-Word Key-Word/Auto-Recognition
  Autohelp: Yes No No Change
  Display mode: Black/White Color Graphics No-Change

  Display of file names for file prompting: Yes No
  Automatic file backup: Yes No

  Automatic load of macro file:
  Automatic load of worksheet:

  Quiet execution of project files: Yes No
  Single-step execution of project files: Yes No
```

Fig. 8.2.
Spreadsheet parameters (second screen).

```
  Default value format
    Select notation: Normal E-Notation
    Select precision: 0 1 2 3 4 5 6 7 8 9
    Currency notation: Yes No
    Commas: Yes No

→ Default column width: 10

F1 Help    F2 Edit text    F3 Blank text    F10 Finished
parameters
Worksheet: (none)    Loc: r1c1              FN:      Font: Standard
PARAMETERS - set spreadsheet parameters
```

Selecting Automatic mode causes the worksheet to recalculate after every entry. This mode may be what you want to use if you are actively using a model. If you are developing a model, however, you may not want to wait for the recalculation or see a screen full of errors just because you have not finished development. In Smart 3.10, if you change the Parameters menu, any new worksheet you create is initialized with Recalculation mode. In SmartWare II, use the Tools Preferences Spreadsheet command to establish the default recalculation mode; to set the recalculation order in SmartWare II, use the Layout Worksheet-Options New-Sheet command.

You always can change your Recalculation mode during a session by executing the Auto-Recalc command on list 5 (see fig. 8.3). In SmartWare II, use the Sheet Calc-Mode command.

If you select Manual recalculation, you must press the F5 key to recalculate your worksheet. You can determine whether your worksheet needs to be recalculated when the symbol **CALC** appears on the status line, as in figure 8.3. In SmartWare II, pressing F5 recalculates only those formulas that depend on cells that have changed. Shift-F5 forces total recalculation of the entire worksheet.

3.10

8.4 Tip: If you select Yes to display recalculation counts, a count of the number of formulas and recalculations appears briefly on the second command line when the calculation is completed.

```
16
17
18
Select option: Automatic Display Iterate Manual
auto-recalc
Worksheet: sample     Loc: r1c2          CALC  FN: 0    Font: Standard
AUTO-RECALC  specifies when formulas are recalculated
```

Fig. 8.3.
Auto-Recalc modes.

The program does not pause for this display, so you must look quickly. (If you need to know the number of formulas, you can always execute the Index command.) After you have created a worksheet specifying the recalculation-counts display, you cannot alter this setting. Unlike the Auto-Recalc setting, this parameter setting has no corresponding command.

8.5 Tip: Set your confidence number at a level appropriate to the commands you expect to be executed at the Spreadsheet command level. *3.10*

Because you want access to all the commands when you are developing a model or a worksheet, you should select confidence level 3. If your system is to be used by novices, you may want to set the confidence level at 1 or 2. During the session, you can use the Confidence command on command list 5 to change your confidence level.

8.6 Tip: The Prompting mode is somewhat independent of the confidence level. *3.10*

If you select Menu, the confidence level governs the commands displayed on each command list. If you select Key-Word or Key-Word/Auto Recognition, the confidence-levels selection of parameters has no bearing. All commands are available in both Key-Word or Key-Word/Auto Recognition, even though you may have selected confidence level 1 or 2.

The Key-Word selection displays the command on the command line as soon as the system identifies the command you are typing. Execution begins when you press Enter. The Key-Word/Auto Recognition option causes the command to be executed immediately when the system identifies the unique initial characters of the command.

The Confidence command, on command list 5, is a combination of Key-Word and Key-Word/Auto Recognition. Confidence levels 1, 2, and 3 invoke menu prompting at the selected level. Confidence level 4 is the same as Key-Word and level 5 is Key-Word/Auto Recognition.

8.7 Tip: Turn off the Autohelp line to speed the operation of your system when you are using a disk-based system. *3.10*

If your Autohelp line is On, the system must access a file to retrieve the explanatory text and display it at the bottom of the screen. This delay is not noticeable on a hard disk system, but on a floppy-based system, the delay can be significant enough to slow you down.

Unfortunately, turning off the Autohelp line does not increase the usable screen area in the way that disabling a window border increases the amount of visible data.

Both

8.8 Tip: If you do not want to be prompted with a popup menu of file names, select No for the option of displaying the file names for prompting.

Not displaying file names may add a degree of security to your application. In Smart 3.10, the selection is found in the Parameters menu; in SmartWare II, execute the Tools Preferences Global command.

Both

8.9 Tip: If you want an automatic backup of each worksheet, select Yes for the automatic-backup option.

You can have your files backed up automatically when you save a changed worksheet that you have loaded from disk. The original copy is renamed with an extension of BWS and the new version is written to a normal worksheet file with an extension of WS. Each time you save the file, the most recent WS copy becomes BWS and the copy in RAM is written to the WS file.

Because successive BWS files are created each time you save your worksheet during a session, specifying automatic backup does not protect you completely against mistakes. If you destroy a portion of your worksheet, you can always reload the original. Even if you destroy a portion of your worksheet and save it, you can reload the backup copy. However, if you destroy a part of your worksheet and save it *twice*, even the BWS file contains your errors.

In Smart 3.10, the selection is found in the Parameters menu; in SmartWare II, execute the Tools Preferences Global command.

Both

8.10 Trick: To recover from a backup file, erase the WS file and rename the BWS file as WS.

To recover from a backup file, you must erase the original WS file and then rename the BWS file with a WS extension. Files with a BWS extension cannot be loaded.

Unload the worksheet before you attempt to load the backed up WS file because you cannot reload an active file. You must perform the Rename command because the BWS file is not recognized as a worksheet.

Both

8.11 Trap: Do not use Save All as you would use the Unload All command.

If you execute the Save command and respond with the worksheet name "All," the current spreadsheet is renamed to ALL and is saved under that name. By contrast, if you Unload All, all open spreadsheets are unloaded (and saved) under their respective names.

Both

8.12 Trap: The commands Unload All (3.10) or File Unload All (SmartWare II) do not automatically save modified worksheets for you, as is the case in the Database module.

In the Spreadsheet module, when you issue the Unload command and have more than one worksheet open, you are prompted:

```
Enter worksheet name:
```

If you answer *All*, you are prompted:

Smart 3.10:	`Are you sure? (y/n)`
SmartWare II:	`Unload all files without saving? (y/n)`

You get this prompt even if none of the worksheets have been modified since the last Save command. If you answer *Y*, all the worksheets are saved again. If you answer *N*, the command is aborted. In the Database module, when you Unload All, all files are unloaded without any further prompts.

8.13 Trick: Use the following project file to display the names of multiple loaded files to enable you to select the file to unload.

SW II

The File Unload command in the Spreadsheet module does not display the names of the loaded worksheets; in the other modules, the names of the loaded views or documents are displayed. Rather than executing the File Display-Active command to view the names of the loaded worksheets, use the following project file to unload one of several loaded worksheets.

```
'Name: Unload
'declare user defined variables
local $files $choice $unload

'list of the currently loaded worksheets
let $files = currfiles(0)

'display popup menu of loaded worksheets and return
location #
screen prompt 15 1 21 80 fgpleasing bgpleasing \
     $files $choice "Select File to Unload"

'get the name of the selected worksheet from number location
let $unload = group($files,$choice)

'force prompt for save before unloading if worksheet modified
reply nothing to 1004

'unload the selected worksheet
file unload $unload
```

To make use of this project file easier, you can redefine the Alt-U key as follows:

```
F8,"Unload",enter,"I"
```

This redefinition executes the Unload project file in memory.

Both

8.14 Tip: To load a macro file automatically, enter the macro file name in the Parameters menu of Smart 3.10, or the Tools Preferences Spreadsheet menu of SmartWare II. Do not enter the file extension.

Include any needed path, subdirectory, or drive designation. If none is specified, the current drive and subdirectory are assumed. If you have similarly named macro files in separate subdirectories, the parameter setting always loads the file by the name from the current directory. If you want to use the same standard set of defined and saved macros from any subdirectory, however, enter a drive and path designation.

Both

8.15 Tip: To load a worksheet automatically, enter the worksheet name in the Parameters menu in Smart 3.10; use Tools Preferences Spreadsheet in SmartWare II.

The worksheet named in this parameter setting is loaded each time you initiate the Spreadsheet module.

An alternative method of loading a worksheet when you begin a session is to use the command-execution entry switch. The command

```
SMART S -ALOAD BUDGET
```

loads the budget worksheet as you enter the Spreadsheet module.

Similarly, you can begin the execution of a project file when you initiate the module. The DOS command

```
SMART  S -PLOADALL
```

executes the Loadall project file as you enter the Spreadsheet module. The first statement of the project file can, of course, load a worksheet for you:

Smart 3.10:	`Load Budget`
SmartWare II:	`File Load Budget`

For more information on Smart entry switches, refer to Chapter 1.

Both

8.16 Trick: Type the file name and extension when loading a worksheet that has a file extension other than WS.

Normally, worksheets have extensions of WS to identify them. When you execute the File Load command (Load in Smart 3.10), the popup window displays the names of the files in the current subdirectory having this extension. The spreadsheet module enables you to use an extension other than WS, however. When you are prompted to enter a file name and the popup window appears, type the name of the file and the extension at the prompt.

After a worksheet with an extension other than WS has been loaded, the worksheet retains this original extension, even though only the file name is shown on the status line. When you save your worksheet, the worksheet is not saved with the normal extension of WS, but rather with the original extension with which the worksheet was loaded. If you are backing up your worksheets, however, the backups will have the BWS extension.

Although you can load a worksheet with an extension other than WS, this does not apply to worksheets with the following extensions:

bws bsp bks

8.17 Tip: Quiet execution suppresses the command display as the project file executes and allows the project file to execute faster. ***Both***

Not only is execution cosmetically cleaner if you do not display the commands, but your project files execute faster. Under quiet execution, however, statements causing errors are not displayed.

Rather than specifying that all project files are to be executed in Quiet mode, you can place the statement *Quiet on* within your project file.

8.18 Tip: Single-step execution is used to cause a project file to pause before executing each command. Do not turn this setting On, however; you will have more flexibility controlling it within the individual project file. ***Both***

This feature can be turned on and off within a project file by the following commands:

Smart 3.10	*SmartWare II*
`Singlestep on`	`Single-step on`
`Singlestep off`	`Single-step off`

When Singlestep is on, you are prompted

```
Execute the following command? (y/n)
```

for each command in the project file. This feature can help you debug even the most complex project files. In SmartWare II, the command uses a hyphen: Single-Step On.

8.19 Tip: The options for value formats define the initial settings for values you enter into the worksheet. ***Both***

The difference between the Normal and E-Notation displays can be seen in figure 8.4. For business applications, you probably want to select Normal Notation. For scientific applications or federal government budgets, select E-Notation.

The Precision selection refers to the number of decimal places. Currency notation refers to the display of your selected currency symbol (for example, the $ symbol). If you select commas, they are inserted between the thousands positions of values. (You have the option of using either commas or periods as decimal separators, depending on your Configure Setting in 3.20 or Tools Preference Global in SmartWare II.)

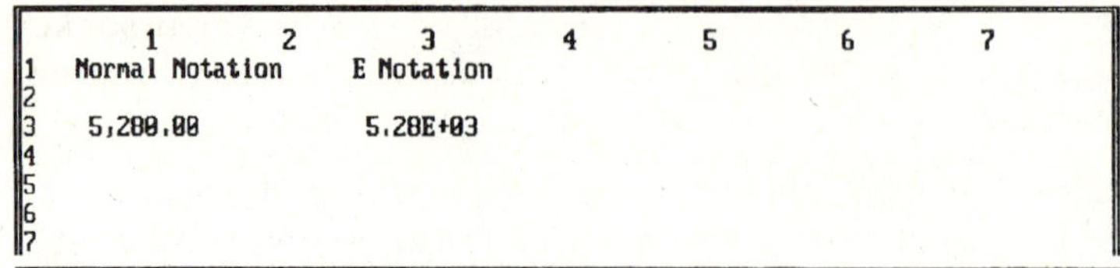
	1	2	3	4	5	6	7
1	Normal Notation		E Notation				
2							
3	5,200.00		5.20E+03				
4							
5							
6							
7							

Fig. 8.4.
Normal versus E-Notation.

Both

8.20 Tip: The default column width is set initially to 10 columns when you install Smart.

Column width refers to actual character positions, including commas, decimal positions, the decimal point, the percent symbol, the minus sign, and dollar signs. If a value is too big for the column, asterisks appear in the cell. You can change the default cell width with the Parameters command in Smart 3.10 and with Layout Worksheet-options New-sheet in SmartWare II. You can change the width of any column with the Width command on command list 3 in Smart 3.10, or by using the Layout Cell-Size Width command in SmartWare II.

Entering Data in the Spreadsheet

There are many ways to enter data into the spreadsheet—some are faster and more efficient than others. This section presents different ways of entering data, both manually and from project files.

Command Mode versus Enter Mode

Both

8.21 Tip: Several data types can be entered from Command mode.

From Command mode, you can press the equal sign (=) to enter a short formula or Alt-F for a long formula. For text, enter a double quotation mark ("). Use the @ symbol to enter a date in the date1 format or the # symbol for the date2 format. A value with a leading currency symbol may be entered with an initial dollar sign.

After you enter your first value from the command level, the system does not return to the command level but remains in Enter mode. Press Esc if you want to return to the command level. (The long-formula editor invoked with Alt-F returns to the command level, however.) If you make a mistake when entering cell contents from the command level, press Esc; you then will be in Enter mode.

Using the Cursor Key or the Enter Key

Both

8.22 Tip: When entering data, except in formulas, you can use the cursor key to advance to the next cell.

You do not have to press Enter before pressing the cursor key. If you are editing a cell, you must use the Enter key or the F10 key to terminate the edit. You cannot use the cursor keys.

8.23 Trick: In a project file, use the Keys command rather than the Cursor Right or Cursor Left commands to skip zero width columns. *SW II*

When you are at the command level, the highlighted cursor block does not enter a cell in a zero width column. Therefore, pressing the right-arrow key causes the cursor to go from column 1 to column 3, skipping a zero width column 2. In a project file, however, the cursor will move into a zero width column. If you want to skip any zero width columns in a project file, use the following command:

```
suspend command
keys Right, F8
```

8.24 Tip: In a project file, use the cursor motion commands rather than the Goto (cell) command to address an adjacent cell—the cursor motion commands work faster. *3.10*

The following is one way to move the cursor down:

```
let %1 = 5
while not (isblank(rc))
     let %1 = %1 + 1
     goto r%1c3
endwhile
```

This method does not work as fast as the following:

```
while not (isblank(rc))
     cursor down
endwhile
```

Use the "cursor down" method in SmartWare II also.

Constructing Formulas with the Cursor Key

8.25 Tip: When entering a formula, you can type the complete formula or use the cursor to help you fill in the necessary row and column numbers. *Both*

The examples in figures 8.5 through 8.8 demonstrate the creation of a formula using the SUM function.

Begin by positioning your cursor in the cell that is to contain the formula. Next, press the equal-sign key (=) to begin the formula entry and enter the beginning of the SUM function, including the opening parenthesis, as shown in figure 8.5.

Fig. 8.5.
Using the cursor keys to enter a formula.

```
9
10
11        7.23
12        9.01
13       10.79
14       12.57
15       14.35
16  ==========
17
18
Enter formula: sum(

Worksheet: sample     Loc: r17c1                FN:       Font: Standard
 ENTER - enter a formula, a value or text into the current cell
```

Next, move the cursor to the top row of the column (row 11) and press F2 to anchor the block (see fig. 8.6). As you move the cursor down to the bottom of the block, the entire block is highlighted (see fig. 8.7).

Fig. 8.6.
Moving the cursor to the top row and pressing F2.

Fig. 8.7.
Moving the cursor to the bottom row.

```
8
9
10
11        7.23
12        9.01
13       10.79
14       12.57
15       14.35
16  ==========
17
18
Enter formula: sum(r11:15c1
F2 Drop anchor   F3 Absolute/Relative
Worksheet: sample     Loc: r15c1                FN: 0     Font: Standard
 ENTER   enter a formula, a value or text into the current cell
```

To complete the formula, enter the closing parenthesis and press Enter (see fig. 8.8). You can create almost any formula using this method, without ever having to type any row or column numbers. If you make an error, such as forgetting the closing parenthesis, the formula editor is invoked so that you can correct your mistake.

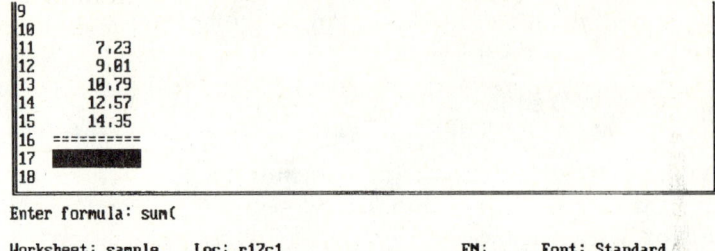

One final note: If you highlight the block from bottom to top rather than top to bottom as shown here, you can save several keystrokes. Start at the bottom row of the block, drop the anchor, and move the cursor up until the entire block is highlighted. Then type the closing parenthesis and press Enter.

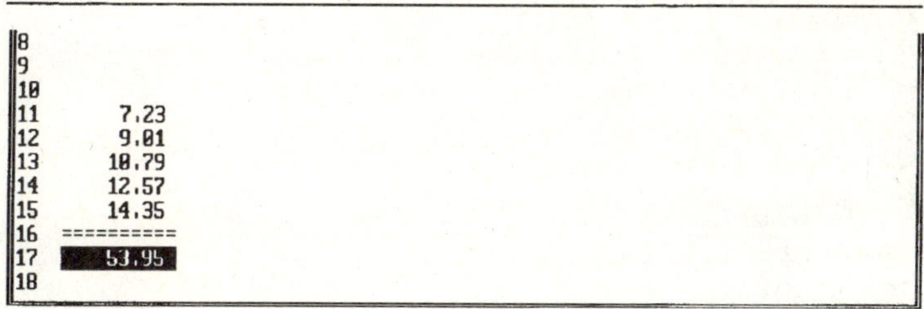

Fig. 8.8. *Completing the formula with closing parenthesis and pressing Enter.*

8.26 Tip: Include additional rows in a formula to allow for future expansion.

Both

In the preceding example, the formula in r17c1 is:

```
sum(r11:15c1)
```

Note that column 15 is the last row in the column containing values to be considered in the formula. If you insert a new row in the middle of the column, the formula is adjusted to include the added row; when you enter a value into the new row, the value is considered in the calculation.

If you insert the additional row immediately before row 16, however, the formula is not adjusted and values in the new row are not included in the calculation. You can, of course, edit the formula to include the new row.

An easier method, and one which is safer and eliminates your having to edit the formula, is to write the original formula as follows:

```
sum(r11:16c1)
```

In this formula, the underscore characters are included in the calculation. Because text entries have no effect on a numerical calculation like this, however, the result is the same as that of the original formula. If you insert a row above the underscore, however, the value in the row is included in the result.

Absolute versus Relative Addresses

8.27 Tip: Use absolute addresses if you plan to copy formulas that include row, column, or cell locations that must not change as the Copy command executes.

Both

The concept of absolute formulas and relative formulas seems to cause some confusion. Figure 8.9 shows a simple example that demonstrates the difference between the absolute and relative formulas. The top window shows the values and formula results. The bottom window shows the formulas themselves.

Fig. 8.9.
Absolute versus Relative formulas.

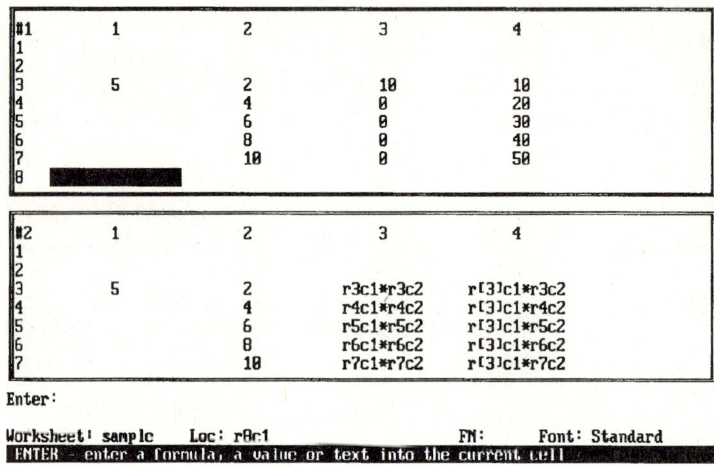

Create the formula in row 3, column 3, to multiply column 1 by column 2. Next, copy this formula down for four additional rows. You get zeros for your result because although the reference to column 2 was adjusted for each new row, the adjustment also was made for column 1. You really don't want that because you want each value in column 2 to be multiplied by the value in row 3 of column 1. You don't want the references to r1c1 to change as you copy the formula to new rows in column 3. Column 4 solves this problem. Notice that square brackets ([ ]) enclose the row number reference for column 1 in the formula for each row in column 4. This square-bracket notation indicates what is called an absolute reference; the brackets mean "do not change this row reference" as the copy is performed.

A marvelous feature of electronic spreadsheets, including the Smart Spreadsheet, is the capability to duplicate formulas and to automatically adjust them for changes in row or column positions. Occasionally, however, you need to specify a particular row or column (or both). In these cases, use the absolute reference notation with the square brackets.

If you are using the cursor keys to help you enter the cell addresses, use the F3 key to toggle the absolute indicators in the cell addresses. Press the F3 key once, and both the row and column numbers are made absolute. Press F3 again, and just the row numbers are absolute. A third press of the F3 key surrounds the column numbers with the square brackets ([ ]) to make them absolute. If you press F3 again, the absolute reference indicators are turned off, and you are back at the starting point.

8.28 Trick: Use the following macro to help you enter a SUM formula into a cell. ***SW II***

```
"=Sum(",Until,")",Enter
```

When you execute the macro while the cursor is on the result cell, move the cursor to the beginning of the block and press F2. Next, move the cursor to the end of the block and type a closed parenthesis ")". The correct SUM formula will be entered into the result cell for you.

8.29 Trick: Omit the entry of the current row or column from a formula if the current row or column is to be included in the formula; the row or column will be inserted for you automatically. ***Both***

If the current cell is r3c4 and you want to enter the formula r3c1/r3c2, for example, you enter *c1/c2*. The resulting formula in the cell is created as r3c1/r3c2, just as if you had typed the whole formula. In this example, the current row is assumed for each cell in the formula.

8.30 Trick: Use the MAKECELL and CELLTEXT functions together to create a formula that adjusts relative to the cell to which the formula is copied. ***Both***

The CELLTEXT function returns a text expression that is an exact representation of the cell contents. This function, however, does not adjust automatically as the cell is copied. In figure 8.10, r1c2 contains the formula

```
celltext("r1c1")
```

As this formula is copied down to successive rows, you can see that the formula does not adjust relative to the row; the formula still refers back to row 1. Column 3 contains the formula

```
celltext(makecell(row,column-2))
```

This formula *does* adjust as it is copied down from row 1; note that the formula displays the text of the values in column 1.

8.31 Trick: Use the INDIRECT and MAKECELL functions to create variable cell addresses. ***Both***

Consider the following formula:

```
Indirect(makecell($row,$col))
```

The MAKECELL function creates a cell address (for example, r5c2) if $row = 5 and $col = 2. The indirect function then displays the contents of the cell at that location. Using these functions is faster than the method of using the Evaluate command in SmartWare II.

Fig. 8.10.
Using Makecell and Celltext together.

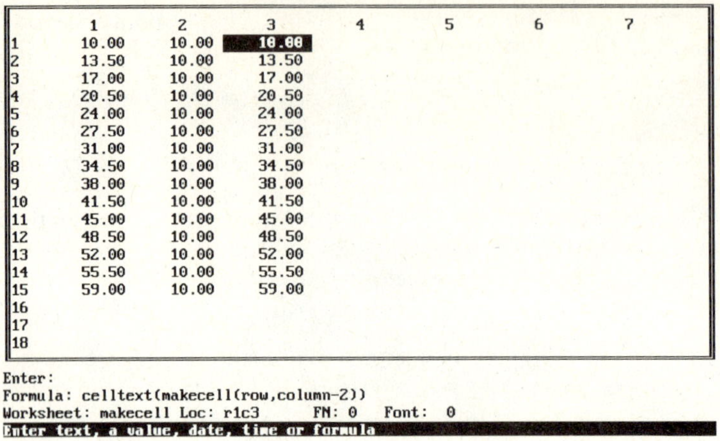

	1	2	3	4	5	6	7
1	10.00	10.00	10.00				
2	13.50	10.00	13.50				
3	17.00	10.00	17.00				
4	20.50	10.00	20.50				
5	24.00	10.00	24.00				
6	27.50	10.00	27.50				
7	31.00	10.00	31.00				
8	34.50	10.00	34.50				
9	38.00	10.00	38.00				
10	41.50	10.00	41.50				
11	45.00	10.00	45.00				
12	48.50	10.00	48.50				
13	52.00	10.00	52.00				
14	55.50	10.00	55.50				
15	59.00	10.00	59.00				
16							
17							
18							

Enter:
Formula: celltext(makecell(row,column-2))
Worksheet: makecell Loc: r1c3 FN: 0 Font: 0
Enter text, a value, date, time or formula

SW II

8.32 Tip: In a project file, use the Evaluate statement to create variable cell addresses.

The following project file uses the Evaluate statement to construct an assignment statement; in turn, the Assignment statement assigns value to a cell. The cell location varies with the contents of the variables $row and $column.

```
public $row $col $value
let $row = 13
let $col = 10
let $value = 61.97
evaluate ( "Let r"|str($row)|"c"|str($col)|" = $value" )
```

In this example, the final statement evaluates as the following:

```
Let r13c10 = $value
```

In Smart 3.10, use parameters to accomplish the same effect.

Entering Text

Both

8.33 Tip: When you are in Enter mode and need to enter a text cell that begins with a number (such as *1st Qtr 1990*, preface your entry with a double quotation mark (").

If you begin the entry with a number, the Spreadsheet interprets the value as being numeric and ignores the remainder of your entry.

Using the F-Calculator

Both

8.34 Tip: Use the F-Calculator to perform a manual calculation and to enter the results into a cell.

If you need to enter the results of a calculation into a cell, you have two choices. You can either reach for your calculator and perform the calculation "off line," or you can use the built- in F-Calculator, have more capability, and save yourself some work as well.

Invoke the F-Calculator with the Alt-K key. This keystroke brings up a full-screen calculator. Enter your formula, however complex it may be. You can use any numbers, mathematical symbols, or Smart functions needed. When you have completed the formula, press the F2 key to display the result on the status line. If the formula needs editing, you can make any needed changes. Press F2 to see the results again.

After you are satisfied with the formula results, press F10 to return to your worksheet. In Enter mode, move your cursor to the cell into which you want to insert the formula results you just calculated and press Ctrl-C. The value appears on the command line; press Enter to complete the entry into the cell.

Make sure you are in Enter mode when you press the Ctrl-C key; the entry will not be accepted in Command mode.

Using Blank Cells

8.35 Tip: Smart spreadsheet entries can be placed anywhere within the 9,999-row by 999-column workspace without performance penalty. ***Both***

Worksheets that are not tightly compacted are possible because Smart does not store blank cells. This method contrasts with some other popular spreadsheet programs on the market, which fill memory more quickly than necessary because blank cells consume RAM.

8.36 Trap: Because a blank cell does not "exist," you cannot preformat the contents. ***3.10***

You cannot specify that a block (or range of cells) is to contain a certain type of data formatted in a particular way. When entering similarly formatted data into a block, use the Value-format or Text-Format commands to establish the formatting characteristics of the new data to be entered. When you move to a new block, change the Value or Text formats for that block.

After data has been entered in a block, the formatting characteristics remain; changing a value does not alter the format. If you decide to change the block format, use the Reformat command.

8.37 Tip: Using a formula of "null" allows you to preformat cells. ***3.10***

Normally, you cannot preformat spreadsheet cells because nothing is there to format. However, if you want to preformat a block of cells, enter the formula *NULL* into the cells and then use the Format command. The format is retained when you enter actual data into the cells at a later time. In SmartWare II, you are allowed to preformat blank cells.

Both

8.38 Tip: Use the following macro to blank just one cell.

Smart 3.10: `abbC` (This is Alt-B,b,carriage return)
SmartWare II: `Alt-B,"b",Enter`

You may want to use Ctrl-Bs (Backspace) as the key to invoke this macro.

Project-File Data Entry

Both

8.39 Tip: Use the Enter command in a project file to enter data into your worksheet.

Some examples of the Enter command in Smart 3.10 are the following:

```
@r1c1 enter value 991
@r2c1 enter date1 1/1/89
@r3c1 enter date2 1/1/90
@r4c1 enter value $123.45
@r5c1 enter text Domestic
@r6c1 enter formula r1c1+r2c1
```

In SmartWare II, the equivalent statements are as follows:

```
at r1c1
enter value 991
at r2c1
enter date1 "1/1/89"
at r3c1
enter date2 "1/1/90"
at r4c1
enter value $123.45
at r5c1
enter text "Domestic"
at r6c1
enter formula "r1c1+r2c1"
```

Each of these statements has the effect of both defining the cell format and entering the literal contents.

Note that in Smart 3.10, the cell address is designated by the `@rRcC` specification at the beginning of the statement. (Capitol R stands for row; capital C stands for cell.) In SmartWare II, use a separate command @ (at), followed by the cell address, as in the following example:

```
at r1c1
```

The first statement, therefore, is interpreted as "Enter the value *991* into the cell at row 1 column 1."

8.40 Tip: To allow for variable input, use the project-processing parameters to enter values, text, or formulas in cells.

Both

In the previous sample statements, the cell values are supplied as literals within the statements themselves. In the following examples from Smart 3.10, parameters are used for variable input:

```
%1   Enter a cell value:
%2   Can I have a date:
%3   How much does it cost:
%4   Which Division:
%5   What is the formula:

@r1c1 enter value %1
@r2c1 enter date1 %2
@r3c1 enter date2 %2
@r4c1 enter value %3
@r5c1 enter text %4
@r6c1 enter formula %5
```

When you want to enter variable values under control of a project file, be sure to use parameters rather than user-defined variables, which will not produce the results you desire. Notice in the fifth line of this example that you can prompt for a formula and have the formula inserted in the cell. When doing this, make sure the worksheet user is acquainted with the ways to write formulas in the Smart Spreadsheet. Of course, the response to the prompt could include the name of a block, and blocks can make the formula somewhat easier for a novice to construct.

The equivalent SmartWare II project file is:

```
public $value $date $cost $division $formula

screen shortinput $value "Enter a cell value:"
screen shortinput $date "Can I have a date:"
screen shortinput $cost "How much does it cost:"
screen shortinput $division "Which Division:"
screen shortinput $formula "What is the formula:"

at r1c1
enter value    val($value)
at r2c1

enter date1    $date
at r3c1
enter date2    $date
at r4c1
enter value    val($cost)
at r5c1
```

```
enter text    $division
at r6c1
enter formula $formula
```

3.10

8.41 Tip: Use the Cursor command to position the cursor at a specified cell and issue a prompt message.

```
@r1c4 cursor Enter Number of Months:
@r2c4 cursor Enter First Date of Month:
@r3c4 cursor Fiscal Year Ending:
@r4c4 cursor Amount of Loan:
@r5c4 cursor Name of Client:
@r6c4 cursor Enter Formula Here:
```

Look for the prompts on the Autohelp line. To make sure the entries are in the desired format, however, you must preface your keyboard-response entry with the appropriate symbolic prefix, just as if you were in Enter mode. Preface a date entry with the @ or # symbols, depending on the desired date format, the dollar field with a $ symbol, and the formula with the = sign. If the text entry begins with a number, you must preface the text entry with double quotation marks.

Because you must remember to use these formatting symbols, this method is not as universally foolproof as the preceding method of using the parameters.

In SmartWare II, use the AT command to locate the cursor at a specific cell.

Both

8.42 Tip: Use the ASK function to embed prompts within your worksheet.

The previous examples provide methods of prompting for data input within project files. If you want the prompt to be embedded within the worksheet itself, you can use the ASK function:

```
ask("Enter the Month Number")
ask("Enter Division Name")
ask("Enter total cost")
```

When you recalculate the worksheet, the prompt message appears on the command line. You then enter the appropriate response, and the next prompt appears. These functions are formulas contained within cells of your worksheet; thus, you do not have a preceding cell address. Because the cells already exist, you can format them in advance so that the results appear as you want. For example, a Dollar field can be reformatted as Currency with two decimal positions.

However, you cannot enter dates or formulas when using the ASK function. If you know the sequential number of a specific date, you can enter the number and have the number displayed in one of the three date formats; however, you probably do not know this number. You are more likely to know an interval number of days, in which case you can use the ASK function within a larger formula:

```
r1c8 + ask("Number of days till maturity")
```

This cell can be reformatted in one of the special date formats.

The ASK function is useful particularly in modeling situations: you are prompted each time you recalculate the worksheet; the prompt is embedded within the worksheet itself; and you do not have to execute a project file. You cannot ignore the prompt, and you need not rely on the correct project file being used. If you enter just a carriage return, however, the resulting function value is zero.

8.43 Tip: Under project file control, you can use the Let statement to enter data into a cell.

Both

The following is an example of using the Let statement for cell assignment:

```
%1  Enter a cell value:
%2  Can I have a date:
%3  How much does it cost:
%4  Which Division:

let r1c1 = %1
let r2c1 = date1("%2")
let r3c1 = date2("%2")
let r4c1 = currency(%3)      'This is text
let r5c1 = "%4"

let r2c2 = days(r2c1)
let r3c2 = days(r3c1)
@r2c2 reformat block rc date1
@r3c2 reformat block rc date2

goto r30c1
goto r1c1
```

This type of data entry initializes each target cell so that any prior formatting characteristics are lost. Note that two types of date cells are created. Date cells in column 1 are in text format and are simply text fields displaying dates. Date cells in column 2 are in date format and contain the sequential number of the date from the beginning of the 20th century, displayed in the date formats. The reformat commands are used to change the display formats. Note that the %4 entered into r5c1 is enclosed within double quotation marks (") because %4 is text. Because the newly entered cells are not immediately displayed, the final Goto statements force the display.

The equivalent project file, using variables instead of parameters, is as follows:

```
input $val1 Enter a cell value:
input text1 Can I have a date:
input $cost How much does it cost:
input $div Which Division:

let r1c1 = $val1
let r2c1 = date1(text1)
let r3c1 = date2(text1)
let r4c1 = currency($cost)      'This is text
let r5c1 = $div

let r2c2 = days(r2c1)
let r3c2 = days(r3c1)
@r2c2 reformat block rc date1
@r3c2 reformat block rc date2

goto r30c1
goto r1c1
```

Notice that the standard variable text1 is used for the date entry, rather than a user-defined variable, so that the date expression is not considered to be numeric.

The equivalent SmartWare II project file is as follows:

```
public $value $date $cost $division $formula

screen shortinput $value "Enter a cell value:"
screen shortinput $date "Can I have a date:"
screen shortinput $cost "How much does it cost:"
screen shortinput $division "Which Division:"

let r1c1 = val($value)
let r2c1 = date1($date)
let r3c1 = date2($date)
let r4c1 = currency(val($cost))     'This is text
let r5c1 = $division
let r2c2 = days(r2c1)
let r3c2 = days(r3c1)
layout format block r2c2 date 1
layout format block r3c2 date 2
```

Both

8.44 Tip: In a project file, use RC to refer to the current cursor row and column; you do not have to specify the actual row and column numbers.

The following project file demonstrates the use of RC to specify the current row and column.

```
global $value x
let $value = 5280
at r1c1
for x = 1 to 10
     let rc = $value
     let $value = $value + 1
     cursor down
end for
```

Note that in the assignment statement, `rc` is specified as the target cell.

8.45 Tip: To enter repeating values throughout a cell, regardless of the cell width, use the backslash key (\). *Both*

In Enter mode, the backslash generates hyphens in the field. Press Enter if you want to accept the hyphens. If you want a different character, type the character and then press Enter. You even can repeat sequences of different characters or spaces across the cell. Figure 8.11 shows some examples.

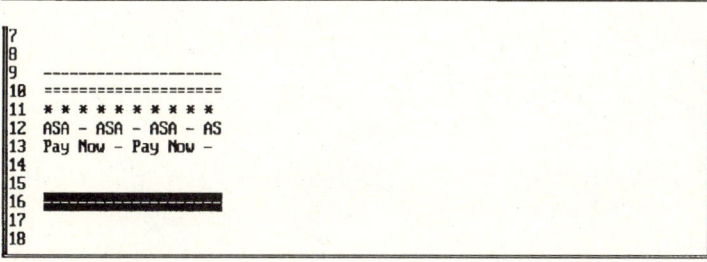

Fig. 8.11. *Repeating cell text contents.*

8.46 Tip: Prevent the destruction of a project file by using the Remember Edit command to display the names of existing project files in the Spreadsheet module before you execute the Remember Start command. *3.10*

The Spreadsheet module does not display the names of your existing project files when you execute the Remember Start command; if you accidentally use an existing project file name, you destroy the contents without any warning. If you display the names of your existing project files by using the Remember Edit command (or the Directory command), you can select an unused name. (The Database *does* display the names of existing project files when you execute the Remember Start command.)

Recalculating the Worksheet

You can recalculate a worksheet manually or automatically; the method you select may depend on the stage of development of the worksheet or the way in which the worksheet is used. If you design a recursive model, you also may specify that the worksheet is to be calculated iteratively.

Both

8.47 Tip: Change the calculation mode as needed, depending on the stage of development of your worksheet.

The Auto-Recalc command in Smart 3.10 on command list 5 has four options—Automatic, Display, Iterate, and Manual (see fig. 8.12). In SmartWare II, Sheet Calc-mode, a fifth option is added—Calc-Order.

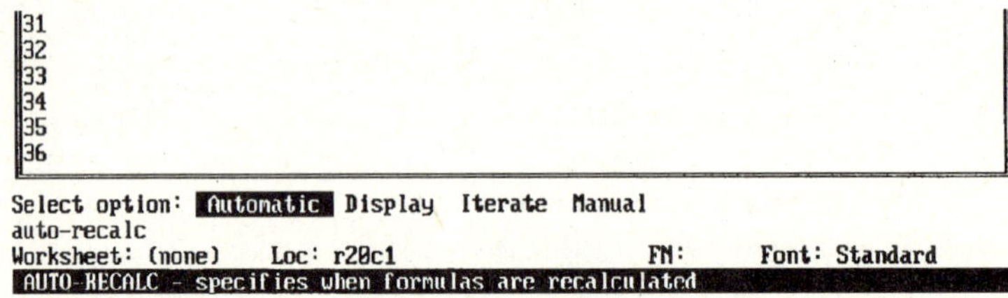

Fig. 8.12.
Auto-Recalc options.

The Automatic option causes your spreadsheet to be recalculated automatically each time you make an entry or a change. You may prefer to select the Manual option if you are in the process of building your worksheet, or if you have many entries to make before a recalculation is necessary.

Both

8.48 Tip: Execute Auto-Recalc Display to remind yourself if you are working in Automatic or Manual mode.

The Display option of Auto-Recalc tells you whether you are in Automatic or Manual recalculation mode (see fig. 8.13).

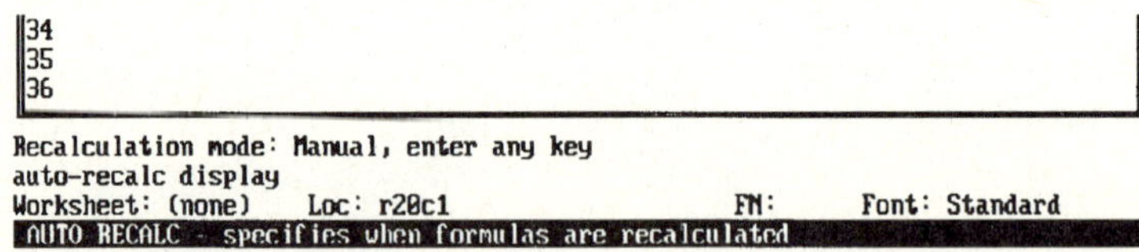

Fig. 8.13.
The Auto-Recalc display.

Both

8.49 Trick: Use the Edit command (Smart 3.10) or Edit-Cell command (SmartWare II) to recalculate just one cell of a worksheet without having to recalculate the entire worksheet.

If you edit the cell (or use the Alt-E quick key) and press Enter, the cell is recalculated; you do not have to wait for the entire worksheet to be recalculated. This trick can be especially helpful if you have a large worksheet.

In SmartWare II, the minimal recalculation feature recalculates only those formulas in which the factors have changed; press F5 for minimal recalculation. Press Shift-F5 to force recalculation of the entire worksheet.

8.50 Trap: Before using the results of the CELLPOINTER function in a project file, be sure to Recalc your spreadsheet. The result of the function changes with the location of the current cell. *SW II*

Even with Automatic recalculation turned on, you have to execute the Recalc command for the CELLPOINTER function to be re-evaluated.

Circular References

8.51 Tip: The calculation Iterate option is used to recalculate your worksheet a specified number of times or until a certain test value is achieved. *Both*

To examine the Iterate option, refer to the example in figure 8.14.

```
        1            2            3            4            5            6            7
1   P = POINTS                               3.00%
2   A = AMOUNT OF CURRENT LOAN              50,000.00
3   B = AMOUNT TO BORROW                    51,546.39
4
5   PROBLEM: HOW MUCH DO YOU NEED TO BORROW (B) TO PAY OFF YOUR
6   CURRENT LOAN (A) IF THE BANK IS GOING TO CHARGE YOU POINTS (P)
7
8   POINT $ =  1,546.39
9   BORROW  = 51,546.39
10  TEST    =      0.00
11
12
13
14
15
16
17
18
Select option: Count Remove Test
auto-recalc iterate
Worksheet: POINTS     Loc: r1c4        CIRC          FN: 0     Font: Standard
AUTO-RECALC - specifies when formulas are recalculated
```

Fig. 8.14.

An example using Iteration.

Typically, you try to avoid circular references within spreadsheets. A circular reference usually means that you have made an error causing one or more cells to refer back to themselves. In most cases, worksheet formulas are unidirectional, having a termination point. Having circular references (as indicated by the `CIRC` flag on the status line in figure 8.14) means that somewhere in your worksheet, a series of formulas is without a termination point.

If you are planning to use the Iterate recalculation option, design your worksheet with circular references. The worksheet in figure 8.14 is such an example.

The problem addressed in figure 8.14 is a simple one, but it demonstrates the subject. Suppose that you plan to refinance your house, and you want to take out a new loan that covers not only the outstanding balance you owe on the existing loan, but also enough to cover the percentage points the bank will charge you on the new loan. The total amount you borrow governs the loan amount needed for the points as well. The more you borrow, the higher the cost due to the points and, therefore, the more you need to borrow. Hence the circular reference.

The worksheet input cells are the points, displayed as a percentage in r1c4, and the current loan amount in r2c4. In the example in figure 8.14, the points are 3 percent and the current loan amount is $50,000.

The calculations for solving the problem are contained in column 2, rows 8, 9, and 10 (see fig. 8.15). Column 2, row 8, contains the amount needed to borrow for the points the bank is charging (r9c2*r1c4). Row 9 is the total amount needed to cover the original loan and the payment of the points (r2c4+r8c2). The circular reference arises from the fact that row 8 references row 9, and row 9 references row 8.

Fig. 8.15.

A worksheet showing formulas.

```
        1           2          3          4          5          6          7
1   P = POINTS                                3.00%
2   A = AMOUNT OF CURRENT LOAN           50,000.00
3   B = AMOUNT TO BORROW                 r2c4/(1-r1c4)
4
5   PROBLEM: HOW MUCH DO YOU NEED TO BORROW (B) TO PAY OFF YOUR
6   CURRENT LOAN (A) IF THE BANK IS GOING TO CHARGE YOU POINTS (P)
7
8   POINT $ = r9c2*r1c4
9   BORROW  = r2c4+r8c2
10  TEST    = r9c2-r8c2-r2c4
11
12
```

Row 10 is the test value that makes the iterative recalculation work. The formula in r10c2 subtracts the original loan amount and the cost of the points from the amount being borrowed. If you calculate this worksheet over and over again, this test value should be zero. This is exactly the condition you establish in the Iterate option of the Auto-Recalc command.

When you select Iterate, the first menu is:

```
Count  Remove  Test
```

To use the test formula in the worksheet as a measure of the iteration, select Test. The next prompt is:

```
Enter name or block reference:
```

In this example, enter *r10c2*. Now you are prompted:

```
Enter delta value:
```

When the amount of change in the block reference field drops below the delta value, the automatic iteration stops. In the example, you entered *.001*, which is 1/10 of one cent.

As a safety precaution, the final prompt is:

```
Enter maximum number of iterations:
```

The rationale for this prompt is explained in the following Tip.

8.52 Tip: Enter a low number for the iteration maximum. *Both*

So that your recalculation does not continue for hours, either because of the complexity of the recalculation or an error on your part, you should enter a reasonable number here. For the example, 99 was used, but 10 probably would have worked as well. Don't set the number too high because you cannot stop the processing after it starts.

After you have entered the maximum amount, the automatic iterative recalculation takes place. If you change either input value, the calculation takes place again.

8.53 Tip: Select the Count option to recalculate a specified number of times. *Both*

Rather than establish a test cell, you can specify that the recalculation is to be performed a particular number of times. Select the Count option of the Auto-Recalc Iterate command. You are prompted:

```
Enter number of iterations:
```

Using the Count option rather than the Test option may be easier (and safer). If you want to see your circular calculation work, set Auto-Recalc on Manual; each time you press the F5 key, you see the results get closer and closer.

In either case, your specified number of recalculations is stored with the worksheet and is performed whenever a recalculation needs to be performed. To remove the automatic iterative recalculation, select Remove from the Iterate menu.

The formula in row 3, column 4 displays the same value as r9c1, the amount to borrow. This example is somewhat trivial because you really don't need the Iterative recalculation to arrive at the answer to the problem. The formula in cell r3c4 is a much easier way of solving the problem. For another example of Iterative recalculation (one without a formula), refer to Appendix B.

8.54 Trap: If used within the referenced data block, the CELL function yields a circular reference. *Both*

The following example yields a circular reference if the formula is used anywhere within the block called Data.

```
cell("width",Data)
```

To avoid the circular reference, the formula with the CELL function must be outside the block.

3.10

8.55 Trick: On a network, if you load a worksheet but are told that the worksheet is in use by another station, look for the W$$ file and erase the file if you are sure that no one else is using the worksheet.

On a network, when you Load a worksheet, a file is created with the same name as the worksheet and with an extension of W$$; this extension denotes that the file is in use and that no one else can load or change the file until you finish. However, if the network goes down, this W$$ file is not erased. When you try to load the file again, the following error message is displayed:

```
Worksheet in use by another station
```

Although you can load the worksheet, you cannot save the worksheet under the current name. If you are sure that you are the only person using the worksheet, unload it and erase the W$$ file. You then can use the worksheet normally.

Both

8.56 Trap: You must manually recalculate a worksheet that references another sheet if that other sheet has changed.

Automatic recalculation does not apply to changes in subordinate worksheets, nor does the CALC message appear. You must execute the Recalc command manually (or press the F5) to recalculate the worksheet.

Both

8.57 Tip: Set Auto-Recalc to manual if you are using a project file to construct a spreadsheet; then use the Recalc command when the construction is complete.

You can construct a spreadsheet using project file commands. If the calculation mode for the sheet is automatic, however, recalculation takes place each time the program changes or adds to the worksheet, slowing execution. Therefore, to execute the project file as fast as possible, set automatic recalculation to manual at the beginning and execute the Recalc command when the construction of the worksheet is complete.

In SmartWare II, use the Sheet Calc-mode Manual command.

SW II

8.58 Trick: In a project file, you can force a total recalculation of your worksheet by using the Suspend and the Keys commands; there is no explicit command to do this.

To force a total recalculation of your spreadsheet from within a project file, use the following two statements:

```
Suspend
Keys sF5,F8
```

The first command suspends the project file; the second command assigns the Shift-F5 quick key to perform the total recalculation and then resumes execution of the project with the F8 key.

8.59 Trap: After a block has been sorted, formulas outside the sorted block do not recalculate when you press the F5 key; you must force a total recalculation with the Shift-F5.

SW II

In figure 8.16, the data in blocks 1 and 2 start out the same; the totals are shown at the bottom of each block. However, block 2 is sorted in descending order, using row 10. Note that the totals for block 2 have not changed, even though the calculation mode is automatic and F5 has been pressed in an attempt to recalculate the sheet.

```
          1          2          3          4          5          6          7
1   Block 1:         1          4          7
2                    2          5          8
3                    3          6          9
4   --------------------------------------
5     TOTAL:         6         15         24
6
7
8
9
10  Block 2:         7          4          1
11                   8          5          2
12                   9          6          3
13  --------------------------------------
14    TOTAL:         6         15         24
15
16
17
18
Menu:  Sheet  Edit  File  Layout  Print  Graph  Tools  Window  Help  Remember
       Quit  New-Directory
Worksheet: sortcalc Loc: r10c1      FN: 0   Font:  0
Blank Copy Delete Edit-Cell Fill Hide Unhide Insert Move Sort ValueCopy
```

Fig. 8.16.

Cells are not recalculated after a sort.

If you press Shift-F5, the formulas for block 2 recalculate to their correct values. Also, when you make a new entry into any other cell in the worksheet, the formulas for block 2 recalculate correctly if you press F5, and automatically if the calculation mode is automatic.

8.60 Trap: When the recalculation mode is set to Row or Column order, the Recalc command does not work from a value upwards through formulas that depend on the value.

SW II

You must force a total recalculation of the worksheet in such a case, but even then, the Shift-F5 key recalculates upward only one formula at a time.

Figure 8.17 shows a series of numbers and formulas; the values are shown in window 1 and the formulas in window 2. The calculation mode is automatic, column order. If you change the value 4 to 104 in r14c1, r8c1 changes to 128; however, only 100 is added to each of the other calculations. Pressing F5 does not force the correct calculations. If you force a total worksheet recalculation, using Shift-F5, the formulas recalculate, but only individually, from bottom to top. You must continue to press Shift-F5 until all the formulas have been correctly recalculated.

Fig. 8.17.
Calculation order can affect results.

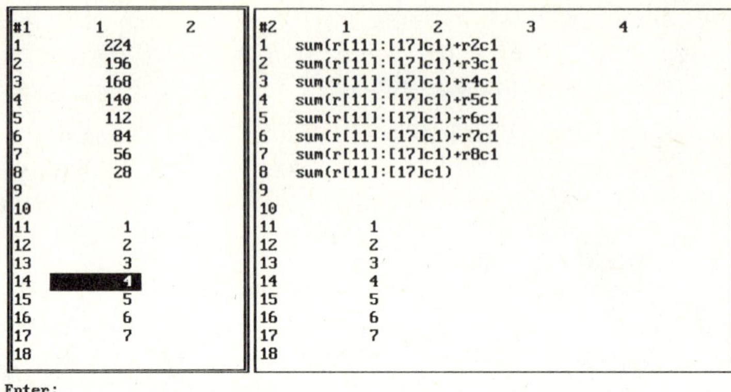

Be careful, therefore, if you change the recalculation order.

Protecting the Worksheet

Both

8.61 Tip: Use the Newname (3.10) or Sheet Newname (SmartWare II) command to protect worksheet templates.

Frequently, you develop a worksheet to use in repetitive models, but you don't want to destroy or write into the original. One way to prevent a problem is to use a project file similar to the following:

```
%1 Enter New Worksheet Name:

load r1099

newname %1
```

Because the file is immediately renamed, a Save command will not overlay the original worksheet. The SmartWare II equivalent is

```
local $name
screen shortinput $name "Enter New Worksheet Name:"

file load "r1099"

file newname $name
```

Both

8.62 Trick: Protect a worksheet template by marking the file attribute as "read only."

Several DOS utility programs, both proprietary and in the public domain, can be used to change the file attribute. After you develop a good model, unload the worksheet, return to DOS, and use one of these utilities to mark the file as "read only." You then can load the worksheet into the Smart Spreadsheet without being able to save any changes. In SmartWare II, you get the warning:

```
Note: No permission to save file under this name.
```

You must use the Newname command to save the file. If you try to save the file under its original name or unload the file, you get the message:

Smart 3.10: `Error closing file`
SmartWare II: `No permission to save file under this name`

Execute the Newname command and save the file again. Alternatively, within the Save command itself, when you are prompted to

```
enter worksheet name
```

type a new name and press Enter. The worksheet is saved under the new name and the current worksheet name is changed.

8.63 Tip: The (Sheet) Lock Protect command provides protection against changes to the contents of a worksheet. ***Both***

If you want to protect the contents of a worksheet against all changes, use the (Sheet) Lock Protect command. Anyone using the worksheet is prevented from changing or even seeing your formulas. Complete protection is provided by locking the blanks, text, and any values you do not want changed before you use the (Sheet) Lock Protect command on the worksheet.

Smart 3.10: Lock Protect
SmartWare II: Sheet Lock Protect

When you protect the worksheet, give the worksheet a new name and save it. From then on, your formulas are hidden from view. As an added benefit, protected worksheets load faster than normal worksheets.

8.64 Tip: The full screen editor (Alt-F) enables you to change a locked formula. ***3.10***

The Edit command, or the quick key Alt-E, however, may not be used to edit a locked formula. To use the Edit command, you must either disable the lock or unlock the formula. In SmartWare II, Alt-F does not allow you to edit a locked formula.

8.65 Tip: Even though you have protected a worksheet, the original still is available to you. ***Both***

A protected worksheet cannot overlay a normal worksheet. If you want to safeguard the original worksheet, copy it to another subdirectory or a floppy disk and then erase the worksheet from the current subdirectory.

Remember, however, that a protected worksheet still may be saved with newly entered values. Simply protecting a worksheet does not solve the problem addressed in the preceding Tip.

SW II

8.66 Trap: If you unload a worksheet to which you have attached a password but have not made any other changes, the password protection will be ignored.

Normally, when you unload a worksheet that has been changed, you get the message:

```
Worksheet has been modified. Save before unloading? (y/n)
```

Although you alter the worksheet by attaching the password, you don't get a prompt asking whether you want to save the worksheet before unloading it, as you do if you change data. To make sure the new password is retained, be sure to use the File Save command to explicitly save the worksheet.

This same problem exists if you remove a password from a worksheet; if you unload the worksheet without specifically saving it, the password still will be attached.

Incorporating Data from the Database

Both

8.67 Tip: Use an external worksheet reference to incorporate into the current worksheet any data that you send from the Database.

When you send data from the Database to the Spreadsheet, a worksheet is created with the same name as the database. How do you incorporate this data into an existing worksheet? The solution to this question is made easy with Smart's capability to reference one worksheet from another.

Figure 8.18 shows two worksheets. The worksheet in the upper window results from a Send Summarized command in the Database. The lower worksheet has been developed within the Spreadsheet module. Whereas the upper worksheet contains only data and no formulas, the lower worksheet contains only text (for the headings) and formulas. The formulas in the body of the worksheet reference individual cells in the upper worksheet (see an example on the command line). The totals and averages also are formulas.

The formulas for the worksheet in window 2 of figure 8.18 are as follows:

Cell	*Formula*
r3c1	sumpers.r2c1
r3c2	sumpers.r2c2
r3c3	sumpers.r2c3
r3c4	r3c2/r3c3

Cell	*Formula*
r4c1	sumpers.r3c1
r4c2	sumpers.r3c2
r4c3	sumpers.r3c3
r4c4	r4c2/r4c3
r5c1	sumpers.r4c1
r5c2	sumpers.r4c2
r5c3	sumpers.r4c3
r5c4	r5c2/r5c3
r6c1	sumpers.r5c1
r6c2	sumpers.r5c2
r6c3	sumpers.r5c3
r6c4	r6c2/r6c3
r7c1	sumpers.r6c1
r7c2	sumpers.r6c2
r7c3	sumpers.r6c3
r7c4	r7c2/r7c3
r8c2	sum(r3:7c2)
r8c3	sum(r3:7c3)
r8c4	r8c2/r8c3

To make this pair of worksheets operate together, first load the upper worksheet—the Send command does this for you. As soon as you load and recalculate the second worksheet, the job is completed. Although both worksheets are displayed simultaneously in two windows, the worksheet you send (window 1) does not need to be seen at all; the referencing formula works just as well with a worksheet that is active but not visible in a window. You now are ready to print.

```
#1       1          2          3          4          5          6          7
1   DEPT       WAGE       DEP
2   ACCT       3,365.86          7
3   DATA         654.34          2
4   MFGR       2,401.45          1
5   MKTG       4,080.59          4
6   SALE       2,626.61          5
```

```
#2       1              2              3            4                5
1   Department     Total Wages     Employees    Average Wage
2   -------------------------------------------------------
3   ACCT              3,365.86            7          480.84
4   DATA                654.34            2          327.17
5   MFGR              2,401.45            1        2,401.45
6   MKTG              4,080.59            4        1,020.15
7   SALE              2,626.61            5          525.32
8   TOTAL            13,128.85           19          690.99
9
Enter:
Formula: sumpers.r2c2
Worksheet: sump2      Loc: r3c2                  FM: 0    Font: Standard
ENTER   enter a formula, a value or text into the current cell
```

Fig. 8.18.

The original data and the formatted worksheet.

Both

8.68 Tip: Use a project file to change a worksheet sent from the Database.

Rather than using a separately prepared worksheet, as seen in the preceding example, you can use the following Smart 3.10 project file to produce the worksheet seen in the lower window of figure 8.18.

```
@r2c1 width 13 columns 1
@r2c2 width 15 columns 3
@r2c2 insert rows 1
@r1c1 enter text Department
@r1c2 enter text Total Wage
@r1c3 enter text Employees
@r1c4 enter text Average Wage
@r1c2 justify right block r1c2:4
@r2c1 enter text \-
@r2c1 copy right single-cell copies 3
@r8c1 enter text Total
@r8c2 enter formula sum(r3:7c2)
@r3c4 enter formula r3c2/r3c3
@r3c4 copy down single-cell copies 5
@r8c2 copy right single-cell copies 1
@r8c3 reformat block rc numeric normal nocommas precision 0
@r7c1 font change OU rows 1
recalc
```

This project file was created using the Remember Start command.

Both

8.69 Tip: Numeric row identifiers are converted to alpha strings in the database Data Cross-Tabs (SmartWare II) or Write Summarized (Smart 3.10) commands.

When you use a numeric field to generate automatic rows, the numbers become alpha strings in the Spreadsheet when you import the resulting file. Use the following SmartWare II project file to convert the alpha strings back to numerics.

```
'insert 2 new columns after the first column
sheet goto cell r1c2
edit insert columns 2

'col 2 becomes the val of col 1 , a true number in formula form

enter formula "val(r1c1)"
edit copy down single-cell copies 73

'column 3 becomes an actual number entry, not just a formula
```

```
edit value-copy right column length 74 copies 1

'get rid of the first 2 columns
sheet goto cell r1c1
edit delete columns 2
```

8.70 Tip: When transferring data from the database to the spreadsheet, use the SmartWare II File Export and Import commands, rather than the Data Send, for a cleaner appearance. In Smart 3.10, use the Write and Read commands.

Both

In a project file, if you do not want to see the spreadsheet data that is being transferred from the database, rather than using the Data Send command, use the File Export command in the Database and the File Import command in the Spreadsheet module. In the Spreadsheet project file, issue Screen Clear and Repaint Off commands prior to the File Import command. The transferred data does not appear on-screen and you have a cleaner appearance to the application.

9

Operating the Worksheet

After you have entered some data and a few formulas, you can expand and work with your worksheet. The topics in this chapter cover tips and tricks to use with the Copy and Move commands. The similarities and differences of these commands also are discussed.

In the section on operating your worksheet, particular emphasis is placed on worksheet block names, the Fill command, Matrix commands, and sorting your data. Numerous project files and worksheets are provided as examples.

Copying Parts of the Worksheet

One of the marvelous aspects of the Smart Spreadsheet lies in the ease with which you can copy portions of your spreadsheet to other areas. You can copy rows, columns, or blocks. When you copy a formula, the cell addresses in the formula are adjusted automatically to reflect relative cell references. (Some exceptions to this feature are covered in this chapter.)

The Copy command of the Smart Spreadsheet can be used to copy not only within the current worksheet, but also from and to other worksheets. Several examples are provided, showing consolidations and the use of this feature when you send data from the Database.

Using Absolute Addresses

9.1 Tip: When using the Copy command, specify absolute addresses if you do not want rows, columns, or cells to change as the Copy command is executed. *Both*

Sometimes you need to specify that some addresses are absolute and do not change as a formula is copied. To specify that a row or column reference is absolute rather than relative, place square brackets ([ ]) around the row or column number, as in the following example:

```
r[3]c1*r3c2
```

As you copy the formula, the row number (3, in this example) does not change. This absolute-reference specification applies to cell addresses in the current worksheet and to other loaded worksheets, as in

```
domestic.r18c[50]
```

Copying a Block of Text

Both

9.2 Tip: The Copy (3.10) or Edit Copy (SmartWare II) commands can duplicate the contents of a portion of a row, a column, or a block of cells.

The options in the Copy command are

```
Down        From        Right
```

Selecting Down or Right signifies that the result is to be contiguous to the current row or column of cells. The From option is used when you want to copy a block of cells to a worksheet area that is not contiguous; only one copy of the source block can be made for each command execution.

When copying Down, you can copy one cell or a number of cells in the row. The prompt is

```
Row         Single-Cell
```

If you specify Row, you are prompted to enter the row length, which is the number of cells in the row that you want to copy. You can enter a number, but it's often easier to use the → key to point to the cells and then press Enter. The Single-Cell choice is an easier way of specifying the Row choice with a length of one.

Similarly, the Right option prompts:

```
Column          Single-Cell
```

In the example in figure 9.1, beginning with row 1 column 1, specify that rows 1 through 10 are to be copied to the right. The highlighted block is created by pressing the ↓ key to pick up the rows of the column that you want to copy. You also can type the number 10 on the command line in response to the prompt

```
Enter length of column:
```

but you have to count the rows on the screen.

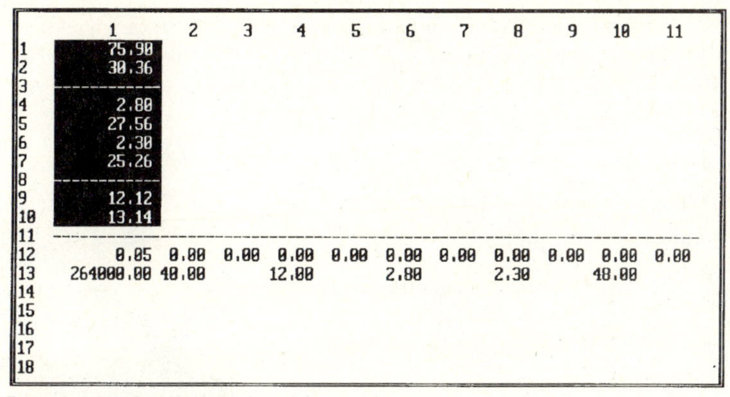

Fig. 9.1.
The prompt for column length.

Similarly, you can answer the next prompt

```
Enter number of copies
```

by moving the cursor to the right or by entering a numerical response on the command line (see fig. 9.2).

```
           1      2     3     4     5     6     7     8     9     10    11
1      75.90
2      30.36
3   ----------
4       2.80
5      27.56
6       2.30
7      25.26
8   ----------
9      12.12
10     13.14
11  ----------------------------------------------------------------------
12      0.05   0.00  0.00  0.00  0.00  0.00  0.00  0.00  0.00  0.00  0.00
13  264000.00 40.00        12.00       2.80        2.30        40.00
14
15
16
17
18
Enter number of copies 10
copy right column length 10 copies
Worksheet: INT6      Loc: r1c11                FN:      Font: Standard
COPY - copy part of the worksheet to another location
```

Fig. 9.2.
The prompt for the number of copies.

9.3 Tip: Use the command editing feature to perform multiple copy commands.

Both

As stated in the preceding tip, you can make only one copy of a source block for each command execution. With the command editing feature, however, you can edit the previous copy command and perform another (Edit) copy command without having to enter the entire command again.

To edit the last command you entered, press Alt-X. The following appears on the command line:

```
Edit command: c
```

in which `c` represents the most recent command you have issued. If you copy a block from r1:3c1 to r8c1 and press Alt-X, the entry on the command line will be

```
Edit command: @r1c1 copy from r1:3c1 to r8c1
```

If you want another copy in r8c3, for example, edit the command by changing `r8c1` to `r8c3` and pressing Enter.

If you want to copy the same block more than once, you can move the highlight to the new cell, edit the r8c1 to rc, and press Enter. Next, move the highlight to the next cell and press F9 and continue until all the copies have been made.

Both

9.4 Tip: To copy to an area of your worksheet that is above or to the left of the original block, or to an area that is not adjacent, you must use the (Edit) Copy From option.

With the (Edit) Copy Down or (Edit) Copy Right commands, you can create multiple copies, as seen in figures 9.1 and 9.2. However, if you need to copy to a portion of your worksheet above or to the left of the initial cell, you must use the From option.

Press the F2 key to "drop the anchor" for the upper left corner of the source block. Use the cursor keys to define the lower right corner and press Enter. Finally, position your cursor on the upper left corner of the new block into which you are copying, and press Enter.

Both

9.5 Tip: Make copying easier by constructing your worksheet from top left to bottom right.

Generally, copying Down or Right is easier than copying From, so if you can work from top left to bottom right, construction of your worksheet proceeds more smoothly.

Both

9.6 Trick: Even if your worksheet has blank rows between formulas, go ahead and copy the formulas down—you can blank out the extraneous formulas easily later.

By copying a formula down, you get formula cells on the rows you do not want. You can use the Edit Blank command to blank out the first cell and then use the

F9 key to repeat the command to blank the other cells. This technique is often easier than using the Copy From command multiple times to copy to each individual cell in which the formula is to be entered.

9.7 Tip: The (Edit) Copy From command enables you to use the F3 key to change from a relative cell address to an absolute address (see fig. 9.3). ***Both***

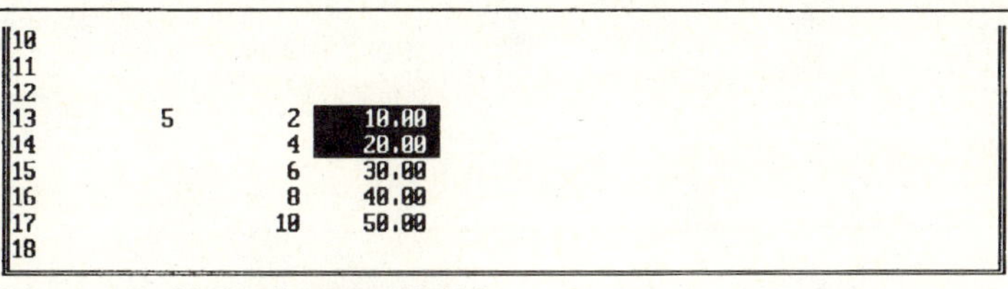

Fig. 9.3.
Using function keys in the Copy command.

When you first execute the (Edit) Copy command, function-key prompts do not appear on the command line, as shown in the figure. To bring forth the function key prompts so that you can use the F3 key to toggle absolute cell references, move your cursor down one cell and then back up. You then can press F3 as needed to insert the square brackets for the absolute references and F2 to "drop the anchor."

9.8 Trick: Temporarily add rows or columns to your worksheet to use the (Edit) Copy command to best advantage. ***Both***

Because the (Edit) Copy command works so easily when you have contiguous blocks, you should try to use the (Edit) Copy command as often as possible. Sometimes, however, using (Edit) Copy may not seem possible.

Consider the example in figure 9.4, showing summary and detail portions of a worksheet. The detail portion has multiple lines (two in this case) that are summarized to create a total for each division. The detail totals are to be recorded within the summary block on rows 1 and 2.

You easily can enter into r1c4 a formula to extract the total from r8c4 for the East Division total. But for the West Division total, you want to be able to copy r1c4 to r2c4. Although this example works with only 2 divisions, copying would become even more important if you have 50 or 60 divisions; you would not want to enter separate formulas for each line in the summary area.

A simple copy command will not suffice here. The formula in r1c4 reads r8c4. If you copy that formula to r2c4, the result is r9c4. Clearly, this result is not what you want; you want the result to be r12c4. In effect, rather than incrementing by one row in the copy command, you want to increment by four rows.

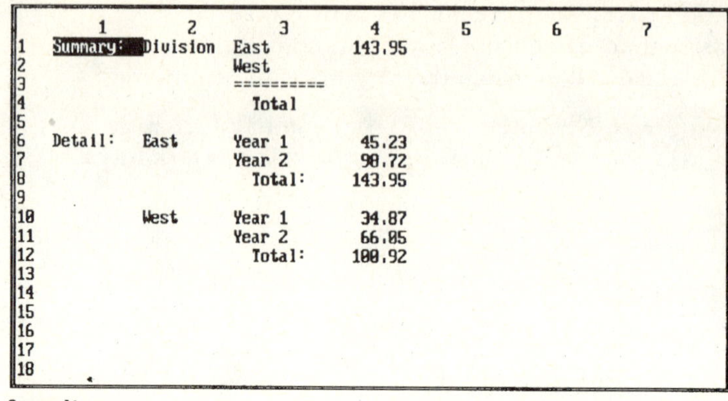

Fig. 9.4.

Copying discontiguous blocks.

The solution to this problem is to temporarily insert three extra rows in the summary area, to copy from r1c4 to r2:5c4, and then to delete the extra rows. Figure 9.5 shows the worksheet with the temporary rows after the copy has been performed and recalculated.

```
        1        2        3           4        5        6        7
1  Summary:  Division  East        143.95
2                                    0.00
3                                   34.87
4                                   66.05
5                      West        100.92
6                      ==========
7                        Total
8
9  Detail:   East      Year 1       45.23
10                     Year 2       90.72
11                       Total:    143.95
12
13           West      Year 1       34.87
14                     Year 2       66.05
15                       Total:    100.92
16
17
18
Command:
Worksheet: discon   Loc: r1c4              FN: 0   Font: Standard
```

Fig. 9.5.

Inserting temporary rows.

The presence of values in rows 2, 3, and 4 is unimportant because the rows are deleted, as shown in figure 9.6.

An example of only two divisions may seem trivial, but if you have many summary line items, this trick can be a significant time saver.

Both

9.9 Tip: Change the format of a value cell before you copy it; the format will be copied, along with the cell.

```
         1          2          3          4          5          6          7
1  Summary:  Division  East          143.95
2                      West          100.92
3                      ==========
4                        Total
5
6  Detail:   East      Year 1         45.23
7                      Year 2         98.72
8                        Total:      143.95
9
10           West      Year 1         34.87
11                     Year 2         66.05
12                       Total:      100.92
13
14
15
16
17
18
Enter:
Formula: r12c4
Worksheet: discon     Loc: r2c4                    FN: 0     Font: Standard
ENTER - enter a formula, a value or text into the current cell
```

Fig. 9.6.
Deleting temporary rows.

Fewer keystrokes are involved in formatting an individual cell, compared to a row, column, or block. By formatting before you copy, you can save time. If the blocks you copy are discontiguous, the time savings can be even greater.

The Effect of Copying to the Destination Block

9.10 Trap: The (Edit) Copy command will overlay the cell contents within the destination block.

Both

Make sure you have enough space to accept the copy of a source block. If there is not enough space, use the Insert command to create some new rows or columns. If you are in doubt, insert extra rows or columns; you can always delete them later if you don't need them.

Remember that, unlike some other electronic spreadsheets, the Smart Spreadsheet does not use extra memory for empty cells, so you need not worry about using up your computer's memory if you have too many empty rows or columns.

Preformatting a Block

9.11 Trick: Preformat a block by copying a block from another worksheet.

Both

Although you cannot preformat a block in the Smart 3.10 Spreadsheet, you can achieve the preformatting effect if you copy a block from another worksheet. The block can be filled with zeros or dummy alpha entries. This method works well when your applications have recurring blocks with the same format.

A simple project file can illustrate this trick:

```
'preformat a block
'copy from another worksheet

%1 Number of Rows:
%2 Number of Columns:

copy from dec3.r1:%1c1:%2 to rc
```

In this example, the worksheet is called dec3, in which the block r1:25c1:25 is filled with zero values at a precision of three decimals. By using this project file, you can copy a portion of this worksheet into your current worksheet to preformat a block of cells. After the copy, cells in the destination block of your current worksheet retain the formatting characteristics from those in the external worksheet.

Remember that, for this trick to work, the external worksheet must be loaded or activated. If you need various formats at different times, you can have several external worksheets, or you may decide to include all of your common formats in one, all-purpose worksheet.

In SmartWare II, you may preformat a block of cells.

Using External References

Both

9.12 Trick: To copy from one spreadsheet to another, use an external reference with the (Edit) Copy command.

You can copy from the current spreadsheet to another active spreadsheet or copy in the opposite direction. For example,

```
Edit copy from r1:10c5:20 to sheet2.r1:10c5:20

Edit copy from sheet2.r1:10c5:20 to r1:10c5:20
```

Both worksheets must be active, but the external worksheet does not have to be in a window.

In SmartWare II, you also may use the File Combine command to either Copy, Add, or Subtract. You may specify that the source is either an entire worksheet, or a block of a worksheet. The source worksheet does not have to be loaded to be able to use this command.

Moving Portions of the Worksheet

The Move (3.10) or Edit Move (SmartWare II) commands can be used to rearrange portions of your worksheet for cosmetic purposes or for ease of use. The formula references are adjusted at the time of the move so that the original formulas still calculate correctly.

Like copying a block, moving a block overlays the destination contents, but moving a whole row or column causes a shift of the remaining worksheet. Unlike the (Edit) Copy command, however, the (Edit) Move command can be performed only within the current worksheet.

The (Edit) Copy Command Compared to the (Edit) Move Command

9.13 Tip: Keep in mind the differences between the (Edit) Copy and (Edit) Move commands. *Both*

The (Edit) Copy command takes the cell contents in the source block and copies them to the destination block, performing relative-address adjustments as the command executes. For example, you can create a formula one time and then make multiple copies of the formula for additional divisions, time periods, line items, and so on.

The (Edit) Move command, on the other hand, is used to rearrange your worksheet to make it better looking or easier to work with. Addresses in the worksheet are changed, but only because the block that you moved is now in a different spot and any cells that referenced this block must now refer to different cell addresses. (Fortunately, you don't have to make the changes yourself.)

9.14 Tip: With the (Edit) Move command, the original source block is converted to blanks. *Both*

With the (Edit) Move command, as with the (Edit) Copy command, the contents of the destination block are overlaid by the source block you have moved. But unlike the (Edit) Copy command, the (Edit) Move command blanks the source block. If the worksheet does not have enough space to accommodate moving the source block, be sure to insert some additional rows or columns.

For example, if you decide that the layout in figure 9.7 looks better than the one in figure 9.6, you can rearrange your worksheet with the (Edit) Move command.

The cell references in rows 1 and 2 of column 4 (the totals for the East and West Divisions) are adjusted automatically to reflect the new locations of the total lines in the detail areas. You do not have to make those changes manually because you are moving a block within the same worksheet.

The Effect of the (Edit) Move Command on External References

9.15 Trap: Cell references to external worksheets are not adjusted automatically when you move blocks in the external worksheets. *Both*

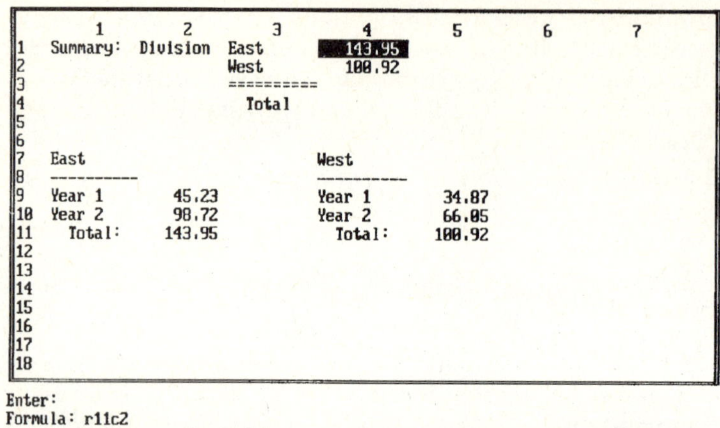

Fig. 9.7.
The worksheet after using the Move command.

Cell references are adjusted if you perform an (Edit) Move command within a single worksheet. If you move blocks in another worksheet that are referenced from your current sheet, however, the adjustments are not made in the current sheet. You can solve this problem by references to block names in external worksheets.

Suppose that you have the detail information from the previous example in one worksheet, and the summary information in another. The formulas in rows 1 and 2 might read:

```
detail.r11c2
detail.r11c5
```

Now, if you move the detail blocks for the divisions around in the detail worksheet, the summary sheet has no means of keeping track of these block movements. The formulas in the summary worksheet are not adjusted automatically to reflect the new locations.

You can solve this problem by using block names. The block names in the detail worksheet can be set up to refer to the total cells r11c2 and r11c5. In the summary worksheet, the formulas in rows 1 and 2 then would read:

```
detail.east
detail.west
```

When you move a block that contains a named cell or block, the name is moved at the same time. Therefore, a reference to the block in the other worksheet always retrieves the desired data.

Both

9.16 Trap: Moving rows and columns within named blocks can yield unspecified results because the block boundaries may not be evident.

For example, if you have a named block with the definition r1:7c1:4 and you move column 1 to column 3, the named block is now r1:7c3:4 because the left margin of the block remains tied to the data in the original column. As shown in this example, blocks covering the same columns yield similarly unpredictable results. Following the movement of column 1 to column 3, for example, the named block r10:16c1:2 will have the definition r10:16c1:3.

Be careful, therefore, if you are moving rows or columns within named blocks.

Operating the Worksheet

Naming a worksheet block can save time when you have to provide a block specification. You can save space when you have only a limited area to provide a series of specifications within a menu and can save headaches, especially when used with external references.

Using Named Worksheet Blocks

9.17 Trick: Use the Name Edit (3.10) or Sheet Name Edit (SmartWare II) commands to view the names of your worksheet blocks. ***Both***

Smart has no explicit command for viewing these names. Use the (Sheet) Name Edit command, as shown in figure 9.8, to view the names or to change the row and column specifications associated with the names.

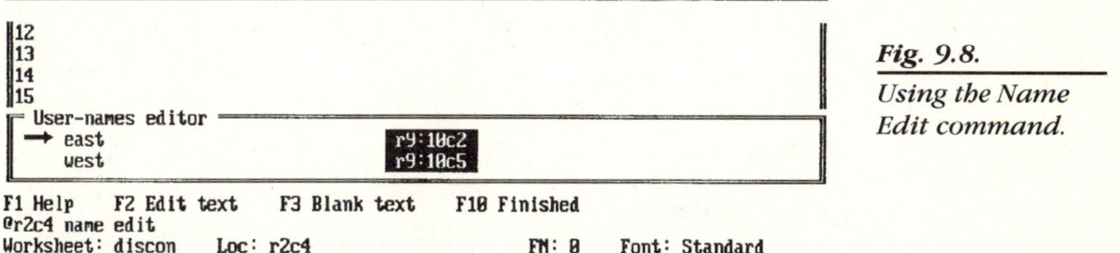

Fig. 9.8.
Using the Name Edit command.

9.18 Trap: Adding a row or column adjacent to any boundary of a named block does not automatically include that row or column in the block. You must edit the block definition manually. ***Both***

If you insert a row or column in the middle of a block defined by a name, the specification is adjusted automatically. Similarly, if you delete a row or column, the definition is adjusted. However, if you add to any boundary of a named block an adjacent row or column that you want included in the block, you must edit the block definition and make the adjustment manually.

9.19 Trap: Using a reserved word for a block name causes an ambiguity that may not be resolved accurately. ***3.10***

The system does not catch the use of reserved words (SUM, for example). If you use a reserved word for a name, the results are unpredictable.

In SmartWare II, many more of the reserved words are trapped, preventing you from using them. For example, if you try to use the name SUM, you get the following error message:

```
Invalid cell or block name
```

Both

9.20 Tip: In the Name Edit (3.10) or Sheet Name Edit (SmartWare II) command, use the F6 key to return temporarily to the worksheet to help you redefine the boundaries of a named range.

Rather than writing down the new range boundaries, you can use the F6 key to display the worksheet. Use F2 to drop the anchor at the upper left corner of the range, move to the lower right, and press Enter. The range is inserted into the edit workspace.

Both

9.21 Trap: If you are not careful, you can define two worksheet blocks with the same name. The two block names, one that references the current worksheet and the other an external worksheet, can accidentally exist simultaneously (see fig. 9.9).

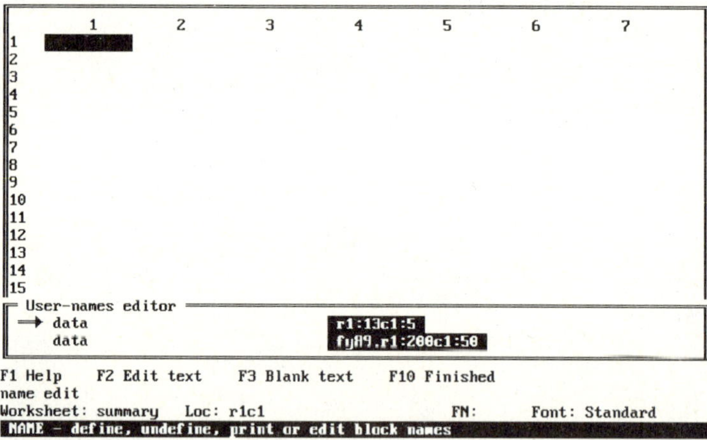

Fig. 9.9.

A worksheet displaying two blocks with the same name.

If you define the first block name, referencing the external worksheet while the external sheet is loaded, you have no problem. Later, however, if the external worksheet is *not* loaded, you can define the *same* block name, referencing just the current worksheet.

In usage, the top name takes precedence, being the definition in the current worksheet. In practice, however, you do not want to use duplicate names. Use the Name Undefine (3.10) or Sheet Name Undefine (SmartWare II) commands to clear up the problem. The first execution of the command undefines the top occurrence. Execute the command again if you want to undefine the second one. If the external worksheet is not loaded, you cannot undefine the block name that references the external worksheet.

9.22 Trap: When you define a new block name using the (Sheet) Name Define command, you receive no warning if you are overlaying an existing name.

Both

To make sure you are not replacing an existing block name, use the Sheet Name Edit (SmartWare II) or Name Edit (3.10) commands to display the current block names and their definitions.

9.23 Trap: Project files that reference block names do not compile unless the worksheet with the named block is current.

SW II

For example, the following print statement contains the name of a block called DATA:

```
print text block data printer draft copies 1
```

Unless you have a current worksheet with a block named DATA, you will get the following error message when you try to compile the project file (or press F10 from the Remember Tools Editor):

```
Undefined variable or function
```

Note that the block name is *not* in quotation marks. To solve the problem, load the worksheet with the named block and then recompile the project file.

Using the Fill Command

9.24 Tip: To create a data series without having to type the series yourself, use the Fill (3.10) or Edit Fill (SmartWare II) commands.

Both

You can fill each of the following options of the (Edit) Fill command:

```
Block      Columns      Rows
```

If you fill columns, you are prompted for the number of columns, the start value, and the increment value. If you are filling rows, you are prompted for the number of rows. To fill a block, select the Block option and specify the block.

The start and increment values do not have to be whole, positive integers. You can use numbers with decimals or negative numbers.

9.25 Tip: In the (Edit) Fill command, each row in a column is filled before the rows in the next column are filled.

Both

For example, a 2 x 2 block is filled in the following order:

1 3
2 4

Using Matrix Commands

Matrix commands are used to perform statistical operations on an entire block (or matrix) of data at one time. Several of these commands are presented in this section. The Matrix Regression command is given particular attention.

The Matrix Transpose Command

Both

9.26 Tip: Use the Matrix Transpose command to change a block filled by column to a block filled by row.

The Matrix Transpose command can effect a transposition after you execute the Fill command. The difference between the two filled blocks can be seen in figure 9.10.

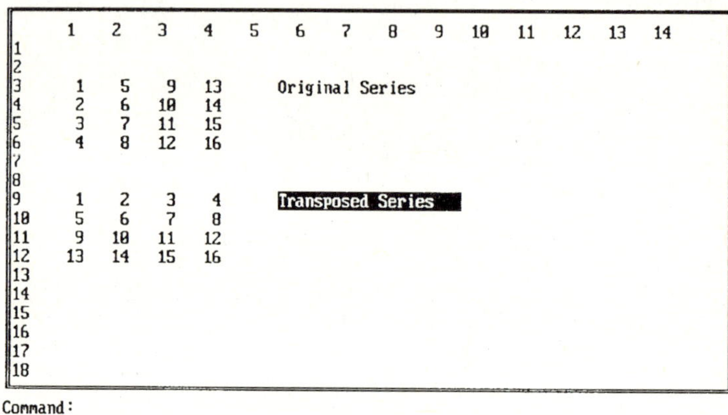

Fig. 9.10. *Matrix transposition of filled data.*

Both

9.27 Tip: You can use the (Edit) Fill command to create a column of dates.

The start value should be the sequential number of the day you want to start with, and the increment value should be 1 for every day, 2 for every other day, 7 for every week, and so on. Use the Reformat (3.10) or Layout Format (SmartWare II) commands to display the numbers in a Date format.

Both

9.28 Tip: Use the F-Calculator to generate the sequential number of a date when filling a block with dates.

Press Alt-K before you begin the (Edit) Fill command; when in the F-Calculator, determine the sequential day number:

```
days("5/25/69")
```

Press F2 to display the number on the command line and F10 to exit from the calculator.

Now execute the Fill command. In response to the prompt

```
Enter start value:
```

press Ctrl-C. This keystroke retrieves the sequential date you determined in the F-Calculator and inserts that date on the command line. Now, continue with the command. When you are done, use the Reformat (3.10) or Layout Format (SmartWare II) commands to change to the Date format display.

The Matrix Parallel Command

9.29 Tip: Use the (Sheet) Matrix Parallel command to perform arithmetic operations with several data blocks simultaneously.

Both

The (Sheet) Matrix Parallel command can be used to add, multiply, subtract, or divide—on a cell-by-cell basis—multiple data blocks. Figure 9.11 shows several examples using this command.

```
     1   2   3   4   5   6   7   8    9          10          11     12  13  14
1    Block #1           Block #2          Result Block
2    ---------------------------------------------------------------
3     1   7  13          5   2  -1          6.000       9.000     12.000
4     3   9  15    +     4   1  -2    =     7.000      10.000     13.000
5     5  11  17          3   0  -3          8.000      11.000     14.000
6
7    23  44  65         65  59  53          0.354       0.746      1.226
8    30  51  72    /    63  57  51    =     0.476       0.895      1.412
9    37  58  79         61  55  49          0.607       1.055      1.612
10
11    1  10  19         10   4  -2         10.000      40.000    -38.000
12    4  13  22    *     8   2  -4    =    32.000      26.000    -88.000
13    7  16  25          6   0  -6         42.000       0.000   -150.000
14
15
16
17
18
Select option: Add Div Mult Sub
matrix parallel r11:13c1:3
Worksheet: (none)      Loc: r11c1                    FM: 0     Font: Standard
MATRIX - perform statistical, matrix, or element operations on blocks
```

Fig. 9.11

Using the Matrix Parallel Command.

The Linear Regression Command

9.30 Tip: Use the (Sheet) Matrix Regression command to create a forecast.

Both

Simply stated in graphical terms, linear regression is an attempt to graph a straight line through a plotted series of numbers so that the line passes as closely as possible to the data points. You probably have tried this by the "eyeball" method at one time or another, but linear regression accomplishes the task more accurately with statistical techniques.

In a linear regression, you always have a variable (or set of observation data points) whose behavior you are trying to predict. This is called the dependent variable because its value depends on other variables whose values you do know (or at least will know with greater certainty). These other variables are called the independent variables.

Both

9.31 Tip: You must have at least one independent variable, but you can have more.

The introduction of additional independent variables may or may not be helpful in the development of your linear-regression model. If the independent variables are related naturally to each other (a condition called autocorrelation), the entry of additional independent variables only confuse the issue.

In this example, the dependent variable is monthly registrations (in thousands) of domestic passenger automobiles, beginning with 1976. Column 2 in figure 9.12 shows the number of registrations from January 1976 to March 1977.

Fig. 9.12.

Monthly registrations of domestic passenger automobiles.

	1	2	3	4	5	6
1			Month	12 Month	Centered	Percent of
2	Month	Cars	Sequence	Moving Total	Moving Average	Moving Average
3	----------	----------	----------	----------	----------	----------
4	Jan 76	677	1			
5	Feb 76	634	2			
6	Mar 76	764	3			
7	Apr 76	804	4			
8	May 76	914	5			
9	Jun 76	937	6			
10	Jul 76	939	7	9,752	812.67	115.55%
11	Aug 76	848	8	9,801	816.75	103.83%
12	Sep 76	749	9	9,884	823.67	90.93%
13	Oct 76	797	10	9,956	829.67	96.06%
14	Nov 76	763	11	9,996	833.00	91.60%
15	Dec 76	846	12	10,097	841.42	100.54%
16	Jan 77	726	13	10,210	850.83	85.33%
17	Feb 77	717	14	10,284	857.00	83.66%
18	Mar 77	836	15	10,463	871.92	95.88%

```
Command list 4:  Activate  Directory  File  Index  Load  Matrix  Password  Read
                 Save  Unload  Write
Worksheet: CAR2       Loc: r1c1                  FN: 0    Font: Standard
MATRIX - perform statistical, matrix, or element operations on blocks
```

The other values in figure 9.12 are the following:

Column 1: Name of month.

Column 3: Sequential month number. (This is used as the independent variable in the linear-regression model.)

Column 4: A 12-month moving total. The value for July 76 represents the sum of the cars registered from January 1976 to December 1976. August is the sum from February 1976 through January 1977.

Column 5: Centered moving average. Column 4 divided by 12.

Column 6: Percent of moving average. Column 2 divided by column 5.

Columns 4 through 6 are used to develop a seasonality model, which is discussed later (see fig. 9.13).

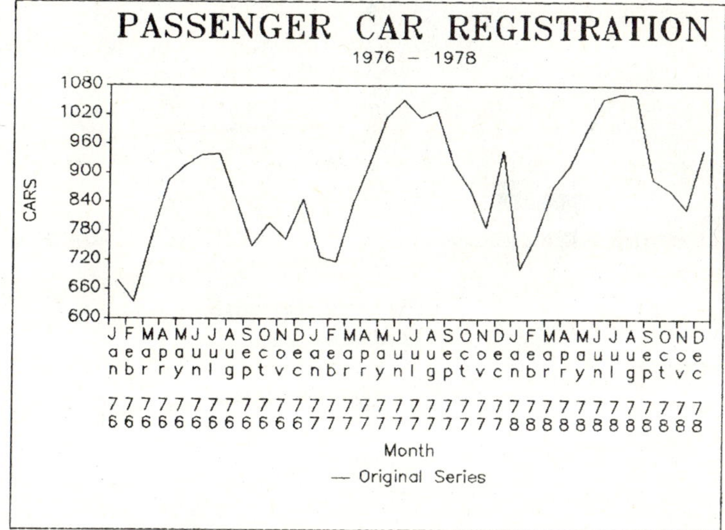

Fig. 9.13.
A graph of passenger-car registrations from 1976 to 1978.

Figure 9.13 is a graph of the dependent variable from 1976 through 1978. Note that there seems to be an increase from year to year; the extent and predictability of this increase can be determined in the linear-regression model. Note also a repetition in the pattern from year to year, leading you to suspect that the data is seasonal. More cars seem to be registered in the spring and summer than in the winter, although each December shows a "spike."

The usefulness of the linear-regression technique lies in the degree to which actual observations correspond to the predicting variables both now and in the future. In the current model, the dependent variable is the number of cars registered; the independent variable is the sequential month number. The assumption, then, is that the number of cars registered is dependent on time and not related to any other factor. The linear regression produces the coefficients of a formula in the format

$$y = a + bx$$

in which y is the number of cars, a is the left intercept (number of cars in month zero of the model), b is the slope of the line (number of cars added each month), and x is the month number. If the model is valid, knowing the month number in the future will enable you to predict how many cars will be registered.

9.32 Tip: To initiate linear regression, invoke the (Sheet) Matrix command.

Both

The Matrix command is found on command list 4 (refer to figure 9.12). In SmartWare II, use the Sheet Matrix command. The Matrix subcommand menu is shown in figure 9.14.

```
13  Oct 76   797      10           9,956          829.67          96.06%
14  Nov 76   763      11           9,996          833.00          91.60%
15  Dec 76   846      12          10,097          841.42         100.54%
16  Jan 77   726      13          10,210          850.83          85.33%
17  Feb 77   717      14          10,284          857.00          83.66%
18  Mar 77   836      15          10,463          871.92          95.88%

Select option:  Aux  Diagonal  Eigen  Invert  Multiply  N-Solve  Parallel
            Regression  Sweep  Transpose  Upper
Worksheet: CAR2       Loc: r1c1                 FN: 0     Font: Standard
MATRIX - perform statistical, matrix, or element operations on blocks
```

Fig. 9.14.

The Matrix Regression command.

Select the Regression option to initiate the Linear Regression command. The first prompt, `Enter matrix block`, is shown in figure 9.15.

```
40  Jan 79   755      37          10,915          909.58          83.01%
41  Feb 79   766      38          10,767          897.25          85.37%
42  Mar 79   922      39          10,585          882.08         104.53%
43  Apr 79   953      40          10,552          879.33         108.38%
44  May 79   988      41          10,574          881.17         112.12%
45  Jun 79   880      42          10,474          872.83         100.82%

Enter matrix-block: r4:39c2:3
F2 Drop anchor    F3 Absolute/Relative
Worksheet: CAR2       Loc: r39c3                FN: 0     Font: Standard
MATRIX - perform statistical, matrix, or element operations on blocks
```

Fig. 9.15.

Selection of the regression matrix block.

Both

9.33 Tip: The dependent variable for a linear-regression model must be positioned in the left column of the matrix block. The independent variables must be positioned in the columns immediately to the right of the dependent variable.

This is the only means of identifying the variables to the model. In figure 9.15, note that column 2 is the dependent variable (cars) and column 3 is the independent variable (sequential month number). Keep in mind that only 36 months are being used in the model; the remaining months help evaluate the model's accuracy.

Both

9.34 Tip: Select a report if you want the statistics that underlie the model.

After you select the matrix block, the next prompt is

```
No-Report        Report
```

When you select Report, you are prompted to enter a name or block reference indicating where the report should be written.

The regression report provides the statistics to indicate the value of the linear-regression model. Although linear regression determines a straight line through the graph of the original series, you may want to know the degree of model validity.

9.35 Tip: Be sure to provide enough space for the regression report. *Both*

If you select the Report option, you must provide an output block with at least 6 columns, 21 rows for standard data, and 1 row for each independent variable.

9.36 Tip: Select an output block for the regression coefficients. *Both*

The last prompt is

```
Enter cell, column vector, or row vector:
```

The computed regression coefficients (a and b in Tip 9.31) are inserted in the designated rows. The best way to answer this prompt is to provide the address of one cell in a column. The intercept is inserted into that cell, and the independent variable coefficients are inserted into each following row in that column.

The regression model then is calculated, and the report and coefficients are generated. Figure 9.16 shows the resulting report.

```
      16             17            18            19           20           21
1                               MULTIPLE LINEAR REGRESSION
2
3   Dependent Variable:
4
5                                           Parameter    Standard     T for H0:
6   Variable                       Mean     Estimate      Error      parameter=0
7
8   Intercept                                 786.20       36.32         21.64
9   Variable  1                   18.50         4.84        1.71          2.83
10
11                               Sum of       Mean
12  Source            DF         Squares      Square      F-Value
13
14  Model            1.00         90966        90966        7.99
15  Error           34.00        387173        11387
16  Total           35.00        478139
17
18  Dependent Mean                            875.72
Command list 4:  Activate  Directory  File  Index  Load  Matrix  Password  Read
                 Save  Unload  Write
Worksheet: CAR2        Loc: r1c16                      FN:       Font: Standard
MATRIX - perform statistical, matrix, or element operations on blocks
```

Fig. 9.16.
A linear regression report.

The calculated coefficients are shown in rows 8 and 9 of column 19. In the example, the intercept of 786.20 means that in month "0" (December 1975), 786,200 cars would have been registered. Each additional month witnesses an increase of 4.84 (thousands).

The F-Value in r14c20 can be considered a measure of confidence in whether the straight line resulting from the linear-regression model accurately reflects a trend. (A statistics book would indicate that with 36 observations [months], an F-Value of 7.99 well exceeds the value of 3.09 needed to provide a 99 percent degree of confidence in the model.)

Similar to the F-Value, the T statistics in rows 8 and 9 of column 21 indicate that both the coefficients fall within the 99 percent confidence limit. If you have multiple independent variables, you would want to discard any variable whose T statistic did not provide the confidence level required.

Both

9.37 Trick: Use the results of a linear regression to develop a forecast.

If you are satisfied that the regression model may accurately reflect the pattern of observations in the sample 36 months, you can begin to use the results of the model.

In figure 9.17, rows 3 and 4 of column 22 contain the computed regression coefficients. (I selected r3c22 as my answer to the final prompt in the regression command.) Ignore columns 24 and 25 for the moment; column 23 has been calculated by adding the intercept to the product of the slope and the independent variable (month):

```
straight line = (slope * month number) + intercept
```

Fig. 9.17.
An application of the linear model.

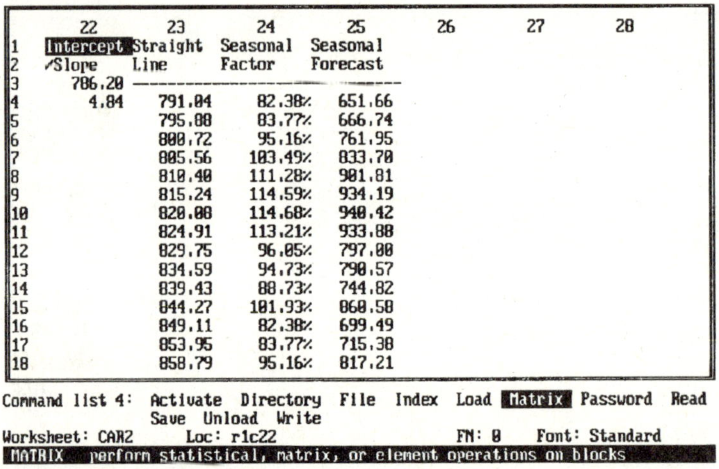

```
      22        23        24        25        26        27        28
1  Intercept Straight  Seasonal  Seasonal
2  /Slope    Line      Factor    Forecast
3    786.20  ----------------------------
4      4.84    791.04    82.38%    651.66
5              795.88    83.77%    666.74
6              800.72    95.16%    761.95
7              805.56   103.49%    833.70
8              810.40   111.28%    901.81
9              815.24   114.59%    934.19
10             820.08   114.68%    940.42
11             824.91   113.21%    933.88
12             829.75    96.05%    797.00
13             834.59    94.73%    790.57
14             839.43    88.73%    744.82
15             844.27   101.93%    860.58
16             849.11    82.38%    699.49
17             853.95    83.77%    715.30
18             858.79    95.16%    817.21

Command list 4:  Activate  Directory  File  Index  Load  Matrix  Password  Read
                 Save  Unload  Write
Worksheet: CAR2      Loc: r1c22                  FN: 0    Font: Standard
MATRIX   perform statistical, matrix, or element operations on blocks
```

By constructing this column, you attempt to predict the number of cars registered by month for each of the 36 months (see fig. 9.18).

Figure 9.18 shows both the original series and the superimposed regression line. (Notice that 1979 is included on the graph for comparison with the trend.)

First, you notice that although the straight line may approximate the actual values, in no way does the straight line come close to reflecting the ups and downs of the original series. The regression line does seem to follow the general upward trend of the first three years, but year 4 (1979) falls short of the forecast.

Both

9.38 Tip: Data beyond the range of the regression model has no effect.

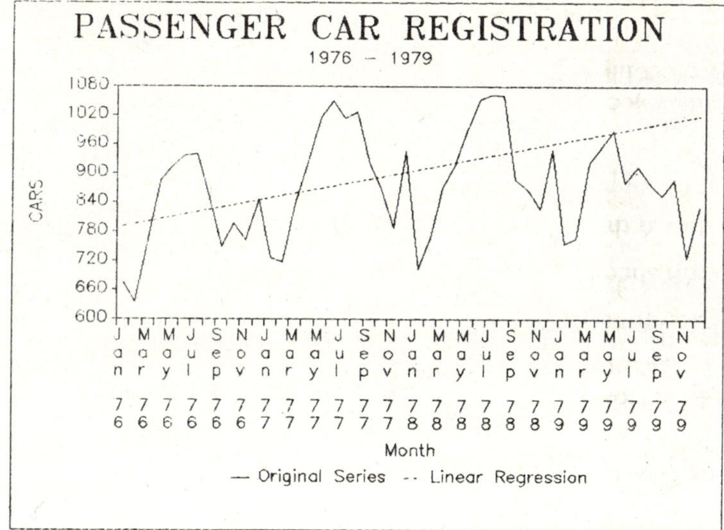

Fig. 9.18.
A graph showing a regression line and the number of cars registered from 1976 to 1979.

Remember that the regression model was developed using only the data from 1976 through 1978; the number of cars registered in 1979 was not included in the calculation. The actual slump in the automotive industry, if there was one in 1979, has no effect on the trend line. Looking at these figures, you must conclude that the model did not do a good job of predicting registrations in 1979, and that automotive registrations may depend on factors other than the sequential month number or growth over a period of time.

9.39 Trick: Develop a seasonal model from the historical data.

Both

Even if there had not been a slump in 1979, the linear-regression model lacks something as a general predictor of automobile registrations. Perhaps the model would be acceptable on an annual basis, but if cars are manufactured according to this forecast, manufacturers would need a huge parking lot to hold all the cars produced in the winter months but not sold until the summer.

Let us address this question of seasonality. By inspection, a pattern seems to exist from year to year. A few simple calculations can help analyze this apparent seasonality.

Note in figure 9.12 that columns 4, 5, and 6 are used to calculate a seasonality factor for each month. Column 4 is a 12-month moving total. For July 1976, the calculation is the sum of the cars from January through December of that year; and for August, the calculation is the sum of February through January of 1977.

Column 5 is column 4 divided by 12; this is a moving average centered within a 12-month period. Column 6 is column 2 divided by column 5, representing a ratio between the actual observation for the month and the moving average. In effect, you are calculating the extent to which the individual observation varies from the 12-month average.

Each month, of course, has its own ratio between the average and the actual observation. The table in figure 9.19 calculates a ratio to be used for all January months, all February months, and so on.

Fig. 9.19.

Calculation of a seasonality index.

	9	10	11	12	13	14	15
1							Adjusted
2	Month	1976	1977	1978	1979	Median	Median
3	------------	------------	------------	------------	------------	------------	------------
4	January		85.33%	77.72%	83.01%	83.01%	82.38%
5	February		83.66%	84.41%	85.37%	84.41%	83.77%
6	March		95.88%	95.45%	104.53%	95.88%	95.16%
7	April		104.28%	100.79%	100.38%	104.28%	103.49%
8	May		113.81%	100.60%	112.12%	112.12%	111.28%
9	June		117.46%	115.46%	100.82%	115.46%	114.59%
10	July	115.55%	112.27%	116.42%		115.55%	114.68%
11	August	103.83%	114.07%	115.76%		114.07%	113.21%
12	September	90.93%	101.60%	96.78%		96.78%	96.05%
13	October	96.06%	95.44%	94.05%		95.44%	94.73%
14	November	91.60%	86.91%	89.40%		89.40%	88.73%
15	December	100.54%	104.61%	102.71%		102.71%	101.93%
16						------------	------------
17						1,209.11%	1,200.00%
18							

Command list 4: Activate Directory File Index Load **Matrix** Password Read Save Unload Write

Worksheet: CAR2 Loc: r1c9 FN: Font: Standard

MATRIX - perform statistical, matrix, or element operations on blocks

Column 14 of figure 9.19 represents the median seasonality index from among the three ratios calculated for each of the similar months in the period 1976 to 1979. Using the median requires that you discard any aberrant values that would distort the calculations. Column 15 adjusts each entry in column 14 so that the sum of the index figures is 1,200, or an average of 100 percent for each month.

Both

9.40 Trick: Apply the seasonal model to the data forecast.

After the seasonality indices are calculated, the indices can be used by applying them back against the regression trend line (see fig. 9.20). Refer to columns 24 and 25 of figure 9.17. Notice that column 24 represents the seasonality indices from figure 9.19; column 25 is the product of column 23 (the straight line from the linear-regression model) and column 24. Column 25, then, is the seasonal, trend-adjusted forecast. Refer to figure 9.20 to see how well reality is represented.

Note that the dashed line, representing the seasonal forecast, has been included on the graph; and the line, for the most part, seems to follow the cyclical pattern from year to year. However, because the seasonality index was applied to the trend line, the seasonal forecast in 1979 came out significantly above the actual figures. In spite of this error of magnitude, the seasonal pattern in 1979 has held up pretty well.

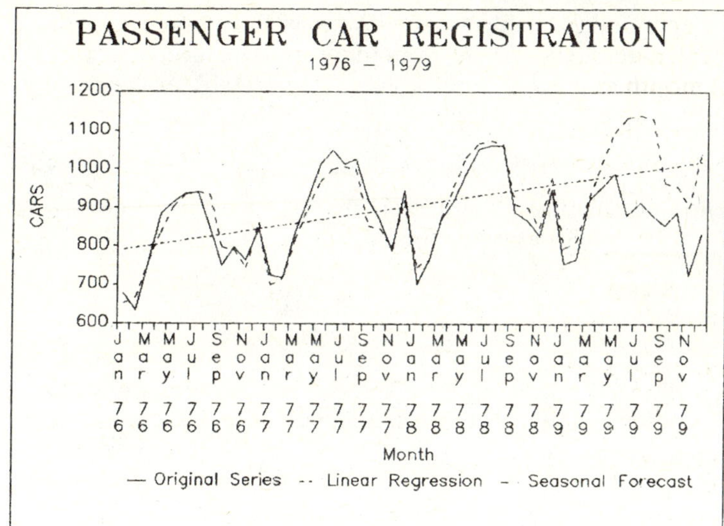

Fig. 9.20.
A seasonal forecast of registrations from 1976 to 1979.

Was 1979 just an "off" year, and would the seasonal, trend-adjusted model be accurate in predicting monthly car registrations in 1980 and 1981? To answer this question, two more years are graphed, as shown in figure 9.21.

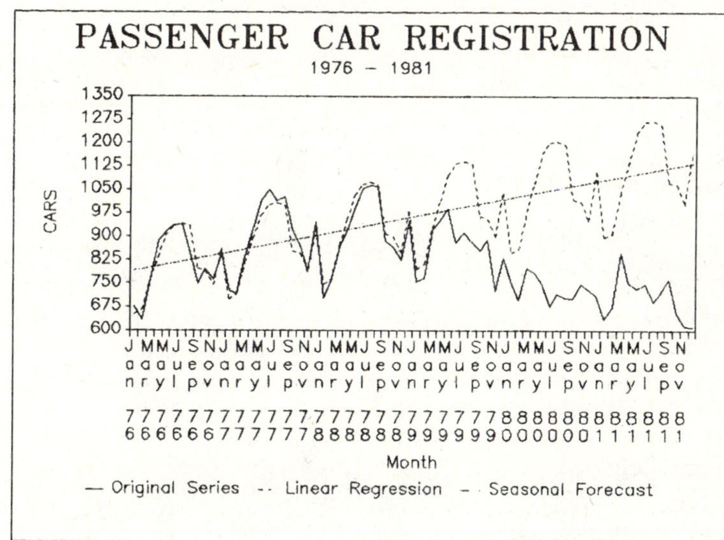

Fig. 9.21.
A seasonal forecast of registrations from 1976 to 1981.

Fortunately, this model was not used to tell General Motors how many cars to produce because, as you can see, beginning in about May 1979, the automotive industry began a steep decline.

Remember, the independent variable in the model is the sequential month number; this assumed that registrations would increase from month to month. Obviously, other factors were at work here, which are best left to the economists in Detroit.

Both

9.41 Trick: Use a formula to calculate the median of three values.

Smart has no function to calculate a median, as shown in column 14 of figure 9.19. The following is the calculation for the median in r4c14:

```
sum(r4c11:13)
-max(r4c11,r4c12,r4c13)
-min(r4c11,r4c12,r4c13)
```

This formula subtracts both the maximum and minimum of columns 11, 12, and 13 from the total of these columns. The result is the figure in the middle—the median. This formula works for a series of three numbers, but you cannot apply the formula to a larger series.

Using the File Combine Command

SW II

9.42 Trap: If a spreadsheet data source in the File Combine command is an unloaded, external worksheet that has not been recalculated, the results may be erroneous.

Because the File Combine command allows the use of unloaded worksheets, it may not be evident that a worksheet has been changed but not recalculated. Using the worksheet in a File Combine command does not recalculate the source worksheet automatically, and therefore may yield false data.

Sorting the Worksheet

Both

9.43 Trap: You cannot sort a calculated text row or column; the results are unpredictable.

The Sort command is used to arrange a block of data or formulas in an order that you specify. Normally, whether you use a value, text, or formula as the sort key does not matter. If you are sorting on a calculated text row or column, however, the sort does not work correctly. The block may not sort at all or may rely on an adjacent numerical column for the sort criteria.

3.10

9.44 Trick: Use the ASC function to convert text to a value to allow a sort using calculated text cells.

To solve the problem of not being able to sort using calculated text cells, create an extra column (or row) that uses the ASC function to convert the first character of the calculated text to the ASCII representation. You then can sort on this ASCII column or row. If necessary, create additional columns for the subsequent text characters; the ASC function can be used only one character at a time.

9.45 Trap: Make calculated text cells left-justified to be able to sort them correctly. *SW II*

If you are using calculated text cells as the sort criteria for sorting a block, make sure the text cells are left-justified; use the Layout Justify command. If the cells are not left-justified, the results are unpredictable.

9.46 Trick: If you run out of memory when trying to perform a large sort, and then break the sort block into smaller pieces, sort the smaller blocks individually and perform the large sort again. *Both*

Presorting portions of a large block makes the final sort much easier for the system to perform. Not as much workspace has to be maintained in RAM.

Forcing Zeros to Blanks

9.47 Trick: Use a project file to force all zeros to be null. *3.10*

Sometimes you may have a worksheet in which you want any zero values to appear as blanks, rather than zeros. You may want to keep the formatting, however, if the cell was preformatted. To make the cell appear blank, replace the "0" with a "null." The following project file can be used to find any zeros and make them null.

```
'find and null all zeros
goto r1c1

label begin

find value 0

if cerror = 1007 then jump alldone
Let rc = null
jump begin

label alldone
beep
message  All Zero's Have Been Nulled .. press any key
```

Note that the test for the command error (*cerror*) branches out of the loop when all zeros have been found. The *cerror* value will be 1007 if the Find command fails to find a zero.

In SmartWare II, when you format numeric cells in SmartWare II, you have the following two options:

```
Show-All  Zero-Blank
```

By selecting Zero-Blank, any cells that are zero will appear as blank.

10

Functions

Spreadsheet functions not only save you time, but they can perform operations you may never be able to do without them. The Smart Spreadsheet has a vast number of functions, many of which are covered in this chapter.

The chapter begins with the LOOKUP functions and a comparison of the Smart and the 1-2-3 spreadsheet versions. (There are important differences.) Next, the discussion moves to error handling, worksheet position functions, and methods of validating the contents of your worksheet.

The DATE and TIME functions are covered in their own section. Finally, numeric and text functions are reviewed with several tips and tricks.

Using the LOOKUP Functions

Use the vertical and horizontal LOOKUP functions to retrieve a value from a table. In a vertical LOOKUP function, the system searches the left column of the table to match the argument; in a horizontal lookup, the top row is searched. The Spreadsheet module includes not only the Smart LOOKUP functions, but also the similar functions from 1-2-3. Vital differences are apparent in the way they work.

Smart versus 1-2-3 LOOKUPS

10.1 Tip: The VLOOKUP and HLOOKUP functions require an exact match in the table if your search argument is numeric. ***Both***

The LOOKUP functions beginning with the @ character do not require an exact match in the lookup table. Functions that don't contain the @ character do require exact matches, however.

The two varieties of LOOKUP functions are distinguished by the presence or absence of the "at" sign character (@). LOOKUP functions with the "at" sign duplicate the Lotus 1-2-3 functions and differ significantly from the "native" Smart functions, VLOOKUP and HLOOKUP. Good reasons exist for using the 1-2-3 functions rather than always using the Smart functions.

Figure 10.1 demonstrates the differences between @Vlookup and VLOOKUP. The functions in column 2 of rows 1 through 5 look up the values of the cells in column 1 of the same rows. (The formulas are displayed in column 4.)

Fig. 10.1.

A vertical lookup without an exact match.

```
         1        2        3        4              5          6        7
1      2.50     4.55            vlookup(r1c1,r[8]:[16]c1:5,2)
2      3.25   Error 8           vlookup(r2c1,r[8]:[16]c1:5,2)
3
4      2.50     4.55            @vlookup(r4c1,r[8]:[16]c1:5,2)
5      3.25     5.29            @vlookup(r5c1,r[8]:[16]c1:5,2)
6
7
8      1.00        A     2.33      8.99      15.65
9      1.50        B     3.07      9.73      16.39
10     2.00        C     3.81     10.47      17.13
11     2.50        D     4.55     11.21      17.87
12     3.00        E     5.29     11.95      18.61
13     3.50        F     6.03     12.69      19.35
14     4.00        G     6.77     13.43      20.09
15     4.50        H     7.51     14.17      20.83
16     5.00        I     8.25     14.91      21.57
17
18
Enter:
Formula: vlookup(r2c1,r[8]:[16]c1:5,2)
Worksheet: lookex     Loc: r2c2                    FN: 0     Font: Standard
ENTER   enter a formula, a value or text into the current cell
```

Notice that the formulas in rows 1 and 2 use the VLOOKUP function, whereas the formulas in rows 4 and 5 use the 1-2-3 version, @Vlookup. The table block is r8:16c1:5 in all cases. The functions in rows 1 and 4 work without any errors. In both cases, the exact value of 2.50 is located in column 1 of the table (row 11) and the value of 4.55 is retrieved from the second column over, which was the amount by which the table was offset.

Both

10.2 Tip: If your application calls for a table lookup in a range of values, use @Vlookup or @Hlookup rather than VLOOKUPor HLOOKUP.

An example of this type of application might be one in which you determine a tax rate as defined by a range of net income values.

As shown in figure 10.1, the differences between the two types of lookup functions become apparent when no exact match occurs in column 1. The VLOOKUP function in row 2 searches for 3.25 in the table but doesn't locate this exact match, so Error 8 occurs.

The @Vlookup function in row 5 behaves differently. If the exact match is not found, the value in the cell immediately preceding the "phantom" row is retrieved. Thus the value of 5.29 is retrieved, as if the search argument had been 3.00 rather than 3.25.

10.3 Trap: To prevent an error from occurring when you use @Vlookup or @Hlookup, sort the table block by the search column or row in ascending order.

Both

If the search column or row is not sorted in ascending order, the @Vlookup and @Hlookup functions produce an Error 8 message, as shown in figure 10.2. Note that even though the value in r4c1 is in the table, the result is an Error 8 message.

```
            1          2          3          4          5          6          7
1         2.50       4.55                 vlookup(r1c1,r[8]:[16]c1:5,2)
2         3.25    Error 8                 vlookup(r2c1,r[8]:[16]c1:5,2)
3
4         2.50    Error 8                 @vlookup(r4c1,r[8]:[16]c1:5,2)
5         3.25    Error 8                 @vlookup(r5c1,r[8]:[16]c1:5,2)
6
7
8         5.00          I       8.25      14.91      21.57
9         1.50          B       3.07       9.73      16.39
10        2.00          C       3.81      10.47      17.13
11        3.50          F       6.03      12.69      19.35
12        2.50          D       4.55      11.21      17.87
13        1.00          A       2.33       8.99      15.65
14        4.00          G       6.77      13.43      20.09
15        4.50          H       7.51      14.17      20.83
16        3.00          E       5.29      11.95      18.61
17
18
Enter:
Formula: @vlookup(r4c1,r[8]:[16]c1:5,2)
Worksheet: LOOKEX      Loc: r4c2                       FN: 0    Font: Standard
ENTER - enter a formula, a value or text into the current cell
```

Fig. 10.2.

A Lookup table block in random order.

10.4 Trip: If you use Smart's VLOOKUP or HLOOKUP functions, the table block doesn't have to be in sorted order.

Both

Even though the table block is in random order in figure 10.2, the value in r1c1 is located by the VLOOKUP function in r1c2. The @Vlookup functions in rows 4 and 5 both fail because the table is not sorted. The VLOOKUP function in row 2 fails, of course, because the match is not found in the table.

Alphabetic versus Numeric Lookups

10.5 Trap: An error results when you use any of the four LOOKUP functions with an alphabetic argument and the functions don't find an exact match in the LOOKUP table.

Both

The VLOOKUP and HLOOKUP functions always must find an exact match in the lookup table. The @Vlookup and @Hlookup functions, however, return the next-lowest value from the table if a numeric argument is used and an exact match is not found. This is not the case with alphabetic arguments. As shown in figure 10.3, the @Vlookup function in r5c2 returns Error 8 because the letter F is not found in column 2. Both the @Vlookup and VLOOKUP functions operate as expected in rows 1 and 4, locating the letter D in column 2 of the lookup table.

Fig. 10.3.

A lookup table with an alphabetic argument.

	1	2	3	4	5	6	7
1	D	11.21		vlookup(r1c1,r[8]:[16]c2:5,2)			
2	F	Error 8		vlookup(r2c1,r[8]:[16]c2:5,2)			
3							
4	D	11.21		@vlookup(r4c1,r[8]:[16]c2:5,2)			
5	F	Error 8		@vlookup(r5c1,r[8]:[16]c2:5,2)			
6							
7							
8	1.00	A	2.33	8.99	15.65		
9	1.50	B	3.07	9.73	16.39		
10	2.00	C	3.81	10.47	17.13		
11	2.50	D	4.55	11.21	17.87		
12	3.00	E	5.29	11.95	18.61		
13	3.50	G	6.03	12.69	19.35		
14	4.00	H	6.77	13.43	20.09		
15	4.50	I	7.51	14.17	20.83		
16	5.00	J	8.25	14.91	21.57		
17							
18							

```
Enter:
Formula: vlookup(r2c1,r[8]:[16]c2:5,2)
Worksheet: lookex2   Loc: r2c2                    FN: 0    Font: Standard
ENTER - enter a formula, a value or text into the current cell
```

Both

10.6 Tip: If you use an alphabetic argument with a LOOKUP function, the Lookup table doesn't have to be in sorted order.

Even if you are using the @Vlookup or @Hlookup functions, which usually require that the lookup table be sorted in ascending order, you don't have to sort the table if your argument is alphabetic (see fig. 10.4).

Fig. 10.4

An unsorted lookup table with alphabetic argument.

	1	2	3	4	5	6	7
1	D	11.21		vlookup(r1c1,r[8]:[16]c2:5,2)			
2	F	Error 8		vlookup(r2c1,r[8]:[16]c2:5,2)			
3							
4	D	11.21		@vlookup(r4c1,r[8]:[16]c2:5,2)			
5	F	Error 8		@vlookup(r5c1,r[8]:[16]c2:5,2)			
6							
7							
8	4.50	I	7.51	14.17	20.83		
9	3.00	E	5.29	11.95	18.61		
10	1.50	B	3.07	9.73	16.39		
11	1.00	A	2.33	8.99	15.65		
12	5.00	J	8.25	14.91	21.57		
13	2.50	D	4.55	11.21	17.87		
14	4.00	H	6.77	13.43	20.09		
15	3.50	G	6.03	12.69	19.35		
16	2.00	C	3.81	10.47	17.13		
17							
18							

```
Enter:
Formula: @vlookup(r5c1,r[8]:[16]c2:5,2)
Worksheet: lookex2   Loc: r5c2                    FN: 0    Font: Standard
ENTER - enter a formula, a value or text into the current cell
```

Note that the results of the functions in rows 1 through 5 are the same as in figure 10.3, even though the table is in a random order. When used with alphabetic arguments, @Vlookup and VLOOKUP work the same way.

Error Handling

This section covers finding errors in your spreadsheet and dealing with the errors after they are located.

10.7 Tip: Error 7 is a "false" error caused by an error in a cell to which the formula refers. *Both*

To correct an Error 7 condition, examine the formula in the cell and correct the formula's error factors. After you correct the formulas in the source cells, the Error 7 condition disappears.

10.8 Tip: Use the Find Error (3.10) or Sheet Find ... Calc-Error (SmartWare II) commands to locate errors on your worksheet and to display an explanation of the errors. *Both*

In Smart 3.10, the Find command, which is on command list 1, has three options:

```
Error     Text     Value
```

Select Error to find any cell errors below or to the right of the cursor's current position. The cursor stops at the next error cell and displays on the command line an explanation of the condition causing thc error (see fig. 10.5). To find the next error, press F9.

```
        1       2        3        4          5          6        7
1          D   11.21             vlookup(r1c1,r[8]:[16]c2:5,2)
2          F   Error 8           vlookup(r2c1,r[8]:[16]c2:5,2)
3
4          D   11.21             @vlookup(r4c1,r[8]:[16]c2:5,2)
5          F   Error 8           @vlookup(r5c1,r[8]:[16]c2:5,2)
6
7
8     4.50          I     7.51     14.17      20.83
9     3.00          E     5.29     11.95      18.61
10    1.50          B     3.07      9.73      16.39
11    1.00          A     2.33      8.99      15.65
12    5.00          J     8.25     14.91      21.57
13    2.50          D     4.55     11.21      17.87
14    4.00          H     6.77     13.43      20.09
15    3.50          G     6.03     12.69      19.35
16    2.00          C     3.81     10.47      17.13
17
18             Error 7
Press F9 to continue search, any other key to halt
Error 8: HLOOKUP/VLOOKUP failed
Worksheet: lookex2   Loc: r2c2               FN: 0    Font: Standard
FIND  Find an error, a value or text item
```

Fig. 10.5.
Finding an error.

If you press F9 and Smart has found the last error cell, the system displays the following message:

```
No error found below current cell
```

The Find Error command cannot locate a cell with an Error 7 condition because such an error is only a result of an error in another cell.

In SmartWare II, the Sheet Find command has an initial set of options:

```
Block    All
```

By specifying Block, you can search for errors (or other contents or conditions) within a selected block of cells. The next set of options is:

```
Calc-Error   Empty   Highlight   Text   Value
```

Select Calc-Error to search for any errors.

Both

10.9 Tip: Use the Edit command to display an explanation of an error condition without using the Find Error command. In SmartWare II, use the Edit Edit-Cell command.

If you place the cursor on a cell displaying an error and execute the Edit command (or Alt-E), you can edit the formula and also display an explanation of the error condition on the second command line. Refer to figure 10.6.

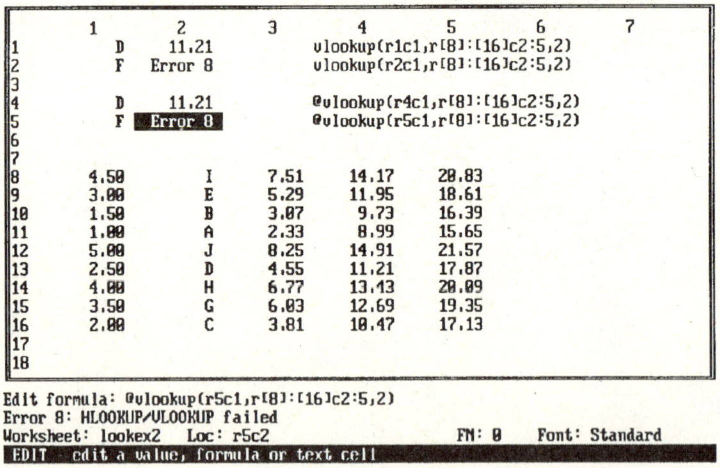

Fig. 10.6.

An error explanation in the Edit command.

```
        1        2         3         4          5          6          7
1          D     11.21              vlookup(r1c1,r[8]:[16]c2:5,2)
2          F   Error 8              vlookup(r2c1,r[8]:[16]c2:5,2)
3
4          D     11.21              @vlookup(r4c1,r[8]:[16]c2:5,2)
5          F   Error 8              @vlookup(r5c1,r[8]:[16]c2:5,2)
6
7
8       4.50          I    7.51     14.17     20.83
9       3.00          E    5.29     11.95     18.61
10      1.50          B    3.07      9.73     16.39
11      1.00          A    2.33      8.99     15.65
12      5.00          J    8.25     14.91     21.57
13      2.50          D    4.55     11.21     17.87
14      4.00          H    6.77     13.13     20.09
15      3.50          G    6.03     12.69     19.35
16      2.00          C    3.81     10.47     17.13
17
18
Edit formula: @vlookup(r5c1,r[8]:[16]c2:5,2)
Error 8: HLOOKUP/VLOOKUP failed
Worksheet: lookex2   Loc: r5c2                    FN: 0    Font: Standard
EDIT  edit a value, formula or text cell
```

Both

10.10 Tip: Use the Iserr function to provide your own error messages.

You may want to control error conditions by substituting different values or displaying different cell contents or messages. In figure 10.7, for example, the word `Missing` is displayed instead of the cryptic Error 8 message. Figure 10.8 shows the formula in r2c2.

```
         1        2        3        4         5        6        7
1        D      11.21              vlookup(r1c1,r[8]:[16]c2:5,2)
2        F    Missing
3
4        D      11.21              @vlookup(r4c1,r[8]:[16]c2:5,2)
5        F    Error 8              @vlookup(r5c1,r[8]:[16]c2:5,2)
6
7
8      4.50          I      7.51     14.17     20.83
```

Fig. 10.7.

Using the ISERR function to trap error codes.

```
Formula Editor
if iserr(vlookup(r2c1,r[8]:[16]c2:5,2)) = 1 then

"Missing" else

vlookup(r2c1,r[8]:[16]c2:5,2)
```

Fig. 10.8.

A formula using the ISERR function.

Using Worksheet Position Functions

The evaluation of worksheet position functions depends on the location of the formula cell in which the function is located.

10.11 Tip: Use the COLUMN or ROW functions to reference the current cell column or row. ***Both***

The key words column or row can be used in a formula to retrieve column or row numbers. Suppose, for example, that you want to display the column and row numbers of your worksheet when you print it. Figure 10.9 shows a sample.

```
      1     2        3         4        5        6        7        8
1          Col 2    Col 3    Col 4    Col 5    Col 6    Col 7    Col 8
2    Row 2
3    Row 3              D    11.21             vlookup(r1c1,r[8]:[16]c2:5,2)
4    Row 4              F   Missing
5    Row 5
6    Row 6              D    11.21             @vlookup(r4c1,r[8]:[16]c2:5,2)
7    Row 7              F   Error 8            @vlookup(r5c1,r[8]:[16]c2:5,2)
8    Row 8
9    Row 9
10   Row 10          1.00        A     2.33     8.99    15.65
11   Row 11          1.50        B     3.07     9.73    16.39
12   Row 12          2.00        C     3.81    10.47    17.13
13   Row 13          2.50        D     4.55    11.21    17.87
14   Row 14          3.00        E     5.29    11.95    18.61
15   Row 15          3.50        G     6.03    12.69    19.35
16   Row 16          4.00        H     6.77    13.43    20.09
17   Row 17          4.50        I     7.51    14.17    20.83
18   Row 18          5.00        J     8.25    14.91    21.57
Enter:
Formula: "Row "!fixed(row,0)
Worksheet: lookex2    Loc: r2c1               FN: 0     Font: Standard
ENTER - enter a formula, a value or text into the current cell
```

Fig. 10.9.

Using the COLUMN and ROW functions.

Both

10.12 Tip: Use the Fixed function to convert a number to a text string.

In figure 10.9, the following formula is used to display the row numbers in column 1 of the worksheet:

```
"Row "|fixed(row,0)
```

You can use the word `Row` to make it clear that this is a row number, and you can append the actual row numbers to that text. To be able to accomplish these tasks, you need to convert the row number to a string. Use the Fixed function to perform this conversion. The arguments to the Fixed function are the value and the number of decimal places.

Validating Worksheet Contents

The functions outlined in this chapter can be used to ensure the validity of your data. The N/A function is useful when you must work with incomplete data. In this section, you learn how to differentiate between blank cells and those cells that contain a blank.

The NA Function

Both

10.13 Tip: Use the NA function to display N/A in a cell not meeting your specified conditions and to cause any calculations using that cell also to display N/A.

In figure 10.10, the NA function is used in columns 4 and 6 to select only the even numbers from column 2. (The MOD function also is used.) In columns 4 and 6, the characters N/A appear.

At the bottom of column 4 is a formula to calculate the value averages in the column. Some column entries are not available, so the result of the AVERAGE function also is N/A. Row 13 of column 6 contains the formula to calculate row sums in that column; the result also is N/A. The formula for row 3 and col 6 can be seen on the command line.

With the exception of the totals, columns 6 and 8 look identical. What is the difference? The formulas for the individual rows in column 8 follow this format:

```
if mod(r3c[2],2) = 1 then "N/A" else r3c[2]
```

Although the characters N/A appear in the cells, the effect on the total calculation is quite different. An actual NA condition, created by using the NA function, causes a resulting formula to be N/A as well. Just displaying the characters N/A as text within a cell, however, does not invalidate the SUM formula and causes Smart to display the sum of the numeric cells in the column.

	1	2	3	4	5	6	7	8	9
1		Average		Average		Sum		Sum	
2		----------		----------		----------		----------	
3		1.00		N/A		N/A		N/A	
4		2.00		2.00		2.00		2.00	
5		3.00		N/A		N/A		N/A	
6		4.00		4.00		4.00		4.00	
7		5.00		N/A		N/A		N/A	
8		6.00		6.00		6.00		6.00	
9		7.00		N/A		N/A		N/A	
10		8.00		8.00		8.00		8.00	
11		9.00		N/A		N/A		N/A	
12		==========		==========		==========		==========	
13		5.00		N/A		N/A		20.00	
14									
15									
16									
17									
18									

```
Enter:
Formula: if mod(r3c[2],2) = 1 then na else r3c[2]
Worksheet: (none)     Loc: r3c6                    FN: 0     Font: Standard
ENTER - enter a formula, a value or text into the current cell
```

Fig. 10.10.

Using the NA function.

If the display of incomplete results are misleading, you should use the NA function. Suppose that you have several corporate entities that report at different times, for example, but you need to print interim reports. Use the NA function to highlight the fact that the results are incomplete in both the detail and the totals. No one then will mistake the totals as being complete.

A cell does not automatically contain an N/A for certain standard conditions within your worksheet. You must specify, in a formula, the conditions that invoke the NA specification.

The ISNA Function

10.14 Tip: Use the ISNA function to test a cell for the NA condition. ***Both***

In figure 10.11, the ISNA function in r15c2 causes Smart to display `Results Incomplete` if the formula in r13c4 results in an NA condition.

The ISNA function returns the value of 1 if true or zero if false. When using this function, you must test for those values.

The ISBLANK Function

10.15 Tip: Use the ISBLANK function to test for blank cells. ***Both***

Figure 10.12 demonstrates the use of the ISBLANK function. The upper window displays the cell results; the lower window shows the formulas.

In the Smart Spreadsheet, a blank cell is not a null cell. Figure 10.12 shows that when testing for blank cells in column 1, the ISBLANK function returns a value of 1 if the cell is blank. In this example, the word **blank** appears if the cell is blank.

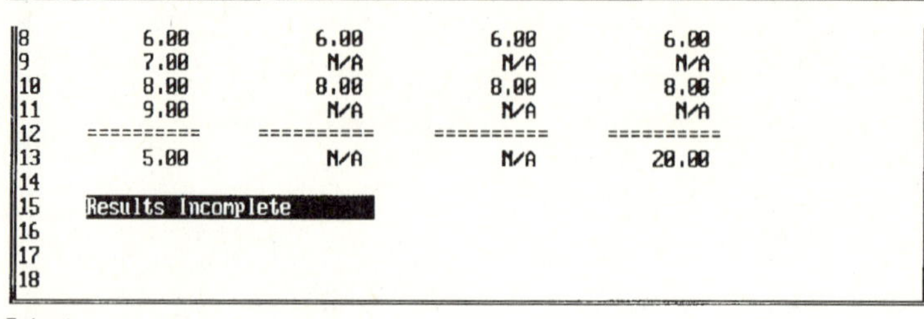

Fig. 10.11.

The ISNA function.

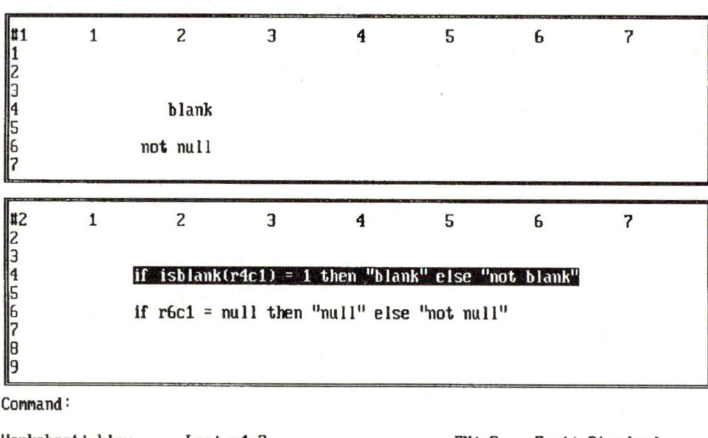

Fig. 10.12.

The ISBLANK function.

The formula in row 6 has no meaning within the Spreadsheet; a cell cannot be null, so the test fails. You must use the ISBLANK function to test for a blank cell.

SmartWare II has a new function called BLANK. If this function is entered into a cell, the ISBLANK function does *not* return true. ISBLANK returns true only if nothing is in the cell.

SW II

10.16 Trap: A cell containing just the function BLANK *is* counted as zero in a count or average function; a cell that actually is blank (containing nothing) is not counted.

In figure 10.13, row 3 in column 1 contains the function BLANK; row 3 in column 3 contains nothing. Note the effect on the averages and the counts.

Both

10.17 Trap: A cell that looks blank may not actually be blank.

A cell tests positive to the ISBLANK function only if the cell has never had contents or if you used the Blank command. If, however, you enter one or more spaces as text within a cell, the cell looks blank, yet tests as not blank when you use the ISBLANK function.

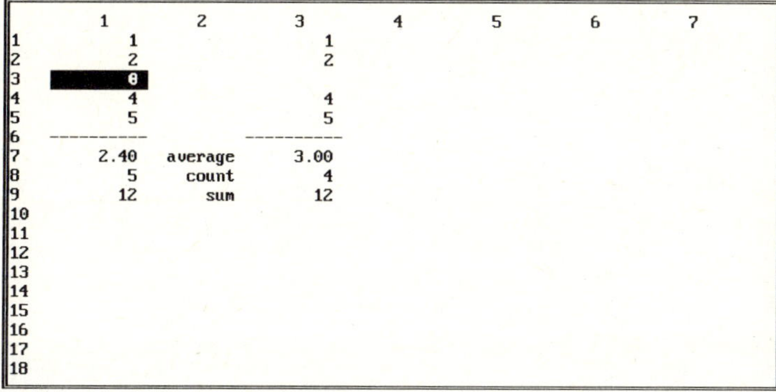

Fig. 10.13.
The effect of blank formula on average and count functions.

10.18 Tip: Use the "contains" operator (!) to test for spaces in a cell. **Both**

The formula in figure 10.14 tests for blank cells by using the ISBLANK function and tests for spaces in cells by using the contains operator (!).

```
Formula Editor
if r2c1 ! " " then "spaces"

else if isblank(r2c1) = 1 then "blank"

else "real"
```

Fig. 10.14.
Testing for blank cells and spaces in cells.

You also can use a test such as

```
if left(r2c1,1) = " " then "spaces" else "real"
```

to test for spaces in cells.

When Smart is in Enter mode, you can visually distinguish a blank cell from one that contains spaces. If a cell contains spaces, the cell type `Text:` appears on command line 2. No cell type appears if the cell is blank.

10.19 Trap: The difference between a blank cell and one that contains a zero may be significant when using the AVERAGE function. **Both**

Sometimes a blank cell evaluates as a zero. When you sum a column of numbers and one cell is a blank or a zero, the sum value is the same (see fig. 10.15). But when you calculate an average, a cell that is zero is counted as an occurrence in the set, whereas a blank cell is not counted. The average figures of columns 3 and 5 in figure 10.14 illustrate this difference.

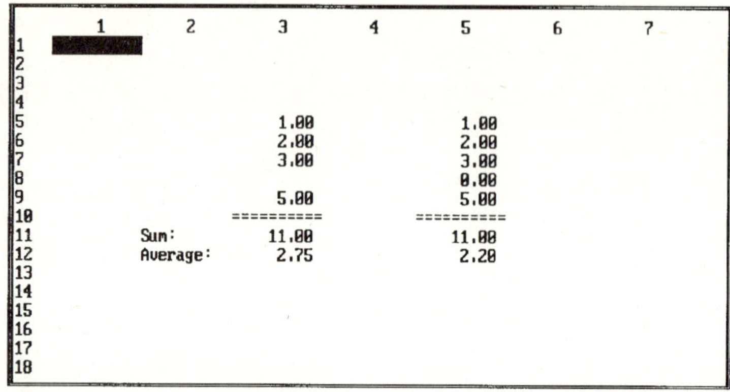

Fig. 10.15.
A blank cell versus a zero cell.

Both

10.20 Tip: Use the Paint command to help debug a worksheet; in SmartWare II, the command to use is Window Paint.

You can use the Paint command for more than just cosmetic purposes. For example, if you find that a column of numbers doesn't total correctly even though the formula in the calculation cell is correct, then a value in the column may have been entered as text rather than as a true value. Use the Paint command to paint all text cells a certain color, and the offending cell will stand out clearly.

In SmartWare II, you also can use the Sheet Audit command to help debug a worksheet.

Using Date and Time Functions

The Smart system contains many functions you can use with dates and times. For the most part, the functions work well, but you need to watch out for some traps and restrictions.

3.10

10.21 Trick: Although Smart 3.10 does not directly support dates beyond the 20th century, there are ways to get around the problem.

Use the following project file to enter dates in the 21st century:

```
input $date Enter date:

if days($date) <= days("12/31/40")
let $numdate = days($date) + 36525
else
let $numdate = days($date)
endif
```

```
let %1 = row
let %2 = column

let r%1c%2 = $numdate

reformat block r%1c%2 date2
```

Using this project file, you can enter a date in the 21st century into any cell. The date will have the usual MM-DD-YY format, so you have to remember that some dates are in the 20th century and others are in the 21st century.

In this project file, you should use a cut-off date before which the dates are to be considered in the 21st century. For example, I decided that all dates on or before 12/31/40 are in the 21st century, and any dates after that are in the 20th century.

In the Smart Spreadsheet, dates actually are maintained as numbers, sequentially assigned beginning with 01/01/00. The Reformat command is used to display dates in one of the three date formats.

In SmartWare II, you do not have this problem because dates beyond the 20th century are supported directly.

10.22 Trap: The Adate function does not correctly display a date in the 21st century. *3.10*

Although the underlying date may have a sequential number well into the 21st century, the ADATE function displays the alphabetic date as if the date is in the 20th century.

10.23 Trick: You can calculate the last day of the current month with the formula in figure 10.16. *Both*

This formula determines the first day of the next month, then uses the ADDAYS function to subtract 1 from that date.

Formatting and Selection Functions

The CELLTEXT function can be used to display text expressions matching one or more cells.

10.24 Trap: The CELLTEXT function doesn't adjust cell addresses automatically within the argument when you perform a copy. *Both*

To make Smart adjust the addresses, use a formula similar to the following:

```
celltext("r"|fixed(row,0)|"c1")
```

Usually, you would write the function as

```
celltext("r1c1")
```

```
Formula Editor
adddays(fixed(month(addmonths(today,1)),0)!

"/01/"!

fixed(@year(addmonths(today,1)),0),-1)
```

Fig. 10.16.
A formula to calculate last day of current month.

Because the cell address is enclosed in quotation marks, it is considered text and therefore is not adjusted as are other types of addresses in a Copy command. If you use a formula as the argument to the CELLTEXT function, as in the first example, the row number changes with the function location, and the entire function argument address is changed.

Both

10.25 Trick: Use the LEN and CELLTEXT functions to determine the width of a column.

If you want to determine how wide a column is, use the following formula:

```
len(celltext("r5c7"))
```

Both

10.26 Tip: Use the Case function instead of a long, complicated if...then...else statement.

The Case function in figure 10.17 calculates the number of days in each month (except for leap years). When the value matches the first argument inside the parentheses, the second argument is returned. For example, if the month number is 4, the number 30 is returned. The Case function can be used when the choices are discrete and can match exactly with the first argument in the parentheses. Note that the dates in the figure are displayed in the Date3 format.

```
12
13
14
15
16    Jan 87    1    31.00
17    Feb 87    2    28.00
18    Mar 87    3    31.00

Enter:
Formula: case r16c3 (2,28) (4,30) (6,30) (9,30) (11,30) else 31
Worksheet: blex        Loc: r16c4                FM: 0    Font: Standard
ENTER - enter a formula, a value or text into the current cell
```

Fig. 10.17.
The CASE function.

Both

10.27 Tip: Combine an if...then statement with a function.

For example, the formula in figure 10.18 calculates the number of days in the month, as was done in figure 10.17, but also determines whether the year is a leap year.

```
Formula Editor
if ( r16c3 = 2 and mod(year(r16c1),4) = 0 ) then 29 else

case r16c3 (2,28) (4,30) (6,30) (9,30) (11,30) else 31
```

Fig. 10.18.

Using `if...then` *with the CASE function.*

If the month number is 2 and the year is evenly divisible by 4, then the year is a leap year and February has 29 days. If these conditions are not met, the CASE function is evaluated.

10.28 Tip: Use the CHOOSE Function if the search value is discrete, begins with zero, and increments by 1.

Both

Rather than using an if...then statement or the CASE function, use the CHOOSE function. Figure 10.19 shows an example.

```
Formula Editor
choose (r16c3, "Error",

"Jan","Feb","Mar","Apr",

"May","Jun","Jul","Aug",

"Sep","Oct","Nov","Dec" )
```

Fig. 10.19.

The CHOOSE function.

The month abbreviation is retrieved by position from the arguments of the function. That is, month 1 retrieves the value in the first position, month 2 from the second position, and so on. (The first argument is the zero position.) If you encounter month 13, the function returns Error 24.

10.29 Tip: Use the SELECT function as a shorthand `if...then...else` statement in which different conditions must be evaluated.

Both

The formula in figure 10.20 calculates a label to be attached to each month in figure 10.21.

In the SELECT function, each set of parentheses contains a condition and a result. The conditions don't have to refer to the same values or fields. The conditions are evaluated in order, and the first condition satisfied determines the result. Therefore, February 1988 is satisfied in the first condition, but February 1987 "falls through" to the next condition.

```
Formula Editor
select

( (mod(year(r16c1),4) = 0 and r16c3 = 2) , "Feb, Leap Year" )

( r16c3 = 2 , "Feb, Regular Year" )

( r16c4 = 30, "Short Month" )

( r16c4 = 31, "Long Month" )

else error
```

Fig. 10.20.
The SELECT function.

```
      1      3      4      5    6           7         8        9
14
15
16   Jan 87   1         31  Jan Long Month
17   Feb 87   2         28  Feb Feb, Regular Year
18   Mar 87   3         31  Mar Long Month
19   Apr 87   4         30  Apr Short Month
20   May 87   5         31  May Long Month
21   Jun 87   6         30  Jun Short Month
22   Jul 87   7         31  Jul Long Month
23   Aug 87   8         31  Aug Long Month
24   Sep 87   9         30  Sep Short Month
25   Oct 87  10         31  Oct Long Month
26   Nov 87  11         30  Nov Short Month
27   Dec 87  12         31  Dec Long Month
28   Jan 88   1         31  Jan Long Month
29   Feb 88   2         29  Feb Feb, Leap Year
30
31
Enter:
Formula: select~~( (mod(year(r16c1),4) = 0 and r16c3 = 2) , "Feb, Leap Year" )~~
Worksheet: datex     Loc: r16c6                  FN: 0     Font: Standard
ENTER - enter a formula, a value or text into the current cell
```

Fig. 10.21.
Creating month labels with the SELECT function.

Unless you are absolutely certain of the search arguments, you should specify an `else` condition following the last set of parentheses.

Numeric Conversion Functions

This section covers several number-handling functions, as well as the 1-2-3 database functions introduced with Version 3.10 of Smart.

VAL and STR

Both

10.30 Trap: The VAL function returns a zero if the argument is a numeric field.

The VAL function is used to convert a number in a text field into a value. If the argument happens to be a numeric field, however, the function evaluates as zero. No error message is displayed.

10.31 Trap: The STR function returns a zero if the argument is a text field. *3.10*

The STR function enables you to convert a numeric cell to a text cell. If the argument is a text cell, the result is a text cell containing the zero character. The lower window of figure 10.22 shows the formulas containing the VAL and STR functions. The upper window shows the formula results. Column 1 contains a numeric 5.00 in row 15 and a text "5" in row 17.

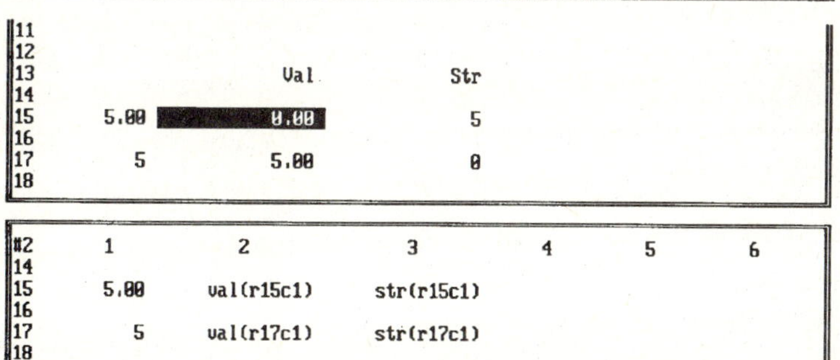

Fig. 10.22. *Misuse of the VAL and STR functions.*

10.32 Tip: Make sure that your variables are initialized to avoid a Variable Not Found error. ***Both***

If you include a variable, make sure the it is initialized with a value when you recalculate your spreadsheet.

Otherwise, Smart displays the error message `Variable Not Found`. To make the entry into a variable, you must execute a project file to perform the assignment. For a complete discussion of parameters, user-defined variables, and system variables, refer to Chapter 14.

Making Block References

10.33 Tip: Use the exclamation point (!) to precede a cell reference in certain 1-2-3 Version 2 functions that require block references. ***Both***

If you want to designate only a single cell as a block when using the functions introduced for 1-2-3 Release 2 compatibility, you must preface the cell reference with an exclamation point (!) to indicate a block reference. If you don't use this prefix, an error results. Functions other than those added for purposes of this compatibility don't require the exclamation point.

Statistical Database Functions

The statistical database functions, introduced with Version 3.10 of Smart Spreadsheet and also available in SmartWare II, enable you to perform the following calculations within a worksheet block:

Average
Daverage: Ignores blanks and text
Davg and @Davg: Ignores blanks; text is zero
Count
Dcount: Ignores blanks and text
@Dcount: Ignores blanks, counts text
Minimum
Dmin and @Dmin
Maximum
Dmax and @Dmax
Standard Deviation
Std and @Std
Sum
Dsum and @Dsum
Sum of Squares
Dsumsq
Variance
Dvar: sample variance
@Dvar: population variance

The calculations are performed only on rows meeting specified criteria. By specifying search criteria, you can treat the worksheet block as a miniature database.

The worksheet in figure 10.23 is an example. The "database" is in the block r1:13c1:11. Note that this block must include the column titles because they are referenced in the criteria block.

The criteria block is in r15:17c1:11, which contains a copy of the column titles in the database block, plus two extra rows. The extra rows are used to hold the criteria for selection of rows from the database.

The statistical functions take the following form:

function(database block, offset value, criteria block)

The *offset value* represents the number of columns to the right of the leftmost column of the database block upon which the operation is to be performed.

In figure 10.23, the criteria are specified as F for SEX and S for MS (Marital Status). The DAVERAGE function calculates the average age of the individuals who are both female and single. Because the criteria are on the same line, both conditions must be met; placement of the criteria on the same line is the

```
      1         2          3   4   5   6   7  8        9    10      11
1  FIRST     LAST       AGE SEX MS  DEP CAR ST      WAGE STATUS   DEPT
2  Rosanna   Ronaldo     52 M   M     3   2 IL    878.75 Y        ACCT
3  Debbie    Linden      29 F   S     1   2 MA  1,403.79 Y        MFGR
4  Michael   Davis       61 M   M     1   2 LA    734.56 2        SALE
5  Julius    Karenski    41 M   D     0   1 KY  1,020.33 2        MKTG
6  Jeff      Harris      34 M   M     4   5 OH    629.23 Y        ACCT
7  LeAnne    Markus      40 F   W     1   1 CO    887.49 2        SALE
8  Marilyn   Lester      55 F   M     4   3 MA  1,516.26 Y        MKTG
9  David     Marzetti    47 M   D     0   1 NC    901.45 2        ACCT
10 Paula     Bernstein   30 F   S     3   3 CA  1,004.56 2        SALE
11 Alfred    Adelson     60 M   M     0   1 CT    956.43 Y        ACCT
12 Ellen     Aliakbari   35 F   S     0   1 NJ    997.66 2        MFGR
13 Howard E. Peters      18 M   S     0   1 LA  1,544.00 1        MKTG
14
15 FIRST     LAST       AGE SEX MS  DEP CAR ST      WAGE STATUS   DEPT
16                           F  S
17
18 Average:     31.33
Enter:
Formula: daverage( r1:13c1:11, 2, r15:17c1:11 )
Worksheet: person       Loc: r18c2                FN: 0     Font: Standard
ENTER - enter a formula, a value or text into the current cell
```

Fig. 10.23.

An example database.

equivalent of a logical "and." When the criteria are on separate lines, the effect is that of a logical "or" (see fig. 10.24).

```
      1         2          3   4   5   6   7  8        9    10      11
1  FIRST     LAST       AGE SEX MS  DEP CAR ST      WAGE STATUS   DEPT
2  Rosanna   Ronaldo     52 M   M     3   2 IL    878.75 Y        ACCT
3  Debbie    Linden      29 F   S     1   2 MA  1,403.79 Y        MFGR
4  Michael   Davis       61 M   M     1   2 LA    734.56 2        SALE
5  Julius    Karenski    41 M   D     0   1 KY  1,020.33 2        MKTG
6  Jeff      Harris      34 M   M     4   5 OH    629.23 Y        ACCT
7  LeAnne    Markus      40 F   W     1   1 CO    887.49 2        SALE
8  Marilyn   Lester      55 F   M     4   3 MA  1,516.26 Y        MKTG
9  David     Marzetti    47 M   D     0   1 NC    901.45 2        ACCT
10 Paula     Bernstein   30 F   S     3   3 CA  1,004.56 2        SALE
11 Alfred    Adelson     60 M   M     0   1 CT    956.43 Y        ACCT
12 Ellen     Aliakbari   35 F   S     0   1 NJ    997.66 2        MFGR
13 Howard E. Peters      18 M   S     0   1 LA  1,544.00 1        MKTG
14
15 FIRST     LAST       AGE SEX MS  DEP CAR ST      WAGE STATUS   DEPT
16                              S
17                           F
18 Average:     35.83
Enter:
Formula: daverage( r1:13c1:11, 2, r15:17c1:11 )
Worksheet: person       Loc: r18c2                FN: 0     Font: Standard
ENTER - enter a formula, a value or text into the current cell
```

Fig. 10.24.

Criteria equivalent to a logical "or."

10.34 Tip: When using a statistical database function, use a formula to select a row from a worksheet block.

Both

If you enter a formula in a criterion field, the selection is based on that formula. In figure 10.25, the following formula has been entered in r16c3 to select only those records in which the age is less than 35:

```
r2c3 < 35
```

The fact that 0.00 appears in r16c3 is unimportant.

Fig. 10.25.

Selection of formula criteria.

```
     1          2          3   4   5   6   7  8        9     10      11
1  FIRST      LAST       AGE SEX  MS  DEP CAR ST      WAGE STATUS   DEPT
2  Rosanna    Ronaldo     52 M    M    3   2 IL     878.75 Y        ACCT
3  Debbie     Linden      29 F    S    1   2 MA   1,403.79 Y        MFGR
4  Michael    Davis       61 M    M    1   2 LA     734.56 2        SALE
5  Julius     Karenski    41 M    D    0   1 KY   1,020.33 2        MKTG
6  Jeff       Harris      34 M    M    4   5 OH     629.23 Y        ACCT
7  LeAnne     Markus      48 F    W    1   1 CO     887.49 2        SALE
8  Marilyn    Lester      55 F    M    4   3 MA   1,516.26 Y        MKTG
9  David      Marzetti    47 M    D    0   1 NC     901.45 2        ACCT
10 Paula      Bernstein   30 F    S    3   3 CA   1,004.56 2        SALE
11 Alfred     Adelson     60 M    M    0   1 CT     956.43 Y        ACCT
12 Ellen      Aliakbari   35 F    S    0   1 NJ     997.66 2        MFGR
13 Howard E.  Peters      18 M    S    0   1 LA   1,544.00 1        MKTG
14
15 FIRST      LAST       AGE SEX  MS  DEP CAR ST      WAGE STATUS   DEPT
16                      0.00
17
18 Average:   1,145.40                          Age:          35.00

Enter:
Formula: r2c3 < 35
Worksheet: person      Loc: r16c3                    FN: 0     Font: Standard
ENTER - enter a formula, a value or text into the current cell
```

Note that the first data row has been selected for measurement in the formula. Don't, however, select the first row of the table—this is the field-title row.

You may combine formula criteria with constant criteria as needed.

Both

10.35 Trick: If you are using a reference to a worksheet cell in a formula criterion, use the absolute cell reference.

The formula evaluation takes place for each row in the database. If you plan on measuring the formula against a constant in a particular cell that doesn't adjust for different rows in the database, be sure to use the absolute reference, as shown in figure 10.26. The reference in the formula in cell r16c3 is to r[18]c10, which contains a constant.

Fig. 10.26.

An absolute cell reference in a formula criterion.

```
     1          2          3   4   5   6   7  8        9     10      11
1  FIRST      LAST       AGE SEX  MS  DEP CAR ST      WAGE STATUS   DEPT
2  Rosanna    Ronaldo     52 M    M    3   2 IL     878.75 Y        ACCT
3  Debbie     Linden      29 F    S    1   2 MA   1,403.79 Y        MFGR
4  Michael    Davis       61 M    M    1   2 LA     734.56 2        SALE
5  Julius     Karenski    41 M    D    0   1 KY   1,020.33 2        MKTG
6  Jeff       Harris      34 M    M    4   5 OH     629.23 Y        ACCT
7  LeAnne     Markus      48 F    W    1   1 CO     887.49 2        SALE
8  Marilyn    Lester      55 F    M    4   3 MA   1,516.26 Y        MKTG
9  David      Marzetti    47 M    D    0   1 NC     901.45 2        ACCT
10 Paula      Bernstein   30 F    S    3   3 CA   1,004.56 2        SALE
11 Alfred     Adelson     60 M    M    0   1 CT     956.43 Y        ACCT
12 Ellen      Aliakbari   35 F    S    0   1 NJ     997.66 2        MFGR
13 Howard E.  Peters      18 M    S    0   1 LA   1,544.00 1        MKTG
14
15 FIRST      LAST       AGE SEX  MS  DEP CAR ST      WAGE STATUS   DEPT
16                      0.00
17
18 Average:   1,145.40                          Age:          35.00

Enter:
Formula: r2c3 < r[18]c10
Worksheet: person      Loc: r16c3                    FN: 0     Font: Standard
ENTER - enter a formula, a value or text into the current cell
```

10.36 Trap: If your database contains extraneous rows, formula criteria don't evaluate correctly.

Both

An extra line, such as a line of hyphens to separate the field names from the data, causes a formula to be evaluated against the line following that which you would expect. Constant criteria, however, evaluate correctly.

Text Functions

Text functions can be used to manipulate and deal with strings. The REPLACE function, introduced with Version 3.10, is described in this section.

The FIND and MATCH Functions

10.37 Tip: Use the FIND function to locate the starting position of a string within a larger string.

Both

The FIND function's format is:

find(string to find, string searched in, start position)

In figure 10.27, the formula in column 3 finds the starting position of the string `man` in column 2, within the larger string `Fishman` in column 1. The first position is number 0, which is why the result of the function is 4 rather than 5.

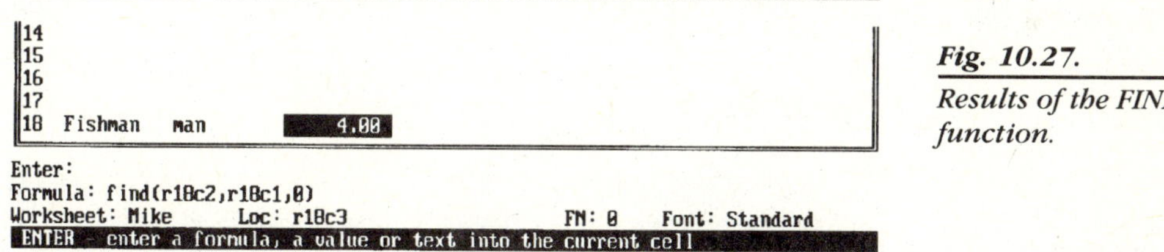

```
14
15
16
17
18  Fishman    man          4.00

Enter:
Formula: find(r18c2,r18c1,0)
Worksheet: Mike      Loc: r18c3              FN: 0    Font: Standard
ENTER - enter a formula, a value or text into the current cell
```

Fig. 10.27.

Results of the FIND function.

To begin at the first position of the string being searched, make sure that the start position is zero, not 1. Error 18 results if the string is not found or if the starting position is out of range.

10.38 Trap: Don't confuse the FIND function with the MATCH function; their purposes are the same, but their results are different.

Both

The FIND function's starting position is zero; the MATCH function's starting position is 1. The order of the arguments is also reversed, so be careful. In figure 10.28, for example, the MATCH function in column 4 is used like the FIND function in column 3, but the result is 5 because the starting position is 1 rather than zero.

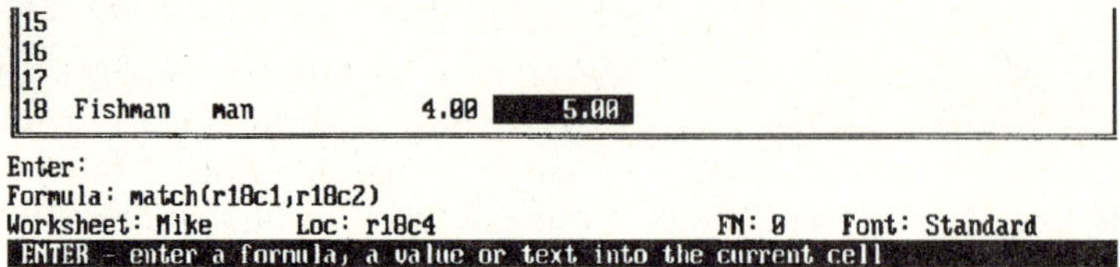

Fig. 10.28.
The FIND and MATCH functions compared.

Substituting Parts of Strings

Both

10.39 Tip: Use the REPLACE function to substitute a portion of a string.

This function handles differing string lengths by deleting a specified portion of the existing string and then inserting the new string. The REPLACE function's format is

replace(t1, n1, n2, t2)

in which

t1 is the existing string

n1 is the starting position in existing string

n2 is the number of characters to delete

t2 is the string to insert

The first position in the existing string is zero. Figure 10.29 shows an example of this function.

```
15
16
17
18  Congress shall make no law respecting an establishment of religion ..
19
20  Congress shall make no ordinance respecting an establishment of religi
Enter:
Formula: replace(r18c1,23,3,"ordinance")
Worksheet: Mike      Loc: r20c1                FN: 0    Font: Standard
 ENTER - enter a formula, a value or text into the current cell
```

Fig. 10.29.
Results of the REPLACE function.

Miscellaneous Functions

Three miscellaneous, but extremely powerful, functions are introduced in this section. The INDIRECT function can be used for indirect addressing, a feature that has been needed in sophisticated worksheets. The CELLPOINTER function can be used to construct worksheet-based menus. And the GOAL function is useful for solving complex equations.

Both

10.40 Tip: Use the INDIRECT function to refer to a cell whose address is in another cell.

Figure 10.30 provides an example. The INDIRECT function in row 20 refers to row 18, which contains the address of the cell in row 16. The contents of the cell in row 16 are displayed in row 20. By changing the cell containing the reference address, you can vary the evaluation of the INDIRECT function. Remember, however, that because the cell addresses within the reference cells are text, the cell addresses are not adjusted automatically if you move or copy them, or if you insert or delete rows or columns.

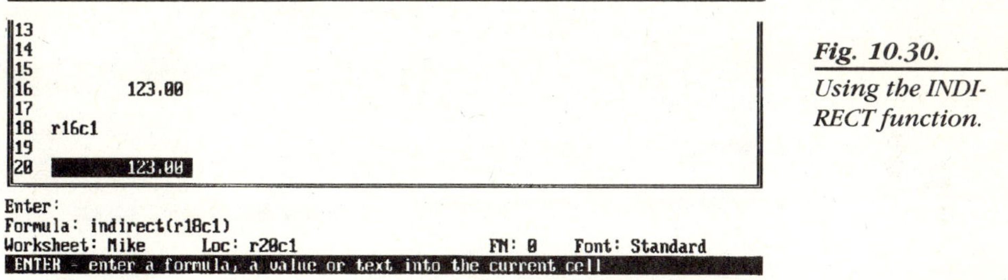

Fig. 10.30.
Using the INDIRECT function.

10.41 Trick: Use the CELLPOINTER function as a menu-selection indicator. ***Both***

The CELLPOINTER function returns a value that is either the row or column number of the cursor's position at the time of recalculation.

The CELLPOINTER function's format is

cellpointer("row")

cellpointer("column")

If your application calls for the user to select from among several choices, the cursor's location can be determined by placing the cursor on the worksheet. (see figs. 10.31 and 10.32).

Figures 10.31 and 10.32 show an example of the use of the Cellpointer function. Figure 10.31 shows a selection menu in column 4 and several numbers in column 1. The result of the summary statistic selected in column 4 is displayed in row 15 of column 1 by positioning the cursor on the desired statistic name and pressing F5 to recalculate the worksheet.

Figure 10.32 shows the formula contained in r15c1. A different formula is used each time, depending on the position of the cursor at the time of recalculation. This technique may be used for constructing worksheet-based menus to make applications as easy to use as possible.

10.42 Tip: Use the GOAL function to solve an equation in one unknown. ***Both***

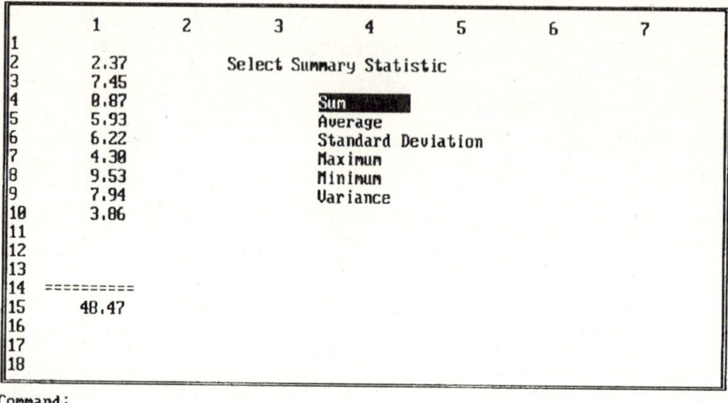

Fig. 10.31.
A menu created with the CELLPOINTER function.

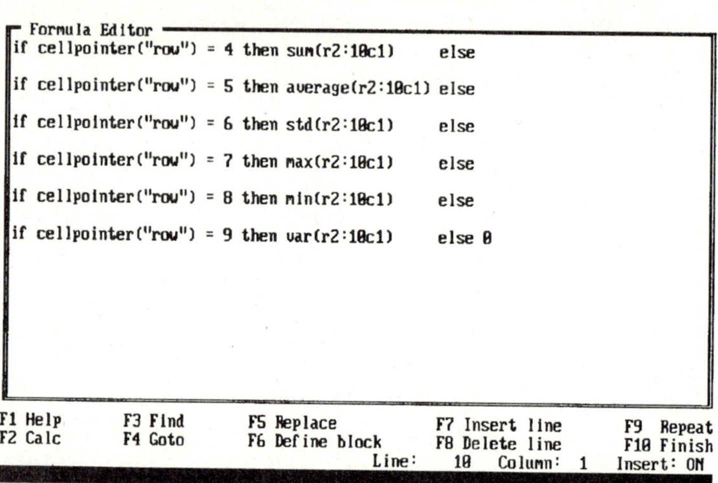

Fig. 10.32.
The formula used with the menu in figure 10.31.

You can use the GOAL function to solve an equation by iteration until the difference in successive calculations is less than 1E-7 (.0000001) or until 20 iterations have been calculated. Although you may be able to rewrite an equation algebraically to solve the equation, using the GOAL function is often more convenient and faster. Figure 10.33 shows a complicated quadratic equation that would take more than a few minutes to solve manually, but the GOAL function solves the equation instantly. The function is shown in row 15, the formula is shown in the command area below, and row 17 contains a formula to verify the GOAL function's accuracy.

In some formulas, the unknown may have more than one possible value. An example is

```
13
14
15  Function:      12.96
16
17  Verify:     5,280.00
18

Enter:
Formula: goal(27, 5280, 3*guess^3 - 7.5*guess^2 + guess )
Worksheet: michael    Loc: r15c2                FN: 0     Font: Standard
 ENTER - enter a formula, a value or text into the current cell
```

Fig. 10.33.

Seeking a goal.

The two possible values for the unknown are -2 and -4. In cases like this, the screen displays an Error 30 message: `No convergence.`

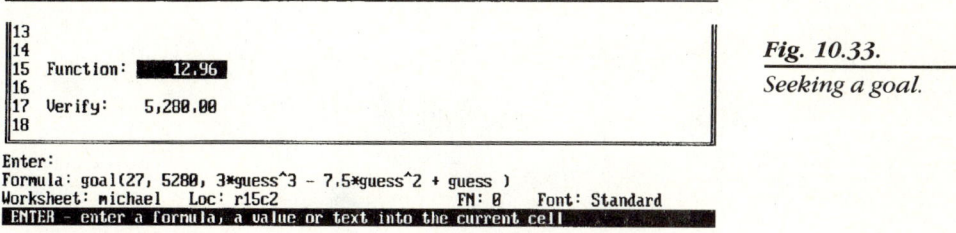

You should try to guess as close to the true unknown value as possible, because only 20 iterations will be performed. If your guess is too far from the actual value, convergence won't be achieved by the 20th iteration, and Error 30 will result.

For safety's sake, you should perform your own calculation to verify the GOAL function until you are satisfied that your formula and constants are within the satisfactory range of a solution.

11

Printing, Reporting, and Integrating the Spreadsheet

No matter how good your spreadsheet model may be, eventually you need to communicate the results to other individuals. This chapter covers tips and tricks to use when printing or reporting from your worksheet. Both the Print and Report commands can direct output to your printer, but they have very different uses and capabilities.

Before printing your worksheet, you can adjust its appearance so that the worksheet is as meaningful as possible. Several tips help you do this.

The output from your worksheet may not be a printed report. You may decide to integrate the results of your work with one of the other Smart modules. Integration, both to and from the Spreadsheet, is the third major topic of this chapter.

Controlling Worksheet Appearance

A successful worksheet is not composed of just numbers, text, and formulas. To make your worksheet as easy to read as possible, Smart provides different type attributes, such as underscoring and boldface, that you can use to improve the appearance of your worksheets.

Underscoring Entries in the Spreadsheet

11.1 Tip: Use the Font Select command to underscore new entries in your spreadsheet. *3.10*

If you want to underscore newly entered items in your spreadsheet, use the Font Select command on command list 2. If you want to retain the standard font, at the prompt

```
Enter new font number:
```

type *U* to activate the underscoring feature and to retain the same font style. If underscoring is already in effect, execute the Font Select command and type *u* at the prompt to turn underscoring off. Note that the uppercase U turns on the underscoring feature, and the lowercase u turns it off.

If you want to switch to a different font at the same time you initiate the underscoring, enter the font number followed by the uppercase U.

Both **11.2 Tip:** Use the Ctrl-U quick key as an easy way to toggle the underscore.

Rather than initiating the Font Select command, you can use the Ctrl-U quick key to turn underscoring on or off for newly entered cells. Press Ctrl-U to turn on underscoring; press this key combination again to turn underscoring off. The current status of underscoring is indicated on the right side of the status line, as shown in figure 11.1.

	1	2	3	4	5	6	7
1							
2				1,000.00		1,000.00	
3		1,000.00		23,452.00		23,452.00	
4		23,452.00		9,876.34		9,876.34	
5		9,876.34		734.56		734.56	
6		734.56		98,763.45		98,763.45	
7		98,763.45		1.00		1.00	
8		1.00		----------		----------	
9	TOTAL:	133,826.35		133,827.35		133,827.35	
10							
11							
12							

Fig. 11.1. *Underscore status indicated on the status line.*

Notice in the figure that `-U` has been appended to the font name Standard. If your monitor lacks the capability to display the underscore, the `-U` is your indicator that underscoring is in effect.

3.10 **11.3 Trap:** Underscores appear under only the values within a cell, not across the entire cell width.

In figure 11.2, the last data entry in column 2 is underscored. Note that only the value itself is affected, not the cell. In this case, the underscore is easily overlooked because the upper values in the column are so much larger than the last figure.

```
     1          2       3        4        5        6          7
1
2                          1,000.00           1,000.00
3               1,000.00  23,452.00          23,452.00
4              23,452.00   9,876.34           9,876.34
5               9,876.34     734.56             734.56
6                 734.56  98,763.45          98,763.45
7              98,763.45       1.00               1.00
8                   1.00 -----------         ----------
9  TOTAL:     133,826.35 133,827.35         133,827.35
10
11
12
```

Fig. 11.2.
Underscore width determined by the width of the value.

In SmartWare II, the underscore spans the width of the column.

11.4 Tip: To underscore across the entire width of a column, press the backslash key while Smart is in Enter mode. **Both**

The backslash key (\) is used to duplicate one or more characters across the column, regardless of its width. If you change the column width, the repeating set of characters still appear across the entire column. Even if you decrease the column width, you never get an overflow condition.

When you press the backslash key, the system defaults to entering the hyphen character (-), as shown in r8c4 of figure 11.2. If you want a different character such as the equal sign, type the character after the backslash. If you want to repeat several characters, type them—the characters will be repeated across the column width. Press Enter after you define your character set within the column. You can create some fancy entries with this capability; see figure 8.11 in Chapter 8 for more examples.

11.5 Tip: Use the REPEAT function to specify the exact number of dash characters to substitute for the underscore. **Both**

The REPEAT function is used to repeat a character a certain number of times. For example, if you want to specify a dashed line to simulate an underscore exactly 10 characters in length, as in column 6 of figure 11.2, the function in row 8 should be

```
repeat("-",10)
```

11.6 Trick: Use several functions together to create a substitute underscore that "floats" with the length of the column total. **Both**

In Tip 11.5, the REPEAT function is used to specify a series of 10 dash characters. Suppose, however, that you *do* want the number of dashes to match the length of the column total. This is similar to the way in which the real underscore underlines only the values in the column in Smart 3.10, but this is a floating "overscore" of the total. To create a floating overscore, use the following formula:

```
repeat("-",len(fixed(r9c6,2))+1)
```

This formula converts the total in row 9 to a string, determines the length of the string, adds 1 to the length (for the comma), and repeats the dash based on the resulting value. Remember that the LEN function works on text entries only, so you must include the FIXED function to perform the conversion.

3.10

11.7 Trap: If you specify actual underscores within your cells, you must use the Report command to print them.

The Print command is intended for quick and easy printing, so do not expect to be able to use special features. When using the Print command, for example, you cannot print underscoring, even though portions of your worksheet are underscored. To print the underscoring, you must use either the Report Normal or Report Enhanced commands.

3.10

11.8 Trick: Use a printer macro in your worksheet to perform underscoring when using the Print command.

The Print command is designed to be a "quick and easy" printing facility; for anything fancy, you must use the Report command. Although you can underscore a cell in your worksheet, you cannot use the Print command to print the underscoring. If you use printer macros, however, you can achieve underscoring with the Print command. To turn on underscoring, put a printer macro in the cell; to turn off underscoring, put another printer macro at the right side of the cell. If the cell contains anything other than text, place the printer macros in cells to the right and left of the cell you want to underscore.

Controlling Column Width

Both

11.9 Tip: To hide a column, set its width to zero.

If you have a column that you don't want to be seen in your output, use the Width (3.10) or the Layout Cell-Size Width (SmartWare II) command to set the column width to zero. The column contents then remain as they are, and even the underlying attributes are retained. The only difference is that you do not see the column. You then can print a contiguous block and effectively hide the column.

Printing the Worksheet

The Print (Smart 3.10) or Print Text (SmartWare II) commands are used for quick and easy printing when you want to get all or part of your worksheet on paper or in a disk file in a hurry. Besides printing the visible contents of the worksheet, you also can print the formulas for documentation purposes.

Printing Formulas

Both

11.10 Tip: Use the Print Formulas command to document your worksheet.

The Print Formulas command enables you to print all formulas on your worksheet or only those formulas in a specified block. If your formulas are long, you can select the Compressed option.

Formulas cannot be printed to a disk file or to the screen. To view formulas on-screen, use the Reformat Formula-display Text command in Smart 3.10 or the Layout Format Formula-Display Text command in SmartWare II.

Selecting Output Destinations

11.11 Trap: Using the Print command to direct output to a disk file does not automatically specify the file extension. *3.10*

If you use the command Print Text...Disk, you are prompted to enter the name of the file into which the output is to be directed. Unlike many other disk-related commands in Smart, this command does not assign a file extension automatically. Therefore, if you specify only a file name, no extension will be assigned. You can specify a file extension of your choice by including the extension as part of the disk file name—for example, VIEW1.TXT.

In SmartWare II, the default extension for the Print Text...Disk command is PRN.

11.12 Trap: You can overwrite a disk file accidentally when you use the Print Text...Disk command. *Both*

If the output file already exists when you use this command, Smart provides no warning prompt. If the output file exists, the command continues executing, and Smart overwrites the target disk file. Use the Directory command to see whether a file of the designated name already exists.

By comparison, when you direct a report to a file in the Database, you are prompted to verify that you want to overwrite an existing output file.

11.13 Trick: Use the FILE Function in a project file to check for the existence of an output disk file when you use the Print Text...Disk command. *Both*

To make sure you don't write over an existing file when using this command in a project file, you can use the following example in Smart 3.10:

```
label begin

%1 File name:

if file(%1) = 1
  beep
  input $yn File %1 exists . . . overwrite it? (y/n)
  if upper($yn) <> "Y"then jump begin
endif

print text worksheet disk %1
```

If the file already exists, the system beeps and asks whether you want to overwrite the file. If you respond with anything but Y, the system prompts you to enter a new output-file name.

In SmartWare II, the equivalent project file is:

```
local $file $yn
label begin

screen shortinput $file "File name and extension:"

if file($file) = 1
  beep
  screen shortinput $yn "File "|$file|" exists . . . overwrite it? (y/n)"
  if upper($yn) <> "Y"
    jump begin
  end if
end if

print text worksheet disk $file
```

Changing Print Line Width

3.10 **11.14 Tip:** The number of characters your printer can print on a line is determined by the Configure setting on the Main menu.

To print as many characters as you need, make sure that you have set the `Characters per Line` setting in the Configure command on the Main menu to the number you need. If you are using compressed print, you may be puzzled to find that your printer doesn't go beyond the limits you are accustomed to—either 80 or 132 columns—even though you clearly can see that there is enough paper. Check your Configure settings—the `Characters per Line` specification is causing the short lines.

3.10 **11.15 Tip:** The Configure setting for `Characters per Line` also controls the maximum number of characters per record in an output disk file created by the Print Text...Disk command.

If you want to print a wide worksheet to a disk file so that you can later use one of the popular print-enhancement products to print the worksheet "sideways" on your dot-matrix printer, you must make sure that the Configure setting accommodates the line length you need. The range for the number of characters per line is from 20 to 255.

SW II **11.16 Tip:** The selection in the Forms Width option of the Layout Worksheet-Options Current-Sheet menu controls the maximum number of characters per record in an output disk file created by the SmartWare Print Text...Disk command.

The longest valid width you can enter is 91.020833333 inches ; anything larger is converted to this number when you save the options. The maximum number of characters you can write to a disk file is 135. If you have selected a printer driver other than generic, the printer control characters also are written to the file.

11.17 Tip: Use the Report command to override the nine lines of top and bottom margins that the Print command inserts. *3.10*

The Print command automatically creates top and bottom margins totaling nine lines. To override this default, use the Report command to specify the amount of data (and margins) each page should have.

The Report Command

The Report command is used when you need formal reports, complete with headings, footings, page breaks, and special formatting. You must create a definition to use the Report command, but the quality of the output is well worth the effort. In SmartWare II, the command is Print Report.

Duplicating a Report Definition

11.18 Trick: To duplicate a report definition in Smart 3.10, use the File Copy command; in SmartWare II, use the Tools File Copy command. *Both*

A Spreadsheet report definition has an extension of RDF. If you want to make a new report that is a slight variation of an existing report, use either the (Tools) File Copy command or the following DOS Copy command:

```
COPY OLD.RDF NEW.RDF
```

Now use the Report Define (3.10) or Print Report Define (SmartWare II) command to change the specifications in the new report.

11.19 Trap: You may not be able to rely on the backup version of your Spreadsheet report definitions. The file extension BDF is used for backup versions of both Spreadsheet reports and Communications settings definitions. *SW II*

If you accidentally erase or damage your report definition, you can recover the most recent backup version by renaming the BDF file so that the file has an extension of RDF. If the BDF file actually is the backup of the communications definition, however, you will not be successful.

Report Headings and Footings

11.20 Tip: If you want a report heading that varies depending on the worksheet contents, use a cell reference rather than text in the heading. *Both*

Sometimes you may want the heading of a report to change from printing to printing, depending on the worksheet contents. Rather than changing your report definition, insert a row-and-column cell reference in the heading specification. When the Report command is executed, the cell contents are inserted into the heading. Figure 11.3 provides an example.

Fig. 11.3.

Using a cell reference in report heading.

```
Report Definition: COMPREP
   Heading

     Justification:  Left  Center
     Line 1:  WATKINS COMPANY DIVISIONAL REPORT
     Line 2:  Pro-Forma 1987 Income Statements
 →   Line 3:  r3c4
     Blank lines after heading:  0  1  2  3
```

Both

11.21 Tip: Enter a cell reference in a report heading by either typing the reference or pressing the F6 key.

If you remember the address of the cell you want, just type the cell reference. If you don't know what cell you want, press F6 to return temporarily to the worksheet. Smart then prompts you to enter a block reference; enter the block as the cell whose contents you want in the heading. The underscoring or boldface characteristics of the heading cells are carried through to the printer output.

Remember that the cell contents aren't entered into the report definition—only the cell reference is entered. The actual cell contents are not retrieved and used until you print the report itself.

Report Width Specifications

3.10

11.22 Trick: Use a block reference in a report heading that exceeds 60 characters in length.

If you type your heading in a report definition, you can use a maximum of 60 characters on the line. If you enter a block reference on the heading specification line, however, the boundaries are limited only by the report margins.

In SmartWare II, the maximum you can type in a report heading definition is 99 characters.

Both

11.23 Trap: If you're using a block reference in a report heading, specify only one cell—Smart ignores all other cells.

When specifying a report heading, press F6 to return temporarily to the worksheet so that you can use the cursor to define the block from which the heading is to be taken. Although you are prompted as though you can supply an entire block, only the first cell in the block is used in the heading. Other cells in the block are ignored.

11.24 Trap: Don't fix the titles of your worksheet if you expect to reference them with the F6 keystroke when defining a report or graph.

Both

If you fix the titles of your worksheet, you are prevented from moving the cursor into these areas. This preclusion still is in effect if, when defining a report, you use the F6 keystroke to return temporarily to the spreadsheet and define a block for use as a horizontal or vertical title block. If you want to use this feature, drop the titles before beginning the Report definition.

11.25 Trap: Don't specify the intersection of the horizontal and vertical title blocks within either title block; a shift in title will result.

Both

When defining a report in the Spreadsheet, you cannot include this area within either the horizontal or vertical title blocks because the alignment of the block with the data will be thrown off. For example, if the vertical title block is one column wide and you include this extra column in the horizontal block, the column headings will shift to the right by one column. The data in column 2 will appear with the heading from column 1, and so on.

11.26 Trick: Use leading spaces to center footings.

Both

Leading spaces preceding a footing cause the footing to be positioned further to the right, one position for each space. The Spreadsheet Report command doesn't ignore or strip out the leading spaces. Because many of the 60 characters allocated for the footing will be blank, however, your centered footing may have to be kept short.

11.27 Trap: If you use a cell reference to select a footing from the worksheet, you can print the footing only left-justified.

Both

Entering leading spaces, as suggested in Trick 11.26, does not work if your cell reference is either the actual row-and-column address or a block name. The leading spaces cause the report generator to treat the cell contents as a literal set of characters rather than as a cell reference or name. You end up with the cell reference itself centered on your report.

11.28 Tip: A heading is centered relative to the form width you declare in the Report definition.

Both

If you declare a form width of 80 characters, the heading is centered on column 40. If you find that your report heading is not centered, check the form width.

Report Output Destinations

11.29 Tip: When you write a report to a disk and give the report a file name, the extension PRN is appended if you don't add your own.

Both

In Trap 11.11, the Print command does not append a file extension when you direct output to a file. The Report command, however, appends the extension

PRN unless you override the extension by supplying your own. In SmartWare II, both the Print Report and Print Text commands default to an extension of PRN if you direct the output to a disk file.

Both **11.30 Trap:** Smart provides no double-check to prevent you from writing over an existing output file with output from the Report command.

If you direct your output to a file and the file already exists, it will be written over. You cannot solve this problem at the command level of Smart. With a project file, however, you can do your own file checking. (See the sample project file in Trick 11.13).

3.10 **11.31 Trap:** Manually advance the paper to top of form if you halt report printing with the F2 key, or the next printing will not begin at top of form.

Normally, the paper advances to top of form at the successful completion of printing a report. However, if you stop the report prematurely, you must advance the paper manually. The paper will not advance automatically to top of form the next time you print a report.

Block and Print Group Specifications

Both **11.32 Tip:** To force certain sections of your report to begin at the top of a page, use the print groups facility.

Each print group begins at the top of a page; you can define a maximum of three print groups within one Report definition. If you need additional print groups, you should define another report.

Both **11.33 Tip:** Individual blocks can be printed within each print group so that you can print discontiguous areas of the worksheet on the same page.

You are able to specify as many report-body blocks as can fit within the number of characters allowed on the block definition line (see fig. 11.4). In Smart 3.10, the maximum is 40 characters; in SmartWare II, the maximum is 99 characters.

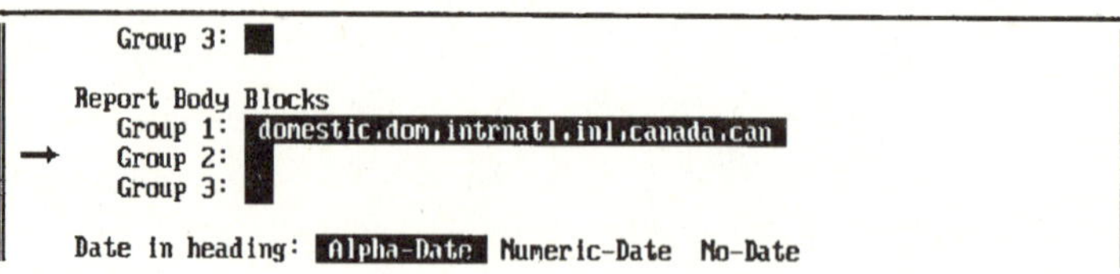

Fig. 11.4.
Report body block definitions.

You can use the row and column block definitions (for example, r5:43c1:23), or you can use a block name you defined with the Name command in Smart 3.10 or Sheet Name in SmartWare II. If the block is to come from a worksheet other than the current one, you must preface the block definition or name with the spreadsheet name, as shown in the figure 11.4. Using block names is one way of reducing the number of characters required to define the print group.

11.34 Tip: If you want to arrange the body blocks vertically, use a comma to separate them within the print group. To arrange the body blocks horizontally, use a semicolon.

Both

In figure 11.4, the blocks are separated by commas. The commas have the effect of placing one block over the other on the report. If you want the blocks to be arranged side by side, enter a semicolon between the blocks.

11.35 Trick: You can use commas and semicolons together to produce some unusual results.

Both

By using the body block definitions shown in figure 11.6, the report in figure 11.7 can be produced from the worksheet in figure 11.5.

```
         1         2         3          4    5    6         7         8
1
2                            Block 1    Block 1   :
3                            Block 1    Block 1   :
4                            Block 1    Block 1   :
5                            Block 1    Block 1   :
6                            -------------------:
7                            Block 2    Block 2   :
8                            Block 2    Block 2   :
9                            Block 2    Block 2   :
10                           Block 2    Block 2   :
11                           -------------------:
12                           Block 3    Block 3   :
13                           Block 3    Block 3   :
14                           Block 3    Block 3   :
15                           Block 3    Block 3   :
16                           -------------------:
17
18
Enter:
Text: Block 1
Worksheet: repsamp    Loc: r2c3                  FN: 0    Font: Standard
ENTER - enter a formula, a value or text into the current cell
```

Fig. 11.5.

A sample worksheet with three blocks of data.

```
     Report Body Blocks
 →     Group 1: block1;block2,block3
       Group 2:
       Group 3:
```

Fig. 11.6.

A multiple body block definition.

```
Block 1   Block 1   :Block 2   Block 2   :
Block 1   Block 1   :Block 2   Block 2   :
Block 1   Block 1   :Block 2   Block 2   :
Block 1   Block 1   :Block 2   Block 2   :
--------------------:-------------------:
Block 3   Block 3   :
Block 3   Block 3   :
Block 3   Block 3   :
Block 3   Block 3   :
--------------------:
```

Fig. 11.7.

A combination horizontal and vertical report.

Note that the semicolon used in figure 11.6 causes block 2 in figure 11.7 to be positioned to the right of block 1. The comma between block 2 and block 3 positions block 3 below block 1 on the report. (Dashes and the vertical bars are included as part of the blocks on the report for purposes of clarity.)

Page Numbering

Both

11.36 Tip: Selecting a starting page number other than 1 prints that number on the first printed page.

If you are printing a report to be included within another publication, you may want the page numbers to mesh with those of the entire work. Rather than having page numbering begin with 1, you can specify that the first page to be printed is numbered as specified within the Report definition.

Both

11.37 Tip: You can use the top and bottom margin setting to control the position of the report's body block on a page.

Although a print group normally is used to begin on a new page, you can control pagination manually by carefully selecting your top and bottom margins. Margins have a range of 0 to 20 rows, so if you can select your margins appropriately, you can force page breaks where you want them.

Changing Report Definitions

Both

11.38 Trick: A report definition can be changed within a project file by using the file access commands Fopen, Fwrite, and Fclose.

Because report definitions are ASCII files, they can be changed easily by a program or the project-processing file access commands. (Try typing or editing an RDF file. You will recognize the contents as being the elements of the Report definition.)

You must be careful, however, to maintain the same data item lengths, because the RDF file is variable in length and the file access commands work by pointer position within the file, not by line. For example, the report's body blocks for print group 1 are specified at line 62 in the file. After you determine the position of the first character in this line, you can use the Fwrite command to overlay the current specification in the file. The length of the string you insert into the file, however, must be exactly the same as the string you are overlaying, because a line-feed character immediately follows the last character on that line. The Report generator balks if you overlay that character.

The following is an example of a Smart 3.10 project file to overlay the contents of a report definition file:

```
input $newblk
let %1 = len($newblk)

fopen "test.rdf" as 1
fseek 1 667
fwrite 1 length %1 from $newblk
fclose 1
```

Remember that although the `fseek` in this file was performed to position 667, this position will vary with the other specifications in the report definition, such as those specifications for headings and footings. You have to determine for yourself the correct position in the file, or you can use a project file like the second one shown in Chapter 6, Trick 6.89.

Before trying this technique, make a backup copy of the RDF file for safety's sake.

11.39 Trick: Change block names so that you can use the same Report definition with several different blocks. *Both*

Suppose that you want to use the same Report definition to print from different blocks at different times. Rather than editing the Report definition, you can change the block definition within your worksheet and then use the unchanged Report definition. Use the Name Edit command on command list 1 to change the definition for a block name.

11.40 Tip: In a project file, change the boundaries of a worksheet block that is used in a report. *Both*

In Smart 3.10, changing a report definition from a project file is impossible; in SmartWare II, it can be done, but this method may be easier.

If the area you want to print may vary, even though you cannot alter the report definition, you can change the size of the named range that the report prints.

In the following examples, the report definition has been developed to print a block called DATA as the body block. If data has been sent from the Database to the Spreadsheet, you may not always know the number of rows. The following two project files determine the number of rows and then change the block definition.

Smart 3.10 project file:

```
'find the last row
goto lower-edge
let %1 = row

're-define the DATA block name
name define DATA r1:%1c1:2

'print report, which uses the DATA body block
```

SmartWare II Project file:

```
local $row

'find the last row
sheet goto lower-edge
let $row = str(row)

're-define the DATA block name
evaluate ( "sheet name define ""DATA"" r1:"|$row|"c1:2" )

'print report, which uses the DATA body block
```

Integrating the Spreadsheet withOther Modules

The Smart Spreadsheet program is excellent by itself, and as a module in the complete Smart system, the spreadsheet shines. The capability to send data from one module to another adds a new dimension to your computing.

This section covers both the sending and receiving of data from other modules of the Smart System.

Using an All-Formula Spreadsheet

Both

11.41 Tip: To incorporate data that is sent from the Database to the Spreadsheet module, use a spreadsheet that consists of formulas only.

When you send data from the Database, a new worksheet containing that data is created, but without any headings, formulas, or formatting. Smart enables you to share data among spreadsheets so that you can load a worksheet consisting of formulas which draw upon the data in the worksheet from the Database.

The left window in figure 11.8 shows the data as it was originally sent from the Database; the right window shows a worksheet with formats and totals. Figure 11.9 shows the formulas used in the right window of figure 11.8.

Note that the detail on the worksheet in window 2 is retrieved from the worksheet sent from the Database. When the Send command is completed, you have only to load this worksheet and then perform the Recalc command to fill the worksheet with the detail data and calculate the totals.

Both

11.42 Tip: Use the following technique to sort a worksheet using date fields if the data has been sent from the database.

If you send data from the database that includes date fields and want to sort using the date column, you cannot simply sort the date column because the database date fields become ordinary alpha fields in the spreadsheet. Sorting by using this type of date column groups all January dates together, then all February dates, and so on. This is because alpha fields, of course, sort from left to right.

```
#1    1         2         3      #2    1          2           3
1  DEPT       WAGE     DEP       1  Departmental Wage Analysis
2  ACCT      3,365.86       7    2
3  MFGR      2,401.45       1    3                 Wage    Number of
4  SALE      2,626.61       5    4  Department     Total   Dependents
5  MKTG      4,080.59       4    5  --------------------------------
6  DATA        654.34       2    6  ACCT       $3,365.86           7
7                                7  MFGR       $2,401.45           1
8                                8  SALE       $2,626.61           5
9                                9  MKTG       $4,080.59           4
10                               10 DATA         $654.34           2
11                               11 ================================
12                               12 Total     $13,128.85          19
13                               13
14                               14
15                               15
16                               16
17                               17
18                               18
Command:
Worksheet: dept       Loc: r16c1              FN:     Font: Standard
```

Fig. 11.8. Formatting data from the Database.

```
#2    1          2          3          4        5        6        7
1  Departmental Wage Analysis
2
3               Wage     Number of
4  Department   Total    Dependents
5  ------------------------------------------
6  dept.r2c1   dept.r2c2 dept.r2c3
7  dept.r3c1   dept.r3c2 dept.r3c3
8  dept.r4c1   dept.r4c2 dept.r4c3
9  dept.r5c1   dept.r5c2 dept.r5c3
10 dept.r6c1   dept.r6c2 dept.r6c3
11 ===============================
12 Total     sum(r6:10c2)sum(r6:10c3)
13
14
15
16
17
18
Command:
Worksheet: deptrep   Loc: r17c1              FN:     Font: Standard
```

Fig. 11.9. A formula-only worksheet.

If you want to sort using date fields that are in text format cells, create a new column with a formula similar to the following:

```
days(r2c1)
```

In this example, the alpha date in row 2 is converted to a number of days, counting from the beginning of the 20th century. After you have this sequential number and have copied the formula down for the rest of the rows, you can execute the sort using this sequential number. Make sure you include the original date cells in the sort block. If you want to display the formulas of numbers as dates, use the Reformat command in Smart 3.10 and Layout Format in SmartWare II.

Both

11.43 Tip: Use the technique of referencing another worksheet if you are using the Read Text (3.10) or File Import (SmartWare II) command to read files created with the Database's Write (3.10) or File Export (SmartWare II) command.

The previous example cites a case in which the Send (3.10) or Data Send (SmartWare II) command is used to send data from the database to the spreadsheet. If you need data from multiple databases or with separate summaries, you must use the Write (3.10) or File Export (SmartWare II) command to create Smart files and read them as text files into separate worksheets within the Spreadsheet module.

After you read the separate text files, you load your formula worksheet that references all the other worksheets. Any formula or function you can perform with the data in the main worksheet can be performed just as easily by referencing the subordinate worksheets. Be sure to preface the cell or block references with the subordinate worksheet name, followed by a period.

Using Project Files To Reformat Data

Both

11.44 Tip: Use a project file to reformat a worksheet you have sent from the Database.

If you use a project file to reformat and perform calculations on data you have sent from the Database, you have a great deal more flexibility than if you just use a "fixed" formula-only worksheet, as demonstrated in Tip 11.41.

You can use the following Smart 3.10 project file to construct the worksheet shown in window 2 of figure 11.8:

```
load dept
@r1c1 insert rows 4
@r1c1 enter text Departmental Wage Analysis
@r3c2 enter text Wage
@r4c2 enter text Total
@r3c3 enter text Number of
@r4c3 enter text Dependents
@r5c1 enter text \-
@r5c1 copy right single-cell copies 2
@r4c1 enter text Department

@r4c1 width 12 columns 1
@r4c2 width 13 columns 2
@r3c2 justify center block r3:4c2
@r3c3 justify right block r3:4c3
@r6c1 goto next-down
let %1 = row
let %2 = %1 + 1
let %3 = %1 + 2
let %4 = %2 - 6
```

```
@r%2c1 enter text \=
@r%2c1 copy right single-cell copies 2
@r%3c1 enter text Total:
@r%3c2 enter formula sum(r6:%1c2)
@r%3c2 copy right single-cell copies 1

@r6c2 reformat columns 1 currency normal commas precision 2
@r6c3 reformat columns 1 numeric normal commas precision 0

@r6c1 sort r6:%1c1:3 ascending using column 1
@r6c1 goto r1c1

recalc
newname deptrep2
save
```

The same project file for SmartWare II is:

```
local $row
at r1c1
edit insert rows 4

enter text "Departmental Wage Analysis"
at r3c2
enter text "Wage"
at r4c2
enter text "Total"
at r3c3
enter text "Number of"
at r4c3
enter text "Dependents"
at r5c1
enter text "\-"

edit copy right single-cell copies 2

at r4c1
enter text "Department"
layout cell-size width 12 columns 1

cursor right
layout cell-size width 13 columns 2
layout justify center block r3:4c2
layout justify right block r3:4c3

at r6c1
sheet goto next-down

let $row = str(row)
cursor down
enter text "\="
edit copy right single-cell copies 2
cursor down
enter text "Total"
```

```
cursor right
evaluate ( "enter formula ""sum(r6:"|$row|"c2)""" )
  edit copy right single-cell copies 1

  layout format columns 1 currency commas minus show-all precision 2
  cursor right
  layout format columns 1 numeric nocommas minus show-all precision 0

  evaluate \
   ( "edit sort r6:"|$row|"c1:3 ascending using column "|"""1""")
  recalc
  at r1c1
  file save "depwage5"
```

Using Parameters in Project Files

3.10 **11.45 Trick: Use parameters as row-substitution designators when utilizing project files to construct a worksheet with data sent from the Database.**

As seen in the project file in Tip 11.44, the following command locates the last line of the data block:

```
@r6c1 goto next-down
```

By setting the parameter %1 to the row number at this location, you can deal with raw data of varying numbers of rows from the Database. The following lines from the project file calculate the needed row references:

```
let %1 = row 'last row of data
let %2 = %1 + 1 'row for underlines
let %3 = %1 + 2 'row for totals
let %4 = %2 - 6 'total number of data rows
```

The value of a parameter that is part of a cell address in a project file determines the effective address. Therefore, the following command enters the double underline on the row whose number is contained in the parameter %2 (11, in this case):

```
@r%2c1 enter text \=
```

The following command sorts the block r6:10c1:3, given that the tenth row is the last row of data:

```
@r6c1 sort r6:%1c1:3 ascending using column 1
```

Before executing the Goto Next-down command, be sure that you have inserted any necessary rows at the top of your worksheet for headings. If you pick up the row number of the last data row before you add headings, the row value will be wrong because no automatic adjustment of parameter values occurs after you insert new rows.

Sorting

11.46 Trap: Numbers sent from the Database don't sort correctly if they originated in alphabetic rather than numeric fields or as the row field in a Summarized Send. *Both*

You can, of course, store numbers in alphabetic fields in the Database. If you want to send these numbers to the Spreadsheet to be used as numbers, however, make sure they are in numeric fields. Even if you don't have the numbers in numeric fields, you can use the VAL function to create new cells that have the values of the text cells. Sorting the cells calculated with the VAL function yields correct results.

Sending and Writing Data from the Spreadsheet

11.47 Tip: Use the Matrix Transpose command to convert rows to columns prior to sending them to the Database. In SmartWare II, the command is Sheet Matrix Transpose. *Both*

When you send a block of data to the Database, the columns become fields and the rows become records in a new database. If you want the columns to become records and the rows to become fields, transpose your block of data by using the Matrix Transpose command.

11.48 Tip: When you send data to the Database, Smart uses certain defaults. *Both*

The fields in the new database are named F001, F002, and so on. Numeric fields are declared as numeric; all other fields are declared as alphabetic. Numeric fields are declared with the appropriate number of decimal positions as displayed in the worksheet. No data types other than alphabetic or numeric are declared automatically.

11.49 Trick: When sending data from the spreadsheet to the Database module, current declarations are used if a database exists. *Both*

If you send data to the Database and a database exists that has the same name as your worksheet, Smart appends the data in the worksheet block to the existing records.

Smart appends the records if the fields and data types match the destination database. You can insert numeric data into alphabetic fields, but alphabetic cells from the spreadsheet create zero values for numeric fields.

In Smart 3.10, if the receiving fields are declared as SSN, Phone, or Date, appropriate data from the Spreadsheet is accepted because these fields are special forms of the alphabetic field type.

Both

11.50 Tip: Use the Write (3.10) or File Export (SmartWare II) command to create a file to be read into a database.

You can create the file in either Text or Smart formats; either can be imported into a database. The Write Text command enables you to create a file in a fixed-column format. If your database exactly matches the field lengths within the external file, you may want to use this format. In SmartWare II, you can export a file in the ASCII format, as well.

The Text format is similar to the following:

```
ACCT 3,365.86 7
MFGR 2,401.45 1
SALE 2,626.61 5
MKTG 4,080.59 4
DATA   654.34 2
```

Smart files probably are better to use, however, because they are delimited with spaces. The delimiters define the fields for the Database Read command, permitting the omission of certain fields and the reading of data whose length varies from that of data within the file.

The Smart format is similar to the following:

```
"ACCT" 3365.86 7
"MFGR" 2401.45 1
"SALE" 2626.61 5
"MKTG" 4080.59 4
"DATA"  654.34 2
```

Both

11.51 Tip: Use the Send Wordprocessor command to transfer data to the Word Processor module; in SmartWare II, the command is Sheet Send.

You must specify the block of data to be sent to the Word Processor. The spreadsheet-formatting characteristics are maintained, as are the calculation results. The document is not given a name automatically; you must use the Newname command. The document type is Document, not Textfile.

Both

11.52 Trap: The worksheet is not recalculated prior to the Send command.

If you make changes to your worksheet, be sure you recalculate before using the Send command. If you don't recalculate, the data sent may be wrong. This trap applies to the Send command when used to send data to either the Word Processor or the Database.

If Auto-Recalc mode is Automatic, you don't have to worry—this problem occurs only when the mode is Manual.

Both

11.53 Tip: You can send Spreadsheet data to be included in a Word Processor document, a graphics file, or both.

Data to be used in a document is transferred one row per line; hard carriage returns terminate every line.

If you select a graph to be sent, the popup menu displays the names of all saved graphs in the subdirectory. The graph doesn't have to relate to the current spreadsheet. After the graph is sent, the graph is listed as the default for the Word Processor Graphics command.

Select `Both` under the Send Word Processor command if you want to send both document data and a graph at the same time.

11.54 Trick: Send your data to the Database module if you need to write a file in the ASCII format; you cannot write a file in ASCII format directly from the Spreadsheet. *3.10*

Although you can write a file in the Smart format directly from the Spreadsheet module, you cannot create a file in the ASCII format. If you need an ASCII file, use the Send command to create a database, then use the Write All command in the Database module to create an ASCII file.

In SmartWare II, you can use the Spreadsheet File Export command to create a file in the ASCII format.

Using the Read and File Import Commands

11.55 Tip: Use the Read command to read files in the Symbolic Link format (SYLK) into your spreadsheet. *Both*

The Smart Spreadsheet now has the capability of reading SYLK files into your worksheet. If Smart cannot convert a formula, the system displays the cell containing the formula and asks whether you want to continue. The unsupported SYLK functions are

INDEX
IRR
LOOKUP
MIRR
PV
FV
NPER
PMT
RATE
SIGN

If you do continue, note the cell because the resulting worksheet will contain the formula results rather than the formula itself.

Interfacing with 1-2-3 Releases 1A and 2.0

Both

11.56 Tip: Use the Read (3.10) or File Import (SmartWare II) command to read 1-2-3's Version 1A and Release 2.0 worksheets into the Smart Spreadsheet.

Beginning with Version 3.10 of Smart, you can read files from either Version 1A or Release 2.0 of 1-2-3. No longer do you have to use 1-2-3 to change 2.0 worksheets back to the 1A format before you read the worksheets into Smart. Figure 11.10 shows the prompt to the Read command that enables you to perform this task.

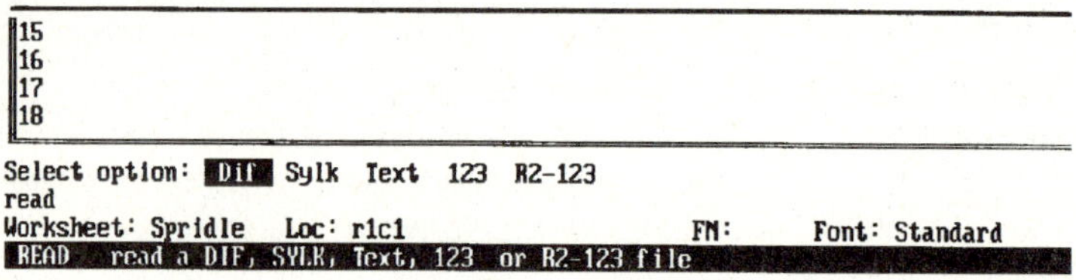

```
15
16
17
18

Select option: Dif  Sylk  Text  123  R2-123
read
Worksheet: Spridle   Loc: r1c1                  FN:       Font: Standard
 READ - read a DIF, SYLK, Text, 123 or R2-123 file
```

Fig. 11.10.
Read command options.

Select 123 for Version 1A or R2-123 for Release 2.0. Keep in mind that 1-2-3 macros are not translated if you read a 1-2-3 worksheet into Smart; macros are inserted as text.

Both

11.57 Tip: Use the Write (3.10) or File Export (SmartWare II) commands to write 1-2-3's Version 1A or Release 2.0 worksheets from a Smart Spreadsheet.

Beginning with Version 3.1 of Smart, you can write 1-2-3 files in formats not only for the 1A version but also for the 2.0 version. Figure 11.11 shows the Write command's secondary menu.

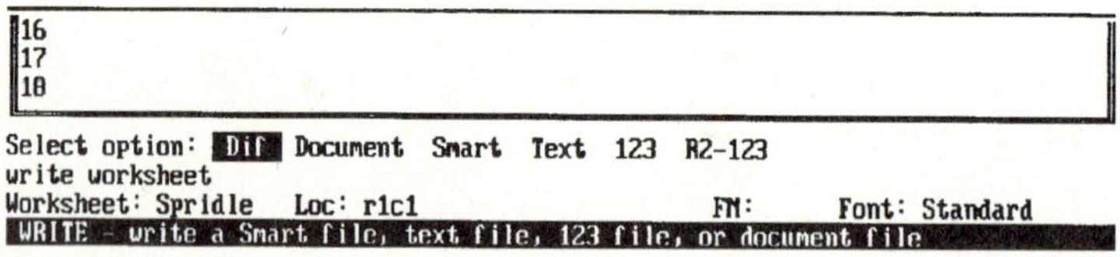

```
16
17
18

Select option: Dif  Document  Smart  Text  123  R2-123
write worksheet
Worksheet: Spridle   Loc: r1c1                  FN:       Font: Standard
 WRITE - write a Smart file, text file, 123 file, or document file
```

Fig. 11.11.
Write command options.

Select either 123 for Version 1A or R2-123 for Version 2.0 of 1-2-3.

12

Graphics

Printing a graph is another way of communicating the results of your spreadsheet to others. The graphics capabilities contained in the Smart Spreadsheet rival those of many stand-alone graphics packages. In addition, you have the advantage of being able to integrate your graph with not only the Spreadsheet itself, but also with a Word Processor.

12.1 Tip: Use Ctrl-G to repeat the most recent Graphics output command. ***Both***

Use the Ctrl-G key sequence to repeat your most recent Graphics display command. In Smart 3.10, Ctrl-G repeats the most recent Generate or Matrix-Print option. In SmartWare II, Ctrl-G repeats the Preview Metafile Hardcopy option.

This quick key can be useful if you are fine-tuning a graph definition and need to switch back and forth between defining and viewing the graph.

Creating Graph Definitions

This section contains several tips and tricks to help you define your graphs easily.

12.2 Tip: Enter a new name for a graph in the Definition screen to create a new version of a definition (see fig. 12.1). ***Both***

Line 1 of the General Graph Definition menu initially displays a graph definition name. If you define an existing graph and change the name on this line, saving the graph definition causes the entire definition to be saved under the new name. Any changes you make are saved under the new name, rather than under the original name.

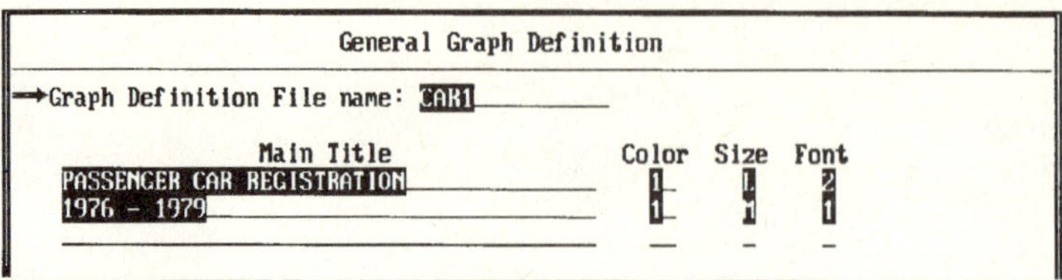

Fig. 12.1.

Using Graph Definition Name.

Both

12.3 Trick: Use the Fwrite command to change a graph definition file.

If you need to change a graph definition file dynamically within a project file, you can use the file-access commands Fopen, Fseek, and Fwrite to write the changes to the graph-definition (GDF) file. Refer to the generalized file-replacement project file in Trick 6.88 in Chapter 6. You also can use the Text-Editor because the file is ASCII. Because the contents of the definition file must be exact, you must take great care when making replacements. Be sure to save a backup of the GDF file until you are certain that your routines in the project file are going to be successful.

Figure 12.2 shows the portion of a graph definition file containing the specifications for the data blocks.

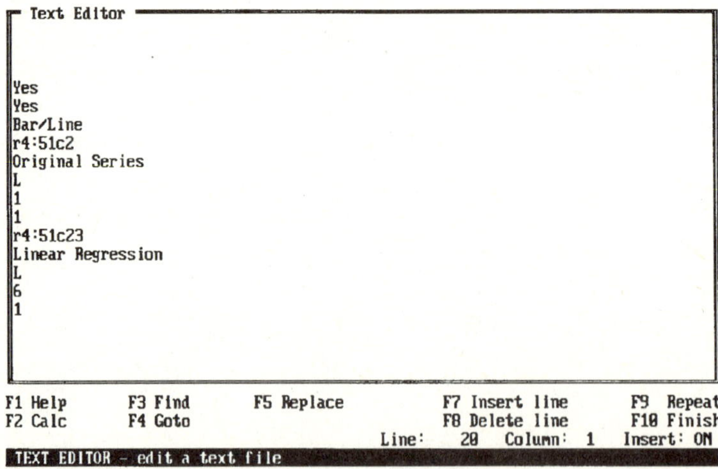

Fig. 12.2.

The contents of a Graph Definition (GDF) file.

Both

12.4 Trick: Copy a graph definition file to create another version.

If you use the File Copy command to create a new graph definition file (with the extension GDF), you then can define the new file and make any changes without affecting the original.

The command is:

```
File Copy OLD.GDF to NEW.GDF
```

12.5 Tip: Use the F6 key to extract cell addresses from the spreadsheet when defining a graph.

Both

Rather than having to remember the cell addresses for the data or title blocks, use the F6 key to return temporarily to the spreadsheet. Locate the cursor at the beginning of the block and press F2; then locate the end of the block and press Enter. You then are returned to the graph-definition menu, and the cell addresses are entered in the original cursor location.

12.6 Tip: Before defining a graph, position the cursor near the blocks to be used in the graph.

Both

Before selecting the Graphics Define command, place the cursor near the cell blocks you plan to reference in the graph. After selecting the command, press F6 to return temporarily to the worksheet so that you can retrieve the cell addresses. By placing the cursor near your data cells before you select Graphics Define, you avoid having to move the cursor to locate the beginning cell of each block. If you are entering the addresses of several blocks, this tip can be a real time-saver.

12.7 Tip: Use the Delete key to clear a block definition.

Both

Unlike other definition screens, in which the F3 or F7 key is used to delete definition-field contents, the Del key is used in the Graphics definition screen.

If you are replacing the contents of a definition field, type the new entry; as soon as you begin typing, the old entry is deleted. If you press the F6 key, the block you retrieve overlays the contents of the definition field.

12.8 Tip: When editing a line of text in a graph definition, the Insert is always OFF. If you want to insert additional text, you must press the Insert key for each line you edit.

SW II

The Insert mode selected on one line does not carry forward to the next line you want to edit. You must continually select the Insert mode for each line you edit if you want to insert additional characters.

In Smart 3.10, you cannot edit lines of text in graph definitions; you must retype them.

12.9 Tip: Use the CELLTEXT or DATE2 functions to create an x- or y-axis data block displaying dates in the Date2 format.

3.10

If you enter dates into a block with the # prefix, the cell values are displayed in the Date2 format. However, the actual values "underlying" the display are sequential numbers representing the number of days from the beginning of the 20th century. If you develop a graph using these dates on either the x- or y-axis, the graph shows these sequential numbers instead of the formatted dates. To display the dates in Date2 format on the graph, create another column with either the DATE2 or the CELLTEXT functions. You then can use this new column as the x- or y-axis data block.

In SmartWare II, this problem has been taken care of; date cells in the axis labels are displayed in the date format.

Graph Operations

This section presents several tips and tricks (and a trap or two) that make generating your graphs easier.

3.10

12.10 Tip: From a graph generated on your screen, return to command mode by pressing the Esc key.

By using Esc, rather than some other character to return to command mode, you avoid having to answer the prompt:

```
Do you wish to save this screen (y/n) ?
```

Both

12.11 Tip: The minimum graph scaling is the lower of a manual selection or the actual data.

If you specify manual scaling of a graph and then enter a minimum figure, you may not get what you select. Smart overrides your choice if you have entered a minimum figure greater than the actual minimum in the spreadsheet. The minimum you enter has an effect only if it is lower than any value on the axis.

Both

12.12 Trick: Use the ROUND function if you are using the value option for label titles and the values themselves are the results of calculations.

Using the ROUND function ensures that values do not overflow their allotted space in the graph. If the values overflow, the labels are filled with asterisks instead of the values you want.

Both

12.13 Trick: Extract a portion of your worksheet so that you can produce a graph if your worksheet is paging to disk.

If your worksheet is so large that Smart is paging to disk, you will not have enough RAM space left to produce a graph. If this happens, copy to a new worksheet that portion of your worksheet needed for the graph and unload (and save) your original worksheet. When you have completed the graph, you then can load your original worksheet.

Unlike the Word Processor, the Spreadsheet has no facility for reserving a portion of RAM for graphics generation.

3.10

12.14 Trick: If you want to save screen files and you have an EGA adapter and screen, set your configuration to the CGA mode.

Because of the very high resolution of the EGA configuration, SCN files are too large to save on disk. By dropping back to a CGA configuration, you are able to save the screens.

3.10

12.15 Trap: Pie chart slices under five percent are not labeled.

In figure 12.3, the January percentage is just slightly under the five-percent mark, and therefore is not labeled.

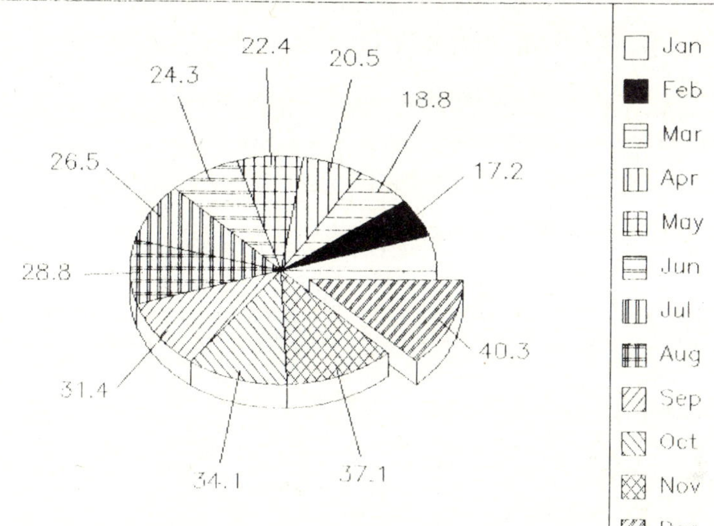

Fig. 12.3.
A pie chart with an unlabeled slice.

In SmartWare II, this problem has been fixed.

12.16 Trap: Do not use actual addresses for data blocks if you plan to change your worksheet, because the location changes will not be reflected in the Graph definition. Use block names instead.

Both

When you adjust cells within your worksheet, the cell addresses in the graph definitions are not adjusted. Therefore, if you enter cell addresses in the row and column format, your graph definition will be in error and will have to be redefined. If you establish names for the data and title blocks, however, the graph definition can always reference the correct blocks, regardless of the blocks' locations on the worksheet.

12.17 Trap: Even though your spreadsheet appears to show valid numbers, you cannot graph the numbers if they are text rather than actual values or formulas.

3.10

It is possible to enter text into a worksheet, thinking that the text is a number. (This can happen if you initially enter text in a cell and then change your mind.) However, you cannot perform calculations on these numbers in order to graph them. If the Graphics Generate command is not graphing all the data, or the error message `no data` appears, check for text values. In Enter mode, the word `text` appears on the command line when you place the cursor on a text cell. Refer to Tip 10.15 in Chapter 10 to find out how to spot test cells easily.

SW II

12.18 Trap: A data block with a blank cell or a text entry generates an error message when you try to create a graph.

The following error message appears when you try to create a graph:

```
Data region contains invalid item
```

In Smart 3.10, blank or text cells are treated as zero values.

Both

12.19 Trap: The graph title may be entered with the F6 key; but the actual title, rather than the address, is substituted on the line.

If the title you want to use is contained within the worksheet, you can save yourself the bother of retyping the title. The title cannot be changed dynamically by changing the worksheet when the graph is run, however, because the actual title, rather than the cell address, is picked up in the graph definition. This also holds true for the main title, footnotes, legends, and axis titles.

Printing Edited Graphs

3.10

12.20 Trap: You cannot use the Matrix Print command to print a graph that you have edited.

To print an edited graph, you must send the graph to the Word Processor and include the graph in a document. If you want to print only the graph, be sure to insert a blank line at the top of the document; otherwise, the graph will not be inserted.

3.10

12.21 Trap: The patterns generated on your screen may be different from patterns printed on your printer.

Because of separate drivers and routines used by the screen and the printer, a pattern that you select for a graph on-screen may be different when directed to the printer with the Matrix Print command. Make notes in your manual or book to remind you of the patterns generated for each selection. You also can print an example of each type of pattern and save the sample graph in your manual or book.

In SmartWare II, the result you get on paper is much closer to the preview you see on-screen.

Histograms versus Bar Charts

12.22 Trap: The Histogram graph does not display bars with negative numbers. *3.10*

A histogram is designed to display a frequency distribution of values within a given population (for example, the number of registered voters by state). If you have a set of values with negative numbers, however, you should use the three-dimensional bar chart instead. Your negative numbers then appear as you expect.

Part IV

The Word Processor

Includes

Using the Word Processor

13

Using the Word Processor

The Smart Word Processor is a delight to use. Even without the integration with the other modules, you cannot go wrong in selecting this module as your primary word-processing software. The ability to incorporate data—or graphs—from the other modules within the body of your word-processing document makes the Smart Word Processing module an outstanding package.

This chapter provides several tips and tricks to help you in your use of the Word Processor. Special attention is paid to footnotes and spell checking.

Starting the Word Processor

This section covers several tips you should know when you configure your system or begin a new Word Processor session.

13.1 Tip: To use the DOS window from within the Word Processor, you must reserve memory with the -R entry switch. *3.10*

The Word Processor allocates all the memory available when you initiate that module. To invoke the secondary command processor with Ctrl-O, sufficient memory must be reserved before entering the Word Processor. For example, type the following entry sequence to set aside 64K of RAM while using the Word Processor:

```
SMART W -R64
```

13.2 Tip: Even if your computer has 256K of RAM, Smart may display the message `Insufficient memory` and `Error loading spell driver.` Check for the use of the -R memory-reservation switch in the Smart initiation command. ***Both***

When you use the -R switch, you are specifying that the Smart System should not use a certain amount of RAM. Typically, you use this switch to reserve a portion of RAM so that you can use Ctrl-O to temporarily invoke a secondary command processor. By using this facility, however, you inadvertently can reduce the available RAM below the amount needed by the Smart Word Processor. If you must reserve this extra memory, you should increase your computer's RAM.

SW II

13.3 Trick: You can take several steps to make additional memory available in the Word Processor.

1. Use Tools Preferences Word Processor to disable the Thesaurus. The additional memory available will be 24,000 bytes.
2. Eliminate any memory-resident programs you may have loaded before initiating the SmartWare II Word Processor session.
3. Use the Layout Fonts Delete command to delete any unused fonts in your document.
4. Use the Tools Preferences Hardware command to select a dot-matrix printer instead of a laser printer.
5. Clear the copy and delete buffers. Use the Alt-Minus Quick key.
6. Work with only one document at a time.

SW II

13.4 Tip: To make additional memory available in the Word Processor module, unload and load your document again.

If you do a lot of document editing, the working memory, known as the "Heap," becomes fragmented in the Word Processor. Although you may not notice a degradation of speed or efficiency, when you try to print or spellcheck a large document, you may get the following error message:

```
Insufficient Memory
```

To clean up the Heap and avoid this error message, save, unload, and load the document again.

Both

13.5 Tip: To display the names of your documents, select `Yes` for the option `Display file names on file prompting` on the Parameters menu in Smart 3.10 or in the Global Preferences menu in SmartWare II (see fig. 13.1).

When you select `Yes` the pop-up menu displays the names of DOC files in the current subdirectory. If you change to a new directory while in the Smart session, the screen displays the document files in that subdirectory. If you want to hide the document names so that a user must know the name of the document before the document can be loaded, select `No` after `Display file names on file prompting`.

```
Word Processor Parameters
→ Confidence: 1 2 3 No-Change
  Prompting mode: Menu Key-Word Key-Word/Auto-Recognition
  Autohelp: Yes No No-Change
  Display mode: Black/White Color Graphics No-Change
  Automatic load of macro file: d:\smart\macs

  Display file names on file prompting: Yes No
  Automatic file backup: Yes No

  Quiet execution of project files: Yes No
  Single-step execution of project files: Yes No

  Character insertion mode: On Off
  Display of page breaks: Visible Invisible
  Display of paragraph markers: Visible Invisible
  Display of tab markers: Visible Invisible

  Justification of paragraphs: Normal Left-Justified
  Left margin: 5
F1 Help    F2 Edit text    F3 Blank text    F10 Finished
parameters
Document: (none)  Pg:1  Ln:1  Ps:11  FN:0    Font: Standard        Insert ON
PARAMETERS  set Word Processor parameters
```

Fig. 13.1.

The first screen of the Parameters menu.

13.6 Trap: On a network, a file with the extension D$$ prevents the loading of a DOC file with the same file name. *3.10*

On a network, a temporary file with the extension D$$ is created to indicate that the corresponding DOC file is in use. If the user's session is terminated abnormally, the D$$ file still exists, even though the file is not actually in use. To allow the file to be used, delete the D$$ file.

13.7 Trick: When entering the Word Processor, use a batch file to select one of several files to be used as the WPPRINT.DEF file for Print Preset. *Both*

The Print Preset selection is in a file named WPPRINT.DEF. This file is read at the time you initiate a Smart Word Processor session. Under different circumstances, you may want to use different settings. If you use a batch file to select one of several files to be used as the WPPRINT.DEF file for the current session, you can use different preset conditions.

The following is an example of a batch file that selects a print-definition file to be used during a Smart session:

```
if #  == #%1 goto badargs
if %1 == m goto M
if %1 == M goto M
if %1 == j goto J
if %1 == J goto J

:badargs
echo You Must Enter M or J
goto alldone
```

```
:M
copy M.DEF WPPRINT.DEF > nul
smart w
goto alldone

:J
copy J.DEF WPPRINT.DEF > nul
smart w

:alldone
```

For additional suggestions on ways to configure your Smart environment for an application, refer to Trick 1.1.

SW II

13.8 Tip: Following certain steps may help you create your documents more quickly and easily because you can have a good amount of overhead even when you are only creating a document.

The longer your document, the more you should follow these steps:

1. Make pagination manual. If you are only adding onto the end of a document, the effect of manual pagination is not noticeable. However, if you are editing a document in the middle, automatic pagination slows you down. Use the Tools Preferences Word Processor command to display the menu for changing this selection.

2. Create a document in standard font so that you can see as much as possible on-screen. A proportional font usually extends beyond the right border of your screen, and you have to use the cursor keys to move back and forth to view your document.

3. Check the spelling. You may have to enable the Spellchecker if you have turned it off to save memory. Use the Tools Preferences Word Processor to enable the Spellchecker.

4. Change to a proportional font, if desired.

5. Change the print options and check your work by printing two or three pages. You do not want to print the entire document if the options are wrong. If you plan to insert section breaks (Layout Section Insert), you want to have the first options correct before you begin duplicating the options for other sections.

6. Working down through the document, insert sections as needed, changing print options as you go. If pagination is to continue from section to section, be sure to change the starting page number to zero in the second section before inserting additional sections.

7. Make pagination automatic again.

8. From the top to the bottom of your document, insert fixed page breaks as needed.

9. Finally, save your document and you are ready to print.

13.9 Trick: Use a Copy and Save command sequence in a project file to avoid the file-name prompt of the Write command. *3.10*

If you use the Write command in a project file, you cannot avoid the prompt for the name of the output document. The following project file can be used to write the remainder of the current document to a second document without prompting for the output file name:

```
copy remainder        'insert text into copy buffer
unload                'unload current document
insert                'retrieve text from buffer
save (filename)       'save document
```

You cannot use the Copy command's Block options because no method exists to record block designations in a Word Processor project file. You can use all other options.

In SmartWare II, this problem does not exist because the command to write the remainder of the current document is:

```
File Export Remainder filename
```

The destination file is included within the command; if necessary, the file name can be a variable.

13.10 Tip: Create a macro to move easily from window to window. *3.10*

Unlike the Database, the Word Processor requires that you first unzoom your screen before you can go to a new window or use the Alt-F7 or Alt-F8 keys to change windows. (In the Database, you can go to another window without first unzooming the screen.) The following macro accomplishes the task for you:

F7Alt-F8F7

This macro performs the unzoom, advances to the next window, and zooms again. If you use the Ctrl-F7 and Ctrl-F8 keys for the macros, you can return consistency with the standard quick keys of Alt-F7 and Alt-F8.

In SmartWare II, you do not have to Unzoom before going to another window in the Word Processor or the Spreadsheet modules.

Editing and Formatting Documents

The following section covers techniques for editing and changing your document. Special attention is paid to the use of footnotes.

Both

13.11 Tip: Use the Alt-R quick key to repeat the most recent Find command. The Global option is ignored.

Rather than executing the Find command from scratch each time, use Alt-R to repeat the most recent Find or Replace command. If you select the Global option (which starts the search from the beginning of the file), that option is ignored when you use the Alt-R quick key. Searches begin at the cursor's current location when Alt-R is used.

Both

13.12 Tip: There are two ways you can check the contents of the copy buffer.

In Smart 3.10 check buffer contents quickly by pressing Ctrl-@, then F2. In SmartWare II, you must successively press the F2 function key or you can press Shift-F2 twice to see the copy buffer.

If the Insert command does not seem to work the way you expect, check the buffer contents by pressing Ctrl-@, then F2. The screen displays the buffer contents on the command line. You may find that the buffer is empty, which would account for the failure of the Insert command.

Both

13.13 Tip: To erase the contents of your Copy/Move and Delete buffers, use the Alt-Minus quick key.

The Alt-Minus quick key erases the contents of both buffers. In Smart 3.10, you must use the minus key on the regular keyboard; the minus key on a numeric keypad does not work for this quick key. In SmartWare II, you may use either minus key. You are protected from accidentally erasing the buffers; if you try to erase either the Copy or Delete buffer, Smart asks you to confirm the erasures individually with the following prompts:

```
Erase copy buffer? (y/n)
Erase delete buffer? (y/n)
```

Press `y` to erase the buffer as prompted.

Both

13.14 Tip: Text inserted into the Copy or Delete buffers loses its formatting characteristics.

When you extract the text using the Insert or the Undelete command, the text assumes the formatting of the paragraph into which the text is inserted. The text acts as if you had just typed it from the keyboard.

3.10

13.15 Tip: Use the Replace command not only to change text, but also to change fonts in your document.

Before you execute the Replace command, select the font you want to apply to the replacement text. When you perform the Replace command, the newly inserted text will match the font you just selected. This technique works not only with numbered fonts, but also with the bold and underscore attributes.

The search text is unaffected by either its original font or the selected font; the search text is located regardless of font.

Using Footnotes

13.16 Tip: Using the Del key to remove a footnote number deletes the footnote, as well.

Both

Smart provides no explicit command for deleting footnotes. If you delete a footnote number from the body of the text, Smart deletes the footnote itself. You can use the Delete command in Smart 3.10 or the Edit Delete command in SmartWare II, but using the Del key is faster.

13.17 Tip: A deleted footnote can be restored.

Both

In Smart 3.10, if you use the Delete command to delete a footnote, you can use the Undelete command to restore the footnote. In SmartWare II, the commands are Edit Delete and Edit Undelete.

Using the Delete command deletes not only the footnote number from the body of the text, but also the footnote itself. Both the number and footnote are stored in the delete buffer. To retrieve them from the buffer, position your cursor and undelete the text.

13.18 Trick: Use the Delete and Undelete commands to copy a footnote in Smart 3.10. In SmartWare II, the commands are Edit Delete and Edit Undelete.

Both

When you use the Delete command to delete a footnote, Smart inserts both the footnote text and the number into the delete buffer. If you immediately undelete the footnote, Smart restores both the number and text. Using the Undelete (or Edit Undelete) command does not clear the buffer, so you can place the cursor at another location in your document and use the command again. Smart then inserts the same footnote, with a new number, at the designated location.

You also can use the Copy command (or Edit Copy command, in SmartWare II) to copy a footnote.

13.19 Trap: When you delete or copy footnotes, the buffer contents do not show the footnote.

Both

Usually, when you delete or copy text, you can press the F2 key until the contents of the Delete and Copy buffers are displayed. If you are deleting or copying only footnotes, however, the contents of these buffers appear blank in Smart 3.10, or show only the footnote number in SmartWare II.

13.20 Trap: When you delete a sentence in the Word Processor, a decimal point in a number within the sentence marks the end of the sentence.

3.10

The end of a sentence in the Word Processor is marked by a period, not by a period followed by a space. Therefore, if you have a sentence that reads, "The cost is 2402.50, plus shipping charges," and you want to delete the sentence, the decimal point is interpreted as the end of the sentence. You have to use the Block mode to delete this sentence.

Other punctuation within the sentence causes problems within both Smart 3.10 and SmartWare II. Consider the following example:

> "What was the result of the meeting?" he asked.

In both versions of the software, the question mark terminates the sentence.

Both

13.21 Trick: You can include printer macros in footnotes for different fonts.

In Smart 3.10, If you want to use different fonts in your footnotes, you can embed printer macros to define those fonts, just as you do in the body of your document. The macros can select underscoring, boldface, or other fonts if your printer supports them. For example, the printer macros in figure 13.2 italicize the book title.

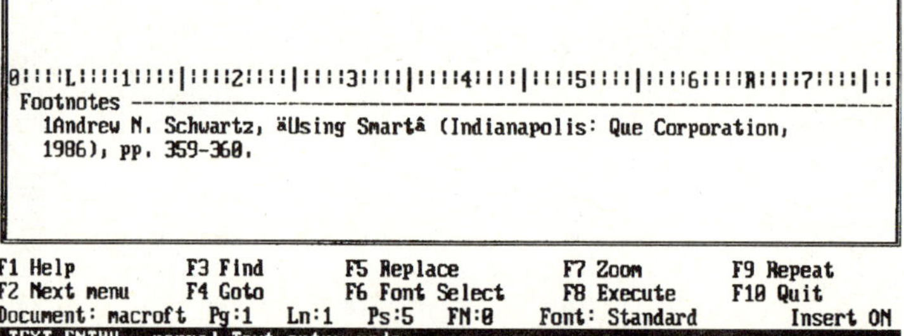

Fig. 13.2.

Printer macros in a footnote.

In SmartWare II, you can specify a font in a footnote by using the following format:

```
%[12bU]The capacity of the 23-A unit
```

The %[] notation delineates the font format. In this example, font number 12 has been selected. Bold is OFF, as indicated by the lower case b, but underscore is ON, shown by the uppercase U.

3.10

13.22 Tip: Selecting printer fonts before entering a footnote does not affect the footnote font.

The footnote font is always the standard font, regardless of what font is selected for the body of your document. To select a different internal printer font, use a printer macro, as outlined in Trick 13.7.

13.23 Trap: If you are printing a footnoted document to a file, superscript fonts for the footnote numbers are eliminated. *3.10*

Because all enhanced print characters are lost when you print a report to a file, the usual superscript fonts that designate footnotes are omitted. When you print your document from the file to paper, therefore, the footnote numbers appear as a normal part of the document body text and footnote text, regardless of whether the footnotes appear at the bottom of the page or at the end of the document.

Reformatting Documents

13.24 Tip: Define a macro to use Ctrl-T for the Reformat command. *3.10*

The Reformat command has no quick key. Since the Ctrl-T key combination currently is unused, you can assign the key as follows:

```
Alt-ZRef  (for confidence level 5)
Alt-Z2R   (for confidence level 3)
```

The Alt-Z in the macro switches the command level, and the remainder of the macro invokes the Reformat command.

13.25 Trick: To reformat a document containing hard carriage returns at the end of each line, you can define a macro to delete the returns. *3.10*

The macro you define should contain a Ctrl-→ (right arrow) followed by a delete. Execute this macro repeatedly until all carriage returns are deleted from the document. Then go back and insert returns where you need them and reformat your document. You cannot use the Replace command to drop the unneeded carriage returns.

13.26 Trick: Use a project file to drop carriage returns from a file so that a Reformat command can be used. *3.10*

Using the file-access commands of the project-processing facility, you can drop carriage returns from a text file. (See Appendix C for an example of such a project file.)

13.27 Tip: Use the %P to replace a carriage return in a document. *SW II*

This is a one-way replacement, however. You cannot replace text in your document with a %P to insert a carriage return.

In a document, a carriage return is displayed as the paragraph symbol. While you cannot replace this symbol directly, you can join individual lines to turn a text file into a document file. To do this, replace a "%P" symbol with either nothing or a space. Be aware, however, that you cannot use the same technique to insert carriage returns. The "%P" symbol is recognized only within the search text specification, not as the replacement text.

Refer to appendix C for project files to convert a text file into a format for use with Smart Version 3.10.

Multiple Columns

SW II

13.28 Trap: In a linked multiple column area, the Edit Sort Column command evaluates the text on only the first line of the entity and ignores any text beyond the first line.

To sort correctly, therefore, text must begin on line 1 of the column item. Any blank lines you need for spacing must appear at the end of the item, not at the beginning. If you have items with identical text on the first lines, the items will sort in an unpredictable sequence unless you enter text that distinguishes between them and make the first lines unique.

SW II

13.29 Trick: Make a second copy of a multiple column area (MCA) to split the column area in two. There is no explicit command to divide an MCA.

After you have created an MCA, if you want single column text in the middle, you cannot split the multiple column area. Copy the entire MCA so that the MCA falls below your newly entered single column text. Next, use the Document Columns Edit command with the Delete option to delete entities from the end of the first MCA and from the beginning of the second copy. Caution: Do not use the Document Columns...Remove command because this will remove the entire MCA.

Using Dictionaries

If you use the Spellchecker, this section will be of importance to you. If you have not purchased the Smart 3.10 Spellchecker yet, this section contains several tips that may affect your decision.

3.10

13.30 Trap: Quit from Smart immediately after adding the Spellchecker to your existing system.

The Spellchecker requires additional memory. If you initiate the Word Processor without the Spellchecker installed, memory for the Spellchecker is not set aside. If you change the Parameters menu to indicate that the Spellchecker is installed and then save the Parameters menu, however, the screen displays several error messages indicating that memory is insufficient. Press F10 and exit Smart. When you enter the Word Processor module again, the necessary memory will be allocated for the Spellchecker.

Both

13.31 Tip: When you add a word to a custom dictionary, that dictionary is added to the options for the current document.

In Spellchecker versions prior to 3.10, even when you added a word to a custom dictionary, you still had to attach the dictionary to the document. The result was that an unknown word was flagged continually, even though the word had been added to the dictionary. In Smart Version 3.10 and SmartWare II, the dictionary is attached automatically.

13.32 Trap: The Word Processor Parameters menu allows you to enter a custom dictionary name longer than 8 characters, but the dictionary cannot be used.

3.10

Custom dictionary names must be 8 characters or less to be valid. If you enter a longer name in the Parameters menu, the name is not rejected and it is attached to new documents. However, you will not be able to use this new dictionary during spell checking—it will have no effect. If you specify a name that is too long in Dictionary Options, when the dictionary attaches to the current document, you get the following error message:

```
Invalid Custom Dictionary name
```

13.33 Trap: The medical and legal dictionaries do not support automatic hyphenation.

3.10

If you purchase the medical or legal dictionary, be aware that these special dictionaries replace the AMERICAN.HY file containing Spellchecker's standard American dictionary. (You cannot use both professional dictionaries because implementing this feature requires that the selected dictionary replace the AMERICAN.HY file.) The AMERICAN.HY file contains syllable breaks for automatic hyphenation, but the professional dictionaries do not; so you must make the choice between having hyphenation or using professional dictionaries.

13.34 Tip: Install a legal or medical dictionary from another source as a custom dictionary.

Both

Rather than purchasing the legal or medical dictionary to overlay the AMERICAN.HY file, you may be able to purchase a list of legal or medical terms on a disk in ASCII format. In Smart 3.10, you then can install this list as a custom dictionary, using the Dictionary Custom Create command. This arrangement enables you to retain the automatic American dictionary hyphenation features, and make industry-specific terms available through the custom dictionary. If you edit the ASCII file to insert commas at syllable breaks, Smart automatically hyphenates the words in the custom dictionary.

In SmartWare II, custom dictionaries are simply ASCII files in the strict ASCII sort sequence. No delimiters are used for syllable breaks because an algorithm is used instead.

Currently, Informix Software does not offer an ASCII file containing legal or medical terms. You must develop your own source for these terms.

13.35 Trick: List a custom dictionary to a file for editing.

3.10

You have no direct way to edit a custom dictionary. You can, however, list the dictionary to a file, edit the file, erase the original dictionary, and then re-create the custom dictionary from the edited file. Although no evidence exists that a custom dictionary loaded in sorted order is more efficient, sorting the file before editing enables you to spot duplicate entries more easily.

Both

13.36 Trick: Select `No` for the option `Correction information` on the Parameters (3.10) or Tools Preferences Word Processor (SmartWare II) menu to prevent the Spellchecker from searching for the spelling of proper nouns (see fig. 13.3).

```
Word Processor Parameters
   Indent: 0
   Spacing: 1
   Tabs: 5,10,15,20,25,30,35,40,45,50,55,60,65,70
   Decimal tabs:

   Spellchecker enabled: Yes No
   Default language: American English French
   Correction information: Yes No
   Custom dictionary hyphenation prompting: On Off
   Auto-hyphenation: On Off
   Default maximum consecutive hyphen breaks: 2
   Default custom dictionaries:
     1: c:\office\office
     2:
     3:
     4:
     5:

 → Reserved memory:

F1 Help    F2 Edit text    F3 Blank text    F10 Finished
parameters
Document: (none)  Pg:1  Ln:1  Ps:11  FN:0   Font: Standard      Insert ON
PARAMETERS  set Word Processor parameters
```

Fig. 13.3.
The second screen of the Parameters menu.

If you select *Yes* for `Correction Information` you indicate that every word not found in the dictionary is to be matched phonetically to find the closest sounding word. Although this feature may be appropriate for words you would expect to find in a dictionary, proper nouns and industry-specific terms are unlikely to be found at all. Furthermore, the Spellchecker is slowed as it performs these spurious searches. If you select *No*, you can choose which words are to be sought in the dictionary by pressing the F7 (3.10) or F8 (SmartWare II) key during the spell-checking operation.

Both

13.37 Trick: To spell-check footnotes, print your document to a file.

Because footnotes are not checked for spelling by the Dictionary command, you need to print your footnoted document to a file and then load the file back into the Word Processor to perform spell-checking. Placing footnotes at the end of a document is easier because you can put your cursor at the beginning of the footnote section and spell-check only the remainder of the document. If you really want the footnotes at the bottom of the pages, load your original document again and change the print options.

Remember that any changes you make to the version of the document printed to the disk file will not be reflected in the original document. However, this is a handy way of having the system find any spelling mistakes for you. You then have to make the corrections manually in the original document.

To use this technique in SmartWare II, select the generic printer in Tools Preferences Hardware to avoid writing the printer control codes into the external file.

13.38 Tip: On a network, custom dictionaries cannot be shared. You get an error message if someone else has loaded a document that uses the same custom dictionary you want to use.

Both

Because custom dictionaries cannot be shared on a network, you may want to consolidate dictionaries from multiple users periodically and redistribute them. In Smart 3.10, use the Dictionary Custom List command to write the custom dictionary to an ASCII file, which then can be edited. Several of these ASCII files may be copied together, the duplicates eliminated, and then rebuilt as a custom dictionary. Use the Dictionary Custom Create command to construct a new custom dictionary from an ASCII file.

In SmartWare II, custom dictionaries are maintained in an ASCII format and can be edited directly using the Tools Text-Editor. Be careful, however, because you must maintain strict ASCII sorting sequence in SmartWare II. Use the Udc-Conv command to sort the file into the correct order and to prepare the file for use as a custom dictionary.

1. Press Alt-X and F8 to provide a blank line so that you can type your own command.
2. Type the following on the command line:

   Udc-Conv `filename`

The file name must include the path, if it is different from the current path. The file must have an extension of UDC, but do not include the extension in the command.

13.39 Tip: Use the Udc-Conv command to prepare a list of words to create a custom dictionary.

SW II

If you have a list of words you want to use as a custom dictionary (perhaps a list you have purchased or brought from another system), the Udc-Conv command should be used to prepare the list for use as a custom dictionary.

Each word should be on a line by itself and the file must have an extension of UDC. The command sorts the entries into the ASCII sequence and removes any commas used as syllable breaks. The longest word may be 22 characters. Refer to the preceding tip for the specific steps to follow when using the Udc-Conv command.

SW II

13.40 Trick: You can use the Tools Text-Editor command to add words to your custom dictionary, but be careful.

In SmartWare II, custom dictionaries are ASCII files maintained in strict ASCII order. You can add words manually to a custom dictionary, but you must make absolutely sure that you maintain the ASCII order, with all uppercase words before lowercase words and set in alphabetical order. If you have several words to add and do not want to maintain the order manually, use the UDC-Conv program to put the dictionary back into shape after you are done.

SW II

13.41 Tip: From the point of view of efficiency, you have no reason to maintain multiple custom dictionaries.

When you spell-check your document, all the custom dictionaries attached to the current document are merged together temporarily. From an organizational point of view, however, having multiple custom dictionaries may be advantageous. You may decide to keep employee's names in one dictionary, industry terms in another, and product names in a third. Different organizations within your company might use the same industry terms, but would not need the same employees' names checked.

Printing Documents

Eventually, you will want to print your Word Processor document on paper. This section gives you several tips and tricks to help make document printing easier and more efficient.

SW II

13.42 Tip: In SmartWare II, printing the current document ([default]) is more efficient than printing the version on the disk, because the disk version actually is loaded into RAM before being sent to the printer.

In Smart Version 3.10, the reverse is true: printing the version of the document on the disk is more efficient than printing the [default]. When you print the [default] in 3.10, the document is written to the disk before the document is printed.

SW II

13.43 Trick: If you print a document to a disk file, the codes necessary for the selected printer are included with the text so that you can print the disk file later "offline."

If your current printer is an HP Series II Laser printer, for example, the printed disk file will contain all the escape sequences and codes this printer requires. Even if your computer does not have access to this type of printer, you can take your printed disk file on a floppy disk over to another computer that **does** have this printer and print the document. Use this command at the DOS level:

```
Copy A:filename.prn PRN
```

This command copies the file from the floppy disk in the A: drive to the computer's printer.

13.44 Trick: Use the Word Processor's features to print a Database report in single-sheet mode. 3.10

The Database doesn't have a single-sheet printing feature, so you need to use the Word Processor to perform this function. Within the Database, print your report to a disk file. Then, in the Word Processor, load the disk file into the current window. You must change the type to Document because you want to specify single-sheet printing with Print Options. Set your top and bottom margins to zero. Make sure that zero blank lines are specified after headings and footings. The page length should be set to the same value as in the Database Report (66 is normal).

In SmartWare II, you can specify manual paper feed in the Tools Preferences Hardware menu from any module; you do not have to use this trick.

13.45 Trick: If your printer has multiple feed trays, embed a printer macro in the heading and footing of the first page to select from the tray with letterhead paper. 3.10

The feed tray selection is controlled by codes sent from your computer to the printer. If you use these codes by invoking them from printer macros in a heading and footing line of the first page of your document, you can feed from the letterhead tray for the first page and from the second-sheet tray for all other pages.

The macro in the heading initiates the selection from the letterhead tray. The macro in the footing starts the selection from the second sheet tray. Any additional text also may be included in the heading and footing. If you use this technique, however, the heading and footing can be printed *only* for the first page.

In SmartWare II, the Print Options menu enables you to select from individual printer bins for each section of the document.

13.46 Trick: If your printer has multiple input trays, use a project file to control tray selection. 3.10

You can use a project file to control the selection of paper feed trays. The following project file, for example, prints the first page from one tray and the remainder from the second tray.

```
Lprint <codes to select from letterhead tray>
Print normal [] printer copies 1 start-page 1 end-page 1

Lprint <codes to select from plain paper tray>
Print normal [] printer copies 1 start-page 2 end-page
```

The pair of square brackets denotes the printing of the current (default) document. If you prompt for a document name using parameter 1, for example, the second line would read:

```
Print normal %1 printer copies 1 start-page 1 end-page 1
```

Refer to your printer manual for the set of codes needed to select from the different paper trays.

This method doesn't depend on the placement of the macros in the headings and footings, so you aren't restricted to using headings and footings on the first page only.

3.10

13.47 Trap: Print Options have no effect on a Textfile.

If your print options are having no effect, check to make sure that you haven't accidentally changed your file from a Document to a Textfile. The notation appears at the left on the status line. If you want the print options to apply, use the Change-Type command on command list 4 to change from a Textfile to a Document.

3.10

13.48 Trap: If you are working on a Textfile (rather than a Document), do not print to a disk file with the same name as the Textfile and an extension of TXT; the computer will lock up.

Because the default extension of a Textfile also is TXT, printing to a disk file having exactly the same name creates a conflict that Smart 3.10 cannot resolve. This situation causes your computer system to freeze.

3.10

13.49 Trick: You can achieve 1-1/2 line spacing by adjusting the lines per inch, the spacing, and the page length of your document.

If you set the lines per inch to 8 and the page length to 88 in Print Options and change the spacing of your document to 2, the result is 1-1/2 spacing between lines. The 4 lines per vertical inch appear to be 1-1/2 spacing, compared to single spacing at 6 lines per vertical inch.

SW II

13.50 Tip: Select Space-Justify on the Hardware Preferences menu for fastest printer operation when printing justified text.

If your text is to be justified, your printer can adjust the spacing on the line in two ways so that the right and left margins align. If you select Micro-Justify, your printer makes very small, in-line spacing adjustments, even if you are printing in the Draft mode. This form of justification can produce a more uniform appearance than space justification, but is more time-consuming. With Space-Justification, complete character spaces are used, as in Version 3.10

Headers and Footings

3.10

13.51 Tip: You can toggle between the Insert On/Off modes when editing a heading or footing line in Print Options.

When you press the Insert key, however, the Insert status key indicator in the lower right of the status line does not change. Don't allow this to prevent you from using the Insert key; the status will change, even though the indicator does not.

13.52 Tip: Change your document's left margin to force footings and footnotes to align with the body of the text. *Both*

The left margins of footings and footnotes always are zero; you cannot change them. If you want the body of your document to line up with the footings and footnotes, you must reformat the document so that the left margin is zero. (Or, before beginning the document, you can establish zero as the default left margin.)

If you do not want the printing to abut the left side of your paper, however, change the following Print Option:

```
Left indent (positions):
```

When you print the document, the entire document shifts to the right by the number of positions you enter at this prompt.

13.53 Trap: Document headings are centered relative to the form width specified in Print Options, not relative to the margins. *Both*

To ensure that your headings are centered, check to see that the form width setting in Print Options is consistent with the margins of your document. The heading should be centered on the form width, not the margins you have selected in the document body. If the heading appears not to be centered when you print your document, adjust either the form width or the margins.

13.54 Trap: Space reserved for headings and footings cannot be used for other text. *Both*

If you specify that headings and footings are to be printed on all but the first page of a document, you cannot recover the unused space on the first page and fill the space with text.

Smart has no facility for printing text in those spaces.

13.55 Trap: Document space is wasted if you specify headings or footings on `First-page-only` or `All-but-first-page`. *Both*

If you specify headings or footings to be printed on just the first page or on all pages but the first, the unused lines on the other pages cannot be filled with text. These lines are wasted and are unavailable for your use. The overall length of your document is unaffected, therefore, by the selection of one of these print options, as compared to printing the headings or footings on all pages.

In Smart 3.10, you can solve the problem by creating the first page as a separate document. In SmartWare II, the first page can be a separate section.

Printer Settings

3.10

13.56 Trap: If your printer supports a proportional font, use only left-justification and avoid tabs for the most uniform output.

With a proportional font, do not try to use Normal justification (right and left) or tabs in your document. Proportional fonts consume space on the printed line relative to the character width. For example, the letter W takes up more room than the letter I.

Different character widths are a function of your printer or font cartridge and are not recognized by the Smart Word Processor—Smart considers all characters to be the same width. Therefore, what may be Normal justification as generated by Smart most likely will be something of a combination of left-justification and Normal when printed on paper. You will not be happy with the results.

Both

13.57 Tip: Use Print Preset to establish default settings for new documents you create. Use Print Options to change the settings for your current document.

The Print Preset and Print Options menus are identical, so confusing their functions is easy. You should establish the settings in Print Preset to represent the default settings you usually want to apply to all new documents you create in the Word Processor.

After you establish these default settings, the settings will apply to any new document each time you enter the Word Processor. If you want to change the settings for an existing document, use the Print Options command. All settings from Preset and Options are stored with the document.

Refer to Trick 13.7 for a method of selecting from among a number of preset configurations.

Both

13.58 Tip: The `Start page number` setting in Print Options is different from `Starting page number` in the Print command.

When you specify `Start page number` in Print Options, the number you enter is assigned to the first document page. You use this feature most frequently when you split a long document into shorter files and you want to maintain consecutive page numbering throughout.

The `Starting page number` selection in the Print command determines the physical page that is to be printed first. If you have exhausted the paper supply or the paper jams when printing your document, for example, you can use the `Starting page number` option to avoid having to begin from the first page to print the rest of the document. If you have printed four pages, you enter 5 when you resume printing. If you only press Enter, the default is 1.

13.59 Tip: When you specify that printing should begin on a page number greater than 1, printing doesn't begin immediately.

Both

Before finding the page on which to begin printing, Smart must pass through the lower-numbered pages. Printing is delayed by the time needed to perform this search.

13.60 Tip: Use a macro to alter Print Options settings.

Both

Because the F10 character can be saved in a macro, you can use a macro to alter your print options. Step through the change one time, noting every keystroke you make. The final keystroke will be F10, which you press to exit the Print Options menu and return to the command level. When creating the macro in 3.10, include the F10 at the end by using the key sequence Ctrl-F10. In SmartWare II, the F10 is entered in the macro editor just as you would enter any other function key.

13.61 Tip: If you have a laser printer, you may need to adjust your page length to prevent text from "creeping" onto successive pages.

3.10

Many laser printers have physical limitations that prevent you from printing on all 66 lines of a standard sheet of paper. For example, the Hewlett-Packard LaserJet printer can print only 60 lines on a page. If you keep the length at 66, on each succeeding page the text is 6 lines further down the page. To reflect the number of physical lines your printer can handle, you should change the page length in Print Options.

13.62 Tip: If you are switching from a dot-matrix printer to a laser printer, change the number of lines per page in the Print Options menu.

3.10

Most laser printers can print only 60 lines per page, but most dot-matrix printers can print 66 lines per page. If the document was created originally to be printed on a dot-matrix printer, the number of lines per page will be wrong. If you try to print the document on the laser printer, the page "creeps" down by 6 lines each page. If this happens, change the Print Options to 60 lines per page. Also, make sure your Print Preset selections are correct for your current printer.

13.63 Trick: To create templates for different types of documents, construct documents containing only print options.

Both

If you frequently create different types of documents with different sets of specific print options, you can create template documents containing only the print options themselves.

When you decide to create a document using one of the templates, load the document containing the appropriate print options, assign the document a new name, and begin entering your document text. Using the Newname command immediately isn't critical, but using Newname prevents you from accidentally overwriting the template with the contents of the document you have just created.

3.10

13.64 Tip: Use the following configuration to print envelopes on a laser printer.

1. Set the left margin within the document at 55.
2. Form length (lines): 45
3. Form width (positions): 80
4. Beginning with line 22, enter the merge variables:

   <<name>>

   <<address 1>>

   <<+address 2>>

   <<city>> <<state>> <<zip code>>

5. Create and Execute a project file with the following statement:

   lprint chr(27);"&l1O"

   This statement resets your HP laser printer for landscape mode.

6. Execute the Merge command to print your envelopes.

On an HP printer, the envelopes must be fed manually, face up, with the right side of the envelope first. For best results, open the rear output tray to minimize paper jams.

3.10

13.65 Trap: You cannot print letter-quality text on a dot-matrix printer while using Smart's fonts.

Smart's fonts are drawn dot for dot in your printer's graphics mode, which is why you have to select Print Enhanced to use the graphics mode. Your printer's letter-quality selection works only in native mode, not in graphics mode. If you need darker print, however, you can print boldface font in enhanced mode.

Both

13.66 Tip: To retain Print Options settings, be sure to save your document.

The print options are retained with the document file. To keep any changes you have made, be sure to save your document. If you change the print options and attempt to unload the document without having issued the Save command, you are prompted:

```
Save modified document first (y/n)
```

Select *y* to retain the print option changes you have made.

3.10

13.67 Tip: You can change orientation and font selection on a laser printer by using a project file.

Use a project file to change orientation and font selection on a laser printer.

```
'Name:                Font

'Purpose:         Select Internal Font and Orientation On
'                      HP LaserJet II

label askorient
input $orient P)ortrait or L)andscape
if $orient      == "P
     lprint chr(27);"&l0O"
elseif $orient == "L"
     lprint chr(27);"&l1O"
else
     jump askorient
endif

label askfont
input $font C)ourier, B)old or L)ine
if $font      == "C"
     lprint chr(27);"(s10h0B"
elseif $font == "B"
     lprint chr(27);"(s10h3B"
elseif $font == "L"
     lprint chr(27);"(s16.66h0B"
else
     jump askfont
endif
```

This project file enables you to select either Portrait or Landscape orientation and select among the three internal fonts: Courier, Bold, or Line.

Merge-Printing

13.68 Tip: Press Enter to select the default data file when executing a Merge File (3.10) or Print Merge File (SmartWare II) command, if you have sent the data from the Database. ***Both***

If you use the Send (3.10) or Data Send (SmartWare II) command rather than writing to a file, Smart creates a temporary file with the extension IFF. This temporary file is retrieved when you select the `[default]` file name in the Merge command.

13.69 Tip: The names of data files with an extension of MRG are displayed in the pop-up window when you execute the Print Merge File command. ***SW II***

When you execute Print Merge File and select either the Enhanced or Draft option, a pop-up window will display the section `[default]` and the name of any file with an extension MRG. You are prompted:

```
Enter the input filename:
```

Move the cursor to the desired data file and press Enter.

To allow the names of data files to be displayed in the pop-up window, create them with the MRG extension. In the Database, when using the File Export command to create a merge data file, type both the name of the file to create and the extension MRG.

Both

13.70 Trick: Rename the temporary IFF file sent from the Database module if you want to save that file.

The IFF file is in Smart format with spaces as delimiters, double quotation marks around alphabetic fields, and a header record containing the field names.

The advantages of using the Send command from the Database, as opposed to the Write command, are that you do not have to remember to erase the external data file and you can make an immediate transfer to the Word Processor module.

After you are working with the Word Processor, if you decide you want to keep the external data file (for example, to print your merged letters the next day), rename the IFF file so that it has the extension MRG. The file then isn't overwritten the next time you send data from the Database.

Both

13.71 Tip: If you use the plus (+) sign to suppress the printing of blank lines when no data exists, a space or a tab character in the field no longer causes a blank line to print.

In versions prior to 3.10 of the Smart Word Processor, a field containing a blank or a tab character was considered nonblank and caused a blank line to be printed. This no longer is true; blanks and tab characters by themselves allow the suppression of the line if the plus sign, enclosed between Ctrl-J and Ctrl-K symbols, is entered before the field name.

Both

13.72 Tip: Smart 3.10 and SmartWare II have different limitations on the number of merge fields.

In Smart 3.10, You can merge up to 20 fields from a file and 18 fields from the screen. The limits do not include multiple uses of the same field within the document. You can, however, use the same field an unlimited number of times within a document.

In SmartWare II, the limit is 50 fields. Each field cannot be greater than 50 characters, and the total of the fields cannot be greater than 1,025 characters.

Both

13.73 Tip: Do not send the same field more than once from the Database to use the field several times in a document merge.

You can use a single field several times, although the field appears only once in each record of the data file. Sending the field more than once would only cause the send and merge processes to run more slowly and decrease the total number of fields that Smart could process in the merge.

13.74 Trick: Use the Text editor to look at the data file if you forget the spelling of the field names when creating a merge document.

Both

The field names are found on the first line of the data file, contained within quotation marks. If you use the Write command (Smart 3.10) or the File Export command (SmartWare II) in the database module, you supply the name of the external file when you execute the command to create the data file. If you use the Send or the Data Send commands, the name of the external file is the same as the name of the database or view, and the extension is IFF.

13.75 Trick: You can select merge field names by using a macro.

SW II

Use this macro to select merge field names and insert them into the body of your document.

```
Alt-Z,Alt-Y,Alt-F8,^Home,Alt-C,Until,F10,"b",Alt-F8,
Alt-I,^Right,^k
```

To be able to use this macro, the assumptions are:

- The merge document is in window 1 and the data file is in window 2.
- Because the Edit Copy command is invoked in window 2, you must move the cursor to the first character of the desired field name and press F2 to drop the anchor. Move the cursor to the last character and press F10. The way this macro is written, you must press F10 at this point, not Enter.

When you use this macro, the field name is copied into your merge document, along with the necessary merge field markers.

13.76 Tip: To circumvent the field-number limit, use the Replace command instead of Merge.

Both

If you want to merge more than the maximum number of fields from the screen within a document, you can use the Replace command to insert designated words or phrases as needed. For example, if you construct your document so that the symbols @1 are to be replaced with field 1, @2 with field 2, and so on, you can perform multiple replacements to effect a merge. In Smart 3.10, under control of a project file, the process can be automated to simulate the Merge command quite closely:

```
%1 Enter Number of Variables:
let %2 = 0

while %2 < %1
     let %2 = %2 + 1
     message Ready for variable %2 .. press any key
     %3 Enter Contents of Next Variable
     replace "@%2" with "%3" options g
endwhile
```

Both

13.77 Trick: Edit the merge data file to eliminate records already processed.

If you must stop in the middle of a merge because of time limitations or an equipment malfunction, you can resume where you left off without having to return to the Database and perform another Query.

Edit the data file containing the names and addresses (or other data you have written to the file), and delete the records already processed. Do not delete record 1, which contains the field names tied to the names within the document. If the file contains more than 255 characters per line, however, you have to use an editor with a line-length capacity greater than that of Smart's Text Editing facility.

Both

13.78 Trap: If a merge produces no results, the first line in the data file may be blank.

If the merge process seems to be working properly but you get no results, the first line of your data file may be blank. Load the file into the text editor and check it. If the first line is blank, delete it. The first line in the data file must contain the names of the fields.

Both

13.79 Tip: To underscore a merged variable, underscore the variable name in the document (see fig. 13.4).

Fig. 13.4.

Underscoring a merge variable.

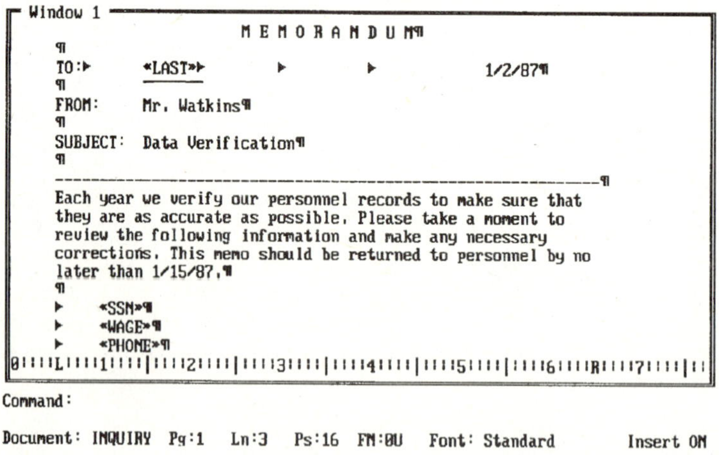

```
Window 1
                    M E M O R A N D U M¶
¶
TO:▸      «LAST»▸        ▸        ▸         1/2/87¶
¶
FROM:     Mr. Watkins¶
¶
SUBJECT:  Data Verification¶
¶
------------------------------------------------------------¶
Each year we verify our personnel records to make sure that
they are as accurate as possible. Please take a moment to
review the following information and make any necessary
corrections. This memo should be returned to personnel by no
later than 1/15/87.¶
¶
▸     «SSN»¶
▸     «WAGE»¶
▸     «PHONE»¶
0::::L::::1::::|::::2::::|::::3::::|::::4::::|::::5::::|::::6:::R::::7::::|::
Command:

Document: INQUIRY Pg:1  Ln:3  Ps:16  FN:0U  Font: Standard       Insert ON
```

Not only will the underscore font specification apply, but any other font designation will affect the merged field. Use the Font Select (3.10) or Layout Font Select (SmartWare II) command just as you would if the field contents were embedded in your file rather than being substituted for the field name. Remember to select Enhanced printing if the Smart fonts are to be used.

13.80 Tip: When printing a merge document and supplying the data values on-screen, you must wait for the printing of the current document to be completed before you type the text for the next document. *3.10*

Most computers have a keyboard buffer that retains several keystrokes you type in advance, even though they may not be called for yet by the program. In most places in the Smart system, you can type ahead into this buffer, and the keystrokes are extracted by the program when they are needed. In the Merge Screen command, however, this buffer is disabled and you cannot type ahead while the document is printing.

If you are seeking speed and efficiency, consider creating your own data file to be used with the Merge command. Use the text editor to create a file in the Smart format, with the field names on the first line. Each successive line contains the data needed for the Merge document. Spaces separate the individual fields, and quotation marks offset the text fields.

13.81 Trap: Your computer freezes if the last line of a merge document contains a field name with a plus (+) sign to suppress blanks and the corresponding field is empty. *3.10*

When performing a Merge, the plus sign suppresses a blank line if the field has no contents. The entry has this appearance:

```
<<+Address2>>
```

However, if this type of entry appears on the last line of the merge document and there is no value for the field, your computer will lock up. You can prevent this problem by inserting at least one blank line at the end of the document, following the merge variable with the plus (+) sign.

13.82 Tip: Use this technique to include the current system date in the body of a merge document. *SW II*

If you include the following in a merge document:

```
<<=today>>
```

the current system date is inserted when you execute the Print Merge command. As with any merge document, the left bracket is inserted with Ctrl-J and the right bracket with Ctrl-K. The equal sign (=) indicates the calculation of a formula.

Inserting Graphics

13.83 Trick: To insert a graph at the top of a document, create a single blank line and then insert the graph on the second line. *3.10*

A graph cannot be inserted at the very top of a document. At least one blank line must separate the top of the graph and the top of the document.

3.10

13.84 Tip: Use the Parameters command to specify the amount of RAM available for the Graphics View and Print Enhanced commands (see the `Reserved memory` setting in fig. 13.3).

If Smart displays the error message `Insufficient memory`, you must set aside a portion of RAM to be used within the Word Processor for generating graphics. This message appears only if you are processing a very large document and including certain types of graphs. Enter the amount `48` or `64`, press F10 to save the settings, and quit the Word Processor session. (The memory reservation takes place only on entry into the Word Processor.) You don't need to quit to DOS; you can initiate another module and then return to the Word Processor.

Note that this memory reservation is not the same as the one made when you use the -R switch to access Smart. The -R switch is used to set aside memory that Smart will not use at all. The memory reservation facility on the Parameters menu of the Word Processor is used by the system for graphics operations only.

Both

13.85 Trap: To print a graph in your document, you must print in Enhanced rather than Normal mode.

Because the printer must "draw" the graph pixel by pixel, you must use enhanced mode. Refer to Trap 13.23 for more information about enhanced printing.

Miscellaneous Tips, Tricks, and Traps

Several additional Word Processor tips, tricks, and traps are provided in this section.

Both

13.86 Tip: To accelerate processing, break up documents into smaller portions.

If needed, the Word Processor uses all available memory for your document. When RAM has been exhausted, the system pages parts of the document to disk, according to the paging path established through the Configure command on the Main menu.

Paging to disk slows the Word Processor. In Smart 3.10, to determine whether your file is paging to disk, press Ctrl-@ and then F2. If disk paging is taking place, the message `ON DISK` appears on the right of the screen. In SmartWare II, press Ctrl-F1 to display the status screen, which indicates disk paging.

3.10

13.87 Trap: Exceeding a practical maximum number of pages in your document can damage some of your previous work.

If you create an 80- or 90-page document, some of your previous work may be destroyed without your knowledge. To prevent this problem from occurring, limit a document to a maximum of 50 or 60 pages.

13.88 Tip: To recover a documen from automatic backup, erase the DOC file and rename the BDC file to DOC.

Both

If you select `Automatic file backup` on the Parameters menu (see fig. 13.1), the most recently saved version of your document is always maintained for you. Document files have DOC extensions and backup document files have BDC extensions. If you must recover a document from its backup, erase the DOC file and rename the BDC file with a DOC extension. When you load the file, you will be loading the backup.

In SmartWare II, you also may have a DAS file if you have elected to backup your documents automatically as you work with them. This selection is made on the Tools Preferences Word Processor menu.

13.89 Trap: Existing backup document files (BDC or DAS) are *not* encrypted automatically when you assign a password to a document.

SW II

If you add a password to a file you have been working with, only the DOC file is encrypted when you save the file to the disk. If backup document (BDC) or automatic save files (DAS) exist, they are not endowed with the same protection. If you save your document twice, however, the second save command overlays the contents of the BDC file. If you invoke the automatic save feature, the first save following the assignment of the password overlays the DAS file.

13.90 Tip: Use the following macro to help you delete outdated documents from your disk and to make light work out of this odious task.

Both

The macro for Smart 3.10 is:

Alt-X	(Display last command, the Load)
un	(Change Load unto UnLoad)
Cr	(execute the command)
Alt-X	(display last command, the Unload)
DelDelDelDelDelDel	(Delete the word "Unload")
File Erase Ctl-Right	(Cursor to the right of the command line)
.??C	(specify both the DOC and the BDC files)
Cr	(execute the command)
Alt-L	(prepare to load another command)

If you display the macro using the Macro View command, the macro should look like the following:

```
axUNCraxDelDelDelDelDelDelFILE ERASE^Ri.??CCral
```

In SmartWare II, the macro is as follows:

```
Alt-Z,Alt-X,Repeat,#5,Right,"UN",Enter,
Alt-X,"TOOLS",Repeat,#5,Right,Repeat,#6,Del,"ERASE",
^Right,Left,Bs,Bs,Bs,"??C",Enter,Alt-L
```

To use this macro, you must have Insert On and you must not execute an intervening command after you load a file. You may page up and down in your document to check its contents and decide whether you want to keep the document, but do not issue a command, such as Find or Goto. The macro relies on the previous command having loaded the document and does not work if the previous command has done anything else. When you decide that you do not need the document any longer, press the key for the macro. The file is unloaded from memory and erased from the disk, and a pop-up window is displayed for you to load another file.

If you do not want to erase the file from your disk, unload the file and load another one you think you want to get rid of. In Smart 3.10, you do not have to unload the file because loading a new file replaces the previous document. In SmartWare II, you should unload the document because multiple documents can be loaded simultaneously.

3.10

13.91 Trick: Use the Newname command to assign a temporary name to a loaded document if you want to store the document in a subdirectory other than the one from which the document was loaded.

You cannot simply load a document from one subdirectory and save the document with the same name in a different subdirectory. When you try to rename the document using the new subdirectory designation, you get the following error message:

```
Filename in use
```

To solve this problem, do the following:

1. Load \sub1\document
2. Newname temp
3. Newname \sub2\document

In this example, a document is loaded from subdirectory "\sub1." The Newname command is used to assign a temporary name and then used again to assign the original name back to the document, but within a different subdirectory.

Both

13.92 Trap: Documents may seem to get lost if you load them from a different subdirectory and do not specify the current subdirectory along with a new name when you save them.

You can load a document from a different subdirectory by specifying the path when you load the document. If you modify the document and want to save it under a new name in your current subdirectory, you must type both the new name and the name of the current subdirectory when you save the document. If you do not specify the current subdirectory, the original subdirectory will be assumed. The file will be saved, but not in the current subdirectory.

13.93 Tip: In the Word Processor, you can selectively unload only the current document. Use the Document Goto command to make current the document you want to unload. *SW II*

If you have several documents loaded and you issue the File Unload command, no prompt appears to ask you which is to be unloaded; the command operates on the current document only.

Unless you want to unload the current document, you must use the Document Goto command to either position the document in the current window or change to the window containing the document you want to unload. (The F7 and F8 keys also may be used to change windows.)

13.94 Tip: Use the Compute command, on command list 2, to perform computations in the Word Processor. *3.10*

You can use the Compute command to compute formulas and sums in the Word Processor. For example, suppose that you are computing the sum of a column of numbers. Press F2 to mark the beginning of the block, move the cursor, and then press Enter to mark the end of the block. The resulting sum is entered into the compute buffer, just as if you had used the F-Calculator. To retrieve the value, press Ctrl-C. If you use commas to separate thousands, the commas appear in the answer.

To compute a formula, write the formula on one line in your document, as you would if using the F-Calculator. Any text in the formula is discarded. You must use the standard arithmetic symbols, but variables or parameters are not permitted in the formula.

An example of a valid formula is

```
$100*18.5000 APR/365 days per year/100*3 days
```

13.95 Trap: Words are not allowed in computation formulas in the SmartWare II Word Processor as they are in Smart 3.10. *SW II*

In SmartWare II, the command to calculate a formula is

```
Document Math Formula
```

If you try to compute the formula in the previous example in SmartWare II, you get the following message:

```
Variable not found
```

If you remove the dollar sign, the formula computes, but the result is incorrect because computation stops at the first non-computational character. In this case, the only portion of the formula that is calculated is 100*18.5000. The result of this calculation is 1850, but if the entire formula is calculated, the answer is 0.01521, as in Smart 3.10. There is no error message that the formula has not calculated completely.

3.10 **13.96 Trick:** Insert trailing zeros in one factor of a formula to specify the necessary degree of precision.

A computation in the Word Processor is carried out to a degree of precision equal to the greatest number of decimal places of any factor. To increase the degree of precision, add trailing zeros as desired. Refer to the previous formula example.

Figure 13.5 shows the calculation of the area of a circle with a radius of 10. Note that the value of PI has been carried out to varying degrees of precision. This degree of precision is reflected in the result of the calculation. In the first calculation, although the value of PI has been entered as 11 decimal places, the result is expressed in only 9 places. In all the other formulas, the degree of precision in the result exactly matches the precision of PI.

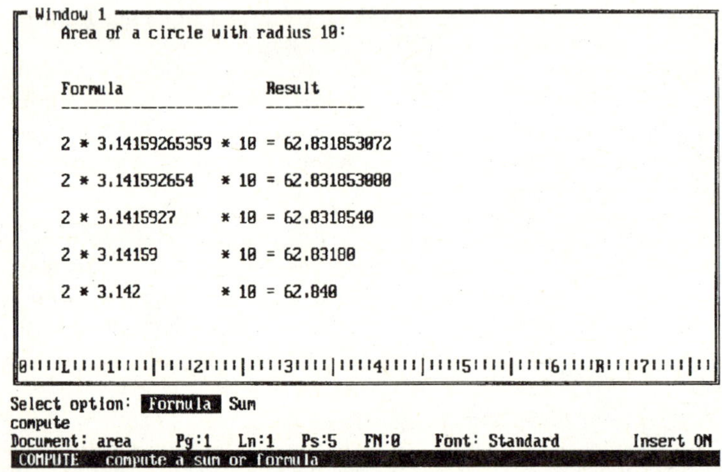

Fig. 13.5. *A formula calculation with varying degrees of precision.*

Depending on the accuracy you require, you should adjust the degree of precision of the formula factors.

3.10 **13.97 Trap:** You can specify only 66 lines using the Draw command.

You cannot alter this limit by changing the lines per page on the Main menu or Print Options; this limit is an inherent system feature.

3.10 **13.98 Tip:** The Word Processor has a limit of 132 print positions.

No matter how many times you change page sizes on the Main menu or Print Options, you cannot override this limit.

In SmartWare II, the limit is 255 characters per line.

13.99 Trap: Using a font in a heading, footing, or footnote does not record its usage within the document, as happens if the font is used within the body of the document. *SW II*

When you execute the Layout Font Remove command, an asterisk (*) indicates fonts that have been attached to the current document, but which have not been used. You can conserve memory if you remove the fonts you do not need. Because any fonts you specify for usage in Print Options (Headings or Footings) or footnotes are *not* marked as being used, a potential problem arises. If you try to print a document from which you have removed a font that is used in a heading, footing, or footnote, you get the following error message:

```
Invalid font number in heading, footing, or footnote text in
section 1.
```

The document does not print. If you want to use the font, you then must use the Layout Font Edit command to reinstate the missing font. Take care to re-establish the font with its original specifications.

13.100 Trick: Although the Word Processor does not adjust the height of a line to accommodate fonts of different point sizes, you can use a formula to calculate the amount of space to allow. *SW II*

In SmartWare II, different fonts can have different heights; the standard font has a height of 12 points, or 1/6th of an inch. There are 72 points per inch. If you use a larger font and do not allow enough space, the letters on one line overlap the letters from the previous line. Use the formula `72/p` to determine the number of lines per inch to use, in which `p` is the point size of the font. If the point size is 12, therefore, 72/12 = 6 lines per inch. If the point size is 9, 72/9 = 8 lines per inch. If you have a font with a point size of 18, for example, the formula is 72/18 point = 4. For this size, you can use either 6 lines per inch at a spacing of 1.5 or 8 lines per inch double spaced. In either case, you print 4 physical lines per vertical inch.

13.101 Trap: The File Erase command can be used to erase the current document (DOC) file. *3.10*

Smart does not prevent you from erasing the disk file of the currently loaded document. (The Database, on the other hand, does prevent you from erasing an open database file from disk.) Be careful if you use this feature. If you erase the disk file and then quit the Word Processor without saving the document, you lose the document altogether. (Refer to Tip 13.88 about automatic backup under the Parameters command.)

In SmartWare II, if you attempt to erase the DOC file of the current document, you receive the following message:

```
File filename.doc is active - Continue with other files? (y/n)
```

The current DOC file cannot be erased.

Both

13.102 Tip: In your macros, use Alt-Y or Alt-Z to alternate between Enter and Command modes, respectively.

To execute a macro from Command or Enter mode, you use either Alt-Z to return to Command mode or Alt-Y to return to Enter mode. If you insert one of these quick keys at the beginning of your macro, you don't have to remember to press Esc to switch modes before executing the macro. You also can use these key sequences in the middle of a macro if you need to switch back and forth between the two modes. If Smart is already in Command mode when it encounters the Alt-Z, the key sequence has no effect. Refer to Tip 13.24 for an example.

SW II

13.103 Tip: When you use a command to overlay an existing disk file, different commands react in different ways.

If you print a document to disk, the following error message appears:

```
File of that name exists. Overwrite? (y/n)
```

Press either *y* or *n* in response to the prompt. If you use the File Export or File Save commands to overlay an existing file, you get the same message.

If you try to rename a loaded document (File Newname), the message is slightly different:

```
File of that name exists. Continue? (y/n)
```

Press *y* if you want to rename the current document.

SW II

13.104 Tip: Going to a marker in a large document is more efficient than going to a location.

When you use the Document References Marker Add command to establish a marker, an internal table is set up that keeps track of the marker locations. Using the Document Goto Marker command uses this internal table and is faster than using the Document Goto Location command to go to a section, page, or line.

SW II

13.105 Tip: Be sure to allow enough space between the decimal tab and the previous regular tab to accommodate the largest number.

Because the tab key is used to advance to both the standard tabs and the decimal tabs, you cannot bypass the standard tabs to get to just the decimal tabs, as you can in Smart 3.10. If there is not enough space between the two tabs, the decimal point does not align with the decimal tab. The following example shows a normal tab at position 20 and a decimal tab at 23:

```
  1.23
 12.34
 123.4
```

The decimal points of the first two figures align, but the decimal of the third figure does not align because there is insufficient space between the decimal tab and the previous normal tab.

13.106 Tip: Make sure your Caps Lock is off when setting an indent on a ruler line; only the lowercase "i" may be used. *SW II*

When using the Layout Ruler Edit command, if Caps Lock is on and you type the letter *I* (rather than *i*), the system beeps at you and you wonder why. You must use the lowercase "i" to indicate an indent position on the ruler line.

13.107 Tip: Deleting a current ruler can cause varying results. *SW II*

If you delete the current ruler while the ruler is not visible, you are asked the following:

```
Are you sure? (y/n)
```

Press either *y* or *n*. If the ruler is visible, however, you are not prompted. The ruler is deleted without any further warning.

Part V

Project Processing

Includes

Project Processing

Communications and Commands Used throughout Smart

14

Project Processing

If you are developing an application to be used by other people, you almost certainly will write portions of the application using the Project Processing facility of the SmartWare Systems. At its simplest level, a project file can contain any statements you otherwise can issue at the command level of Smart. Project Processing, however, involves much more.

Within a project file, you can control the order of execution of the various statements. The change of order can be conditional, based on the values of variables, fields, or cells, or the change of order can be absolute. Your project file can test for certain conditions or prompt the user for variables; these methods can make a given project file more widely applicable.

If you are just beginning to work with project files, use the Remember Start command to help you build a project file. As your expertise grows, you may decide to write all your project files in the Word Processor instead of the project-file editor of the module to which the project file applies. (The Word Processor gives you more features than the editor.)

The wealth of information in this chapter results from the creation of hundreds of project files and should help you to develop your own files successfully.

Creating a Project File

14.1 Tip: Use the backslash (\) to mark a continuation line in project files.

Both

If your command line is too long to view in the project-file editor, you can use the backslash (\) to indicate that the current line is to be continued on the following line of the file. You can continue multiple lines in this fashion. At least one space should separate the backslash from the last command on the line.

SW II

14.2 Tip: Project file statements may be continued for a maximum of 50 lines or 1,000 characters, whichever is achieved first.

Continue a project file line with a backslash (\) at the end of the physical line. If the logical line exceeds the limits, the following error message appears:

```
Line is too long
```

You should break the statement into shorter segments so that you don't violate the limitations.

Both

14.3 Tip: Only the first line of a multiple line project file statement is displayed on the command line if an execution error occurs.

A long project-file statement may be continued onto a second line if you place the backslash character (\) at the end of the first line. If an execution error occurs, however, only the first line is displayed. This first line may not reveal what caused the error; be sure to check the second or any successive lines in your project file for the error condition.

3.10

14.4 Tip: In project files, use field names rather than numbers to document your work and guard against errors caused by file changes.

By using field names (such as [lastname]) instead of field numbers (such as [3]), you can make your project files easier to read and better documented. In addition, you do not have to change your project files if you alter a file at a later time and cause field numbers to change. If you build a project file with the Remember Start command and type a field name instead of using the cursor and Enter keys, the name is inserted in the file.

If you convert to SmartWare II, you must use field names because explicit field numbers do not exist.

3.10

14.5 Trick: Use an editor other than the Remember Edit to create or edit large project files.

Other text editors may have more capabilities, such as the ability to move or copy ranges of lines.

For example, you can use the Textfile mode of the Word Processor to edit a project file. Make sure you use the Textfile mode, and not the Document mode because you want pure ASCII text. You must specify the file extension, such as PF3. You also must use the Remember Compile command to create the compiled version after you return to the module in which the application will run.

In SmartWare II, the Remember Tools Editor has the complete capability of copying, moving, and deleting blocks of lines.

SW II

14.6 Tip: Even after executing the Remember Tools Delete command, you still may be able to recover most of your project file.

When you execute the Remember Tools Delete command, the PFx (source) and RFx (compiled) files are erased from the disk. However, the BPx (backup) file is not erased by this command. If you accidentally delete the wrong project file, use the Tools File Rename command to change the name of the BPx file to the PFx file and then edit the file to insert your latest changes. You will be back in business!

Be aware, however, that in Smart 3.10, even the backup file is erased by the Remember Delete command.

Using the Beep Command

14.7 Tip: Use the Beep and Message commands together to send an audible signal and a message.

Both

Although the Beep command can cause your computer to beep and display a message, the message disappears immediately. To signal the user and to pause project-file processing to enable a user to read the message, use the following combination:

```
beep 2
message "No Open Matter Files ... press"| \
     " any key to continue .."
```

Note that quotation marks are required because this is a SmartWare II project file.

14.8 Trap: You cannot deactivate the system beep within a project file because the project-file command Beep is executed in place of the command-level Beep.

3.10

At the command level, the Beep command toggles the activation of the system beep. Issue the command, and the audible error tone is deactivated; execute the command again, and the tone is turned on again.

In a project file, however, the Beep command is used to issue a tone immediately to alert the operator. The Beep statement in a project file does not turn off the system beep as the Beep statement does at the command level.

In SmartWare II, you can use the Beep ON and Beep OFF commands to enable and disable the beep.

Error Handling

14.9 Tip: Some commands generate undocumented CERROR codes.

3.10

Many commands, in addition to those documented in the manual, generate CERROR codes if the command fails. The actual CERROR code is not important; a CERROR code greater than zero indicates a command failure. The test should be in the following format:

```
if cerror > 0 then ...
```

Be sure to test for the CERROR immediately following the command. For an example, see the following Trick 14.10.

Figure 14.1 shows a project file to trap and display the CERROR code generated when you use the Fread command to read beyond the end of a file.

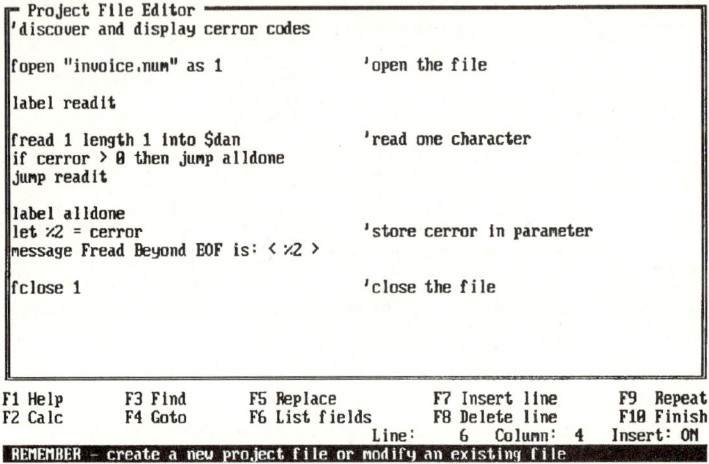

Fig. 14.1. A CERROR code trap.

Although some commands generate CERROR codes, either documented or undocumented, a great many commands do not generate error codes to which a user has access.

In SmartWare II, Appendix A of the Project Processing manual has a complete list of the error codes. Checking for a nonzero CERROR code usually is sufficient, although instances have occurred in which the code should have been zero but was not.

Both

14.10 Trick: Check CERROR codes immediately following the command you want to check for error conditions.

If a command fails, a nonzero CERROR code may be generated. Because many commands either generate new CERROR codes or clear the old code, you must check the CERROR code on the next statement. If you need to store the code, you can assign the code to a parameter or user-defined variable for reference later in the project file.

SW II

14.11 Tip: Use Reply ON Char rather than the temporary command Reply Char to prevent filling the reply buffer.

If the same reply code is used repeatedly without having been "used" by the following statement, the reply buffer fills and the following error message appears:

```
Reply buffer is full
```

This error occurs if more than 22 Reply conditions are active at one time. If you specify Reply ON Char for the same code, only one entry needs to be made into the reply buffer. The Reply status then applies throughout the current project file and any subordinate programs.

Adding Comments

14.12 Tip: A single quotation mark (') can be used to delimit a comment line in a project file. ***Both***

Rather than using the Comment command, you can use a single quotation mark at the beginning of the line to mark a comment.

14.13 Trick: You can use a single quotation mark (') to mark a comment on the right side of some project-file statements. ***Both***

You can enter a comment on the right side of the line only for some types of statements. You cannot use this technique if the statement is open-ended, with an optional entry as the last item. You cannot place a comment on the right side of a Find statement in the Smart 3.10 Database, for example, because the last entry may be an option. You also cannot use a comment if you have a project-processing IF statement, because these statements can continue for an indefinite length, depending on their complexity.

Generally, you are safe in using a comment on a command line that contains a known number of items or words. You must be somewhat careful, however, because the possible maximum command length and its elements can govern the starting position of the comment. Some commands do not tolerate a comment at all. For example, if you place a comment on the line

```
unload screen %1
```

the command fails with an error message `File not found`, no matter where the comment is located. No fixed rule exists on the placement of end-of-line comments because this feature was not designed originally to be used in Smart 3.10.

14.14 Trap: Do not place comments on DOS Window statement lines; comments are interpreted by DOS as a part of the command and cause an error. ***3.10***

Because DOS, unlike the Smart project-processing facility, has no facility for accommodating comments on the right side of a command line, you should not place comments on the right of these DOS Window commands. Comments are not stripped out before being passed to DOS and they cause DOS errors.

Compiling Project Files

Both

14.15 Tip: In Smart 3.10, compile project files without line numbers after you have debugged the files. In SmartWare II, use the Remember Tools Compile No-Debug command.

Project files compiled without line numbers run faster, load more quickly, and do not open the PFx file (thus minimizing the number of open files). To compile without line numbers, use the Remember Compile command on command list 5 in Smart 3.10. If project files are compiled without line numbers in Smart 3.10 or in the No-Debug mode in SmartWare II, the Quiet Off and Singlestep On commands have no effect.

SW II

14.16 Tip: Use the Debug Off statement to force a project file to be compiled in the No-Debug mode, even when compiled from the editor.

If your first statement in the project file is Debug Off, the entire project file is compiled in the No-Debug mode. You do not have to recompile your project files separately to convert them to No-Debug.

SW II

14.17 Tip: Use the undocumented **$_pfcp** Smartpoke variable to control whether project files are compiled with Debug On or Off.

Usually, when you create a project file using the Remember Tools Editor and press F10, the default mode of compilation is Debug On. If you reset the `$_pfcp` Smartpoke variable from a value of 1 to a value of 0, the default is changed to Debug Off. This change remains in effect for the duration of the SmartWare II session, but reverts to Debug On when you begin a new session. The command is

```
SmartPoke $_pfcp 1
```

Spreadsheet-Related Topics

Both

14.18 Tip: Use the Cursor command to prompt and enter cell contents in spreadsheet cells within a project file.

The Cursor command can be used to enter cell contents directly, without first having to place an Input command into a variable:

```
@r1c1 Cursor Enter the Amount:
```

To be sure of the desired target cell type, use the additional command-type modifier:

```
@r1c1 Cursor Value Enter the Amount:
```

Valid type-modifiers are Value and Text. Note that in SmartWare II, the @r1c1 notation may not be used. Use the AT statement preceding the Cursor command to indicate the cell location.

14.19 Tip: Use the Enter Formula command to enter a formula into a worksheet cell.

Both

A formula can be entered from within a project file by using a statement in the following format:

```
@r1c3 Enter Formula r1c1 * r1c2
```

Using the Enter Formula command is the only way to enter a formula into a worksheet from within a project file.

14.20 Trick: In Smart 3.10, use a combination of a standard text variable and a parameter to enter a true date into a worksheet cell. In SmartWare II, use a variable.

Both

The following sequence of commands can be used to enter a true date in a worksheet cell in Smart 3.10:

```
Input text1 Enter Beginning Date:
Let %1 = text1
@r5c5 Enter date2 %1
```

By entering the initial value into a text variable, you ensure that the entry is not treated as a numerical expression. The conversion to a parameter permits the use of parameter substitution on the third line. The result is a numerical cell displayed in the DATE2 format. This type of cell can be used in date functions and calculations.

In SmartWare II, the same project file would be:

```
local text1
screen shortinput text1 "Enter Beginning Date:"
at r5c5
Enter date2 text1
```

14.21 Trap: If you use a Let statement rather than an Enter statement to assign a date to a spreadsheet cell, you cannot use the result in a date calculation or function.

3.10

The following statements are not equivalent:

```
Let r1c7 = date2("8/20/71")
@r1c1 enter date2 "8/20/71"
```

The first example enters a text string into the cell. The string is in the DATE2 format but cannot be used in date calculations or functions. The second example enters a numeric value into the cell; the value is the number of days from the beginning of the 20th century to the date specified. The cell contents are displayed in the DATE2 format, however. You can use this type of cell in any calculation or date functions.

Both

14.22 Trick: In Smart 3.10, use a combination of a standard text variable and a parameter to prompt for and to enter a formula in a worksheet. In SmartWare II, use a variable.

The following statements prompt for a formula to be entered in a worksheet in 3.10:

```
Input Text1 Enter the Test Formula:
let %1 = text1
@r1c1 Enter Formula %1
```

By prompting for the original formula to be entered in the text1 variable, you ensure that your response is not evaluated as an expression. The conversion of the variable to a parameter permits substitution on the command line in line 3.

In SmartWare II, use the following set of statements:

```
local $formula
screen shortinput $formula "Enter a formula:"
@ r10c3
enter formula $formula
```

Editing Project Files

Both

14.23 Trick: Use Alt-F2 to erase the entire project file's contents within the Editor.

If you want to delete the entire file, use the Alt-F2 key sequence. The F8 key can be used to delete a single line.

Both

14.24 Trick: Use the Alt-F3 key to read another project file into the current edit workspace. This is a good way to make a copy of an existing project file or to assemble a larger program from smaller ones.

When you press Alt-F3, you are prompted for the file to read. You must type both the file name and extension. The file you specify is inserted prior to the current cursor position.

SW II

14.25 Tip: If you want to create a copy of a project file while editing the file, press Alt-W. You also can write out just a portion of the program.

When you press Alt-W, you are prompted for the name of the file to create. Type the name, including the extension, and press Enter. If you want to write just part of the file, press Alt-C and highlight the section as if you were going to copy the lines, then press Alt-W. Press Esc to abort the copy.

Database-Related Topics

Both

14.26 Tip: Use the Lock-record command to accelerate multiple- assignment statements in a Database project file.

If you are performing assignment statements in several successive fields of a record within a project file, you can accelerate project execution by placing the Lock-record command immediately before the first assignment statement. The purpose is to hold the assignments' results in a working buffer in RAM until you proceed to another record or close the file. Without the lock-record statement, the entire record is written to the database buffer for each assignment.

The longer the records and greater the number of assignments, the more time you save by using the Lock-record command. If the file is small and only one or two assignments are being made, however, this statement actually may slow processing.

14.27 Tip: On a network in the Database module, if you lock and update a record, you must write the record before you can go to another view. *SW II*

The following is an example:

```
Lock-Record
Data Update Only-One
Write-Record
Data Goto View "person2.vw"
```

14.28 Trap: You must make sure your file is ordered sequentially if you enter a blank record in a project file and then perform an assignment statement. If the file is ordered by a Key or an Index, the assignment will affect the wrong record. *3.10*

The purpose of entering a blank record is to make assignments to fields in that record. If the file is ordered sequentially, assignments made immediately following the blank-record entry affect the fields in that record. If the file is not ordered sequentially, assignments affect an indeterminate file record, but certainly not the one you want.

14.29 Tip: When deleting a record in a project file, make sure the record is not deleted already. If the record already is deleted, you activate the record again because the Delete command is a toggle. *3.10*

To make sure you do not accidentally activate the record, use the following statement:

```
If deleted = 0 then delete
```

In SmartWare II, you do not have this problem because the commands Data Delete Yes and Data Delete No force a record to be either deleted or active.

14.30 Trick: Use a project file to insert double quotation marks into an alpha field if you really, *must* have them there. The practice may be dangerous, however. *3.10*

The normal Enter or Update commands do not allow the entry of double quotation marks into an alpha field from the command level. But if you really *must* have them, you can use the following project file:

```
let [field] = chr(34)|[field]|chr(34)
```

The `chr(34)` represents a quotation mark. The danger you run is that you may have unexpected truncation of the field and unspecified results (garbage, for example) if you write the fields to an ASCII file. SmartWare II does not prevent the direct entry of double quotation marks into an alpha field through the normal Data Enter command.

3.10

14.31 Trap: To advance to the next record in a Database project file, use the command Goto Record Next. If you tend to write English more often than project-development language, however, you may be tempted to write Goto Next Record.

This second form sounds more logical, but the command does not work and does not yield an error message during the compile process or during execution.

Both

14.32 Tip: Use the screen print (SmartWare II) command or menu Print command (Smart 3.10) in a project file to display your progress as a project file goes from record to record of a database.

Sometimes you want to know what record you are on, but you want to have Repaint Off so that the job runs as fast as possible. You can use the following SmartWare II code in a project file:

```
screen clear 7 0
while record <= records
     screen print 5 5 7 0 \
          "Current Record: "|str(record)|" out of "|str(records)| \
          " Completed: "|format(record/records,"2r%")
     data goto record next
end while
```

In Smart 3.10, use parameters to display the record count and percentage.

3.10

14.33 Tip: Do not update your database keys unless you absolutely have to; you can save processing time by not updating them.

The Key Update command obviously takes time to execute—time you may not want to waste. If you can accomplish your tasks without updating the keys, you can save this time and speed up your application. The following is an example of a way to avoid the key update:

```
%1 Last Name:
let $cerror = 0
find [last] equal "%1" options
if cerror <> 0
     key update
     find [last] equal "%1" options
     let $cerror = cerror
```

```
endif
if $cerror <> 0
     beep
     message Last Name %1 not found .. press key
     jump addemp
endif
```

The normal tendency is to ensure that the keys are updated before performing an optimized Find command. As shown in this example, however, you can avoid updating the key if the appropriate record is found. Only if the record is not found should you update the key to make sure that the name *really* is not in the file.

14.34 Trick: Check to see if the DBU file exists to determine if a database has been loaded. *3.10*

In Smart 3.10, you have no direct way to determine if a database currently is loaded. When a database is opened, however, a DBU file is created, which stores the record numbers of any records that have been updated or entered. If this DBU file exists, the file probably is open. If you forget to update the keys of the database before you unload it, the DBU file exists even if the file is not loaded, so this method is not foolproof. On a network, DBU files always exist, so this technique cannot be used in this situation.

Any command that creates a database fails if the database is loaded or exists. Make sure that the resulting database is unloaded and does not exist on the disk. The following is an example of a check for the existence of the DBU file to determine if a database is loaded:

```
if file("ledtemp.dbu") = 1 then unload file ledtemp
if file("ledtemp.db") = 1 then utilities erase file ledtemp
relate predefined ACCLED intersect ledtemp
```

14.35 Trick: On a network, you can use the renaming of a file as a means of communicating between users. The name of the file can indicate a status or permission level. *Both*

In a network application, you sometimes do not want two users to do the same thing at the same time. You would like to have one wait until the other finishes. Although there is no direct way you can send a wait message to another user, the following Smart 3.10 project-file code shows you how.

```
while file("invoice.yes") = 0
     wait .1  Waiting for permission
endwhile

file rename invoice.yes to invoice.no
     'perform processing here
file rename invoice.no to invoice.yes
```

In this example, the program continues to loop until the file `invoice.yes` exists. For even greater security, you can use a random number as the name of the file:

```
let %1 = int(uniform(10000)+1)
file rename invoice.yes to %1
     'perform processing here
file rename %1 to invoice.yes
```

Here, the signal file is renamed temporarily to a random number and renamed back again after the processing has concluded.

3.10

14.36 Tip: In a Database project file, if you omit the sort direction, "ascending" is assumed.

The full sort command is:

```
SORT NOW indexname FIELDS [field1;field2] ASCENDING
```

If you want an ascending sort, you can omit the direction at the end of the command. Of course, if you want a descending sort, you must have the word "descending" at the end of the command.

Executing Project Files

Both

14.37 Tip: Use the Execute command to run another project file and to return control to the current project upon completion. Use the Transfer command to run a second project without returning control.

If your application runs multiple project files in succession, you can use the Execute command or the Transfer command to run a second project from the first. Use the Execute command if you want control to return to the first file; use Transfer if you do not.

3.10

14.38 Trick: Execute project files "in-memory" from the command level of Smart.

If you type the words `in-memory` after the name of a project file at the command level of Smart, the whole project file is loaded into RAM prior to execution. Use of this option accelerates project-file execution. This option at the command level of Smart is the same one offered when executing a project file from within another project file. Note that the project file must be smaller than 64K and that sufficient RAM must be available for loading the project file.

You must spell out completely the words `in-memory` for this feature to take effect. If you abbreviate, you get no error message, but you do not achieve the desired result of executing the project file entirely in memory.

Both

14.39 Tip: Run all project files in-memory, whenever possible, especially if you are on a network. This is advisable even if your project file has no looping or repetitively executed statements.

If you do not execute a project file in-memory, but rather from-file, each statement must be read individually from the RFx file to be executed. Although the loss of speed due to disk access may not be noticeable on a stand-alone computer or with a small project file, accessing the RFx file repeatedly from the file server on a network definitely would slow the execution of the program.

14.40 Tip: You should deliberately execute a project file from-file if, in the course of execution, you want to perform a command that cannot run if not enough memory is available.

Both

For example, loading a spreadsheet worksheet, resetting hardware preferences, or using the Memalloc command to allocate memory all consume working memory. When you execute a project file in-memory, the entire program is loaded into memory before execution begins. If this does not leave you with enough memory to do the rest of the job, however, you must run the program from-file.

14.41 Tip: Use the following macro to execute all your project files in-memory.

SW II

```
Alt-Z,F8,until,enter,"I"
```

This macro issues the F8 function key to Execute, waits for you to select the project file from the pop-up menu, and issues the "I" for in-memory after you press Enter. An appropriate key to use for this macro might be the Shift-F8 key.

14.42 Tip: Project files compiled without line numbers and with Quiet On reduce the number of open files.

Both

If Quiet is On and the project file has been compiled without line numbers, the source file (PF1, PF2, or PF3) is not accessed during project execution. Only the object file (RF1, RF2, or RF3 file) is used for execution. Therefore, the number of open files is reduced. In Smart 3.10, this feature can be important when your project is running on a network or when you are not using the -FVIRTUAL switch on a single-user system.

14.43 Tip: Use the following project file to compile all your project files with Debug-Off.

SW II

```
public $projects $count

let $projects = getfnames("*.pf3",1)
let $count = 1

while group($projects,$count) <> null
     remember tools compile no-debug group($projects,$count)
     let $count = $count + 1
end while
```

14.44 Trap: If the current project file is executed from within another project file, do not use the Execute command to resume processing of the first file.

Both

If you execute project file 2 from within project file 1, control automatically returns to file 1 on completion of project file 2. Do not include in file 2 a command to execute file 1; if you do so, two versions of file 1 will be open simultaneously, and execution of file 1 will begin with line 1 instead of the line following the one that executed file 2.

3.10

14.45 Tip: If you want a project file to be executed in-memory when you enter a module, use the -a entry switch. If you use the -p switch, the project is executed from-file.

To execute an initial project file in-memory, your batch file should contain the -a switch, as in the following example:

```
-aExecute Loadall in-memory
```

The -a is used to specify a command to be executed immediately upon entering Smart. The following examples use the -p entry switch:

```
-pLoadall
-pLoadall in-memory
```

In either of these instances, the Loadall project file executes line by line from the file.

In SmartWare II, if you use the -oe entry switch, a project file you execute with the -p entry switch is run in-memory.

SW II

14.46 Tip: Project files written originally for one module can be executed from within another if the files do not contain module-specific commands.

Of course, because the extensions of the RF files indicate the module, RF files written for another module do not appear in the pop-up window. You must type both the name and the extension of the RF file you want to execute.

SW II

14.47 Tip: Develop a collection of your own functions and load them into memory when you initiate a SmartWare II session.

By having your favorite functions in memory at all times, you are able to access them from any project file, query, or report. The functions execute quickly because they are memory-resident. The possible disadvantage is that the more you have in memory, the greater the possibility that you will run out of RAM for other portions of the application. To load a project file in memory, use the Remember Tools Load command.

File-Access Commands

3.10

14.48 Trick: Performing a Fread command beyond the end of a file generates a CERROR code.

The Fread command performs no explicit test for end-of-file conditions. A CERROR greater than zero, however, is an indication of having reached the end of file. In fact, the CERROR is 3, but as long as you test for a value greater than zero, you will be fine.

An Fread command beyond the end of the file in SmartWare II does not generate a CERROR code. Test for an end-of-file by using the EOF function.

14.49 Trap: Fseek does not generate an end-of-file CERROR code as does Fread. ***Both***

Performing an Fseek command beyond the end of the file does not generate an end-of-file CERROR code. Use an Fread command to check for end of file.

14.50 Trap: The Fwrite command writes unpredictable results if the string length does not match the length specified in the command. ***Both***

If the string is shorter than the specified length when you use the Fwrite...Length command, possibly nothing is written to the file or the remainder of the file may be deleted beyond the last character in the variable. For best results, make sure that the length of the actual string matches the specified length.

14.51 Trap: Fwrite does not generate an end-of-file CERROR code as the Fread command does. ***Both***

Performing an Fwrite command beyond the end of the file does not generate an end-of-file CERROR code. Use an Fread command to check for end of file.

14.52 Tip: Create a compact fixed-format external file, using the Fwrite command, along with the FIXED and LEN functions. ***Both***

Although you can use the Write (3.10) or File Export (SmartWare II) commands to create a fixed-format file from the database, you always have at least one blank column between each field. If the field name is longer than the field width, you have more spaces. As an added problem, you also have the field names in the first record of the file. The following is an example of a file written in the mixed format.

Last Name	SSN	Status	Dependents	ST
Ronaldo	345-98-7593	1	3	IL
Linden	498-48-3980	1	1	MA
Davis	239-87-8876	2	1	LA

If you need to transmit a data file in a fixed format to your company's mainframe computer, reading is easier and transmit time is lessened if you can get rid of the extra blanks and the unneeded first line. The following SmartWare II project file uses the Fwrite command to write an external file in a fixed format:

```
tools file erase "sample.txt"
fopen "sample.txt" as 1
data goto record first
```

```
while record <= records
     fwrite 1 from format([last name],"l10")      | \
                   format([ssn],"l11")            | \
                   format([status],"l1")          | \
                   format(str([Dependents]),"r2") | \
                   format([st],"l2")
     data goto record next
end while
fclose 1
```

In the FORMAT function, the numeric fields are right-justified and the alpha fields are left-justified. Compare the resulting file to the preceding example:

```
Ronaldo   345-98-75931 3IL
Linden    498-48-39801 1MA
Davis     239-87-88762 1LA
```

Notice that no extra blanks exist between the fields; the only blanks are due to the fixed format.

In Smart 3.10, the equivalent project file is:

```
fopen "sample.txt" as 1
goto record rec-number 1
while record <= records
   fwrite 1 from [last]|repeat(" ",10-len([last])) | \
                 [ssn]                                | \
                 [status]                             | \
                 repeat(" ",2-len(str([dep])))|str([dep]) | \
                 [st]
   if record = records then break
   goto record next
endwhile
fclose 1
```

Note that in this program, blanks are appended onto the right of the [last] field because that field is left-justified and onto the left of the [dependents] field because that field is right-justified.

3.10 **14.53 Tip:** Execute an Fclose command before the Fopen command to make sure that the file has not been left open from a previous project file.

If the external file has been left open from a previous project file, the Fclose command closes the file. If the file already is closed, the statement has no effect.

In SmartWare II, you cannot close a file that is not open, and closing a file is unnecessary because all files opened with the Fopen statement are closed at the conclusion of the project file.

3.10 **14.54 Trap:** If you Fwrite to a file that has not been opened, the command fails but you receive no error message.

Make sure you Fopen your output file before you attempt to write to the file. You receive no error message or CERROR code generated if the file has not been opened.

14.55 Tip: Use the Fwrite command to create a batch file containing several DOS commands. Next, execute the batch file with one, rather than several, Command /c commands. (In SmartWare II, use the Tools OS command.)

Both

If you execute all the DOS commands at one time in the batch file, the execution of your project file is cleaner because the screen does not blank and repaint with each command. The following project file is an example:

```
fopen "sample.bat" as 1
fwrite 1 from "dir *.doc"
fwrite 1 from "type catalog.txt"
fclose 1
tools os "sample"
```

As an added advantage, your project file runs faster.

14.56 Tip: Use a concatenation of constants and variables to construct an argument to the Tools OS command, which will vary during the execution of a project file.

SW II

If you want to display a list of the project files in various different subdirectories, for example, use the following project file:

```
public $dir
screen shortinput $dir "Subdirectory:"
Tools OS "Dir "|$dir|"\*.pf* /p"
```

In response to the prompt, enter the name of the subdirectory, preceded by the backslash or a drive letter and backslash, if needed. You cannot and should not use the Evaluate statement with the Tools OS command.

14.57 Tip: Use the following project file to print to a file, in much the same way you use the Fprint command to print to the printer.

3.10

```
'Name:                  Fprint
'Purpose:               Write messages into file fprint.prn
'Calling Sequence:      let $fprint = "Any Message"
'                       execute fprint in-memory

quiet on
fclose 1
fopen "fprint.prn" as 1

'initialization
let $top = 32000         'est. max file size in bytes
let $bottom = 0
let %1 = $top / 2        'initial seek location
```

```
let $char1 = " "

'find the end of the file by binary search method
label nexchar
fseek 1 %1
fread 1 length 1 into $char1

if round($top,0) <> round($bottom,0)

    if cerror = 0                            'still within the file
       'we are low
       let $bottom = %1
       let %1 = %1 + ($top - %1) / 2
  else                                       'beyond the end of the file
       'we are high
       let $top = %1
       let %1 = %1 - (%1 - $bottom) / 2
   endif
   jump nexchar
endif

let %1 = round(%1,0)

fseek 1 %1
fread 1 length 1 into $char1
   if asc($char1) = 26                       'check for Ctrl-Z EOF marker
   let %1 = %1 - 1
   endif

fseek 1 %1
fwrite 1 from $fprint                        'write the message
fclose 1

clear $char1 , $fprint , $top , $bottom
```

This project file enables you to print to a file instead of to the printer. Note that the end of the file is located by a binary search; if you try to Fread beyond the end of the file, the CERROR code is not zero. The project file also checks for the Ctrl-Z end-of-file marker, which is generated by some programs. The Fwrite command does not generate the Ctrl-Z, but if you use the Text Editor and save the file (F10), Ctrl-Z is written at the end of the file.

In SmartWare II, the task is even easier because you can seek directly to the End of File (EOF):

```
'Name:                    Fprint
'Purpose:                 Write messages into file fprint.prn
'Calling Sequence:        let $fprint = "Any Message"
'                         execute "fprint" in-memory
external $fprint
local $char1 $seek

  fopen "fprint.prn" as 1
```

```
fseek 1 EOF                          'get to end of file

fposition 1 into $seek               'position number
let $seek = $seek - 1                'back up 1 position
fseek 1 $seek
fread 1 length 1 into $char1         'read the last character
if asc($char1) = 26                  'check for Ctrl-Z EOF
 fseek 1 $seek                       'back up - over write
end if

fwrite 1 from $fprint                'write the message
fclose 1                             'close the file
```

Note that these project files are designed to be executed from another project file, in which a message or line of text is assigned to the variable $fprint.

Using IF Statements in Project Files

14.58 Tip: IF statements in project files are of four types.

Both

The first type, which is available in Smart 3.10 only, takes the form:

```
if (logical expression) then (command)
```

This format allows for the execution of one command if the expression is true. An example is

```
if [material] = "gravel" then jump slump
```

The second type is similar to the first, except that multiple commands can be issued if the logical expression is true:

```
if <logical expression>
            <command1>
            <command2>
end if
```

An example using this format is

```
If cerror = 3716
     beep 2
     message "Applicant Not Found ... "| \
             "press any key to continue ..."
     jump askapp
end if
```

Note that in this format, the word THEN is not used, the commands are specified on separate lines, and the keyword END IF designates the end of the list of commands. (In Smart 3.10, there is no space between END and IF.)

Neither format 1 nor format 2 specifies an ELSE condition to be executed if the logical expression is not true. For this specification, use the third format:

```
if <logical expression>
                <command1>
                <command2>
else
                <command3>
                <command4>
end if
```

In this format, you can specify multiple commands to be executed if the condition is true and multiple commands to be executed if the condition is not true.

Note that each command occupies a separate line by itself, and the keywords ELSE and END IF are on separate lines.

The fourth format takes the following form:

```
if <logical expression 1>

             <command1>
             <command2>
elseif <logical expression 2>
             <command3>
             <command4>
else
             <command5>
             <command6>
end if
```

In this format, you can specify commands to be executed if the evaluation of any one of a number of logical expressions is true. The evaluation of the first true expression causes the execution of the commands immediately below the expression.

Any subsequent expressions are not be evaluated, even though they may be true. Therefore, the order in which you enter the logical expressions and the associated commands is important because the set of expressions is evaluated from top to bottom.

3.10 **14.59 Trap:** The compiler usually is very specific that each IF must have a corresponding ENDIF. However, the compiler does not catch a misspelling of ELSEIF.

Examine the following example:

```
If $yn = 1
     beep
elseif $yn = 2
     beep 2
ELESIF $yn = 3
     beep 3
else
     beep 4
endif
```

If $yn = 3, this condition is not be recognized and you hear 4 beeps. If $yn = 2, however, you hear 2 beeps, and then see the following error message:

```
Unknown command
```

Processing then continues with 3 beeps.

14.60 Tip: In an IF series of statements, both the ELSEIF and ELSE are optional. In Version 3.10, if you use this fourth form of the IF, the ELSE is mandatory.

SW II

For example, the following is acceptable:

```
If $yn = 1
     beep
elseif $yn = 2
     beep 2
end if
```

If you try this in Smart 3.10, you get the following error messages when you try to compile the program:

```
Unresolved label: if1
Unresolved label: endif1
```

In Smart 3.10, if no ELSE condition really exists, you can solve the problem by inserting an ELSE statement that consists of only a comment.

14.61 Tip: Use an IF statement when verifying a true or false condition.

Both

Smart's true or false functions return 1 if true and 0 if false. Test for the 1 or 0 with an IF statement:

```
if isnumber($amount) = 0
     jump askamt
end if
```

You also can test for a non-zero numeric variable with the following:

```
if $amount
     jump askamt
end if
```

In an IF test, a variable evaluates TRUE if the value is numeric and not zero, but false if the value is zero, or null, blank or text.

14.62 Tip: When used in a formula, the IF facility has a different form from the one used in project processing.

Both

The format of the IF facility in a formula has the following format:

if (logical expression) then (expression 1) else (expression 2)

Note that here you can specify both THEN and ELSE together. The project-processing command does not support this structure, however. A formula containing an IF condition can appear in a calculation in the Spreadsheet, in a calculated field or a query in the Data Manager, or in a calculation of a variable, cell, or field contents in a project file. IF statements also can be specified in the F-Calculator.

Both

14.63 Tip: Use the UPPER function to test responses.

If you are prompting for a yes/no answer within a project file with a statement similar to the following:

```
input $yn Another Invoice (y/n) ?
```

one way to check the response is

```
if $yn = "Y" or $yn = "y" then jump begin
```

If you use the UPPER function, however, you can avoid having to check for uppercase and lowercase separately:

```
if upper($yn) = "Y" then jump begin
```

You also can use the double equal sign to test for equality regardless of case:

```
if $yn == "y" then jump begin
```

In SmartWare II, you cannot use the first form of the IF statement specifying `then`. Also, use the Screen Shortinput command instead of the Input command.

Both

14.64 Trick: Use the CASE function instead of a series of IF conditions.

Using the CASE function may be easier than several IF statements:

```
let $amount = if (case [dept] ("ACCT",1) \
     ("DATA",1) else 0) = 1 then 3394 else 6621
```

Figure 14.2 shows an equivalent statement using a compound IF condition.

```
Project File Editor
let $amount =  if ([dept] = "ACCT") \
               or ([dept] = "DATA") \
               then 3394 else 6621

let %1 = $amount

message The Amount is: < %1 >
```

Fig. 14.2.
An assignment statement using compound IF conditions.

3.10

14.65 Trap: In an IF statement in a Project file, you cannot use the IF...THEN...ELSE format.

No error is displayed if you try to use an IF...THEN...ELSE format in a project file for statement execution control; the THEN choice always is selected. For example, the following is an illegal statement:

```
if [dept] = "ACCT" then let $pct = 5.2 else 4.7
```

The proper format for such a statement would be:

```
if [dept] = "ACCT"
     let $pct = 5.2
else
     let $pct = 4.7
endif
```

14.66 Trap: If an IF statement tests multiple conditions and some of the condition expressions are incomplete, only the complete expressions are evaluated and no error message is issued. *3.10*

The following formula may look correct and may be tempting to write because it is easier, but the formula is incorrect:

```
let $amount = if [dept] = "ACCT" or "DATA"  \
     then 3394 else 6621
```

The correct way to write this formula is:

```
let $amount = if [dept] = "ACCT" or \
     [dept] = "DATA" then 3394 else 6621
```

Note that the full condition after OR must be specified.

14.67 Tip: When you use the Tools File Erase command in a project file, if the file does not exist, you do not get an error or a prompt to continue, as happens from the command level. *SW II*

Because you do not get an error, you do not have to check whether the file exists before you issue the command. Although no error message is displayed, if you want to check whether the command was successful, a CERROR code of 209 is generated.

14.68 Trap: The File Erase command sometimes does not work successfully. Use another command to erase a file, such as Query Undefine. *3.10*

Occasionally, the File Erase command fails to erase a file successfully, and you may receive the following message:

```
File filename.ext is active.
```

Apparently, an internal switch failed to reset. To erase a file, use one of the other commands that delete a file. For example:

```
if file("rogcon.dat") = 1
     query undefine rogcon.dat
endif
```

Although the subject file is not a query definition, you can use this command to erase the file. This command usually is more successful than the File Erase command.

Using the INCHAR and NEXTKEY Functions

Both

14.69 Tip: Function keys, cursor keys, and Ctrl- and Alt-key combinations can be captured by a project file by means of the INCHAR and NEXTKEY functions.

In Smart 3.10, these special keys or combinations of keys are not represented in ASCII codes; the code returned is the product of an "extended" code and the number 256. (The extended code is usually the scan code of the primary key you press, but this is not always true.) If you press the ↑ (up arrow) key, the extended code is 72, which, when multiplied by 256, yields 18432.

The complete list of the extended ASCII codes is found in Appendix B of the system section of the Smart 3.10 manual or in Appendix G of the IBM BASIC manual.

An example of the use of this facility can be found in the Browse project file in Appendix A of this book.

In SmartWare II, test for INCHAR by inserting the name of the key within braces:

```
case inchar
     when {F3}
          beep 3
     when {F4}
          beep 4
     when {enter}
          sound 200 .5
end case
```

3.10

14.70 Trick: Use the INCHAR function and a combination of project file commands to display a blinking cursor to simulate regular screen input.

```
let $partno = null
menu clear 7 0
menu print 8 5 7 0 PART NUMBER:

label prt2
let %2 = 9
let %1 = 18

label prt1
     let %9 = "_ "
     menu print 8 %1 %2 0 %9
     call wait
if nextkey = 0 then jump prt1

let $key = inchar

if  $key = 256*68     'F10
     jump alldone
elseif $key = 13          'CR
```

```
        if $partno = null
            beep 2
            jump prt1
        endif
        'process the part
    elseif $key = 8             'backspace
        if %1 = 18 then jump prt1
        let %1 = %1 - 1
        let $partno = left($partno,%1-18)
        jump prt1
    else
        if %1 = 30 then jump prt1
        let %9 = chr($key)
        let $partno = $partno|"%9"
        menu print 8 %1 15 0 %9
        let %1 = %1 + 1
        jump prt1
    endif

    end

    procedure wait
    if %2 = 0
        let %2 = 9
    else
        let %2 = 0
    endif

    let $wait = 0
    while $wait < 5
        let $wait = $wait + 1
        if nextkey > 0 then jump kantwait
    endwhile
    label kantwait
    return

    label alldone
```

The wait count is set to 5 in this example; decrease the number if you want a faster cursor flash.

In SmartWare II, use the Locate command to display one of three different cursor types at a specified location.

Jumping to a Project File Statement

14.71 Tip: You cannot jump to a label that is a parameter variable. *3.10*

The argument of a Jump command must be an actual label in your project file. If you attempt to use a parameter, you cannot exit Edit mode with a successful project file compilation. The following error message appears:

```
Unresolved label: %1
```

3.10

14.72 Trap: Project file labels are case-sensitive, so all references must match exactly to be recognized by the project-processing facility.

The uppercase spelling of a project file label is different from the lowercase spelling. If you decide at the outset that you are going to use one case or the other for labels, you will not run into problems later.

3.10

14.73 Trap: Make sure that you do not mistakenly use the Goto command instead of the Jump command in a project file. You will not receive an error message warning you of the mistake.

To get to a label in a project file, you must use the Jump command. If you forget and use the Goto command instead, you do not get an error message during the compilation of the project file or during execution. The command simply has no effect.

Using Let Statements in Project Files

Both

14.74 Tip: For text and values, a Let statement can be used interchangeably with an Enter statement in Spreadsheet project files.

The following pairs of statements are equivalent:

```
let r1c1 = "HEFF"
enter text HEFF

let r5c5 = 5088
enter value 5088
```

If you enter text with the Enter Text command, do not use quotation marks. Even if the text is two or more words, the text is entered correctly without the quotation marks. In fact, quotation marks appear in the cell if you enclose the text within them.

Both

14.75 Tip: The Let command is optional in an assignment statement.

In a project file, the following two statements have identical results:

```
let $amount = 6621
$amount = 6621
```

You may choose to use Let for clarity.

Both

14.76 Tip: Use an external reference to assign a field value to a file in a window other than the current window.

You can assign a value to a field in a window other than the current window by using a statement similar to the following:

In Smart 3.10, the format is:

```
let maillist.[country] = "Jordan"
```

In SmartWare II, both the view and field names must be enclosed within the brackets:

```
let [maillist.country] = "Jordan"
```

Without this capability, you have to go to the window containing the destination file, perform the assignment, and return to the original window again. The external reference can be used on only the left side of the equation, not the right.

14.77 Trap: When an assignment statement within a Database Manager project file makes an external reference, the destination record is indeterminate unless the destination file is in a window. *3.10*

The destination file must be in a window if the correct record is to be addressed, because there cannot be a record pointer for a file not in a window. After a file is removed from a window, the current pointer is lost and the file reverts to a sequential order. For a record to be considered "current," however, the file need not be visible; the window of another file may be zoomed.

14.78 Trap: When assigning a text literal to a user-defined variable, only 80 characters at a time may be assigned, even though a variable may contain 1,000 characters of text. If the text string is longer, the remainder is discarded. *3.10*

The following type of statement assigns a maximum of 80 characters:

```
let $description = "Long Description"
```

If the string you want to assign actually is longer than 80, you can append to the variable as follows:

```
let $description = $description | "remainder of description"
```

14.79 Trap: You must restrict user-defined variables to 1,000 characters, the specified maximum. Any characters beyond this limit are discarded without warning. *3.10*

The maximum size of a user-defined variable is 1,000 characters. If you exceed this limit, any additional characters are ignored, and you receive no error message.

14.80 Trick: Be careful about multiple variable assignments on the same line of a project file—they may not mean what you expect. *SW II*

Suppose that you have the following expression:

```
let X = Y = Z
```

This actually means let X = logical(Y = Z); therefore, if Y = Z then let X = 1, else let X = 0 .

Consider, however, the following statement:

```
let X = let Z = Y
```

This means that the value of Y is assigned to the variable Z, and the value of Z is assigned to X.

SW II

14.81 Trick: Double the use of quotation marks if you need to include quote marks within text.

The quotation mark (") cannot be used on its own because the quotation is used to offset text. By doubling up the quotation marks, however, you can include the quote marks within the text itself. For example,

```
"""Fish"""
```

yields

```
"Fish"
```

The result includes the quotation marks. If you want just quote marks by themselves, you use:

```
let $quote = """"
```

This is equivalent to either of the following statements:

```
let $quote = chr(34)
let $quote = chr({"})
```

Direct Printing from a Project File

Both

14.82 Tip: Use the Lprint command to send special codes to your printer.

Rather than using a printer macro, you can use the Lprint command from a project file to send special codes to your printer. Any text entries must be enclosed in double quotation marks. You can send ASCII characters by using the CHR function. Remember to separate entries on the print line with semicolons.

Because the Lprint syntax is similar to that of the BASIC language, using an Lprint command is usually straightforward because many printer manuals provide examples in BASIC.

For example, to quickly eject an additional page from your printer, use the following project file:

In SmartWare II:

```
Open-Printer
Lprintraw chr(12)
Close-Printer
```

In Smart 3.10:

```
lprint chr(12)
```

On some printers, at the completion of a report, you must eject another piece of paper. Sometimes you have to push several buttons on the printer, and, of course, you must wait until the report has finished printing. With this short project file, the ejection of the additional page is accomplished easily. If the printer has a buffer, the project file completes execution before the printer has finished printing the report.

14.83 Trick: Use a Database Report Form instead of the Lprint command to print formatted output. ***Both***

In much the same way that you can merge prompted input with a word-processing document, you also can use a Report Form to "fill in the blanks" where you have calculated fields. In fact, none of the data needs to be derived from the file at all; each calculation can be based on a variable.

Figure 14.3 shows the format of a Report Form designed for just such a purpose. Notice that each calculation is simply a user-defined variable. The last calculation is a concatenation of `"Dr."` and the doctor's name.

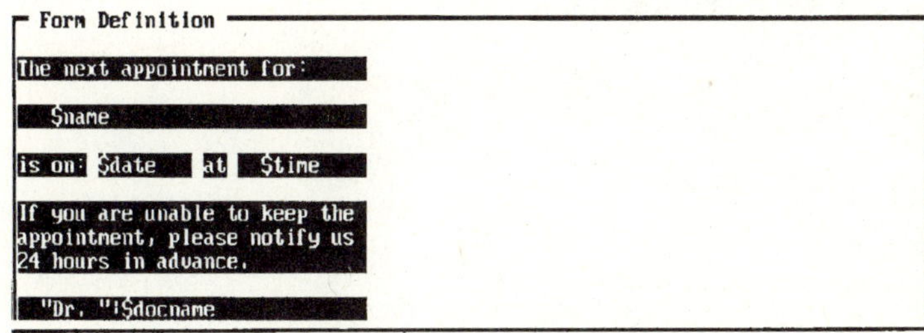

Fig. 14.3.
A Report Form for formatted output.

Figure 14.4 shows a Smart 3.10 project file that prompts for the variables and executes the report. If you plan to use this technique in SmartWare II, the variables must be declared Public, but they do not have to be locked. Figure 14.5 shows the final output.

One word of caution: If you want to print only one copy of the form, make sure your data file is ordered by an index with just one entry. Even though the form may not reference any data in the file, the report is printed once for each record.

14.84 Trick: Use a combination of functions to align decimals when you use the Lprint command. ***Both***

The following statement can be used to align decimals for the Lprint command.

In Smart 3.10, use the following:

```
repeat(" ",10-len(fixed($val,2)));fixed($val,2)
```

```
Project File Editor
'print form instead of lprint commands
'similar to word processor merge

input $name Patient Name

input $date Appointment Date

input $time Appointment Time

input $docname Doctor's Name

report print form printer

F1 Help      F3 Find      F5 Replace       F7 Insert line      F9  Repeat
F2 Calc      F4 Goto      F6 List fields   F8 Delete line      F10 Finish
                                     Line:   1  Column:  1     Insert: ON
REMEMBER  create a new project file or modify an existing file
```

Fig. 14.4.

A project file to execute the formatted form report.

```
The next appointment for:

        Danielle Rahn

is on: 5/24/87  at 10:30 A.M.

If you are unable to keep the
appointment, please notify us
24 hours in advance.

                    Dr. Edwards
```

Fig. 14.5.

Formatted output.

This series of functions determines the length of the number and pads the remainder of the "field" (10 characters, in this case) with blanks.

In SmartWare II, use the following:

```
format($val,"2r10")
```

The argument to the Format option specifies 2 decimal positions, right-justified in a field of width 10.

3.10 **14.85 Trick:** You can print a field that is not available on the current screen if you use the Lprint command.

Even if a field is not on the current custom screen, you can use the Lprint command to print the field. Although this may represent a convenient feature, this feature also can be a potential security weakness.

Using Menu and Screen commands

14.86 Trick: To hide an entry in the Menu facility, set the foreground and background to the same colors.

Both

If you want to prevent the display of an entry (such as a password) in response to Menu Input, the entry does not appear if you make both the foreground and background colors identical. An example is the following:

```
menu input 5 10 17 17 3 $pass
```

On most monochrome monitors, color 17 results in a solid block.

14.87 Trap: Do not try to enter a value into the last position of the input field generated by the Menu Input statement—the last position cannot be used.

Both

For example, a field length of 1 generates an apparent input field width of 2. This 2nd position is unusable. If you try to enter something into the 2nd position, the system beeps. You must use the left arrow to move the cursor back into the usable portion of the field.

14.88 Tip: You can invoke the Calculator within your project file and then insert the result into a Screen Input field.

Both

An example of a project file in SmartWare II is:

```
global $value
screen clear 7 0
tools calculator
screen input 5 10 0 7 5 $value
keys look,result
```

The final statement in this example inserts the result of the calculation in the field. Within the calculator, you must remember to actually perform the calculation (F5), rather than just pressing F10 to exit. If you forget, the result of the previous calculation is used.

14.89 Tip: Create a project file to display a message and prompt for a Yes/No response.

Both

If you have an important question that *must* be answered, you can create a project file to display a message with a box around it, flash the screen, and prompt for the answer.

```
'NAME:          MSG
'PURPOSE:       Flash a message to be answered by Y or N
'VARIABLES:     Set $msg equal to your message.

external $msg $yn
local $flash $len per3 per4
```

```
clear $yn
let $flash = 9                          'screen intensity toggle
screen clear 7 0
let $len   = len($msg)                  'length of message
let per3   = 40 - $len/2 - 4            'starting position of box
let per4   = 40 + $len/2 + 5            'ending position of box

while $yn <> "Y" and $yn <> "N"         'must be Y or N
 while nextkey = 0                      'wait for a key stroke

  screen draw box 7 per3 12 per4 $flash 0      'draw the box
  let $flash = abs( $flash - 9 )               'toggle the character color
  screen print 9 40-$len/2 $flash 0 $msg       'print your message here
  SCREEN PRINT 10 38 7 0 "(y/n)"

  milli-wait 25                            'vary the wait to taste
 end while
 let $yn =  upper(chr(inchar))             'read the key pressed
end while
```

To use this SmartWare II project file, you would have a project file like the following:

```
public $msg $yn
let $msg = "Print Monthly Reports"
execute "msg" in-memory

if $yn = "Y"
     execute "monthly" in-memory
end if
```

The message continues to flash until you press either Y or N.

Both

14.90 Tip: Use the following statement in Smart 3.10 to clear the entire 25-line screen within a project file.

```
menu clear box 1 1 25 80 0 0
```

In SmartWare II, use this statement:

```
screen clear box 1 1 25 80 0 0
```

This statement clears the entire screen, including the status line at the bottom.

Both

14.91 Tip: Print over the borders of your screen to provide additional information and enhance appearance.

For example:

```
screen clear box 1 1 25 80 7 0
screen print 1 32 7 0 "╣ Open New Job ╠"
data update
```

Notice in figure 14.6 that this example prints on the first line of the screen, which overlays a portion of the border. Here, the message appears during the execution of the Update command. Note that the graphics characters have been inserted using the appropriate ASCII numbers on the numeric keypad. To type the character "╣," hold down the Alt key and type the number 185 on the keypad. When you release the Alt key, the character appears.

╣ Open New Job ╠

SSN	LastName	FirstName	Ag	Sex	M	DE	CA	Street	City	ST
345-98-7593	Ronaldo	Rosanna	52	F	M	3	2	546 Olive Hill	Oak Park	IL
498-48-3980	Linden	Debbie	29	F	S	1	2	409 Pleasant St	Amherst	MA
239-87-8876	Davis	Michael	61	M	M	1	2	180 Lewis Ave.	Covington	LA
208-23-0300	Karenski	Julius	41	M	D	0	1	18 Olive St.	Louisville	KY
887-63-5498	Harris	Jeff	34	M	M	4	5	1201 Horton Rd.	Lyndhurst	OH
598-44-5922	Markus	LeAnne	48	F	W	1	1	14 Crumpet Ave.	Alamosa	CO
876-33-0989	Lester	Marilyn	55	F	M	4	3	6 Greenville St	Yarmouth	MA
987-65-7653	Marzetti	David	47	M	D	0	1	20 Grayln Dr.	Wilmington	NC
387-59-8374	Steffans	Charles	25	M	M	2	2	44 Center Drive	Brunswick	ME
498-34-5998	Bernstein	Paula	30	F	S	3	3	18 Worcester St	Beaumont	CA
776-39-8763	Adelson	Alfred	60	M	M	0	1	14 Spring St.	Hartford	CT
345-54-2287	Aliakbari	Ellen	35	F	S	0	1	2171 University	Westfield	NJ
198-03-3024	Peters	Howard E.	18	M	S	0	1	10 Dennis Drive	Winnfield	LA

Social Security Number
View: person2.vws   Window:1   Rec:1 (1)
Add new records or update existing records

Fig. 14.6.
Overlaying the window border.

14.92 Trap: In a Menu Clear Box statement, if you accidentally specify an upper left row that is greater than the lower right row, you get some very strange results. *3.10*

For example, consider the following command:

```
Menu Clear Box 10 2 6 79 7 0 no-border
```

Note the statement tries to clear from row 10 to row 6, which of course is backwards. When this command executes, the entire screen clears, no error message is displayed, and, after a long pause, the project file continues.

14.93 Trick: Use a combination of functions to align decimals when you are using the Menu Print command. *3.10*

Figure 14.7 shows two columns of numbers displayed using the Menu Print command. Notice that the decimal points in column 1 are not aligned but that they do line up in column 2.

Fig. 14.7.

Using Menu Print with and without decimal alignment.

```
8384.4557          8384.4557
3785.9261          3785.9261
3.6952                3.6952
6130.0236          6130.0236
3289.9252          3289.9252
2524.7906          2524.7906
405.3898            405.3898
1740.4001          1740.4001
6290.3358          6290.3358
3444.1038          3444.1038
7213.6289          7213.6289
1661.7097          1661.7097
1060.5674          1060.5674
4527.4616          4527.4616
1322.5979          1322.5979
3504.1415          3504.1415
```

If you are printing variable information on the screen, you must use a project file parameter (see also Tip 14.101). Unfortunately, the Menu processing facility does not have a decimal alignment feature—therefore, the result in column 1.

The project file in figure 14.8 was used to create the illustration in figure 14.7.

Fig. 14.8.

A project to demonstrate decimal alignment.

```
Project File Editor
'demonstrate use of fixed fields in menu print

menu clear 7 0
let %1 = 2

label nextline
let text1 = fixed((rand*100)^2,4)              'a random number
let %1 = %1 + 1                                'line counter
let %2 = text1                                 'must display parameter
let %3 = repeat(" ",10-len(text1))|text1       'repeat Alt-255

'print floating number and aligned number
menu print %1 15 9 0 %2
menu print %1 40 9 0 %3

if %1 <= 17 then jump nextline
```

The trick to the decimal alignment in the project lies in printing column 2 as a text field, preceded by a series of blank characters. (An actual blank is not used; use the Alt-255 character.) The number of blank characters with which to pad the front end of the text number is determined by the length of the number.

In line 10, the length of the text number is subtracted from 10; this derived value then is used to repeat the blank character, onto which the text number then is concatenated. Therefore, the total of the number of blank characters and text number characters is constant. If the number has six characters, the number is printed preceded by four blank characters. If the number has nine characters, only one blank character is printed before the number.

If you use this technique, make sure that your value has a fixed number of decimal positions because the overall length of the numbers includes the numerals to both the right and the left of the decimal point.

14.94 Tip: Use parentheses around an expression in a Screen Print command if the expression may seem ambiguous. *SW II*

For example, the following expression cannot be compiled due to ambiguity about the use of the word `format`:

```
screen print 10 10 7 0 format(Today,"Dyyyy")
```

This is confused with the following form of the Screen Print command:

```
screen print 10 10 7 0 Format "Dyyyy" Today
```

In this case, you must use parentheses:

```
Screen print 10 10 7 0 (format(Today,"Dyyyy")) .
```

Of the above examples, the first cannot be compiled, the second displays the date in the DATE2 format `7/19/1990`, and the third displays just the year in the four-digit format `1990`

14.95 Trick: Use the commands Screen Save and Screen Restore to display a randomly moving message on-screen to call attention to something important. *SW II*

The following project file displays a message with a box around it, indicating that the program has completed:

```
local $message $fromrow $fromcol
screen clear 7 0
screen draw box 5 10 11 70 9 0
screen print 8 19 0 9 \
     "JOB COMPLETED ... PRESS ANY KEY TO CONTINUE"
screen save 5 10 11 70 $message

while nextkey = 0
     screen clear 7 0
     let $fromrow = int(uniform(13)+1)+1
     let $fromcol = int(uniform(18)+1)+1
     screen restore $fromrow $fromcol $message
     milli-wait 2000
end while
```

For an even greater impact, you can use the Beep or Sound commands in addition to the display.

In Smart 3.10, because the Screen Save and Restore commands are not available, you have to use parameters, such as the following:

```
while nextkey = 0
     menu clear 7 0
     let %1 = int(uniform(13)+1)+1
```

```
        let %2 = int(uniform(18)+1)+1
        let %3 = %1 + 6
        let %4 = %2 + 60
        let %5 = %1 + 3
        let %6 = %2 + 9
        menu draw box %1 %2 %3 %4 9 0
        menu print %5 %6 0 9 \
         JOB COMPLETED ... PRESS ANY KEY TO CONTINUE
        wait 2
endwhile
```

In Smart 3.10, to stop the display, you have to hold down a key longer than in SmartWare II because the Wait command in 3.10 consumes a keystroke and delays key recognition by the NEXTKEY function.

Command Line Substitution

Both

14.96 Tip: Use parameters for project-file command-line substitution in Smart 3.10. In SmartWare II, use variables.

When a parameter is used in a Smart 3.10 project file, two stages of evaluation take place. In the first stage, the contents of the parameter are substituted for the parameter itself on the command line, in much the same way that you would read the command. Therefore, if

```
%1  = "van Horn"
```

the statement:

```
find [last] equal "%1" options f
```

becomes:

```
find [last] equal "van Horn" options f
```

after the initial evaluation. In the second stage, the command line is executed and the Find command, in this case, attempts to locate `van Horn`.

The evaluation of parameters may go only two levels deep; for further discussion of this point, refer to Trap 14.110.

In SmartWare II, use a variable to substitute for the portion of a statement that is not part of the command structure:

```
local $name
screen shortinput $name "Employee Name:"
data find [LastName] equal $name options "f"
```

You cannot, however, use a variable as a substitute for an actual part of the command. The following project file will not compute:

```
local $option
screen shortinput $option "Equal Greater-Than Less-Than:"
data find [LastName] $option "Markus" options "f"
```

In this case, you must use the evaluate statement:

```
local $option
screen shortinput $option "Equal, Greater-Than, Less-Than:"
evaluate ( "data find [LastName] "|$option|""""|"Markus"| \
      """"|" options "|""""|"f"|"""" )
```

Read further about the Evaluate statement in this chapter.

14.97 Tip: Parameters cannot be used to alter the message in a command to prompt for a parameter. *3.10*

You cannot execute the following:

```
%1 Field Name:
%2 Value for %1 field:
find [%1] equal "%2" options
```

The second prompt appears as:

```
Value for %1 field:
```

If you want to vary a prompt for a parameter, you must use the Input command with a variable.

```
%1 Field Name:
Input $value Value for %1 field:
let %2 = $value
find [%1] equal "%2" options
```

14.98 Tip: A parameter can contain a maximum of 25 text characters. *3.10*

The maximum number of characters that may be contained in a parameter (%0 to %9) cannot exceed 25. If you need to store longer text, use either the text1 or text2 variables, which can store 100 characters each, or user-defined variables, which can store 1,000 characters.

14.99 Tip: Although a parameter can contain only 25 characters, you can concatenate parameters to display longer information. *3.10*

The following statements demonstrate the use of this technique:

```
let %1 = [description]
let %2 = mid([description],26,25)
menu print 5 10 0 7 The description is: %1%2
```

In this example, a description field up to 50 characters in length can be displayed on-screen.

3.10 **14.100 Tip:** Use parameters in Message and Menu Print commands in a project file.

For a screen display that varies, you must use parameters (rather than user-defined variables) in Message and Menu Print commands. Some examples are:

```
message Customer Code %2 Not Found . . . press any key
menu print 10 10 7 0 The Total is: %5
```

3.10 **14.102 Tip:** For most text operations, parameters must be enclosed in double quotation marks (").

Figure 14.9 demonstrates the use of the double quotation marks surrounding text parameters.

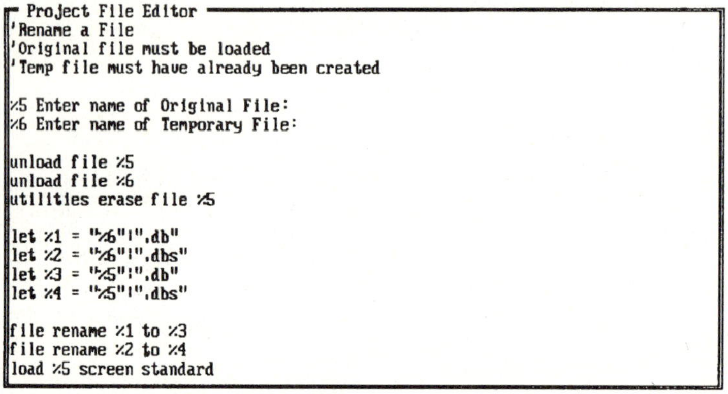

```
Project File Editor
'Rename a File
'Original file must be loaded
'Temp file must have already been created

%5 Enter name of Original File:
%6 Enter name of Temporary File:

unload file %5
unload file %6
utilities erase file %5

let %1 = "%6"|".db"
let %2 = "%6"|".dbs"
let %3 = "%5"|".db"
let %4 = "%5"|".dbs"

file rename %1 to %3
file rename %2 to %4
load %5 screen standard
```

Fig. 14.9.
A project to "rename" a database.

If you do not use quotation marks around an alpha string, you generate the following error message:

```
Bad syntax
```

If the contents of the parameter are numeric and you want to maintain the numeric quality in the variable, do *not* use quotation marks.

3.10 **14.102 Trap:** If a parameter contains a number, the parameter is considered "numeric" and cannot be considered text.

Consider the following statement:

```
let %1 = "1"
```

Normally, you would think that with quotation marks around the number, the parameter would be text. With a user-defined variable, this would be true. But with a parameter, if the content is a number, the parameter is considered to be numeric.

This becomes a problem in some project files if you are trying to test the value of an alpha field that contains a numeric. For example, if you have an alpha field that contains numeric account numbers, you may be tempted to write the following:

```
%1 Enter account number:
if [account] = %1
     beep
endif
```

This example would not work because the alpha account number in the file (301, for example) would not be equal to the numeric value 301. To solve the problem, you may be tempted to write the following:

```
if [account] = "%1"
```

This would not help you either because `%1` would not evaluate to "301", but simply to the literal "%1". The way to solve the problem is to use the STR function, which converts a number into a string:

```
if [account] = str(%1)
```

This converts the number 301 into the string "301" and allows a comparison to the alpha field [account].

14.103 Tip: Use parameters to construct a file name from today's date. *3.10*

If you want to save a worksheet with today's date, use the following:

```
let %1 = date2(today)
let %1 = replace("%1",2,1,"-")
let %1 = replace("%1",5,1,"-")

save %1
```

The file name will be in the format: mm-dd-yy. The slash character (/) cannot be used because this is not allowable within a DOS file name.

14.104: Use parameters to substitute portions of cell addresses in the spreadsheet. *3.10*

In the following example, note the use of the parameters to allow the substitution of the row and column numbers of a cell address. The parameter value is substituted prior to execution.

```
let %1 = 5
let %2 = 10
goto r%1c%2
```

When the Goto command is executed, the command is evaluated as

```
goto r5c10
```

14.105 Tip: Use parameters and variables to transfer data from one module to another. *3.10*

The values assigned to parameters and variables are maintained when you invoke another Smart module. If you want to clear a user-defined variable from memory, however, use the Clear command.

3.10

14.106 Tip: Save your parameters in user variables if you run out of parameters and need more.

Because project processing has only 10 parameters, you may find that you need more parameters in a complicated situation. You can save their contents in user-defined variables in order to conserve usage. The following procedure saves all 10 parameters in user variables:

```
procedure savepar
        let $per0 = %0
        let $per1 = %1
        let $per2 = %2
        let $per3 = %3
        let $per4 = %4
        let $per5 = %5
        let $per6 = %6
        let $per7 = %7
        let $per8 = %8
        let $per9 = %9
return
```

You may need to initialize and assign a value to all 10 parameters at the beginning of your project file. For example, use the following:

```
let %9 = null
```

If you execute one of the assignment statements in the procedure for a parameter that does not contain a value, the user variable contains the literal name of the parameter. For example, after the statement:

```
let $per9 = %9
```

if `%9` is not assigned a value, the contents of the `$per9` variable literally would be "%9".

3.10

14.107 Trick: Use parameters for command variability.

In a project file, you may want to perform different functions, depending on the answer to a prompt. One way to handle this is to use a parameter to control the execution (see fig. 14.10).

Depending on the answer provided, either the Fsort1 or Fsort2 definition is used. (Be sure to check that the answer to the parameter is either 1 or 2 before proceeding to the Sort command.)

3.10

14.108 Trick: Use parameters to simulate arrays of variables.

If you append a parameter to a variable name, the result can be a set of variables that acts like an array. For example, the variable

```
$div%1
```

evaluates as $div1 if %1 is 1 and $div5 if %1 is 5. Because parameter substitution is made before statement execution, this technique works effectively. The parameters do not have to be numeric; alpha codes work just as well. Do not make the combination of the prefix and the parameter contents longer than 10 characters, however, because this is the maximum length of a variable name.

```
Project File Editor
'using a parameter to select a definition

label asktype
%1 Sort by (1) Last Name or (2) Zip Code
if %1 = 1 or %1 = 2 then jump oktype
beep
message Wrong Selection ... press any key to continue
jump asktype

label oktype

'perform fsort1 or fsort2
sort predefined fsort%1 index ind1

order index ind1
```

Fig. 14.10. *Using a parameter to select a definition.*

You can create multidimensional arrays as well:

```
$div%1%2
```

This technique can be used when, for example, you are accumulating totals for multiple divisions for multiple years. The %1 parameter can represent the division abbreviation and %2 can represent the year.

14.109 Trap: Parameters are evaluated down to only the second level; attempting to bring about evaluation below that level causes errors. *3.10*

Take care in specifying parameters because they are evaluated down to only the second level.

The following project file illustrates an illegal use of parameter substitution:

```
let %1 = "fname"
if $name = [%1] then jump alldone
```

This represents 3 levels of evaluation. The first level is from the %1 to "fname"; the next level is from the [fname] to the actual field contents in the database, and the third level is the comparison of the field contents to the variable $name. You can overcome this restriction by breaking the second statement into two:

```
let %1 = "fname"
let %2 = [%1]
if $name = %2 then jump alldone
```

SW II

14.110 Tip: Unless you really need to, do not use the Evaluate statement because Evaluate slows project file execution.

Even if you have to use several IF...ELSEIF...ELSEIF...ELSE...END IF statements, this is faster than using an Evaluate statement to accomplish the same task.

Compare the following two partial examples of project files. The first example uses an evaluate statement, and the second uses an IF...ELSE...END IF series of statements.

Example 1:

```
while $counter > 0
     if mod($counter,2) = 0
          let $yesno = "yes"
     else
          let $yesno = "no"
     end if
     EVALUATE ( "data delete "|$yesno )
     let $counter = $counter - 1
end while
```

Example 2:

```
while $counter > 0
     if mod($counter,2) = 0
          data delete yes
     else
          data delete no
     end if
     let $counter = $counter - 1
end while
```

The first example takes more time to execute than the second one.

Procedures and Functions in Project Processing

3.10

14.111 Trap: Make sure your procedures are isolated logically to prevent them from being executed accidentally.

A procedure begins with the Procedure command and ends with the Return command. The only way to execute procedure code legitimately is by using the Call statement. Make sure the command immediately before the beginning of the procedure is a statement that affects execution order, such as jump, end, quit, stop, or the Return command of a previous procedure. You do not want in-line code to fall through into a procedure, although no error trap exists to prevent this from happening and unpredictable results will occur.

14.112 Tip: In a project file, the main section of code stops when a function is encountered, even if there is no END MAIN statement.

SW II

In Smart 3.10, you always should have a statement to prevent the accidental execution of a procedure at the end of the main section of code. This statement can be END, STOP, JUMP, or any other statement that prevents the main code from running into the procedure. In SmartWare II, the encounter of a function statement signals the end of the MAIN section, just as if you had the statement END MAIN. Therefore, the MAIN and END MAIN statements are optional.

14.113 Trap: Always exit procedures through the Return statement to avoid unpredictable execution sequences.

3.10

Each time you execute a procedure in a project file with a Call statement, the return address is maintained. Execution of the Return statement causes a branch to that address. Because nested procedures can be executed, the return addresses are "stacked." If you jump out of a procedure without removing the address from the stack by passing through the Return statement, the next time you execute a procedure, the wrong address is pulled from the stack. Needless to say, this can wreak havoc with your project files.

14.114 Tip: Within a procedure, you can jump to the first line by using the Jump (procedure-name) statement as if it were a label. Consider the following example:

3.10

```
let $accum = 0
goto record rec-number 1
call accum
end
procedure accum
let $accum = $accum + [wage]
if record <> records
     goto record next
     jump accum
endif
return
```

You do not have to declare an additional label at the beginning of the procedure if you want to jump to the beginning. From outside the procedure, however, you must use the Call statement; you cannot Jump to the procedure.

14.115 Tip: When declaring a function in a project file, make sure you use the phrase "End Function" rather than just the Smart 3.10 phrase "Return." If you use only the Return statement, you'll think you have a disk problem.

SW II

If you forget, you get the following error message:

```
Unexpected End of File
```

This message leads you to believe you have a hard disk error. Not true—you just need to change your thinking to the SmartWare II statement. Change "Return" to "End Function" and you will be fine.

SW II

14.116 Tip: In the declaration of a function, the number of arguments of the function must be stated in parentheses; if there are no arguments or only one, use the parentheses alone.

For example, if you have a function that requires four arguments, the declaration must state the number of arguments:

```
global writit(4)
```

All uses of the function in your project file must specify four arguments, within parentheses, separated by commas. If you have functions without arguments or with only one argument, you may declare them with just the parentheses:

```
global upname()
```

When using the function, you must specify the function name and use the parentheses, but without any argument inside the parentheses.

SW II

14.117 Tip: Declare functions as Global if you want to use them in the current project file only. Declare functions as Public if you also want to use them in projects that are executed from the current project file. If you want to Load a project file function into memory for use from the command level, the function must be declared as Public.

You cannot lock a Public function, however. After a project file function is loaded into memory, the function is available for the duration of the current module session, until you either unload the function or quit to another module. If you want to use the same function in a later module, you must load the function into memory while within the module.

Using Quiet Settings

Both

14.118 Tip: Turn Quiet Off to help debug project files.

When the Quiet setting is turned Off, each command is displayed on the command line as it is executed. If an error occurs, the statement causing the error is displayed. (If you compile your project files without line numbers, the Quiet setting has no effect.)

Both

14.119 Tip: The Quiet setting carries over to the next project file.

If Quiet is turned On in one project file, Quiet still is on in the next project unless it is explicitly reset to Off. To guarantee the setting, you should deliberately set Quiet On or Off at the beginning of your project file.

Both

14.120 Top: Turn Quiet Off at certain places in your project file to help debug difficult code.

If certain portions of your project file are giving you trouble, you can selectively turn the Quiet setting On when certain sections of code are entered, or even in accordance with logical condition. The statement Quiet Off can be executed as the result of the evaluation of a logical expression in an IF statement. When the condition changes, you can turn Quiet On for speedier and cleaner project-file execution.

14.121 Tip: Turn the Quiet setting On for faster processing.

Both

If you place the statement

```
quiet on
```

at the beginning of a project file, your project runs faster because each statement does not have to be displayed on-screen and the source file (PFx) does not have to be referenced during execution. Even if Quiet is Off and the source file is not present, the effect is as if Quiet is On.

Testing for the End of a Data File

14.122 Tip: Use the functions Record and Records to test for the end of file in Database Manager project processing.

Both

The Record function returns the current logical record number; Records returns the total number of records in the current order. Therefore, by testing

```
if record = records
```

you can take appropriate action on an end-of-file condition.

Editing Project Files

14.123 Tip: Use the F2 (3.10) or F5 (SmartWare II) function key to calculate an expression on the top line of your file in the project file editor. Figure 14.11 shows a project file that uses this comparison.

Both

Just as pressing the calculate key in the Calculator displays the result, the same key can evaluate an expression on the top line while you are in the project file editor. The top line is the first physical line in the file, not counting any blank lines.

You can develop a complex formula on the top line and check the formula by using the calculate key. Remember, however, that you must write the formula as if you were in the Calculator, not a project file statement. For example, the formula should not be written as

```
let $value = (formula)
```

but simply as the formula itself. When you determine that the formula is correct, use the F8 key to delete the formula and place it in the buffer, position the cursor where you want to insert the formula, and press F7. The formula will be retrieved from the buffer. Now add the assignment phrases, such as

```
let $value =
```

to the beginning of the formula.

Fig. 14.11.

A project file to calculate and display a total.

```
Project File Editor
Comment  ********  ACCUMULATE FIELDS THROUGHOUT A FILE  *********
repaint off
%9 Enter Field Name:
Let %3 = 0
Goto Record Rec-number 1

While Record < Records + 1
Let %3 = %3 + [%9]
If Record = Records Then Jump Alldone
Goto Record Next
Endwhile

Label Alldone
Menu Clear 7 0
Beep 2
Menu Print 10 5 7 0 Total of %9 is: %3
Message Press <SPACE> To Continue ...
Repaint
```

Both

14.124 Trick: Use the Word Processor to create a project file.

If you find that the inability to move or insert entire blocks of lines is a problem in Smart 3.10 Remember Edit mode, you can use the Smart Word Processor to create and edit a project file. Create a text file with a carriage return at the end of each line. You then can use all Word Processor facilities.

When you finish editing, save your work, specifying one of the following file extensions:

Extension	*Module*
PF1	Spreadsheet
PF2	Word Processor
PF3	Database
PF4	Communications (SmartWare II)
PF6	Communications (3.10)

Return to the module in which you want to execute the project file and compile it, using the Remember Compile command on command list 5 in Smart 3.10 or Remember Tools Compile in SmartWare II. Initially, compile with line numbers or in the Debug mode. After all the bugs are out and you are into production, you can compile without line numbers, or No-Debug.

Both

14.125 Trick: Use the F8 and F7 keys to duplicate lines in the Remember Edit mode.

Pressing F8 deletes the current line and inserts the line in a buffer. If you want to move the line to another location, position the cursor on the line before which the deleted line is to be inserted and press F7. Pressing F7 does not clear the buffer; you therefore can use this capability to duplicate a line any number of times. To delete a line without placing the line in the buffer, use the Ctrl-Y key combination.

In SmartWare II, you can copy multiple lines using the Alt-C to copy and Alt-I to insert.

14.126 Tip: Use the Alt-F3 key combination to append or insert project files. *Both*

You can build project files in sections and append them while in the Remember Edit mode. Position your cursor on the line before which you want to insert the contents of another project file and press Alt-F3. At the prompt

```
Read:
```

enter the name of the project file you wish to insert. You must include the extension PFx, in which x is a number corresponding to the current Smart module. If you wish to append another project file to the end of the current one, your cursor should be one line beyond the last line of the current project file.

14.127 Tip: Use the Alt-F3 combination to make a copy of a project file. *Both*

If you want to make a different version of an existing project file, use the Remember Edit command and specify the name of the project file you want to create. The project-file editor is initiated with a blank screen. Press Alt-F3 and, at the prompt for the file name, enter the name of the project file you want to copy. You must include the extension PFx, in which x represents the number of the Smart module. The project file is read into the editor workspace. Make your changes and then press F10 to save your work.

14.128 Trick: Use the Remember Start command to form the basis for a larger project file. *Both*

With the Remember Start facility, you can record a large portion of your project file by executing the necessary commands with Start mode active. When you record all you can, finish the project-file recording (Remember Finish) and edit the file, adding prompts and other specific project-processing commands.

Repainting the Screen

14.129 Tip: Set the Repaint command to Off in the Database to retain menus on-screen, speed operation, and provide a cleaner looking application. *Both*

With the Repaint option set to Off, the screen is not repainted for each record or when opening and closing files. Thus you can retain menus on-screen during execution, providing a cleaner and more informative screen. In addition, your application runs faster because the time needed to repaint the screen is eliminated.

3.10

14.130 Trap: Repaint is turned back when you restart a project file after suspending it.

Frequently, having Repaint Off not only makes the execution of a project file better looking, but also speeds up the processing because the screen does not have to be repainted. If execution of the project file is suspended, however, the Repaint mode will be On when you resume execution. To avoid this situation, insert the Repaint Off command within the project file so that the command is encountered after suspension, as in the following example:

```
repaint off
goto record rec-number 1
while record <= records
     if [dept] = "ACCT"
          beep
          suspend
         repaint off 'repaint turned off again
     endif
     if record = records then break
     goto record next
endwhile
repaint
```

Note that Repaint is turned Off again, following the Suspend command.

Both

14.132 Trick: To display the screen contents, perform a Repaint command after setting Repaint On.

Setting Repaint to On does not repaint the screen immediately; it means that the new display will be visible the next time the screen is repainted. To cause an immediate screen refresh, issue the Repaint command after issuing Repaint On.

3.10

14.132 Trap: If the Order command is to take effect, you must use the Goto Record Rec-Number 1 option after an Order Index command while the Repaint option is Off.

If you do not use the Goto Record Rec-Number 1 command when the Repaint option is Off, the Order command doesn't always work. Even if you currently do not have Repaint Off but you possibly will turn Repaint Off in the future, you should adopt the practice of going to record 1 after every Order by Index or Key command so that you do not have to go back and change your project files. If you don't, you suffer the invalid results of accessing incorrect records after the Order command. As harmless as the Repaint command seems, in this case the Repaint command can have some serious side effects.

Singlestep Settings

14.133 Tip: Set the Singlestep option On for debugging complicated project files. *Both*

The command in Smart 3.10 is:

```
Singlestep On
```

In SmartWare II, use the following:

```
Single-Step On
```

Place this statement at the beginning of a project file to cause the system to pause before the execution of each command. This facility is useful if you are having trouble tracing the execution pattern of a long project file. If just a portion of a project file is complex, you can turn the Singlestep option On for just that section and turn the option Off later. Unless you turn Singlestep Off, it remains on for the next project file within the same module. If you move to another module, the Singlestep option is controlled by the setting in the Parameters menu.

14.134 Trick: Use conditional logic to turn Singlestep On for certain sections of a project file. *Both*

Rather than having Singlestep turned On all the time, you may want to turn it on for only certain conditions, as in the following Smart 3.10 project file:

```
If [dept] = "ACCT" and [wage] > 850 and [sex] = "F"
      singlestep on
end if
```

Halting Project-File Execution

14.135 Tip: The Stop, End, Quit, and Suspend commands can each be used to control termination of a project file. *Both*

The Stop command causes all project files to cease and returns control immediately to command level.

The End command causes only the current project file to be terminated. If the file containing the End command is invoked with an Execute command from another project file, control is returned to that project file.

In Smart 3.10, the Quit command terminates the project and Smart as well, returning control to the DOS level. This command is equivalent to pressing F10 and Quit. In SmartWare II, the command is Quit Quit.

The Suspend command can be used to halt project-file execution temporarily and return control to the Smart command level. Suspend is equivalent to pressing Ctrl-Z and S to suspend. Be careful while you are in this Suspend mode, because any changes you make may cause the project file to go awry when it resumes. If you go to a different window, for example, the project file may fail when it starts again because the file cannot locate a referenced field. If you use this facility, take care that you reset the crucial elements of the application.

In SmartWare II, you can specify suspension in either the command or entry modes by the following:

Suspend Command
Suspend Enter

SW II

14.136 Trick: Use Ctrl-Z to stop a project file immediately after the conclusion of the Suspend mode and before any more statements are executed.

If you press Ctrl-Z while still in the Suspend mode, the system beeps as if an error has occurred. When you press F8 to resume execution, however, you are prompted:

```
Cancel or suspend execution? (c/s)
```

Press `C` to cancel the project file. This same trick works if you press Ctrl-Z while you are in the Trace Suspend or if the project file is prompting for input.

Using Variables in Project Files

3.10

14.137 Tip: Use the ISNUMBER function to check for a numeric response.

If you are using a user-defined variable to accept a response and want to verify that the response is numeric, use the ISNUMBER function:

```
label askamt
Input $amount Enter Amount of Check:
if isnumber($amount) = 0 then jump askamt
```

3.10

14.138 Trap: The default value for a variable is numeric zero if you press Enter, Esc, or F10 in response to a prompt. Use a text variable to validate the response if zero may be valid.

In a project file, the Input and Menu Input statements are used to prompt the user to enter a value into a variable. Normally, you type the value and press Enter.

```
label askinput
input $value Enter value:
```

If you mistakenly press Enter, Esc, or F10, the value of the variable is set to zero. If zero never will be valid, you can check this and re-prompt. But if zero may be valid and you want to distinguish between a zero response and either Esc, F10, or Enter, use text1. Any of these last three responses by themselves will set text1 equal to Null.

```
label askinput
let text1 = null                    'initialize as null

while text1 = null                  'dont allow Esc, F10 or Enter
     input text1 Enter value:  'which create null
endwhile

'allow simply a zero, but not any alphabetics
if ( text1 <> "0" and val(text1) = 0 )
     jump askinput
else
     let $value = val(text1)
endif
```

In this example, a zero by itself is allowable, but F10, Esc, and Enter are not. If you enter an alphabetic word, the VAL function returns a zero, but this also is disallowed.

14.139 Tip: Dynamically declare variables as they are needed for accumulation in a project file; use a master variable to keep track of the variable names. 3.10

If you need to accumulate values in a project file, but you do not know in advance the variable names, you can dynamically declare variables as they are required.

```
let $vars = null                              'list of dept codes
goto record rec-number 1

while record <= records
     let %1 = [dept]                          'department code
     if $vars !! [dept]                       '1st time for this department?
          let $vars = $vars | [dept] | "/" 'add to dept list
          let $%1 = 0                         'initlize at zero
     endif
     let $%1 = $%1 + [wage]                   'accumulate the wage
     if record = records then break
     goto record next
endwhile
```

Note that the $vars variable keeps track of each new department code encountered in the file. Each time a new department is encountered, the code is added to the list until the $vars variable looks like this:

```
ACCT/MFGR/SALE/MKTG/DATA/
```

For each new department, a variable is established ($ACCT, for example) and initialized at zero. Finally, the wages are accumulated in the appropriate department variables.

3.10

14.140 Tip: Test for the existence of a variable by using the ISERR function.

If you do not know whether a variable exists, use the following coding:

```
if Iserr($variable) = 1
     'variable does not exist
endif
```

The ISERR function returns 1 if an error occurs. In this example, the nonexistence of a variable is such a condition.

3.10

14.141 Tip: User-defined variables can contain 10 times as much text as standard text variables.

A standard text variable (text1 or text2) can contain a maximum of 100 characters. A user-defined variable, when used to contain text, can hold a maximum of 1,000 characters.

Both

14.142 Tip: For flexibility, use variables in queries.

Within a query, you can enter a variable name on the right side of the equation:

```
[lastname] = $lname
```

If you supply a value to `$lname` within the project file, when you execute the query, the value is substituted for the variable in the query definition. You cannot use Smart 3.10 parameters in query definitions, however, nor can you perform a substitution on the left side of the equation in a query definition.

3.10

14.143 Tip: There are two standard text variables and two standard numeric variables, but the number of user-defined variables is limited only by the amount of RAM in your computer.

The standard text variables are TEXT1 and TEXT2; the variables that can hold only numbers are called VALUE1 and VALUE2. A variable that you declare must start with a dollar sign ($) and can have a name length of 10 characters. (Actually, the variable name can extend to 80 characters, but only the first 10 are recognized by the project-processing language.) A user-defined variable can contain either text or numbers.

Both

14.144 Tip: Clear variables you no longer need.

In Smart 3.10, if you don't clear variables, they remain active. Active variables consume RAM and reduce the effective working space. The Clear statement by itself can clear all user-defined variables. To clear specified variables from RAM, issue the Clear statement, followed by the variables' names, separated by commas.

In SmartWare II, declaring variables as Local, Global or Public controls their duration in RAM. A locked, Public variable continues to exist even after the termination of the project file.

14.145 Tip: In a project file, if a variable already exists by having been declared in a previous project file, declaring the variable again does not clear it or have any other effect. *SW II*

No discernible disadvantage exists to declaring an existing variable again. If project file "A" declares a variable and then executes project file "B", which also declares the same variable, no problem exists. The variable is not cleared, nor is any additional memory consumed. If you want to clear a variable, use the Clear statement.

14.146 Tip: A variable assumes a value of numeric zero after the variable is declared and before a value has been entered into the variable. *SW II*

The Clear command also assigns a value of numeric zero to an existing variable. If the variable is not public and not locked, the variable is erased from memory after the project file has completed and you are returned to the command level of the module.

14.147 Tip: Variable names cannot begin with a number; you must use a letter or a special character ($,#, or _) as the first character. *SW II*

If you try to use a number, the following error message appears:

```
Missing name
```

You get this error message when you try to compile the program.

14.148 Tip: Array variables may contain a mixture of text and numbers; all of the elements do not have to be of the same type. *SW II*

For example, you can have the following array variable:

```
$wage[2,13]
```

In row 1 of this array, you can insert the name of the employee, and in row 2, that employee's wage. To avoid confusion, however, you may want to use two variables, such as: $name[13] and $wage[13].

14.149 Trick: If you want to clear all but one or two of your user-defined variables, assign them to the system variables TEXT1, TEXT2, VALUE1, or VALUE2 and then issue the Clear statement. *3.10*

The Clear statement, by itself, clears all user-defined variables from memory—you do not have to specify the names of the variables. The Clear statement does not, however, clear the system variables. Therefore, you can store the values of four user variables safely in the system variables, and then issue the Clear statement without having to name each user variable. Be aware, however, that the two text variables can hold a maximum of only 100 characters each, but user variables can hold 1,000 characters.

14.150 Tip: Clear array variables to make more memory available. *SW II*

Clearing an array variable sets each element to zero and also frees memory within the module. When you use an array variable, a separate set of pointers keeps track of the location of the individual elements in memory. The fewer the elements having actual contents, the fewer pointers are needed. When you clear the array variable, none of the elements have contents and no pointers or value locations are assigned.

Although you can assign a value of zero to each element of an array within a FOR...END FOR loop, these zeros are considered "values," and therefore the pointers and value locations are established. Numerically, the value of zero within a cleared array is identical to a value of zero assigned with a LET statement, but in the second case, the memory usage is greater.

SW II

14.151 Trick: In a project file, Quit to the current module to reallocate system memory and unfragment variable assignment locations.

Variables are located in memory when values are assigned to them. If you use the Clear statement in a project file, or if some of the variables are not locked, the locations to which they were assigned now are available for usage. Some of the empty locations are small, and others are large, depending on the previous contents. If you Quit to your current module, any system-locked variables are repositioned contiguously at the beginning of free memory, without leaving any unused areas. The commands are as follows:

Quit Database
Quit Spreadsheet
Quit Communications
Quit Wordprocessor

Even from the command level, you can Quit to your current module. Press Alt-X to display the most recent command, press F8 to clear the line, and then type the appropriate command.

3.10

14.153 Tip: Variables at the beginning of the alphabet are accessed more rapidly than those at the end of the alphabet.

User-defined variables are stored in RAM in alphabetical order. If the names of your most frequently used variables start with letters near the beginning of the alphabet, those variables are accessed faster than variables whose names are found towards the end of the alphabetic sort order.

3.10

14.153 Trick: Add a zero to a numeric variable or parameter if the variable or parameter might be null.

If you are assigning a value to a parameter or variable from a source that might be null, add zero to the variable or parameter to make sure it is not null, as in the following:

```
let %1 = [ohqty]
let %1 = %1 + 0
if  %1 = 0 then jump nostock
```

In this example, if the `[ohqty]` field is null (has never contained a value), adding a zero to the parameter permits testing the parameter for a zero condition. If you are using the parameter in an incrementing calculation such as

```
let %1 = %1 + [ohqty]
```

make sure the `%1` is not null when you begin or you will get an error.

14.154 Trick: Use Text1 or Text2 for entering a number that is to be used as text. *3.10*

A number entered into the variables Text1 or Text2 always is considered to be text. If you enter a number into a user-defined variable or a parameter, the result is numeric, and comparison to text fields or use in text expressions becomes more complex than necessary.

14.155 Trap: Do not use a user-defined variable to accept a Social Security number in a project file, because the Social Security number will be evaluated as a subtraction calculation. *3.10*

If your project file has the statement

```
Input $ssn Enter SSN:
```

the result is a numeric value resulting from the subtraction of the second two SSN elements from the first. To accept an SSN, use a standard text variable to guarantee that the result is accepted as a text string:

```
Input text1 Enter SSN:
```

14.156 Trap: Comparison of a number in an alpha field to a number in a parameter or user-defined variable cannot be performed accurately without the use of a conversion function. *3.10*

When you enter a number into a parameter or a user-defined variable, the result is numeric and cannot be compared directly to a number stored in an alpha field. To perform the comparison, use a FIXED function to convert the numeric variable:

```
if [zip] = fixed($zip,0)
```

or use a VAL function:

```
val([zip]) = $zip
```

14.157 Trap: A number can be stored in a user-defined variable either as a value that you can use in a calculation or as a text string. Use the FIXED or VAL functions to convert from one usage to the other. ***Both***

Because a user-defined variable can contain either text or numbers, a number can be entered in either of these two formats, yet have different capabilities. If you enter a value

```
let $total = 6621.99
```

the number can be used in a calculation. However, if you enter a string

```
let $total = "6621.99"
```

the appearance is the same, but the variable cannot be used in a calculation. To convert from a numeric to a string, use the FIXED function:

```
let $textot = fixed($total,2)
```

The VAL function converts a string to a numeric value:

```
let $valtot = val($total)
```

3.10

14.158 Trap: Errors in Date functions cause the project file to terminate; use these functions at the beginning of your project.

If you perform a date conversion using the DATE2 function near the beginning of a project file, you can catch any errors before the project has progressed very far. By using the statement

```
let $fdate = date2($fdate)
```

you cause the project file to terminate at the beginning, rather than at the end, if an error occurs. Avoiding this problem is especially important if you have just issued a prompt for a user to enter a date from the keyboard. There is no function to validate a date field and to perform error checking within the project file.

In SmartWare II, use the ISDATE function to trap any date errors.

Both

14.159 Trick: If you enter a date into a variable, use the DATE2 or FORMAT function to convert the date to the standard format.

If you have the following Smart 3.10 statement:

```
Input $fdate Enter Current Date:
```

and the response is returned as 1/1/88, you can use the following statement to convert the response to the standard eight-digit date format:

```
let $fdate = date2($fdate)
```

In SmartWare II, you also can use the FORMAT function to accomplish the same effect:

```
let $fdate = format($fdate,"Dmm/dd/yy")
```

The result is 01/01/88.

3.10

14.160 Tip: Use this project file to check for valid dates in response to an Input or Menu Input statement in a project file.

```
'Routine:  ISDATE
'Purpose:  Validate a date in mm/dd/yy or mm-dd-yy format
'          February leap years are validated.
'Call:     Date must be in text1 variable
'Return:   $Isdate returns 1 for valid date, 0 for invalid date

    let $isdate = 1                       'initialize as valid date

'check if slash (/) or dash (-) is used
if text1 ! "/"
    let $sep = "/"                        'uses slash
elseif text1 ! "-"
    let $sep = "-"                        'uses dash
else
    let $isdate = 0                       'error - uses neither
endif

if $isdate = 0 then jump baddate

'extract month ($mm), day ($dd), and year ($yy)

let $br1 = match(text1,$sep)              'position between month and day
let $br2 = match(text1,$sep,$br1+1)       'position between day and year

let $mm = val(left(text1,$br1-1))                  'month
let $dd = val(mid(text1,$br1+1,$br2-$br1-1))       'day
let $yy = val(mid(text1,$br2+1))                   'year

'check valid ranges

'month must be from 1 to 12
if ($mm >=1 and $mm <= 12) then jump testyr
jump baddate

label testyr
'year must be from 0 to 99 (1900 to 1999)
if ($yy >= 0 and $yy <= 99) then jump testday
jump baddate

label testday
'test the day
                                          'for february
if $mm = 2
   if $yy/4 = int($yy/4)
       let $maxday = 29                   'maximum is 29 if leap year
   else
       let $maxday = 28                   'maximum is 28 if not leap year
   endif
else
                                          'months other than february
   let $maxday = case $mm (9,30) (4,30) (6,30) (11,30) else 31
endif

'test if day within the allowable range
if ($dd >= 1 and $dd <= $maxday) then jump alldone
```

```
label baddate
let $isdate = 0                                  'set switch to indicate bad date

label alldone
```

The ISDATE project file checks for valid dates. You may use either slashes (/) or dashes (-) in the response; leading zeros are not required. Only the valid months are acceptable, and each month is checked for the proper maximum number of days. Leap years also are checked. The variable $isdate will be 1 if the date is valid, or 0 if the date is invalid.

This ISDATE project file is called from another project file as follows:

```
label askdate
input text1 Enter Date:
execute isdate in-memory
if $isdate = 0
     beep
     message Invalid date .. press any key ..
     jump askdate
endif
```

In SmartWare II, you do not need this project file because the ISDATE function may be used to test for a valid date.

3.10

14.161 Tip: Create a project file to check for the type of response to a prompt, testing whether it is numeric, text, or an F10 or Escape.

```
'Name:           ISVALUE
'Purpose:        Validate Text1 response as a number or zero
'Call:           Text1 contains a response
'Return:         $isvalue = 0 : Text
'                $isvalue = 1 : Valid Numeric
'                $isvalue = 2 : Valid Text .. see $valvar below
'                $isvalue = 3 : Carriage Return or F10

let $valvar = "XZ"
let $isvalue = 0

if text1 = null
   let $isvalue = 3

elseif $valvar ! upper(left(text1,1)) and len(text1) = 1
   let $isvalue = 2

elseif text1 = "0"
   let $isvalue = 1

elseif left(text1,1) = "." and len(text1) = len(str(val(text1)))-1
   let $isvalue = 1

elseif len(text1) <> len(str(val(text1)))
   'no operation
```

```
elseif val(text1) = 0
   'no operation

elseif isnumber(val(text1)) = 1
   let $isvalue = 1

else
   'no operation

endif
```

In a project file, it is often important that a response to an Input statement be a value or text. This project file can be used to check for the type of response and will return a code that you can test.

This ISVALUE project file can be called from another project file as follows:

```
label askwage
input text1 Enter wage:
execute isvalue in-memory
if $isvalue <> 1
     beep
     message Invalid entry .. press key
     jump askwage
endif

let $wage = val(text1)
```

Notice that the input must be into TEXT1; be sure to assign the contents of text1 to a user variable after you have validated the entry.

14.162 Tip: Any Lock commands must be issued within the main section of a project file. If you do not have a main section, the Lock statements must fall after the declaration statements. *SW II*

Statements that Lock variables always must be issued after the statements which declare them. Consider the following statement:

```
Public $amount $dept
```

If you want to lock these variables, use either of these statements after the declaration:

```
Lock System Public
Lock System $amount $dept
```

A Lock statement must be within the main section of a project file, if you have one.

14.163 Tip: In the Suspend mode of a project file, all variables are available through Remember Tools Trace regardless of whether they are Public, Global, or Local. Public variables do not have to be locked. Only the Public variables are available in the calculator, however. *SW II*

Normally, for a Public variable to be available at the command level, you must have locked the variable within the system or the module. Because the project file has not completed while you are in the suspend mode, however, not only the Public variables, but also the Global and Local variables are available through Remember Tools Trace. Only the Public variables may be used in the calculator. At the completion of the project file, only the locked Public variables continue to be available.

SW II

14.164 Tip: To conserve RAM memory, declare variables as Global or Local, if possible, rather than Public. While developing the application, however, you may want to keep the variables as Public and Locked.

Local and Global variables apply to only the project file in which they are declared. Because these classes of variables cannot be Locked, you cannot check their contents at the completion of the program. You can declare these variables as Public, however, and Lock them while you are developing the application. After all the bugs (if any) are out of your program, you can go back and change selected variables to Global or Local, to save RAM.

SW II

14.165 Trap: If you have a global variable in the main section of code and a local variable with the same name in a function, you cannot access the global variable in the function.

Local variables are usable only within the section in which they are declared. They take precedence over any other variable with the same name. If you want to access a global variable within a function, you must not use a local variable of the same name in the function.

SW II

14.166 Tip: Use Local and Global variables instead of Public variables for reasons of speed and memory usage.

Local and Global variables consume less memory because there is less overhead. Local and Global variables are erased when they are not needed any longer—when the section in which they were declared terminates. Local and Global variables are also accessed faster than Public variables, because of the way they are stored and addressed in memory.

SW II

14.167 Tip: Use the Key Define command in a project file to define a macro key that uses the contents of a variable; you cannot use an Evaluate statement to create a Key statement which changes when the program executes.

The following macro prompts and changes the title of a table report.

```
public $title

screen shortinput $title "Enter title:"

'add quotation marks around the title
let $title = chr(34)|$title|chr(34)
key define "#1000" $title
```

```
print report modify "artwork"
keys "tt",down,look,#1000,enter,f10,f10,f10
```

Note that the Key Define statement establishes the value of the numbered macro as the contents of the $title variable. After being established, the macro is used in the Keys statement. In addition to the macros numbered 896 through 1023, you also may use any key combination available on your keyboard, whether or not the key combination currently is a macro.

14.168 Tip: You cannot define a macro within a project file by using the Tools Macros Edit command; you must use the Key Define command. *SW II*

If you have the command Tools Macros Edit within a project file, you are prompted:

```
Press key to edit:
```

This prompt occurs regardless of the Keys statements following the command in the program. You must use the Key Define command, as shown in the preceding tip.

14.169 Tip: Use the Tools Macros Clear All command in a project file to clear all macros. To clear an individual macro, however, you must use the Key Remove command. *SW II*

If you want to clear an Alt-F1 macro, for example, use the command

```
Key Remove "Alt-F1"
```

If you try to use the command Tools Macros Clear One, you are prompted:

```
Press key of Macro to remove:
```

Any key you press is accepted, whether or not it is a macro key. If you press the correct key, the macro is cleared. If you press a nonmacro key, no error message appears.

14.170 Tip: A Keys statement must immediately follow a command that calls for keyboard input; you must not have any intervening commands. *SW II*

For example, the following statements change a report definition to a width of either 8.5 or 14 inches in the Spreadsheet:

```
if $count < 10
     Print Report Define "SUMMARY.RDF"
     keys ^end,up,up,up,up, "8.5",Enter,F10
else
     Print Report Define "SUMMARY.RDF"
     keys ^end,up,up,up,up, "14",Enter,F10
end if
```

The following series of statements does *not* work, however:

```
Print Report Define "SUMMARY.RDF"
if $count < 10
     keys ^end,up,up,up,up, "8.5",Enter,F10
else
     keys ^end,up,up,up,up, "14",Enter,F10
end if
```

The statements between the `Print Report Define` and the `keys` commands violate the use of the Keys command. In this second example, the report definition is displayed on-screen and the program pauses for further action.

SW II

14.171 Tip: Use the Keys command to respond to a prompt for keyboard input. If you want to initiate action, you must use the Suspend command prior to the Keys command.

The Keys command may be used to provide a response to a prompt or a menu as if you had typed the response from the keyboard. In the Database module, for example, following a Data Query command, you probably want to have a Keys Esc command so that the pop-up information window is cleared and the project file continues without manual intervention. The Keys command alone, however, cannot be used to initiate action or activity. If you want to execute the Data Query, for example, you cannot use the following:

```
keys "dqe",Enter,"i",Enter,Esc
```

If you want to use the Keys command to execute a Data Query, rather than using the command, you have to do the following:

```
suspend command
keys "dqe",Enter,"i",Enter,Esc,F8
```

Don't forget the F8 at the end to terminate the Suspend mode and resume execution of the project file.

SW II

14.172 Trap: When editing a variable in the Remember Tools Trace facility, variables are not assumed to be text, as they are when prompting for them in a project file.

For example, if a variable called $begdate has a current displayed value of 05/05/40 and you want to change the value to 12/10/89, you must place quotation marks around the new entry to indicate that the entry is text: "12/10/89". If you do not use quotation marks, the value of the variable will be 0.013483, which is 12 divided by 10 divided by 89. Similarly, if an alpha variable contains a numeric code, be sure to use quotation marks, or you will change the variable to numeric.

SW II

14.173 Tip: When adding variables to the list to be displayed when you execute Remember Tools Trace, you cannot specify several names on one line.

To add variables, press F3. You may specify all variables (use *) or type them individually by name. After typing each name you specify, press Enter. If you try to save time and specify several names on one line, using a space between them, nothing happens. If you separate the names with a comma (no space), the string of text is accepted and displayed in the variable list window, but there is no other effect. No shortcuts are available; you must enter the variable names individually.

14.174 Trap: There is no field verification when defining a project file Trace condition in the Database module. *SW II*

When you execute the Remember Tools Trace command and press F6, you can edit, add, or remove the breakpoint condition on which the trace screen is to be displayed. Type 2 enables you to type the conditional statement. If you use a field in the condition, the system does not check to see if the field is valid; you must be careful to type the name of the field carefully. If the field is mistyped, no error message appears and the Trace mode is not invoked when your intended condition is satisfied.

14.175 Trap: The Escape, F10, and Enter keys terminate the prompt generated by the Screen Input command. Escape, however, aborts the prompt. If you establish a default value, you can make sure that you have a valid entry. *SW II*

If you set the variable equal to an unacceptable value, you can distinguish between an intended entry and an Escape. Refer to the following example:

```
local $date

let $date = "dummy"
screen clear 7 0

while not (isdate($date))
     screen print 5 10 7 0 "Enter Date:"
     screen input 5 22 0 7 10 $date today
end while
```

Note that the default for the display is the function TODAY. If you press Enter or F10, today's date is entered. You also may supply another date of your choice. If you hit an Escape, because "dummy" is not a valid date, the program will prompt again. Note that you cannot check whether the response is equal to {Escape}.

14.176 Trap: Pressing Enter in response to the Screen Input command may enable invalid defaults to be accepted, even if they violate the mask. *SW II*

Consider the following:

```
local $defdept $dept
let $defdept = "acct"
clear $dept
```

```
screen clear 7 0
screen print 5 10 7 0 "Department Code:"
screen input 5 27 0 7 4 $dept mask "*4au" $defdept
```

In this example, the default value is "acct", but mask specifies that the four characters must be uppercase alpha. If you press Enter, the lowercase characters are accepted. If you decide to reject the default and type your own code, however, the code must correspond to the mask.

SW II

14.177 Trick: The Screen Menu command in a project file can be used to create a numeric variable, rather than text. All other screen input commands create only text variables.

In SmartWare II, most of the project-processing commands to enter data from the keyboard create only text variables, even if the response is numeric. In those cases, if you want the variable to be numeric, you must convert the variable within the program:

```
let $value = val($value)
```

The Screen Menu command, however, creates a numeric variable directly:

```
local $value
screen clear 7 0
screen menu 5 10 5 70 9 0 0 9 1 \
"1 2" $value "Select 1 or 2: "
```

In this example, the variable $value is numeric and has a value of either 1 or 2.

SW II

14.178 Tip: In a project file, when using the Screen Menu command, the items in the list are displayed in Proper case in the pop-up menu, rather than their original case.

Consider the following project file:

```
public $list , $choice , $title

let $list = "DETAIL-INVENTORY SUMMARY-INVENTORY ORDER- STATUS \
            Backorders Company-Transfers Goods-Damaged \
            Work-in-Progress Productions-Delayed"

let $title = "Select Desired Report:"

screen clear box 9 3 16 77 9 0
screen menu 10 5 15 75 9 0 9 17 1 $list $choice $title
```

Notice that the entire first line of the list has been written in uppercase. Figure 14.12 shows the screen display generated by this project file:

In the display, those items from the first line are shown in proper case. The hyphen between the words of an individual menu item capitalize each word, even if the words originally were written entirely in lowercase.

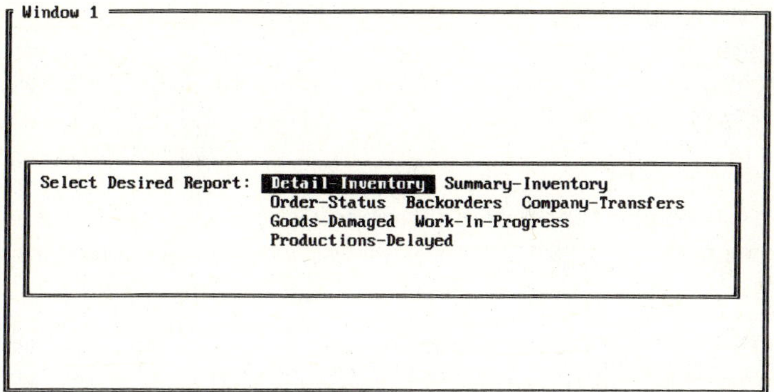

Fig. 14.12. *A screen menu display in proper case.*

14.179 Tip: When using the Screen Menu command, initialize the choice selection number variable at zero to test if an Escape is pressed. *SW II*

Normally, pressing Escape in response to the Screen Menu command aborts the prompt and allows the program to continue. If you want to make sure the prompt is answered, use the following technique:

```
public $list , $choice , $title

clear $choice

while $choice = 0
  let $list = "Detail-Inventory Summary-Inventory Order-Status \
               Backorders Company-Transfers Goods-Damaged \
               Work-in-Progress Productions-Delayed"

  let $title = "Select Desired Report:"

  screen clear box 9 3 16 77 9 0
  screen menu 10 5 15 75 9 0 9 17 1 $list $choice $title
end while
```

If Escape or F10 is pressed, rather than Enter, the value still is zero and the Screen Menu command is executed again.

14.180 Trick: User variables that are locked can be used in response to prompts at the command level. *SW II*

At the command level, you usually select from names that appear on a pop-up menu or you type the response. If a user variable contains the name you want to use, but the variable has been locked, you can use the variable in response to the prompt. (The variable must be locked to cause it to exist at the command level.)

For example, the File Load command in the database requires you to enter a view name. If the variable contains the name of the view you want to load, press Alt-x to display the most recent command, press F8 to clear the line, and type the following:

```
file load custom-view $filename
```

In this case, the variable $filename contains the name of the view you want to load. A macro can be created to perform these steps to make them easier and quicker to execute.

SW II

14.181 Trick: In the calculator or on line one of any of the various editors, you can both create and assign a value to a project-processing variable.

For example, type the following formula in the calculator and press F5:

```
let $dept = "ACCT"
```

The $dept variable thus is created, if it did not exist already, and the value of "ACCT" is assigned to it. The variable becomes public and locked within the module, but not within the system.

Caution: In a project file, you cannot unlock a variable created this way.

15

Communications and Commands Used throughout Smart

This chapter covers the Communications module and those commands that are common to all the modules.

Commands Used throughout Smart

The commands that are common to all the Smart modules are covered in this section, rather than separately in the individual module sections of this book.

Windows and Borders

15.1 Trick: To display more windows or data on-screen, disable the border of each window. *Both*

In the Database, removing the borders makes displaying a greater amount of data in each window possible. In the Spreadsheet and Word Processor, you can display more windows if you remove the borders. You cannot remove the borders in the Communications module, however (see Tip 15.66).

15.2 Tip: Move your cursor horizontally if you are splitting your window vertically, or move your cursor vertically if you are splitting horizontally. *Both*

In some modules, you are not prevented from moving your cursor the wrong direction, but when you press Enter, you get one of the following error messages:

```
Window too small
Marked area too small to split
The specified area is too small to split
```

3.10

15.3 Tip: You cannot go from window to window in the Smart 3.10 Word Processor or Spreadsheet while in the Zoom mode; you first must Unzoom your screen.

In the 3.10 Database, you can change windows while in Zoom. In SmartWare II, you can go to a new window while zoomed in any of the modules.

The DOS Window (Secondary Command Processor)

Both

15.4 Trap: Some DOS commands issued while in the secondary command processor have only a temporary effect.

If you invoke the secondary command processor with Ctrl-O, some commands that you issue are effective only in the DOS window; their effect is lost when you return to Smart. For example, a change of the current drive, directory, or path has no effect when you exit back to Smart. Even if you return to DOS, these previous changes will be lost. Environment settings are temporary only while within a secondary command processor. If you erase a file, however, this physical change will have a lasting effect.

Both

15.5 Trap: DOS commands executed with Command /C or Tools OS default to the directory from which you entered Smart, not a directory to which you have changed within Smart.

If you change subdirectories within Smart, you must be careful if you execute operating system commands (DOS) using Tools OS or Command /C because these commands will not execute within the new Smart subdirectory. From the DOS viewpoint, you never left your original subdirectory.

As an example, if you change directories, you get different results from the following two SmartWare II commands:

```
Tools OS "dir *.*"
Tools Directory Display "*.*"
```

The Tools OS command shows the names of the files in your original subdirectory; the Tools Directory Display command displays the files in your current subdirectory.

File Commands

Both

15.6 Trap: Use file extensions when executing the File command because no standard extensions are assumed.

The File operations (Erase, Rename, and Copy) require the use of file extensions. For example, the following Smart 3.10 command:

```
file erase *.IDX
```

erases all index files. In SmartWare II, the command is Tools File Erase*.IDX.

15.7 Trap: You cannot access the File command in the Data Base Manager from confidence level 4 or 5 because the abbreviation for the File command is identical to that of the File-Specs command. *3.10*

The File and File-Specs commands begin with the same first four letters, so the command interpreters at confidence levels 4 or 5 cannot distinguish them. To execute the File command in the Data Base Manager, you must return to confidence level 3. Using the DOS Window Ctrl-O key sequence to invoke a secondary command processor may be faster than switching to level 3, performing the commands, and switching back again. If you are selecting a New-Directory, however, you must use the File command.

15.8 Trick: Execute the File commands from confidence level 5 by typing the full command from the keyboard. *3.10*

Press Alt-X to display the most recent command, if any. Press F8 to erase the line and then type the File command. To erase a file named IND1.IDX, for example, type

file erase ind1.idx

Similarly, you can execute any of the other File commands. Be sure, however, to include the word "to" in the Copy and Rename commands:

```
file copy qnow.dfq to mine.dfq
```

15.9 Trap: The File command's New-Directory option (Tools Directory New-Directory for SmartWare II) doesn't change the current directory available through the DOS Window. *Both*

Although you change to a new directory with the File New-Directory command, the directory available through the DOS window remains unchanged. This is true whether you use Ctrl-O to invoke the DOS window or the Command (Smart 3.10) or Tools OJ (SmartWare II) statement of a project file. The File New-Directory command temporarily changes the application data path specification found in the Main menu Configure command, but doesn't perform a DOS CD or CHDIR (change directory) command.

15.10 Trap: The File New-Directory command doesn't issue an error message if you specify a directory that doesn't exist or you misspell the name. *3.10*

Take great care when using the File command to change to a new directory, because Smart doesn't display an error message if the directory you specify doesn't exist. Smart accepts the entry. If you try to load a file, however, the directory appears completely empty. If you execute the Directory command with the *.* specification, Smart responds

```
No matching files, enter any key.
```

Only if you quit to another module and then return to the current one do you see the following error message:

```
Invalid application data path
```

3.10

15.11 Trap: The File New-Directory command affects only the current module; you therefore should initiate a new module before changing the directory.

Suppose you are working with the Data Base Manager and want to initiate the Spreadsheet within a different subdirectory. Change to the Spreadsheet first and then execute the File New-Directory command. If you change the directory first, the change is not reflected in the Spreadsheet when you initiate that module.

SW II

15.12 Trick: Use the following project file to help you change directories:

```
'Name:                          Newsub
'Purpose:                       Change Subdirectories

global readin()
global $choices $title $which

label main
     let $title = "Subdirectories"
     readin()
     screen prompt 3 25 18 55 fgpleasing
bgpleasing \
            $choices $which $title
     if $which > 0
            tools directory new-directory
     group($choices, $which)
     end if
end main

function readin()
     local $first
     fopen "c:\util\direct.txt" as 1
     let $first = " "
     while $first <> ""
            fread 1 into $first
            let $choices = $choices & $first
     end while
     fclose 1
end function
```

To use this project file, you must create a file that contains the names of the possible subdirectories to which you want to change. Use the text editor. In the example, the file is called `c:\util\direct.txt`. Be sure to specify the path so that you can use this project file from many different subdirectories.

To make this project file even easier to use, you can include the file on the Main menu of SmartWare II, using the Optional Menu Keywords feature.

15.13 Tip: If you change your directory to a different drive, the new drive is not assumed for subsequent directory changes. ***Both***

When you use either File New-Directory (Smart 3.10) or Tools File New-Directory (SmartWare II) to change to a different drive, the original drive still is assumed if you change your directory again. In DOS, when you change to a different drive, the new drive is assumed until you change back to the original drive. In Smart, however, the original drive is always assumed, so you must specify the drive letter when you change directories again if you want to stay on the same drive.

15.14 Trap: When you use the File New-Directory command, the selection applies to the current module only. When you switch modules, the default directory in the Configure menu is used. If this selection is blank, the home directory is assumed. If you return to the previous module, the subdirectory does not change if the directory specification in Configure is blank. ***3.10***

If you want to remain in the same directory in a Smart session when going from module to module, do not specify a subdirectory in Configure, but change to the desired directory before beginning the Smart session. Alternatively, in a project file, you can execute the following:

```
Jump Spreadsheet project-file c:\sub2\Ssproj
```

In the project file `SSproj`, begin with the following statement:

```
File New-Directory c:\sub2.
```

Another way to solve the problem is to specify, in the Configure menu, that all modules default to the same subdirectory. Each time you change to a new module, the system reverts to the specified subdirectory.

Finally, you can have different configuration menus for individual applications. The selection of subdirectories can be application-dependent. If you have the file called CONFIGUR in the subdirectory from which you begin the Smart session, the application path settings within the configuration will be used for the duration of the session. Of course, you still can use the File New-Directory command within a module to change subdirectories temporarily.

15.15 Tip: The Tools File Copy command overlays existing files without an error message, which is in contrast with Smart 3.10. ***Both***

Just like DOS, the Tools File Copy command overlays existing files without a message. In Smart 3.10, however, if you try to use the File Copy command to copy into an existing file, you get the following error message:

```
File already exists
```

In Smart 3.10, you must erase the destination file before you can create a copy with the same name.

SW II

15.16 Trip: If you use the Tools File Erase command to try to erase a nonexistent file, you are prompted to continue, but this has no meaning.

If the file you are trying to erase does not exist, you are prompted:

```
File filename.ext not found - Continue with other files? (y/n)
```

You must press either `y` or `n`, but in either case you are returned to the command level. No actual continuation of the command occurs.

SW II

15.17 Trick: Use the Tools File Rename command to move a file from one subdirectory to another. This is faster than using the Tools File Copy command.

The Tools File Rename command may be used to change the name of a file in its current subdirectory and change the directory tables to reassign the file to a different subdirectory on the same physical drive. For example,

```
Tools file Rename "NANCY.WS" to "\CROSSE\DALLAS.WS"
```

assigns the file `NANCY.WS` to the `\CROSSE` subdirectory under the name `DALLAS.WS`. Because the file simply is renamed, the command does not take any longer with a large file than with a small file.

To use this feature, the file must remain on the same physical disk drive. If you want the file on a different drive, you must use the Tools File Copy command.

SW II

15.18 Tip: The asterisk wild card (*) operates differently in the Tools File commands than in DOS.

In the Tools File Rename command, wild cards are not allowed. For example, if you try to execute the following command:

```
Tools File Rename "john.*" to "jack.*"
```

you get the error message:

```
Invalid filename
```

In the Tools File Copy command, you may execute the following commands without error:

```
Tools File Copy "C:*.*" to "A:"
Tools File Copy "*.*" to "\temp"
```

You may not, however, execute the following:

```
Tools File Copy "STL*.B01" to "*.001"
Tools File Copy "STL.*" to "\util\BOS.*"
```

In the Tools File Erase command, wild cards are allowed.

15.19 Trap: Smart does not prevent the creation of files having the same names as reserved DOS devices: LPT1, LPT2, COM1, COM2, PRN, CON, AUX.

Both

Do *not* use these names for any files you may create. Various problems will occur and may interfere with the operation of other commands.

Input Screens

15.20 Trick: Edit Input Screen definitions in the Text-Editor rather than using the Input-Screen Define command.

Both

Editing an Input Screen definition directly may be faster than using the Define option. (An Input Screen file has the extension ISx, in which x is a number representing the individual module.) Before trying to edit your definition, make a backup copy of it. By examining the Input Screen definition file contents, you also can find the names of the parameters and variables loaded during execution.

Figure 15.1 shows an example of a simple Input Screen that accepts two values.

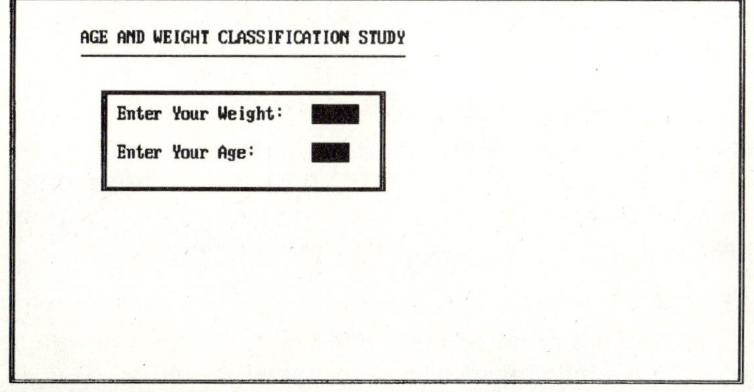

Fig. 15.1. *A sample input screen.*

The following is the code that generates the screen in figure 15.1:

```
1 7 0
2 713 7 0Enter Your Weight:
```

```
2 913 7 0Enter Your Age:
2 3 9 7 0AGE AND WEIGHT CLASSIFICATION STUDY
4 4 9 443 7
3 734 4 0 7$weight
3 934 4 0 7$age
4 6111141 7
```

An input-screen definition has four types of records; the record type is listed in the first column. The entries are very similar to those used when building Menus in project processing.

Type 1 is the first record. The data represents foreground and background colors.

Type 2 represents text. The data is the beginning row and column numbers, the foreground and background colors, followed by the actual text entries.

Type 3 records are input items; the beginning row and columns numbers are followed by the length of the input item and the foreground and background colors. The variable or parameter is the final entry on the line.

Type 4 represents a box or a line. The numbers represent the upper left row and column numbers, the lower right location, and the foreground color.

Both

15.21 Trick: Print the Input-Screen definitions for documentation purposes and to record the variable and parameter names created.

Input-Screen definitions are text files, so you can print them for inclusion in your system documentation. If you forget what variables or parameters were created by the Input Screen, you can refer to the printed documentation.

Both

15.22 Trick: Input screens are not module-dependent.

The file extension of an input screen indicates the module in which the screen was developed. The extension is in the format ISx, in which x is the module number. In fact, you can execute an input screen from any module by supplying the input screen file name and extension at the following prompt:

```
Enter input-screen filename:
```

In Smart 3.10, you can display a pop-up menu of the names of all your input screens, regardless of the module in which you created them, enter

```
*.IS*
```

at the prompt and press F5.

3.10

15.23 Trick: Use two variables in the Input Screen facility to get around the 25-character variable limit.

If you need more than 25 characters, you can define 2 adjacent fields, each of which can contain a maximum of 25 characters. Then, in your project file, you can concatenate the two variables into one longer variable.

15.24 Trick: You can "slide" text entries to the right when designing an Input Screen.

Both

If insert mode is active, you can move text entries to the right for alignment purposes. Therefore, if you purposely begin the entry to the left of the desired final destination, you can slide text to the right by pressing the space bar. You cannot slide text to the left by using the Del key, however.

Note that this capability to slide text to the right doesn't apply to all screen-design facilities. For example, you cannot slide text to the right when designing a custom screen in the Smart 3.10 Data Base Manager.

15.25 Trap: When you are editing an input screen, overlays can occur if you are not careful. You should delete an entry before changing it.

Both

Several text entries or prompts can appear in the same location on an input screen. This arrangement,however, is usually more confusing than helpful. If you need to use the Input-Screen command to edit a custom screen, you should delete the offending entry and then enter the correction instead of trying to overlay the current contents. Otherwise, you may end up with unpredictable results.

Macros and Quick Keys

15.26 Tip: A macro can contain an F10 keystroke and therefore be used to change menus that require an F10 for termination.

Both

To insert an F10 in a Smart 3.10 macro, you press Ctrl-F10. You can use several F10s if necessary—for example, several F10 keystrokes are needed if you are using a macro to change a report definition.

When you are editing a macro in SmartWare II, you type *F10* within the body of the macro.

15.27 Trap: If you edit a macro containing an F10 keystroke, Smart deletes all characters to the right of the first F10 (and the F10 itself), and macro editing terminates immediately.

3.10

An F10 in a macro acts like the F10 you use to terminate the original creation of the macro. If you edit the macro, therefore, the first F10 that Smart encounters terminates the editing and you lose all keystrokes to the right of the F10. Make sure that your macro definition is correct initially so that you don't have to edit it. If you need to see the macro, use Macro View rather than Define.

15.28 Tip: In macros, use Quick Keys rather than the commands they represent.

Both

Quick keys can be executed in Command or Enter mode in the Spreadsheet or Word Processor. By using a Quick Key in a macro, you can use the macro in either Command mode or Enter mode—you don't have to invoke Command mode and access the correct command list.

3.10

15.29 Tip: Because no recording mode exists for creating macros, you should write down each keystroke you plan to enter.

Run through the steps you plan to perform with a macro, taking care to write down each keystroke you use. Do not forget carriage returns and cursor-arrow keys because they, too, must be entered into the macro. When created, a macro can be changed, but you cannot insert anything into or delete anything from the middle of the macro. You can, however, erase from the end and rebuild the macro.

3.10

15.30 Tip: One macro cannot invoke another.

The keystrokes with which you initiate the execution of a macro take on their original meaning if they are issued within a second macro. The only way to execute a macro is by pressing the proper key sequence on the keyboard.

Both

15.31 Tip: Before creating a macro, test the keystroke to make sure the key is not currently used.

To avoid superseding an existing quick key, you should test a particular keystroke before assigning the keystroke to a macro. The prior assignment of the key as a quick key should be immediately evident, indicating that you should select a different key sequence for your macro.

Both

15.32 Trick: You can execute a project file from a macro.

Because the execution of a project file can be represented by a series of keystrokes, you can initiate a project file from a macro. (In Smart 3.10, however, you cannot execute a macro from a project file.) To execute a project file from a macro, include the quick key F8, followed by the project name and a carriage return. Although you may be tempted to include the cursor keystrokes to select the project from the pop-up menu, the position of the project names in the menu change if you try to add a new project file, and you would have to change the macro.

Both

15.33 Trick: Use a macro to pass arguments to a project file.

By including within a macro the arguments entered on the execution line of a project file, you can simulate the passing of arguments—the keystrokes of the responses are queued in the computer's input buffer.

For example, the following Smart 3.10 macro passes two arguments to the project file called HEFF:

```
F8HEFFCrMTCCrFl1ACr
```

This macro is explained as follows:

F8	Execute
HEFF	Name of project file
Cr	Enter
MTC	Response to first prompt
Cr	Enter
Fl1A	Response to second prompt
Cr	Enter

You must remember to include carriage returns (represented by Cr) in the macro.

The following is the same macro in SmartWare II:

```
F8,"heff",enter,"i","mtc",enter,"Fl1a",enter
```

15.34 Tip: Use Alt-Z or Alt-Y in your Smart 3.10 Word Processor or Spreadsheet macros to alternate between Command and Enter modes. Use these keys in any module in SmartWare II.

Both

So that you can execute a macro from either Command or Enter mode, you should include an Alt-Z in your macro to return to Command mode or an Alt-Y to return to Enter mode. Inserting one of these quick keys at the beginning of your macro spares you from having to remember to switch modes manually with the Esc key before executing the macro. You also can use these keys in the middle of a macro if you need to alternate between modes.

If Smart is already in Command mode when the system encounters the Alt-Z, the key sequence has no effect.

15.35 Tip: Use the following macro to avoid having to specify "In-Memory" each time you execute a project file.

SW II

```
Alt-Z,F8,Until,Enter,"I"
```

The macro displays a pop-up window showing the names of your project files. Select the file you want and press Enter. A good key for this macro is Shift-F8.

15.36 Tip: Use multiple quotation marks in a macro to enclose a string in quotes.

SW II

The following macro enters the string "St. Louis" (including the quotes) in a spreadsheet cell:

```
Alt-Y,"""""St. Louis""",Enter,Alt-Z
```

All literals in macros must be contained within quotation marks.

15.37 Trick: Include comments in your macros so that other people know what they do.

SW II

The usage and purpose of a macro can be documented if you use a comment. Text enclosed within quotation marks between two COMMENT words in the macro is ignored and may help explain the macro. Use comments sparingly, however, because they consume RAM memory. The following macro may be used in the Word Processor module to unload and erase the current document.

```
Comment,"UNLOAD AND ERASE CURRENT DOCUMENT",Comment,
Alt-Z,Alt-X,Right,Right,Right,Right,Right,"un",Enter,Alt-X,
"tools ",Repeat,#5,Right,Repeat,#6,Del,
"erase",^Right,Bs,".*""",Enter,"fl"
```

If you use this macro, make sure you do not execute any other command after you load the document, and make sure your insert key is On.

SW II

15.38 Tip: You cannot record a macro while in the Suspend mode from a project file.

You get the following error message:

```
Remember not allowed while project executing or sus-
pended
```

You can create a macro by editing it and typing entries from the keyboard, but you cannot record the keystrokes.

SW II

15.39 Tip: You can include macro control terms in macros as well as in the Keys statement in project processing. The control terms give you additional control over the operation of your macro.

For example, you can include Until,Enter in a macro:

```
F8,Until,Enter,"i"
```

The macro pauses until you press Enter. You can type any other keystroke, but when you press Enter, the Enter key is processed and the macro continues. This macro also may be used to execute a project file in-memory. Until you press Enter, you may move the cursor to the name of the project file you want, or you may type the name.

SW II

15.40 Trick: When editing a macro, single-digit user entries (text or numbers) do not have to be enclosed within quotation marks. If the text is longer than one digit, however, you *must* use quotation marks.

If you create the following macro, for example, you can save the macro without an error message:

```
"tpd",down,up,1,Enter,F10
```

When you view the macro, you find that the macro has been transformed into:

```
"tpd",down,up,"1",Enter,F10
```

Notice that the quotation marks have been added around the user text "1". If the value had been 10 instead of 1, however, the following error message would have appeared:

```
Unrecognizable character at line 1 column 15
```

15.41 Trap: When repeating a number of keystrokes in a macro, if you forget to use the pound sign (#) before the number of repetitions, the number is interpreted as an ASCII character value. *SW II*

The format to use when you want to repeat a number of keystrokes is the following:

```
Repeat,#n,keystroke
```

Here, the n is the number of times to repeat, and keystroke is the actual keystroke to repeat. For example, if you want to perform 8 down arrows, the macro is:

```
Repeat,#8,down
```

The ASCII value of the number 8 is 56.

Zooming Windows

15.42 Tip: Create a macro to advance easily from window to window when working with the Word Processor or Spreadsheet. *3.10*

Unlike the Data Base Manager, these two modules require that you first unzoom your screen before you can go to a new window or use Alt-F7 or Alt-F8 to change windows. The following macro accomplishes the task for you:

```
F7Alt-F8F7
```

This macro performs the unzoom, advances to the next window, and zooms again. You can use the Ctrl-F7 and Ctrl-F8 keys as the macro keys for this formula.

15.43 Tip: Press Alt-X to display the most recent command. The command is displayed on the second command line. *Both*

You can use Alt-X to enable you to check your most recent command. For example, you may need to remind yourself of the name of the index you created. You also can edit the command and press Enter to issue the command again.

Even if you are in the middle of building a new command, you can press Alt-X to display the previous command. Press the Esc key to resume building your new command, or press Enter to execute the command displayed by the Alt-X.

Functions

3.10

15.44 Trick: The three bit evaluation functions BITAND, BITOR, and BITXOR are available in Smart 3.10 as well as SmartWare II—they are not documented in Smart 3.10, however.

These three functions compare the two numeric arguments on a bit-by-bit basis, yielding a number whose binary makeup is derived from the following set of rules.

BITAND

The resulting bit is 1 if the corresponding bits of the argument numbers are both 1.

BITOR

The resulting bit is 1 if either of the corresponding bits of the argument numbers is 1.

BITXOR

The result is 1 if one and only one of the corresponding bits of the argument numbers is 1. The result is 0 if both bits are the same, either 1 or 0.

Figure 15.2 demonstrates the use of these three functions.

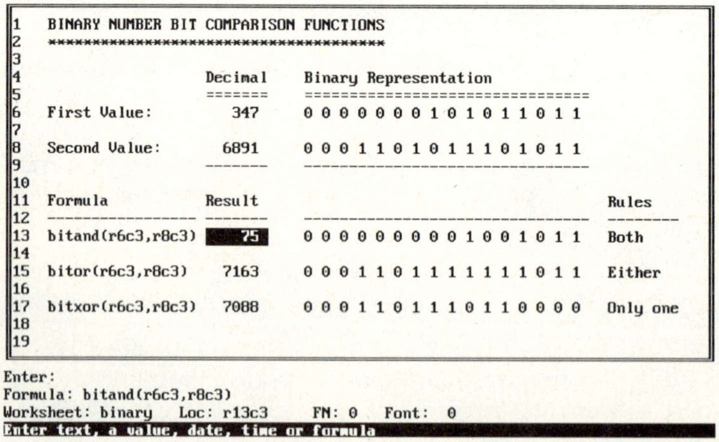

Fig. 15.2.
Binary number bit comparison functions.

```
1    BINARY NUMBER BIT COMPARISON FUNCTIONS
2    **************************************
3
4                          Decimal    Binary Representation
5                          =======    ===============================
6    First Value:            347      0 0 0 0 0 0 0 1 0 1 0 1 1 0 1 1
7
8    Second Value:          6891      0 0 0 1 1 0 1 0 1 1 1 0 1 0 1 1
9                          -------    -------------------------------
10
11   Formula               Result                                         Rules
12   -------------------   -------    -------------------------------    --------
13   bitand(r6c3,r8c3)        75      0 0 0 0 0 0 0 0 0 1 0 0 1 0 1 1    Both
14
15   bitor(r6c3,r8c3)       7163      0 0 0 1 1 0 1 1 1 1 1 1 1 0 1 1    Either
16
17   bitxor(r6c3,r8c3)      7088      0 0 0 1 1 0 1 1 1 0 1 1 0 0 0 0    Only one
18
19
Enter:
Formula: bitand(r6c3,r8c3)
Worksheet: binary   Loc: r13c3     FN: 0   Font:  0
Enter text, a value, date, time or formula
```

SW II

15.45 Trick: By using a negative number, you can represent a date before January 1st, 1900.

The smallest number that can be used is -657,435, which represents January 1st in the year 100. Date chronology this far back is somewhat inexact, however, due to the adoption of the Gregorian calendar by the British Empire on 9/15/1752. If you are tracking dates after this time, however, you may accurately use negative numbers.

15.46 Tip: Use a combination of the ISERR, DATE2, and LEN functions to check for a valid date. *3.10*

If you prompt for a date, you cannot always be sure the date is valid. This technique helps you guarantee that the entry is a valid date:

```
label askdate
input text1 Enter your birthdate:

if iserr(date2(text1)) = 1 or len(text1) < 6\
or val(text1) = 0
     beep
     message Bad Date ...
     jump askdate
endif
```

This technique is shorter, but not as foolproof as the ISDATE project file in Chapter 14.

15.47 Trap: Using the ADDMONTHS function yields unusual results if the months vary in length. *Both*

Consider the following examples:

```
addmonths("12/31/87",-1) = 11/30/87

addmonths("2/29/88",-1) = 1/29/88
```

If you go back to a short month from a long month, the function yields the highest day possible. But if you go back from a short month to a long month, the day of the month remains the same.

15.48 Tip: The EXACT function works with numeric cells, contrary to the documentation. *SW II*

The purpose of the EXACT function is to determine if two strings are identical:

```
exact(r4c1,r4c2)
```

the result of the function is 1 if the cells are equal and 0 if they are not. This function operates correctly on text and numeric fields and cells.

15.49 Tip: Use the FILE function to check for the use of device driver names in effect. *SW II*

The format is:

```
file("\dev\drivername")
```

This function returns 1 if the driver name is in effect or 0 if the driver name is not in effect. If you are using Quarterdeck's QEMM386, for example, you can check for its use by the following:

```
file("\dev\QEMM386$")
```

Other device names you can check for are:

EMMXXXX0	(expanded memory in effect)
@!NETW!@	(Novell NetWare)

Several utility programs on the market display other DOS device names in use on your own computer.

SW II

15.50 Tip: Use the File function to check for the existence of a subdirectory.

The following command returns 1 if the subdirectory "Dallas" exists:

```
file("c:\dallas\nul")
```

If the subdirectory does not exist, the function returns 0. Note, however, that this technique does not work on a Novell network.

SW II

15.51 Trap: The arguments to the FORMAT function are case-sensitive.

To specify a date, for example, the elements of the date must be lowercase:

```
format("7/21/89","Dmm/dd/yy") = 07/21/89
```

The following example uses uppercase:

```
format("7/21/89","DMM/DD/YY") = MM/DD/YY
```

The data type letter "D" may be in either upper- or lowercase.

SW II

15.52 Trick: To specify a comma as a thousands separator in the FORMAT function, you also must specify the precision.

For example:

```
format(10000,"2,r10") = 10,000.00
```

The arguments indicate that the number is to have 2 digits to the right of the decimal, a comma as a thousands separator, and right-justified in a field width of 10. However, consider the following example:

```
format(10000,",r10") = 10000
```

In this example, the thousands separator is ignored when the precision is not specified.

SW II

15.53 Tip: The GETFNAMES function provides a limit of 1,000 characters to text, but it is possible to exceed this limit without warning.

Partial file names are not included, so the total number of characters may be less than this limit. If the text exceeds this limit, no error message or other warning is provided.

15.54 Trick: Use the INT function to round a non-integer value up to the next highest integer by converting the argument to a negative number.

Both

The INT function normally is used to return the integer value of a number with decimal digits. For example:

```
INT(5.1) = 5
```

If you have a situation in which you want to always return the *next higher* integer, however, you can use the INT function of the negative number:

```
-1*INT(-1*5.1) = 6
```

Although the formula INT(5.1) + 1 will work in this case, you get the wrong answer if the argument already is an integer:

```
INT(5) + 1 = 6
```

Be careful not to use the @INT function because the functions round negative numbers differently:

```
@INT(-5.1) = -5
```

15.55 Trap: The ISDATE function returns 1 even if the argument is blank, null, or zero, indicating a valid date.

SW II

Use the following project file to prompt for a date:

```
local $date
clear $date

     while isdate($date) = 0 or val($date) = 0
          screen shortinput $date "Enter date:"
end while
```

15.56 Trap: The PHONEX function cannot be relied upon to distinguish between homonyms or even between some words that are similar.

SW II

The function generates a code that can be used to determine if words sound alike. However, consider the following examples:

Word	*Phonex Code*
right	15000
write	3992
rite	15040
write	3992
wrote	3992
rote	15040
rot	15040
rite	15040

Both

15.57 Tip: The PROPER function capitalizes the first letter of a word following a dash, but not other special characters.

Text	*Proper Conversion*
break-in	Break-In
(fifth floor)	(fifth Floor)
arms&legs	Arms&legs
arms+legs	Arms+legs
"jules"	"jules"

SW II

15.58 Tip: The undocumented function SPSYMMAP returns special characters used throughout the SmartWare II system.

The arguments to the function are numbers in the range 0-64. Figure 15.3 displays these characters.

The types of symbols are paragraph marks, tabs, mail-merge characters, keep marks, and so on.

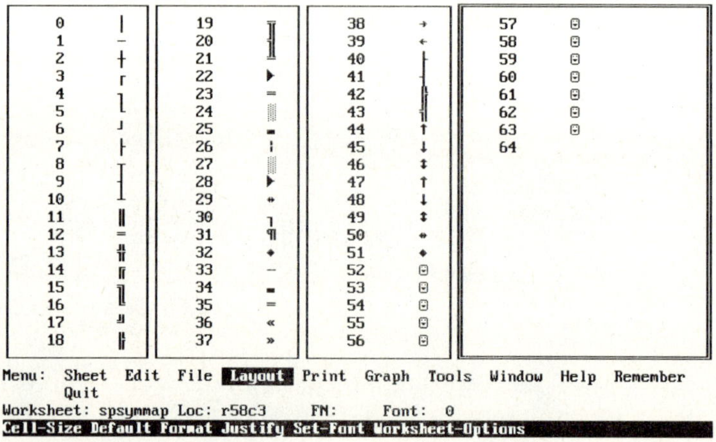

```
Menu:  Sheet  Edit  File  Layout  Print  Graph  Tools  Window  Help  Remember
       Quit
Worksheet: spsymmap Loc: r58c3     FN:     Font:  0
Cell-Size Default Format Justify Set-Font Worksheet-Options
```

Fig. 15.3. *SPSYMMAP function characters.*

Both

15.59 Trap: On some computers, the TIME function occasionally generates an invalid time.

This problem does not occur on all computers, so you can test yours with the following project file:

```
while minutes(time) > minutes("05:")
    screen print 5 10 7 0 time
end while
```

Occasionally, the TIME function generates a time with seconds of 60, as in 10:17:60. This really should be 10:18:00. The MINUTES function does not accept this invalid format and yields the following error message:

```
Bad time
```

If you have a project file that is waiting for a specific hour, the solution is to use either left(time,3) or left(time,6), as in the following:

```
while minutes(left(time,3)) > minutes("05:")
```

When you use either of these left functions, the seconds are ignored.

15.60 Tip : Use the TRIM function to drop multiple blanks from not only the beginning and end of a string, but also from the middle. *SW II*

The following function:

```
trim("   Spaghetti     and      Meatballls    ")
```

yields:

```
"Spaghetti and Meatballs"
```

The PrtSc Key

15.61 Trap: Make sure you have access to your printer. *3.10*

If you don't have a printer and accidentally hit the Shift-Print Screen key sequence, you risk freezing your machine, having to reboot, and losing data in RAM. In the Spreadsheet and Word Processor modules, you lose the work you had devoted to the current worksheets or documents. In the Data Base Manager, if you have to reboot the system, you can lose your Updates and newly Entered records. The file itself also could be damaged.

Fonts

15.62 Tip: Copy any newly rasterized fonts from your home subdirectory into the system subdirectory for more widespread usage. *SW II*

When you use the Tools New-Font command to create a rasterized font file, the file is not written automatically to the system subdirectory—the file goes into your home subdirectory. If you want to use this font file within applications started from other subdirectories, or if you are on a network and want to share the font file, copy the file to the system subdirectory.

The Communications Module

Several tips and tricks relating to the Smart Communications module are contained in this section.

Both

15.63 Trap: Don't run memory-resident programs that access time-dependent interrupts; communications timing problems can occur.

Some memory-resident programs that access time-dependent interrupts cause problems with Smart's Communications module. Examples include programs that create clock displays and some implementations of "turbo speed" software.

Both

15.64 Tip: Use Esc or F3 to switch between Command mode and Terminal mode.

To execute just one command, press Esc to display the command list. Smart returns to Terminal mode as soon as you execute the command. If you want to execute several commands in succession, press F3. After you finish executing your commands, press F3 again to return to Terminal mode.

Both

15.65 Tip: If you want Smart to answer an incoming call, set the switches on your modem so that auto answer is Off.

Because the Communications module answers incoming calls through software rather than relying on the modem's inherent hardware facilities, you should set your modem's auto answer switch to Off so that the modem doesn't answer the call. Smart then can perform that task.

3.10

15.66 Tip: The Communications module no longer supports the Border command.

Because of the addition of the VT100 and VT52 terminal emulation modes, the capability to remove the border from the Communications module's windows has been dropped.

Both

15.67 Tip: No DOS MODE command is needed because the Smart Communications module writes directly to the serial port and doesn't go through DOS.

Smart writes directly to the hardware, so a computer that differs greatly from the IBM PC configuration may not work well with the Communications module, even though the computer may be running MS-DOS.

3.10

15.68 Trap: Don't confuse the two types of keyboard-redefinition commands in the Communications module: Keyboard Macros and Macros.

The macros you define and use at the command level of the Communications module work just like macros in any other module. You can define a set of keystrokes to be issued when you press a defined key sequence. You cannot use these macros, however, if Smart is in terminal mode. When working in this mode, you must use Keyboard Macros, which are defined on command list 2. In a Keyboard Macro, you define a set of keystrokes that are sent over the communications line instead of controlling local system operation.

3.10

15.69 Trick: To send a carriage return without a line feed, use the CHR function to establish a user-defined variable.

When using the output statement, you usually send a carriage return and line feed at the end of the line. You can suppress these characters by placing a semicolon at the end of the line. If you want to send only a carriage return, define a user-defined variable:

```
$cr = chr(13)
```

Your output line then can be as follows:

```
output "text";$cr;
```

Capturing and Storing Data

15.70 Trap: When using the Data Get Line Variable command to store the result of data sent with the Data Output command, a carriage return is appended to the variable. *SW II*

If you look at the contents of the variable in the calculator, you see a symbol that is a single musical note with an open flag. This is the representation of a carriage return character—ASCII 13. The carriage return character does not create a problem if you are using the Data Match command. If you must compare the contents of the variable to another variable or text, however, you will have to strip off this extraneous character:

```
let $code = left($code,len($code)-1)
```

15.71 Tip: You do not need to erase an existing file if you are receiving a file and want to keep the same name. *SW II*

The Data Receive command overlays an existing file without an error. You do not need to use the Tools File Erase command prior to receiving a data file.

15.72 Tip: If the capture buffer becomes full, the screen displays the error message `Out of Memory`. You must save and clear the buffer to continue capturing to it. *Both*

Even though you save the buffer contents to a file, you still must perform the extra step of clearing the buffer. Saving the buffer doesn't clear the buffer automatically.

15.73 Tip: If you frequently experience a buffer-full situation, capture the output directly to a file rather than to the buffer. *Both*

If you have enough disk space, you don't have to stop periodically to save the buffer to a file and then clear the buffer. Your communications process won't be much slower because the process of writing to a hard disk generally is considerably faster than the process of receiving information over communications lines.

15.74 Tip: Capture information to a buffer so that you can review the terminal session. *Both*

After capturing information to a buffer, you can view the buffer contents on-line, reviewing what may have scrolled across your screen too quickly to read. Initiate the process of capturing to the buffer by executing the Capture Buffer Begin (Smart 3.10) command or Data Capture Buffer Begin (SmartWare II) command. Capture Buffer View enables you to look at the buffer contents while you still are connected to the remote computer. You can use the F5 key to toggle the capturing on and off. For a quick view of the buffer contents, use Alt-V.

3.10

15.75 Trap: Repeated use of the Capture File Begin command may overlay the contents of a file. Use the F7 toggle key to append information to an existing file.

When you press F7 the first time, Smart prompts you for the file name. Press F7 again, and Smart suspends the capturing of information. When you want to resume, press F7. The information is appended to the existing file.

With Smart in command mode, however, you run the risk of overlaying your original file contents because the Capture Buffer Begin File command asks for a file name, even on repeated execution. Smart destroys the original file contents if you provide the same file name. If you press Enter, the most recent capture file is appended.

In SmartWare II, if you begin capturing to a file that already exists, you have the option to overwrite or append to the file.

SW II

15.76 Trap: If you append to an existing file with the Capture Buffer Save command and an end-of-file (EOF) mark appears at the end of the file, the new data is inaccessible.

When you use the Capture Buffer Save command and append to an existing file that has an EOF mark, the new buffer information is written *following* the EOF mark. Although the new data is actually written to the file, you are not able to use the data because the EOF mark is interpreted by DOS as the end of file, and nothing after that will be processed by a program, or even the DOS TYPE command. To append to an existing file, use the Capture File command.

Dialing the Modem

Both

15.77 Tip: Dialing your modem requires that the sum of the number of data bits and parity bits be at least 8.

If you establish your Settings at 7 data bits and no parity, your modem's Dial function doesn't work, although the system appears to be dialing.

3.10

15.78 Trap: If you establish your settings as seven data bits without any parity, communications appear to proceed, but in fact nothing happens.

You must specify a parity setting if there are fewer than eight data bits. If you don't, the system may appear to be working correctly, but nothing happens. And no error message appears to tell you that something is wrong.

15.79 Trick: You can use the Communications module's Dial (Smart 3.10) or Connection Dial (SmartWare II) command as an automatic dialer for voice communications. *Both*

Use the Voice option to initiate a call for voice communications. If the phone number is busy, the number of redial attempts is governed by a setting in your profile.

15.80 Trick: Use the Goto (Smart 3.10) or Set-Terminal Goto (SmartWare II) command to switch between Carrier and Voice communications to talk to or communicate with the distant party. *Both*

You may need to talk to the individual on the other end of the line before you begin data transmission. Select Voice as the Dial option to engage in voice communications. After you finish talking, use the Goto Carrier command to initiate data communications. Both parties must execute this command at the same time.

15.81 Trick: Edit the Param6 file to switch on the debug capabilities of the Communications module. *3.10*

Change the last character of the Param6 file from 0 to 1 to turn on the Communications module's debug facility. As you dial a call, four lines appear on-screen:

Line	*Meaning*
1:	Codes sent by Smart to the Modem
2:	What Smart expects to receive back from the Modem
3:	Actual characters returned from the modem
4:	The wait time in hundredths of seconds

Figure 15.4 shows a sample display of this Debug mode.

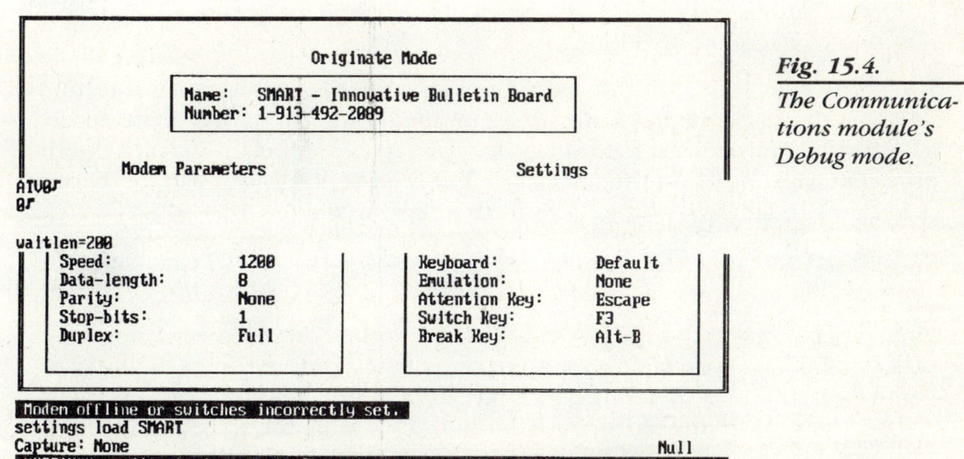

Fig. 15.4.

The Communications module's Debug mode.

When you edit the Param6 file, make sure you don't introduce an extra carriage return at the end of the file. After you track down all your communications problems, reset the final character in the Param6 file to 0. You must quit and re-enter the Communications module for the change to the Param6 file to be recognized. The Param6 file is read only upon initiation of the module.

In SmartWare II, to create this same display, select *yes* for the selection Display Modem Commands/Results in the Tools Preferences Communications menu.

Both

15.82 Trap: The Communications settings revert to a Null Modem configuration if editing the settings is unsuccessful. If the Null Modem is selected when you dial, the already connected error message appears.

If a hardware configuration prevents your modem from being properly initialized, the selection reverts to the default of 1 (null modem). When you try to dial, the already connected error message appears because the null modem is in effect. Correct the hardware problem, and edit your settings again to select the correct modem.

Using Files in Communications

Both

15.83 Trick: Use a Format definition to reformat a multiple-record file into a single record.

To select specific fields from a file for input into another module, you can use a Format definition with the Send command (Data Send in SmartWare II) in the Communications module. You also can create a physical record from multiple records appearing in repeating groups in the source file.

In the Communications Module, the Format command (Data Format in SmartWare II) can be used to change a data file that has been transmitted to you and to restructure the file for use in the Database. Even if you are not using Communications, this feature can be used to change the structure of external files that you acquire on a disk.

Use of this capability is not restricted to files received over a communications link; you can use a file from any source as the input. Therefore, if you receive a file in ASCII format that looks like a "report," you may be able to pick out the important data by using the Format definitions. You also can use the Format definitions to create multiple lines from one source line.

Both

15.84 Trick: Use the Fread and Fwrite project-processing commands to supplement the use of formats when translating ASCII files.

If the repetition within a file is consistent, the Format definition enables you to pick out the fields you want to send to one of the other modules. If, however, you have extra lines (headings, footings, and so on), you may not be able to isolate them with the Format definition. By using the Fread and Fwrite commands within a project file, you can Fread each line from a source file, examine its contents, and Fwrite the line to a destination file if you want to keep the line. If you want to discard a line, Fread the next line without writing the unneeded line.

Profiles and Settings

15.85 Tip: If you don't have access to your modem, use the Profile Define command rather than the Settings Edit command to prevent the definition from reverting to the null-modem condition. *3.10*

The Profile Define command enables you to establish your settings without actually loading them for execution. The effect is similar to that of using the Settings Edit command, but some settings are not saved if the modem is not ready when Settings Edit is exited. Specifically, the modem type defaults to 1 (Null Modem). If you access your modem later and try to load these settings, you get the message `Already connected`—and you wonder why (see Trap 15.25).

15.86 Tip: Include the drive and subdirectory path when defining the modem in your terminal settings. *SW II*

Although a list of available modems is displayed when you press the F6 and is inserted into the menu when you press Enter, this is not sufficient for proper operation. When you attempt to load the settings, you get the following error message:

```
Modem definition not found. Check pathname and/or Modem name.
```

To prevent this problem, follow these steps while still creating the definition. After the modem name has been inserted into the definition menu, move the cursor to the right and into the field. Now type the drive and path of the subdirectory in which SmartWare II is installed. For example, you might use the following text to precede the modem definition:

```
c:\smartii\
```

The entire modem definition would look like this for a Hayes, 2400 baud modem:

```
c:\smartii\cmmodem Hayes 2400
```

Now press Enter to finish and F10 to save your work.

15.87 Tip: Use the Settings Save command to retain any changes you made to a communications definition. The changes are not saved automatically when you leave the Communications module. *3.10*

You expect settings changes to be saved for you when you Quit the Communications module, because spreadsheet and word processing document changes are saved for you when you leave those modules. This is not true, however. You must explicitly save the Settings changes if you want to retain them.

Both

15.88 Tip: Specify a prompt character if you want your computer to wait for a prompt before transmitting the next line.

If you should not transmit until the remote computer issues a prompt character, you can specify the prompt within the Settings menu. You can enter multiple characters and even nonprinting characters, using the ASCII decimal representation preceded by a backslash. For example, suppose that the ready symbol and the prompt of the remote system are

```
;
C>
```

Your prompt specification would appear as shown in figure 15.5.

Fig. 15.5.

A prompt specification.

```
Communication Profile
   Select Character Delay: 0
      0) No Delay
      1) Wait for Echo
      #) Delay Time in 1/10 seconds
   Select Line Delay: 0
      0) No Delay
      1) Wait for CR
      2) Wait for User
      3) Wait for Prompt
      #) Delay Time in 1/10 seconds
→     Prompt to wait for: ;\13\10C>
   End of File delay time (seconds): 360
```

Both

15.89 Tip: Because no provision is provided for creating a settings definition similar to an existing definition, copy an existing definition to create one like it.

Using the Tools File Copy command (SmartWare II) or File Copy (3.10), copy one of your existing communications definitions to a new name, and then edit the definition for the changes you need to make. Remember that the file extension of a communications definition file is UCP.

Emulating VT100 and VT52 Terminals

3.10

15.90 Trap: The definition files for the VT100 and VT52 terminals must be available in your Smart subdirectory, even though you don't use them.

When you install Smart, these definition files are copied automatically into your subdirectory. If you decide to erase them, an error message appears for each file as you initiate the Communications module. Because your computer searches for these files, starting the Communications module takes longer if they aren't present. But otherwise, not having these files causes no harm.

15.91 Tip: If you need to operate in the traditional half-duplex mode, establish your settings as Full Duplex with Forced Local Echo to avoid potential communications problems. *3.10*

Smart Communications' Half Duplex setting enables you to use your computer as a half-duplex host machine. If you specify Half Duplex mode for communication with a half-duplex computer at the other end, the echo may cause unspecified results—some remote machines accept this with no problem, however. You are better off selecting Full Duplex with the Forced Local Echo if you need to communicate in half duplex.

15.92 Trap: Select Xon/Xoff protocol for emulating the ANSI, VT100, VT102, or VT52 terminals to prevent the remote computer from sending characters faster than your computer can receive them. *Both*

The Xon/Xoff protocol should be used when your system should send (and the other system can recognize) an Xoff character, which indicates that transmission should cease until your system can catch up. An Xon character then initiates further transmission. When using the special terminal emulations, you must select this option in your settings.

15.93 Trap: In VT100 emulation mode, use F5 rather than F3 to toggle between Command mode and Terminal mode. *Both*

Usually, you press the F3 key to toggle to Terminal mode. Because F3 has a special function in VT100 emulation, however, you must use F5 to switch back and forth between Terminal and Command mode.

15.94 Tip: Use the Transfer-Time command to determine how long file transmission takes (see fig. 15.6). In SmartWare II, the command is Data Xfer-Time. *Both*

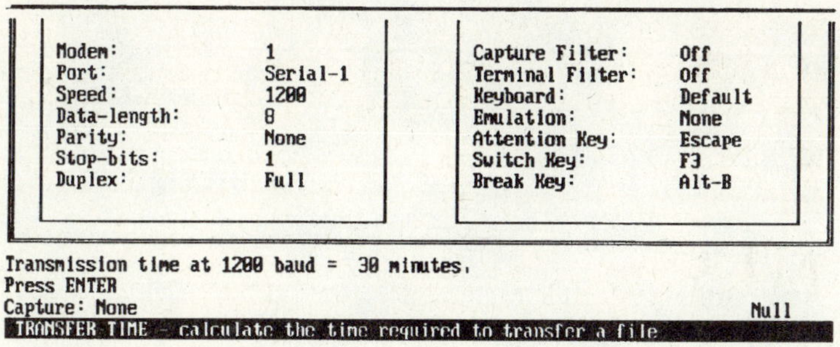

```
Modem:          1                 Capture Filter:   Off
Port:           Serial-1          Terminal Filter:  Off
Speed:          1200              Keyboard:         Default
Data-length:    8                 Emulation:        None
Parity:         None              Attention Key:    Escape
Stop-bits:      1                 Switch Key:       F3
Duplex:         Full              Break Key:        Alt-B

Transmission time at 1200 baud =  30 minutes.
Press ENTER
Capture: None                                               Null
TRANSFER TIME - calculate the time required to transfer a file
```

Fig. 15.6.
The transfer-time message.

By measuring the file size against the current baud rate, the system can determine how long file transmission will take. You may decide that sending the file on a disk by mail or courier service would be less expensive, depending on the urgency of the situation and the cost of the long-distance call. Remember, too, that if the telephone line is noisy, as is more likely to happen over long distances, the Xmodem protocol may have to perform multiple transmissions for each block.

Database Project Files

Appendix A contains several useful project files that you can use when developing applications or that demonstrate important points mentioned in the chapters on the Database.

Project Files To Delete All Records from a Database

The following project files will delete all records from a database. The first version is for Smart 3.10, and the second is for SmartWare II.

Smart 3.10:

```
'procedure will save screens in the .dbs file
'assumes that the file is loaded

%1 ENTER DATABASE FILE NAME:

unload file %1
let %2 = "%1"|".DB"
let %3 = "%1"|".DBS"

file rename %2 to KILL.DB
file rename %3 to KILL.DBS

activate kill screen standard
create file %1 fixed-length no-password matching file kill

unload file KILL
unload file %1

file erase KILL.DB
file erase %3
file rename KILL.DBS to %3
```

```
load %1 screen standard
beep 2
wait 60 All Records Have Been Deleted...
```

SmartWare II:

```
local $file
file unload all
tools file erase "kill.*"
screen shortinput $file "Database name:"

file create "kill" similar standard-view $file no-password
keys "rd",Enter,"kill",Enter,"fn",F10

file unload all
tools file erase $file|".db"
tools file rename "kill.db" to $file|".db"
if file($file|".key") = 1
     tools file erase $file|".key"
     tools file rename "kill.key" to $file|".key"
end if

file load standard-view $file|".vws"

beep 2
wait 60 "All Records Have Been Deleted from "|$file
```

Project File To Find and Change a Date in a Smart 3.10 Report Heading

```
label askfile
%1 Enter Name of report file
let %2 = "%1"|".dfr"
if file(%2) = 1 then jump okfile
beep 2
message File < %2 > does not exist ... press any key ..
jump askfile

label okfile
fopen "%2" as 1
let %3 = 0

label askdate1
input $nowdate Enter Existing Date in file:
if days($nowdate) = 0 then jump askdate1
let $nowdate = date2($nowdate)

label askseek
let %3 = %3 + 1
if %3 < 2000 then jump noteof
beep 3
message End of file at < %3 > ... press any key ...
jump alldone
```

```
label noteof
fseek 1 %3
fread 1 length 8 into $date
if $date = $nowdate then jump askdate2
jump askseek

label askdate2
input $newdate Enter a new date to place in file
let %5 = $newdate
if days($newdate) > 0 then jump writit
message You Entered < %5 > .. check entry ..
jump askdate2

label writit
fseek 1 %3
fwrite 1 length 8 from date2($newdate)
fseek 1 %3
fread 1 length 8 into $date
let %4 = $date
message New date is < %4 > ... press any key
message Seek position is < %3 > ... press any key

label alldone
fclose 1
```

Forcing Generation of a New Form in a Smart 3.10 Combination Report

If you absolutely must have a form at the top of the page of a combination report, even if the table overflows onto successive pages, here is a way to create the report.

The trick relies on—you guessed it—good old Alt-255, which prints a blank on my printer but is not recognized as being different from any other printing character by the Smart Database. Smart does not treat the Alt-255 as a blank.

You need two additional fields; let's take the Dept field as the example in this case. In my detail Personnel file, in addition to the regular DEPT field, which is alphanumeric and four bytes wide, I have a five-byte alpha field called SUPDEP. Data is entered into this field in the following project file.

In my Department file I have, in addition to the regular DEPT field, a five-byte field that contains the four characters of the Department, plus an additional character that is either blank or Alt-255. There are two records in the Department file for each department; one has the trailing blank in the extra field, and the other has the trailing Alt-255. It is this extra field that is used as a key to order the file for the reporting.

The trick is to enter into the SUPDEP field in the detail file the DEPT code, followed by either a trailing blank or a trailing Alt-255. In my project file, the first page of detail data has a trailing blank; the next page has a trailing Alt-255. By specifying the maximum number of lines I want to allow on a page (I set mine at 40), I can test whether the page is full and change the trailing character.

Of course, if the actual DEPT field changes, then the first four characters of the SUBDEP field change, as does the trailing character.

You will see that I sort the data before generating the SUBDEP field to make sure that all like departments are grouped together. Within each department, you can sort by any additional fields you want.

Subtotals on your report can be at either the end of the page level (when you break on SUBDEP) or at the real department level. If you want to break on just the real department, you have to include that field in the table, of course. If you want to hide the DEPT field, refer to my suggestions in Chapter 6.

This method of forcing page breaks and form generation is awkward and time-consuming. However, if you need the capability, this is one way of solving a current shortcoming of the Smart Database's reporting facility:

```
'force page breaks to display form

sort predefined dept index ind1 'dept order
order index ind1
goto record rec-number 1

let $dept = [dept]                'initialization
let $maxline =  40                'max lines/page
let $linecount  = 0
let $blank = "  "                 'blank
let $alt255 = " "                 'Alt-255
let $break = $blank

label newrec
if [dept] <> $dept then call newpage
if $linecount = $maxline then call newpage
let $linecount = $linecount + 1
let [subdep] = [dept]|$break
if record = records then jump alldone
goto record next
jump newrec

procedure newpage
let $dept = [dept]
let $linecount = 0
if $break = $blank
        let $break = $alt255
else
        let $break = $blank
endif
return
```

```
label alldone

link 2 field [subdep]
report print deptrep printer
```

Series of Smart 3.10 Project Files To Construct and Execute a Query

The following project files demonstrate a method of developing Query definitions entirely from menus. A new user could answer the prompts to have the Query developed but know nothing about the structure of the Query itself.

Project File 1

This first project file is the primary "driver" for the series:

```
'primary project file
quiet on
goto window 1
goto file applicant screen AP1

execute qdev in-memory
query predefined qdev index ind1
if cerror <> 3003 then jump okq
beep 2
message No Applicants Match Your Search     ... press any key
jump alldone

label okq
order index ind1
print file report [2;3;4;5;6;1;17;14] printer

label alldone
order key [ssn]
quiet off
```

Project File 2

The following project begins the development of the Query definition and executes each of the subordinate projects. Note that the file QDEV.DFQ is opened as the output file; this is the Query definition file. Observe also that the tilde characters must be inserted in the definition file to mark carriage returns.

```
'qdev   project file.

if file("qdev.dfq") = 1 then file erase     qdev.dfq

fopen "qdev.dfq" as 1fseek 0
fseek 0
```

```
fwrite 1 from "not (deleted) and~"
fwrite 1 from "([status] = "|chr(34)|" "|chr(34)|"~"
fwrite 1 from " or [status] = null) ~"
fwrite 1 from " and (days(today) - days([appdate]) <= 60 ) and ~"

label begin

execute fldsel in-memory
fwrite 1 from $fldsel

execute relation in-memory
fwrite 1 from $rel

execute value in-memory
fwrite 1 from $value

execute logic in-memory
  if $logic <> "done"
          fwrite 1 from $logic
                  jump begin
endif

close 1
```

Project File 3

The following project file is used to select the fields to be used in the Query. Note that a menu of the fields is provided to the user.

```
'fldsel project file. field selection.

label begin
clear $choice
menu clear 7 0
menu print 1 31 9 0 FIELD SELECTION
menu print 2 31 9 0 ---------------

menu print 4 10 9 0 1    SSN                2 Last Name          3 First
menu print 5 10 9 0 4     MI                5 Sex                6 Race
menu print 6 10 9 0 7    Birth Date         8 Address1           9 Address2
menu print 7 10 9 0 10   City               11 State             12 Zip
menu print 8 10 9 0 13   Phone              14 Date Applied      15 Source
menu print 9 10 9 0 16   Location Apply     17 Job Wanted        18 Not Wanted
menu print 10 10 9 0 19 Recent Job          20 Nearest Location  21 Relatives
menu print 11 10 9 0 22 Prior Employment23 Monday Start          24 Monday End
menu print 12 10 9 0 25 Tue Start           26 Tuesday End       27 Wed. Start
menu print 13 10 9 0 28 Wed Start           29 Thurs Start       30 Thurs End
menu print 14 10 9 0 31 Fri Start           32 Friday End        33 Sat. Start
menu print 15 10 9 0 34 Sat. End            35 Sunday Start      36 Sunday End
menu print 16 10 9 0 37 Screening           38 Interviewer       39 2nd Intervw.
menu print 17 10 9 0 40 Date of Hire        41 Job Hired Into    42 Location Hire
menu print 18 10 9 0 43 Status
menu print 20 28 9 0 Enter:
menu input 20 35 9 17 2 $choice
```

```
if $choice < 1 or $choice > 43 then jump begin

let $fldsel = "["|fixed($choice,0)|"] "
```

Project File 4

In this project, the user selects the relational operator to be used. The choices are listed in the menu.

```
'relation selection

'relational operators
label begin
menu clear 7 0
menu DRAW box 2 20 8 59 9 0
menu print 3 29 9 0 RELATIONAL OPERATORS
menu print 5 29 9 0 --------------------

menu print 7 35 9 0
menu print 10 22 9 0 1. EQUAL TO
menu print 11 22 9 0 2. GREATER THAN
menu print 12 22 9 0 3. LESS THAN
menu print 13 22 9 0 4. GREATER THAN OR EQUAL TO
menu print 14 22 9 0 5. LESS THAN OR EQUAL TO
menu print 15 22 9 0 6. NOT EQUAL TO
menu print 16 22 9 0 7. CONTAINS
menu print 17 22 9 0 8. DOES NOT CONTAIN
menu print 18 22 9 0 9. COMPARE, IGNORING CASE
menu print 20 28 9 0 Enter:
menu print 20 35 9 17 1 $choice

if $choice < 1 or $choice > 9 then jump begin

let $rel = case $choice (1,"= ") (2,"> ") (3,"<  ") (4,">= ") \
 (5,"<= ") (6,"<> ") (7,"! ") (8,"!! ") (9,"== ")
```

Project File 5

Value selections are entered in this project.

```
'value selection
label begin
clear $value
menu clear 7 0
menu DRAW box 2 20 8 59 9 0
menu print 3 31 9 0 VALUE SELECTION
menu print 5 31 9 0 ---------------
menu print 7 35 9 0
menu print 10 27 7 0 ENTER VALUE:
menu input 10 40 9 0 10 $value

let $value = chr(34)|$value|chr(34)|" "
```

Project File 6

The logical operators AND or OR are entered in this last project file.

```
'logical operators
label begin
menu clear 7 0
menu DRAW box 2 20 8 59 9 0
menu print 3 32 9 0 LOGICAL OPERATORS
menu print 5 32 9 0 -----------------
menu print 7 35 9 0
menu print 10 22 9 0 1. AND
menu print 11 22 9 0 2. OR
menu print 12 22 9 0 3. No More

menu print 20 28 9 0 Enter:
menu input 20 35 9 17 1 $choice

if $choice < 1 or $choice > 3 then jump begin

let $logic = case $choice (1,"and~ ") (2,"or~ ") (3,"done") else "none

if $logic = "none" then jump begin
```

Project File To Simulate the Browse Command

Smart 3.10:

```
quiet on
let %9 = chr(25)
let %8 = chr(24)

browse fields [1]

label retry
menu clear box 22 1 23 80 0 1 no-border
menu print 22 2 14 1 Enter = select
menu print 22 19 11 1 %8 = prev rec \
     Pg Up = previous screen Ctrl Home = first rec
menu print 23 10 14 1 record
menu print 23 19 11 1 %9 = next rec \
     Pg Dn = next screen Ctrl End = last rec

$key = inchar
if not($key = 18432 or $key = 20480 or $key = 13 or $key = 18688 or \
     $key = 20736 or $key = 30464 or $key = 29952)
  jump retry
endif

if $key = 18432
     goto record previous
     jump retry
```

```
elseif $key = 20480
     goto record next
     jump retry
elseif $key = 18688 and record - 20 > 0
     %0 = record - 20
     goto record rec-number %0
     jump retry
elseif $key = 18688 and record - 20 <= 0
     goto record rec-number 1
     jump retry
elseif $key = 20736 and record +20 <=records
     %0 = record + 20
     goto record rec-number %0
     jump retry
elseif $key = 20736 and record +20 > records
     %0 = records
     goto record rec-number %0
     jump retry
elseif $key = 30464
     goto record rec-number 1
     jump retry
elseif $key = 29952
     %0 = records
     goto record rec-number %0
     jump retry
endif

browse off
```

SmartWare II:

```
'Name:                              Browse
'Purpose:                           Browse a file

PUBLIC $key

LABEL retry
SCREEN CLEAR box 22 1 23 80 0 1 no-border
SCREEN PRINT 22  2 14 1 "Enter = select"
SCREEN PRINT 22 19 11 1 \
    chr(24)|" = prev rec   Pg Up = previous screen  Ctrl Home = first rec"
SCREEN PRINT 23  2 14 1 "F10 = end"
SCREEN PRINT 23 19 11 1 \
    chr(25)|" = next rec   Pg Dn = next screen      Ctrl End  = last  rec"

    $key = inchar

    IF $key = {up}
       DATA GOTO RECORD PREVIOUS
       JUMP retry
  ELSEIF $key = {F10} or $key = {cr}
       JUMP alldone
```

```
  ELSEIF $key = {down}
     DATA GOTO RECORD NEXT
     JUMP retry
  ELSEIF $key = {PgUp}
     suspend
     keys PgUp,F8
     JUMP retry
  ELSEIF $key = {PgDn}
     suspend
     keys PgDn,F8
     JUMP retry
  ELSEIF $key = {^Home}
     suspend
     keys ^Home,F8
     JUMP retry
  ELSEIF $key = {^End}
     suspend
     keys ^End,F8
     JUMP retry
  elseif $key = {right}
     suspend
     keys right,F8
     jump retry
  elseif $key = {left}
     suspend
     keys left,F8
     jump retry
  else
     jump retry
  END IF

  LABEL alldone
```

Project FilesTo Simulate the Find and Data Find Commands

Smart 3.10:

```
quiet on
let $cnt = 0

%1 Enter the information to find:
%2 Select Option: E)qual G)reater-Than L)ess-Than P)artial
%3 Enter Options: I)gnore case W)hole words only

label find

find [first] %2 "%1" options %3

if cerror = 3002 and $cnt = 0 beep
         menu print 22 1 7 0 End of search, data not found \
         press any key
         $nomore = inchar
elseif cerror = 3002
```

```
        beep
        menu print 22 1 7 0 \
             No more occurrences of data, enter any key
   $nomore = inchar
   else
   $cnt = $cnt + 1
   repaint
   beep
   menu print 22 1 7 0 Data found in [first], continue search (y/n)

   label continue
   $found = inchar
     if not($found = 78 or $found = 89 or $found = 110 \
      or $found = 121 )
      jump continue
     endif

   if $found = 78 or $found = 110
   end
   elseif $found = 89 or $found = 121 or record <> records
   repaint off
     goto record next
     jump find
 endif

 endif

 goto record previous
 repaint on
 end
```

Smartware II:

The following is one version of a Data Find project file that is an approximate translation of the Smart 3.10 version:

```
local $cnt $info $choice $type $option $typelist $optionlist
local $found $nomore

clear $cnt
let $typelist      = "Equal Greater-Than Less-Than Partial"
let $optionlist    = "Ignore-case Whole-Words-Only"

screen shortmenu 1 $typelist $choice
let $type = group($typelist,$choice)

screen shortinput $info "Enter the data search item:"
let $info = chr({"})|$info|chr({"})

screen shortmenu 1 $optionlist $choice
let $option = group($optionlist,$choice)
let $option = chr({"})|left($option,1)|chr({"})

 label find
```

```
evaluate ( "data find [first name] "|$type|" "|$info|" options "|$option )

     if cerror = 3716 and $cnt = 0
   beep
   screen print 22 1 7 0 \
        "End of search, data not found - press any key"
         let $nomore = inchar
 elseif cerror = 3716
      beep
      screen print 22 1 7 0 \
               "No more occurrences of data, enter any key"
     $nomore = inchar
 else
     let $cnt = $cnt + 1
     repaint
     beep
     screen print 22 1 7 0 \
         "Data found in [first name], continue search (y/n)"

   label continue
   let $found = inchar
       if not($found = {N} or $found = {Y} or $found = {n} \
       or $found = {y} )
       jump continue
    end if

   if $found = {N} or $found = {n}
       stop
   elseif $found = {Y} or $found = {y} or record <> records
       repaint  off
       data goto record next
       jump find
   end if
 end if

 data goto record previous
 repaint on
```

The following example takes advantage of other features of SmartWare II to simplify the task of executing the Data Find command in a project file:

```
suspendone command
keys "df",F2,"first name",enter
```

In this example, the Data Find command is executed within the project file through the field name selection. At the conclusion of the one command, control is returned to the remainder of the project file.

Project File to Add a Record To an Index

Smart 3.10:

```
'Name:  ADDREC
```

```
fclose 9
let %5 = $file|".idx"                          'open index file
fopen "%5" as 9

fseek 9 0                                      'get # of records
fread 9 length 1 into $lsb
fread 9 length 1 into $msb
let $totrec = asc($msb)*256 + asc($lsb)        '# of records

let $value  = $totrec + 1                      'add 1 record
call lsbmsb

fseek 9 0                                      'write record count
fwrite 9 length 1 from chr($lsb)
fwrite 9 length 1 from chr($msb)

let $value = $precord                          'convert to base 256
call lsbmsb

'plug the new record number into the index file
let %2 = 60 + 4 * ( $totrec + 1 )
fseek 9 %2
fwrite 9 length 1 from chr($lsb)
fwrite 9 length 1 from chr($msb)

fclose 9
clear $value , $totrec , $lsb , $msb
end

'*******  P R O C E D U R E S  **********

'Convert $value to base 256 in 2 bytes.
'Maximum count is 65535

procedure lsbmsb
     let $msb = int($value/256)
     let $lsb = mod($value,256)
return
```

The ADDREC program should be called from another project file similar to the following:

```
input $precord Physical record number:
let $file = "ind1"
order sequential
execute addrec in-memory
order index ind1.idx
```

Note that the index file "ind1" is built into the calling project file; change this as necessary because the variable $file will accept the name of any index file. The index must exist for this database before it is used in this procedure.

The total number of records in the index cannot exceed 65535, because this is the maximum positive number that can be stored in 2 bytes.

This program will work on index files created as a result of a Query command, but may not work on index files created by a Sort of small databases.

Note that the file number used in the procedure is 9, and that the parameters are numbers 2 and 5. The physical record number is inserted into the $precord variable, which is used in the ADDREC project.

B

Iterative Recalculation in the Spreadsheet

The example in this Appendix demonstrates the use of the iterative recalculation capabilities of the Smart Spreadsheet. Ordinarily, you would think that a worksheet with a circular reference would have been defined in error. However, some calculations, by their nature, feed back into themselves. If the objective can be defined so that the change of a cell becomes smaller and smaller, then the iterative recalculation mode of the Smart Spreadsheet can be used to solve the problem.

The example represents a trivial game, but it provides a demonstration of this capability.

Have you ever played the game in which you're told to guess a number between, say, 1 and 100? The fastest way to guess the answer is to select the number at the middle of the range, so you start by guessing 50. If that guess is too low, your next guess is 75. If that guess then is too high, you guess 67 or 68. On each guess, you split the difference defined by your preceding guesses. This technique is called a binary search.

The following example is just such a game, using the Auto-Recalc Iterate option to perform the multiple guesses. Figure B.1 shows the worksheet with the numbers, and figure B.2 shows the underlying formulas.

If you know your powers of 2, you should be able to determine the maximum number of passes needed to find the value. Set the Auto-Recalc to Manual, and try to verify your answer.

To find the answer in the range 1 to 100,000, the maximum number of passes will be 17 because

$2^{17} = 131,072$

Fig. B.1.

Iterative recalculation example (values).

```
     1           2              3              4          5          6
1  FIND A NUMBER BETWEEN 1 AND A HIGH VALUE
2  ========================================
3
4                 Original             New
5                    Range           Range
6             ------------------------------
7  Low:                  1       8,888,888
8  High:        99,999,999       8,888,888
9
10 Number to find:               8,888,888
11 Computer tries this:          8,888,888
12 Test difference:                      8
13
14
15 Instructions: Enter the high value in r8c2, and
16               the search value in r10c3.
17
18
Command:

Worksheet: CIRCSAMP  Loc: r1c1        CIRC          FN: 8    Font: Standard
```

Fig. B.2.

Iterative recalculation example (formulas).

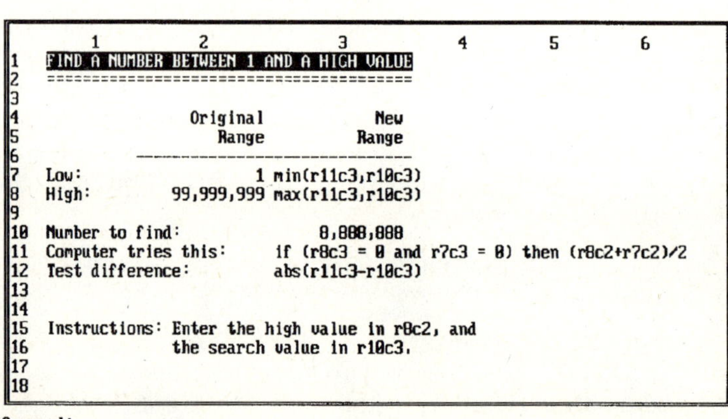

```
     1           2              3              4          5          6
1  FIND A NUMBER BETWEEN 1 AND A HIGH VALUE
2  ========================================
3
4                 Original             New
5                    Range           Range
6             ------------------------------
7  Low:                  1 min(r11c3,r10c3)
8  High:        99,999,999 max(r11c3,r10c3)
9
10 Number to find:            8,888,888
11 Computer tries this:       if (r8c3 = 8 and r7c3 = 8) then (r8c2+r7c2)/2
12 Test difference:           abs(r11c3-r10c3)
13
14
15 Instructions: Enter the high value in r8c2, and
16               the search value in r10c3.
17
18
Command:

Worksheet: CIRCSAMP  Loc: r1c1        CIRC          FN: 8    Font: Standard
```

Word Processor Project Files

The project file in this appendix, and the associated Input-Screens, can be used to prepare a text file for entry into the Smart Word Processor. Carriage returns are stripped from the file, and some minimal formatting is accomplished for you. You will need to "hand-tailor" the resulting document to introduce your own paragraphs and other formatting characteristics.

CONVERT.PF2: The Main File

```
'PROJECT FILE TO STRIP CARRIAGE RETURNS FROM TEXTFILE

singlestep off
quiet on

'Default reformat parameters. Margins, indent, spacing:
%2 = 10
%3 = 70
%4 = 0
%5 = 1

clear

input-screen load intro     'Load intro screen, pause for keystroke.

input-screen load filename  'Get text file and desired document name.
                            'Return error message
                            'and stop.
if not(file(%9))
     call bad filename
     repaint
     end
endif

%8 = "%8.doc"               'Assign the DOC extension to filename.
if file(%8)                 'Check for an existing named document
     call existing document
```

```
     repaint
     end                     'Return error message and stop.
endif
%8 = left("%8",len("%8")-4)'Remove .DOC from filename

if file("oldfile.txt")       'Check for existence of OLDFILE.TXT
call oldfile exists
     repaint                 'Return error message, clear screen
     end                     'and stop.
endif

input-screen load format     'Get desired format for new document.

file copy %9 to oldfile.txt'Make copy of text file.
fopen "newfile.txt" as 1     'Open output file.
fopen "oldfile.txt" as 2     'Open existing text file for reading.

%6 = 7                       'Print progress message
%7 = 0                       'in blinking video stored in %6 and %7.
label top
menu print 10 17 %6 %7 Conversion in Progress...... Do NOT Interrupt!
value1 = %6
%6 = %7
%7 = value1

fread 2 into $var            'Read line from source, check EOF.
if cerror <> 0 then jump out
if len($var) < 1 then jump top
if mid($var,len($var),1) = "." 'Check for end of sentence (eos).
$var = $var|"  "             'Add 2 spaces if eos
else 'or
$var = $var|" "              '1 space if not eos.
endif
     while mid($var,1,1) = " " 'Remove leading spaces from line.
     $var =  right($var,len($var)-1)
     endwhile
%9 = len($var)
fwrite 1 length %9 from $var      'Write the line without cr/lf
jump top
label out
$eof = chr(26)
fwrite 1 length 1 from $eof'Write end of file marker.
fclose 2                     'Close the files.
fclose 1

load newfile.txt             'Load text file.
change-type                  'Change to document file.

reformat document %1 left %2 right %3 indent %4 spacing %5
save %8                      'Save.
file erase oldfile.txt       'Clean up text files
file erase newfile.txt       'used in conversion.
beep 3
end

procedure oldfile exists
menu clear 9 0               'Error message exist OLDFILE.TXT
menu print 8 15 15 9 A textfile by the name of "oldfile.txt" already exists
menu print 10 15 15 9 on your drive. Please rename or erase that file.
menu print 12 15 15 9 It will be used by this program.
```

```
menu print 15 15 15 9 Press any key to continue....
message
return

procedure bad filename
menu clear 9 0          'Error message for bad input filename.
menu print 8 15 15 9 A text file by that name is not found in the current
menu print 10 15 15 9 directory. Please check the file name and extension
menu print 12 15 15 9 and try again.
menu print 15 15 15 9 Press any key, then execute project again.
message
return

procedure existing document
menu clear 9 0          'Error message for duplicate document name.
menu print 8 15 15 9 A document by that name already exists. Please rename
menu print 10 15 15 9 that document or choose a different name.
menu print 15 15 15 9 Press any key, then execute project again.
message
return
```

FILENAME.IS2: Called by CONVERT

```
111 0
2 41211 0A copy of your text file will be made before conversion.
2 51211 0Your original file will remain unchanged.
2 81211 0Enter the name of the text file with extension. (name.ext)
3103212 0 7%9
2131211 0What should the document be named?
31532 8 0 7%8
```

FORMAT.IS2: Called by CONVERT

```
111 0
2 3 615 0Please select the format you wish your document to have:
5 7 6 76215 911 0%1 Normal Left-Justified Right-Justified Centered
210 615 0Please enter the Left Margin:
2104215 0Please enter the Right Margin:
212 615 0Please enter the Indent:
2124215 0Please enter the Spacing:
2 5 615 0Justification:
31037 215 9%2
31074 215 9%3
31237 215 9%4
31274 215 9%5
215 615 0If you do not enter a number in any of the above options, a default
216 615 0value will be assumed. Left margin - 10. Right margin - 70.
217 615 0     Indent      - 0.  Spacing     - 1.
2162715 0: Left Margin - 10.  Right Margin - 70.
```

INTRO.IS2: Called by CONVERT

```
111 8
2 7 911 8This program will remove the hard carriage returns from your
2 8 911 8text file and reformat it as a SMART document. In order to
2 9 911 8accomodate various text file formats, all blank lines will be
210 911 8removed and paragraphs will not be preserved. You will need
211 911 8to insert the carriage returns necessary to separate paragraphs
212 911 8after the conversion.
214 911 8IMPORTANT NOTE: During the conversion, two text files will
215 911 8be opened for read and write. If the program is terminated
216 911 8by the user these files will not be closed properly and will
217 911 8be damaged!!
2 43411 8INTRODUCTION
```

Index

@ character, with LOOKUP functions, 359-360
@Hlookup function (SS), 360-363
@Vlookup function (SS), 360-363

A

absolute address
  copying formulas, 309-311
  vs relative address, 309-312
  with Copy command (SS), 333-334
absolute cell reference, with worksheet cells, 378
Activate (DB) command (3.10), 81-82
Adate (3.10) function (SS), 371
ADDMONTHS function, 533
aligning decimals, Menu Print command (3.10), 485-486
all-formula spreadsheet, 398
alpha fields (3.10), 37
  advancing to next field (SW II), 153
  case recognition (3.10), 127
  editing display width (SW II), 44-45
  entering data, 145
  Form report (3.10), 212
  masks (SW II), 51-53
  number in, 274-275
  quotation marks (3.10), 461
  reforming, 151
  sorting ranges in query, 275-276
  special (3.10), 235
  with query (3.10), 270-271
  wrapping, 197
  wrapping calculated (3.10), 198-199
alphabetic key fields, trailing blanks, 113-114
alphabetic vs numeric lookups, 361-363
alphanumeric fields, 68-72
  reforming, 150
  saving disk space, (SW II), 69-72
AMERICAN.HY file, 427
ampersand (&) symbol, calculating items in a report, 199
AND operator, 266-268
Append (F7) key, 540
applications, customizing configuration, 12
arguments
  FORMAT function, 534
  in functions (SW II), 496
  macros to pass to project files, 528-529
  project files, 469
  SYMMAP function, 536
array variables (SW II), 505
ASC (3.10) function (SS), 356
ascending sort, (DB) project files, 464
ASCII
  character 13 (SW II), 539
  character values, macros (SW II), 531
  files
    importing, 234
    reading into editors, 18
    report definitions, 396
    translating, 542-543
  sorting sequence, with key fields (SW II), 52
ASK function (SS), 316-317
assignment statement, 474-478
  Database Manager project files (3.10), 479
AST Rampage memory board, 17
asterisk (*) wild card, with File commands, 524

AT statement (PP), 458
audible signal, sending, 455
Auto mode (3.10), 169
Auto-Recalc Display command (SS), 320
Autohelp line, with disk-based system (3.10), 301-302
automatic dialer, 541
AUX DOS files, 525
AVERAGE function (SS), 369-370

B

background colors, 483
backslash key (\)
    duplicating column characters, 387
    mark continuation line, 453
backup document files, erasing (SW II), 443
backup file, recovering from, 302
bar charts (3.10), 413
bar menus (SW II), 49-53
    positioning entries (SW II), 49-50
    uppercase entries (SW II), 49
batch files, 28-30
    DOS commands, 469
    executing, 469
BDF file extension (SW II), 391
Beep, (PP) command, 455
binary number bit construction, 532
BITAND function, 532
BITOR function, 532
BITXOR function, 532
blank cells, formatting contents (3.10), 313
blank field (SW II), 273
blank records (3.10), 461
    entering in networks (3.10), 164
    entering in read-only custom screen, 151-152
blanks, dropping form string (SW II), 537
block definition, clearing, 409
block specifications, report, 394-396
blocks, worksheet
    defining names, 344-345
    editing definition manually, 343
    moving in external worksheets, 341-342
    preformatting, 339-340
    reserved words with (3.10), 343-344
    viewing names, 343
book, overview, 1-7
Border (CM) command (3.10), unsupported, 538
borders
    removing, 519
    to print over, 484-485
    window, 96
BPx (backup) file (PP), 455
braces {}, with alpha field mask (SW II), 51
break field (3.10), 64
breakpoints
    assigning (SW II), 208-209
    counting NULL entries, 210
    defining, 207
    double-spacing records, 207
    editing (3.10), 209
    hiding (SW II), 207
    inserting, 209
    minor fields, 210-211
    order of declaration, 207-208
    printing (SW II), 211
    Result Line Label (SW II), 211-212
British pound currency symbol, 24
Browse command (DB), 93-95
    project file to simulate, 554-556
Browse All (DB) command, 38
Browse mode, 94-95
    memory requirements (SW II), 95
buffers, 539
    reply, filling (SW II), 456
    word processor text, 422
BWS file extension, 302

C

calculated fields, 53-62, 198-201
    adding to existing file (SW II), 53
    alpha field size (SW II), 61
    as substitute for counter field, 68
    as switch factor, 59-60
    bypassing with jump rule (SW II), 62
    CASE function vs IF statement, 60-61
    changing NULL variable to BLANK (SW II), 58
    changing view (SW II), 58
    defining in YYMM format, 56-57
    defining with IF statements, 60
    editing (3.10), 58-59
    error checking (3.10), 56
    FETCHFIELD function (SW II), 61-62
    grouping dates by week, 57
    including on custom screen (3.10), 55
    left-justification (SW II), 224-225
    Let statement in project file, 59
    locating on custom screens, 158
    manually calculated view field (SW II), 62
    NA function (SW II), 63
    omitting from screen display (3.10), 54

positioning, 53-54
recalculation mode, 53
recursive calculation (3.10), 55
Replace feature of Query (DB) command, 59
replicating (SW II), 62
report, 217-218
right-justification (3.10), 224
syntax errors, 56
targeting a transaction, 141
used as link in a Lookup retrieval (3.10), 166
using variables in calculations, 57-58
vs query, 59
writing to output file (3.10), 137
calculated text cells, sorting (SW II), 357
calculation fields, using DBS_Conv program on 3.10 files, 54-55
Calculator, invoked in project file, 483
Call statement (3.10), 494-495
calls, incoming, 538
capitalization, PROPER function, 536
Caps Lock key (SW II), 449
capture buffer, 539
Capture Buffer Begin (CM) command (3.10), 540
Capture Buffer Save (CM) command (SW II), 540
Capture Buffer View (CM) command, 540
Capture File (CM) command (SW II), 540
Capture File Begin (CM) command (3.10), 540
Capture on/off (F5) key, 540
carriage returns
replacing with %P (SW II), 425-426
stripping from text files, 563-565
without line feed, 538-539
case-sensitive, 474
arguments, 534
labels, project file (3.10), 478
Case function (SS), 372
CASE function, 60-61, 474
CELL function (SS), 323
CELLPOINTER function (SS), 321, 381
cells
addresses
extracting, 409
parameters (3.10), 491-492
blank, 313-314
calculated text, sorting (SW II), 357
contents, entering, 458
entering repeating values, 319
preformat (3.10), 313-314
recalculating, 320-321
references, moving blocks in external worksheets, 341-342
testing blank looking, 368-369
CELLTEXT function (SS), 311, 371-374, 409-410
CERROR code, 466-467
undocumented (3.10), 455-456
testing, 455-456
characters
ASCII, 531, 539
prompt, 544
special, 536
speed sent, 545
Characters Per Line option, 23
charts, bar (3.10), 413
CHOOSE function (SS), 373
CHR function (3.10), 538-539
clear statement (3.10), 505
Close command (DB), 97
codes
CERROR, 466-467
3002, 127-128
testing, 455-456
undocumented (3.10), 455-456
font-selection, 30
printer initialization, 26-27
colon (:), with field range (3.10), 132
color rule, creating (SW II), 48-49
COLUMN function (SS), 365
columns
hiding, 388
specifying, 318-319
COM1 DOS files, 525
COM2 DOS files, 525
combination reports, 225-230
creating embedded table, 226, 228-229
defining breakpoint fields (3.10), 226-227
duplicating fields, 230
linking fields (3.10), 225
marking table records (SW II), 225-226
new forms (3.10), 549-551
printing breakpoint fields (3.10), 227
printing table fields (SW II), 226
table overflow (SW II), 225
comma, as thousands separator, 534
command, display, suppressing, 305
command failure, 455-456
command line, project file statement displayed, 454
command line substitution, 488-494
parameters (3.10), 488-489
variables (SW II), 488-489
command-type modifier, 458
Command (SS) mode, 306

Command mode, switch to Terminal mode, 538, 545
COMMAND.COM file, 19
commands
  3.10
    Activate (DB), 81-82
    Border (CM), unsupported, 538
    Browse (DB), 94
    Capture Buffer Begin (CM), 540
    Capture File Begin (CM), 540
    Compute (WP), 445
    Copy (SS), 333-334
    Copy (WP), 421
    Create (DB), 36-38
    Create File Similar or Matching (DB), 88-89
    Cursor (SS), 316
    Delete (DB), 176
    Delete (WP), 423
    Dial (CM), 541
    Draw (WP), 446
    Edit (SS), 320
    Enter Blank (DB), 91, 239-241
    Fclose (PP), 468
    File Copy (DB), 258-259
    File Copy (SS), 391
    File Copy, 220, 523-524, 544
    File Erase (DB), 118, 185
    File Erase (PP), 475
    File Erase (WP), 447
    File Erase, 521
    File-Specs (DB), 35
    Fill (SS), 345
    Find (DB), 123-130
    Find Error (SS), 363
    (Find...Partial), 127
    Font Select (SS), 385-386
    Fopen (PP), 468
    Format (CM), 542
    Fprint (PP), 469-471
    Fread (DB), 77
    Goto (CM), 541
    Goto (PP), 478
    Goto Record Next (DB), 129, 164, 462
    Goto Record Rec-Number (PP), 500
    Graphics View (WP), 442
    Init-Sequences, 26-27
    Jump (PP), 478
    Key Organize (DB), 105, 109
    Key Update (DB), 90, 92, 107, 141, 462-463
    Keyboard Macros (CM), 538
    Link (DB), 99, 101-102
    Load (DB), 83
    Lookup (DB), 167-174
    Macros (CM), 538
    Menu Print (DB), 92
    Menu Print (PP), 485-486, 490
    Merge (DB), 40
    Merge File (WP), 437
    Message (PP), 490
    Name Edit (SS), 343-344
    Newname (SS), 326
    Newname (WP), 444
    order (PP), 500
    Order Sequential (DB), 109
    Parameter (DB), 53
    Parameters (WP), 442
    Print (DB), 187-188, 190, 462
    Print (SS), 389
    Print Enhanced (WP), 442
    Print...Report (DB), 39
    Printer-Setup Init-Sequences 26-27
    Printer-Setup Printer-Codes, 25, 27-28
    Profile Define (CM), 543
    Query (DB), 163, 177-178, 260-295
    Query Undefine (PP), 475
    Query...Neither (DB), 285
    Read (DB), 147
    Read (SS), 331, 406
    Read Text (SS), 400
    Relate (DB), 37-38, 112, 130-132, 178
    Relate Define (DB), 136-137
    Remember Compile (PP), 454
    Replace (WP), 422-423
    Report (DB), 178, 188, 191, 244
    Report (SS), 391
    Report Undefine (DB), 231
    Save (WP), 421
    Send (CM), 542
    Setting Save (CM), 543-544
    Settings Edit (CM), 543
    Sort Now (DB), 116-117
    Transaction (DB), 138, 179
    Transfer-Time (CM), 545-546
    Undelete (WP), 423
    Unload All (SS), 302
    Update (DB), 159-160
    Utilities Alter-Count (DB), 65
    Utilities Alter Count Renumber (DB), 65
    Utilities Concatenate (DB), 144-148
    Utilities Duplicates Delete (DB), 180-181
    Utilities New-Password File Password (DB), 88

Utilities New-Password Screen (DB), 89
Utilities New-Password Screen Password (DB), 88
Utilities Purge (DB), 184
Utilities Restructure (DB), 38, 66, 142-148
Width (SS), 388
Write (DB), 236, 241
Write (SS), 331, 404, 406
Write All (DB), 147, 244
Write/Send Summarized (DB), 255
Write Summarized (DB), 245, 258
Write Summarized (SS), 330-331
Auto-Recalc Display (SS), 320
Beep (PP), 455
Browse (DB), 93-95
Browse All (DB), 38
building, 531
Close (DB), 97
Configure, 12, 19-20, 22
Create File (DB), 87
Create Screen (DB), 87
Cursor (PP), 458
Data Browse Off (DB), 95
Data Capture View (CM), 540
DOS
COPY, 278-279
executing from Smart, 11
MODE, 22-23, 538
Edit Copy From (SS), 336-337
Edit Move (SS), 341-343
End (PP), 501-502
Enter Formula (SS), 459
Enter text (PP), 478
Execute (PP), 464-465
file access (SS), 396
File, 520-525
File-Access (PP), 466-471
File Combine (SS), 356
File Copy (SS), 408
File Display-Active (DB), 84
File New-Directory, 521-523
File Rename (DB), 276
File-Specs Key-Fields (DB), 106-107
Find (DB), 111
Find...Equal (DB), 127
Font, 26
Fread (PP), 466-467, 542-543
Fseek (PP), 467
Fwrite (DB), 261-262
Fwrite (PP), 467-469, 542-543
Fwrite (SS), 408
Goto (DB), 82
Goto Window (DB), 98
Graphics Define (SS), 409
Graphics Generate (SS), 412
Graphics output (SS), 407
Index (DB), 84
Key Add (DB), 104
Key Organize (DB), 113
Linear Regression (SS), 347-356
Link (DB), 103
Load (DB), 80
Lock-record (DB), 164, 460-461
Lprint (PP), 480-482
Matrix Parallel (SS), 347
Matrix Print (SS), 412
Matrix Transpose (SS), 346, 403
Menu, 483-488
Message (PP), 455
overlaying an existing disk file (SW II), 448
Paint (SS), 370
Print (DB), 39
Print File...Report (DB), 189
Print Formulas (SS), 388-389
Print Screen (DB), 246
Print Text...Disk (SS), 389
Print...List (DB), 188
Query (DB), 59, 66-67, 118
Query...Screen (DB), 129
Quit (PP), 501-502
Read (DB), 233-234
Read (SS), 405
Relate (DB), 65
Relate...Subtract, 114
Remember Start (PP), 453, 499
Repaint (PP), 499-500
Report Form Label (DB), 190
Save (DB), 89-90
Save All (SS), 302
Screen, 483-488
Send (DB), 249-250
Send Wordprocessor (SS), 404
(Sheet) Lock Protect (SS), 327
Sheet Matrix (SS), 349-350
Sheet Name Define (SS), 345
Sort (DB), 115, 118
Split (DB), 97
Split Horizontal (DB), 96
Split Vertical (DB), 96
Stop (PP), 501-502
Suspend (PP), 501-502

SW II
- Capture buffer Save (CM), 540
- Capture File (CN), 540
- Connection Dial (CM), 541
- creating, 14-17
- Cursor Right/Left (SS), 307
- Czbreak Off (DB), 92
- Data Browse (DB), 62, 95
- Data Browse Fields (DB), 62, 94
- Data Browse Off (DB), 62
- Data Capture Buffer Begin (CM), 540
- Data Cross-Tab (DB), 201, 251-252, 258, 260
- Data Cross-Tabs (SS), 330-331
- Data Delete Record (DB), 176, 180
- Data Find (DB), 123-130
- Data Format (CM), 542
- Data Get Line Variable (CM), 539
- Data Goto Table (DB), 290
- Data Goto Window (DB), 99
- Data Goto Window Next (DB), 99
- Data Match, (CM), 539
- Data Output (CM), 539
- Data Query (DB), 59, 163, 177-178, 260-295
- Data Query Now (DB), 276-277
- Data Receive (CM), 539
- Data Relate (DB), 114, 130-132, 178
- Data Send (CM), 542
- Data Send Wordprocessor Data (DB), 242-243
- Data Transact (DB), 138, 179
- Data Utilities Append (DB), 143-148
- Data Utilities Change-Count (DB), 65
- Data Utilities File-Fix Data (DB), 90
- Data Utilities File-Fix Data-File (DB), 37, 78
- Data Utilities Information (DB), 35-36, 50, 106
- Data Utilities Purge (DB), 184-185
- Data Utilities Recalc-All (DB), 53
- Data Xfer time (CM), 545-546
- Delete Item Field (DB), 42
- Document Goto (WP), 445
- Document References Marker Add (WP), 448
- Edit-Cell (SS), 320
- Edit Copy (SS), 334, 339, 341
- Edit Delete (WP), 423
- Edit Fill (SS), 345-346
- Edit Undelete (WP), 423
- File Activate (DB), 81-82
- File Create (DB), 89, 236, 241, 243-244
- File Export (SS), 331, 404, 406
- File Import (DB), 233
- File Import (SS), 331, 400, 406
- File Load (DB), 80
- File Modify (DB), 43
- File Password (DB), 88
- File Save (DB), 89-90
- File Unload All (SS), 302-302
- Fread (DB), 36
- Key (PP), 514
- Key Define (PP), 512
- Key Organize All (DB), 184
- Key Remove (PP), 513
- Keys (SS), 307
- Layout Cell-Size Width (SS), 388
- Layout Ruler Edit (WP), 449
- Lock (PP), 511
- module specific, 466
- Order Change Index (DB), 118
- Order Key Add (DB), 104
- Order Manual (DB), 294
- Order Sort (DB), 118
- Order Sort Now (DB), 116-117
- Print Merge File (WP), 437
- Print Report (DB), 178, 188, 191
- Print Report Remove (DB), 231
- Print View (DB), 187-188
- Print View Report (DB), 39, 190
- Recalc (DB), 62
- Remember Tools Compile No-Debug (PP), 458
- Remember Tools Delete (PP), 454-455
- Remember Tools Editor (PP), 454
- Remember Tools Load, (PP), 466
- Remember Tools Trace (PP), 511-512
- Reply ON Char (PP), 456-457
- Screen Input (PP), 515-516
- Screen Menu (PP), 516-517
- Screen Print (DB), 462
- Screen Print (PP), 487
- Screen Restore (PP), 487
- Screen Save (PP), 487
- Sheet Calc-mode Manual (SS), 324
- Sheet Find...Calc-Error (SS), 363
- Sheet Name Edit (SS), 343-344
- Sheet Newname (SS), 326
- Sheet Send (SS), 404
- Terminal Goto (CM), 541
- Tools Directory Display 520
- Tools File Copy (CM), 523-524, 544
- Tools File Copy (DB), 72, 258-259

Tools File Copy (SS), 391
Tools File Erase (CM), 521, 524
Tools File Erase (DB), 118-119, 185
Tools File Erase (PP), 475
Tools File Rename (CM), 524
Tools File Rename (PP), 455
Tools Macros Clear All (PP), 513
Tools New-Font, 537
Tools OS, 13, 469, 520
Tools Text-Editor (WP), 430
Udc-Conv (WP), 429
Window Split Horizontal (DB), 97
Window Split Vertical (DB), 97
Window Zoom (DB), 98
Transfer (PP), 464
Utilities Concatenate (DB), 120
Utilities Purge (DB), 66
Windows and Borders, 519
Zoom (DB), 97
comment line, delimiting (PP), 457
comments
adding to project file, 457
DOS window statement lines, 457
in macros (SW II), 529-530
communications definitions, 544
Communications module, 6, 519-546
computation formulas (SW II), 445
Compute (WP) command (3.10), 445
COMSPEC environment variable, 19
CON DOS files, 525
concatenated field (3.10), 55
confidence level, spreadsheet, 301
configuration files, 12
Configuration menu, 19-22, 523
Configure command, 12, 19-20, 22
Configure menu, 390, 523
Connection Dial (CM) command (SW II), 541
control terms, macro (SW II), 530
CONVERT.PF2 file, 563-565
Copy (3.10) command (SS), 333-334
Copy (3.10) command (WP), 421
COPY command (DOS), 278-279
Count option (SS), 323
counter fields, 64-68
as invoice numbers, 65
changing count values, 65
concatenating files, 66
deleting records, 66
incrementing, 64
selecting in relate definition (3.10), 137
sequential numbering, 67-68
using Query for permanent value storage, 65-66
Create (DB) command (3.10), 36-38
Create Box subcommand (DB), 85
Create File (DB) command, 87
Create File Similar or Matching (DB) command (3.10), 88-89
Create or Edit Calculation (DB) subcommand (SW II), 42
Create or Edit Rule, (DB) subcommand (SW II), 42
Create Screen (DB) command, 87
Create Screen Editor (3.10), 84
Cross-Tab definition
criteria overlap (SW II), 252
using expert mode (SW II), 251
currency symbols, British pound, 24
current column, specifying, 318-319
current record, pointer location (3.10), 128-129
current row, specifying, 318-319
current view, reading name (SW II), 36
cursor, display blinking (3.10), 476-477
cursor key, constructing formulas, 307-309
cursor-movement keys, viewing windows, 98
Cursor (PP) command, 458
Cursor (SS) command (3.10), 316
Cursor Right/Left (SW II) command (SS), 307
custom dictionary
adding words, 426-427
creating, 429
installing legal/medical dictionaries, 427
listing to a file (3.10), 427-428
maintaining multiple (SW II), 430
naming conventions (3.10), 427
custom screens
adding notes to (SW II), 86-87
assigning field values (3.10), 165
assigning passwords, 87-88
blanking text (3.10), 86
changing field order, 85-86
concealing (3.10), 84
deleting fields (3.10), 86
designing, 154
displaying
fields (3.10), 94
help information, 154-155
user messages (3.10), 166-167
drawing boxes, 84-85
field ranges with, 86
hiding Lookup source file fields (3.10), 166
including new fields (3.10), 147

locating calculated fields, 158
naming conventions (3.10), 82-83
omitting destination fields (3.10), 170
order-entry, 156
using additional, 154
viewing calculation results, 156-157
custom view
deleting fields (SW II), 42-43
in sort functions (SW II), 115
Czbreak Off (DB) command (SW II), 92

D

D$$ file extension (3.10), 419
DAT file extension, 258
data
arranging in database, 102
bits, modems, 540
changing order, 118-122
combining file (3.10), 167
confusing import file types, 237
database, incorporating into worksheet, 328-331
database, sending to spreadsheet, 250-251
deleting, 176-185
entering in alpha fields, 145
entry message, adding to fields, (SW II), 41
exporting in fixed format (SW II), 242
file
attaching to a view (SW II), 74-75
modifying (SW II), 42
receiving (SW II), 539
testing for end, 497
numeric field, exporting editing characters (SW II), 242
path, specifying with (-d) entry switch, 12
preventing accidental loss (SW II), 43
reading from an external source, 233
safeguarding, 89-90
sorting, 114-118
storing, 539-540
summarized, writing to file, 245-248
transferring (3.10), 491-492
types, changing (3.10), 145
Data Browse (DB) command (SW II), 62, 95
Data Browse Fields (DB) command (SW II), 62, 94
Data Browse Off (DB) command (SW II), 62, 95
Data Capture Buffer Begin (CM) command (SW II), 540
Data Cross-Tab (DB) command (SW II), 201, 258, 260
Data Cross-Tabs (SS) command (SW II), 330-331
Data Cross-Tab command
creating view field (SW II), 251-252
maximum field length (SW II), 252
numbered column titles (SW II), 252
omitting summary type (SW II), 251
periods in column titles (SW II), 252
single output row (SW II), 251
summarizing data (SW II), 252-253
Data Delete Record (DB) command (SW II), 176, 180
Data Find (SW II) command (DB), 123-130
Data Find command project file to simulate, 557-559
Data Format (CM) command (SW II), 542
Data Get Line Variable (CM) command (SW II), 539
Data Goto Table (DB) command (SW II), 99, 290
Data Goto Window Next (DB) command (SW II), 99
Data Match (CM) command (SW II), 539
Data Output (CM) command (SW II), 539
Data Query (DB) command (SW II), 59, 163, 177-178, 260-295
Data Query Now (DB) command (SW II), 276-277
Data Receive (CM) command (SW II), 539
Data Relate (DB) command (SW II), 114, 130-132, 178
Data Send (CM) command (SW II), 542
Data Send Wordprocessor Data (DB) command (SW II), 242-243
Data Transact (DB) command (SW II), 138, 179
Data Utilities Append (DB) command (SW II), 143-148
Data Utilities Change-Count (DB) command (SW II), 65
Data Utilities File-Fix Data (DB) command (SW II), 90
Data Utilities File-Fix Data-File (DB) command (SW II), 37, 78
Data Utilities Information (DB) command (SW II), 35-36, 50, 106
Data Utilities Purge (DB) command (SW II), 184-185
Data Utilities Recalc-All (DB) command (SW II), 53
Data Xfer time (CM) command (SW II), 545-546
database
creating new versions (3.10), 37
creating summarized, 245-246
erasing (3.10), 185
exiting, 90

keys, updating (3.10), 462-463
merging data with word processor, 437
multiple, report definitions (3.10), 220-225
ordering by keys, 120-121
project files, 464, 547-560
re-creating (3.10), 220
report, printing in single-sheet mode (3.10), 431
safeguarding data, 89-90
sort order (SW II), 260
summarized, creating, 250-253
topics (PP), 460
verify loaded (3.10), 463
Database module, overview, 3-4
Database project files, 460-461
Database Report Form, 481
date
as filename (3.10), 491
changing in report heading (3.10), 548-549
entering into variable, 508
fields
evaluated equal to Null (3.10), 274
importing date in string format (SW II), 235
sorting prior to sending to spreadsheet, 259-260
with query (3.10), 263-266
negative numbers to set (SW II), 532-533
project file to prompt (SW II), 535
style, changing display order, 24-25
testing validity (3.10), 508-510
Date function, 370-371
errors (3.10), 508
DATE2 (3.10) function, 281, 409-410
DATE2 function, 508, 533
Days function (3.10), 264-265
dBASE files
importing, 234
writing deleted records, 241-242
writing summarized (3.10), 245
dBASE III files, creating, 241
DBS files (3.10), 37
DBS_Conv program, 54-55
DBU file, 113, 463
debug capabilities, (CM) (3.10), 541
Debug mode (3.10), 541-542
Debug Off statement (SW II), 458
debugging project files, 496-497, 501
decimal tabs, spacing (SW II), 448-449
decimals, aligning, 481-486
default
directories, modules, 523
values (SW II), 515
definition files
VT1OO terminal (3.10), 544-545
VT52 terminal (3.10), 544-545
delete status indicator (SW II), 180
Delete (DB) command (3.10), 176
Delete (WP) command (3.10), 423
Delete (F8) key, 144
Delete Block (DB) subcommand (SW II), 42-43
Delete Item Field (DB) command (SW II), 42
Delete Item Field (DB) subcommand (SW II), 41, 43
Delete key (SS), 409
destination file
designating as driver or driven, 139
invoking lookup definitions (3.10), 168
file, physical order same as source file, 146
detail files, creating, 241-244
detail lines, Table report, 203-204
device drivers names, FILE function (SW II), 533-534
DFR file extension, 220
DFW file extension, 258-259
DFX file extension, 137
Dial (CM) command (3.10), 541
Dial option, 541
dictionaries, using, 426-430
directories
changing, 520-522
drives, 523
with modules, 522
project file to change (SW II), 522
disk-based system, turning off Autohelp line (3.10), 301-302
disks, writing report to, 393-394
Display file names on file prompting option (WP), 418
DOC file, erasing (3.10), 447
Document Goto (SW II) command (WP), 445
Document References Marker Add (SW II) command (WP), 448
documents
1-1/2 line spacing (3.10), 432
assigning temporary name (3.10), 444
changing fonts, 422-423
changing left margin, 433
creating templates, 435
editing/formatting, 421-423
fonts (SW II), 447
header positioning, 433
including current system date (SW II), 441

inserting graphics, 441-442
markers in (SW II), 448
merge-printing, 437-441
page limitations, 442
paging to disk, 442
printing, 430-432
graphs, 442
justified text (SW II), 432
merged (3.10), 441
to a file (3.10), 425
to disk file, 430-431
recovering from automatic backup, 443
reformatting, 425-426
saving, 436
specifying
headings/footers on first page only, 433
subdirectory when saving, 444
underscoring a merged variable, 440
DOS commands
executing from Smart, 11
temporary effect, 520
with Command /C, 520
with Tools OS, 520
DOS, directing printer output, 23
DOS files, reserved
AUX, 525
COM1, 525
COM2, 525
CON, 525
LPT1, 525
LPT2, 525
PRN, 525
DOS MODE command, 538
DOS window, 11, 13
reserving RAM memory, 13
statement lines, comments, 457
using from within word processor (3.10), 417
using with two floppy-disk systems, 19
DOS Window (Secondary Command Processor), 520
dot-matrix printers, printing letter quality text (3.10), 436
double quotation marks, parameters (3.10), 490
Draw (WP) command (3.10), 446
drive path, modems, (SW II), 543
driven files
identifying, 138-139
vs driver files (3.10), 194-195
driver file
deleted records (SW II), 142
identifying, 138-139
marking for deletion, 140
vs driven files (3.10), 194-195
driver record, preventing deletion, 140
drives, changing directories, 523
dummy fields, 104
writing to fixed format file (3.10), 247-248
dummy view field (SW II), 46-47
Dupe (SW II) option, 217
Duplicate (3.10) option, 217
duplicating lines, 498

E

Edit (SS) command (3.10), 320
Edit-Cell (SS) command (SW II), 320
Edit Copy (SS) command (SW II), 334, 339, 341
Edit Copy From command (SS), 336-337
Edit Delete (WP) command (SW II), 423
Edit Field (DB) subcommand (SW II), 42
Edit Fill (SS) command (SW II), 345-346
Edit Move command (SS), 341-343
Edit Undelete (WP) command (SW II), 423
ELSE statement, 473
end of file (EOF)mark (SW II), 540
end-of-file conditions, 467
End (PP) command, 501-502
END MAIN statement (SW II), 495
Enter (SS) mode, 306
Enter Blank command (3.10), vs writing data to file, 239-241
Enter Blank (DB) command (3.10), 91
Enter Formula (SS) command, 459
Enter mode, terminating (3.10), 153
Enter statement, 478
to assign a date (3.10), 459
Enter Text (PP) command, 478
Enter/Update function keys (SW II), 41
entry switches
-a (3.10), 466
-a, 13-14
-d, 12
-e, 12-13
-f (SW II), 18
-FVIRTUAL (3.10), 18, 81
-n, 14
-oe, 14
-p (3.10), 466
-p, 13-14
-r, 13
-R (WP), 417-418
envelopes, printing on a laser printer (3.10), 436

environment variables, COMSPEC, 19
EOF function, 467
Erase line (F8) key, 460
error handling, 455-457
error messages
    not displayed, 521
    splitting windows, 519
error rule (SW II), 48
Error 7 condition, correcting, 363
Esc key, switch modes, 538
Escape, (F10) key, 515
Evaluate statement, 489, 494
    creating variable cell address (SW II), 312
EXACT function (SW II), 533
exclamation point (!), with cell reference, 375
Exclusive mode (SW II), 78
Execute, (PP) command, 464-465
execution errors, project file statements, 454
expanded memory
    installing, 17
    reserving use, 12-13
expressions, tested (3.10), 475
external file, fixed format, 467-468
external reference, assign fields, 478-479

F

F-Calculator, 313
    generating worksheet sequential date, 346-347
    using, 149-150
Fclose (PP) command (3.10), 468
FETCHFIELD function (SW II), 61-62, 158, 181-182, 284, 293
    with calculated field (SW II), 61-62
field formats, 235-238
field input masks, displaying (SW II), 36
field mask
    alpha (SW II), 51-53
    excluding ranges (SW II), 52-53
    non-conforming field value (SW II), 52
field names
    matching case (3.10), 143
    project files (3.10), 454
    source file vs destination file (3.10), 147
    with query definitions (3.10), 260-263
field range, defining relations (3.10), 132
field rules (SW II), 45-49
    color, creating (SW II), 48-49
    declaring order (SW II), 47-48
    error (SW II) 48
    jump
        bypassing mandatory field (SW II), 45
        to next record (SW II), 46-47
        validating field entries, 45-46
    specifying complete field names (SW II), 47-48
fields
    adding data entry message (SW II), 41
    adding to tables (SW II), 74
    advancing between, 152-154
    alpha (3.10), 37
        advancing to next field (SW II), 153
        case recognition (3.10), 127
        Form reports (3.10), 212
        special (3.10), 235
        wrapping, 197
        wrapping calculated (3.10), 198-199
    alphanumeric, 68-72
    assigned with external reference, 478-479
    assigning values when transferring, 143
    available Confidence Level 1 (3.10), 36
    blank (SW II), 273
    break (3.10), 64
    calculated, 53-62, 198-201
        left-justification (SW II), 224-225
        report, 217-218
        right-justification (3.10), 224
        writing to output file (3.10), 137
    changing
        confidence level (3.10), 36
        input order (SW II), 42
        input order (SW II), 43-44
    concatenated (3.10), 55
    counter, 64-68
        selecting in relate definition (3.10), 137
    data entry messages with (SW II), 50
    date, importing date in string format (SW II), 235
    declaring, 38-45
    defaulting to pop-up menu (SW II), 50
    deleting (SW II), 42-43
        duplicate (3.10), 181-182
    displaying with custom screen (3.10), 94
    dummy, 104
    dummy view (SW II), 46-47
    dummy, writing to fixed format file (3.10), 247-248
    effects of automatic return, 152-153
    extracting with lookup definition (3.10), 168
    Form report (3.10), 212
    hiding Lookup source file (3.10), 166
    inverted (3.10), 37
    inverted, Find command with, 130

key, see key fields
link
combination report (3.10), 225
specifying multiple, 133-135
with file transactions, 139-140
linkage, retrieving (3.10), 172
linking, 101-102
mandatory (SW II), 49
bypassing (SW II), 45
escaping from entry (SW II), 155
temporary entry, 154-155
masking restrictions (SW II), 152
maximizing output when printing, 39
modifying views (SW II), 41-42
moving location (SW II), 42
multiple, declaring (3.10), 37-38
multiple search, 129-130
naming, (3.10), 38
naming conventions, 39
null (3.10), 272-273
NULL numeric, converting to zeros (3.10), 145-146
positioning, 38
printing multiple columns, 189-190
printing unavailable, 483
project processing
assigning default value (SW II), 40
viewing (SW II), 40
read-only, with Lookup facility (3.10), 173-174
recovering from inadvertent deletion (SW II), 45
referring by numbers (SW II), 39
reforming, 150-151, 198
relation, specifying in output file, 137-138
repeating, setting values, 163
replacing with query (3.10), 280-281
replicating (SW II), 72-73
returning to first in Browse mode, 94
reverting to unbrowsed mode, 95
running-total (3.10), 63-64
selecting (SW II), 41-42
specifying label, 217
trailing blanks in names (3.10), 39-40
transferring to a file (3.10), 143
validating entries with Lookup facility (3.10), 172
vertical bar (|) in quick reports, 187-188
view (SW II), 54
ZIP code, 68
file access commands (SS), 396
file attributes, read-only, 326-327
file buffer, writing to disk, 89
file extensions
BDF (SW II), 391
BWS, 302
D$$ (3.10), 419
DAT, 258
DFR, 220
DFW, 258-259
DFX, 137
GDF (SS), 408
MRG (SW II), 437-438
PRN (SS), 393-394
PRN (WP) 430-431
RPT, 231
TXT (WP), 432
UCP, 544
use in execution, 520
VW (SW II), 78
VWS (SW II), 78
file operations, 520
file types, external, 234-235
File-Access (PP) commands, 466-471
File Activate (DB) command (SW II), 81-82
File Allocation Table (FAT), 89
File Combine command (SS), 356
File command (CM), 520-525
File command (DB), 521
executing from confidence level 5, 521
with asterisks, 524
File Copy command, 220, 258-259, 391, 408, 523-524, 544
File Create (DB) command (SW II), 89
File Display-Active (DB) command, 84
File Erase (CM) command (3.10), 521
File Erase (DB) command (3.10), 118, 185
File Erase (PP) command (3.10), 475
File Erase (WP) command (3.10), 447
File Export (DB) command (SW II), 243-244, 236, 241
File Export (SS) command (SW II), 331, 404, 406
File Import (DB) command (SW II), 233
File Import (SS) command (SW II), 331, 400, 406
File Load (DB) command (SW II), 80
File Modify (DB) command (SW II), 43
File New-Directory command, 521-523
switching modules, 523
File Password (DB) command (SW II), 88
File Rename command (DB), 276
File Save (DB) command (SW II), 89-90
File-Specs (DB) command (3.10), 35
File-Specs Key-Fields command (DB), 106-107

File Unload All (SW II) command (SS), 302-303
FILE function (SS), 389-390
FILE function (SW II), 533-534
FILENAME.IS2 file, 565
filenames, DOS, reserved, 525
files
  accessing from main menu, 12
  activating, 81-82
    with Goto (DB) command, 82
    without displaying, 81-82
  adding fields (3.10), 116
  AMERICAN.HY, 427
  appending (SW II), 540
  appending data (3.10), 147
  ASCII, 234, 542-543
  backing up, 79
  backup document, erasing (SW II), 443
  backup, recovering from, 302
  batch, 28-30
  BPx (backup) (PP), 455
  breaking links (3.10), 101
  chaining (SW II), 74
  changing
    calculated fields to view (SW II), 237-238
    confidence level (3.10), 36
    subdirectories, 524
  checking for number of records, 133
  closing, 468
  combining, 130-132
  combining data (3.10), 167
  COMMAND.COM, 19
  configuration, 12
  consolidating password prompting, 82
  CONVERT.PF2, 563-565
  creating, 35-38
    Confidence Level 1 (3.10), 36
    standard views (SW II), 73
  data (SW II), 74-75, 539
    modifying (SW II), 42
    preventing accidental loss (SW II), 43
  dBASE, importing, 234
  DBS, (3.10), 37
  DBU, 113, 463
  deleting all records (3.10), 179-180
  detail, creating, 241-244
  DOC, erasing (3.10), 447
  DOS, reserved, 525
  erasing nonexistent (SW II), 524
  executing project files from, 465
  exporting, defined query to select records (SW II), 243
  external, 467-468
  FILENAME.IS2, 565
  fixed format, using dummy fields (3.10), 247-248
  fixed, importing, 234
  fixed-length vs variable-length (3.10), 37
  Fixed Text, writing to (3.10), 246-247
  FORMAT.IS2, 565
  identifying transaction driven, 138-139
  identifying transaction driver, 138-139
  IFF, 438
  importing password protected (SW II), 237
  in communications, 542-543
  index, erasing, 118-119
  inserting, 460
  INTRO.IS2, 566
  key (SW II), 78, 90, 105
  linking (3.10), 99-102
    with field length (SW II), 74
  loading, 75-78
    from alternative subdirectories, 80-81
    from several subdirectories (3.10), 79
    in Exclusive mode (SW II), 78
  macro, loading, 304
  minimizing open (3.10), 91
  name, 463
  network limitations, 17-18
  open, 465
  opening, 468
  ordering
    by index, 119
    by field, 124
    multiple (3.10), 121-122
    sequentially, 121
  paging path, 23-24
  Param6 (3.10), 541-542
  PFx (source) (PP), 455
  PIX, 27
  PRINTDM.DSC, 29
  printing documents to, 425, 430
  printing reports to, 188
  printing to, 469-471
  PRINTWP.DSC, 29
  PRINTxx.DSC, 25
  project, see project files
  reading into spreadsheet, 405
  recovering dead spaces (SW II), 37
  reformatting, 542
  relating two files into a third, 130-138
  replicating (SW II), 72-73
  report definitions (3.10), 220

restricting access (3.10), 89
reverting to unbrowsed mode, 95
RFx (compiled) (PP), 455
screen, saving (3.10), 410
SMART, importing, 234
SMART.MNU, 14-17
sort-definition (3.10), 115
SW II, QNOW.DFQ, 276
temporary, repeating data (3.10), 162-163
text
reading into editors, 18
writing to, 236-237
transaction destination, 139
unloading lookup definitions (3.10), 167
unopened, 468-469
viewing, 93-95
VIRTUAL.DVR, 18, 81
WPRINT.DEF, 419-420
writing to vs Enter Blank command (3.10), 239-241
Fill (SS) command (3.10), 345
Find command (DB), 111, 123-130
Find command project file to simulate, 557-559
Find Error (3.10) command (SS), 363
FIND function, 379-380
Find...Equal command (DB), 127
Find...Partial command (3.10), 127
fixed files, importing, 234
fixed format file, using dummy fields (3.10), 247-248
fixed-length vs variable-length files (3.10), 37
Fixed function (SS), 366
FIXED function, 467, 507-508
Fixed Text file, writing to (3.10), 246-247
floppy disk system, paging path, 24
font-selection codes, overriding, 30
Font command, 26
Font Select (SS) command (3.10), 385-386
fonts (SW II) 537
document (SW II), 447
letter-quality, 25-26
proportional (3.10), 434
Table report (SW II), 198
footers
changing document left margin, 433
reserved space, 433
toggling between Insert On/Off modes (3.10), 432-433
footings, report, 391-392
footnotes
copying, 423
deleting, 423
font macros, 424
spell-checking, 428-429
Fopen (PP) command (3.10), 468
forecasts
creating, 347-348
linear regression, 352
foreground colors, 483
Form reports
alpha fields (3.10), 212
centering text, 218-219
defining, 212-219
emphasized type, 217-218
labels, 213-217
ringing printer bell, 217
specifying fields (3.10), 212
underscore font (SW II), 219
formal report
creating, 191-195
double-spacing, 195
driver vs driven files, 194-195
form specifications, 193-194
page length specifications, 192-193
page overflow (3.10), 195
table specifications, 193-194
Format (CM) command (3.10), 542
Format definition, 542
FORMAT function, arguments, 534
FORMAT.IS2 file, 565
formats, field, 235-238
formatted output, printing, 481
formatting functions (SS), 371-374
forms, new, in combination report (3.10), 549-551
formulas
calculating point size space (SW II), 447
calculating the median of three values, 356
changing locked, 327
computation (SW II), 445
constructing with cursor key, 307-309
copying, 309-311
copying worksheet, 336-337
entering in worksheet, 460
including rows in, 311
inserting trailing zeros (3.10), 446
printing worksheet, 388-390
with statistical database functions, 377-378
Fprint, (PP) command (3.10), 469-471
Fread (DB) command (3.10), 77
Fread (DB) command (SW II) 36
Fread (PP) command, 466-467, 542-543
Fseek (PP) command, 467

function keys, SW II
  Enter/Update, 41
  Text-Editor, 36
  to duplicate lines, 498
functions, 532-537
  @Hlookup (SS), 360-363
  @Vlookup (SS), 360-363
  Adate (SS), 371
  ADDMONTHS, 533
  ASC (SS), 356
  ASK (SS), 316-317
  AVERAGE (SS), 369-370
  BITAND, 532
  BITOR, 532
  BITXOR, 532
  Case (SS), 372
  CASE, 60-61, 474
  CELL (SS), 323
  CELLPOINTER (SS), 321, 381
  CELLTEXT (SS), 311, 371-374
  check valid date (3.10) 533
  CHOOSE (SS), 373
  CHR (3.10), 538-539
  COLUMN (SS), 365
  combining (SS), 387-388
  combining an if...then statement, 372-373
  Date (3.10), 508
  date2, 508
  Date (SS), 370-371
  DATE2, 281, 409-410, 533
  Days, 264-265
  declaring in project file (SW II), 495-496
  encountered in project files, 495
  EOF, 467
  EXACT (SW II), 533
  FETCHFIELD, 61-62, 158, 181-182, 284, 293
  FILE, 389-390, 533-534
  FIND (SS), 379-380
  Fixed (SS), 366
  FIXED, 467, 507-508
  FORMAT, 534
  formatting (SS), 371-374
  GETFNAMES, text limits, 534
  Global (SW II), 496
  GOAL (SS), 381-383
  HLOOKUP (SS), 359-363
  INCHAR, using, 476-477
  INDIRECT, 311-312, 380-381
  in memory, 466
  INT, 535
  ISBLANK (SS), 367-370
  ISDATE (SW II), 535
  Iserr (SS), 364-365
  ISERR, 504, 533
  ISNA (SS), 367
  ISNUMBER (3.10), 502
  LEN, 467, 533
  LOOKUP (SS), 359-363
  MAKECELL (SS), 311
  MATCH (SS), 379-380
  NA, 63, 366-367
  NEXTKEY, using, 476-477
  numeric conversion (SS), 374-379
  PHONEX (SW II) 535-536
  project processing, 494-496
  PROPER, 536
  Public (SW II), 496
  Record, 497
  REINVERT, 130
  REPEAT (SS), 387
  REPLACE (SS), 380
  ROUND (SS), 410
  ROW (SS), 365
  SELECT (SS), 373-374
  selection (SS), 371-374
  statistical database (SS), 376-379
  STR (SS), 374-375
  SYMMAP, undocumented, 536
  TABLECOUNT, 47
  text (SS), 379-380
  three bit evaluation (3.10), 532
  Time (SS), 370-371
  TIME, 536-537
  to align decimals (3.10), 485-486
  Trim (3.10), 282-283
  TRIM (SW II), 537
  UPPER, 474
  VAL, 374-375, 507
  VLOOKUP (SS), 359-363
  worksheet position (SS), 365-366
Fwrite command (DB), 261-262
Fwrite command (PP), 467-469, 542-543
Fwrite command (SS), 408

G

GDF file extension (SS), 408
GETFNAMES function, text limits, 534
global
  variables, 512
  functions (SW II), 496
GOAL function (SS), 381-383

Goto (CM) command (3.10), 541
Goto (DB) command , 82
Goto (PP) command (3.10), 478
Goto Record Next (3.(DB) command (3.10), 129, 164, 462
Goto Record Rec-Number (PP) command (3.10), 500
Goto Window (DB) command, 98
graph definition
- actual address for data blocks, 411
- copying, 408
- editing (SW II), 409
- changing, 408
- creating, 407-410

Graph Definition menu (SS), 407-408
Graphics Define command (SS), 409
Graphics Generate command (SS), 412
Graphics output command (SS), 407
Graphics View (3.10) command (WP), 442
graphics, inserting in documents (SW II), 441-442
graphs
- creating an x or y axis data block (3.10), 409-410
- histogram (3.10), 413
- minimum scaling, 410
- naming, 407-408
- pie chart slices under five percent (3.10), 410-411
- positioning cursor, 409
- printing edited (3.10), 412
- printing in documents, 442
- returning to command mode (3.10), 410

greater-than (>) symbol, 267, 271
greater-than operator, 126-127

H

half duplex, communicating in (3.10), 545
half duplex mode (3.10), 545
hardware configuration, modem, 542
Hardware preferences menu (SW II), 432
headers
- reserved space, 433
- toggling between Insert On/Off modes (3.10), 432-433

heading lines, Table report, 204-205
headings, report, 391-392
help information, displaying on custom screen, 154-155
histogram graph (3.10), 413
HLOOKUP function (SS), 359-363
homonyms, PHONEX function (SW II), 535-536

I

IBM character set, 24
IBM PC AT
- initiating a Smart session, 14
- Intel Above Board, 17

IF facility, in formulas, 473-474
IF statements
- defining calculated fields, 60
- project files, 471-475
- true/false condition, 473

if...then statement, combining with a function, 372-373
IF...THEN...ELSE statement, 474
IFF file, 438
illegal statement, 474-475
INCHAR using, 476-477
index
- as a substitute for a key (3.10), 138
- files
  - erasing, 118-119
  - reusing, 119
  - using with keys (3.10), 119-120
- ordering, 179
- ordering source file, 144
- project file to add record (3.10), 559-560
- to omit deleted records, 144

Index (DB) command, 84
INDIRECT function (SS), 311-312, 380-381
information, captured to buffer, 539-540
Init-Sequences command, (3.10), 26-27
input mask specifications, displaying (SW II), 36
input screens (3.10), 526
- modules, 526

Input-Order (DB) subcommand (SW II), 86
Input-screen definitions
- printing, 526
- records, 525-526

Input Screen facility, variables in (3.10), 526
Input screens, 525-527
- editing, 527
- editing definition, 525
- sliding text entries, 527

Insert (F7) key, 143
INT function, 535
Intel Above Board, 17
interrupts, time dependent, 538
INTRO.IS2 file, 566
inverted fields (3.10), 37

Find command with, 130
ISBLANK function (SS), 367-370
ISDATE function (SW II) 535
Iserr function (SS), 364-365
ISERR function, 504, 533
ISNA function (SS), 367
ISNUMBER function (3.10), 502
Iterate option (SS), 321

J

jump rule (SW II), 45
bypassing calculated fields (SW II), 62
to next record (SW II), 46-47
validating field entries (SW II), 45-46
Jump (PP) command (3.10), 478
Jump statement (3.10), 495

K

key combinations
Alt-255 (3.10), 84, 549-551
Alt-B, 94
Alt-F (Full Screen Editor), 327
Alt-F2 (Erase project file contents), 460
Alt-F3 (Append/Insert), 499
Alt-F3 (Insert file), 18, 460
Alt-K (F-Calculator), 149-150
Alt-Minus (WP), 422
Alt-R (Repeat command) (WP), 422
Alt-V (Buffer view), 540
Alt-W (Copy file) (SW II), 460
Alt-X (Display command), 73, 336, 521, 531
Alt-Y (Alternate modes), 529
Alt-Z (Alternate modes), 529
Ctrl-A (Lookup mode), 169-170
Ctrl-G (Graphics), 407
Ctrl-O (DOS window), 11, 13, 520
Ctrl-Right Arrow, 36
Ctrl-U (Underscore), 386
Ctrl-Z (Stop), 92, 118, 502
Shift-F5 (Global Recalculation) (SS), 320
Shift-Print Screen (3.10), 537
key fields
adding, 113
alphabetic, trailing blanks, 113-114
changing values (3.10), 106-107
declaring as first field, 38
defining, 103
deleting, 105
eliminating sorting, 104-105
finding next (3.10), 127
indexing (3.10), 112-113
length constraints, 105-106
locating, 123-124
maintaining in same case (SW II), 105
mandatory uses, 110
multiple (3.10), 103-104
ordering driven file (3.10), 141-142
ordering files, 124
preventing duplicates (3.10), 174
searching by abbreviation, 124-125
speeding up commands, 110
updating (3.10), 107-108
viewing names, 106
vs sort, 111-112
with ASCII sorting sequence (SW II), 52
key files (SW II), 90, 105
indexing (3.10), 112-113
repairing damage to (SW II), 78
updating network (3.10), 109
vs sort, 111-112
Key Add command (DB), 104
Key Define (PP) command (SW II), 512
Key Organize (DB) command (3.10), 105, 109, 113
Key Organize All (DB) command (SW II), 184
Key Remove (PP) command (SW II), 513
Key Update (DB) command, 90, 92, 107, 141, 462-463
Keyboard Macros, (CM) command (3.10), 538
keys
cursor-movement, viewing windows, 98
Delete (SS), 409
deleting prior to importing (SW II), 237
Esc (Switch modes), 538
F3 (Switch modes), 538, 545
F5 (Capture on/off), 540
F5 (Recalculate) (SS), 320
F5 (Switch modes), 545
F7 (Append), 540
F7 (Duplicate line), 498-499
F7 (Insert), 143
F8 (Delete), 144
F8 (Duplicate line), 498-499
F8 (Erase line), 460
F9 (Repeat), 158-160
F10 (Escape), 515
F10 (Quit), 90
F10 (Save), 543
F10 (Terminate menu), 527
lookup (3.10), 55

Print Screen, 136
PrtSc (3.10), 537
quick, 527-531
SW II, Caps Lock, 449
Keys (PP) command (SW II), 514
Keys (SS) command (SW II), 307
Keys statement (SW II), 513-514, 530
keystrokes
recording in macros (3.10), 528
repeated in macro (SW II), 531
testing, 528

L

labels
blank line suppression, 216
calculated view fields (SW II), 215
continuous pin-fed, 216
creating, 190
Duplicate option, 217
Form report, 213-217
including literals, 214-215
inserting text (SW II), 215
label blocks, 216
printing
combination reports (3.10), 216
multiple, 213-214
on laser printer, 216-217
project file (3.10), 478
specifying fields, 217
LAN User Access modules, 31
laser printers
adjusting page length (3.10), 435
creeping text (3.10), 435
printing envelopes (3.10), 436
printing labels, 216-217
Layout Cell-Size Width (SW II) command (SS), 388
Layout Ruler Edit (WP) command (SW II), 449
Layout Worksheet-Options Current-Sheet menu (SW II), 390
legal dictionary (3.10), 427
LEN function, 467, 533
less-than (<) symbol, 267, 271
less-than operator, 126-127
Let statement
assign a date (3.10), 459
entering data in a cell, 317-318
LET statement, project file, 478
letter-quality fonts, 25-26
line-length option, 23
line numbers, compiling project files (3.10), 458
linear-regression, dependent variable, 350
Linear Regression command (SS), 347-356
link fields
combination report (3.10), 225
effects of case on Relate command, 135-136
effects of Lookup facility (3.10), 171
specifying multiple, 133-135
with file transactions, 139-140
Link (DB) command, 99, 101-103
linkage field, retrieving (3.10), 172
links
macro for multiple simultaneous file (SW II), 99-101
multiple key fields, 103
Load (DB) command (3.10), 80, 83
local variable, 512
Lock (PP) commands (SW II), 511
Lock-Record command (DB), 164, 460-461
logical conditions, with query definition, 268
look definitions, unloading (3.10), 167
lookup definitions
automatic vs manual mode, 169-172
data retrieval from source-file record, 168
extracting fields (3.10), 168
loading (3.10), 168-169
selective lookups (3.10), 170
source files (3.10), 169
lookup key, defining (3.10), 55
lookup mode, turning off (3.10), 169-170
Lookup (DB) command (3.10), 167-174
Lookup Definition screen (3.10), 166
Lookup setting, file applications (3.10), 171
LOOKUP functions (SS), 359-363
Lprint (PP) command, 480-482
Lprint statement, aligning decimals (3.10), 249
LPT1 DOS files, 525
LPT2 DOS files, 525

M

macro control terms (SW II), 530
macro editing, terminating, (3.10), 527
macro file, loading, 304
macro keys, define, 512-513
macros, 527-531
alternating between Enter and Command modes, 448
blanking a cell, 314
calculate a field value during data entry (SW II), 150
clearing (SW II), 513

comments in (SW II), 529-530
deleting outdated documents from disk, 443-444
editing (SW II), 530
enclosing a string (SW II), 529
entering a SUM formula into a cell (SW II), 311
erasing (3.10), 528
executing (3.10) 528
executing project files, 528-529
footnote fonts, 424
keystrokes, testing, 528
multiple simultaneous file links (SW II), 99-101
printer, 25, 27-28
printing headers and footers (3.10), 431
quick keys, 527
recording in Suspend mode (SW II), 530
recording keystrokes (3.10), 528
repeating keystrokes (SW II), 531
Table report printer (3.10), 204
to alter Print Options settings, 435
to change windows (3.10), 531
to correct Lookup link-field errors (3.10), 172
to delete hard carriage returns (3.10), 425
to execute project files (SW II), 465
to move from window to window (3.10), 421
to pass argument to project file, 528-529
to repeat entries in records, 158-159
to select merge field names (SW II), 439
to supply passwords under control of a project file, 75
to underscore in a worksheet (3.10), 388
to use Ctrl-T for the Reformat command (3.10), 425
viewing (3.10), 527
with F10 key, 527
Macros (CM) command (3.10), 538
Main menu, 19-20
MAKECELL function (SS), 311
mandatory fields (SW II), 49
bypassing (SW II), 45
escaping from entry (SW II), 155
temporary entry, 154-155
master variable (3.10), 503
MATCH function (SS), 379-380
math coprocessor, preventing use on IBM PC AT, 14
Matrix Parallel command (SS), 347
Matrix Print command (SS), 412
Matrix subcommand menu, 350
Matrix Transpose command (SS), 346, 403
medical dictionary (3.10), 427
memory
allocation, variables, 506
expanded, 12-13, 17
project file, 465
RAM, reserving for DOS window, 13
resident programs, 538
specifying available RAM for graphics (3.10), 442
with variables (SW II), 505-506
menu (PP) commands, using, 483-488
Menu Clear Box statement (3.10), 485
Menu facility, hiding entries, 483
Menu input statement, 483
Menu Print (DB) command (3.10), 92
Menu Print (PP) command (3.10), 485-486, 490
menus
bar (SW II), 49-53
Configuration, 19-22
Configure, 390, 523
Graph Definition (SS), 407-408
Hardware preferences, 432
Layout Worksheet-Options Current-Sheet, 390
Main, 19-20
Matrix subcommand, 350
Parameters, 152, 299-300,419, 427
pop-up (SW II), 49-53
Print Options (WP), 434-435
Print Preset (WP), 434
Printer-Setup Printer-Codes, 21-22
retaining, 499-500
Settings, 544
Tools Preferences, 13
Tools Preferences Communications, 542
Tools Preferences Global, 13
Tools Preferences Hardware, 22
merge document
including current system date (SW II), 441
printing (3.10), 441
merge-printing, 437-441
Merge (DB) command (3.10), 40
Merge File (WP) command (3.10), 437
merged variable, underscoring in documents, 440
Message command (3.10), 455, 490
messages
A view is already ordered by this index file, 122
Already connected (3.10), 543
Bad syntax (SW II), 263, 274-275, 490
Cannot assign value to field (SW II), 282
Cannot find data for field, 114, 170-171
Cannot repeat field in first record, 160
Data-file already exists, 132

Data region contains invalid item (SW II), 412
Destination file already exists (SW II), 258
displaying user (3.10), 166-167
Error closing file (3.10), 327
Error loading spell driver, 417
Error reading data-file (SW II), 109
Error reading dBASE file, 242
Expression too complex (3.10), 262
field data entry (SW II), 50
Field is not on current view (SW II), 196
File already exists, 258, 524
File contains un-updated records (3.10), 108
File contains unmerged records (3.10), 141
File filename.ext is active (3.10), 475
File in use by another station (3.10), 109
File is active - Continue with other files?, 447
File not found (PP), 457
File of that name exists. Continue (SW II), 448
File of that name exists. Overwrite? (SW II), 448
Filename in index file does not match (SW II), 121
Form and table will overlap on table overflow, 225
Incorrect command syntax (3.10), 83
Insufficient memory, 417, 442
Invalid application data path, 522
Invalid cell or block name, 344
Invalid field (SW II), 262
Invalid field entered, 94, 132
Invalid field in equation for calculated field, 56
Invalid field in sort definition file, 115
Invalid filename, 524
Invalid font number in heading or footnote text, 447
Invalid LET or command target (SW II), 63
Invalid rule on field (SW II), 48
Key value for data-file already exists (SW II), 151
Label overlaps first break field, 211
Line is too long (SW II), 454
Mandatory entry Please enter something into field, 155
Marked area too small to split, 519
Missing name (SW II), 505
Modem definition not found (SW II), 543
Move would cause line overflow, 197
moving, display, 487-488
No data-file in current window (SW II), 262
No error found below current cell, 364
No matching files, enter any key, 522
No Rows or Automatic-Rows have been defined, 251
Note: No permission to save file under this name, 327
Out of memory, 539
Page file creation failure, 23-24
Path not accessible, 24
Press Enter to add at current break position, 208
project file to display, 483-484
Record must be locked to do assignment (3.10), 164
Remember not allowed (SW II), 530
Reply buffer is full (SW II), 457
Saved definition does not match command parameters, 253
Screen used in definition not open (3.10), 136
Some data may be lost when files is restructured, 43
Someone else may be using this file (3.10), 184
The specified area is too small to split, 519
Too many files open (3.10), 81
Trying to total an alpha calculation (SW II), 200
Unable to modify Data-file (SW II), 42
Unexpected end of file, 185, 495
Unknown command, 473
Unrecognizable character (SW II), 531
Unresolved label: %1 (3.10), 477-478
Unresolved label: endif1 (3.10), 473
Unresolved label: if1 (3.10), 473
Variable not found (SW II), 286, 445
Window too small, 96, 519
Worksheet has been modified Save before unloading, 328
Worksheet in use by another station, 324

MODE command, DOS, 22-23

modems
auto answer off, 538
data bits, 540
defining in terminal settings (SW II), 543
dialling, 540-542
hardware configuration, 542
parity settings (3.10), 540
profiles, 543-544
settings, 543-544

modes
alternating, 529
Auto, 169
Browse, 94-95
Command, 306, 538, 545
Debug (3.10), 541-542

Enter, 306
Exclusive (SW II), 78
half duplex, 545
No-Debug, project files, 458
Prompting, 301
Quiet, 305
Remember Edit, 498-499
Recalculation, 299-300
suspend (SW II), 511-512, 530
switching, 538
Terminal, 538, 545
Textfile (WP), 454
module specific commands (SW II), 466
modules
changing directories, 522
input screens, 526
LAN User Access, 31
transferring data between (3.10), 491-492
Move Item Field (DB) subcommand (SW II), 41
MRG file extension (SW II), 437-438
multiple
databases, report definitions (3.10), 220-225
fields, declaring (3.10), 37-38
file views, 73-75
files, sort definition (3.10), 116

N

NA function (SS), 63, 366-367
Name Edit (SS) command (3.10), 343-344
named worksheet blocks, 343-345
negative numbers, to set early dates (SW II), 532-533
networks
assigning printer ports, 22
D$$ file extension (3.10), 419
entering a blank record (3.10), 164
file names, 463
file opening limitations, 17-18
files, loading in Exclusive mode (SW II), 78
importing data in single user mode (SW II), 239
loading files (3.10), 76-77
loading worksheets (3.10), 324
multiple simultaneous file links (SW II), 100-101
query with, 287-288
renumbering counter fields (3.10), 65
sharing custom dictionaries, 429
updating
key files (3.10), 109
records (3.10), 164
Newname (SS) command (3.10), 326
Newname (WP) command (3.10), 444
NEXTKEY using, 476-477
No-Debug mode, compiling project files, 458
non-integer values, rounding up, 535
non-zero numeric variable, testing, 473
null fields (3.10), 272-273
null values, changing to a unique value (3.10), 146
Null Modem setting, 542
NULL numeric fields, converting to zeros (3.10), 145-146
numbers, as text in variables (3.10), 507
numeric cells, EXACT function (SW II), 533
numeric conversion functions (SS), 374-379
numeric fields, 68-72
as sort field, 117-118
calculating (SW II), 200
commas in (3.10), 244
default values, 197
displaying sum (SW II), 191
dollar signs in (3.10), 244
Find command operators, 126-127
imported files width (SW II), 234-235
including commas (3.10), 68-69
sizing (SW II), 196
numeric parameters (3.10), 490-491
numeric row identifiers, converting to alpha strings, 330-331
numeric variable, 506-507, 516
numeric vs alphabetic lookups, 361-363

O

operations, file, 520
operators
AND, 266-268
greater-than, 126-127
less-than, 126-127
OR, 266-268
partial, 125-126
options
Characters Per Line, 23
Count (SS), 323
Dial 541
Display file names on file prompting (WP), 418
Dupe (SW II), 217
Duplicate, 217
Iterate (SS), 321
line-length, 23
Partial (DB), 254-255

Password (DB), 87-89
singlestep, 501
Start page number (WP), 434-435
Whole Words Only, 125-126
OR operator, 266-268
Order (PP) command (3.10), 500
Order Change Index (SW II) command (DB), 118
Order Key Add (DB) command (SW II), 104
Order Manual (DB) command (SW II), 294
Order Sequential (DB) command (3.10), 109
Order Sort (SW (DB) command (SW II), 118
Order Sort Now (DB) command (SW II), 116-117
output file
loading after Relate (3.10) command, 133
specifying relation fields, 137-138
overlays, Input screens, 527

P

page numbering, report, 218, 396
paging file path, 23-24
paging, using RAM disk card, 17
Paint command (SS), 370
Param6 file, edit (3.10), 541-542
parameter variable (3.10), 477-478
Parameter (DB) command (3.10), 53
parameters
command variability (3.10), 492
concatenating (3.10), 489
evaluation (3.10), 493
in command line substitution (3.10), 488-489
numeric (3.10), 490-491
project file, 402
saved in user variables (3.10), 492
search-string (3.10), 128
spreadsheet, setting, 299-306
text characters (3.10), 489
to construct filename (3.10), 491
to control execution (3.10), 492
to simulate arrays of variables (3.10), 492-493
to substitute parts of cell addresses (3.10), 491
Parameters menu (3.10), 152
Parameters menu (SS), 299-300
Parameters menu (WP), 419, 427
Parameters (WP) command (3.10), 442
parentheses
in expressions (SW II), 487
in functions (SW II), 496
parity settings, modem (3.10), 540
Partial (DB) option (3.10), 254-255
partial field list, reading, 238-239
partial operator, 125-126
Password option (DB), 87-89
passwords
assigning to custom screens, 87-88
naming conventions, 87
project file, 88
screen, 87-89
PFx Source) files (PP), 455
PHONES function (SW II), 535-536
PIX file, 37
pop-up menus (SW II), 49-53
moving around in, 77-78
positioning entries (SW II), 49-50
updating contents (SW II), 50-51
writing contents to file (SW II), 50
ports, printer, 22
pound sign (#) in macros (SW II) 531
print group specifications, report, 394-396
Print (DB) command (3.10), 39, 187-188, 190, 462
Print (SS) command (3.10), 389
Print Enhanced (3.10) command (WP), 442
Print File...Report command (DB), 189
Print Formulas command (SS), 388-389
Print Merge File (SW II) command (WP), 437
Print Options menu (WP), 434-435
Print Preset menu (WP), 434
Print Report (DB) command (SW II), 178, 188, 191
Print Report Remove (DB) command (SW II), 231
Print Screen command (DB), 246
Print Screen key, 136
Print Text...Disk command (SS), 389
Print View (DB) command (SW II), 187-188
Print View Report (DB) command (SW II), 39, 190
Print...List command (DB), 188
Print...Report (DB) command (3.10), 39
PRINTDM.DSC file, 29
printer
codes
initial, 26-27
testing, 27
directing output through DOS, 23
drivers, selecting, 21
fonts, selecting (3.10), 424
ports, assigning, 22
settings, 434-437
Printer-Setup Init-Sequences command (3.10), 26-27
Printer-Setup Printer-Codes command (3.10), 25-28
Printer-Setup Printer-Codes menu, 21-22

printers
 macros, 25, 27-28
 multiple input trays (3.10), 431-432
 overriding font-selection codes, 30
 proportional fonts (3.10), 434
 selecting with batch files, 28-30
 serial, 22-23
 setting characters per line, 23
 switching between, 21-22
 writing to, 20
printing
 documents, 430-432
 from project files, 480-482
 graphs (3.10), 412
 merge documents, 437-441
 over borders, 484-485
 reports, 230-232
 worksheets, 388-391
PRINTWP.DSC file, 29
PRINTxx.DSC file, 25
PRN DOS files, 525
PRN file extension (SS), 393-394
PRN file extension (WP), 430-431
procedures
 exiting (3.10), 495
 isolated (3.10), 494
 project processing, 494-496
Profile Define (CM) command(3.10), 543
profiles, modems, 543-544
programs
 DBS_Conv, 54-55
 memory resident, 538
 TRANSLAT (SW II), 122
project files, 36, 50-51, 62-63, 67-68, 75-76, 91-97, 453-518
 adding records to existing index (3.10), 122
 advancing to next record (3.10), 462
 alpha field (3.10), 461
 append/insert, 499
 arguments to vary, 469
 assigning values to repeating field, 160
 avoiding multiple password prompts (3.10), 147-148
 backslash (\), 453
 blank records (3.10), 113
 changing
  a calculated field (3.10), 162
  a custom screen (3.10), 84
  existing database structure (3.10), 91
  worksheet block boundaries, 397-398
 checking existence of output file, 133
 clearing Query summary from screen, 291-292
 code, wait message, 463-464
 command-line substitution, 488
 comment line, delimiting, 457
 comments, adding, 457
 compiling, 91, 458
 continuation line, 453
 continuing automatically (SW II), 148
 copying, 460, 499
 created with word processor, 498
 create variable cell address (SW II), 312
 creating, 453-455
  summarized report (3.10), 248-249
 cursor motion commands (3.10), 307
 database, 460-461, 547-560
  sorting, 464
 Database Manager (3.10), 479
 deactivating system beep (3.10), 455
 debugging, 496-497, 501
 declaring variables (SW II), 505
 defining, 515
 delete status indicator (SW II), 180
 deleting Order Change Index commands (SW II), 122
 determining if a screen is zoomed, 97-98
 direct printing from, 480-482
 display progress, 462
 displaying
  multiple loaded files (SW II), 303
  recalculated values (SW II), 62-63
  sum of any numeric field (SW II), 191
 documenting query definition (3.10), 279-280
 documenting work, 454
 editing, 454, 460-464, 497-499
 entering formulas, 459
 erasing contents, 460
 executing, 464
  from-file, 465
  from macro, 528-529
  Link command (3.10), 102
 execution, halting, 501-502
 field names (3.10), 454
 for entry of double quotation marks (3.10), 461
 forcing recalculation (SW II), 324-325
 forcing zeros to blanks (3.10), 357
 function encountered (SW II), 495
 isolating current record (SW II), 293-294
 IF statements, 471-475
 in memory (SW II), 530
 in memory, executing (3.10), 464-466

indexing keys (3.10), 112-113
inserting, 460
invoking Calculator, 483
key capture, 476
key fields, declaring (SW II), 495-496
Keys command vs Cursor Right/Left command, 307
labels, 477-478
laser printer page orientation (3.10), 436-437
Let statement with calculated field, 59
LET statement, 478-480
macro to execute in memory (SW II), 465
macros to pass arguments to, 528-529
macros to supply passwords, 75
modules, changing (SW II), 466
moving between records (3.10), 165
multiple, 464
multiple assignments, 164
opening, 468
overlay contents of a report definition, 396-397
parameters, 402, 490
parameters to control (3.10), 492
passwords with, 88
pausing printer between report pages, 230-231
preventing duplicate key-field entries (3.10), 174-175
purging deleted records from a file, 182-184
query definition specifications (SW II), 294
rebuilding keys (SW II), 109
record entry codes (SW II), 151
records, deleting (3.10), 461
recovering deleted, (SW II), 454-455
reformatting data, 400-402
run in memory, 14, 464-466
search-string parameter (3.10), 128
sequential numbering, 67-68
simulating the Browse command (DB), 93-96
singlestep for debugging, 501
single-step execution, 305
splitting windows, 96-97
spreadsheet, 478
spreadsheet cells, 458
statement
execution errors, 454
jumping to, 477
length (SW II), 454
quotation marks w57
testing for open database (3.10), 77
to change directories, (SW II), 522
to change a worksheet sent from the Database, 330
to check database record, 462
to check for response to prompt (3.10), 510-511
to check for valid dates (3.10), 508-510
to clear screen, 484
to compile with Debug-Off (SW II), 465
to display message, 483-484, 487-488
to drop carriage returns (3.10), 425
to eject page from printer, 480-481
to enter true date in cell, 459
to execute batch file (SW II), 469
to generate screen display, 516
to list (SW II), 469
to print to a file, 469-471
to prompt date (SW II), 535
to rename a database, 493
to test TIME function, 536-537
to turn Repaint Off, 500
to update pop-up menu contents (SW II), 50-51
to write external file, fixed format, 467-468
types of IF statements, 471-472
updating FAT (SW II), 90
validating code entries (3.10), 172-173
without line numbers, 465
word processor, 563-566
worksheet data entry, 314-319
Project Processing (PP) 453-518
fields
assigning default value (SW II), 40
viewing (SW II), 40
functions, 494-496
procedures, 494-496
variables, 41, 518
prompt character (CM), 544
Prompting (SS) mode, 301
PROPER function, 536
proportional fonts (3.10), 434
protocols
emulation, 545
Xmodem, 546
PrtSc key (3.10), 537
Public function (SW II), 496

Q

QNOW.DFQ file (SW II), 276
query
alphabetic field range test, 275
AND operator, 266-267
AND operator for two different fields, 267-268

applying index to custom view (SW II), 294-295
beginning with if, 271
changing fields unavailable in current view (3.10), 282
constructing from a project file (3.10), 286
controlling order of evaluation, 271-272
copying definitions, 278
date specifications (3.10), 263-266
Days function (3.10), 264-265
deleting/activating records, 284-287
deleting already deleted records (3.10), 284-285
documenting definitions, 278-280
FETCHFIELD function (SW II), 284, 293
field names with (3.10), 260-263
formula writing techniques, 271-277
ignoring deleted records, 278
isolating current record, 293-294
key date field (SW II), 265-266
key order of a view (SW II), 292
keys statements (SW II), 293
listing where condition, 269
logical condition with where condition 268-269
logical conditions with, 268
manual (3.10), 287
matching variable data type to field data type, 275
meeting conditions, 267
modifying, 262-263
multiple replacements (SW II), 283-284
network, 287-288
numbers in alpha fields, 274-275
physical order of database, 276
project files
    to construct (3.10) 551-554
    to execute (3.10) 551-554
range of dates (3.10), 266
records, changing active status, 284
replace facility, 280-284
replacing
    dates (SW II), 281-282
    fields (3.10), 280-281
    read-only field (SW II), 282
    records, 285
    values in index/database (3.10), 282
saving Query Now definition, 276
selecting
    current file/view, 262
    records (SW II), 277
sequential, 269-270
size limitations (3.10), 262
sorting alpha field ranges, 275-276
special alpha fields (3.10), 270-271
specifying blank/null text (3.10), 273-274
speeding up, 268-270
testing (SW II), 270
    definition, 277
    for cerror, (SW II), 292
trailing blanks (3.10), 291
trim function (3.10), 282-283
updating keys (3.10), 282
user-defined variables (3.10), 286
using record number (SW II), 270
utilitized fields (3.10), 274
variables with, 285-286
varying referenced field, 261-262
variables, 504
Query (DB) command (3.10), 59, 66-67, 163, 118, 177-178, 260-295
Query by Example (QBE), 288-291
    browsing fields (SW II), 290
    clearing field contents (SW II), 288
    combining with view expression (SW II), 289
    editor selecting records (SW II), 266
    multiple summary statistic specifications (SW II), 289
    optimized search (SW II), 269
    quotation marks with alpha field (SW II) 288
    selecting records, 290-291
    view expressions (SW II), 288
    viewing selection criteria (SW II), 288
Query Undefine (PP) command (3.10), 475
Query...Neither (DB) command (3.10), 285
Query...Screen command, vs Find command (DB), 129
quick keys, 527-531
    Ctrl-O (Tools OS), 13
    in macros, 527
quick reports
    creating, 187-191
    default field widths, 189
    field names, 188-189
    printing to file, 188
    specifying print line width, 190
    vertical bar (|) in fields, 187-188
Quiet (SS) mode, 305
Quiet settings, 496-497
Quit (F10) key, 90
Quit (PP) command, 501-502
quotation marks (SW II), 480
    in alpha field (3.10), 461

macros (SW II) 529-531
mark comments, 457
parameters (3.10), 490
with QBE alpha field (SW II), 288

R

RAM
disk card, 17
memory, conserving, 512
variables, 504
ranges, excluding from field mask (SW II), 52-53
read-only fields
replacing with query (SW II), 282
with Lookup facility (3.10), 173-174
read-only file attribute, worksheet template, 326-327
Read (DB) command, 147, 233-234
Read (SS) command, 331, 405-406
Read Text (3.10) command (SS), 400
Recalc (DB) command (SW II), 62
Recalculate (F5) key (SS), 320
recalculation
Count option (SS), 323
displaying (3.10), 300-301
iteration maximum, 323
mode
calculated fields, 53
set to Row/Column order (SW II), 325-326
Recalculation mode (SS), 299-300
Record function, 497
records
advancing
at command level (3.10), 170
between, 152-154
appending to existing file, 144-145
automatic conditions (3.10), 169
blank (3.10), 461
changing key values (SW II), 153
checking number in file, 133
current, pointer location (3.10), 128-129
deleting (3.10), 461
/activating with 284-287
active (3.10), 179-180
duplicate fields, 181-182
existing (SW II), 180
from database, 547-548
disallowing duplicate keys (SW II), 151
displaying active status, 188
double-spacing with breakpoints, 207
entering, 149-152
in read-only custom screen, 151-152
in temporary file (3.10), 163-164
repeating values automatically, 160-162
importing deleted (SW II), 238
Input screen definition, 526
isolating, 114
lock/update (SW II), 461
marking for deletion, 48-49, 176
moving between (3.10), 165
preventing deletion, 177-178
processing deleted, 176
project file to add to index (3.10), 559-560
rejecting deleted from Lookup facility (3.10), 172
repeating data, 158-164
repeating values (3.10), 159-160
selecting for Query by Example (QBE), 290-291
temporary deletion, 178-179
terminating Enter mode (3.10), 153
updating, 149-152
in networks (3.10), 164
with standard view (SW II), 153-154
visually locating in Browse mode, 150
recursive calculation (3.10), 55
regression
coefficients, 351-352
report, 350-351
REINVERT function, 130
relate definition
as template, 137
assigning names to fields, 138
changing (3.10), 136-137
relate definition
creating (3.10), 137
printing, 136
screen-dependent (3.10), 136
Relate (DB) command, 37-38, 65, 112, 130-132, 178
Relate Define (DB) command (3.10), 136-137
Relate...Subtract command, 114
relation fields, specifying in output file, 137-138
relative address, vs absolute address, 309-312
relative cell address, changing to absolute address, 337
Remember Compile (PP) command (3.10), 454
Remember Edit mode, 498-499
Remember Start (PP) command, 453, 499
Remember Tools Compile No-Debug (PP) command (SW II), 458
Remember Tools Delete (PP) command (SW II), 454-455

Remember Tools Editor (PP) command (SW II), 454
Remember Tools Load, (PP) command (SW II), 466
Remember Tools Trace (PP) command (SW II), 511-512
Repaint (PP) command, 499-500
Repeat (F9) key, 158-160
REPEAT function (SS), 387
repeating fields, setting values, 163
Replace (WP) command (3.10), 422-423
Replace Activate Query definition, 178
REPLACE function (SS), 380
reply buffer, filling (SW II), 456
Reply ON Char (PP) command (SW II), 456-457
report definitions
  changing, 396-398
  creating similar (3.10), 220
  duplicating, 391
  erasing, 231
  saving file/screen names (3.10), 194
  screen name case-sensitivity (3.10), 194
report heading/footing, 391-392
Report (DB) command (3.10), 178, 188, 191, 244, 391
Report form
  moving blocks (SW II), 230
  for formatted output, 481
Report Form Label command (DB), 190
Report Undefine (3.10) command (DB), 231
reports
  block reference (3.10), 392
  block specifications, 394-396
  calculated fields, 217-218
  changing number of fields in a file (3.10), 201
  combination, new forms, generating (3.10), 549-551
  combination, see combination reports
  default file extension (RPT), 231
  Form, see Form reports
  formal see formal reports
  headings, changing date (3.10), 548-549
  manually advancing paper when printing, 394
  output destinations, 393-394
  page numbering, 396
  previewing a print job, 190
  print group specifications, 394-396
  printing, 230-232
  printing multiple (3.10), 231
  quick, see quick reports 187-191
  regression, 350-351
  Table see Table report
  values, displaying Not Available (3.10), 199-200
  width specifications, 392-393
  writing to disk file, 231
  writing to disks, 393-394
Result Line Label, breakpoints (SW II), 211-212
Return statement (3.10), 495
RFx (compiled) files (PP), 455
ROUND function (SS), 410
ROW function (SS), 365
rows
  automatic generation in numeric fields (SW II), 256-257
  duplicating portions, 334-335
  including in formulas, 311
  specifying, 318-319
  unique, case sensitive, 256
RPT file extension, 231
ruler line, setting indent (SW II), 449
rulers, deleting (SW II), 449
rules, field (SW II), 45-49
running-total fields (3.10), 63-64

S

Save (3.10) command (WP), 421
Save (F10) key, 543
Save All command (SS), 302
Save command (DB), 89-90
screen contents, displaying, 500
screen files, saving (3.10), 410
screen input, simulate (3.10), 476-477
Screen (PP) commands, 483-488
Screen input field, inserting calculator result, 483
Screen Input command (SW II), 515-516
Screen Menu (PP) command (SW II), 516-517
Screen Print (DB) command (SW II), 462, 487
Screen Restore (PP) command (SW II), 487
Screen Save (PP) command (SW II), 487
screens
  custom, 82-87
  Input, 525-527
  Lookup Definition (3.10), 166
  naming conventions (3.10), 82-83
  passwords with, 87-89
  project file to clear, 484
  repainting, 499-500
  viewing names (3.10), 83-84
search-string parameter (3.10), 128
seasonal model
  applying to data forecast, 354-356

developing from historical data, 353-354
Secondary Command Processor (DOS Window), 520
SELECT function (SS), 373-374
selection functions (SS), 371-374
Send (CM) command (3.10), 542
Send (DB) command, 249-250
Send Wordprocessor command (SS), 404
sequential queries, 269-270
serial printers, selecting ports, 22-23
Setting Save (CM) command (3.10), 543-544
settings changes, saving (3.10), 544
settings, modems, 543-544
Settings Edit (CM) command(3.10), 543
Settings menu, 544
Sheet Calc-mode Manual (SS) command (SW II), 324
Sheet Find...Calc-Error (SS) command (SW II), 363
Sheet Lock Protect command (SS), 327
Sheet Matrix command (SS), 349-350
Sheet Name Define command (SS), 345
Sheet Name Edit (SS) command (SW II), 343-344
Sheet Newname (SS) (SW II), 326
Sheet Send (SS) command (SW II), 404
Singlestep settings, 501
Smart System
configuring, 19-25
entering, 12-17
installing, 12
networking, 30-31
SMART files, importing, 234
SMART.MNU file, 14-17
Smartpoke variable, 458
Social Security number, in project file (3.10), 507
sort, database project files, 464
sort definition
creating, 114-115
dependency on field numbers (3.10), 116
file (3.10), 115
multiple files (3.10), 116
multiple views (SW II), 116
sort
halting in progress (3.10), 118
selecting sequence, 115
using custom view (SW II), 115
vs key fields, 111-112
Sort command (DB), 115, 118
Sort Now (DB) command (3.10), 116-117
source files
hidden retrievals (3.10), 166
lookup definiteness (3.10), 169
ordering by index, 144
ordering by key (3.10), 146
special characters, 536
evaluating with Lookup facility (3.10), 174
Spellchecker
adding to existing system (3.10), 426
proper nouns with, 428
spell-checking footnotes, 428-429
Split command (DB), 97
Split Horizontal command (DB), 96
Split Vertical command (DB), 96
spreadsheet
see also worksheet
blank cells, 313-314
changing print line width, 390-391
circular references, 321-325
column width, 388
confidence number (3.10), 301
converting source blocks to blanks, 341
copying between, 340
cursor key vs enter key, 306-307
data entry, 306
default settings (3.10), 299-300
directing output destinations, 389-390
entering text, 312
error handling, 363-365
Error 7 condition, 363
external references, 340-343
extracting cell address, 409
formulas only, 398
graphing text numbers, 411-412
incorporating into database, 398
iterative recalculation 561-562
reading database files, 400
reading Lotus 1-2-3 V 1A/Release 2.0 files, 406
sending data to
database, 250-251, 405
word processor, 404
sending/writing data from, 403-405
setting parameters, 299-306
sorting database data, 403
Symbolic Link format (SYLK), 405
topics, 458-460
underscoring entries, 385-388
using F-Calculator, 313
writing Lotus 1/2-3 V 1A/Release 2.0 files, 406
Spreadsheet module, overview, 5-6
standard view
modifying fields (SW II), 42
updating records (SW II), 153-154
Start page number option (WP), 434-435

statement lines, DOS window, comments, 457
statements
  assignment 474, 478
  AT (PP), 458
  Call (3.10), 494-495
  clear (3.10), 505
  Debug Off, (SW II), 458
  END MAIN (SW II), 495
  Enter, 459, 478
  Evaluate, 489, 494
  IF...THEN...ELSE, 474
  illegal, 474-475
  in project files (SW II), 454
  Jump (3.10), 495
  Keys (SW II), 513-514, 530
  Let (3.10), 459
  LET, 478
  Menu Clear Box (3.10), 485
  Menu input, 483
  multiple assignment, 460-461
  project file, jumping to, 477
  Return (3.10), 495
statistical database functions (SS), 376-379
Stop (PP) command, 501-502
STR function (SS), 374-375
strings
  enclosing in a macro (SW II), 529
  substituting with REPLACE function, 380
subcommands
  Create Box (DB), 85
  SW II
    Create or Edit Calculation (DB), 42
    Create or Edit Rule (DB), 42
    Delete Block (DB), 42-43
    Delete Item Field (DB), 41
    Delete Item Field (DB), 43
    Edit Field (DB), 42
    Input-Order (DB), 86
    Move Item Field (DB), 41
subdirectories, 79-81
  changing, 520
  creating, 12
  existence of, 534
  path for modem (SW II), 543
  searching (SW II), 80
summarized data, writing to file, 245-248
summarized database, creating, 250-253
summarized definition
  changing (3.10), 253-254
  changing to an option (3.10), 253-254
  specifying row order (3.10), 255
  testing, 257-260
  undefining (3.10), 257-258
  unique row field (3.10), 256
summary definition, storing field numbers (3.10), 246
Suspend (PP) command, 501-502
Suspend mode
  project file (SW II), 511-512
  recording macros in (SW II), 530
Switch modes (F3) key, 538, 545
Switch modes (F5) key, 545
switches, entry, see entry switches
Symbolic Link format (SYLK), 405
symbols
  < (less-than), 267, 271
  > (greater-than), 267, 271
SYMMAP function, undocumented, 536
system beep, deactivating (3.10), 455
system documentation, 526

T

table definition
  insert/delete temporary calculation, 196
  moving fields, 197
table linkage, delete status indicator (SW II), 180
Table report
  breakpoints, 207-212
  case sensitive field names (SW II), 196
  creating a variable heading (3.10), 224
  defining, 195
  double space records, 205-206
  double-spacing, 195
  entering text, 205-206
  field selection, 196-198
  heading lines, 204-205
  headings (SW II), 202-203
  leading blanks in table footings, 224
  multiple print lines, 203-206
  No Justification setting, 197
  printer macros (3.10), 204
  printing secondary table lines, 206
  proportional fonts (SW II), 198
  reforming fields, 198
  sizing numeric fields (SW II), 196
  summary types (SW II), 209-210
TABLECOUNT function (SW II), 47
tables
  adding fields (SW II), 74
  positioning fields (SW II), 73
templates

document, 435
relate definition, 137
worksheet, 326
temporary file
repeating data (3.10), 162-163
to enter new records (3.10), 163-164
terminal session, reviewing, 539-540
Terminal Goto (CM) command (SW II), 541
Terminal mode, switch to Command mode, 538, 545
terminals, emulation, 545
Terminate menu (F10) key, 527
termination, of project file, 501-502
text
centering Form report, 218-219
characters, in parameters (3.10), 489
copying blocks in worksheet, 334-336
editors, files, reading, 18
entering in spreadsheet, 312
entry, moving, 527
file
writing to, 236-237
preparing for Smart, 563-566
print options (3.10), 432
functions (SS), 379-380
literal, assigned to user-defined variable (3.10), 479
variables, 459, 502-503
with quotation marks (SW II), 480
Text editor, viewing data files, 439
Text-Editor function keys (SW II), 36
TEXT1 variable (3.10), 504
TEXT2 variable (3.10), 504
Textfile mode (WP), 454
three bit evaluation functions (3.10), 532
time dependent interrupts, 538
Time function (SS), 370-371
TIME function, 536-537
Tools Display Display command, 520
Tools File Copy command, 72, 258-259, 391, 523-524, 544
Tools File Erase command, 118-119, 185, 475, 521, 524
Tools File Rename (PP) command (SW II), 455, 524
Tools Macros Clear All (PP) command (SW II), 513
Tools New-Font command (SW II), 537
Tools OS command (SW II), 13, 469, 520
Tools Preferences Communications menu (SW II), 542
Tools Preferences Global menu, 13
Tools Preferences Hardware menu, 22
Tools Preferences menu, 13
Tools Text-Editor (WP) command (SW II), 430
Tools Text-Editor, creating QBE Query definition (SW II) 289-290
Transaction (DB) command (3.10), 138
transactions
defining (3.10) 140
executing predefined (3.10), 141
matching case of field names (3.10), 143
naming conventions (3.10), 141
targeting into a calculated field, 141
Transactions (DB) command (3.10), 179
Transfer (PP) command, 464
Transfer-Time (CM) command (3.10), 545-546
TRANSLAT program (SW II), 122
trim (DB) function (3.10), 282-283
TRIM function (SW II), 537
true/false conditions, IF statement, 473
TXT file extension (WP), 432
type modifiers, 458

U

UCP file extension, 544
Udc-Conv (SW II) command (WP), 429
Undelete (3.10) command (WP), 423
undocumented
function, SYMMAP, 536
variables (SW II), 458
unique rows, case sensitive, 256
UNIQUE search
altering order of file (3.10), 259
available RAM (3.10), 259
Unload All (3.10) command (SS), 302
update, of database keys (3.10), 462-463
update records (SW II), 461
Update (DB) command, (3.10), 159-160
UPPER function, test results, 474
user defined variables, text contained (3.10), 504
user entries, macros (SW II), 530-531
user variables (SW II), 517
Utilities Alter-Count (DB) command (3.10), 65
Utilities Alter Count Renumber (DB) command (3.10), 65
Utilities Concatenate (DB) command (3.10), 120, 144-148
Utilities Duplicates Delete (DB) command (3.10), 180-181
Utilities New-Password File Password (DB) command (3.10), 88

Utilities New-Password Screen (DB) command (3.10), 89
Utilities New-Password Screen Password (DB) command (3.10), 88
Utilities Purge (DB) command (3.10), 66, 184
Utilities Restructure (DB) command (3.10), 38, 66, 142-148

V

VAL function (SS), 374-375, 507-508
valid date, checking (3.10), 533
VALUE1 variable (3.10), 504
VALUE2 variable (3.10), 504
variable assignments, multiple (SW II), 479-480
variable cell address, creating, 311
  with Evaluate statement, 312
variable-length vs fixed-length files, 37
variable names, keeping track of (3.10), 503
variables
  $_pfcp, undocumented (SW II), 458
  access time (3.10), 506
  adding to display list, 514
  as Table report heading (SW II), 202
  clearing, 505
  default value (3.10), 502-503
  editing, 514
  environment, COMSPEC, 19
  global, 512
  in command line substitution (SW II), 488-489
  in Input Screen facility (3.10), 526
  in project files, 502-518
  in queries, 504
  linear-regression dependent, 350
  local, 512
  master (3.10), 503
  names, 505
  non-zero numeric, 473
  numeric, 504, 506-507
  parameter (3.10), 477-478
  project processing, 41, 518
  simulated by parameters (3.10), 492-493
  Smartpoke, 458
  testing for (3.10), 504
  text (3.10), 502-504
  to enter true dates, 459
  user-defined, 479, 504, 538-539
  user, to save parameters (3.10), 492
  value (SW II), 505
  with calculated fields, 57-58
  with query, 285-286
vertical bar (|), with field range (3.10), 132
view field, defining as Manual (SW II), 54
view tables, positioning fields (SW II), 73
views
  attaching data file (SW II), 74-75
  changing order (SW II), 121
  creating, 35-38
  current, reading name (SW II), 36
  modifying, (SW II), 41
  multiple file, 73-75
  project processing fields (SW II), 40
  sort definition (SW II), 116
virtual-file facility, 17-18, 81
VIRTUAL.DVR file, 18, 81
VLOOKUP function (SS), 359-363
VT100 emulation mode, switching modes in, 545
VT100 terminal definition file (3.10), 544-545
VT52 terminal definition file (3.10), 544-545
VW file extension (SW II), 78
VWS file extension (SW II), 78

W

wait message, project file code, 463-464
Whole Words Only option, 125-126
Width (3.10) command (SS), 388
wild cards, asterisk (*), 524
Window Split Horizontal (SW II) command (DB), 97
Window Split Vertical (SW II) command (DB), 97
Window Zoom (SW II) command (DB), 98
windows
  changing, 99, 520
  closing, 97-99
  DOS, 11, 13
  error messages, 519
  macros to change (3.10), 531
  minimum sizes, 96
  moving between (3.10), 421
  splitting, 96-97, 519
  to display more, 519
  turning off border, 96
  viewing multiple, 98
  zooming, 97-99, 531
Windows and Borders command, 519
word processor
  buffers, inserted text, 422
  calculating point size space (SW II), 447
  changing document fonts, 422-423
  checking contents of the copy buffer, 422
  computations in (3.10), 445

copying footnotes, 423
deleting
footnotes, 423
rulers (SW II), 449
sentences (3.10), 423-424
displaying document names, 418-419
document creation tips (SW II) 420-421
editing merge data file, 440
erasing buffer contents, 422
footnotes, deleting, 423
headers/footers, 432-433
memory requirements, 417-418
merge field limitations, 438-439
merging database data, 437-438
multiple columns, 426
page limitations, 442
print limitations (3.10), 446
project files, 563-566
repeating Find command, 422
starting, 417-421
suppressing blank lines when printing, 438
underscoring a merged variable, 440
unloading current document, 445
using dictionaries, 426-430
using DOS window (3.10), 417
to create project files, 498
Word Processor module, overview, 6
worksheet
see also spreadsheet
adding temporary rows/columns, 337-338
automatic backup, 302
blocks, defining with same name, 344-345
cell reference to select a footing, 393
cells, testing blank looking, 368-369
centering headings, 393
changing calculation mode, 320
changing value cell prior to copying, 338-339
circular references, 321-325
constructing from top left to bottom right, 336
copying
area above or to left of original block, 336
blocks, 334-336
discontiguous blocks, 338
formulas, 336-337
parts of, 333-340
default column width, 306
defining block names, 345
extracting to graph when paging to disk, 410
file extension other than WS, 304-305
fixing titles, 393
formulas, entering, 460
incorporating database data, 328-331
initial settings for value formats, 305-306
loading, 304
loading on worksheets (3.10), 324
locating errors, 363-364
making block references, 375
manual recalculation, 324
moving rows/columns within named blocks, 342-343
named blocks, 343-345
position functions (SS), 365-366
preformatting blocks, 339-340
printing, 388-391
protecting, 326-328
recalculating, 319-323
redefining boundaries of a named range, 344
referencing current cell column/row, 365
rows, duplicating, 334-335
safeguarding original, 328
sorting, 356-357
sorting database data, 398-399
templates, protecting, 326
title block intersection, 393
unloading (SW II), 328
use leading spaces to center footings, 393
viewing block names, 343
WPRINT.DEF file, 419-420
Write (DB) command (3.10), 236, 241
Write (SS) command (3.10), 331, 404, 406
Write All (DB) command (3.10), 147, 244
Write/Send Summarized (DB) command (3.10), 255
Write Summarized (DB) command (3.10), 245, 258
Write Summarized (SS) command (3.10), 330-331
Write summarized definition, selecting wrong options (3.10), 253

X

Xmodem protocol, 546
Xon/ Xoff protocol, 545

Z

ZIP code fields, 68
Zoom command (DB), 97
Repaint Off effects on 8088 computer, 98-99
Zoom mode, changing windows (3.10), 520
zooming windows, 531

Computer Books From Que Mean PC Performance!

Spreadsheets

1-2-3 Database Techniques	$29.95
1-2-3 Graphics Techniques	$24.95
1-2-3 Macro Library, 3rd Edition	$39.95
1-2-3 Release 2.2 Business Applications	$39.95
1-2-3 Release 2.2 Quick Reference	$ 7.95
1-2-3 Release 2.2 QuickStart	$19.95
1-2-3 Release 2.2 Workbook and Disk	$29.95
1-2-3 Release 3 Business Applications	$39.95
1-2-3 Release 3 Quick Reference	$ 7.95
1-2-3 Release 3 QuickStart	$19.95
1-2-3 Release 3 Workbook and Disk	$29.95
1-2-3 Tips, Tricks, and Traps, 3rd Edition	$24.95
Excel Business Applications: IBM Version	$39.95
Excel Quick Reference	$ 7.95
Excel QuickStart	$19.95
Excel Tips, Tricks, and Traps	$22.95
Using 1-2-3, Special Edition	$26.95
Using 1-2-3 Release 2.2, Special Edition	$26.95
Using 1-2-3 Release 3	$27.95
Using Excel: IBM Version	$29.95
Using Lotus Spreadsheet for DeskMate	$19.95
Using Quattro Pro	$24.95
Using SuperCalc5, 2nd Edition	$29.95

Databases

dBASE III Plus Handbook, 2nd Edition	$24.95
dBASE III Plus Tips, Tricks, and Traps	$24.95
dBASE III Plus Workbook and Disk	$29.95
dBASE IV Applications Library, 2nd Edition	$39.95
dBASE IV Programming Techniques	$24.95
dBASE IV QueCards	$21.95
dBASE IV Quick Reference	$ 7.95
dBASE IV QuickStart	$19.95
dBASE IV Tips, Tricks,and Traps, 2nd Ed.	$24.95
dBASE IV Workbook and Disk	$29.95
R:BASE User's Guide, 3rd Edition	$22.95
Using Clipper	$24.95
Using DataEase	$24.95
Using dBASE IV	$27.95
Using FoxPro	$26.95
Using Paradox 3	$24.95
Using Reflex, 2nd Edition	$22.95
Using SQL	$24.95

Business Applications

Introduction to Business Software	$14.95
Introduction to Personal Computers	$19.95
Lotus Add-in Toolkit Guide	$29.95
Norton Utilities Quick Reference	$ 7.95
PC Tools Quick Reference, 2nd Edition	$ 7.95
Q&A Quick Reference	$ 7.95
Que's Computer User's Dictionary	$9.95
Que's Wizard Book	$ 9.95
Smart Tips, Tricks, and Traps	$24.95
Using Computers in Business	$22.95
Using DacEasy, 2nd Edition	$24.95
Using Dollars and Sense: IBM Version, 2nd Edition	$19.95
Using Enable/OA	$29.95
Using Harvard Project Manager	$24.95
Using Lotus Magellan	$21.95
Using Managing Your Money, 2nd Edition	$19.95
Using Microsoft Works: IBM Version	$22.95
Using Norton Utilities	$24.95
Using PC Tools Deluxe	$24.95
Using Peachtree	$22.95
Using PFS: First Choice	$22.95
Using PROCOMM PLUS	$19.95
Using Q&A, 2nd Edition	$23.95
Using Quicken	$19.95
Using Smart	$22.95
Using SmartWare II	$29.95
Using Symphony, Special Edition	$29.95

CAD

AutoCAD Advanced Techniques	$34.95
AutoCAD Quick Reference	$ 7.95
AutoCAD Sourcebook	$24.95
Using AutoCAD, 2nd Edition	$24.95
Using Generic CADD	$24.95

Word Processing

DisplayWrite QuickStart	$19.95
Microsoft Word 5 Quick Reference	$ 7.95
Microsoft Word 5 Tips, Tricks, and Traps: IBM Version	$22.95
Using DisplayWrite 4, 2nd Edition	$24.95
Using Microsoft Word 5: IBM Version	$22.95
Using MultiMate	$22.95
Using Professional Write	$22.95
Using Word for Windows	$22.95
Using WordPerfect, 3rd Edition	$21.95
Using WordPerfect 5	$24.95
Using WordPerfect 5.1, Special Edition	$24.95
Using WordStar, 2nd Edition	$21.95
WordPerfect QueCards	$21.95
WordPerfect Quick Reference	$ 7.95
WordPerfect QuickStart	$19.95
WordPerfect Tips, Tricks, and Traps, 2nd Edition	$22.95
WordPerfect 5 Workbook and Disk	$29.95
WordPerfect 5.1 Quick Reference	$ 7.95
WordPerfect 5.1 QuickStart	$19.95
WordPerfect 5.1 Tips, Tricks, and Traps	$22.95
WordPerfect 5.1 Workbook and Disk	$29.95

Hardware/Systems

DOS Power Techniques	$29.95
DOS Tips, Tricks, and Traps	$24.95
DOS Workbook and Disk, 2nd Edition	$29.95
Hard Disk Quick Reference	$ 7.95
MS-DOS Quick Reference	$ 7.95
MS-DOS QuickStart	$21.95
MS-DOS User's Guide, Special Edition	$29.95
Networking Personal Computers, 3rd Edition	$24.95
The Printer Bible	$29.95
Que's Guide to Data Recovery	$24.95
Understanding UNIX, 2nd Edition	$21.95
Upgrading and Repairing PCs	$29.95
Using DOS	$22.95
Using Microsoft Windows 3, 2nd Edition	$22.95
Using Novell NetWare	$29.95
Using OS/2	$29.95
Using PC DOS, 3rd Edition	$24.95
Using UNIX	$24.95
Using Your Hard Disk	$29.95
Windows 3 Quick Reference	$ 7.95

Desktop Publishing/Graphics

Harvard Graphics Quick Reference	$ 7.95
Using Animator	$24.95
Using Harvard Graphics	$24.95
Using Freelance Plus	$24.95
Using PageMaker: IBM Version, 2nd Edition	$24.95
Using PFS: First Publisher	$22.95
Using Ventura Publisher, 2nd Edition	$24.95
Ventura Publisher Tips, Tricks, and Traps,	$24.95

Macintosh/Apple II

AppleWorks QuickStart	$19.95
The Big Mac Book	$27.95
Excel QuickStart	$19.95
Excel Tips, Tricks, and Traps	$22.95
Que's Macintosh Multimedia Handbook	$22.95
Using AppleWorks, 3rd Edition	$21.95
Using AppleWorks GS	$21.95
Using Dollars and Sense: Macintosh Version	$19.95
Using Excel: Macintosh Version	$24.95
Using FileMaker	$24.95
Using MacroMind Director	$29.95
Using MacWrite	$22.95
Using Microsoft Word 4: Macintosh Version	$24.95
Using Microsoft Works: Macintosh Version, 2nd Edition	$24.95
Using PageMaker: Macintosh Version	$24.95

Programming/Technical

Assembly Language Quick Reference	$ 7.95
C Programmer's Toolkit	$39.95
C Programming Guide, 3rd Edition	$24.95
C Quick Reference	$ 7.95
DOS and BIOS Functions Quick Reference	$ 7.95
DOS Programmer's Reference, 2nd Edition	$29.95
Oracle Programmer's Guide	$24.95
Power Graphics Programming	$24.95
QuickBASIC Advanced Techniques	$22.95
QuickBASIC Programmer's Toolkit	$39.95
QuickBASIC Quick Reference	$ 7.95
QuickPascal Programming	$22.95
SQL Programmer's Guide	$29.95
Turbo C Programming	$22.95
Turbo Pascal Advanced Techniques	$22.95
Turbo Pascal Programmer's Toolkit	$39.95
Turbo Pascal Quick Reference	$ 7.95
UNIX Programmer's Quick Reference	$ 7.95
Using Assembly Language, 2nd Edition	$29.95
Using BASIC	$19.95
Using C	$27.95
Using QuickBASIC 4	$24.95
Using Turbo Pascal	$29.95

For More Information,
Call Toll Free!

1-800-428-5331

All prices and titles subject to change without notice. Non-U.S. prices may be higher. Printed in the U.S.A.